BRUSHES WITH HISTORY: AN AUTOBIOGRAPHY

Brushes with History

An Autobiography

KRISHNA KUMAR BIRLA

PENGUIN
VIKING

VIKING
Published by the Penguin Group
Penguin Books India Pvt. Ltd, 11 Community Centre, Panchsheel Park, New Delhi 110 017, India
Penguin Group (USA) Inc., 375 Hudson Street, New York, New York 10014, USA
Penguin Group (Canada), 90 Eglinton Avenue East, Suite 700, Toronto, Ontario, M4P 2Y3, Canada (a division of Pearson Penguin Canada Inc.)
Penguin Books Ltd, 80 Strand, London WC2R 0RL, England
Penguin Ireland, 25 St Stephen's Green, Dublin 2, Ireland (a division of Penguin Books Ltd)
Penguin Group (Australia), 250 Camberwell Road, Camberwell, Victoria 3124, Australia (a division of Pearson Australia Group Pty Ltd)
Penguin Group (NZ), 67 Apollo Drive, Rosedale, North Shore 0632, New Zealand (a division of Pearson New Zealand Ltd)
Penguin Group (South Africa) (Pty) Ltd, 24 Sturdee Avenue, Rosebank, Johannesburg 2196, South Africa

Penguin Books Ltd, Registered Offices: 80 Strand, London WC2R 0RL, England

First published in Viking by Penguin Books India 2007

Copyright © Krishna Kumar Birla 2007

ISBN-13: 978-0-67008-129-5   ISBN-10: 0-67008-129-9

Typeset in Sabon by Mantra Virtual Services, New Delhi
Printed at Thomson Press, Noida

Dedicated to my father Dr G.D. Birla
a man of great nobility who was
a '*Karmayogi*'
a follower of the teachings and philosophy of
Srimad Bhagavad-Gita
a devotee of Lord Krishna
a man who regarded Mahatma-ji as father
and whom the Mahatma regarded as a friend and mentor
a visionary who established a large number of industries
and thus contributed significantly to the nation's
wealth and prosperity
who as a philanthropist and firm believer in
education and technology
as paths to progress and awakening of the nation
established the Birla Education Trust
and the Birla Institute of Technology and Science—
the two biggest educational foundations of the country
a patriarch who taught his children to tread on the
righteous path—
to such an exalted father who lived the life of a '*Karmayogi*'
my respectful obeisances
'*Koti Koti Pranams*'

Contents

Foreword

The relations between Dr K.K. Birla's family and the Congress party date back to the tempestuous days of India's freedom struggle. Dr Birla's father, the late G.D. Birla, was an important associate of Gandhi-ji's and the family played a major role in the battle for India's independence.

Of the members of his generation in the family, Dr K.K. Birla has been the most active in carrying on his father's connection with public life. He was a member of Parliament for many decades and has always seen himself as an industrialist with an obligation to keep up his father's traditions.

He was a close associate of Indira Gandhi's and even when things got rough for Indira-ji, he remained true to his principles and to their friendship. He knew Rajiv-ji well and I have always regarded him as being part of the Congress family.

I am delighted to learn that he has finally penned his autobiography. Very few people have the range of experience that Dr Birla has. His life encompasses many eras and many areas. There cannot be many industrialists who can write about the growth of Indian business through the twentieth century. And there cannot be many other people with as great an acquaintance and friendship with the most important figures of post-independence India. In that sense, he has truly been a witness to history.

His relationship with the media has also been significant. The late G.D. Birla became involved in the *Hindustan Times* at the behest of Gandhi-ji and, under his stewardship, the paper became the voice of the nationalist movement, a counterpoint to the British-owned English papers that dominated pre-independence India. Over the last several decades, Dr K.K. Birla has transformed the *Hindustan Times* into one of modern India's leading newspapers with new editions all over the country.

All this is part of his commitment to public life. In that sense, he represents a generation of industrialists who saw their task as nation building and were not interested in vulgar displays of wealth or in showing off their assets.

His own personality—low-key, dignified and always unwilling to throw his weight around or to draw attention to himself—is an example of the values that his generation often embodied.

I have known Birla-ji personally for many years. He has been a steadfast friend, always ready with a word of advice or a bit of encouragement. His dignity and his old-world charm have always served as a source of reassurance that no matter how quickly India changes, the old values are still around.

I hope his memoirs will reflect the man himself.

If they manage to do that, they will be invaluable reading.

New Delhi   Sonia Gandhi
14 April 2007

Introduction

I had lunch with K.K. Birla the very first time I met him. Two decades ago, shortly after I had taken over as editor of *Sunday*, Aveek Sarkar, my then boss, told me that 'K.K. Babu'—as everyone in Kolkata called him—had expressed a desire to see what I was like. Aveek was due to have lunch with K.K. Babu the following fortnight. Could I come along?

I had met other members of the Birla family before. Shortly after moving to Kolkata, I had been fortunate enough to have been invited home for dinner by B.K. Birla (K.K. Babu's younger brother), and I knew various members of the next generation of Birlas, chiefly K.K. Babu's nephews Aditya, Ashok, Sudarshan and Chandrakant.

But K.K. Birla was different. He was the one Birla that all journalists knew about. He owned the *Hindustan Times*, Delhi's biggest and most powerful paper. Just as his father G.D. Birla had befriended Mahatma Gandhi, so K.K. Birla had become a friend and confidant of, first, Indira Gandhi and, then, her son Rajiv (who was prime minister when we met). He had spent several years in Parliament and his interest in political affairs was said to be even greater than his focus on his own business empire.

Aveek was a friend of many Birlas and—I think it is probably fair to say—a bit of a fan. 'The thing to remember about the Birlas,' he once told me, even as I swallowed rapidly, 'is that they are the royal family of India.'

Certainly, our visit to K.K. Birla's office in a building that headquartered the Birla businesses was treated as something of an occasion. Aveek was quite specific: we were to be exactly on time—K.K. Babu hated unpunctuality of any kind.

When the man himself appeared, he was not unlike the many pictures of him that I had often seen in the newspapers—but three things stood out. The first was that he was impeccably tailored, in an almost English, Savile Row sort of way. The second was that he managed to combine warmth and formality. He was friendly and seemed happy to see us. But there was still a certain reserve, a kind of measured formality about him. And the third was that he came to lunch with an agenda. Sitting on his left at the dining table, I was intrigued to see that he frequently referred to a handwritten list of subjects titled 'Points to be discussed with Sh Aveek Sarkar and Sh Vir Sanghvi'. As lunch went on and we talked about many things, from the circulation of the *Telegraph* and the *Hindustan Times* to the fate of the government, I was a little taken aback to see that he moved the conversation effortlessly from subject to subject, making each shift seem entirely natural—even though we followed the exact agenda that he had brought to the lunch, in exactly the same order in which he had written it.

*

I was to meet K.K. Babu again—and again. At first, Aveek and I went to joint lunches. But, within a year or so, he was decent enough to start inviting me on my own to lunch in Kolkata and at Birla House in Delhi.

I had just turned thirty and was struggling to turn *Sunday* around and to make sense of national politics. K.K. Babu had a grandson who was only a little younger than me and he was one of India's most powerful people. Yet, he treated me like an equal. He never patronized or talked down to me; never acted as though he knew much more than I did (which, of course, he did); and never contradicted me when I was saying things that he must have known were wrong.

Each lunch would follow the same pattern. There would be a tray of fruit juices and a few snacks. Then, we would go to the dining table to eat almost exactly the same meal each time: asparagus soup served with puris, followed by a vegetable cutlet with four thick-cut French fries and a vegetable *au gratin*; followed by rice and two gravy vegetable dishes (one of which was always made with potato) and then gulab jamuns for dessert. Coffee would be served in the sitting area once we had left the table and K.K. Babu would always have the decaf version.

At each lunch, he brought along a pad with a handwritten agenda, though within a few years we had begun to get along well enough for him to deviate from that agenda. After a few such lunches, I became careful of how loosely I spoke because if an agenda subject cropped up again after a few months and I shot my mouth off, he would look up and say, 'But Vir, I remember that the last time we discussed this, you said something quite different ...'

Did he keep notes? I began to wonder. Did he summon his secretary after each lunch and dictate a summary of what had transpired? Otherwise, how could he always remember what I had said?

The lunches confirmed my original impressions. He was always impeccably tailored (Jermyn Street or Savile Row, as I was later to discover). He was terrifyingly punctual. Sometimes, his schedule would include an appointment that went from 10.23 to 10.47. A minute was a long time to keep K.K. Babu waiting.

His entire life was organized with breathtaking efficiency. Was he planning to be in London soon? 'Yes, Vir,' he would respond instantly, 'I am booked on the British Airways evening flight on the 28th of next month. I shall be in London for one day. Then my wife and I will go to Geneva for a few days. On the 3rd we return to London ...'

As the lunch menu suggested, he was a creature of habit. He always stayed at Grosvenor House on Park Lane in London. His father had first taken him there before the war (the Second World War, naturally) and he had grown accustomed to a particular suite. As he sometimes stayed in London for months, I once asked if he got Grosvenor House—which had long since ceased to be the grand hotel patronized by G.D. Birla—to give him a good rate. He did not understand the question. I persisted: 'They've come down a little in the world,' I said. 'You could probably get a huge discount.'

He looked alarmed. 'A discount?' he asked. 'Oh no, I *never* ask for a discount.'

He stayed there for months, paying full rack rate for a suite. Small wonder then that each time he went, the entire senior staff of the hotel lined up to welcome him. And in 2007, when the property was finally refurbished, they asked him to inaugurate the new tea lounge officially in front of an invited audience of lords, ladies, MPs and corporate tycoons.

*

As fate would have it, around five or six years after I started lunching with K.K. Babu, I became friends with his daughter Shobhana and his son-in-law Shyam. They quickly became my closest friends and through them I met other members of the Birla family, chiefly Shobhana's two older sisters and their husbands.

K.K. Babu was pleased at this development but it did nothing to alter the terms of his relationship with me. We still met for lunch on our own. Shobhana and Shyam would be invited to lunches and dinners of their own. Of course, we would often meet socially at family celebrations or gatherings at Shobhana and Shyam's but our lunches continued to take place in a bubble, completely outside of any family relationship. Moreover, I always had the impression that his fabled discretion ensured that he never repeated a word I said to anyone, even my closest friends—his own daughters and sons-in-law.

But that, I was to learn, was K.K. Babu's way. He is capable of great love and affection, and dotes on his children and their families. And yet, that mixture of warmth and formality continues. Shobhana and he will write letters to each other. She will rarely drop in on him unannounced. If she is five minutes early for lunch with him, she will drive around the block till it is time. She knows, she says, that he plans his days with meticulous care and detail, and that even a five-minute disruption can wreak havoc on his schedule.

Even with friends, he is capable of mixing the formal with the affectionate in ways that never cease to surprise me. In 1996–97, when I was undergoing a certain degree of personal turbulence, he found out about it through sources of his own (Shobhana, I would guess) even though I would never have dreamt of raising the subject.

One evening, after we'd finished with dinner and the handwritten agenda had been completed, he sipped his decaf coffee contemplatively and then gently asked if I was okay. Was there anything he could do? He had heard that I was without a car. Would I like to borrow one of his? And so on.

Naturally, I refused all his generous offers of help, but the memory has stayed with me. He raised the subject once or twice again but always gently and with tact. Once the crisis had passed and I was okay, he never once mentioned it again.

*

In 1999, when the editorship of the *Hindustan Times* fell vacant, Shobhana decided to offer it to me. Though I grabbed the opportunity—journalistic jobs don't come much bigger than this—both she and I were more apprehensive than either of us let on to the other. It is never easy for close friends to work together and more difficult when one friend becomes the other's boss.

Only K.K. Babu seemed unperturbed. His chief consideration was for Aveek Sarkar, who was going through a bad patch of his own. He did not want it to seem, he said, that the *HT* was stealing me from Aveek. After all, it was because of Aveek that we first met. I assured him that I had spoken to Aveek and he had told me that this was a great career opportunity and that I should not even consider turning down the job.

K.K. Babu was reassured. He had lunch with Aveek, was relieved to find that my former employer had not treated the job offer as evidence of bad form, and wished me luck. He was sure that I would enjoy working at the *HT*, he said warmly.

Some of my friends were less convinced. Even though I told them I had met K.K. Babu at least once every month for thirteen years, they maintained that I did not realize what I was getting into. It was one thing to be friends with the Birlas; quite another to work for them.

I was regaled with stories about K.K. Babu's tendency to interfere in editorial matters, to give instructions to his editors, to ask the paper to hire his favourites and to dictate editorials. How would I cope with all this? Not only did he have a business empire to promote, he was also an active politician and a member of Parliament.

I heard the sceptics out but never, not even for a second, did I think that I would have a problem. You cannot know a man for over a dozen years and not have some sense of him and his eagerness to do the right thing.

I was right.

In all my years at the *HT* (four as editor and then as editorial director), never did I come across a single instance where K.K. Babu interfered in the editorial policy. Not once was I asked to do something that I did not want to.

This is not to say that he did not have his own political views. There were many occasions when he disagreed strongly with the stands I took. Often his own views were at total variance with the editorials, which are supposed to reflect the entire paper's (including the owners') view of events. But he always took the line that as long as Shobhana, whose paper it now was, had no objection, his own views were no more than those of a reader. Which is a nice thing to say, especially when you are chairman of the company.

Often, he would send me his own position in writing. But it would always end with the following standalone paragraph: 'However, these are my personal views. It is entirely up to you to decide what the paper's policy should be'.

When we met again, I would discuss his position and tell him why I disagreed. Frequently, he was unconvinced. But never did he expect me to change my mind.

It couldn't have always been easy for him. During my time as editor, the BJP was in power and he was a close personal friend of A.B. Vajpayee and L.K. Advani. On many occasions, they complained to him. A particular columnist had written disparagingly of the prime minister. A beat reporter was biased. The paper was too hostile to the BJP, thanks to the prejudices of its editor (me!).

He faithfully relayed these comments to me. But not one columnist was dropped. Not one reporter had his beat changed. And not one story was rewritten. No matter how loud the complaints, he always stood up for his editor.

This was more difficult to do when he disagreed completely with me. On the Gujarat riots, for instance, he felt the paper was right to condemn the state government. But when I took to referring routinely to Narendra Modi as a mass murderer, he felt that a) this was overkill, and b) the paper had some obligation to take note of Modi's success as an administrator. I disagreed. Perhaps Modi was a good administrator. But then, Mussolini got the trains running on time. Hilter revived German industry. But so what? A mass murderer remains a mass murderer no matter what else he does.

He thought I was being too cussed and too harsh and thousands of readers agreed with him. But these remained dinner table disagreements. I was free to write what I wanted in the paper. And, indeed, I don't think I've ever written a sentence where 'Narendra Modi' is not accompanied by the phrase 'mass murderer'.

No one at the *HT* has tried to stop me and that is to K.K. Babu's eternal credit.

*

This autobiography has been in the works for many years. True to his methodical nature, K.K. Babu has diligently worked on it, section by section, setting himself a mental deadline for completing it—and, naturally, sticking perfectly to that deadline.

As this piece is being written—shortly before the book goes to press—nobody other than the editors at Penguin and I have read it. K.K. Babu's family has treated its publication with some trepidation. Their concern has been with K.K. Babu's legendary frankness.

I am actually quite pleased by the frankness. Too many autobiographies pull their punches or soften the truth with hypocrisy and doublespeak. And all too often, billionaires hire ghostwriters to devise polished voices for them.

One of the strengths of this book is that it is written in its author's own distinctive voice. It is not an image-making exercise and it has no subtext, no hidden agenda.

K.K. Babu has written the book for the best reason of them all: because he likes writing and because he enjoys telling stories.

The editors at Penguin wondered why there was so little about the business. Though this is not widely known, K.K. Babu inherited very little from his father on the grounds that as he had no sons, he had no one to leave it to. His two biggest successes, Zuari and the money-spinning Chambal, are entirely his own creations. When he took charge of the *Hindustan Times*, it made no money at all. Now, thanks to Shobhana's management skills, it has combined editorial excellence with massive profitability.

So, why is there so little on management techniques about the business of making money? Largely, I suspect, because business has never really been K.K. Birla's passion. He has inherited his father's entrepreneurial skill and so has found it easy to make his billions. But he is the only one of the Birlas to have inherited G.D. Birla's interest in public life and his deep commitment to the politics of India.

His real passions have to do with public life, with public personalities and with his conceptions of the public good. It is those passions that this book reflects.

And certainly, he has been a witness to history, retaining a ringside seat from which to watch India transform itself from a democratic experiment into a potential superpower.

Few people have known the makers of modern India so closely. Fewer still have been privy to their secrets, their hopes and their fears. The strength of this book lies in the anecdotes and in the stories that offer us an insider's view of life at the very top in India. It is a slice of history, written by a man who participated in the shaping of modern India and knew the principal players intimately. It is an invaluable guide to the history of the twentieth century and is quite indispensable for the serious student of modern Indian history.

Though Penguin's editors sought to impose some kind of chronological timeline on the narrative, this is not a traditional autobiography. When you read it, try and imagine that somebody is speaking out the words. See it less as a simple story and more as an after-dinner conversation with a well-connected, well-travelled and well-informed man who is sharing the stories of his life and times with you.

And the story of his life is often the story of India.

*

Why is this book being published now? K.K. Babu once told me that he would wait till his beloved daughter Shobhana got into Parliament—an ambition that probably meant much more to him than it did to her—before sending the manuscript to his publishers. He broke with family tradition to pass his companies on to his three daughters but Shobhana's nomination to the Rajya Sabha has been the one event that he feels was most like passing the torch on. The billions and the companies matter less to him than his passion for public life. And now that a third generation of Birlas has kept the tradition going, he feels that the book has found an appropriate ending.

But of course, he's not ready to retire yet. Possessed of the energy of a man forty years younger than he—renewed by a heart bypass operation that has left him even fitter and with a greater zest for life—he continues to take a benign interest in all his businesses, flying from Kolkata to Lucknow to Goa to Madhya Pradesh to Delhi to check on the health of his companies. He remains the single most painstaking reader of the *Hindustan Times*. Nothing misses his eagle eye—not one proofing error or even a tiny story that rival papers found room for but which the *HT* ignored. He will still call or fax me from whichever part of the world he is in to give me his opinion of my column or to compliment me on a food piece he has enjoyed.

But for several months of the year, he will abandon the heat of the Indian plains and escape. He will go to his house in Mussoorie and play bridge with old friends. He will take his wife shopping to the best stores in New York. He will walk by the shores of Lake Geneve. Or he will mark his copy of the *HT*, sitting on a bench in Hyde Park.

Over the last few years, I have met him often in London. He is entirely at home in that city. More surprisingly, he has managed to transform even the most upmarket corner of England into a great Birla House-on-the-Thames. At a three-star Michelin restaurant, I watched astonished as the chef recreated that familiar menu of soup, vegetable cutlet and four thick-cut French fries. And no matter where in Mayfair he goes, they always seem to know him.

Pandit Nehru used to joke about himself that perhaps he was the last Englishman to rule India. In much the same sort of way, K.K. Babu is the last Englishman to run a major industrial empire in India.

He stands for the old world, for the traditional courtesies, for the decency of a bygone era and for a very English punctuality and meticulousness.

But he also stands for a very Indian warmth, affection and deep friendship. And embedded deep within the two worlds of K.K. Birla is his passionate love for the country that made him.

New Delhi

June 2007

Vir Sanghvi

Advisory Editorial Director,

HT Media Limited

Preface

I was born on Monday, 11 November 1918, at Pilani in Rajasthan at 6.51 in the morning on the holy day of Gopashtami (Samvat Kartik Shukla 8, 1975). It happened to be a historic day too as the agreement of Armistice for the First World War was signed on that date.

When I grew up, along with business, I also took a lot of interest in politics. Father was deeply involved with the political developments in the country. As he was in close touch with all the top leaders of the country and very close to Bapu, the atmosphere in the family was deeply influenced by the struggle for freedom and the upsurge of national politics. I grew up in such an atmosphere. By the time I was only twenty-two years of age I had come to know most of the national leaders as also the leading political personalities of Bengal.

I was only thirteen when Pandit Motilal Nehru died in 1931. However, I got an opportunity of meeting him once in Kolkata when, during his visit to that city, he was invited by father to an afternoon tea. When Motilal-ji arrived at our residence Birla Park, father asked me to touch his feet as per our tradition which I did, receiving his blessings. I have had the rare privilege of having met all the members of the Nehru–Gandhi family starting from Motilal-ji, to Jawaharlal-ji, Kamala-ji, Indira-ji, Rajiv, Sonia-ji and Rahul. I do not think there are many people alive today who have had this distinction.

I am nearly ninety years old now. I can see how conditions have changed dramatically from those days—from the early 1920s to present-day India. There are not many people alive today who remember Mahatma-ji's march to Dandi, popularly known as 'Dandi Yatra', Gandhi's call for satyagraha in 1930, then his call to the British to Quit India in 1942, after which all the top leaders of the country were arrested from our house in Mumbai—Birla House—and subsequently how we were blessed with independence that came like soothing dew from heaven.

I remember when, to visit Pilani, my birthplace, one had to go to Sadulpur, a town in the then princely state of Bikaner and from there travel 24 miles on a 'rath' driven by bullocks which took about eight hours. I remember the time when a daily worker in a village in India earned only 25 paise a day and one in the city earned only Re 1 per day. I remember graduates could be hired for Rs 100 per month and the principal of a college was very happy if he received a salary of Rs 250 per month. I remember the time when wheat was sold at 13 seers to a rupee (one seer is equal to approximately 2.2 pounds) and cow milk at 25 paise a seer.

As a record of the dramatic changes that have taken place, I did want to write my autobiography, which covers my childhood to my years as a senior citizen, how I entered politics, my close association with Indira-ji and other leaders, my entry into Parliament and my membership for three successive terms in the Rajya Sabha ending on 9 April 2002. I am also happy my darling daughter Shobhana entered the Rajya Sabha as the President's nominee. To be nominated to the Rajya Sabha by the President is a rare distinction.

As a Congress (I) member of Parliament, I worked under Rajiv and Sonia-ji's directions for all of eighteen years and though I am no longer an MP, I am still a lifelong member of the Congress and a member of the All India Congress Committee.

Sonia-ji is a personality of remarkable ability. Without knowing anything about politics (she was dragged into it owing to drastic circumstances), she has done wonderfully well. Today she commands a unique position in the country as she is the binding force for all the Congress members. If the Congress has come out successful and formed the coalition UPA government, it is purely owing to the personality of Sonia-ji. With BJP's reputation having completely gone down, and with Atal-ji's advancing age and there being no clear leadership within the BJP, the Congress is the only party which can lead the country. I have no doubt that in the next general elections, the Congress will be re-elected with a clear majority under the leadership of Sonia-ji.

After having won the general elections held in 2004 and after the Congress was in a position to form a government, for Sonia-ji to have declined the prime ministership, was commendable indeed. Sonia-ji acted like a seasoned stateswoman.

These musings have prompted me to write this autobiography. I am very grateful to Smt Sonia Gandhi for having agreed to write the Foreword of this book. I have had the privilege of working as a member of Parliament for three consecutive terms spanning eighteen years as a member of the

Congress party, first under the leadership provided by the late Rajiv Gandhi and subsequently by Sonia-ji. At the time of my retirement from Parliament, Sonia-ji sent me a very charming letter stating inter alia:

'I would like to convey to you my deep appreciation of the great distinction with which you have served the Nation, Parliament and the Congress Party, during your long tenure as a Member of the Rajya Sabha.' Continuing, she said, 'You brought stature and honour to the institution of Parliament with your dignified and dedicated commitment to your responsibilities.' I can never repay the debt of gratitude for the kind words that Sonia-ji has written for me in her letter.

I am also grateful to Shri Vir Sanghvi for having agreed to write the Introduction to explain what the book is about.

I have known Vir for over thirty years now. He is a man of great character, very honest and sincere, and undoubtedly one of the finest writers of the English language. He is a man of vision and his analytical power is supreme. His style is excellent and his writing flows extremely well in whatever he contributes. All his articles are therefore read with keen interest. I have known Vir since he was in Kolkata working with the Ananda Bazar group much before he shifted to Delhi. Gradually the acquaintanceship with Vir went on ripening and today Vir has become like a member of the family to me. I also thank all my friends and acquaintances and my secretaries D.K. Neogi, Kamal Sen and Jyotsna Sud who have worked very hard in the preparation of my autobiography. I hope this work of mine will be received well by the public.

Krishna Kumar Birla

PART I

MY EARLY YEARS

A Banyan Tree Takes Root

Rajasthan, earlier called Rajputana, was made famous by the Rajputs, a valiant race claiming ancestry from the sun and moon gods and also a chivalrous people. The other group which made a mark in Rajasthan was the business community, popularly known as the Marwaris. Living in harsh conditions in Rajasthan, where water is found 120 feet below ground level and harvests are meagre, toiling hard to make the desert and the arid soil productive, the community became strong and sturdy.

The business community was confined to Rajasthan till the sixteenth century. As Akbar's Commander-in-chief Man Singh, raja of Amber, conquered and subjugated distant areas of the country, the business community went with him to regions outside its homeland. In course of time, it spread throughout the country. Wherever they went, members of the community went with small means but through business acumen and diligence earned good money and fame and founded business establishments away from the home province.

About 200 km from Jaipur, in what is popularly referred to as the Shekhawati region, is a village called Pilani. Perhaps its earlier name was Palelgarh. In a fight between the local Thakur and a Jat going by the name Pilania, the latter fought with great courage. To commemorate this feat of bravery, the name of Palelgarh was changed to Pilani. That is the popular legend about the origin of Pilani.

Pilani is the village to which our forefathers migrated from village Budholi—one branch of the family went to Nawalgarh and another came to Pilani. The Birla family belongs to the Vaishya caste and are Maheshwaris, a small community.

Our generation can be traced to our forefather Jaimal-ji who lived in the early eighteenth century. There is no record of how we got the surname Birla. The popular belief is that one of our forefathers was a man named

Behad Singh. The name in course of time got corrupted and became Beheda, then Behdla, next Bedla and finally Bidla or Birla. Even now our name is spelt in Hindi as Bidla; it is only in English that it is spelt as Birla.

Among the business community of north India there are three main groups—Agarwals, Oswals (who are Jains) and Maheshwaris. The Agarwals and Oswals are large groups; the Maheshwaris are much smaller in number but well knit. There is an interesting story about their origin.

During the eighth century, seventy-two Suryavanshi Kshatriya groups— Pratihars—of Rajasthan, decided to become Vaishyas. The legend goes that they became Vaishyas inspired by Lord Shiva. Mahesh being another name of Shiva, they named their new community Maheshwari. These seventy-two groups were the progenitors of the same number of lineages amongst the Maheshwaris.

A well-knit community, the Maheshwaris invariably do their best to organize various types of social services—schools, colleges, libraries, hospitals, dharmashalas and the like—which look after the welfare of all communities. For building these social service institutions, money was collected only from the Maheshwaris but once these institutions were established, they were for the good of all communities. The three largest concentrations of Maheshwaris are in Indore, Jaipur and Kolkata. In each of these places, there are more than twenty Maheshwari institutions rendering yeoman service to society.

Before I proceed further, I should like to give a brief background of the Birla family. The family tree of our ancestors may be traced to Jaimal, the great grandfather of Shobharam. Shobharam was the grandfather of my grandfather Raja Baldeodas. Thus, I am in the seventh generation after Jaimal. Not much is known about Jaimal. After his death, his son Bhudarmal, a businessman of repute, settled down in Pilani. His son Udairam was also a successful businessman. The eldest son of Udairam was Shobharam.

If we take each generation's lifespan to be about thirty years, Jaimal must have been born around 1710, shortly after the death of Aurangzeb and the dissolution of the Mughal Empire. Jaimal had six children. His son Bhudarmal, who is the direct ancestor of our branch of the family tree, had four children and his son Udairam had three sons. Thus, Shobharam had two other brothers.

Business was poor and the family wealth got depleted because of the large number of children that Jaimal, Bhudarmal and Udairam had. Shobharam's share of the patrimony, therefore, was small. He did not do well in business and had to seek employment. He had only one son, Shivnarayan, my great-grandfather.

Shivnarayan, unlike his father, was an enterprising man who was prepared to take risks, for he had confidence in himself. He did well in business. Shivnarayan had only one son—Baldeodas, my grandfather. Baldeodas was born in 1863. He grew up in Pilani. When he was nine years of age, his Yajnopavit (sacred thread) ceremony was performed at Pushkar with great fanfare. He got married at the age of twelve.

In those days, child marriage was prevalent throughout India. Twelve or thirteen years was regarded as the right age of marriage for boys, ten or eleven years for girls. For three or four years after the wedding, the girl would stay with her parents. After that the boy would go to his father-in-law's place for another ceremony called *muqlawa*. After this, the husband would return with his wife to his father's place.

A year or two after the wedding, Baldeodas went to Mumbai and started working with his father. They started a firm in 1879 called Shivnarayan Baldeodas. Baldeodas flourished in business. He was as good as his father in trading, if not better.

The principle of futures trading which Baldeodas adopted was to move with the market, never against it. Thus, in case the trend was bearish one should sell; if bullish one should buy. His motto was that in case the market was bearish one should also adopt the same attitude. 'Never swim against the tide' was the principle he followed, and this proved to be very beneficial. Baldeodas had four sons and three daughters. His sons developed their own separate identities as businessmen. All the sons were brilliant in their own ways. More about them later.

My grandmother lived mostly in Pilani, though from time to time she visited Mumbai. In any case, Baldeodas visited Pilani every three or four years. He conducted business even from Pilani but as there was no post and telegraph office nearby, telegraphic messages were flashed from Jhunjhunu through heliograph.

Baldeodas thought that since his father was already in Mumbai, there was no point his conducting business from there as well. So he took his father's permission to start his own business in Kolkata. Towards the end of the nineteenth century, Baldeodas went to Kolkata and commenced operating from there. Baldeodas prospered, making a name for himself through his acumen, straightforward business dealings and limpid honesty. He became friendly with the Chamaria family of Howrah. Baldeodas established his business centre, called *gaddi*, at Kaligodam and started a firm named Baldeodas Jugal Kishore. This gaddi still exists.

In course of time, Baldeodas started trading in other commodities also like silver and oilseeds. In course of time when his sons grew up, they too started businesses in Kolkata—except my uncle Rameshwar Das, who settled in Mumbai. Cleverest in forward trading was perhaps my uncle Jugalkishore.

Baldeodas was not only a man of character but also endowed with a strong sense of piety. The welfare of others was his passion. In 1899, there was an unprecedented famine in Rajasthan. Shivnarayan and Baldeodas started giving free food to all. There was another famine in 1905. To help the distressed, Shivnarayan arranged for a tank to be constructed at Pilani which has never run dry even during the severest drought. Even now, people say that the tank never dried up owing to the good deeds performed by the ancestors of the Birlas, meaning Shivnarayan and Baldeodas.

*

When Shobharam had gone to Ajmer in search of a job, he worked in a firm controlled by a family called Ganeriwal where he was a munim (accountant). I heard from my grandfather that Shobharam so impressed the Ganeriwals by his honesty and sincerity that they started treating him like a member of the family and the younger generation of the Ganeriwal family was, in fact, instructed to be guided by his advice. His annual salary was Rs 300 but he was, in effect, a partner and got a share of the profit. Shobharam died in 1859.

His son my great-grandfather Shivnarayan, was a lad of sixteen at that time. The head of the Ganeriwal family suggested to Shivnarayan that he take the place of his father, who had died quite young. Shivnarayan, however, was of a different mettle. He told the Seths that he would prefer to do his own independent business. To discourage him from this resolve, the Ganeriwals said that Shobharam owed a lot of money to the Ganeriwal family. Shivnarayan had enormous self-confidence. He not only resisted all the persuasions of the Ganeriwal family to join their firm but declared that if his father owed money to the family, he would pay back every pie with interest. He requested the Ganeriwals to provide him with a statement showing the amount his father owed them. The Ganeriwal Seths did this, sure that the money Shobharam owed could never be repaid and Shivnarayan would one day have to return to Ajmer and accept service or partnership with them in order to repay his father's debts. Shivnarayan took the statement, came back to Pilani, and carefully kept it in the safe. He took some money from his mother in Pilani and, after offering prayers at various temples, left for Mumbai.

Going to Mumbai in those days was full of hazards. One had to travel on camelback for days together. There was danger of getting waylaid by dacoits. The practice was to travel during the daytime on camels and to spend the night at a dharmashala. A well-built camel could trot up to sixty miles a day. To journey such a distance, not only did the camel have to be robust but the rider too had to be made of sturdy stuff.

Shivnarayan went to Mumbai in 1860 and commenced business. The Birla family regards 1860 as the year when the business house was established. That is why the Birla centenary was celebrated in 1960.

Great-grandfather Shivnarayan (about 1905)

Shivnarayan journeyed on camelback to Khandwa in Maharashtra and then took the train to Mumbai. The business community in those days consisted mostly of Gujaratis, Bhatias, Parsis and, of course, the British. The Rajasthanis had just started going to Mumbai, and those who were already established there took it upon themselves to arrange for the accommodation of others of the community so that food and lodging were conveniently available.

Shivnarayan, after reaching Mumbai, plunged into business. In those days, much trading and speculation used to be done in opium. China was a large purchaser of opium, India was an exporter. Shivnarayan started trading in opium and later in cotton too. There was a firm called Cheniram Jesraj which had a gaddi in Mumbai. Shivnarayan commenced his business from a corner of this office. Within a short period, Shivnarayan earned good profits. By this time, Ahmedabad too had been connected to Mumbai with a rail link. After a few years in Mumbai, Shivnarayan returned to Pilani via Ahmedabad. From here onwards one had to resort to camelback—that is, travel by road.

In Pilani, Shivnarayan constructed a fine haveli. He also constructed a Shiva temple and had a well dug. The water of the well was delicious. News circulated through the village that Shivnarayan had earned his money by hard work and honest means and the sweet water of the well was the reward for his probity. By now Shivnarayan had earned sufficient money, so he went to Ajmer, checked the account of his father with the Ganeriwals, and repaid the entire amount with interest. He did not raise any question about the accuracy of the amount; whatever figure the Ganeriwals had jotted in their statement as due, Shivnarayan paid. Having made the payment, he asked the Ganeriwals to give him a receipt of full and final settlement of all the dues. This the Ganeriwals did. Shivnarayan returned to Pilani and kept this paper very carefully in his safe.

Life has its ups and downs. The Ganeriwals, who were once a flourishing family, fell into desperate straits after a few years. They lost money heavily and all their businesses had to be wound up.

When a man falls into misfortune he endeavours to get money by any means, fair or foul. Many years had elapsed since Shivnarayan had squared up the account of the Ganeriwals. The Ganeriwals probably thought that after such a long lapse of time it was very unlikely that Shivnarayan would still have the receipt which they had given him. Unannounced, they suddenly turned up in Pilani, having heard by that time that Shivnarayan was doing well financially. Shivnarayan was surprised but extended proper hospitality to them. The Ganeriwals said that they had still to receive some money against Shobharam's dues. Shivnarayan was astonished. He showed the Ganeriwal family the receipt they had given him and enquired how they could make such a claim since it clearly proved they had received full payment. Shivnarayan realized that the

Ganeriwal family was in difficulties. He told them that the proper course would have been to say openly that they were in financial trouble. He could then have helped the family, owing to his old connections with it. The attitude and method adopted by them were, to say the least, reprehensible. Nonetheless, Shivnarayan gave the crestfallen Ganeriwals a sum sufficient to help them tide over their predicament. In course of time, during the 1930s, some members of the Ganeriwal family sought service under father and worked in one of our textile units over a considerable period.

Shivnarayan's fame spread to the entire neighbourhood. Pilani, which was earlier called 'Pilani of the Banyan Tree' because there was a banyan tree of enormous size there, was now called Pilani of the Birlas. During the days of Shivnarayan, Pilani was a village of not more than 1,500 inhabitants. Shivnarayan travelled to many places on pilgrimage. He gradually retired from business.

Shivnarayan had only one son, my grandfather Baldeodas, and a daughter Jhimi, who married into a Churu family. Baldeodas had four sons—Jugalkishore, Rameshwar Das, Ghanshyam Das and Braj Mohan.

By the time my father Ghanshyam Das was six years old, Shivnarayan was a man of considerable financial means. He thought it proper to start a school for the education of his grandsons—Rameshwar Das and Ghanshyam Das—where other children of the village could also study. Thus a pathshala (school) was established in 1901. This pathshala, in course of time, evolved into the Birla Education Trust and Birla Institute of Technology and Science—BITS.

It is surmised that Shivnarayan developed tuberculosis in his last days. It was the year 1909. His grandson Rameshwar Das was with him at Pilani, his son Baldeodas in Kolkata. Rameshwar Das wrote to Baldeodas informing him about Shivnarayan's failing health. Shivnarayan advised Baldeodas not to return to Pilani. Baldeodas was in Kolkata in connection with the wedding of his daughter—my aunt Jaydevi. Shivnarayan wrote to Baldeodas in a philosophical vein, saying that the body is after all mortal, and it would not be right to return in haste. He asked Baldeodas to return only after all the work had been completed. He died at the age of seventy-two.

Shivnarayan was a man of strong will and determination. He was thrown into the vortex of the wide world at the tender age of sixteen. He ignored the offer of the Ganeriwal Seths, where Shobharam was working, to take the position of his father. Without worrying about the numerous risks involved, he embarked on the career of a businessman and trader and made a success of it. He was a pious man and did his utmost to organize public welfare activities. As stated earlier, he constructed a temple, dug a well, constructed a tank and established a pathshala. That apart, any needy person approaching him never returned empty-handed.

In those days, it was customary in our family to give a male child a spartan upbringing. The idea was to initiate a son into a hard and disciplined life to strengthen him to take life's pitfalls in his stride. This was the regimen adopted by Shivnarayan for Baldeodas and later by Baldeodas for his sons. Shivnarayan always adopted a very stern and taciturn manner towards Baldeodas. Even when Baldeodas grew to full manhood, Shivnarayan invariably spoke to him with perceptible severity, though inwardly he loved his son deeply. His favourite, however, was my uncle Jugalkishore. He never denied any wish of young Jugalkishore. In his later days, Shivnarayan gradually gave up business and led a retired life till his death in 1909. He was the founder of the House of Birlas.

2

Varanasi: The Golden Years

After Shivnarayan's death, my grandfather Baldeodas performed the *shradh* ceremony as a dutiful son. He also distributed foodgrain to thousands of needy people. He went to Varanasi to perform the shradh for the peace of his father's departed soul; here a reputed astrologer told him that he would live no more than fifty-five years.

My grandfather, after a few years, decided that the best course for him was to shift to Varanasi. He made Varanasi his headquarters in 1916 and was to die in 1956 when he was ninety-three years old. He lived there for forty years.

Notwithstanding the fact that he took the forecast of the astrologer seriously, grandfather was a very pragmatic person. He knew that his children were all grown up and fully established. He was also aware that his sons had made a name for themselves.

Jugalkishore, Ghanshyam Das and Braj Mohan were living in Kolkata, while Rameshwar Das resided in Mumbai. All the sons were well settled and had achieved name and fame. His daughters were all married. Grandfather, therefore, decided that irrespective of what the astrologer had predicted, he might as well retire from active life. The prophecy of the astrologer was not the only reason for his shifting to Varanasi; he thought that since his children had grown up and were able to look after their businesses, he should leave them alone to live their lives separately. Grandfather was a man of wisdom. Had the astrologer's forecast been the only factor influencing his decision to withdraw from business, he would have returned to Kolkata after the forecast proved to be wrong. But Baldeodas was a man who wanted his sons to flourish independently and the best way to do that was for him to live in a place away from his sons' headquarters. So he shifted to Varanasi. But often, he would leave the holy city to attend to family functions. When my elder brother Lakshmi Niwas got married at Kishengarh and my cousin Gajanan got married at

Jabalpur, grandfather went to both places to attend the weddings.

At Kashi (the other name for Varanasi), a plot of land was acquired on the bank of the Ganga and two buildings were constructed at Lalghat on either side of the lane. The buildings were joined by an overbridge. Lalghat was thoroughly repaired and turned into an enchanting ghat.

In 1918, the title of Rai Bahadur was conferred on him. Lord Chelmsford was then the viceroy of India. Subsequently, the title of Raja was also conferred on him. He was, therefore, called Raja Saheb by everyone. That apart, Maharaja Madhav Singh, the ruler of Jaipur, invited him to Jaipur and conferred great honours on grandfather.

For the first few years after Baldeodas settled down in Varanasi, he took part in important family functions. He participated in the wedding of my elder brother Lakshmi Niwas which was celebrated at Kishengarh in 1927. Lakshmi Niwas's father-in-law was the Diwan of Kishengarh state, and a right royal reception was accorded to our family. The wedding party was headed by my grandfather. Next year he went to Jabalpur to participate in the wedding of another grandson, my cousin Gajanan. That wedding was in the famous Malpani family of Jaipur who played a very important role in the political and social life of Madhya Pradesh. In those days, the Malpanis were one of the richest Rajasthani families. I still have a recollection of the innumerable elephants and chariots with which the *baraat* was received in Jabalpur and taken in a procession to the house where it was accommodated.

As Baldeodas advanced in age, he stopped attending all family functions and ceremonies. He preferred to remain exclusively in Varanasi except during summer when the city sweltered in the heat owing to its ghats made of stone. Then he would sometimes shift to Haridwar for the two summer months. In his later years, he made only one trip outside these two places and that was to Uttarkashi sometime in the early 1940s. He was in Haridwar at that time; from there he and grandmother went to Mussoorie. After spending a couple of days at Mussoorie they went to Uttarkashi, reaching there on the fourth day. I and my cousins, Madhav Prasad and Ganga Prasad, accompanied them.

In the last few years of his life he stopped going even to Haridwar and remained happily confined to Varanasi only.

His day started very early in the morning at 4 o'clock, in fact even earlier than that. He would go to the Ganga for a purifying dip in that sacred river.

The water of the Ganga was polluted even in those days, much as it is now. As I said earlier, Baldeodas was a very practical man. He wanted to have his bath in clean uncontaminated water. So he purchased a boat and had a special platform constructed, with a ladder of six or seven steps that could be attached to the boat. The boat would be rowed by two boatmen and taken to midstream where the platform would be attached to the boat so as to form a small makeshift ghat. This platform, with steps, had railings and wire netting on all sides so that there was no danger of anyone falling into the Ganga. From this platform, grandfather would take his bath in the holy river.

After the bath he would come back, perform his puja and have something to eat. He took his meal at 11 a.m—a simple affair of chapatis and vegetable curries.

In the later years, on the advice of father, he even gave up chapati

Grandfather Raja Baldeodas Birla in the early 1930s

and curry and would take only fruits, dates and milk. After finishing his meal he would lie down on a soft mattress or sofa for a short nap. Anyone wanting to meet him could do so after he finished his breakfast or around noon, after he woke up from his siesta.

In the morning, after breakfast, his assistant would read out all the important news from the newspaper *Aaj* of Varanasi, which was and still is a fine paper. It is remarkable that in spite of his advancing age grandfather kept abreast of whatever was happening in the world. Exactly at 1.45 p.m., he would leave the house for our garden or *bagicha*, as it was called. Grandfather never carried a watch. If he did so in his younger days, I am not aware of that fact. In Varanasi, at least, he did not keep a watch, but he did give a pocket watch to the servant. He had two faithful retainers—Mangu and his nephew Bhana. Even when it was fiercely hot or heavily raining, grandfather would stick to his routine. So punctual was he that people jokingly remarked that they could set their watches on the basis of his movements during different parts of the day.

Grandfather used to visit the garden in a car. He had two cars at Varanasi—one for the members of the family who would visit him, the other for himself. During World War II, when petrol was in short supply, so gracious and considerate was he towards other members of the family that he would opt for a horse-drawn carriage and leave the car for use by the members of the family. In the garden, grandfather would stroll for about forty-five minutes. This practice he kept up right through his life till even two days before his death. He would always say that the more you expose the body to physical exertion the greater will be its resilience to keep you in good health. If, on the contrary, you try to lead a life of comfort and indolence the body will not respond to your needs and will not remain healthy.

In the later years, once he fell down and fractured a bone of one leg. This made him lame in that leg. All the same, he continued his constitutional stroll with the support of a servant. He was a keen enthusiast of keeping the body fit. (If I have acquired this quality, I have inherited it from my grandfather.)

After a walk, grandfather would bathe in the garden. There was no bathroom in the garden. He would sit down in the open on a slightly raised plank of wood—*patta*, as it is called in Hindi. After the bath he would spend an hour in the company of pundits. Such a stickler was he for punctuality that the pundits knew exactly when they should reach the garden. He participated in religious discourses with the pundits. He would present to them his interpretation of the Bhagavad Gita. He would keep the Gita open before him, select a shloka and offer his comments. What grandfather said was invariably so full of depth that the pundits could not but shower praise on him. He would expound on the atma, paramatma, the philosophy of karma yoga and allied spiritual matters. After spending an hour or so with the pundits, he would return home. Finishing his meal, he would lie down on the overhead bridge connecting our two houses during the summer months, and in his mattress during the winter months. This was grandfather's daily routine, which he meticulously followed. Even if on some days he was not all that well, he stuck to his routine.

Grandfather was a firm believer in God. He was not particular about being a devotee of Vishnu or Shiva, Rama or Krishna. He believed in God, and God to him was all in all. He called God Narayana.

Grandfather was so pragmatic that he appeared to be ultra-modern in outlook. Once there was a wedding in the family. At this time, my phoopha-ji (father's sister's husband) Narsinghdas was critically ill. It was a matter of life and death. My father and uncle were deeply perturbed. Should they postpone the wedding? But all the ceremonies prior to the actual wedding had already been performed and only the wedding ritual remained to be completed. Father always consulted grandfather in all matters where he had any doubts about anything, and so telephoned him. Father explained that on the one hand the wedding of his grandson Sudarshan was about to be solemnized, on the other his own brother-in-law—grandfather's son-in-law—was at death's door. What was the right thing to do? Grandfather, who had a solution for every problem, advised father to proceed with the wedding, adding that if the worst happened to Narsinghdas, grandfather should not be informed about it till the wedding was over.

What excellent practical advice! Narsinghdas died, as was feared, before the wedding could be solemnized, but as directed by grandfather, father informed him about his brother-in-law's death only after the wedding was over.

Grandfather was a man of dogged determination. In his younger days he used to smoke. He came from a village and in villages people rarely smoke cigarettes. They smoke bidis, the chillum or the hookah. Grandfather liked to smoke the chillum. Perhaps he smoked bidis too. One day, father told him that smoking was a bad habit. Grandfather had affection for all his children but the greatest faith he had was in father. He would never discard any advice that father gave. When father told him one day that smoking was harmful, grandfather then and there decided to stop smoking. It is well known that those who smoke cannot give it up easily. But as far as grandfather was concerned, the deed was as good as done the instant he made up his mind. It is quite possible that for the first few days he felt the urge to take a few puffs at the chillum. But he was a man of great mental strength and indomitable will. And having given up smoking, he never looked back.

He was dedicated to leading a disciplined life. He kept to his daily routine of life right until two days prior to his demise. He died in 1956. All his sons—father and my uncles—had reached Varanasi in time. I was in Kolkata at that time and along with a large number of our friends rushed to Varanasi. I could not join the funeral procession but I was able to reach Manikarnika Ghat in time where the last rites were performed.

Grandfather's piety inspired him to establish many institutions in Varanasi for the benefit of the public which will keep his name and fame alive.

Reproduced below is a copy of a letter from my grandfather. The letter is dated *Chaitra Krishna 9, 2002* or some time in 1945. In those days the practice was to send a letter on papers the width of which used to be only about four-and-a-half inches and the length thirteen to fourteen

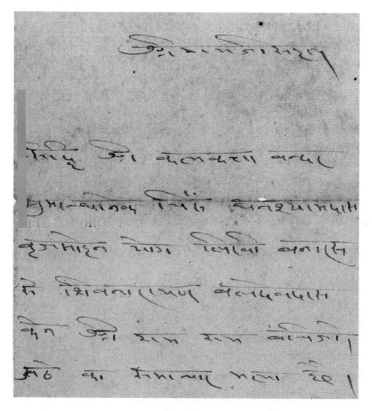

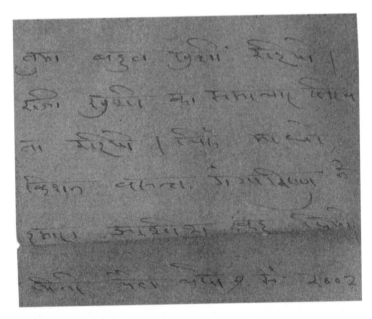

inches. Grandfather dictated this letter and one Kamla Prasad Munshi, a trusted man of grandfather, who was like a head clerk, took down the dictation.

This chapter on my grandparents will not be complete without something about my grandmother, Yogeshwari Devi. Her daily life was also routine-bound. She would get up around 5 a.m. By that time, grandfather had finished his bath in the Ganga. She would go in the boat used by my grandfather to midstream to have a dip in the holy river.

Grandmother had her morning meal at 11 a.m. and dinner around 7 p.m . In between, she took a few snacks.

Grandfather gave the same advice to grandmother as he gave us, that is, to keep the body fit and healthy. For healthy thoughts, for peace and tranquillity of mind, a healthy body is essential. His regimen to keep fit was to walk every day in the garden. Grandmother devotedly walked every day also. She did not go to the garden, preferring to walk in the veranda of our house. There was no fixed time for grandmother's walk. Whenever she got an opportunity to walk, she did so. Around 3 p.m., she would listen to religious stories and legends from the Puranas or Ramayana and other religious books. There were two Ayurvedic vaidyas with grandfather; they had been deputed by father to look after him. One was called Harideo. He hailed from Pilani and his family had produced many vaidyas. The other was Bansidhar Joshi who had passed an examination of the Ayurvedic medical system from Banaras Hindu University. Both were capable vaidyas. Harideo, however, was brusque in his speech. Grandmother did not like him. Bansidhar-ji, on the other hand, was a polished person and served grandmother devotedly. He would recite from the religious books to which grandmother would listen, making queries from time to time.

Both grandfather and grandmother were charitable by nature. They always gave alms to the poor and gur to the cows. That apart, in the morning, grandmother would ask the servants to feed crows and kites. Badas of dal which used to be made for feeding them would be thrown to the crows and kites in the morning. So accustomed did the crows and kites become to this sumptuous feed that they would turn up in flocks for the feast. A servant would throw the badas up in the air and the crows and the kites would intercept them in the air itself.

During the rainy season, my grandparents would distribute umbrellas to the poor and during the winter, shawls. On many occasions, grandfather would personally select people to whom shawls were to be given. There would be a huge gathering of the poor and the needy outside our house. Grandfather stood on the veranda and pointed out to the servants standing below the deserving needy to whom he felt such shawls or chaddars were to be given.

Another person who served grandmother devotedly and selflessly was a trader from our village Pilani named Hariram Khaitan. Grandfather was very fond of him. He visited grandmother three or four times a week and would spend two three hours with her. His business was in Benarasi sarees. Whenever grandmother wanted to purchase Benarasi sarees she would do so only from him.

Grandfather was sanyas by temperament. If there was any dirt anywhere he would not take notice of it. Even if he noticed it he would not speak to anyone about it. Nothing, however, escaped grandmother's notice—she had very keen eyes. She had a sharp tongue too. She would immediately rebuke any servant who erred. But in her heart of hearts she was very gentle and if anyone was in difficulty, she would always try to help him. Even though she was greatly devoted to grandfather, she had a personality of her own. Maaji, as she was called, was feared, respected and loved by all the employees and all our acquaintances.

After grandfather's death, my youngest uncle BM was keen that grandmother should spend the rest of her days with him in his Kolkata house. Grandmother did come to Kolkata after grandfather's death and stayed there for some time. But her heart was in Varanasi. She said that it would be very unfortunate if, after having lived for so many years in Varanasi and after having taken *Kashivas* she were to die away from Kashi. Considering her determination, the entire family came round to her views and agreed with grandmother that she should go back to her beloved city. Father and uncle instructed the members of the family that someone should always remain with grandmother to look after her.

Grandmother was a distinct personality all her own. She died at the ripe old age of 100. After the death of both, the servants and the people of Varanasi remembered grandmother as much as they remembered grandfather. Her individuality and identity were such that she endeared herself to one and all.

There was a break in the monotony of grandfather's daily routine since he would go to our garden at 1.45 p.m. and return at 6 p.m., but as far as grandmother was concerned she was confined all the time to her bedroom and to the veranda where she took a stroll. Grandmother had shifted to Varanasi in the year 1916, along with grandfather and left for her heavenly abode in 1963. Varanasi was her home for forty-seven years. She never left the house except when, in the morning, she went to the Ganga to have a dip in the holy river. Barring the occasions when grandfather or grandmother would go out of Varanasi in the early years of their life, she spent her entire life in that one room and the veranda. It was a remarkable sacrifice. How easy it is to get bored and tired of spending all one's time in one room! But grandmother, devoted as she was to grandfather, passed her time there without a murmur or any protest whatsoever. She considered grandfather's companionship as sufficient compensation for the astonishing sacrifice.

I was very fond of Varanasi. It was so peaceful when grandfather and grandmother lived there, it had an atmosphere of complete serenity and tranquillity. I would visit Varanasi to be with my grandparents once every three months. I would go in the morning and have a dip in the Ganga. I was a good swimmer and so would cross the Ganga and re-cross it. Then I would go to grandfather around 10.30 in the morning. At 11 a.m., when grandmother had her meal, I would eat with her. After the meal I too would retire and attend to correspondence. Around 12.30 or 12.45 p.m., I would again go to grandfather and spend about an hour with him. After grandfather left for the garden, I would spend an hour or an hour and a half with grandmother. I too would listen to religious *katha*s which Vaidya Bansidhar-ji would recite or just discuss general matters with grandmother.

Grandfather had appointed an excellent doctor from the city to visit

Grandparents Raja Baldeodas and Rani Birla in the 1950s

grandmother every day. Dr Ram Kishore was deeply dedicated to grandmother. A fine doctor and an equally fine person. Grandmother liked him. Dr Ram Kishore would spend an hour with her. The actual physical examination did not take him more than five minutes. That over, he would sit with grandmother and chat with her.

Around 4 p.m., I would go back to my room, complete the correspondence, leave in the car at 4.30 p.m., and get down at some place or other for a walk. I, along with Vaidya Bansidhar-ji, would sometimes go to our garden, or the Banaras Hindu University, or Sarnath, or even at times the Cantonment area in Varanasi. I would walk for 45–50 minutes. On the way to these places, I would chew a few *maghai paans* for which Varanasi is famous. Returning by 7 p.m. and finishing puja, I would have dinner at which Vaidya Bansidhar-ji would join me. I would then spend another hour or an hour and a half with grandfather. This was my daily routine—a very relaxed and uneventful routine indeed.

Whenever I departed from Varanasi, grandfather, a man of strong will, gave us leave to go without any display of emotion. Grandmother, however, loving lady that she was, would always try to persuade me to prolong my stay and defer my departure. Only after I explained to her that I had pressing business to attend to, would she very reluctantly permit me to go. Before departure, she would apply a *roli* with rice on my head. We were expected to have our caps on. To keep a cap on at the time of departure from one's house was considered auspicious.

Grandfather was a philosopher and had a very rational outlook. But grandmother was keen that traditions were respected. Departure from Varanasi had to be on an auspicious day. If we were going west, we had to leave on Monday, Wednesday or Saturday; if east, on a Tuesday, Friday or Sunday. If for any reason it was difficult to follow this ancient custom, an alternative arrangement was made. I have no doubt the practice of leaving home on certain days for going north, south, east and west has a historical background.

In fact, right till the time when Lord William Bentinck eradicated thuggee from this country, the roads were not safe. There was always the danger of highway robbery, theft and the like. Besides, when people travelled on foot or by horses or carts, the roads would sometimes cut through dense forests inhabited by wild animals. Considering the dangers and risks involved, the elders, in their wisdom, must have evolved this convention so that, for the sake of safety, people, instead of travelling in small parties, went in a convoy. I think that is how the system of travelling in certain directions on certain days came into vogue. Be that as it may, sometimes owing to the exigencies of work we had to leave on a day which was not regarded auspicious to travel in a particular direction. There was a simple solution in the Rajasthani communities to this difficulty. If I were required to travel in some direction on a day which was not auspicious for going in that direction, the practice was that on an earlier day which happened to be auspicious for going in that direction, a coconut wrapped in a towel would be placed at a specially selected spot between our house and the railway station or the airport. This meant that symbolically I had departed on the previous day. Next day, I had to pick up the coconut on my way out. The whole exercise was called the *prasthana*. Our ancestors were really sagacious and practical people.

Life even now in Varanasi is peaceful. In those days it was much more so. A very noticeable spirit of fraternity prevailed amongst the people who lived in a mohalla. There was no ego amongst them. We lived in Mohalla Lalghat, and we were always accessible to anyone of that mohalla. Varanasi has always been a centre of very refined culture. There were a large number of Sanskrit pathshalas in Varanasi, mostly run by people of the business community of Varanasi and also of other parts of the country. The ambition of old people was to spend their last days in Varanasi. It was said that Bhagwan Shankar gave *mukti* to people who died there. The life of Varanasi was in its galis (lanes). To board a car, one had to come out to the main road from a gali.

From our house in Varanasi, we had to walk seven or eight minutes before we could get to the car. The elder servants in Varanasi addressed us as *bhaiya* or *bhaiya-ji*—an address that combined intimacy and deference. That was the culture of Varanasi city where cordiality and peace ruled. Enjoying the company of my grandparents and pandits, taking a bath in the Ganga and visiting places of interest near Varanasi constituted the most relaxed and lovable days of my life in that city, even though I could spend only five days or so on each visit. Visiting Varanasi four times a year meant twenty days spent annually at Varanasi. The holiness of Varanasi, India's sacred city, soothed the heart. Even the business community took life easy. Habitually, members of the community too would take a dip in the Ganga every morning. They went for outings in the evening, *sair* as they called it, and spent some time in *akhara*s engaged in wrestling or performing on the bank of the Ganga our ancient exercises of *dand* and *baithak*. In their social intercourse, they were conspicuously polite to each other.

Apart from saree, Varanasi was renowned for its maghai paans (betel leaf). These paans are not grown in Varanasi. They come from Magadh in Bihar. In Varanasi, almost everyone chewed paan. Shopkeepers sold paan of various types. When I used to visit Varanasi, the price of the paan started from four paisa, and a paan with all types of masalas could cost up to Rs 2. People would pop the paan in their mouth and not chew it for an hour or so. That was the Varanasi way to go about relishing a paan.

Another trade was to make gold and silver leaves. This work was also done in various lanes of Varanasi. In our own lane, too, gold leaves were prepared. Skilled artisans would beat the gold till it became wafer-thin. Preparing these leaves was quite an art.

One always saw cows roaming about in the lanes of Varanasi. The owner of the cow would milk the cow in the morning and, in the evening, give it some fodder. During the day he would leave the cows free in the lanes to eat whatever came their way. In the evening again he would tie up the cow in his house. Apart from the cows, sometimes there were bulls also moving about everywhere. One had to be careful of the oxen roaming the streets and lanes of Varanasi like maverick cattle.

Close to Varanasi is Ramnagar, a native state as it was called in those days. The Maharaja of Ramnagar, also called Kashi Naresh, was held in very high esteem in Varanasi. Ramnagar was famous for its Ram Leela. The Ram Leela was performed in Varanasi in every mohalla. Sometimes we also went and watched the performance. The best Ram Leela, however, was held in Ramnagar under the patronage of the Maharaja.

When I visited Varanasi as a young boy along with my tutor Pandit Udit Mishra, I would call on the famous people of Varanasi. I remember having met Dr Bhagwan Das who was a great scholar and philosopher. I met, sometimes along with Pandit-ji, Pandit Ayodhya Singh Upadhyay 'Hari Oudh'. He was regarded one of the best poets of his time and distinguished himself by writing *Priya Pravas*.

Driving in Varanasi was always a problem. I do not know how our driver, a man called Chhedi, did it. While Delhi was famous for its tonga (horse-drawn carriage), Varanasi was for its ekka. This was a smaller vehicle compared to the tonga. Only a couple of people could sit comfortably in an ekka unlike the tonga which could accommodate five or six. Varanasi had its own unique culture.

The duration of my stays was short, but I always looked forward to such visits to Varanasi. Nothing could be more conducive to the peace and happiness of my mind than receiving the blessings of grandfather and grandmother. Visits to the temples of Varanasi, the garden, and a dip in the Ganga gave me mental peace. Far away from the din and bustle and hubbub of the madding crowds of cities like Kolkata and Delhi, the serene atmosphere of Varanasi acted like balm on my mind.

3

Father: A Great Person

It is always difficult for a son to write objectively about his father. It is even more difficult when one is blessed, as I was, with a father who became a legend in his lifetime. A true-to-life depiction of the legend might appear exaggerated to the uninitiated; on the other hand, if I attempt to modestly tone down the various superlative qualities he possessed, I will suffer twinges of conscience for having played down the endearing traits and achievements of a great and noble person.

Ghanshyam Das Birla was the embodiment of honesty, courage, equanimity, justice, nobility and wisdom. Above all, he was a karmayogi who believed in purity of thought and action, who believed the means to be as important as the end.

He started his own business—trading in commodities (both ready and future)—like my great-grandfather Shivnarayan and my grandfather Baldeodas. He discovered that it was a highly speculative and hazardous enterprise. So, after consulting both my grandfathers, he commenced business as a broker. Such was his personal acumen and charm that he made an immediate impact. He earned a fabulous income in the very first month. My grandfather was delighted. In those days, most brokers were semi-literate, with no idea about the general conditions of the economy. They could not express themselves properly in English or Hindi. Father, on the other hand, even at that young age, was fast shaping up as an intellectual. He soon won the respect of the business community, both Indian and foreign. Being a man of vision with a sharp mind, he saw that the growth and prosperity of the country depended upon industrialization. He was determined to start industries in India.

At the young age of twenty-five, in 1918 (the year I was born), father entered industry. It was entirely due to the lead given by father that, in course of time, our house became one of the two leading business houses in the country and made India prosperous. What was more satisfying to father was his unremitting endeavour to encourage others to start enterprises. He believed this alone could bring prosperity to the country. This was his greatness.

He was also a fine orator. He could speak well both in English and Hindi. He was constantly required to speak at public and social functions, at the general meetings of the Federation of Indian Chambers of Commerce and Industry (FICCI) and other gatherings of businessmen. He was also an excellent conversationalist and those who came in touch with him felt they were in the presence of a great man.

Father was also a superb writer. He contributed several articles in English and wrote a number of books in Hindi. Among his books, *Bikare Bichar Ki Bharoti* makes interesting reading. His *Krishnam Vande Jagat Gurum* was acclaimed by the Hindi literary world as a masterpiece.

Success in business was only one of the offshoots of father's vision and idealism. What he cherished most in life were higher values. At a very young age, he made a deep study of the Bhagavad Gita and followed the philosophy of karmayoga. Father also devoted himself to the study of the Upanishads, Valmiki's Ramayana and admired Tulsidas's Ramcharit Manas. Whenever he had an occasion to speak, be it a public address or a private conversation, he quoted extensively from these great epics and scriptures. But the message of the Gita formed the core of his life. He discovered that the Gita epitomized the philosophy of the Upanishads and Vedic scriptures. He could find answers to all human problems in the Gita.

Father attached great importance to values in life such as honesty, sincerity, and truth. I remember an incident when I was studying in Hare School, Kolkata. Drawing was one of the subjects in Class VIII and father, who had a great liking for the fine arts, engaged a special tutor for me and my cousin for private coaching.

One day, the school drawing teacher gave us some homework. We finished our task and showed it to our private tutor, who touched it up extensively. For all practical purposes, it became the tutor's drawing rather than ours. When we showed our homework to the drawing teacher at school, he was pleasantly surprised at the excellent work. He praised me and my cousin in the presence of the entire class, much to the envy of the other boys.

At home, we joyfully told father how our work had been extolled in school. To impress on father how clever we were, we proudly gave out the secret of our achievement. Father was very distressed. He said what we had done amounted to cheating; he instructed us to go and confess the truth to the headmaster. Trembling with fear, we confessed everything. The headmaster not only condoned our fault but was also full of praise for father. He had not come across any case where the parent of a student had compelled his son to make a clean breast of an act of dishonesty like this and said that only a truly great man could have done it.

One book—the Gita—and one person—Gandhi-ji—influenced father's life to an extraordinary degree. There was another strong influence in his life: my mother. She was only twenty-six when she died of tuberculosis in 1926. Mother was a lady of remarkably noble disposition. She was totally devoted to father and remained a source of strength to him until the last.

Father came in touch with Gandhi-ji for the first time in 1916 when he was only twenty-two. Gandhi-ji was visiting Kolkata after having acquired an enormous reputation for his new political philosophy of non-violent non-cooperation. At their very first meeting, Gandhi-ji had a tremendous impact on father for his limpid honesty, child-like simplicity, and radiant moral sublimity. Gandhi-ji too was greatly struck by his young admirer. A shrewd judge of men, he immediately discovered that father was no ordinary person. He saw in him a man of rare qualities and rectitude in whom he could freely confide his deepest thoughts. This, in fact, he did.

Before long, father's acquaintance with Gandhi-ji developed into a deep bond such as exists between father and son. There were no barriers of formality between the two. Each spoke to the other frankly and father felt completely at ease in Gandhi-ji's presence. He would constantly put questions to him and forcefully argue his point; he would accept what Gandhi-ji said only after he was fully convinced. Many a time Gandhi-ji changed his views under the influence of father's opinions. That is why as early as 1924, Gandhi-ji wrote to father that he regarded him as one of his mentors.

Father's correspondence with Gandhi-ji started in 1916. Mahatma-ji's earliest communication to father is dated 7 February 1924. Gandhi-ji would take assistance from father whenever funds were needed. On 7 August 1925, Gandhi-ji wrote to father: 'I had praised your action in contributing Rs 1,00,000/- to the Deshbandhu Memorial Fund....'

Mahatma-ji was highly impressed by father's nobility and generosity. On 16 March 1927 he wrote: 'I have great faith in the goodness of yourself and all your brothers. Rich people like you can be easily counted on one's fingers—you are so gentle, so humble. I want these two virtues to multiply manifold in your case in order to use them for the good of the country.'

In an interesting letter addressed to Mahadev Desai, Mahatma-ji's secretary concerning a donation of Rs 75,000, father wrote on 10 January 1928: 'I leave the matter entirely at the discretion of Mahatma-ji. If he is not very much pressed for money I would suggest that preference should be given to such schemes which may accelerate the speed of attaining Swaraj'.

Gandhi-ji's correspondence with father was like that of a father to a son. He wrote about his own health and would constantly advise father on health matters. Often these expounded into philosophical thoughts. In his letter of 31 May 1927, he wrote:

I do take as much care of my health as I deem necessary for its preservation. Malaviya-ji does not do so. He has a great faith in Ayurvedic treatment and his self-confidence is so great that despite his weakness and illness, he is resolved to live up to 75. May God make his resolution good.

The truth is that a man's reason follows in his activities. There is little free scope for human efforts in such matters. One's duty is to strive and one must perform it; but for one and all, a time comes when all efforts become futile and, fortunately and in the interest of conservation of human efforts, God has not given anyone the knowledge of the last moment. Then why should we worry for this inevitable thing? The affairs of the country depend upon neither Malaviya-ji, nor Lalaji (i.e. Lala Lajpat Rai), nor me. All are mere instruments and, as for myself, I believe that a good man's work really begins after his death. Shakespeare is not right in saying:

The evil that men do lives after them;
The good is oft interred with their bones.

Evil is never so long-lived. Rama is alive and we purify ourselves by repeating his name. Ravana is gone, and gone are also with him his evils. Even a wicked man does not remember Ravana. No one knows the real Rama of his age. The poet has told us that in his own age he, too, was subjected to accusations. But all the imperfections of Rama were burnt with his body and we today worship him only as a divine being; and certainly the extent of Ram Rajya was not so great when he was physically alive as it is now.

I do not write this as a highly philosophical statement or for pacificatory consolation. But I want to say emphatically that we should not at all grieve over the death of one whom we consider a saintly man; also that we should have a firm faith that it is only after his death that his true work commences, or rather begins to bear fruit. What were considered to be his great achievements during his lifetime would pale into insignificance before the future ones. Of course, it is our duty to follow, up to the extent of our capacity, the good steps of those whom we respect as saints.

The extent of Mahatma-ji's confidence in father can be seen in his letter of 10 April 1930: 'I am sure you will do all you can to promote the cause of salt struggle, prohibition, and boycott of foreign cloth.'

Gandhi-ji wanted father's help in abolishing untouchability in the country. He started the Harijan Sevak Sangha for that purpose and asked father to become its president. As president of the Harijan Sevak Sangha, father worked very hard. In those days, a large number of Harijans were converting to Christianity in Travancore, as they were not permitted entry in Hindu temples. Father met the Maharaja of Travancore and had a successful discussion with him on this matter. Father wrote to Mahatma-ji on 27 June 1936: 'I have been definitely promised by the Maharajah and Maharani that they would throw the temples open and make the announcement during the next birthday anniversary of the Maharajah.'

Father also met the Maharaja of Mysore. In the same letter father says: 'I had a talk with Maharajah of Mysore also who said that he was quite ready to admit the Harijans in his Durbar and he would consult his advisers.'

These were striking achievements.

On 2 December 1930, Gandhi-ji wrote a letter to father which will be found to be of special interest:

This letter is about Jayaprakash Narayan. He hails from a distinguished family of Bihar and is the son-in-law of that province's great worker, Brijkishore Babu. Till now he has been with Pandit Jawaharlal in the Congress office. He studied in America for seven years. Now that his mother is dead, he feels the need to earn something. His requirements will be covered by Rs. 300 per month. Jayaprakash is a qualified young man. I would like him to be employed somewhere under your auspices with a monthly salary sufficient enough to meet his needs. The rest he will tell you himself.

Jayaprakash-ji met father in accordance with Gandhi-ji's directions. Father appointed him as his secretary. He worked in that capacity for a few years. We were all children in those days but we also came to know Jayaprakash-ji well. Soon father and all of us realized that with his humility, child-like simplicity, transparent honesty and high sense of duty and intense patriotism, Jayaprakash-ji would rise high in the political scenario of the country. He was like any other member of our family. In fact, in 1977, when Indira Gandhi lost the elections and the Janata Party came to power and Morarji Desai became the prime minister, the then government wanted to harass me in a number of ways. Jayaprakash-ji stood by me.

Though very close to Mahatma-ji, father was frank enough to differ with him and express it boldly. Father was looking after the work of Harijan uplift entrusted to him by Gandhi-ji. After consulting Gandhi-ji, father made Dr Bidhan Chandra Roy the president of the Bengal Anti-Untouchability Board. Some people who were not friendly with Dr Roy suggested that Satish Dasgupta or Dr Suresh Banerjee would have been a better choice for the position. Gandhi-ji then wrote to Dr Roy suggesting that he make way for either of them. Dr Roy, a man of dauntless courage, wrote frankly to Mahatma-ji on 12 December 1932:

> You will allow me to mention that the position of the Presidentship of the Bengal Board was not of my seeking and I now know that Mr. Birla had, after consultation with you and with your approval, selected me as President. Now that you do not feel so sure and want me to withdraw, I gladly do so. I am writing to Mr. Birla today offering my resignation. It is not a matter of self-abnegation for me, because I have never in my life occupied any place or position for a moment when those who have it in their gift desired that I should not continue to do so.

Father agreed completely with Dr Roy and felt that injustice had been done to him. He wrote to Mahatma-ji that Dr Roy was right. Gandhi-ji was then at Yeravada Central Prison in Pune. He wrote to father on 15 December 1932: 'Now, as to the Bengal organisation, I fear that I have committed a grievous blunder. I overrated my influence with Dr. Bidhan. I am sorry because I have given him pain; and I am sorry because I have placed you in an awkward position. He will survive the pain; you will surmount all awkward difficulty; I shall not easily forget my folly.'

Father, as stated earlier had supported the stand of Bidhan Babu. He wrote in his letter dated 21 December 1932 to Mahatma-ji:

> There is no question of my being placed in an awkward position.
> If you put me even in a more awkward position, you can do so
> with pleasure. But even now I do not agree with you that your
> mistake was confined to overrating your influence on Dr. Bidhan.
> In fairness to Dr. Roy, I must say that he could not have helped
> feeling hurt .... I think you should not have chosen Dr. Roy for
> sacrifice. This, in my opinion, was your mistake. And I felt surprised
> when I saw your first letter to Dr. Roy, as constitutionally you are
> almost incapable of making such mistakes.

Father, though a businessman, was very much in politics. He was not a
member of any political party but he was close to all the top leaders of
the country. Father also knew all the people in the UK like the foreign
minister or Secretary of State who had something or the other to do with
India.

Some time in July 1932, Gandhi-ji decided to go on fast unto death in
jail on the issue of Harijan franchise. Father sent telegrams to several
people including Sir Samuel Hoare who was then the Secretary of State
for India. Father said in his telegram:

> CRISIS IS SO SERIOUS THAT I THINK IT MY DUTY TO SEND YOU
> THIS CABLE. IN MY HUMBLE OPINION SITUATION COULD BE
> SAVED IF GOVERNMENT WOULD REALLY BE HELPFUL. FIRST OF
> ALL GANDHIJI WITH IMPORTANT LEADERS SHOULD BE RELEASED
> WITHOUT LEAST DELAY. GANDHIJI'S PRESENCE OUTSIDE WILL
> BE VERY HELIFUL IN ARRIVING AT A PACT WITH DEPRESSED
> CLASSES. THIS PACT SHOULD THEN BE CONFIRMED BY
> GOVERNMENT. THIS MAY LEAD TO OTHER IMPORTANT
> CONSTITUTIONAL SOLUTIONS. EARNESTLY IMPLORE NO TIME
> SHOULD BE LOST IN RELEASING GANDHIJI.

Father knew also Winston Churchill (prime minister of Britain in 1940–
45 and 1951–55). Churchill invited him for lunch on several occasions.
After a lunch in 1935, father remarked in a note he prepared: 'A most
remarkable man. As eloquent in private talk as he is in public speech.'
Father tried to remove Churchill's many misgivings about India and kept
him informed about our standpoint.

He was also very friendly with Sir John Anderson (later Lord Waverly), who was the governor of Bengal in the early 1930s, took assistance from him and would often persuade him to speak to the viceroy to prepare the ground for the latter to understand Mahatma-ji's mind.

Father recorded in his diary in April 1932 after a meeting with the governor:

> Gandhi-ji was rushed into things by Lord Willingdon. The Viceroy was not a man of imagination. Hailey was one. He was another. Lord Willingdon had no sympathy with Gandhi-ji. He did not know him and did not understand him. Sir John asked whether Gandhi-ji was a practical man. I said, immensely. He said that Findlater Stuart had said that he was not very practical. I said for a western mind it was somewhat difficult to understand a philosophical mind like that of Gandhi-ji.

This was how father worked to bridge the gap between Mahatma-ji and the British. He kept Gandhi-ji fully informed about his efforts and he greatly appreciated father's role.

The personal relationship between Gandhi-ji and father can be seen from father's letter dated 16 March 1933 addressed to Mahatma-ji, where he says: 'I see that you are annoyed for my delaying the operation on my nose. But I could not help it. There is not a good surgeon in Delhi and I could not afford to stay in Kolkata.'

This did not satisfy Mahatma-ji. He chided father for neglecting his health. He wrote to father on 23 March 1933:

> I have your letter and the cuttings. Unless you make time for the operation I know you will never have the time. This always happens with busy people and therefore, it is necessary to consider matters of health as real matters of business. I do not write this as a philosophic truth, but as a practical truth which I have enforced in my own life and in that of others. I hope therefore, that you will set apart a month or so for the treatment and make an appointment with the doctors beforehand with the fixed resolution of keeping that appointment.

In 1942, the Congress Working Committee debated and passed the Quit India resolution in Birla House, Mumbai. Father and my uncle Rameshwar Das were both in Mumbai at that time, playing host to Gandhi-ji. In order not to cause any harassment to father at the hands of the British,

Gandhi-ji offered to leave Birla House and get the resolution passed elsewhere. Father would not hear of it. He said that he was not afraid of the consequences and that Gandhi-ji should continue to stay at Birla House; the resolution was ultimately passed on 8 August 1942. The next day, 9 August, Gandhi-ji was arrested.

Apart from Mahatma-ji, father knew all the important leaders of India like Sardar Patel, Pt Motilal Nehru, Jawaharlal-ji, Madan Mohan Malaviya-ji, Raja-ji, Lala Lajpat Rai, Rajendra Babu (Rajendra Prasad), J.M. Sengupta, Dr Roy, and other luminaries.

Highly impressed by the pragmatism of Sardar Patel, father had great respect for him. They were very close friends. Even in the 1930s, whenever father went to Mumbai he would frequently meet the Sardar, mostly at Birla House. They would sometimes take a short walk at Marine Drive or Chowpatty in which my brothers, cousins and I joined even though I was a mere boy at that time. After the walk I remember all of us would drink coconut water.

Whenever Sardar Patel came to Delhi, he invariably stayed with us at Birla House. This friendship only blossomed after Sardar Patel became the deputy prime minister. Sardar Patel knew that father had dinner at 7.30 p.m. and after finishing all his engagements got ready an hour before dinner. At this time the Sardar would often drop in at Birla House without any prior appointment and the two discussed various political matters. Father too visited Sardar Patel frequently.

After Gandhi-ji's assassination, Pandit-ji became the supreme leader of India. Many people thought that since the Sardar and father were very close, Pandit-ji would be cold towards father. Some petty people did try to poison Pandit-ji's mind in this regard. But Pandit-ji was too large-hearted for such pettiness. Nothing affected his relationship with father, who had known Pandit-ji since the 1920s.

On 8 January 1942, Jawaharlal-ji wrote a very interesting letter to father. World War II was on and there was a shortage of petrol. Pandit-ji said that owing to lack of petrol he was finding it difficult to move out by car and so would like to use a bicycle. He wrote: 'I, therefore, propose to revert to my old habit of using a bicycle. I do not want, as far as possible, to buy a foreign cycle. I had hoped to be able to get the New Hind Cycle but it does not appear to be available in the market. Could you kindly let me know where I can get it?'

Father immediately arranged to despatch two cycles, made in our factory, to Pandit-ji.

That father and Pandit-ji were close could be seen from a letter that father wrote on 13 January 1942 offering his views on the demand of the Muslims for the partition of India and creation of Pakistan. Father said in his letter:

> Any partner in a business, if he is not satisfied with the partnership, I suppose, has a right to demand separation. The separation, of course, has to be on an equitable basis; but I cannot conceive how anybody could object to it. It is no doubt a very gigantic affair and may not perhaps, in practice, be found an easily workable proposition. But it is all the more necessary then that we should not show our reluctance in offering the solution on which the Muslims insist. I would, of course, make a condition that they will get only what is their due and, where we disagree, a machinery, constituted for the purpose, will decide about the alignment of the *new frontier and the exchange of populations if that be necessary.*

This is exactly how things worked out when Partition took place.

Father sent donations every year to the Prime Minister's Relief Fund on the occasion of Pandit-ji's birthday. Pandit-ji would acknowledge them with gratitude. For example, on 17 November 1956, Panditji wrote: 'I received your letter dated 14th along with a cheque of Rs 67151/-. Many thanks to you. You have sent a big amount. I feel slightly embarrassed but you have sent it with affection. Hence I shall try that it is put to good use, particularly for children.'

One day, when father was discussing economic matters with Pandit-ji, he said that it was a shame that the country had to depend on imports for its aluminum requirements whereas there was a lot of scope for producing aluminum within the country. Pandit-ji suggested that father put up an aluminum plant in Uttar Pradesh. That is how Hindalco was born.

Father had cordial relations with Indira-ji (Indira Gandhi) too. In early September 1967, Indira-ji made an appeal for donation to the Prime Minister's Relief Fund. Father sent an amount of Rs 50,000 (a big amount in those days). Indira-ji replied: 'Thank you for your donation of Rs 50,000 towards the Prime Minister's National Relief Fund. Yours was the first cheque to arrive. As usual, your response towards such a public cause has been prompt as well as generous.'

Father also knew Gurudev Rabindranath Tagore well, though there was not much correspondence between them. In 1936 one of the institutes at Santiniketan called Visva Bharati Samsad was in financial difficulties.

Gurudev wanted to arrange a ballet in Kolkata to raise money for the Samsad. When Gandhi-ji came to know about it he spoke to father, who gave an anonymous donation of Rs 60,000 to the Samsad.

In 1926, the British government offered a knighthood to father. Father declined it. Father wrote in his notes: 'Bapu strongly approved my action in declining the Knighthood.' Gandhi-ji said: 'If you have to decline a title, it is not necessary either to treat the Government as your enemy or to consider titles as something evil, though I do regard them as evil, placed as we are.'

Father knew that to lead an active life good health was very important. He acquired considerable knowledge about Ayurvedic medicines and always kept a small chest of around forty small bottles containing various medicines.

Like Gandhi-ji, father conducted many experiments on his food and diet and often consulted him about his experiences. For him walking was

Pilani, 1953: Jawaharlal Nehru, then prime minister, at Birla Institute of Technology and Science with my father Dr G.D. Birla, me and my brothers L.N. and B.K.

the best exercise and he never missed out on this for a single day all his life. He was also a good swimmer and could cross and recross the Ganga at Varanasi. Besides, he was an excellent rider. At Pilani, he kept about twenty horses and would go out riding for hours together.

My father was also a good musician and was blessed with a melodious voice. He could play the harmonium well and knew most of our classical ragas. He preferred to sing only bhajans, mostly from *Ashram Bhajanavali,* a book which contained selected bhajans from many Indian languages and also some psalms from the Bible. These bhajans were compiled under Mahatma-ji's guidance.

Bravery and courage formed a part of father's character throughout his life. In the late 1920s, there was a riot in Kolkata when hundreds of Hindus and Muslims were killed and many started fleeing from their homes. Father, then in his early thirties, toured various mohallas at great personal risk; he rescued Hindus from Muslim localities and Muslims from Hindu neighbourhoods. Hindus and Muslims both expressed their gratitude to father and paid tribute to his courage. This trait manifested itself in him throughout his life.

His stature attained nobler heights with advancing years. He came to be respected by all sections of the people—businessmen, politicians, staff and workers of our organizations and by the poor and needy. He would reach office at 10.30 a.m. and work till 4 p.m. His memory, intellect and power of judgement remained keen even in old age. He continued to write till the end and also accepted speaking engagements. He surprised his audience by the clarity and logical sequence of his thought, power of expression, and fluency in oratory, in spite of his age. In his daily routine, over an hour was set apart for meeting people who sought his advice and solutions to their problems. All who came to him with their problems went back fully satisfied, with admiration and respect for him.

Father had always been careful about his health. He knew that unless a man kept physically healthy he would not be able to make any contribution to business, society or to national causes. He therefore exercised every day and took brisk daily walks.

Father suffered a heart attack in December 1977. Though he soon recovered, the doctors cautioned him to be careful throughout his life as his heart had been slightly affected. It was a mark of his exemplary courage that, in spite of such discretion emphasized by the cardiologists and the pleadings of Basant Kumar and his wife Sarala, father undertook the pilgrimage to Kedarnath in 1982 when he was eighty-eight years old. The car could not go right up to Kedarnath. One had to walk or travel in a Dandi or ride on a pony for thirteen kilometres. Father insisted on walking for he had strong will power. Basant Kumar and Sarala, both deeply devoted to father, were with him all along and assisted him in this strenuous walk. I have not seen any couple as devoted to their father as they were.

In January 1982 my youngest uncle Braj Mohan (BM) died of heart trouble. Father was very attached to uncle. Uncle, in fact, then was the only surviving brother father had—two of their siblings having expired earlier. In late 1981 uncle had had some heart trouble and so was admitted in one of our hospitals constructed by him. All the members of the family prayed for uncle's recovery, but the doctors had warned us very frankly that uncle's was a difficult case. Father had a sixth sense that uncle's demise was only a question of a few more days. Such was father's attachment to uncle that when he was in hospital, father consulted all the members of the family, particularly Gangaprasad, uncle BM's son, about leaving Kolkata. He knew that if he remained in Kolkata he would not be able to bear the shock if the worst were to happen to uncle BM. Father then left Kolkata.

In January 1982 uncle BM died. Father, of course, rushed back to Kolkata as soon as he got this news. After uncle BM's demise, father was heart-broken. Medha M. Kudaisya, who has written father's biography *The Life and Times of G.D. Birla*, undoubtedly the best biography, has very ably described father's mental and physical condition. She quotes from a book written by father titled *Bapu: A Unique Association*.

The spotless standard of Yama's troops
Comes before my eyes be-dimmed by age
And fighting a losing battle with diseases
This mortal frame doth droop day by day.

We were all hoping that in spite of the shock he suffered, father would continue to live and bless us for a few more years. But it appeared as if father had lost interest in life. All his business friends and associates had passed away much earlier. As for the political friends whom father deeply respected, Mahatma-ji, Sardar Patel and Rajendra Babu were long gone. Father was always friendly with Pandit Jawaharlal Nehru and a special relationship with Pandit-ji sprang up after the demise of Mahatma-ji and Sardar Patel.

Pandit-ji also developed great warmth for father, as most of his contemporaries—Sardar Patel, Rajendra Babu, Rafi Saheb, Pandit Govind Ballabh Pant, Bidhan Babu—had all passed on. Pandit-ji died in 1964.

With Pandit-ji's demise all the important political figures of that period were gone. After Pandit-ji's death father felt very lonely and completely cut himself off from public life.

Father would still do his yogic exercises and walking; he would still recite the Srimad Bhagavad Gita and ponder over the sayings of Bhagwan Shri Krishna. He would constantly review the working of his units like Hindalco, Grasim and Mysore Cements. He was eighty-eight and fully prepared to leave this world like a 'yogi'. Once, after uncle BM's death, father told me, 'Krishan, I do not know how many years more God will grant me.' I told father that I was sure that God was always with him and that all his children—sons and daughters, nephews and their spouses—prayed to God that he remain active for another five years so that they continued to receive his aashirwad. This is what I desired and prayed for from my heart as did all the other members of our family. But we all knew that father's health was deteriorating. He passed away on the morning of 11 June 1983 in London.

Father regularly visited Zug in Switzerland during the summer months where one of our companies had a house. Father preferred to stay there when he was in Zug. In the natural beauty of Switzerland father always found peace and calm. Usually one or two executives from our companies would be with him as well as Murlidhar Loyalka and his wife. At Zug father would spend some time examining the working of the companies that were directly under him. The rest of the time he would walk or converse with those who accompanied him. At night Indian food was cooked for him. For some of the dishes he would give guidance as to how they were to be prepared. It was a carefree life in Zug. He would also visit Mussoorie once a year when my wife and I were there and stay for about a week or so. My wife Manorama would very meticulously and devotedly look after him. He certainly found serenity in the divine land of the Himalayas.

During his visit to Zug in 1983, father went to London for a short stay. On 11 June he went for his morning walk, as usual. Two of our senior executives—Nandlal Hamirwasia, president of Mysore Cements and a great favourite of father's and Sushil Kumar Sabu, a senior executive of Gwalior Rayon—were walking with him. Park Towers Apartments, where father stayed, was just two minutes away from Piccadilly. Father walked along Piccadilly, reached Piccadilly Circus and had entered Regent Street when he felt uncomfortable. Both the executives immediately hailed a taxi and came back to the apartment with father who was having a breathing problem. They put him on a sofa which was near the lift. They also immediately sent for an ambulance. The ambulance arrived within minutes. The medics made father comfortable and massaged his chest. They reached Middlesex hospital by 9.35 a.m. The doctors and nurses, who had been alerted, were anxiously waiting and did their best to energize the heart, but father breathed his last at 9.45 a.m.

My cousin Gangaprasad and his wife Nirmala were already in London when father expired. They had in fact reached Park Towers as soon as they heard about father's condition. Almost all of the rest of the family reached London within the next twenty-four hours. Father had expressed a desire earlier that in case he were to die in any foreign country, his cremation should be done there. He did not want his body to be embalmed and brought back to India. In accordance with his wishes, father was cremated at Golders Green Crematorium in North London on 13 June. Hundreds of people gathered at the crematorium to pay homage to father. In Bharatiya Vidya Bhawan in London, there was a highly respected pandit, Pandit Mathoor Krishnamurti, who knew Sanskrit and all our rituals very well. He recited Vedic mantras and the shlokas from the Bhagavad Gita which father loved and respected. Members of the family sang *Ramdhun* and *Raghu Pati Raghava Raja Ram*.

After father's cremation his remains were gathered in an urn. They were brought to India and taken to Century Bhawan in Mumbai where people from all parts of India assembled to pay their last respects. The urn was also taken [...] of our schools and [...] large number of v[...] the ashes were take[...] and I immersed a [...] members of the fa[...] Gangotri and scatte[...]

Chowdhury Ch[...] other members of the family. I was in Delhi at the time of father's demise and after hearing the news Charan Singh-ji came within half an hour to Birla House. Though we have had our political differences, he was a very warm-hearted person and a man of great character and ability. President Zail Singh in his letter of condolence dated 11 June 1983 said, 'His death is a grave loss to the country and removes from the national scene one of the most illustrious and dynamic sons of India who may well be called a true *Karmayogi*.' He even telephoned me in London. Later, when we returned to India, Indira Gandhi sent Rajiv on her behalf who called on me and other members of the family in Delhi. Rajiv in his letter of 12 June 1983 to me said, 'The contribution he made in helping to build India's industrial base will be his lasting memorial.' Indira Gandhi issued a statement to the press where she said that the country had lost a veteran who would be missed in public life. Among many others who wrote to me was Shri N.T. Rama Rao, the then chief minister of Andhra Pradesh. Smt. Mahadevi Verma wrote a letter to Basant Kumar and his wife Sarala. Mrs Margaret Thatcher, who was then the prime minister of the United Kingdom, also wrote a letter to Basant Kumar. Former British prime ministers Harold Macmillan and James Callaghan also expressed their condolences as did many other public figures such as Lord Listowal and Lord Fenner Brockway. The *Times*, London, described him as 'one of the most influential of Indian businessmen who also played a role in the financing of Gandhi's movement for Indian independence'.

J.R.D. Tata also sent a message:

DISTRESSED LEARN OF THE PASSING AWAY OF YOUR DISTINGUISHED FATHER WHOM I HAD KNOWN AND HELD IN HIGH ESTEEM FOR OVER FIVE DECADES. ON BEHALF OF MY COLLEAGUES IN TATAS AND MYSELF I SEND YOU AND THROUGH YOU TO ALL MEMBERS OF YOUR FAMILY OUR DEEPEST SYMPATHY AND CONDOLENCES IN YOUR BEREAVEMENT.

Fidel Castro, President of Cuba, also sent me his condolences. All the ministers of the Government of India sent condolence messages as did a large number of governors and chief ministers of states. Many foreign industrialists like D.M. Roderick, chairman of US Steel, also wrote to me. All told, I received about 1450 letters of condolence.

The following statement was made in the Lok Sabha at its sitting of 26 July 1983 by the Speaker of the Lok Sabha, Shri Balram Jakhar, while deeply mourning father's loss:

A friend of the Father of the Nation, Shri Birla was associated with the freedom struggle. He accompanied Gandhiji to the Round Table Conference in London. He devoted himself to the cause of political freedom and economic development of the country.

A devout nationalist, parliamentarian, deeply religious, philanthropist and interested in art and culture, he was a man with a vision. He was the founder of numerous educational, scientific and technological institutions, hospitals and welfare organizations etc.

He was scholastic by nature and the University of Rajasthan conferred on him the Doctorate of Literature and the Banaras Hindu University awarded him Doctorate of Laws.

Shri Birla passed away in London on 11 June 1983 at the age of eighty-nine years.

The greatest memorials to father's hallowed memory are the various industries that he established to create wealth and employment opportunities for the people as well as the various institutions—schools, colleges, hospitals, research institutes, temples—that he set up throughout the country, particularly the autonomous institution BITS at Pilani—to serve the people of the country, to spread knowledge and to lay the foundations to make the country strong and rich. These are standing monuments to his many-sided genius. He became a legend in his lifetime and the legend lives on.

4

My Nephew Aditya

Aditya, my nephew, was the son of my younger brother Basant Kumar and Sarala. Aditya was born in Delhi on 14 November 1943. He was an impressive baby and both my wife and I instantly developed an immense liking for him. Father was overjoyed at his birth. He now had two grandsons. Just as my wife and I took a great liking for Aditya, he also developed deep affection and respect for both of us. In his childhood he would call me Kintho Baba and continued to do so throughout his student life. It was only after he joined business that he started calling me Babaji.

It is beyond the scope of this book to write about Aditya's life. What I desire to do is write about Aditya's personality.

After he completed his BSc degree, it was felt by the family that Aditya should acquire a degree from a prestigious American university. He had been a brilliant student and it was not difficult for him to get admission in the Massachusetts Institute of Technology (MIT) from where he qualified in chemical engineering.

My wife and I used to visit America once or twice a year. Whenever we did so, we would look up Aditya at Boston. He was a diligent student and passed his examinations with credit. Two of his friends, Ashwin Kothari and Om Bhalotia, also studied with him at MIT. In course of time, they also came to address me as 'Babaji'.

Aditya was married to Rajashree in 1965, a charming girl who too, like Aditya, developed a deep respect for my wife and me.

Father took an immense liking to Aditya. Even when he was a young lad, it became evident that he would achieve greatness in life. As Aditya grew up, father's love for him deepened. He loved Aditya even more than Basant Kumar and decided that he would leave all his companies to Aditya, which he ultimately did.

After joining business, Aditya branched out independently, establishing enterprises overseas. He started a spinning unit at Bangkok called Indo Thai Synthetics Co. Ltd, which was established in 1969. The mills did very well. Aditya devised his own method of management and control. From the seed that he planted in Bangkok, his efforts blossomed into success abroad as well as in India. Aditya was able to establish seventeen industrial units in five countries. He did the family proud. He was a gem of a person.

Aditya was a very pragmatic businessman.

He was a great thinker and visionary. Hindalco, one of our flagship companies, was involved in a number of litigations with the Government of India. Aditya decided that to fight so many cases was a waste of energy which could be better harnessed in more gainful activities elsewhere. It was a complete reversal of the policy of Durgaprasad Mandelia, father's right-hand man and like a family member to us. Aditya thought it was much better to settle the points of dispute between Hindalco and the government on the basis of give and take rather than carry on litigation. N.K.P. Salve was the minister-in-charge in those days. Aditya had a number of sittings with Salve and was able to sort out matters. Salve, who is a friend of mine, said that he was amazed at the brilliance and pragmatism shown by such a young man. The matter was resolved and as a result Hindalco started doing well.

Aditya was a man with a very lovable character. He was true to his friends and looked after all his people. Not only that, he would endeavour to do his best to assist anyone who approached him for help. He was magnanimous to a fault in his treatment of all his friends, staff and well-wishers. A man of great sincerity and integrity, he enjoyed a high reputation for his moral excellence and firmness of resolve, the two most essential traits of a strong and unimpeachable character. All those who came in touch with him were impressed by his personality. A number of ministers in the government, with whom Aditya interacted, told me how profound an impression he had left on them. He was a good friend of Rajiv Gandhi. Though eminently successful, Aditya shunned publicity.

On many an occasion, people from FICCI, including my nephew Sudarshan Kumar, approached me with the request that Aditya be made a member of the executive committee of FICCI. When I conveyed the proposal to Aditya, he was not at all enthused by the idea. On my persuasion he did join it, but could hardly attend any meeting. He said: 'Babaji, I have joined the executive committee of FICCI on your directions but my heart is not in it.'

I will give another instance of Aditya's warmth towards me. Some time in December 1993 I received a new year gift from one of his major companies along with his card. I sent him a reply on 4 January 1994. It was a simple letter:

My dear Aditya,
I have to thank you for the lovely New Year gift sent by you. I very much appreciate your warmth towards me.

Yours affectionately,
Krishna Kumar

To this, I got a reply on 3 February 1994 from Aditya. The letter is full of warmth and affection:

Pujya Babuji,
On my return, I saw your letter of 4th January in which you have written that you appreciate my warmth towards you.

I have always had the highest of respect, admiration, love and affection for you. In several ways, you are like a Father to me. I am fortunate to have your blessings and guidance and I know that not only you but Badi Ma also has great love and affection for me.

Through this difficult period of the past few months the way you have cared for me, has overwhelmed me. You have stood by me and have given me great courage by your concern, anxiety and advice.

Your frequent calls and anxious enquiries made me realise how deep your love and affection is for me. I hope, I will continue always to receive your and Badi Ma's blessings and guidance.

My respectful Pranams.

Affectionately,
Aditya

Aditya's companies did so well because his method of working was very effective. He once told me: 'Babaji, even when a company gives an excellent performance I always ask the managers to make some extra effort so that the performance can further improve.' And that is what always happened. He was a very popular figure and all those who came in touch with him developed a great respect and warmth for him. He was snatched by the cruel hands of destiny at the young age of fifty-two years. He expired at Baltimore in the United States on 1 October 1995. His body was brought to India. The funeral procession in Mumbai was attended by over 5,000 people. Many wept.

Aditya will always be remembered for his lovable nature, for his abilities and character. I feel that after father, he was the most illustrious person born in our family.

It is a matter of great satisfaction for the entire family to find that Kumar Mangalam, son of Aditya, has turned out to be as brilliant as his father. The working style of Kumar Mangalam is different from that of his late father. Kumar Mangalam has evolved his own method of organizing the companies which he has inherited from his father. He has very effectively guided the affairs of these companies and has acquired some other corporate organizations as well. That Kumar Mangalam would turn out to be an outstanding leader became clear when he sent a letter to all his senior executives soon after Aditya's sad and untimely demise. Kumar Mangalam was only twenty-eight years of age when he sent this letter:

16 October 1995

My dear ...

I am writing this letter not to a Senior Executive of a Large, Prosperous and Growing Multi-national Corporation but to an elder and respected member of the family.

This has been a big blow and shock to all of us, which we can never fully overcome.

The Nation has lost a Nation builder. The Group has lost its beloved leader, 'Babu', as you fondly and respectfully call him.

I have lost my father, who was ideal in every respect, whom I will deeply love and respect forever and ever.

In the building of this empire, you have worked shoulder to shoulder with Pujya Papa, sharing with him both good and bad times. He enjoyed your respect, total commitment and love. He in turn loved and trusted you immensely. In this time of distress, we must remember that we have to put our best foot forward, work in unison as a team and strive hard to fulfil his dream in a way that he will be proud of us.

I am confident that with your support to me, we will together, succeed in furthering his vision of a dynamic, large multi-national corporation striving for excellence, based on the solid foundation of strong business ethics and morals.

I will be in touch with you personally over the next few days in order to ensure no delays and effective decision making.

Life and work must go on—this is how he wanted it to be. However we must never forget that his presence will continue to be with us, forever guiding and protecting us.

With warm personal regards,

Yours sincerely
Kumar Mangalam Birla

5

In a Happy Village

Father was merely thirteen in 1907, when he got married to Durga Devi. She was the daughter of Mahadev Somani of Chirawa, about fourteen kilometres from Pilani. Hundreds of people went in the baraat to Chirawa. Some travelled on camels, some by *rath* and some on horseback. People went there according to their convenience, so that a constant stream of people travelled from Pilani. The wedding was solemnized with great pomp and show, as was the practice in those days.

My elder brother Lakshmi Niwas was born in July 1909. Soon after his birth, Durga Devi died. Father's second marriage was solemnized in 1912. My mother Mahadevi belonged to the Karwa family, an eminent household of Sardar Sahar, a town in the then state of Bikaner. The Ka was had business interests in Assam. They were agents large areas in Assam of the Assam Oil Company of Digboi and t u had a large number of petrol pumps allotted to them. They were fairly wel -c o people.

In the 1940s and right up to the end of the twentieth ce 11 , whenever people asked my date of birth and came to know that it was November 1918, they congratulated me on having been born on a d vhen peace was restored in the world after the First World War. Such c r tulations keep coming even today from old-timers, whenever the to know my birth date.

Being the first son of my mother Mahadevi, there was great rejoicing on my birth. My grandparents gave gifts to pandits and Brahmins and offered puja in temples.

In those days, the ladies of our family mostly stayed in Pilani, though occasionally they would visit Kolkata or Mumbai to spend some time with their husbands. Just prior to my birth we had shifted to a house on Zakaria Street in Kolkata. Before we took this house, father used to stay in our gaddi at Kaligodam. There it was a kind of community living. Father did not have any room to himself. He would take his food in the *basa,* a sort of dhaba. Such a dhaba used to be run by one or two cooks where meals could be had at a reasonable price. There were common toilets and, as their number was small, people had to wait their turn. Father too had to stand in the queue but owing to his position people would often give him precedence in using the facilities.

I was not a handsome child. I was very dark and had an unkempt appearance. People say that after I grew up and shifted to Bengal my complexion and features changed. As I was very dark at the time of my birth, I was given the name Krishna. This name served the twin purpose of satisfying the conventional practice of naming a child after one of the gods in the Hindu pantheon, mine being in adoration of Bhagwan Krishna and the other of symbolizing my dark complexion.

Till 1922, I lived mostly in Pilani with mother. In 1921 we acquired a house in Rainey Park, Kolkata, where Basant Kumar was born. After 1922, mother started living in Kolkata.

My sister Chandrakala was two years older than me. She was a girl of very strong will. An interesting incident shows how strong-willed she was. Our haveli was the largest not only in Pilani but also amongst the neighbouring villages. In our haveli there were many chawks—spaces in the centre surrounded on all sides by rooms or verandahs. They had a beauty of their own. Being open to the sky, the ladies of the household who often congregated in the chawks could, for some time at least, get some respite from the feeling of claustrophobia caused by the confinement for most of the time indoors. That apart, being open to the sky, the chawks helped to provide plenty of sunlight and fresh air.

Above the chawks, there was a net fixed and spread over the entire open space. One day Chandrakala Bai and I were playing on the first floor when something slipped from her hand and fell on the net above the chawk. The net must have been about ten feet above ground level. Chandrakala Bai asked me to pick it up for her. I was then a child of only, perhaps, three. Chandrakala Bai told me that she would help me. She caught hold of my feet and lowered me head and hands foremost. With her hands holding my legs and my face and arms down towards the net, I tried hard to catch hold of the object but did not succeed. She chided me for my failure. At her bidding I made another attempt to get the object, then told her that it was not possible. Chandrakala Bai became furious and said that if I could not fetch the object she would throw me down. This she did. I fell on the net but it could not bear my weight and gave way. I fell to the ground floor. Fortunately, owing to the net, my fall was not as severe as it could have otherwise been. All the same, I suffered a fracture in one leg. Mother and the other ladies rushed in when they found me lying on the floor. Mother immediately shot off a letter to father, who was in Kolkata, about the incident. There were no qualified medical practitioners in the villages. The 'doctor' who examined me could not do anything. Two or three others were called but they too failed in their efforts to set the bone properly. Ultimately a doctor called Dr Gulzarilal, who had a medical diploma and was bold and pragmatic, set the bone in position and bandaged my leg. I recovered after four or six weeks. I still have mother's letter to father about my injury as well as father's reply thereto.

The first three or four years of my life in Pilani were spent in playing with children of the village. I was under the charge and care of a servant called Hira Jat. He was born around 1850 and joined our service some time in the 1860s. Hira was the first servant our family employed. Though short of stature, he was quite courageous. In those days, for a young child the dress was half pant and shirt but after I was four I was taught how to wear a dhoti.

(From left) Me, younger brother Basant Kumar, cousins Madhav Prasad, Ganga Prasad, Girdhar Das Kothari and Ganga Bai in 1928

Whenever I went out of the haveli, Hira would accompany me. He would often recite stories and tales of his own bravado. He was not afraid of thieves or dacoits who were quite numerous in those days. Hira, however, overestimated his strength. Hence, in ordinary bouts he was nearly always beaten. And yet he was always ready to show his prowess and never got demoralized.

There were many other servants who were very loyal and were like institutions in themselves. Their forefathers also worked with us.

Daan Nai was a barber with a majestic appearance. He would put on a pugree just as people of the Vaishya community did. There were no fixed duties for him but he got liberal salary from the haveli. He would cut the hair of all the members of the family as required. He would cut others' hair also. In the evening, Daan Nai would come and light up all the hurricane lanterns.

Though caste-wise he was placed low, *nais* were regarded as a very clever community. Perhaps this was because, while cutting hair, they could converse with members of the family. In medieval Rajasthan and perhaps right up to the end of the nineteenth century, whenever there was need to find a suitable match for a boy or a girl, the work would be entrusted to the family purohit and barber. They went to several towns or villages to find a match as directed. Daan Nai would proudly say that he or his father had arranged matches in our family too.

Then there was Rupa Brahmani. Young widows who did not have any encumbrance would try to find some work or other and for a Brahmin widow there was no better job than to work as a mishrani, fulfilling sundry duties in the kitchen. She would not do the cooking but supervise all the work connected with the pantry such as looking after the milk supply, its distribution to various people, making curd and attending to the kitchens and stores. She would also help the mistress of the house in making papads, pickles, and other preserves. When I was a boy of seven or eight, Rupa was in her sixties. The ladies of the house would address her as '*the*', Rajasthani for the Hindi word '*aap*' and would not address her as '*toon*', the Rajasthani word for the Hindi '*tum*'. Whenever a family lady would introduce Rupa to any guest, Rupa would proudly say, '*Ain ghar ko choon khatan mannain tees baras ho gaya*' (I have been eating the food of this house for the last thirty years).

Bhimji was a Rajput in his late sixties. He was required to sit near a door that led into the preserve of the ladies. He too would have no work except to go from time to time to the village for *peda*s or some other sweets.

Surjan Singh was a Rajput *durwan* who looked after us children. He was totally honest and sincere. A forthright person, he would say what he felt; he was a kind of uncut diamond. When we went out in the evening to play in the sand dunes, he accompanied us.

We had four horsemen, two Muslim and two Rajput. The Muslims were actually Rajputs who converted to Islam. They regarded themselves superior to other Muslims and were proud of having Rajput blood in their veins. Rajputs too regarded them as their brethren. Rahim Khan was the ablest amongst the horsemen. He was like a courtier to father and uncle Rameshwar Das. When father went out for riding, Rahim would accompany him. He had the liberty of freely conversing with father and uncle.

Every well-to-do family in Rajasthan, amongst the Vaishya community, had a *nohra*, a kind of open space in which were tied camels, horses and cows. We had two nohras—one for the cows, bullocks and camels and the other for the twenty horses in our stable.

We were regarded as the richest family in the whole of Shekhawati, but more than that people respected us as they knew that we stood by them whenever they faced problems such as drought. That people respected us and held us in great esteem and affection pleased us the most.

When I was four, father and mother thought that I may as well start going to school. The school to which I was sent was our own, established by my great-grandfather for the education of his grandsons. The only subject taught in it were Hindi and arithmetic. Before I joined, my teacher Pandit Jokhi ram was called to our house. Puja was performed. I offered my *pranam* to Jokhi Ram-ji and was admitted.

The village teacher called arithmetic *patti pahada*. Thus, Jokhi Ram-ji taught addition, subtraction, multiplication and division and also pahadas or counts from two to twenty. The idea was to teach a boy pahada up to the *bora*. That apart, children were also supposed to learn *pouna* (i.e. three-fourths of a figure), *sawaiya* (one-and-a-quarter), *duoda* (one-and-a-half times) and *adhaiya* (two-and-a-half times). More advanced learning would include *huntha* (three-and-a-half times of each figure), *douha*, (four-and-a-half times), *poncha* (five-and-a-half times) and so on. Most boys were supposed to learn up to *adhaiya*.

We were also supposed to learn many formulas. In those days, the measurement of weight was in seers and maunds and currency in rupee, which was divided into 16 annas. A seer had 16 *chhatak*s and a rupee 16 annas. One formula, for example, was that in purchasing anything by quantity, whatever be the value in rupees per seer, the worth of the same quantity in chhataks was the same in annas. By way of illustration, if an item costs five rupees a seer, cost of one chhatak would be five annas. Likewise, many formulas or *gurus* were taught. The idea was that a boy should be able to make day-to-day calculations mentally as far as possible. Only in complicated cases was he permitted to use slates.

Jokhi Ram-ji, judged by the standards then prevailing, was regarded a good teacher. He had his own method of teaching. He would put a question to the boys, those who could answer would raise their hands. One of them would be called by Jokhi Ram-ji to whisper into his ear what the answer was. The boy was not supposed to speak loudly to prevent others from hearing the answers. He was, therefore, supposed to convey the answer to the teacher in a whisper. The problem was how to indicate whether the answer was correct or not. There was a simple method which Jokhi Ram-ji adopted, prevalent in all the other schools in the villages. If the answer was correct, Jokhi Ram-ji would merely nod his head. If the answer was incorrect he would slap the boy.

Jokhi Ram-ji was supposed to teach me alphabets and counting for a few days before teaching more complicated things like gurus. However, when I went to class on the first day and saw what was happening I got frightened. After midday I claimed I had an upset tummy and said I wanted to go home.

We were not permitted to return to our homes till evening, but who could stop the son of the Seths? Jokhi Ram-ji permitted me to go. The durwan was posted outside to take me home. Father was not at Pilani but mother was there. She got very annoyed when she found that I had craftily returned home. After school was over she sent for Jokhi Ram-ji and told him not to listen to my excuses in future.

In this manner and in such an environment I studied for two years. I do not remember whether any exam was held; perhaps there was none. The boys were automatically promoted to the next class. It was in Class III that the study of English was introduced, I learnt it for a few months. After mother shifted to Kolkata, my school days were over until many years later when I joined Hare School.

6

Rustic Charms

In the late 1910s and early 1920s, Pilani was a peaceful and sleepy little hamlet, sparsely populated, with a population of about 4,000. The people had plenty of time for leisure. They were mostly engaged in agriculture, which totally depended on the whims of the weather gods. However, as a large number of people belonging to the trading community had migrated to different parts of India and were doing well, trading activity on a fairly large scale was carried on in the villages. Trading gave employment to a large number of people. The shopkeepers and the wholesalers thrived fairly well. There were many other classes of people engaged in other professions such as *halwai*s (confectioners), builders, shoemakers, washermen, sari printers, goldsmiths, carpenters, weavers and others who did work to meet the needs of the villagers. As most wares were brought into the village by these Rajasthanis who had settled all over India, the villagers were quite prosperous.

In part times, some of the villages of Rajasthan have made arrangements for irrigation, deepening the sand in illit pure years. In those days this was not possible, as there was no electricity in the villages. As part of the desert area, Pilani's water level was very low, about 90 feet or so below ground level. During summer months, the farmers depended on rains for growing crops. If the rains were good, people had a good harvest and thanked God Almighty for the bounty. But, usually, in a four-year cycle they were blessed with a good harvest only once; for the other three years they had either an average crop or no crop at all.

In a year when there was no crop there would be shortage of grass and even fodder. People would then send away their cattle to the neighbouring states so that the animals could survive. During such times the poor people would look to us—the people with money—to help them by sending their cattle to green pastures. Our family readily responded to the needs of the people as part of its social duty. As a result, our ancestors were respected not only for their riches but also for wise use of wealth for the society in times of need.

If the summer months were dry and rainfall poor, people would still do some cultivation through irrigation with water drawn from the wells. But the wells perforce being deep, the hardy villagers of Rajasthan had to use a pair of bullocks to draw water from them. This was done in quite an ingenious manner.

Bullocks were made to draw water by pulling a rope to a distance of about 90 feet. The other end of the rope was tied to a large leather bucket. One person would stand near the well and another would drive the bullocks. There was a wooden contraption to draw the water and a seat for the man who drove the bullocks. In order to facilitate the bullocks trotting while pulling a heavy load of water in large leather buckets, an ingenious device was contrived. The ground on which the bulls were to trot was given a slope which made it easier for them to walk even while pulling a load. The bulls would tug at the rope as they trotted on the ground and when the buckets with water surfaced at the top, the man near the well, instead of shouting, would sing a melodious '*Pani aayo re* (water has come)'. The man sitting behind the bullocks would then immediately rein in the animals, untie the ropes and allow the bullocks to walk back to the top of the well. This is how irrigation with well water was resorted to in those days.

Rajasthan roads were bad. My father was the first person to travel by car from Delhi to Pilani. Driving in the desert in those days was an adventure. At a number of places, the wheels of the car would get bogged down in sand dunes. It would take quite some time before the wheels could be freed and the car start on its way again. It was difficult for drivers from outside Rajasthan to negotiate the car through the sandy deserts. Father normally went to Pilani by train up to the nearest railway station and then drove down to Pilani. But in his younger days he sometimes ventured out in a car for Pilani. On the border of Rajasthan, the drivers would be changed and local drivers engaged to complete the journey. Actually, in dexterity as drivers, they were no match for the drivers of Delhi or Kolkata. However, given the makeshift desert tracks with sand dunes obstructing forward movement ever so often, they were the best drivers for the desert.

Usually, however, we travelled by train. In those days we got down at a village called Rajgarh in the then Bikaner state. The name of the station was Sadulpur. If the trains reached in the evening, we would spend the night at a dharmashala, and resume our journey from Sadulpur to Pilani the next day in bullock-drawn chariots called raths. Elders travelled on camels or horses. The distance of 24 miles between Sadulpur and Pilani took seven to eight hours to cover. That too was quite an adventure.

Rajasthan had three specialities not found in other parts of the country. First, the camel. In those days it was regarded as a ship of the desert. Though the horse, which is a much speedier animal, is more useful for short distances, for long journeys there is no equal of the camel. It is a very hardy animal and can easily carry two people on its back. It can do without water while journeying distances for many days and travel thirty or forty miles with great ease. Once a man had to come to Pilani on urgent work. He travelled all the way from Bhiwani to Pilani, a distance of about ninety miles almost non-stop, except for taking a break for food. Though the camel is found in some other parts of the country also, it is never used as the main beast of burden as it was in Rajasthan.

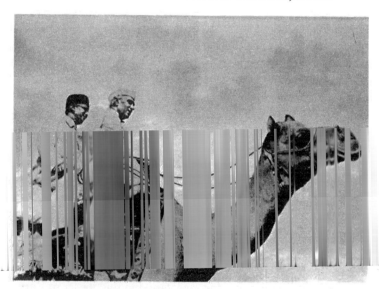

Pilani, 1950: Jawaharlal Nehru rides a camel with my father

The next speciality of Rajasthan is the peacock, a very beautiful bird. It is regarded as a very sacred bird in Rajasthan. No one would even think of harming it. Due to its bulk, it cannot fly long distances. It is a peaceful bird and is an emblem of Rajasthan. Its feathers are exquisitely pretty, of a greenish blue colour and, according to legend, Lord Krishna's crown was made of peacock feathers. It has a very large fan-like tail marked with blue and green eye-like spots.

The third speciality of Rajasthan is its sand dunes. One sees nothing but sand all around, except where cultivators have been able to grow some crop with the help of deep well-water irrigation. In the desert area, villages are few and far between.

As the people of Rajasthan have to toil for their living in excessive heat and cold, they have become sturdy. The people of Rajasthan are decent human beings. They are very warm-hearted and charitable by nature. Even today they are less corrupt and more humane than those of surrounding areas.

The crime rate in those days was low. Women were safe and could go anywhere they liked without fear of molestation. Dacoities did take place in some areas. But even the dacoits respected women. Barring those areas, the other areas were completely peaceful. There was always some jealousy amongst the villagers. This sometimes led to crime. Low-level party politics was also prevalent but on the whole the atmosphere was tranquil and peaceful.

Though untouchability has been the curse of Hindu society, the evil was not that pronounced in Pilani or surrounding areas. That does not mean that people would unhesitatingly touch those whom we now call scheduled castes. But it is certainly a fact that all these people were treated with a degree of civility which permitted fraternizing with them. To give an instance, our family sweeper and shoemaker were known as Bhikla Bhangi and Tulia Chamar. They were always treated kindly by us and, in turn, prided themselves in being higher placed compared to others in their own community because they worked for us.

Pilani had many temples. Of the main temples, one was adjacent to our haveli. Though it was not constructed entirely with donations from our family, our ancestors had certainly contributed large amounts of money towards its construction some centuries back, and also towards its upkeep. The priest of the temple was called Swami-ji. In those days, Swami Charan Das-ji was the priest of the temple. He was a person of saintly disposition with a smattering of Ayurvedic knowledge. Every evening, he would go round the village and examine any ill person free of charge. He took count of the patient's pulse, as this is considered a very specialized job. Swami-ji would then put queries to the patient and prescribe medicines, which would be given free. He did not ask for any fee, but if anyone did give money—as many did—he accepted the sum and used it for the upkeep of the temple and maintenance of its functions.

In case anyone came to the temple hungry, Swami-ji would serve chapati, a vegetable dish and dal. On many an occasion, dust was found mixed in the flour. But nobody minded this aberration on the part of the Swami-ji as he provided the bounty with great warmth and affection. He was held in high esteem. Swami-ji had two disciples—Govind Das and Surjan Das. Surjan Das too practised as a vaidya. He was slightly worldly by nature. In case he got any money from his practice it would, of course, be used for the temple, but if there was surplus cash he would lend the sum and earn interest. This money too would be spent on the temple.

Govind Das was handsome and possessed a very commanding personality. He was tall and had an athletic figure. He was just like a member of the family to us. Whenever father went to Pilani, Govind Das would be constantly with him. Father was fond of riding. Govind Das too would ride with him. He was also a good shooter. Attired in his Rajasthani turban, he looked very impressive and could be immediately spotted in a big gathering owing to his towering height. When father went to England for the first time, he took four people with him. One was Parasnath Sinha, father's secretary, equally proficient in Hindi and English. Later, he became managing director of the *Hindustan Times* for some time. Apart from Parasnath-ji, father took Govind Das, a cook and a servant.

Govind Das was a courageous man. He was dauntless. Once one of our distant relatives, Ram Kumar Birla, tried to commit suicide by jumping into a well because he was suffering from ill health and wanted to end his fe ing. This happened after everybody had retired for the night. [text obscured] slept by [text obscured] kumar's side and that night the [text obscured] Ram [text obscured] was not in bed. [text obscured] father [text obscured] father [text obscured] that Ram [text obscured] was missing. Father wanted to [text obscured] again [text obscured] he se[text obscured] jasthan, people were experts in [text obscured] ng [text obscured] py [text obscured] his footprints in the sand. Ram [text obscured] at was [text obscured] the w[text obscured] where he had jumped. When Ram [text obscured] was jumping into the well, he found [text obscured] very painful, and so repeating [text obscured] when father, along with Govind Das, and some other people reached the well, they discovered that Ram Kumar was still alive. Father said that someone should go down into the well with the help of ropes and bring him up. No one volunteered. Father then said that if no one went, he himself would go down the well. Hearing this, Govind Das came forward. He was lowered into the well with the help of ropes and rescued Ram Kumar. Such was his courage.

In those days, every big village had a witch or *dakan*, as she was called. Pilani's witch was Barjali. She was called Barjali Dakan. She could visit any house; nobody dared stop her. To whichever house she went, she was offered sweets and some money. When she went to a house, the children were immediately whisked away as it was a common belief that if the dakan took a fancy to any child she would kill him or her with the help of her mystic powers and then play with the child in the dead of night. Barjali would sometimes come to our haveli and we children would at once be sent out by mother and other ladies of the house. When grandmother was there, she tackled Barjali. Of course, Barjali was no witch. She was ugly to look at and exploited her looks for material gain. It paid to act as a witch in terms of money, food and deference from all and sundry.

Another distinctive trait of Rajasthan was the presence of what we call in Hindi or Rajasthani *khoji* or tracers. Theft takes place in every part of the world. But in India, particularly in Rajasthan, where there were no proper roads except in towns, if any theft took place in a village, the next day people would flock to the burgled house. Khojis were put on the job and they tried to trace out the footsteps which might have led the thief to the house and away from it, suspecting those footprints to be those of the thief. They would then follow those footprints to guide them to where the thief lay in hiding. Now this art is dying mainly because metal roads have replaced most of the sandy tracks of villages in large parts of the country.

I remember when we were children, thefts took place at our house twice over a period of one year. This, in spite of the fact that there were durwans always on duty at the main gate. The thief, it was clear, carefully watched the movement of the durwans and then scaled the wall of our garden house from a point where no watch was kept. The theft was detected the next day. The articles stolen were worth more than a few thousand rupees. However, it was not a question of monetary loss but of prestige, of loss of face. That theft could take place in the house of a reputed family like ours and the thieves go undetected and, therefore, unpunished was unthinkable. Immediately thereafter, under instructions from my father, about ten people were sent on horses after the thieves to apprehend them. I believe in one instance the khojis felt there were two thieves involved. Having carefully studied the footprints of the thieves, they started from Pilani in hot pursuit.

The thieves were also aware that they would be followed. So they tried to mislead their pursuers in every possible manner. For example, when they came to firm ground they entered the area from one side and exited from some corner which could not be easily noticed. The people who were following were temporarily nonplussed. They circled the ground to find out from where the thieves had entered the spot and left for their next destination. On the third day, our team was able to reach the village where the thieves had taken shelter. Perhaps that was their hideout. When our people reached the village, they initially met with resistance from the villagers who, in spite of knowing the fact that it was a clear case of theft, were siding with the thieves out of neighbourly feeling. Our people, however, did not leave the village, but fetched the police from the nearest police station. Under police escort and assisted by our people, the thieves were brought back to Pilani. They were kept outside our garden house for two to three hours as exhibits to satisfy the curiosity of the local people who had assembled to jeer at them. Subsequently, they were taken into custody by the police.

The second theft followed within a month of the first and the same endeavours and processes were repeated to book the thieves. After that, there was no more theft as the story soon got around that no one who committed theft at our house could go scotfree.

Pilani was a happy village like most of the other villages of Rajasthan. It was a village of Jaipur state ruled by the maharaja, who was held in high esteem by his subjects. Peace and tranquillity reigned everywhere. There was no hustle-bustle of city life. People had plenty of time at their disposal. There was time for gossip. People would get up early and bestir themselves for their daily avocations shortly after 9 a.m. Shopkeepers ____ commen_ ____ ___ ___ farmers would go to their fields, halwais ___ start pr_ ___ ___ and swe_ts, wor_ in their s_op_ _ ir ir houses as ___ de_ectabl_ _eat wer_ in _ct prepa_d _t ei_ _s_ _ Pilani v ___ or s_an_ _ac_ an_ po_ s. Cow__ds _ al_ e _ e cattle t_ ___ g_ unds _ nd t ey w_u_ _etu_n i__ _e __ n_ _u_ _ sunset. ___ we_ding t _ir _ay _nd _cking u_ lu__ _il_ _rr ing to _h_ ___ is _ el_ a s_ _ht _o be sa__ _red and _ _n _ _u_ _o__ns. I_ wa ___ ke_ by co__ple_ _cal_ n a_ _ unruff_ _ q_ _t de_
Throughout the country this time is described as Godhuli Bela and is regarded as the most auspicious time of the day. Tributes have been paid to this hour in verse and in prose by writers of all ages. For a traditional wedding, usually the muhurat (auspicious time and hour) is to be ascertained by a pandit but Godhuli Bela is regarded as an all time propitious hour when a wedding can take place without any question of a laborious search for the right moment to tie the knot.

Festivals like Holi and Diwali were celebrated with elaborate pomp, éclat and show. Fireworks were displayed in the villages of Rajasthan on both these occasions. Untrammelled by the debasing influences of modern civilization, the people were simple in heart and habit.

Labour was very cheap in those days. A man would get one *chowani* (a quarter of a rupee) for his daily wages. The prices of goods were unbelievably low. Wheat would sell at 13 seers a rupee or Rs 3 a maund. Milk was sold at the rate of four seers per rupee and the price of ghee was about a rupee per seer. Living was cheap and people led an unostentatious life. So whatever they earned was adequate to meet their needs. There was no electricity in the villages. In fact, one of the daily routines of one of the servants of our house was to light up twenty hurricane lanterns, one for each room. Even a hurricane lantern was regarded as an article of great innovation and luxury, since oil lamps had the tendency of getting extinguished. A firm bond of friendship and fellow feeling existed amongst the people. Such was Pilani.

Those were the golden days which will never return. Today the country is much richer; it has more facilities but the purity of heart, fellow feeling, good fellowship and the natural urge to help others were unique characteristics of the people of those days, which are conspicuous by their absence today.

7

In the Shadow of Tragedy

In Kolkata, our family stayed in a house in Rainey Park that we had purchased and renovated. Earlier we stayed at Zakaria Street, a Muslim locality. Whenever there was a communal riot in the city, we had to live in constant tension. Once, during one of these riots which probably took place around 1920, our house was surrounded by a riotous Muslim mob. We had many faithful servants including a brave durwan from upcountry named Ashta Singh. Whenever the house was in danger of being attacked, our servants immediately locked the entrance to the house. Ashta Singh would then take a gun and resort to blank fire. My eldest uncle Jugalkishore too was there. Father, however, was not there. Uncle, being a kind and soft hearted man, tried to dissuade Ashta Singh from firing but it would not be best same since our lives were in danger. He fired in the air to frighten and disperse the mob. We were saved in this way.

After this incident, father thought it wise to change our residence. We therefore decided to move to Rainey Park, where Birla Park was born in 19 .

Because the family was expanding, it was thought proper to construct another house. Land was, therefore, purchased at Gurusaday Road, which, in those days, was called Store Road. The land belonged to a member of the Tagore family. Father purchased a large plot of land, so large that we played football in the open space when we grew up. Four tennis courts were marked out on the lawns where father, uncle and other friends would play tennis. When we brothers and cousins grew up, we too started playing tennis on these courts.

We shifted to the new house some time in 1922 and named it Birla Park. I was a child of four when we shifted. I have clear remembrance of its construction. Mother often visited the house in its construction stage along with some other ladies of the household. Mother would often take me with her. It was a large mansion and the entire family lived in this house.

Some time in the late 1930s, Bhai Lakshmi Niwas shifted to another house. The rest of the family, consisting of uncle Jugalkishore, father, uncle Braj Mohan and my aunt and we, the brothers and cousins, continued to stay in Birla Park. In 1953, Braj Mohan also shifted to another house, which is called Birla House. Only we two brothers—Basant Kumar and myself—and cousin, Madhav Prasad, with our wives and children and father (who stayed in Delhi but visited Kolkata quite frequently) were left to live in Birla Park. The house seemed too large, so we two brothers and Madhav Prasad decided to build our own houses. But we also decided that, respecting the closeness amongst the three of us, we would stay near each other. Thus, in 1955, another complex arose. We named it Birla Park, after the palatial building in which we were living. We donated the old Birla Park to the Government of India for establishing an industrial museum. It is now called The Birla Industrial and Technological Museum.

After I shifted to Kolkata permanently, father had to think about my education and Basant Kumar's. Madhav Prasad, who was earlier living in Mumbai, also joined us.

In those days, father did not believe much in school or university education. It was only by the time my nephew, Aditya, grew up that father had changed his views. Initially he was of the view that in schools the students care more for passing exams than applying their mind to acquire knowledge. Father engaged tutors to coach me, but I did not make much progress under them.

I was too young at that time to have any opinion on whether or not I was getting a proper education. But viewing the matter now, I feel that the education of all of us in the younger generation was neglected.

My mother developed tuberculosis some time towards the end of 1924. She was at first moved to Ranchi as it was hoped that since the climate was bracing and invigorating, the change would do her good. It was a vain hope and, as was feared, there was no improvement in her health. In March 1925, father decided to shift mother to Solan, which is a hill station near Shimla. So deeply attached was father to mother that he delegated the authority of managing some of the units under his management to uncle BM (Braj Mohan), with the idea that father may not be burdened with the day-to-day problems of the mills but be free to devote most of his time to taking care of mother. Father then was a young man of thirty-two and uncle only twenty years old.

Tuberculosis was a disease with no cure in those days and father realized that mother had only a few months more to live. Being a very loving husband full of admiration and attachment for mother, father was determined to spend as much time as possible with her so that she may not feel his absence.

From Kolkata, father and we brothers and sisters left for Solan. On the way to Kalka falls Mughalsarai. My grandparents came to Mughalsarai station to meet us and and offer their blessings. Grandmother, out of affection, travelled with us till the next station. On the way, she came to know that tuberculosis was a contagious disease. So she offered to take me, my sister Chandrakala and Basant Kumar to Varanasi with her. Basant Kumar was only four. He started crying when grandmother asked him to get down. Father, always extremely fond of Basant Kumar, told grandmother that the boy would accompany him to Solan.

Chandrakala and I stayed at Varanasi for about a fortnight. After that we were sent to Kolkata to be with my uncle and aunt.

Shortly thereafter, my aunt, who was not well, went to Mussoorie and uncle sent me with her. From Mumbai, another aunt of mine—Madhav Prasad's mother—joined us there. My cousin Ganga Prasad, his sister Ganga and Madhav Prasad's elder brother Gajanan all went to Mussoorie. We stayed at a house called Charlie Ville, just above the Savoy Hotel.

Living was cheap in Mussoorie, but travelling to the place was cumbersome. From Kolkata to Dehra Dun in those days took two nights and one day. From Dehra Dun there was no motorable road to Mussoorie. One had to go to a small town called Rajpur from where one had to go in dandis (a kind of palanquin) or on horse back to Mussoorie. This involved five to six hours of trudging or steep mountain paths.

I had a good time at Mussoorie in the company of my cousins and sister. Mussoorie was a lovely hill station in those days. The surrounding were then far more full of verdure than they are today. There were no jarring sights of limestone quarries and hardly any felling of trees threatening the ecology of the region. The town was fully electrified but the houses had commodes which were cleaned by a sweeper. I did not like the use of commodes at all. In Pilani, when we were children we would go to sand dunes for the purpose.

There were three good hotels at Mussoorie—the Savoy, Charlie Ville and Hakman. They were at best equivalent to the three-star hotels of today. The hotel industry was still in its infancy. Most of the hotels were poorly managed, furniture was shabby, bathrooms were dirty and food poor.

The gentry that frequented Mussoorie in those days was the aristocracy comprising the cream of society. The middle class hardly existed. Only ruling princes, zamindars and businessmen could afford the luxury of regularly visiting hill stations during holidays. Princes of native states would quite often go to the hill station. The maharaja of Kapurthala had a house in Mussoorie even in those days which was regarded as the finest house in town. Though Mussoorie was part of the then British India, rajas and maharajas acted as if Mussoorie was part of their state. I remember once a maharaja was travelling in a rickshaw in Mussoorie when a coolie crossed the road. The maharaja was furious. How could a coolie cross the road when he was travelling in a rickshaw? This was a bad omen. He stopped the rickshaw and asked the coolie to go back to his original position.

The English gentry too would regularly visit Mussoorie in large numbers. In the evenings it presented a very colourful pageant. One could see fashionably clad Indian ladies riding rickshaws and crowding the shops in the markets at Kulri and Library. There were exclusive rendezvous of European ladies too. On the roads one saw plenty of rickshaws with liveried pullers.

Whereas the rich people swarmed Mussoorie during the summer months, the economic condition of the hill people was very miserable, providing a devastating contrast. They lived huddled in small tenements. Their only source of livelihood was employment. In spite of such hardship, people were contented, which might be due to the rich visitors giving the poor employees lavish tips at the time of their departure from the hills to the plains.

Though I had entered my seventh year, no system for my education had as yet been arranged. I had not joined any school nor was there any good tutor appointed to teach us. Mirza Maharaj, a member of our purohit family, was asked to teach us. His knowledge of Hindi was poor. He could not write correct Hindi and did not know how to spell words. The Indian languages give you no spelling headaches—you write what you speak. Yet most people made spelling mistakes. This was the drawback of Mirza Maharaj too, and soon it became evident that he could not teach us Hindi. He only taught us tables from two to twenty and said that after we had mastered these he would teach us tables from twenty-one to forty and so on.

Mirza Maharaj would, every day, write down the tables of three, four or five. We were asked to write the tables twelve times each on twelve slates—a total of 144 times. This really required five to six hours' work. Mirza Maharaj would set the tables and then doze off for a sound sleep. The task set for us young children was very hard but at the end of the day those particular tables were fully memorized. Even to this day I remember them.

In the evening, we would go out for a round of Mussoorie in our rickshaws. This routine continued for about twenty days. Meanwhile at Solan, mother, who very much loved me, became restless over my absence. Father sent a telegram that I should be sent to Solan immediately. It was clear that mother did not have many more months to live. Father put up a brave face but so intense was his love for mother that behind his courageous exterior he was full of gloom. But in spite of that he prepared himself to face mother's departure.

Tuberculosis being a contagious disease, we were permitted to go to mother only once or twice a day for five minutes each time. This was another matter for mother to be distressed over, that she could not meet her own children freely. However, she understood the reason and knew that it was for the good of the children that they were being kept away from her. After some time, seeing mother's gloom, father permitted us to spend more time with her, but from a distance, so that we did not contract the disease. A doctor from Kolkata was with mother throughout her stay

Mother Mahadevi Birla, who died in 1926

at Solan. Not that we could do much against tuberculosis, a dreaded disease.

Gloom pervaded the atmosphere in Solan. Father found solace in turning to religion and getting involved more and more in politics. Our entire family was religiously inclined. In Solan, in order to overcome this gloom, father had also engaged the services of a disciple of Vishnu Digambar-ji, the eminent vocalist.

Let me digress a little. Vishnu Digambar-ji was one of the best vocalists that India has produced. He had a very melodious voice. He could keep an audience spellbound with his singing. As Digambar-ji advanced in age, he took to singing bhajans (devotional songs) of Surdas, Tulsidas, Meerabai and other devotees. Father requested him to spare one of his disciples to recite bhajans so that religiosity pervaded the atmosphere. Father felt, rightly in my opinion, that to lift the pall of gloom, there was no better remedy than singing bhajans, which helped create an aura of tranquillity. Vishnu Digambar-ji spared one of his disciples called Dhundhi Raj for the purpose, who sang bhajans in the morning and in the evening. There is no doubt that the ambience had become intolerably melancholy owing to the impending departure of mother from our midst, which everyone knew was now only a matter of months. Our religious outlook brought peace and solace.

At Solan, many members of the family came to meet mother. She bore her suffering with magnificent fortitude. Mother was a lady of great mental and moral strength. God provided her with strength and peace of mind. Though ill and fully aware that her days were numbered, her satisfaction was that her children could not have got a better father. She was confident that after her demise father would look after the children, imparting training like a father and providing love like a mother.

At Solan, I met Pandit Udit Mishra. Pandit-ji hailed from Kuri, a village near Varanasi. He was engaged to teach Basant Kumar and me all subjects except English. He spent the first few days in trying to establish a rapport with Basant Kumar.

Pandit-ji was working as a correspondent of the paper *Aaj* of Varanasi when he came in touch with father. He had interviewed father for his paper. He also contributed a weekly column, *Gao ki Chitthi* (village letter), disseminating news of rural areas around Varanasi. He wrote well.

Father thought Pandit-ji was a fit person to look after the education of his children, more so as he himself was busy in politics owing to his close association with Mahatma-ji, Madan Mohan Malaviya, Lala Lajpat Rai,

Jawaharlal Nehru and others, apart from the time that he spent in looking after mother. It was a result of Pandit-ji's teachings that I acquired the habit of working hard which I retain to this day.

We stayed at Solan till October 1925. Sometimes we went to Shimla for a day or two where too we had taken a house on rent. But Solan being regarded as a more healthy place, we stayed there most of the time.

When it became very cold in Shimla and Solan, we shifted to Delhi. In the case of tuberculosis patients, it has always been considered advisable to keep the patient away from the dust, din and bustle of the city. Father therefore rented a house at Okhla. We stayed at Okhla for about three months. Father religiously endeavoured to keep the atmosphere of the place as placid as possible. In Delhi again all our relatives came to meet father—and mother for the last time.

Mother's condition deteriorated by the day. She expired on 6 January 1926. I believe it was early in the morning when the recitation of '*Raghupati Raghav Raja Ram Patit Pavan Sita Ram*' reached my ears. We were woken up and told that mother was no more. Basant Kumar, being very young, completely broke down. I too was shattered. Chandrakala was similarly devastated. My younger sisters were too young, but seeing others weeping they too began to cry. Though a child of seven years, I was strong-minded and so did not weep. However, I remember very distinctly that I could not sleep that night.

Father endured the loss very courageously. He was prepared for this and did. His faith in God and closeness to Mahatma ji helped him to bear his loss with greater equanimity

*

Father engaged an English lady, Mrs Burke, to teach us English. She was engaged, as far as I recollect, around the year 1927 and continued with us till early 1932. Mrs Burke was English by birth, a widow whose only son had died many years back. We were fortunate to have Mrs Burke to coach us because she was so dedicated. She taught us grammar, English literature, composition, essay writing for about two hours every day.

All told, studies took up eight hours a day. Of this, Mrs Burke would take up two hours and Pandit-ji six. As Mrs Burke had no family, she would accompany us wherever we went. She would not stay with us, but we made arrangements for her to stay in a hotel whenever we travelled outside Kolkata. When we visited Pilani during the winter months, Mrs Burke stayed in a tent pitched for her in the garden of our house. After we joined school in 1932, she preferred to join an old women's home run by an English charity of Delhi.

Father was constantly travelling. As I have written earlier, after mother's death, he grew very restless; though outwardly he appeared calm and composed, he could never forget mother. His unease was reflected in his constant travels. He could not stay at one place for more than a few days. He would stay in Kolkata perhaps for about a week or ten days in a month, and for the rest keep travelling—going to Delhi and Gwalior where we had textile mills or to Mumbai. The company of uncle RD (Rameshwar Das) was very enjoyable for him. Father, therefore, very consciously decided, while keeping an overall watch over our progress in studies, to entrust our upkeep, education and all else to uncle BM.

In the morning, the first thing we did was to offer our pranams (greetings) to father and uncles JK and BM by touching their feet. Father, being a traditionalist, fully approved of this method of showing respect to elders. Uncle BM, being more modern in outlook, did not quite like this ritual. After getting ready, we would have a cup of milk. We were not free to drink tea. Thereafter Pandit-ji would take us to the Victoria Memorial quite early, around 7 a.m. or 7.30 a.m. We would play at Victoria Memorial for about half-an-hour or so and then, sitting on mattresses, two of which would be spread under the shade of a tree, we would be taught by Pandit-ji till about 9.30 a.m or 10 a.m. Pandit-ji hailed from Varanasi, and that itself commandeered respect. Besides, his personality, communication skill and erudition brought him renown. Soon it became well known that the children of the Birlas come every morning to Victoria Memorial. Children of other people who also came for their walk played with us.

Returning to our house—Birla Park—around 10 a.m. , we would take our bath and then our meals around 11 a.m. After about one-and-a-half hours, we would resume our studies around 1.00 p.m.. Then, after a short recess for snacks, Pandit-ji would take us to the garden of Birla Park around 2.30 p.m. where we would study till 5 p.m. In between, Mrs Burke would teach us. Pandit-ji was fond of the outdoor life. I had all along been a lover of nature.

Around 5 p.m., we would disperse and play games. We were fond of tennis and football. I personally was very fond of climbing trees. I could climb any type, including coconut trees. I would sometimes climb a tree and sit on its branches for half-an-hour or so.

In the evening, after sunset, we would all get ready for dinner and, after dinner, chat with elders. We did not have any fixed time for dinner until it occurred to father that it was better to fix a time. This proposal was approved by all the members of the family. The time fixed was 6.45 p.m. for us children and 7.30 for adults. Separate timings for children, however, did not last for long. Everyone is fond of children and so was father. Hence after some time we all started having dinner together at 7.30 p.m.

Father would, from time to time, find out from Pandit-ji how we were doing in our studies, and he was satisfied with the progress we made.

After dinner, when in Kolkata, we would all assemble in what was called the 'gaddi'. Here father would lie down on the sprawling mattress filled with cotton covered with large clean white sheets.

Having wide contacts and being active in the business, social and political life of the country, many people would come to meet him. Those who were close to us had standing invitations to join us at dinner. Hence during dinner there would always be four or five guests who were close to father taking food with us. Others too who did not come for dinner would

Jaipur, 1928: Me, Basant Kumar, Madhav Prasad and Ganga Prasad with tutor Pandit Udit Mishra and Mahant Govind Das

join us at the gaddi for gossip and casual discussions. At 9 p.m. we all had to retire.

By now, father who was greatly under the influence of Mahatma-ji, started wearing khadi. He taught us children also to spin yarn with a hand device called *takhli*. Father too would spin yarn in this manner or spin on a charkha. We all became experts in spinning yarn with takhli.

Father or uncle would send us to a hill station, usually Mussoorie, every summer. Usually we would go to a hill station with Bhai-ji Lakshmi Niwas but sometimes uncle and aunt would take us with them. If, on any occasion, there was no family elder to accompany us, we would go on our own with Pandit-ji to look after us. Once during the summer of 1931 when we went to Mussoorie, my elder cousin, Gajanan, also came to Mussoorie with us. Amiable, frank, an excellent tennis player, Gajanan Bhai-ji's motto was to enjoy life wherever he was. He was very fond of the Western style of life. Under his influence at Mussoorie we started visiting a skating rink to practise roller skating. Gajanan Bhai-ji would also send for Indian sweets. There was nothing wrong in that but Pandit-ji, old-fashioned and traditionalist as he was, did not like it. He wrote a poem on this practice more in the form of lampooning it. Here are some lines from a few stanzas which I still remember:

Rink mein jane lage khane lage chamcham magha
Namak mirch talak videshi bhav deshi ka bhaga
Kahan hai takali tumhari aur khaddar ka sneh
Bhoomi jo jarkhez thi ab vahan rahe reh.

We did not stop going to the rink for skating as we thought there was nothing objectionable in enjoying ourselves by learning skating. But we liked Pandit-ji's poem and naughty as we were, we started reciting it. Pandit-ji struck his head with his hands in utter disgust over our mischief.

During our sojourns in the hill stations, we would usually take long walks. In Mussoorie too, I remember, Pandit-ji taught us under the shade of trees on the Mall between the Library and the Company Bagh. On our walks, we often met a Christian missionary. Pandit-ji often conversed with him. They became good friends even though Pandit-ji was a devout Hindu and the other a staunch Christian. Once the missionary had to go down to the plains for a fortnight. When he came back, Pandit-ji saw him walking on the Mall. They rushed towards each other and embraced warmly. Pandit-ji was a remarkable man, one who knew how to make friends and honour friendship.

Madhav Prasad, who was three months senior to me, was the leader of our group. We studied the same textbooks, and there always was healthy rivalry between us in studies.

In those days, the government was guided by what was good for Britain irrespective of how it affected the economic fortunes of India. The Companies Act and Income Tax Act were not comprehensive but simple to comply with. Even if there were any infringement of any act, the department concerned would not take any serious note of it.

Whenever father came to or left Kolkata, we would all go to receive him or see him off at the station. Many staff members and a large number of Oriya servants would also accompany us to the station. Going to the station so frequently affected our studies, but since we were not in a school, who cared?

That is how I spent my early boyhood until 1931 in a carefree manner. Life was idyllic. We enjoyed the love of all our elders—father, uncle and aunt, my brother Lakshmi Niwas, my sister-in-law Sushila Devi and so many others.

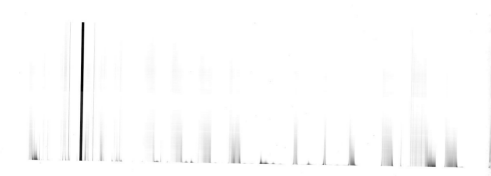

8

School and College

Father believed in imbibing the spirit of learning at the feet of good teachers where a student tried to get to the bottom of the matter of his enquiry, enrich his knowledge of the subject and become a master in the real sense of the term. We did not agree with father, but side by side I would like to admit that the standard of education in those days was very poor; 90 per cent of graduates did not know how to write good English at a time when English was a compulsory subject in schools and colleges! Whenever we wrote an essay on any subject, it was corrected by our home tutor. Father would later point out how poor the corrections were. No wonder father had a dislike for conventional school education. I marvel at how ahead he was of his times in his critique of our pro-Western colonial system of education.

In 1932, however, uncle BM asserted himself. In many ways, he was more pragmatic and advanced than father. He was firmly of the view that instead of leaving the children solely under the care and mercy of home tutors, who would decide what they would study, it was much better that they got admitted in a school and had a set of books as prescribed by the education department of the state government or by some recognized governmental institutions. Uncle also felt that we would mature by rubbing shoulders with boys of our age.

After prolonged persuasion by uncle, father agreed that we get admitted to a school. The question then was: which one? St Xavier's School was at that time regarded as the best in Kolkata, as it is perhaps even now. But father, an ardent follower of Gandhi-ji, did not want us to go to a school where the atmosphere was highly anglicized. We then thought of a school in Ballygunge, but they had no vacancy. The choice was then limited to Hindu School or Hare School. We heard much in praise of Hare School. David Hare (1775–1842), its founder, was a great educationist and a pioneer in the spread of education in Bengal. He was one of the few Englishmen of those days who really loved India. Hare, along with two other Englishmen—Justice Edward Hyde and East Wilson—and Raja Ram Mohan Roy, did pioneering work in the spread of education in Bengal, for social welfare, and the eradication of evil social practices. He established the School Book Society and the Kolkata School Society. The former organization published books prescribed in schools and the latter established schools in and around Kolkata.

So we got admitted to Hare School. This was some time towards the end of March or early April in 1932. Madhav Prasad and I were in fact slightly over-age for Class VIII, but this could not be helped. For appearing in the matriculation exam, a student had to study for two consecutive years in school. We were also found somewhat weak in certain subjects for Class IX.

It took us some time before we could adjust ourselves to the routine of school life. Unfortunately, none of us could speak Bengali, though I was over thirteen years old. Hare School had a special class of Hindi for non-Bengali students who wanted to take Hindi as a vernacular. English was compulsory. A student was required to take Bengali, Hindi or Urdu as the second language. We took Hindi as the second language since our mother tongue was Hindi.

The teachers at Hare School taught us well and were very liberal in outlook. At times, in case they spoke in Bengali, we would request them to explain in English also as we did not fully understand Bengali. No student ever minded this favour shown.

I made friends amongst the Bengali-speaking and Hindi-speaking boys. I participated in sports. I was good at football, though I never represented either my school or my class in sports. My cousin Girdhar was the best amongst us in sport as he played good football, hockey and tennis.

When the results of the examination held in May 1932 were declared, it was found that both Girdhar and I did very badly. The comment by the class teacher on our reports both in respect of Girdhar and myself was 'Not Good'. Madhav did much better than either of us. In the remarks on his report it was stated 'Expected to do much better in future'. The classes had begun in January whereas we got admitted only in March. Thus we had studied only for a few weeks before we could appear in the first examination without adequate time for preparation. Madhav Prasad's good performance only after a short period of regular schooling naturally evoked the remark from teachers that they expected him to do much better in the subsequent examinations. It was creditable that Madhav Prasad did well in the examinations after only a short period of school attendance. He was given a big pat on his back for his performance by father and uncle.

I was regarded as a mediocre student and had, in fact, accepted that Madhav Prasad was a better student. Hence the results did not come as a surprise or dampener.

After we got admission in school, Mrs Burke retired but Pandit-ji carried on teaching us, as he could give us lessons in all the subjects other than English. After the first terminal examination, Pandit-ji paid special attention to us. He also visited the school and met the various teachers. He declared to all the teachers that under his tutorship both Madhav Prasad and I would do much better than other students and even said that in the next examinations we would be at the top.

Then came the second examination which was held in August 1932. When the results were published, there was a surprise in store for everyone. I astounded everyone by securing better marks than Madhav Prasad. This amazed all the members of the family because Madhav Prasad was recognized as a better student. He looked upon my unexpected good showing in the examination as an affront. He was deeply annoyed and mildly jealous. He openly declared that in the annual examination he would do much better than I and would put me in my place. A sense of acute competition and one-upmanship immediately seized us.

The fact that I did better than Madhav Prasad completely transformed me. Until then, I was playing second fiddle to him. But the fact that I got better marks than he in the second term, put new zeal in me. I thought I could do it! I had no doubt in my mind that in the annual examination Madhav Prasad would beat me hollow. Madhav Prasad also publicly threw a challenge to me for the final exams of Class VIII. I really worked hard. I refused to be content with studying the textbooks that were prescribed; I purchased other books too on the subject of study in order to widen my horizon of knowledge. For Sanskrit grammar I purchased books on grammar which were taught in college. But in spite of my assiduous work, I suffered from an inferiority complex.

In December 1932, the results came out; I did much better than Madhav Prasad and the margin by which I beat him was more than the margin by which I had beaten him in the second terminal examination. I still remember that in Sanskrit I got 88 per cent. My teacher was a pandit named Dakshina Ranjan Bhattacharya. We called him Dakshina Babu. He was slightly eccentric. Half the time his teaching consisted of gossiping and regaling his students with all types of tales. After the results of Class VIII were out, Dakshina Babu remarked after seeing my answers, 'Nirbhool' (no mistakes).

Father was very happy when the final results for Class VIII were announced. I stood seventh in the class and did much better than was expected of me. It came as a surprise to the entire family that I could do better than Madhav Prasad.

I remember, soon after the results were announced, I went to Varanasi to meet grandfather. Father happened to be there at the time. He explained to grandfather what high marks I had obtained. Grandfather, however, was indifferent to the niceties and implications of scoring high marks in examinations. He only remarked that he would judge my abilities after a few years by seeing how I fared in business. At any rate, it got established that I was a good student too and I continued to do well in studies throughout the rest of my scholastic career.

Now my transformation was complete: I became very confident of myself. It must be said to the credit of Madhav Prasad that he was sporting enough to concede defeat. However, he was the pace setter.

In May 1933, we brothers and cousins went to Delhi to spend time with father in accordance with his wishes. While we were still in Delhi, it suddenly occurred to him that he would like to have Basant Kumar and me close to him. As an afterthought he felt that it would be better to have Madhav Prasad and me in Delhi as we were in the same class and so would find each other's company useful. Madhav Prasad and I vehemently opposed the idea. Father, however, had made up his mind. He said there were good schools in Delhi which we could join.

As chance would have it, I was at that time down with fever, suffering from acute bronchitis. However, Madhav Prasad's name and mine were submitted to Modern High School, Barakhamba Road, for admission.

Modern High School was regarded as one of the top schools in India. It was run by some leading citizens of Delhi. With father's name and influence, getting admission was no problem.

Since I was down with fever at that time, I could not attend on the first day. Madhav Prasad did—and came back highly disappointed. We had got used to the quality of school life in Kolkata where the Hindi-speaking and the Bengali boys maintained a certain cultured level of behaviour. That refinement was completely missing in Delhi. The boys were aggressive and appeared to be insolent and boorish. To those familiar with their way of life and conversation, they may not have appeared impudent; but coming as we did from Bengal, that is the kind of impression we formed. Madhav Prasad, after his first day's experience in school, returned home very upset. He was almost in tears and declared that he would not go to school the next day.

In those days, Calcutta University boys could matriculate as private candidates. Father, therefore, withdrew us from the school and arranged private tuition for us. Tutors started coaching us with the help of prescribed textbooks. We were able to find good teachers for English, Hindi and Sanskrit, but for Mechanics no teacher came up to standard. Many teachers were interviewed and were found to be lacking adequate knowledge of the subject. Ultimately a teacher named Ramchandra-ji was engaged. He was a good teacher and an upright individual.

After completing the course by October or November 1934, we decided to shift to Kolkata for a few months before appearing in the exam. We got good guidance in Kolkata. Pandit Udit Mishra was there to give the final polish to our knowledge of Hindi and Sanskrit.

In those days, private students had to pass an internal test first. It was said that the test for the private students was very stiff because the University authorities wanted to discourage students from not attending school. Madhav Prasad and I became nervous at the prospect. A child ultimately takes recourse to confiding in a parent when confronted with any type of anxiety or fear. For a boy, his father is his God who will never fail him. We had supreme faith in father. So we approached father and acquainted him with our apprehensions about the test. Father understood our problem and promised to try to help us.

Shyama Prasad Mookherjee was the vice chancellor of Calcutta University in those days. He was a good friend of father's. Father gave him the facts of the case. Father explained that earlier we had been students of Hare School. Could we be permitted to appear in the test of Hare School instead? Shyama Prasad Mookherjee said that he would have no objection if the Hare School authorities agreed to it.

We approached the headmaster of Hare School. As my younger brother Basant Kumar and my cousin Ganga Prasad were still studying in Hare School and as we had a good record of studies, the headmaster readily agreed to our request. We sat for the test and easily passed.

Then came the exam. There were seven papers, each of 100 marks. A few weeks after the exam, Shyama Prasad Babu came to our house at Birla Park. He told father that one boy from the family had done extremely well. He said he did not remember the name but everyone could guess who it was. The results were soon out. I received 569 marks out of 700 or 81.3 per cent. In those days, any student getting more than 75 per cent marks got a star from the University. I, therefore, received a star. I stood eleventh and was the recipient of a number of congratulations from members of the family, friends, relations, father's friends and executives. As usual, there were some sceptics also. When the news got around that I had done so well, these 'non-believers' spread a rumour that the Birlas had bribed the University authorities!

*

In March 1935, father took us to Varanasi to arrange for our yajnopavit, the sacred thread ceremony. Father could think of no saintlier person than Pandit Madan Mohan Malaviya, founder of Banaras Hindu University and its vice chancellor. Malaviya-ji Maharaj, as we used to address him, had a truly venerable disposition. He was a very devout Hindu but never a fanatic. We all respected him and held him in high esteem. He was just like a family elder to father.

On father's request, Malaviya-ji immediately agreed to perform our yajnopavit. A large number of pandits were invited for the feast. After the ceremony he became my guru, my preceptor, and had to give me a mantra, a maxim epitomizing what we should do and what we should not do in life. Such a maxim is whispered into the ear in confidence outside everyone else's hearing. He put a towel over our heads and then spoke to me for five minutes as to how I should conduct myself in life. I considered myself very fortunate to have a guru like Malaviya-ji who resembled our ancient rishis.

Malaviya-ji also taught us how to perform sandhya, a short prayer offered to God in the morning and in the evening. He taught me the Gayatri Mantra as well, one of the most sacred mantras in the Hindu scriptures.

From that day, I started performing sandhya every morning. This continued for about a year. But as this exercise took time—about 10 minutes—I gave it up after some time. I also stopped reciting the Gayatri Mantra.

Whenever I visited Varanasi I would call on Malaviya-ji. I would spend about twenty minutes or half-an-hour with him. During one of the visits to Varanasi, Malaviya-ji asked me whether I was performing sandhya, and reciting the Gayatri Mantra. I replied in the negative.

Malaviya-ji was happy that I spoke the truth as there was no one to check the veracity of my statement. He then said that even if I did not perform sandhya, I should recite at least the Gayatri Mantra in the morning and in the evening. Then he said that since he had given me the yajnopavit, he was very sad that I was not reciting the Gayatri Mantra. I promised him that I would henceforth recite the Gayatri Mantra without fail, in the morning and in the evening. How many times was left to my discretion. Since then I have been regularly doing so.

*

After matriculating, I went to Delhi to join college. I wanted to continue my studies in Kolkata, but I knew that father would not feel happy as he would like me to stay with him in Delhi.

Father, in fact, wanted Madhav Prasad and me to join the family business immediately. Madhav Prasad was agreeable. Much against father's wishes, I ultimately joined a college. I was the first member of the Birla family to go for higher education.

In Delhi in those days there used to be three colleges with a name—St Stephen's run by missionaries, Hindu and Ramjas. Ramjas College was regarded as not of the same standard as the Hindu College or St Stephen's. St Stephen's College was regarded as better, but highly anglicized. People with nationalistic views preferred Hindu College.

Since we had not yet attained independence, I thought that being a son of G.D. Birla, who was a close associate of Mahatma-ji, it would not be proper for me to join St Stephen's College. Hence I joined Hindu. Then arose the question of deciding the choice of subjects. I opted for Intermediate Science (ISc) where the subjects were English, chemistry, physics and mathematics.

I was the recipient of two scholarships—one from the Delhi University and the other from the Hindu College. The scholarship amount of Delhi University was Rs 20 a month and of the Hindu College Rs 18. In 1935, this was a sizeable sum. I did not keep the money for myself but gave it to needy deserving students.

After joining Hindu College, I soon realized that I made a mistake in joining a college in Delhi. The Intermediate Science courses of the Delhi University were basically for students who took science in their matriculation examinations in the Delhi University. In Calcutta University, there was no such subject as pure science for matriculation. Having no background of science, I found physics and chemistry very difficult subjects; the latter had so many formulae for chemical reactions and equations. All the same, I was confident that with hard work I would be able to pick up the threads of both physics and chemistry and do well in the examinations.

But a problem confronted me, which diverted my attention from studies.

My sister Chandrakala had married into the Daga family of Jalpaiguri. My brother-in-law, Bansidhar Daga, was regarded a leader in the tea business. With father's encouragement, he opened a hosiery factory in Delhi around 1933. In 1935, Bansidhar-ji decided to go back to Kolkata. His heart was always in the tea industry. The question then was: who would manage the business?

Father asked me to look after the Daga hosiery factory along with my studies and made me its managing director. I was reluctant, but on father's insistence I accepted the assignment. Every day, therefore, I had to spend two hours at the Daga factory. Including the time required for coming from and going to the factory, it consumed two hours forty five minutes of my time every day.

Science subjects are very difficult, certainly not as manageable as the subjects in the humanities stream. My studies started suffering.

That apart, as father was in Delhi, a large number of people—both businessmen and politicians—would come and stay with him at Birla House. I was expected to receive them at the station when they arrived and see them off when they departed. This further taxed my time.

At any rate, I studied very hard. I was still regarded as a good student in my college. I passed my Intermediate Science examination in 1937. When the results were announced, I, surprisingly, occupied the seventh position in the university and I topped in maths. But though I did well in c, my foundation remained weak. I had concentrated only on those portions of the textbooks from where I was expecting questions to be set. It was clear that father did not attach much value to academic studies. Otherwise he would not have asked me to look after the Daga hosiery factory or to receive guests at the station. Father stuck to his view and refused to attach any importance to formal studies in school and college, though later, by the time my nephew, Aditya, grew up, he had changed his views.

In retrospect, I think it was a mistake on my part to have taken the science course. Had I taken economics and English it would have been much better. Both these subjects would have been very helpful in my business career.

9

The Mahatma Saves Me

After ISc, I wanted to graduate. Father, however, would have none of it. He said enough was enough; no more studies for me. It was, therefore, decided that I would join business immediately after the exams were over.

Before I could do so, I fell seriously ill. I caught a chill and, in spite of medication, my condition worsened. The best doctors available in Delhi were consulted. But my condition did not improve. I continued to run a low temperature and had a virulent cough.

I hold an umbrella over Mahatma-ji to protect him from the sun
as he enters Birla House, where he used to stay

At that stage, father consulted Dr B.C. Roy. Bidhan Babu, as he was popularly known, was definitely the best physician in the country in those days. He was not only our family doctor but also a family friend. Bidhan Babu was quick in diagnosis and excellent in treatment. He gave me some medicines and also asked me to put on some kind of perforated cover over my nose. On this cover some medicines were applied which Bidhan Babu thought were good for the lungs.

In spite of the treatment, the affliction did not show any sign of abating. Both temperature and cough persisted. Father got very worried. It was suspected to be tuberculosis (TB). This is what all the doctors, including Bidhan Babu, felt.

In those days, there was no cure for TB. Father had already lost his wife, my mother, to it. He could not countenance the idea of losing a son to the same fell disease. He, therefore, decided to consult Gandhi-ji. Side by side, father also made arrangements for me to proceed to Switzerland and be treated there. The general impression was that if at all TB could be cured, it was in Switzerland. When Mahatma-ji heard about my affliction, he advised that I be sent to Almora, renowned for its invigorating climate. Gandhi-ji's advice meant that he accepted the responsibility for my health. Without losing any time, father arranged to send me to Almora. I was old enough to look after myself. I took a few trusted persons with me.

Chilkapata House was in a secluded area of Almora. From the main road one had to descend on foot about 300 ft to reach Chilkapata House. There was no other house nearby and from there a fine view of the surrounding mountains and valleys was available. Before leaving for Almora, father cautioned me not to get bored and said that I would be required to stay there for about five months, which I did.

With me there was B.D. Sharma, who was a professor of English in Ramjas College, and who gave me private tuition. At my request, he resigned from the college and joined me as a companion. Another teacher who used to teach me was Ratanlal Jaiman. He did not leave his service, but during school holidays, he would visit me. Muralidhar Dalmia, chief executive of Birla Cotton Mills and a man of great ability and organizational capacity, also visited me during my stay there. I also took Govind Das from Pilani with me. I had a car chauffeured by Jes Raj, a barber from Pilani who was deeply attached to me. There was a cook, my personal servant, and a couple of others.

After reaching Almora, I gradually started improving. Father and I felt that this was owing to the blessings of Gandhi-ji. Our theory was that when Gandhi-ji realized that father, who was so close to him, would be completely shattered if he lost me, he gave his most sincere blessings. Within two months my temperature normalized. I was required to send a telegram every day to father about my temperature and pulse rate. Father would go through them carefully, as can be seen from the following anecdote.

There was a rivulet from Chilkapata House down below in the valley. One day, out of sheer bravado I decided to trek here. Ratanlal, whom we used to call Master-ji and who was as reckless as I was, accompanied me. The rivulet seemed to be very near our house, but actually it took us quite some time to reach it. It was five hours before I returned. I had expected to complete the whole trek to and fro in about an hour-and-a-half. But in the hills, with zigzag paths to traverse, a trek takes much longer even though it appears that the destination is quite close by.

I had just recovered from the illness. To undertake such a journey was nothing but foolhardiness on my part. But that was characteristic of a wild youth like me.

That day my temperature shot up and so did the pulse rate. When I sent the usual telegram to father, he got very worried. He immediately flashed me a wire. When I sent him the explanation he was greatly relieved, but also got annoyed and chastised me for my recklessness.

I had gone to Almora around mid-April 1938 and came back to Delhi about the middle of September, fully recovered. I attribute my recovery to Gandhi-ji's blessings. Father too must have felt the same way.

*

After my illness, graduation was out of the question. Hence I had to join business.

To run a business successfully, one has to be well-versed in accounts. Ever since the days of grandfather, every member of the family understood accounts well. It was felt—rightly, in my opinion—that a man with a competent background in accounts could not be cheated in business. Father felt that there was no royal road to gaining proficiency in accounts except to sit with the chief accountant and to personally prepare and write the accounts books—cash book, ledgers and journal. Father felt that if a man was a good accountant he could organize any work which had to deal with finances. He used to tell us a story about his own young days when he started the jute mills. Not having any technical experience, he was at his wits' end to know what to do and how to manage the mills. An elderly friend advised father not to worry about the technical side of the work. The friend suggested that he make an estimate of what the monthly production in value should be, and what expenses, exercising the greatest amount of economy, should be, and then deduce the expected profit. This friend told father that if he was strong in financial control, he could manage any industrial unit.

Always keen to learn, father immediately realized the precious value of the advice that was given to him and started the famous *parta* system of accounting for which our family and our organization have acquired fame. Father developed the system with such finesse that it could provide a daily profit and loss statement of the performance of the unit concerned. This daily profit and loss sheet would not directly show what the day's profit was. It would merely indicate, as compared to the parta, the amount of gain and loss under various heads. Thus, the daily report had several columns showing daily income earned or loss suffered by the unit in production and raw material consumption and expenses compared to the parta. The statement would thus show in which direction the company was losing compared to the target, and where it was gaining. In this way, attention of the management was diverted to the areas where the unit was losing money. Efforts were then made to analyse the causes of poor performance of the unit and to improve its performance to achieve the target. This system found favour with father all through his life. Even now it prevails in a number of our units.

Father put me in Kesoram Cotton Mills to learn accounts. There was a certain Shanti Lal Mehta who was the number two man in the accounts department there. Shanti Lal was a very able person. He mentioned to me that he was going to start his own practice as a chartered accountant and so would be with us only for a year or so. He took great pains to acquaint me with the intricacies of accounts.

In accounts there are three main books—cash book, ledger and journal. I started with the cash book and made every day's cash entries at the end of the day with the help of vouchers. After I mastered the technique of writing the cash book, I started writing the ledger, which is more difficult. It took me some time to pick up the art of writing the ledger. Then came noting the entries of the cash book and the ledger in the journal. After I had mastered all the three books of accountancy, I started learning how to make the balance sheet. This was a most difficult task. To make a balance sheet, the balance of each account of the journal had to be calculated. If there was a difference in debits and credits, the whole process had to be rechecked. There were no calculators in those days: all the calculations had to be done schoolboy style. It was a tedious job, but essential. I was fast in calculations. Hence I could prepare the balance sheets quicker than many others.

The whole exercise gave me a very thorough background in understanding the significance of each entry in a balance sheet. In case the balance sheet did not tally and there was a difference, we would spend hours trying to spot where the discrepancy lay. After toiling for hours, when a correct balance sheet finally emerged, it was a matter of profound satisfaction to all concerned.

Within six months, I had become proficient in accounts. At the end of six months, father tested me, posing a number of questions. He was satisfied with my knowledge. This was the end of the training so far as accounts were concerned. The question was what I was to do next.

Father thought that if I acquired some knowledge of the technical side of the workings of a textile unit it would stand me in good stead in managing the textile business. He selected Panchu Babu to give me lessons on the technical side of a textile unit. A south Indian, Panchu Babu was the cost accountant at Kesoram Cotton Mills. He was neither a technician nor did he have any accountancy background. He was, however, an able man and had a good knowledge of both accountancy and the working of a textile unit. He became adept in both, and started teaching me about the spinning side of a textile unit. That was in 1938. After that, he gave me an elementary idea of the weaving side. In the five months I spent with him, he taught me the ins and outs of the technical side of spinning and weaving, such as what are reeds and picks, dents, ends, flanged bobbin, spinning, the difference between warp yarn and weft yarn, ring frames, sizing, drawing frames, what should be the number of twists for various counts, how the sizing machine worked, and so on. I still have the notes I made in an exercise book.

What Panchu Babu taught me was the theory of spinning, weaving and sizing. I did not have the opportunity of going to Kesoram Cotton Mills in Kolkata to learn the practice followed in the mills. Father then sent me to Jiyajeerao Cotton Mills at Gwalior which was one of the best managed units in our organization. Not only that, late Durgaprasad Mandelia, who was the most senior manager under father, was in charge of this mill.

Durgaprasad was an outstanding executive. He was a great organizer and a born leader. He enjoyed the full confidence of father. He belonged to Pilani. His father was Gouri Dutt-ji, who used to look after our zamindari (landholding, with revenue collection responsibility) at Ranchi.

Father did not have any liking for zamindari but having one was a sort of status symbol in those days. That apart, my grandfather and my eldest uncle, Jugalkishore, loved having a zamindari. We, therefore, purchased one in an auction in the late 1910s. Since 1923 or 1924, I remember this zamindari near Ranchi and how Jugalkishore, who was very fond of Ranchi, would visit the place quite often and numerous peasants from our zamindari came to meet him to narrate their tales of woe. The plight of the farmer was very bad in those days. There were hardly any irrigation facilities. There was no mechanical farming. The Indian farmer was very backward indeed. Bullocks were used for farming. They were not fed well, and so were very lean and thin. Indian farmers were very poor and were always in debt. Jugalkishore was a saintly person. He would listen to their grievances and sufferings and try to mitigate their hardships as much as possible. In the majority of cases, he would forgo the dues that were receivable from the cultivators.

I stayed in Gwalior in 1939 for three months and got thorough training under Durgaprasad. We were born in a family of businessmen, and finance was in our blood, just as chivalry is in the blood of a Rajput, Maratha, Gorkha, Sikh or Jat. In Gwalior, I got training in stores, time-keeping and the technical side. I learnt the names of hundreds of items used in textile mills, such as shuttles, bobbins, picking, picking band, temple, weft fork holder, lease rod, drop box pickers, weft pern, reed hields, not to speak of items which are used in every factory like bolts and nuts, screws, files etc. Durgaprasad asked me to try to remember who the important manufacturers of important items were, what was the volume of their consumption, what their rates were, and all other details. Not only that, to give me a thorough grasp of the technical side, he asked a fitter to open a carding engine, which is an important machine in a spinning unit, to explain the names of each part and then to reassemble the carding engine in my presence. I could not have found a better guide.

In spite of my good memory and diligent attitude, I must confess that I could have done a better job than what I did. The reason was that I was still keen to study and acquire a degree. I made enquiries and was told that I could appear as a private student from the Punjab University for Hindi Prabhakar (which was equivalent to BA honours in Hindi). I was fond of Hindi and had stood second in Hindi in Calcutta University, scoring 80 per cent marks in matriculation, the highest having been obtained by my cousin Madhav Prasad—81 per cent. So I decided to go in for Hindi Prabhakar.

Punjab University, however, had a rule that only domiciled students could appear as private students. Fortunately, we had a mill at Okara, of which father was the chairman. This helped me to be considered a student of Punjab. After some persuasion, the university authorities agreed that I could appear as a private student. Now the problem was to find someone who could privately teach me Hindi. Durgaprasad said that he knew a good man called Durgaprasad Shastri, a very scholarly person with a fine command over both Hindi and Sanskrit. Shastri was a Vaishya by caste, but, having obtained various degrees, including the Shastri degree from one of the universities, he was not only called Shastri-ji but was many times taken to be a Brahmin. Shastri used to stay at Jhansi. It was, therefore, arranged that he would come every day to Gwalior from Jhansi by train, teach me for a couple of hours from 8 p.m. and return to Jhansi the next morning. This was a good arrangement. I found Shastri to be a splendid teacher and a man of great erudition. He took great pains to coach me. Back in Kolkata, I continued my studies. I discovered to my pleasant surprise how specialized and vast Hindi poetic literature was. I learnt various types of poems and *alamkaras* (metaphors). In 1940, I passed with honours and stood seventh in Punjab University.

The Sarda Act passed in 1929 prescribed the minimum age of marriage to be eighteen years for boys and fourteen for girls. In my generation in the Rajasthani business community, this was accepted as the age at which a boy was to get married. Madhav Prasad, in fact, was married soon after he attained the age of eighteen.

When growing up, I had no desire to get married before the age of twenty. Also, having recovered from a serious disease, which was perhaps TB, I was not expected to marry till it was established beyond any doubt that there was no danger of a relapse and that I was perfectly healthy. By the end of 1939, one year after my recovery, father and uncle started looking around for a suitable match for me. Many offers came, but they were rejected. In some cases, the girl had 'no personality'; in others the girl was considered 'ultra-modern'. Father wanted to find a bride for me who would be of a sober disposition, educated and a 'home-maker'. The search continued. I was at Seohara in early 1940 and there I got the news that father had selected a bride for me, subject to my final approval.

Ultimately, I got engaged in Varanasi with the blessings of grandfather and grandmother. The wedding took place on 3 July 1941. I was almost twenty-three years old, considered quite a ripe age for a bridegroom in our community. My wife Manorama had received education at home. She could speak English, Hindi and Bengali fluently. In fact she spoke Bengali much better than I did.

Kolkata, 3 July 1941: Our wedding. Manorama's grandfather
Rai Bahadur Mangtulal Tapuriah can be seen in the picture

My wife came from the Tapuriah family, one of the aristocratic families
of Kolkata. Her great father—Rai Bahadur Mangtulal—was a man of
very refined tastes. He was a remarkably intelligent and witty person,
elegant and polished. He was fond of good clothes, loved to live in style;
in short he was a thoroughly sophisticated gentleman.

By God's grace ours has been a happy marriage. In all my activities I
have received total support and encouragement from my wife. She is
mobility personified. All the members of both our families—Birla and
Tapuriah—as also our friends and well-wishers, solicit her advice and
guidance whenever there is any problem. She is very witty and possesses
a charming personality. If I have been able to render any service to the
community at large, it is mostly owing to the inspiration I have received
from her.

10

My Early Business Ventures

We had two major companies in Kolkata under our management. Birla Jute Mills was under Madhav Prasad and Kesoram Cotton Mills was being looked after by Basant Kumar, both under father.

Father's thinking was that as the textile industry was the most developed industry in the country at that time, the manufacture of textile machinery should prove to be very profitable. It was a good idea but, unfortunately,

Author with his father Dr G.D. Birla in the early 1950s

its implementation was fraught with problems. If we desired to manufacture textile machinery we should really have sought a good collaboration arrangement and not gone it alone. The best textile machinery manufacturer in those days was the British group, Platts. Father sounded them out for technical collaboration or a joint financial venture. India— a part of the British Empire—was a highly profitable market for Platts. They had no intention of sharing their knowledge or profits with an Indian entrepreneur. Any other person would probably have waited for better times till a collaboration agreement was reached. The spirit of entrepreneurship and adventure would not permit father to do that. A very enterprising man, he did not mind facing problems. If the Platts were reluctant to sign an agreement with us, father decided he could, and would, go it alone. He was determined that we should manufacture textile machinery ourselves.

There was an Austrian named K. Stolba, an able and efficient engineer in our employment. Under father's instructions, he drew up a blueprint for this project. The entire concept was the outcome of a spirit of bravado. The project was put under my charge. I had no idea whatsoever of running an engineering unit. When I told father about the problems which I envisaged, father related to me what he did when he was a young man. Father did work wonders when young. Such was his self-confidence that he would take a plunge into any risky venture, whereas a cautious person m or ferre to walk on trodden ground. I though to embark on this tur v thou proper know-how would be a rash and hazardous ent iki g. At ny rate, a father had deci ed tha ve had to proceed t e p oject here was no looking b ck. A comp ny was registered n t r me d Textile M achinery Cor por tion L d , which was later ng t Tex aco Ltd., now a high-rank ng eng ineering concern at ka i. his w s my first b g venture. The and wa purchased at my cti n the rthern su urb of Belgharia. Placing orders for all the machineries needed, erection of factory sheds and buildings and so on were all done under my directions.

Father was, no doubt, there to guide me, but guide was all he did. He did not participate in the execution of the work or its management. All decisions were left to me.

Father's method of training was to give the maximum possible freedom to his people and limit his presence only to the task of guiding and assessing the results. He always reminded me of a trainer who teaches young boys how to swim. The ideal trainer would have a boy learn swimming by himself by making him follow a few commands. He would certainly make sure that the boy did not drown but, otherwise, he would leave the boy free to splash about in water, keep afloat, and move forward.

I was a young man of only twenty-one, but had a clear idea of the risks involved. As a young man, father had succeeded in whichever business he did. He started his business career as a broker for hessian or jute goods. Later, he started a jute mill and several textile mills. All these industrial units performed excellently. However, they were all consumer industries. There is a big difference between a consumer industry and a capital goods industry. In a consumer industry, like textiles or jute goods, there is a market even for products of inferior quality. The life of a finished product of a textile unit, like a dhoti or a chaddar (sheet), for example, is a few months or a year or so at the most. In the capital goods industry, the life of the finished product like spinning units is fifteen or twenty years. Hence, if the design and workmanship of capital goods are not up to the mark, that becomes a permanent headache for the customer. This is what I tried to explain to father. He did not agree with this view. I, therefore, made frantic efforts to find a suitable foreign collaborator.

In those days, Japanese textile machines were little known in this country. Only three foreign manufacturers of textile machines were known to textile mills in India—Platts of England, Reiters of Switzerland and Saco Lawal of the United States. We sounded out Reiters and Platts. Reiters showed reluctance to enter into any kind of collaboration. I again approached Platts. They were absolutely unwilling to consider any collaboration agreement with any company in India. I expressed my misgivings to father. But he was a man of great determination and ever willing to undertake a risky venture, quite unlike uncle BM who was on the cautious side.

We started with the manufacture of looms in Texmaco and, in spite of heavy odds, manufactured ten looms. We tested these looms. In finish and performance they were below the quality of imported looms, but since they were made without any foreign collaboration and solely with the help of Indian technicians and indigenous Indian skills, there was an atmosphere of quiet satisfaction and optimism in the management. Father was very happy and commended my performance.

While we were applying our mind to increasing the manufacturing capacity of our factory, the Second World War erupted. Texmaco factory was taken over by the government under an agreement with us, by which the government met all the expenses, including depreciation and gave us a certain amount of money every month as profits. The agreement was negotiated by me. I found the profit that was offered to the company for taking over its factory was highly inadequate. Ultimately, I approached Sir Evan Jenkins who was the private secretary to the viceroy (Lord Wavell). Jenkins was a very fair-minded person. He accepted all my arguments and then agreed to allow a decent profit to Texmaco. I continued my friendship with Jenkins even after he retired.

I was not satisfied with the Texmaco situation. I knew that manufacturing textile machines requiring a high degree of precision and skill without foreign collaboration was a Herculean task. I told father that the line which he had selected for me (manufacture of textile machines) was very hazardous. In reply, father gave me a lecture on what could be and should be done. I had no doubt in my mind that what father was saying was of academic significance and to venture into the manufacture of textile machinery alone was like striking one's head against a wall. Uncle, as I mentioned earlier, was more practical. He entirely agreed with me and discussed my problems with father.

Uncle had earlier started a paper mill in Orissa called Orient Paper Mills. It was well planned and well managed. Uncle had also laid down certain systems of management. Orient Paper Mills was the biggest industrial unit under uncle. As a lot of his time was being taken in the management of the mills, he was looking for a family member to take charge of the three sugar mills under him which, in comparison, were smaller units. It was, therefore, decided that, unlike Madhav Prasad or Basant Kumar who were completely under father, I was to work under two family members and under uncle. Uncle was very fond of me and immensely confident in me. He felt very happy that I would be reducing his burden in respect of the management of the sugar mills. I had rather more responsibility in respect of Texmaco and uncle in respect of sugar industry.

The sugar units were tiny factories which, in course of time, grew into huge mills. It is not my intention to dilate on the expansion of my business. I would not like to bore the readers with such an account. But before I conclude this chapter I would like to say a few words about the *Hindustan Times* with which I have been closely connected.

The *Hindustan Times* was started in 1924 and incorporated as a joint stock company in 1927 by Pandit Madan Mohan Malaviya. Father was one of the co-promoters of the *Hindustan Times* along with Malaviya-ji, Lala Lajpat Rai and a few others. When the company was floated, father was the biggest shareholder. He also financed the purchase, and arranged the capital required to run the company. I am reproducing separately the minutes of a meeting of the board of directors of the paper.

A meeting of the Board of Directors of the Hindustan Times was held on 15th march 1929, at 2.30 p.m. in the room of the Legislative Assembly Chambers, Nationalist Party. The following Directors were present:—

1. Pandit M. M. Malaviya   (Chairman)
2. Mr. Ghanshyamdas Birla
3. Mr. M. R. Jayakar
4. Lala Baij Nath Syal

The following business was transacted:—

1.   Resolved that the salaries of Mr. J. N. Sahni & K. D. Kohli, Editor & Manager be raised by Rs. 50/- & Rs. 100/- respectively with effect from the 1st January 1929.

2.   Resolved that the shares be issued in the name of Pandit M. M. Malaviyaji for the sum of Rs. 7,575/- received through him or in the name or names of persons advised by him.

3.   Resolved that share of Rs. 1000/- lying in the name of a friend of Pandit M. M. Malaviya be issued in the name of Pt. M. M. Malaviya or in the name or names of persons advised by him.

4.   Resolved that the purchase of the Motor Car for Manager be approved.

5.   Resolved that the shares may be allotted to the following for the amounts noted against their names:—

    1. Seth Ghanshyamdas Birla Rs 500/=   50 shares
    2. Lala Shri Ram, Delhi Cloth Mills , 200/=   20 "
                                                   ─────
                                                    70

10-f-   70

3. Mr. Suraj Kumar Ajmere   Rs. 100/=   1 Share
4. Mr. Hari Parshad Ajmere   Rs. 200/=   2 ' "
5. Mr. Ghisoo Lal Dhanopia Ajmere Rs. 200/=   2 ' "
6. S. Makhan Singh Lahore Cantt. Rs. 500/=   10 ' "
7. Mr. Ajmeri Parshad Ajmere   Rs. 100/=   1 ' "
8. Mr. Manji Ram Rathore Ajmere Rs. 100/=   1 ' "
9. R.B. L. Mitha Sugar, Lahore. Rs. 1000/=   10 ' "
10. Mr. Keori Lal Sethi, Jaipur Rs. 100/=   2 ' "

Total   99

6. Resolved that in view of the present financial
condition of the Hindustan Times and to raise more
capital the Hindustan Times, Ld., should be reconstructed
and a meeting of the shareholders be immediately
called for the purpose.

M. M. Malaviya
Chairman

A meeting of the Board of Directors was
to be held on the 5th March 19.., @ 2.3 p.m
in the room of the Nationalist party, Assembly Chambers
but was adjourned on % of lack of quorum.

M. M. Malaviya
Chairman

I came to know more about the *Hindustan Times* in 1933 when I shifted to Delhi. In the early days of the paper, Parasnath Sinha was in charge of the paper.

Parasnath-ji, who hailed from Bihar, was engaged by father in the early 1920s as a tutor to Lakshmi Niwas. Thereafter, he became father's secretary. For some time he was also sent to Brajrajnagar to look after Orient Paper Mills but that assignment was not to his liking. He was a man of literary tastes and was remarkably proficient in both English and Hindi. He was a very honest and upright man. He could write well in both the languages. His knowledge of economics too was good.

The management of the company was being looked after by father. In the earlier years, Malaviya-ji was looking after the editorial side of the paper. However, in the early 1930s, father took over complete charge of the paper. In 1936, he appointed Parasnath-ji as the managing editor—in charge of both the management and editorial side of the paper. Parasnath-ji managed the paper very efficiently.

Parasnath-ji suffered from high blood pressure which, in those days, caused great suffering and mental agony to the victim. High blood pressure affected the heart and the kidneys. Father, therefore, thought it best to lessen the workload and responsibility of Parasnath-ji by appointing him as an adviser and making Devdas Gandhi the managing editor of the paper. Gandhi-ji was not very fortunate in his sons, except Devdas. Although Gandhi-ji never spoke to father about Devdas, being close to him, father thought that he should try to find a suitable assignment for Devdas.

Devdas was managing editor from 1937 to 1957. Like Parasnath-ji he managed the paper well. Father was the chairman of the *Hindustan Times* and so Devdas would often visit our house in New Delhi to consult him about the policy and the management matters. As my headquarters was also in Delhi I came in close touch with Devdas.

Devdas died in 1957 of heart failure. The *Hindustan Times*, though it had acquired quite a reputation for its bold and fearless editorials, was still in its infancy. Its daily circulation was 60,322 when Devdas died and the total annual turnover was Rs 80.61 lakh with gross profit at Rs 3.97 lakh.

Father had no time to run the paper and to attend to its problems. Father knew I was fond of politics and enjoyed meeting people. So he asked me to look after the paper. I joined the *Hindustan Times* as a director in 1957 and started looking after it since then. In course of time, the *Hindustan Times* grew in strength and became one of the premier

English dailies of the country. It has the highest circulation of English language dailies in north India. Its turnover has increased from Rs 87.17 lakh in 1957–58 when I took charge to Rs 323.11 crore in 1999–2000. I am still the chairman and am guiding the overall policy of the paper though it is my daughter, Shobhana, who is running the show.

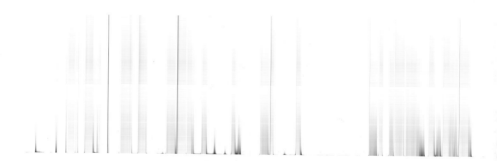

11

Widening My Horizons

Along with business, I took active interest in social welfare as well as
the activities of the associations of industries or chambers, like FICCI
and its affiliates. I took active interest in the Indian Chamber of Commerce,
Kolkata—one of the topmost chambers of commerce in the country. At
the same time, I got myself inducted into the activities of FICCI, first as
an invitee and later as a member of the committee. In course of time, as
my business activities proliferated, the government nominated me to a
number of bodies. I was nominated to the Central Advisory Council of
Industries for many years (along with J.R.D. Tata) and also to the Board

With J.R.D. Tata at a meeting of the Industrial Consultative
Committee

of Trade. I was also a member of the National Railway Users Consultative Committee for quite a few years. This body met from time to time to consider problems faced by the public and industry.

The Central Advisory Council of Industries was an important body. Its function was to advise the government about the problems faced by industries and offer suggestions for the growth of gross domestic product (GDP), industrial production and improvement in balance of trade. As this was the most important body to advise the government on the economy, there were many other industrialists who were aspirants for nomination. On behalf of industry, Tata used to be the first speaker and I used to be the second. The Council continued to function for a number of years and what the representatives of industry said received close attention from the Government of India.

During my active association with FICCI, I toured the country, addressing businessmen. I was a member of all important delegations that called on any minister, including the prime minister. For a number of years I was also a member of the Council of Scientific and Industrial Research (CSIR). I was, for a number of years, a member of the National Integration Council and, thus, came in touch with all the chief ministers of the states and leaders of all political parties. I was also a member of Industrial Credit & Investment Corporation of India (ICICI), which was started in 1955 by my father, Kasturbhai Lalbhai, and other leading industrialists. ICICI, where the majority of the shares at present were held by government bodies, was then an institution in the private sector. It is interesting to note how a private sector organization became a public sector unit.

The shares of ICICI owned by business houses were held by several private sector insurance companies such as New India Assurance, Ruby Insurance and others. With the nationalization of general insurance in 1972, the majority of the shares of ICICI got devolved on the public sector, and ICICI thus became a public sector institution. As I have mentioned, ICICI was started by some businessmen as an institution in the private sector to help industrialists in setting up new industries in the country or modernizing the existing plants. Father was one of the promoters. Our group had a sizeable percentage of the shares. The general understanding was that there would always be one person from our group as a director of ICICI. After some time, father retired and I was taken in as a director in 1959. I continued as director even after ICICI became a public sector company after the nationalization of the general insurance industry in 1972.

In 1977, fresh elections were held in the country. The Congress (I) suffered a crushing defeat as a result of the Emergency imposed in 1975. Morarji Desai, with the support of Jayaprakash Narayan, became prime minister. Indira Gandhi was badly defeated; I stood by her. A lot of pressure was exerted on me to ditch her. I stuck to my decision. In early 1979, I was asked by Jagdish Saxena, who was then chairman of the Industrial Development Bank of India (IDBI) and, in that capacity, a director of ICICI too, to resign from ICICI, which I did. Saxena was a good friend of mine. After a board meeting of ICICI which I had attended he took me aside and said that the high-ups in the government desired that I should resign. Their main ground was that I had stood by Indira Gandhi even after her defeat in the election. I immediately submitted my resignation without any argument.

I was also a member of a number of business councils and was, for several years, chairman of the Joint Business Council of the United States and India as also of the Joint Business Council of India and Japan.

This tenor of life continued right till 1984 when I got elected to the Rajya Sabha as an Independent candidate supported by the Congress (I). Our family has been in politics since the late 1910s. Father came in touch with Gandhi-ji in 1915 and played a pivotal role in the struggle for independence. Owing to father's involvement, there was a general atmosphere of interest in politics in the family. Mahatma-ji always stayed with us and before independence, all the important leaders, such as Malaviya-ji, Sardar Patel, Rajendra Babu, Raja-ji and K.M. Munshi, used to stay with us.

Once I was elected to the Rajya Sabha, I got actively embroiled in politics. However, I continued to look after my business interests with as much vigour as in the past. But I resigned from all the business bodies and have not taken any active interest in these bodies since. For some time, though, I attended a few meetings of FICCI out of loyalty to this great organization which was founded by my father along with other industrialists and which had been nurtured thereafter by other members of our family, notably by my uncle BM and my elder brother Lakshmi Niwas.

Before I got elected to the Rajya Sabha, and when I was actively involved in business, I knew most of the secretaries, additional secretaries and many of the joint secretaries to the Government of India. I would quite regularly invite them for lunch or for drinks. I also knew the governor and the deputy governors of the Reserve Bank of India, chairmen of important banks, the General Insurance Corporation (GIC), Life Insurance Corporation (LIC), etc. After 1984, I drastically reduced my circle of acquaintances, contacts and friends in the government and business. Now I know very few secretaries. A large number of businessmen of my time have either retired or died. I know very few of the new generation of businessmen.

With these words, I would like to bid farewell to writing about my business and private life and go on to say a few words about the milestones and the watershed of my political career.

*

As mentioned earlier, I was actively involved in politics from a young age. Apart from my business activities, interest in politics played a crucial role in my public life.

Gandhi-ji had started staying with us in Delhi since the mid-1930s. Father would personally look after his comforts and needs and I assisted him. There would be prayers in the morning and in the evening. Members of the public were not allowed to join these *prarthana*s but anyone known to Gandhi-ji or our family was welcome. It was not always possible for me to join the morning prarthana but I regularly attended the evening one. Whenever Gandhi-ji visited Birla House in Delhi, father kept him company even during his walks inside the compound. I often followed them during these walks. Thus, I could hear, first-hand, discussions about the contemporary socio political happenings of the country that were going on in politics.

Barring Jawaharlal-ji, almost all the top political leaders stayed with us whenever they were in Delhi. So I came to know all the leaders they lay. This contact naturally diminished somewhat after I shifted to Kolkata in 1940. However, I had the opportunity to develop acquaintances with the leaders of Bengal, as Kolkata had become our headquarters after 1937.

In Bengal, Muslims were in the majority before independence and so, after 1937, the chief ministers of Bengal were Muslims. The first chief minister or premier of undivided Bengal was A.K. Fazlul Haq, whose tenure was from April 1937 to March 1943. After that, a short spell of governor's rule followed. Then Khawaja Sir Nazimuddin became the chief minister. There was again another spell of governor's rule for about a year from 31 March 1945 to 23 April 1946. After that H.S. Suhrawardy became chief minister.

It was during the days of Suhrawardy that the Kolkata killings of 1946 took place. In these riots the Muslims were worst hit, even though the chief minister was a Muslim. Its repercussion was felt in Noakhali, where Hindus were butchered and their women raped on a mass scale. This led to Gandhi-ji visiting Noakhali in November 1946, where he stayed for four months.

Though a devout Hindu, I was secular in my outlook. Whether a chief minister or a minister was a Hindu or Muslim did not matter much in my relations with them. The Muslim chief ministers did not belong to the Congress party. They were, therefore, as a rule, inimical towards the Congress. All the same, they were always polite and helpful with me. I maintained cordial relations with all the top leaders of the Congress and also with important leaders of other parties.

Prafulla Chandra Ghosh

Dr P.C. Ghosh or Prafulla Babu, as we called him, was a long-standing friend of mine. I had known him since the late 1930s. He was a man of simple habits and limpid honesty. He possessed a sterling character and was a true Gandhian in his outlook. He became the first Congress chief minister of West Bengal after independence and remained in power from 15 August 1947 to 23 January 1948.

Dr P.C. Ghosh's most outstanding performance was the way he tackled the twin menace of hoarding and black marketing. During raids on big centres of hoarding, he accompanied the police raiding party to ensure it was conducted properly. It is said that during one such raid on a flour mill, Prafulla Babu was very simply attired. He could go incognito as his face was not familiar to the people. During the raid, therefore, he was offered a bribe. Prafulla Babu had the man who offered the bribe immediately arrested. But such forthright tactics soon had their repercussions. In January 1948, a majority of the Congress members of the legislative assembly (MLAs) wrote to Governor Rajagopalachari expressing their lack of confidence in the chief minister who, they felt, had earned the government notoriety. Raja-ji had no option but to dismiss Dr Ghosh's cabinet and install Dr B.C. Roy (Bidhan Babu) as chief minister.

Prafulla Babu became president of the Harijan Sevak Sangha in West Bengal. Though twenty-nine years senior to me in age, he took a great liking for me. We would discuss politics and although on many points we differed in our vision, I always admired his honesty and simplicity.

Dr B.C. Roy

Bidhan Babu became chief minister in January 1948. Under his leadership, the Congress won three successive elections in West Bengal in 1952, 1957 and 1962. He remained chief minister for fourteen years till his death in 1962. During this long stint, he remained the unchallenged and undisputed leader of the Congress in West Bengal.

Bidhan Babu's long tenure was undeniably the result of his extraordinary administrative ability and keen depth of perception of the

Author with Dr B.C. Roy, chief minister of West Bengal, 1955

practical niceties of a problem. He was a visionary. No wonder he could bequeath such legacies as Durgapur and Salt Lake City to the economically crippled state of West Bengal. I actively helped Bidhan Babu in all the three elections that he contested in 1952, 1957 and 1962. I moved about freely across the booths with other Congress workers. I would speak to many Hindi-speaking people, mostly from my community (Rajasthani) to organize votes for Bidhan Babu.

After Chittaranjan Das, Bidhan Babu was the greatest leader that Bengal has produced. Even at the height of his practice, Bidhan Babu would give free medical advice for two hours every morning in his chamber to the poor and the needy, without charging any fee. People want a leader to be strong, not mild and docile like a sheep which can do neither harm nor good. If there is a strong person like a banyan tree, people get shade under it. For this reason Bidhan Babu, being a powerful person, who feared not even Mahatma-ji and Jawaharlal-ji, enjoyed immense popularity. People felt that as long as he was the chief minister, the state would do well under his leadership.

Before 1948, Bidhan Babu practised as a physician. He acquired name and fame as one of the foremost physicians of India, excellent in diagnosis and treatment. He was our family physician since 1930 or 1931 and was, indeed, like a member of the family. He had a loud and forceful voice, as soon as he entered our house his presence became felt. He would visit us frequently, and during the pre-independence days, apart from medical advice for which he might have been called, he would always spend 30–45 minutes discussing the political situation of the country in general and of Bengal in particular with father or uncle.

Owing to his highly successful career and reputation as a physician, he became a medical consultant of most of the top leaders of the country, especially of Gandhi-ji. So imposing was his personality that except for Mahatma-ji, he addressed all the other leaders of the country by their first names.

Bidhan Babu was also a great humanitarian and cared a great deal for the poor. Even after he became chief minister, he kept up the practice of examining patients for free for two hours every morning.

After he became the chief minister, we would consult him for medical advice only when we felt it was absolutely necessary. My uncle BM, for example, was a heart patient. He had other doctors to treat him but the overall advice was taken from Bidhan Babu.

I will narrate an interesting anecdote concerning Bidhan Babu and myself. I once fell ill and did not get any benefit from the medicines prescribed by a doctor. I decided to go to Bidhan Babu and meet him at his residence where he could examine me. After making an appointment I went to his house at around 7 a.m. But even after I disclosed my identity, the durwan refused to let me enter the house, saying that the saheb was still in his bedroom on the first floor and had not come down. I pleaded with the durwan and told him that I had come by appointment and was prepared to sit in the waiting room till Dr Roy was ready to receive me. But the durwan would not listen. I drove away in my car in search of a telephone. Fortunately there was a pharmaceutical store which had opened early. I went into the shop and requested the shopkeeper to permit me to use the telephone. I telephoned Bidhan Babu and told him what had happened. He was furious and asked me to come immediately. I went in and this time the durwan was very respectful. He immediately took me to Dr Roy, who gave the durwan a piece of his mind followed by a tight slap. I was a hot-blooded person in those days and thought that the durwan deserved punishment. The poor man went away, highly crestfallen. After some time tempers cooled. After Dr Roy had examined me, I told him that it was good that he had chastised the durwan but that he should now forgive him. Dr Roy said that the durwan did deserve the punishment but that he would pardon him. He immediately called the durwan again and gave him Rs 100 and gently admonished him. The durwan had learnt a lesson. Everyone involved in the incident was satisfied.

In 1961, Bidhan Babu made me the sheriff of Kolkata. I was not even consulted about the matter. He did not think it necessary to consult me as he was like a family elder. It was only when I read the newspapers that I knew I had been made the sheriff. At the same time, my telephone started ringing with all my friends and well-wishers congratulating me. I immediately telephoned Bidhan Babu to thank him. When he came to the

Kolkata, 1961: Me as sheriff

telephone, and before I could say 'hello' to him, he said 'Good morning, Mr Sheriff! How are you?'

Whenever any of my business concerns in West Bengal had any problem I would go to Dr Roy with a short note on the matter. He would go through the note, call the concerned officers immediately, and give directions for its solution across the table.

Bharat Ratna, the highest honour in the country, was conferred on him in 1961. Bidhan Babu was a bachelor and, after a brief illness, died on 1 July 1962, on the same date that he was born in 1882. About a million of his countrymen joined the funeral procession. In his death, West Bengal lost a great personality who had become a legend in his time.

Kalipada Mookerjee

Kalipada Mookerjee, a minister in Dr B.C. Roy's cabinet, was a well-liked person and a go-getter. He was above parochialism and was very popular with the business community. Though he was much older than I, we were very close friends and held near-identical views on all topical matters. Whenever I had any problem I would always approach Kalipada Babu, even if it was not connected with his ministry. So close were we that he would take up the matter with other concerned ministers and try to help me. He was a very helpful type of person and so people from all walks of life would approach him with all kinds of problems. Unfortunately, he suffered from high blood pressure. In those days there was no proper treatment for this and it claimed his life in 1962.

Prafulla Chandra Sen

I had known Prafulla-da since 1950. I had also been dropping in at Writers Building or at his residence to discuss current affairs. Sometimes, people approached me in case they had any problem. If I was satisfied that it was a good case, I would plead it with Prafulla-da who would invariably accept my advice. The same thing continued after he became the chief minister. I do not remember even one case where he disregarded my advice.

Three or four years prior to his death, his health broke down and he became very fragile. I visited him often during this time. He never asked for any monetary assistance. That was part of his greatness. But from time to time I contributed something to take care of his medical expenses and other needs. His needs were few and I thought it my duty to look after his scanty requirements. Some members of the family looked after him. I was one of his few friends left to think and care for him during his last days.

Atulya Ghosh

Atulya Ghosh, or Atulya-da as he was commonly known, was a powerful leader of West Bengal. I came to know him around 1955. My association with him continued right up to his death in 1986. Atulya Babu would go out of the way to help a friend. Till he retired from politics, he would collect funds for running the West Bengal Provincial Congress Committee and for elections. He had a personal liking for me and treated me with great warmth and respect.

In fact, he was an all-India leader and though he never joined any government, he wielded tremendous influence. Atulya Babu was a grass-roots worker and a mass leader. With his wide contacts throughout West Bengal, he could effectively control the party. Atulya-da was one of those leaders who did not place his own interest before that of the people.

Atulya Babu's lack of formal education—he left school to join the non-cooperation movement at the age of fifteen—was more than made up by voracious private reading. A powerful speaker with a direct approach, he developed himself as a writer too. His rise to a position of power began with the agitation, on the eve of independence, for the partition of Bengal, in which he played an active and crucial part. Once Atulya-da and I were travelling together from Delhi to Kolkata in a plane. He was seated in front of me. After some time he could not resist looking back ward to see me. I went to his seat. He showed me with great pride a Hindi book which he was reading. He said: 'Krishna Kumar Babu, I am trying to pick up Hindi as without Hindi no politician can become a good leader in this country.'

Atulya Babu played a leading role on the national scene too. He reached the height of his career till the setback suffered by the Congress in West Bengal and several other states in the 1967 elections. Till then he was regarded as one of the kingmakers along with K. Kamaraj, N. Sanjiva Reddy and S. Nijalingappa, the triumvirate who were all known as members of the so-called 'syndicate'. But it is a measure of his innate political astuteness that after his 1967 defeat, he realized that the post-independence brand of Congress politics with which he was closely associated was coming to an end. The man who had remained in politics throughout his life needed a powerful will to withdraw from politics. This is what Atulya-da did. He withdrew from active politics and devoted himself to social work.

We three sons of Ghanshyam Das Birla:
Laxmi Niwas, me and Basant Kumar
in the 1930s

My father being conferred the Padma
Vibhushan by Dr Rajendra Prasad, then
President of India, in 1957

Visiting Pilani at the time of drought in 1973 to organize relief work

My brother Basant Kumar, I and our wives pour milk at Har-ki-Pauri at Haridwar after father's ashes were immersed in the holy Ganga

Jawaharlal Nehru visits Birla temple accompanied by my uncle J.K. Birla and Goswami Ganesh Dutt, a religious leader

With Jawaharlal Nehru, then prime minister, at BITS, Pilani, in 1953

An autographed picture of
Indira Gandhi taken in 1976

An autographed picture of the
Dalai Lama

My wife garlands Indira Gandhi when she came for a private dinner with us.
My daughter Shobhana looks on.

Taking a round of Texmaco factory in December 1953 with
Jawaharlal Nehru, then prime minister

Indira Gandhi at a private dinner with us during a visit to Kolkata in the 1950s

Rajiv Gandhi paying condolences, on behalf of his mother, on the demise of my father in June 1983

With S. Radhakrishnan, then vice president of India, at BITS, Pilani, in 1956

Dr Manmohan Singh, then Governor of the Reserve Bank of India,
paying floral tributes to my father's ashes in June 1983

I welcome Atal Bihari Vajpayee, then prime minister, on the occasion of the
75-year celebrations of the *Hindustan Times* in 1999

As sheriff of Kolkata, I received Queen Elizabeth II during her 1961 visit

With President Bill Clinton at a banquet hosted for him by the then
President, K.R. Narayanan, March 2000

Dr B.C. Roy, then chief minister of West Bengal, introduces me to Nikita S. Krushchev, secretary, Communist Party of USSR, and Nikolai A. Bulganin, chairman of the council of ministers, during their visit to Kolkata in 1955.
A visit to Texmaco was cancelled due to security reasons.

Delivering the speech as president of FICCI for the year 1974–75

National Leaders Whom I Knew

I had the good fortune to come in contact with most of the national leaders of my father's time.

Dr Rajendra Prasad

My acquaintance and relationship with Dr Rajendra Prasad or Rajendra Babu, as he was popularly known, dates back to 1931. I was then a young boy of thirteen, living in Kolkata. Rajendra Babu was a friend of father and whenever he visited Kolkata, he would invariably stay with

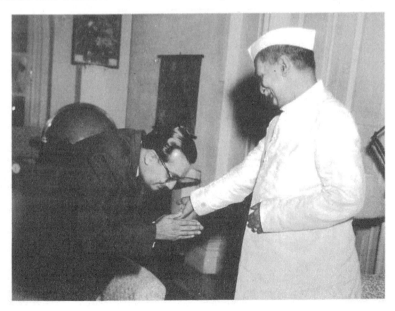

New Delhi, 1950: With Dr Rajendra Prasad after he became the first President of India

us. I have rarely come across a man of such great integrity and simple habits as Rajendra Babu. He would have serious discussions on political affairs with father and yet find time for the children in the family; he would stroll with us for a few minutes whenever he stayed with us and even find time to exchange a few words with us.

Rajendra Babu was born in 1884 in an obscure village situated in north Bihar. He started practice as a lawyer in his youth and achieved success. In his later life, however, he became an embodiment of Gandhian principles. In whatever he did or said he never swerved from the Gandhian path.

He was to Gandhi-ji, to quote Sarojini Naidu, what John was to Christ. Gandhi-ji himself once said of him: 'There is at least one man who would not hesitate to take the cup of poison from my hands.'

Before becoming President, Rajendra Babu used to visit Pilani, our ancestral home. As he was an asthma patient, Pilani's dry and bracing climate suited him very well. He would stay there for days together, spending his time in reading and meeting people. He was also very fond of chess and played the game with village grandmasters. Even after becoming President, Rajendra Babu visited Pilani twice. That apart, whenever any of his acquaintances from Pilani went to Delhi, they could always meet Rajendra Babu; the doors of the Presidential residence were always open to them.

Rajendra Babu was very fond of me. When he stayed at Birla House in New Delhi before Independence, would look after me under father's directions. This made us quite close to each other. I discussed politics with him and, after he became President, we also discussed the economic situation in the country along with other topics. As I was not yet in active politics, our discussions were just conversation. Rajendra Babu cared for people and would enquire about my welfare and that of my family along with the business I was running. He was an apostle of honesty, and full of love for mankind and the indigent.

Pandit Govind Ballabh Pant

I knew Pandit Govind Ballabh Pant, a diplomat, a statesman, a giant amongst parliamentarians and a towering personality, well. He was born in Almora in September 1887. His ancestors were from Maharashtra and had migrated to the Kumaon region of Uttar Pradesh (now Uttaranchal) in the tenth century, under the patronage of the then rulers. Pant-ji possessed all the qualities of leadership.

In the 1937 UP Assembly elections, the Congress party won by a big majority and Pant-ji was unanimously elected chief minister. As chief minister, he showed great administrative acumen and introduced many useful reforms. He was instrumental in having the zamindari system abolished in the state. After the end of the Second World War, when elections were held for the provincial legislatures in 1946, Pant-ji was again chosen as the leader of the victorious Congress party in UP and once more became chief minister.

Following the untimely death of Sardar Vallabhbhai Patel, Pant-ji was asked by Jawaharlal Nehru to join the Union Cabinet. Pant-ji was reluctant to leave UP but, on being pressed by Pandit-ji, he had no choice but to join the Cabinet in 1954. He was given the important portfolio of home affairs which he held for over six years. In spite of his age and ill health he proved himself equal to the task and died in harness on 7 March 1961.

I first came in touch with Pant-ji in the early 1930s. He was close to

New Delhi, 1940s: With Gobind Ballabh Pant when he came to stay at Birla House

father and stayed at Birla House whenever he visited Delhi. From 1939, when I started looking after our sugar mills, I had to go to Lucknow frequently. I used to stay at Carlton Hotel. Pant-ji did not like my staying at the hotel, but I did not like to be confined to the chief minister's bungalow as I had to meet numerous people, sometimes late in the evening. I tried to excuse myself but Pant-ji would not listen. I then had to start staying with him.

Pant-ji also insisted that unless I was dining out at the invitation of a friend, I must have my meals with him. I used to stay two or three days in Lucknow during each visit. Pant-ji insisted that I have at least one dinner with him—so fond was he of me. Over dinner, Pant-ji would ask me all types of questions, about the sugar industry, the general condition of the economy, political happenings in Bengal (before Partition) and West Bengal (after Partition). He would ask me what I thought of the various leaders of Bengal like Dr B.C. Roy, P.C. Sen, Prafulla Ghosh, Kalipada Mookerjee and others. All these people were men of consequence and my friends. They were all people of character and I spoke highly of them. The Communist Party, in those days, was almost non-existent.

While dining with Pant-ji, I came to know his children quite well too. I came in touch with Krishan Chand (K.C. Pant), called Raja by people close to him. I was impressed by his personality, clarity of mind and power of expression. He was a brilliant boy and is certainly a bright politician.

When Raja got married at Naini Tal, Pant-ji informed me well in advance himself that I must attend the wedding. The bride's house was situated at quite a high altitude. The car could not go there and one had to walk up it. Pant-ji offered to arrange a dandi or pony for me. I assured him that would not be necessary. Pant-ji also offered to arrange for my stay at Naini Tal. But that also was not necessary as K.M. Munshi, governor of UP at that time, was a close friend of mine. I stayed at the Government House, attended Raja's wedding, and returned to Delhi.

Pant-ji was a very religious man. When he was in Delhi, he would invite me to dinner almost once every fortnight. I remember especially one such occasion. After I reached his house around 9 p.m., he said he was feeling rather tired and expressed his desire to go out for a drive with me for about twenty minutes. By the time we returned, it was quite late. Pant-ji was sorry that dinner would be served so late. Suddenly, after alighting from the car, Pant-ji looked up at the sky and discovered that the moon was not as bright as it should have been. He asked his attendants what had happened to the moon. His attendants replied that it was a night of lunar eclipse. Pant-ji felt very embarrassed that I would be further delayed for dinner and asked me somewhat hesitantly if I could wait another hour till the eclipse was over. Devout Hindus do not have dinner during the eclipse. According to them, the moon god is tormented from time to time by two demons—Rahu and Ketu—for revealing their identity when the mythical ocean was churned and nectar found. I do not believe in such mythological stories but Pant-ji, being a pious Hindu, never ate during the time of an eclipse. I had no choice but to acquiesce with his suggestion. It was almost midnight by the time we at last sat to have our dinner. But I did not mind this delay at all as I knew that Pant-ji treated me like a member of the family.

Pant-ji's food was very simple. There would be three vegetable curries. There was hardly any fried food like samosa, dahi-wada or kachori. He was however very fond of eating mixed fruit with cream.

There is an interesting episode connected with the sudden and completely unexpected arrival of the Dalai Lama in India. When the Dalai Lama escaped from Tibet in March 1959, a problem arose for the Government of India. Where was he to be put up? Jawaharlal Nehru, who was then prime minister, asked Pant-ji if he could arrange for our house at Mussoorie, Birla House, to be placed at the Dalai Lama's disposal, without any inconvenience, till alternative arrangements could be made. Pant-ji spoke to father and said that Pandit-ji was very particular that we should not be disturbed unless we could conveniently leave Birla House. Father wrote to Pandit-ji saying that Birla House was at the disposal of his daughter-in-law (my wife) and that he would write after enquiring from her, which he did. Father then enquired of my wife whether we could conveniently vacate the house for the Dalai Lama till alternative arrangements were made.

My wife used to go to Mussoorie every year, as she does even now, and stay there for four months. It was certain that vacating the house would cause a lot of inconvenience to her. She asked me what reply she should give father. I told her that before I gave my view I would like to know hers. She said that the Dalai Lama had come as a refugee to this country and so we should try to help the holy leader. I entirely agreed with her.

We stayed at Charle Ville hotel, later to be The Academy. The government offered us free accommodation at the hotel. I said that was not necessary. We took one wing of the hotel and shifted there. When the Dalai Lama came to India, at the request of the Government of India, we vacated our house for His Holiness.

When the Dalai Lama shifted to our house, my wife and my cousin Gangaprasad's wife, Nirmala, went to meet him to offer their good wishes and respects. During this visit J.S. Mehta, our foreign secretary, was there. He was somewhat rude to them and said, rather loudly, that these ladies, for security reasons, should move out. My wife felt very unhappy and reported the matter to me. I knew J. S. Mehta's father, Mohan Singh Mehta, a renowned educationist at Udaipur. During one of my meetings with Pant-ji, I narrated to him what happened at Mussoorie. Pant-ji was furious. Immediately, he sent for his secretary and told him to ask Mehta to meet him any day convenient to him. After a few days when Mehta

Mussoorie, March 1959: Dalai Lama with my wife when he stayed at Birla Niwas. Also seen are Shobhana as a baby and my nephew Chandrakant

met Pant-ji, he told him that he had heard that some officer was very rude to my wife and her sister-in-law and asked Mehta to find out who that officer was.

Mehta panicked. Again without naming him, Pant-ji expressed his annoyance and irritation at the behaviour of this officer, and asked Mehta to enquire into the matter and report to him since he was there at the time the incident took place. The next day, Pant-ji sent for me and related what transpired between him and Mehta. Such a man was Pant-ji—able and shrewd, fair-minded but tolerating no nonsense from subordinates in the administration.

Pant-ji died on 7 March 1961. He was a towering personality, a man of great warmth and affection, and his death was a great loss to Pandit-ji.

Chandra Bhanu Gupta

Chandra Bhanu Gupta, or CB as he was known to friends and admirers, was born in 1902 and hailed from Lakhimpur Kheri in UP. He was drawn into the vortex of the freedom struggle at an early age and, owing to his organizational ability, rose to be one of the top leaders of UP in the Nehruvian era.

He became famous as a brilliant strategist and fund raiser for the party. He also collected funds for other causes such as the Bihar earthquake of 1934, the Motilal Nehru Memorial Society with which he remained connected till the end, and for the Acharya Narendra Dev Memorial Library.

I came in touch with Chandra Bhanu-ji some time in 1940. Initially, this was a mere acquaintanceship. CB was imprisoned and went through a period of incarceration like all the other national political leaders during the Quit India movement. When Pant-ji became chief minister of UP for the second time in 1946, Chandra Bhanu-ji was taken in as his parliamentary secretary. Soon after that, we became intimate friends. Whenever he visited Kolkata, he would stay at our house.

Chandra Bhanu-ji was the chief minister of UP from 1960 to mid-1963, when he had to resign under the Kamaraj Plan. In April 1969, when the Congress split, he joined the Congress (O). In 1977, the Congress (O) party merged with the Janata Party and he became its treasurer. He was offered the post of minister, but he declined.

Chandra Bhanu-ji was a right-of-centre man in politics. He was a great critic of Nehru, who, in turn, was always suspicious of him. The only reason for this dislike was that Chandra Bhanu-ji did not agree with Pandit-ji's idea of socialism. That apart, he was such a powerful person in the Congress party in UP that an overwhelming number of Congress MLAs owed their first loyalty to Chandra Bhanu-ji and only then to Pandit-ji. Pandit-ji could not tolerate this in UP, the largest state of India which he regarded as his *karmabhumi* (theatre of action). The question was how to get rid of Chandra Bhanu-ji.

Kamaraj was very close to Pandit-ji. A very shrewd man, he advised Pandit-ji in 1963, that all the Congress chief ministers, barring a few, should be asked to resign so that all the state governments could be reorganized. Most of the chief ministers were not in favour of this Kamaraj Plan. Chandra Bhanu-ji was not willing to resign. He was astute enough to see through the ploy of Kamaraj to which Pandit-ji had become a party and understood that this was just an exercise to get rid of people whom Pandit-ji did not like. He, therefore, declined to resign. He was then assured by an emissary of Pandit-ji that the resignation was only a formality and that after submitting his resignation he would be renominated as chief minister. Chandra Bhanu-ji himself told me this story. So he resigned and, as was feared by him and his friends, he was not renominated by the Congress high command.

Chandra Bhanu-ji again became chief minister in 1967 but that was only for a very short period as his government was defeated following Charan Singh's breaking away from the Congress to form his own party. The Congress split of 1969 brought a trauma to his political career. He remained loyal to Morarji Desai and, after Indira Gandhi won in the tussle with Morarji and his allies, he was in political wilderness for some time. When Indira-ji became prime minister, Chandra Bhanu-ji continued to play the role of her critic just as he did with Jawaharlal-ji.

Once in early 1973, Indira-ji sent for me. She said that she had heard that I was the closest friend of C.B. Gupta and so I should try to see that he left Morarji's camp and joined her. She said she would give him full support in UP politics. As I was a common friend of both Indira-ji and Chandra Bhanu-ji, I tried hard to bring about a reconciliation, but Chandra Bhanu-ji's ideologies were too different from those of Indira-ji's and he declined to desert Morarji's camp.

When Morarji became the prime minister, Chandra Bhanu-ji again emerged as a powerful leader. Morarji sounded him out on whether he would like to accept a ministry under him, but since Chandra Bhanu-ji was in poor health at that time, he declined Morarji's offer. He died on 11 March 1980.

Chandra Bhanu-ji was somewhat annoyed when I became close to Indira-ji, but that did not sour our personal friendship. He was a man of strong and assertive character. Though a bachelor, there was never any scandal about him. He was a fund raiser of great ability and whatever amount he collected was all for the party. No accusation of embezzlement could be hurled at him. He dressed simply and his lifestyle was totally unostentatious.

Whenever I was in Lucknow, I always had one dinner with Chandra Bhanu-ji. On one such occasion, he indulged in a self-deprecating joke. He said: '*Arey bhai, aapne kuchh suna? Gali gali me shor hai*, C.B. Gupta *chor hai*' (Have you heard? It is being said that in every lane there is talk that C.B. Gupta is a thief), and simultaneously started laughing. He could say this as he was known to be a man of the utmost moral rectitude.

As a minister and chief minister, he proved to be a very able and just administrator. If anyone went to him with any problem he would immediately have it looked into. So long as the Congress was undivided, he was the uncrowned king of UP. However, when the Congress split in 1969, a majority of his followers gradually deserted him and joined Indira-ji's camp. This is not surprising as most of the politicians side with the winner. They know that is where their interests lie. Chandra Bhanu-ji then kept himself busy in organizing his party and in looking after the Motilal Nehru Memorial Society.

Of the various politicians with whom I came in touch, Chandra Bhanu-ji was undoubtedly one of the most honest persons. He was a man of high principles and did not change sides for political gains. He was a very able administrator. My relationship with him was like that of brothers.

Morarji Desai

I came to know Morarji-bhai in the late 1940s. When he became the chief minister of Bombay Presidency in 1952, I got to know him better. As chief minister, Morarji-bhai completely overhauled the police administration and introduced far-reaching land reforms. He was a successful chief minister. When Bombay Presidency was bifurcated into two states—Gujarat and Maharashtra—Morarji-bhai did not want to go to Gujarat as chief minister. He expressed this to Pandit-ji, who called him to Delhi in November 1956. He served as a minister under Pandit-ji in charge of various ministries.

No amount of calumny or criticism could deter Morarji-bhai from following his predetermined line of action and speaking out his mind. He was fearless and spoke frankly what he thought to be right. He was an ascetic in personal life and a strong protagonist of prohibition, khadi and yoga. He had complete faith in God. He believed in the philosophy of karmayoga and once said to me that even if he were to be afflicted by malignancy he would regard it as the fruit of his own karma (fate) and would not blame anybody for it. Stepping into the 100th year of his life, he died in Mumbai on 10 April 1995.

I came to know Morarji-bhai intimately only after he shifted to Delhi in 1956. He was a man of lofty principles and rigid in his views. If he took a certain stand, he hardly ever strayed from it. His inflexibility sometimes made even his friends desert him. Undeterred, he clung to his views. At one

My wife and I with our daughters Nandini and Jyotsna with
Morarji Desai, November 1956

time father was also very friendly with Morarji-bhai but his uncompromising stubbornness made father also distance himself from him. He was junior to father in politics, and so father was not prepared to regard Morarji-bhai as his senior. Father was close to Mahatma-ji and Sardar Patel. So in father's view, Morarji-bhai was much junior to him in the political hierarchy. Morarji-bhai's habit was to preach sermons. This was all right for people like me but not for a person of father's stature.

In fact, in the 1930s, father went to Ahmedabad to meet Mahatma-ji when Morarji-bhai was a very junior leader. Mahatma-ji sent him to the railway station to receive father and deputed him to look after father's comforts while he was in Ahmedabad. When father went from the railway station to Mahatma-ji's ashram, he left the luggage in the care of Morarji-bhai to carry to the ashram.

Before the Congress split I was quite close to Morarji-bhai. When the Congress split in 1969, I kept myself aloof. By 1973, I had become very close to Indira-ji.

I would still meet Morarji-bhai but he knew I was close to Indira-ji. So I was always suspect in his eyes. His son, Kanti, a friend of mine, tried to help me get along with his father whenever there was any problem faced by my industries.

In the late 1960s when Morarji-bhai was finance minister, I went to him about a problem connected with his ministry. It was a clear case of harassment by his ministry. T.P. Singh (father of ex-bureaucrat N.K. Singh) was then the finance secretary. He was a friend of mine. Sometimes we played cards together. But for some reason or the other I was being unnecessarily harassed. Morarji-bhai did not hesitate to phone the finance secretary in my presence to look into the matter. Such was the awe in which he was held by his officers that when I later met TP, he was a completely changed man.

Now let me relate what happened to me in the late 1970s when Morarji-bhai became the prime minister. We had a coffee estate in the Billigiri Hills of Karnataka. The performance of the chief executive was not up to the mark. When, in spite of repeated chances being given to him, his performance did not improve, he was asked to submit his resignation. He reluctantly did so. Simultaneously, he sent a letter to the income tax authorities that the books of account of the estate were manipulated!

Suddenly, the Central Bureau of Investigation (CBI) raided our coffee estate and seized the books of account. When I got the news I approached Morarji-bhai. I explained that the coffee estate was completely exempt from corporate tax. That apart, I said that if our profits were suppressed it was certainly a case for the state government to investigate as we had to pay agricultural tax. Where and how did the CBI come into the picture? Morarji-bhai opined that in case the books of account were manipulated it was certainly a case for the CBI to investigate, irrespective of whether the company was paying income tax or not. Even if the company was not required to pay any tax and if the books were not properly maintained, it was a fit case for the CBI to probe. I was not satisfied with this answer and frankly told Morarji-bhai that I was being needlessly harassed and the only reason for this harassment was my friendship with Indira-ji. I then went to H.M. Patel, who was at that time the finance minister. I had known him ever since he was finance secretary in the government. He agreed with me that it was a clear case of harassment. Patel then said that he would speak to Morarji-bhai, which he did. The CBI ultimately dropped the case.

During the Emergency, Morarji-bhai was arrested along with other Opposition leaders. Two years later, when elections were held in 1977, the Janata Party swept into power and Morarji-bhai became prime minister. Whenever I sought an interview, he readily gave me time. But he was always cold. After his government fell in 1979, he shifted to Mumbai where I hardly met him.

Twelve years elapsed. During this period there was no communication between Morarji-bhai and myself. Some time in 1991, when he was about ninety-five years old, I thought I should at least meet him before he died. I telephoned Kanti who, as I have said, was a friend of mine and sought an appointment to meet Morarji-bhai. Kanti immediately arranged a meeting. Health-wise, Morarj-bhai was all right but owing to age he had become very weak. He was lying in bed when I met him. I was with him for about ten minutes. I could see that he had become very feeble. His voice sounded frail. But his brain was sharp and clear as always.

Respectfully, I touched his feet. After enquiring about his health, I said I had come to meet him for a special purpose. I said to Morarji-bhai that I knew that after 1972 I had lost his affection. I added that I had never hidden the fact from him that I was in Indira-ji's confidence. I told Morarji-bhai that though politically I was with Indira-ji, I always regarded him as a man of very high morality and principle. I said that I had always held him in high esteem and, barring politics, carried out his instructions. I said I had always tried to be fair and honest in life and that if unintentionally I had offended him on any occasion, or for any reason, I now sought his blessings and forgiveness. These words were spoken with folded hands and with the greatest of humility and sincerity. Morarji-bhai was profoundly touched by my words. He wholeheartedly blessed me. Before taking his leave I made a deep bow and touched his feet. He repeatedly patted me on my head and again and again bestowed his blessings on me. I always thought of him as a person of saintly disposition, of high moral character, a virtuous personality, a very superior being. To have received blessings from such a towering eminence gave me great satisfaction.

Lal Bahadur Shastri

I came to know Lal Bahadur Shastri in 1946 when Pant-ji became the chief minister of UP for the second time. Lal Bahadur-ji was then his parliamentary secretary. As I visited Lucknow very often in connection with the problems of the sugar industry, I met him quite frequently.

From the early 1950s, Lal Bahadur-ji began to function from Delhi. This gave me greater opportunity of meeting him. He acquired fame when, in 1956, he accepted moral responsibility for a major railway accident and resigned from the position of railway minister. However, Pandit-ji took him back into the Cabinet again in 1957.

In 1964, on the death of Pandit-ji, Lal Bahadur-ji became the prime minister. Though a man of sterling character, he did not look impressive. Lean and thin, he seemed to have a weak personality. The majority of Indians at that time thought that Lal Bahadur-ji would not make a good prime minister.

I maintained my contact with Lal Bahadur-ji and whenever I sought an appointment he would find time to meet me, even if he had a busy schedule.

After he suffered a heart attack, doctors advised him to take a regular walk. Many times, therefore, Lal Bahadur-ji asked me to meet him during his prescribed constitutional. We would walk together for about 10–15 minutes, after which I would take leave of him. My relationship with Lal Bahadur-ji was very informal. Others, he met in the drawing room.

People thought that, coming after the towering personality of Pandit-ji, Lal Bahadur-ji would make a poor prime minister. However, in 1965, during the Indo-Pakistan war, he provided inspiring leadership. India defeated Pakistan and Lal Bahadur-ji's stock rose sky-high. He was a very clear-headed person and articulated his views on social and political problems with perfect clarity. This had a great impact on the Indian people.

Wherever he did not grasp the intricacies of a problem he would not hesitate to say so and would ask people who met him to explain the gist of the matter so that he could take some decision in the matter.

Pragmatism rather than dogmatism appeared to be the guiding principle of the Cabinet under his leadership. He was always conscious of the problems of poverty and unemployment. He laid emphasis on strengthening the defences of the country and in honouring the man behind the plough.

Lal Bahadur-ji was utterly simple and unassuming in manner; kind and gentle in his dealings; and devout in character. He instinctively kept out of factional politics and remained uninvolved in the bickering within the party. He listened to every point of view and made his own decisions firmly. Though he belonged to a non-vegetarian family, he was a vegetarian himself and did not smoke or drink. He was so modest in his behaviour that he came to be looked upon by the masses as one of them.

Lal Bahadur-ji was one of those few leaders who, though born in poverty, have won recognition by dint of their talents and sacrifice. He gave of his best for the service of the country and did not desire publicity. From nine years in prison to a spell of nineteen months and two days as prime minster, he has an unblemished record of personal honesty in both private and public life, of ceaseless striving for national welfare. Under his leadership the Indian masses acquired a sense of full and vibrant nationhood.

Jayaprakash Narayan

Jayaprakash Narayan was like a member of the family to me. I came in touch with him when I was a young boy. After completing his education he was in search of employment. He had not joined politics at the time. His father-in-law, Brijkishore Prasad, was well known to Gandhi-ji. Gandhi-ji wrote to father on 2 December 1930, suggesting that he give Jayaprakash-ji some plan n

Gandhi-ji wrote o 6 June 9 fro Poor Jail: 'Jayaprakash infor s me that, alt ug d re o ecru ing a y ew peop : jus

With Jayaprakash Narayan in the late 1960s

now, he will be absorbed somewhere because of my recommendation. I certainly hold that Jayaprakash is an able young man but I do not wish that a post be created where none exists today.'

Jayaprakash-ji met father in accordance with Gandhi-ji's directions. Father appointed him as his secretary. Jayaprakash-ji worked in that capacity for a few years.

We were all kids in those days. Jayaprakash-ji lived for some time at our house at Birla Park in Kolkata. So we came to know him well. Soon all of us realized what a gem of a person he was. With his great humility, childlike simplicity, limpid honesty, high sense of duty and intense patriotism, we knew Jayaprakash-ji would make a mark and rise high in the political firmament of the country.

Even after Jayaprakash-ji left father and joined politics full time, his relationship and friendship with me continued. On numerous occasions he wrote to me. Some of our correspondence is in this book.

When Indira-ji lost the elections in 1977 and the Janata Party came to power, Morarji-bhai, though himself a man of high principles, could not check other ministers from harassing me. I only casually informed Jayaprakash-ji about this. He stood by me.

Even after Jayaprakash-ji joined active politics, I maintained my contact with him. He had great warmth for me. He would quite often visit Kolkata. Whenever he did so, he would inform me in advance. I always offered to meet him where he stayed but he preferred to meet me in my house. Jayaprakash-ji truly was a person who believed in the philosophy of 'Vasudhaiva kutumbakam (all the people of the earth are like members of a family). He was noble to the very core. He was a socialist by nature and no one was his enemy.

As I have already indicated, owing to my earlier close association with Indira-ji some of the Janata Party ministers took delight in trying to harass me. A non-bailable warrant was issued against me but I was abroad at that time and so the warrant could not be served on me.

I then approached Jayaprakash-ji and sought his help in the matter. The question I put to him was: 'Why should I be harassed purely because I am a friend of Indira Gandhi?' As usual, Jayaprakash-ji was very kind and warm towards me and solicitous of my welfare. He said that it would be a grave mistake on the part of the Janata Party members or ministers if they persisted in their efforts to harass me.

Though he could not personally intervene to prevent my harassment, I derived great moral courage and solace from the fact that I had his goodwill. Owing to his failing health, Jayaprakash-ji realized that his end was drawing near. He died on 8 October 1979. That I was able to maintain my contact with him till the very end was a source of comfort to me.

Dr Ram Manohar Lohia

Dr Ram Manohar Lohia belonged to the Vaishya community. The family hailed from Rajasthan and settled in Uttar Pradesh. His father migrated to Mumbai. Ram Manohar-ji got his PhD degree from Berlin University. Coming back to India, he applied for a teaching assignment in Banaras Hindu University. Failing to get it, he joined my uncle, Rameshwar Das, as his secretary. Uncle was highly impressed by his personality and honesty.

In 1934, uncle sent him to our New Swadeshi Sugar Mills in Champaran district of Bihar as a management trainee with the ultimate aim of making him the chief executive. He went there, but within a few days he decided to join politics. He joined the Congress Socialist Party, which was formed in 1934. He was arrested a number of times. He also participated in the Quit India Movement and went underground. He eluded the police for some time but was eventually arrested in May 1944. Ram Manohar-ji continued to take part in active politics. He was elected to the Lok Sabha in 1963. A severe critic of the Nehru family, he was a powerful speaker and wrote a number of articles and books on socialism and the social conditions of the country. This brilliant man of strong conviction died in October 1967.

I came in touch with Ram Manohar-ji in the 1940s. I was never as close to him as I was to Jayaprakash—yet I did meet him quite frequently. He had the ability to draw people towards him and even today there are many people in politics who call themselves Lohiaites. Mulayam Singh Yadav, for example, is a staunch Lohiaite.

Though I did not come much in touch with Ram Manohar-ji, I could always feel the pervading power of his personality. Whenever I met him, he was courteous.

Rafi Ahmed Kidwai

Rafi Ahmed Kidwai began his career as a private secretary to Motilal Nehru and virtually became a member of the Nehru family. When the first popular Congress government was formed in Uttar Pradesh in 1935, Rafi Saheb was appointed minister of land revenue.

I came in touch with Rafi Saheb in 1939. However, it was just an acquaintanceship. When he became the food and agriculture minister at the Centre, I came closely in touch with him and our acquaintance matured into friendship.

When Rafi Saheb shifted to the Centre, I started meeting him quite frequently. Though he was always courteous, I could sense that he was cold towards me. It was not difficult for me to assess the reason for this frigidity.

In fact, when the Congress won the Assembly elections in Uttar Pradesh in 1935, by a thumping majority, Pant-ji and Rafi Saheb were each desirous of becoming the chief minister. Rafi Saheb was closer to Pandit-ji, but the majority of the Congress MLAs were in favour of Pant-ji. True democrat that he was, Pandit-ji decided in favour Pant-ji. Though Rafi Saheb joined the Uttar Pradesh Cabinet, bickering between him and Pant-ji continued.

Pant-ji found, amongst the younger MLAs, Chandra Bhanu-ji to be very dynamic. In a way, Panti-ji patronized Chandra Bhanu-ji to fight his battle with Rafi Saheb. I was close to Pant-ji and even closer to Chandra Bhanu-ji. Rafi Saheb was well aware of my proximity to both. Hence, whenever I met him in Delhi, though I found him outwardly courteous, his reticence and coldness towards me were quite apparent.

One day I thought I should have a straight talk with Rafi Saheb about this awkward state of affairs. I asked him point-blank why he was always so cold and indifferent towards me. Rafi Saheb did not reply. I knew the reason and so I told him frankly: 'Rafi Saheb, perhaps you are cold towards me because I am close to Pant-ji and C.B. Gupta.' Again, there was no reply. I made it clear that I would never give up my friendship with Pant-ji and Chandra Bhanu-ji but added that I would feel greatly privileged if I could enjoy his friendship also at the same time. I assured Rafi Saheb that I would not play the role of a tattletale between him on the one hand and Pant-ji and Chandra Bhanu-ji on the one other. I said that the tussle between them was their private matter. As far as I was concerned, I assured him that I would remain as loyal a friend to him as I was to Pant-ji and Chandra Bhanu-ji. I further pointed out that if he found that I had betrayed his trust in any way he could stop meeting me. This course was always open to him, I asserted. This talk had the desired effect on Rafi Saheb. He felt that I was speaking sincerely, and consequently the wall of coldness between us thawed and we became good friends.

I steadfastly kept his confidence in me and never divulged a word of what passed between Rafi Saheb and me either to Pant-ji or to Chandra Bhanu-ji. I also convinced them that whatever they said to me would never be conveyed to Rafi Saheb. Thus I became a common friend. I, in fact, became an honest broker to try and bring about a rapprochement between Rafi Saheb and Chandra Bhanu-ji. Unfortunately, so diametrically opposed were they in their outlook that I did not succeed.

In course of time, when Rafi Saheb came in close contact with me, our relationship blossomed into intimacy. I would meet Rafi Saheb once or twice every week. Whenever I visited him, I found a number of people sitting in the waiting room and/or his secretary's room to meet him. Rafi Saheb would invariably ask some of those people to meet me and would request me to give them monetary assistance or employment.

During one such visit, Rafi Saheb called a young woman who was waiting in his secretary's room. He introduced the lady to me and said she was closely related to Purshottam Das Tandon, a well-known leader of the Congress party. He requested me to give a donation to some institution that was being run by her. I agreed. After the lady left, I asked Rafi Saheb how he was helping Tandon-ji's relation though it was well-known that they held divergent views on all political and social issues. Rafi Saheb said that politically they were in opposite camps but that did not affect their mutual admiration, respect and personal relations. This was the type of man that Rafi Saheb was. His personal relationship always remained above politics and he was always keen to help those who approached him.

When Rafi Saheb became the minister of food and agriculture in 1952 the food situation difficult. He introduced decontrol of food grain sale in the face o opposition from critics and succeeded, by and large, in achieving . The sugar industry, too, was under the food ministry. Rafi Saheb often consult me on matters concerning this industry.

One day, Rafi for me to discuss an important policy matter connected with t industry. Sugar was a totally controlled commodity in those days. He wanted to discuss the question of fixing a fair price for sugar. Rafi Saheb was confident that I would give him correct and sound advice. Though I was myself an industrialist, he was certain my advice would be such as to take care of the interests of both the industry and the consumer. So he apprised me of the thinking of his ministry in the matter. I told Rafi Saheb that the department's suggestions would adversely hit the sugar industry. Rafi Saheb said that he could not wait more than a day before he took action and that whatever suggestions I had to offer should be given to him in the form of a note that very day.

Time was, indeed, of the essence. All the same, I sat down to prepare the note after cancelling all my other engagements. On completing the job, I met Rafi Saheb the same evening at his house and submitted my note which he went through in the most minute detail in my presence. He said he was happy with the note, and barring one or two points, all the other suggestions given by me were accepted by him. I was fortunate to enjoy his confidence and trust to that extent.

While describing Rafi Saheb's friendship and liking for me, I am reminded of an incident concerning a bizarre story which ended on a note of pathos and high tragedy. It concerned a young Hindu.One day Rafi Saheb summoned me urgently. I was actually in the midst of a meeting. I quickly wound up the meeting and went straight to his residence.A despondent-looking young man was sitting near Rafi Saheb. Rafi Saheb asked me to employ the man in one of my companies. This was not an unusual request as earlier, too, Rafi Saheb had asked me to employ some people. After speaking to me, Rafi Saheb asked the young man to wait outside his room. He told me with a glum face that he thought it proper to apprise me that the young man whom he was asking me to employ had earlier attempted to commit suicide and might make yet another attempt to do so. I was taken aback on hearing this, and told Rafi Saheb of my reluctance and reservations about employing a person of such unstable mind in my organization. Rafi Saheb said that he had weighed the matter seriously and decided to make every possible effort to save the life of the young man by arranging for his employment, as he considered that to be a possible way of saving the man's life. In this, Rafi Saheb said, he needed my assistance. I naturally enquired of Rafi Saheb the reason for the young man attempting to end his life. It appeared that the young man was in love with a girl, but because the girl belonged to another caste, his parents were not willing to give their consent to their son marrying her.

This incident happened over forty years back when Hindu society was very closed, orthodox and rigid in its mores. Arranged marriages were then the prevalent practice. Girls were kept under strict surveillance by their parents or guardians so that love marriages could hardly ever take place. When I suggested Rafi Saheb's personal intercession with the parents, he told me that such an endeavour had been made but the parents had remained adamant. I pressed the point further and said that the parents should have become wiser after the attempted suicide by the young man. To this Rafi Saheb stated that even the attempted suicide by the young man could not soften the parents who said that they would rather lose the son than permit him to marry a girl outside their caste! I thought nothing could be more absurd and abominable than this. I finally asked Rafi

Saheb whether I should have a talk with the parents. Rafi Saheb said that would be of no avail. When he who had known the parents for a number of years could not alter their rigid stand, where was the possibility of my succeeding? The logic of Rafi Saheb's argument was irrefutable.

Even after hearing all this, I said that I would not like to engage such a person because if he committed suicide while in our employment, it would cause me great embarrassment. Rafi Saheb however said that in case anything happened, no blame would devolve on me. With great reluctance, I agreed to engage the man.

I asked that youth to meet me in Kolkata. When he met me there I told him about the job and said that in case he had any difficulty he could always meet me. I absorbed him in one of our companies in Kolkata. I also spoke to the chief executive of the company and narrated to him the whole story about this employee's background. I cautioned him about the possibility of the man again attempting to commit suicide and asked him to be very tactful in dealing with him.

Every month, I asked the young man to meet me and tell me if he had any problems. In fact, if any month the man did not phone me, I would send for him. Things went on all right for a few months. In course of time, this man got attached to me. One day, of his own accord, he even wrote me a letter wherein he showered praises on me for having given him an opportunity to work in my company and for showing consideration towards him. I kept the letter carefully in my file.

One day, suddenly a [illegible] of the [illegible] rang me and said that [illegible] had [illegible] suicide. He also told [illegible] who lived in Muzaffarnagar, had [illegible] the body of the deceased be flown [illegible] executive [illegible] make all the necessary arrangements [illegible] parents.

This happened at a [illegible] was [illegible] d. The Kolkata–Delhi sector in those days was being served by an airline company belonging to the Sahu Jains. Our chief executive made arrangements for the body to be flown to Delhi.

Rafi Saheb happened to be in Kolkata at that time. I immediately went to see him after hearing about the young man's suicide, taking with me the letter which the deceased employee had written to me, extolling my 'virtues'. I told him about the tragic incident. Rafi Saheb said he had already heard about it. I also showed him the letter which the man had written to me. Rafi Saheb went through it and said that the young man had in fact told him about my kind disposition towards him as also my concern for him. I told Rafi Saheb that all the arrangements to send the body to Delhi, in accordance with the wishes of the parents of the deceased man, had been completed.

However, a sudden unforeseen obstacle marred the plans. Just about two hours before the departure of the plane, my chief executive telephoned me and said that the airlines authorities were having second thoughts about transporting the body to Delhi. I was surprised to hear this. I immediately spoke to Rafi Saheb over the phone. Rafi Saheb told me that he would go to the airport to personally intervene in the matter and asked me also to rush to the airport. I acted accordingly. By the time I reached the airport, Rafi Saheb had also arrived. I found him giving a strong sermon to the airlines people about their insensitivity to human feelings. The airlines people were very apologetic and immediately agreed to carry the body to Delhi.

That typifies the human side of Rafi Saheb's character. He felt for people as if they were his own kith and kin.

Rafi Saheb did not keep good health. He was a heart patient but in his zeal to serve people he often ignored the advice of his physicians. He died of cardiac arrest in October 1954 at the age of sixty. Thus ended the career of a person who will go down in history as one of the most ardent and dedicated builders of modern India, who cared much for his friends, followers and countrymen.

Madhavrao Scindia

Madhavrao Scindia, maharaja of Gwalior, was the patriarch of the royal house of the Scindias. He was the son of the late Maharaja Jiwajirao Scindia and Rajmata Vijaya Raje Scindia. Jiwajirao was the son of Maharaja Madhavrao Scindia.

Our relationship with the royal family of Scindias dates back to the early 1920s. My father was then a young man in his late twenties. Father was a dynamic personality and had a wide range of contacts. One day, at a party, he met Maharaja Madhavrao, popularly called Madho Maharaja, who was then the ruler of Gwalior. The maharaja was highly impressed by father, and invited him to start some industry in Gwalior. Father agreed.

The people of Gwalior state were very poor. Even so, Gwalior was regarded as an important state. In the 1920s, the state of Jaipur, from where our family hails, had a revenue of about Rs 1 crore. Gwalior's revenue was approximately Rs 3 crore; by that standard Gwalior was a 'big' state. Madho Maharaja was an enlightened ruler. He administered the state ably and was very popular with his subjects.

After surveying the state of Gwalior, father decided to set up a textiles unit there. Accordingly Jiyajeerao Cotton Mills Ltd was established in 1921. Madho Maharaja extended full moral and other support to father in the establishment of this mill. The mill was named after his son Jiwajirao.

As a consequence of this mill being established, the economy of the state improved swiftly. Father and Madho Maharaja became good friends. Father would visit Gwalior every three or four months and every time he went there he was invited to lunch or dinner by Madho Maharaja. Father used to tell me many stories about Madho Maharaja. Father had once sent him a letter. There was no acknowledgement or reply for an entire month. Father was a man of great self-respect, and he stopped meeting Madho Maharaja, who soon realized the reason for this interruption in their friendship. To make up, he invited father for dinner. Whenever the maharaja invited father to dine with him, some of his ministers would be present. Before dinner he took father aside and said: 'Birla-ji, I realize I made a mistake in not replying to your letter. But tell me, how could you, a senior person, make the mistake of stopping your visits to meet me?' Both again became friends.

Once father narrated another interesting incident. Maharaja's senior executives was

trivial errors. Mad

hunting

rulers. The

side. Tiger hu

(a platform on

machan

the elephant

elephants was, before organized. The tiger is a ferocious, certainly a very powerful animal. There was no one on foot. That could be dangerous as the tiger, in case its bloodthirsty instinct was roused, could have caused havoc. It could be fatal to human life. Hence everyone was on elephants. Madho Maharaja asked the sardar to sit next to him on the elephant. The sardar felt very proud that such honour was being shown to him. When they reached the thick forest Madho Maharaja suddenly pushed the sardar down from the elephant. He fell with a thud on the ground and started shouting: 'Maharaja, Maharaja, why this punishment?' Madho Maharaja said to the sardar: 'I had heard that you torture and bully your people. A strong virile man like you should now try to bully the tiger. I would like to watch the fun.' The sardar was taken aback. He immediately asked for Madho Maharaja's pardon and promised to treat his people kindly and generously in future. Thereupon, he was taken back on the elephant.

Another incident related to the resident commissioner at Gwalior. During the British Raj, the government of India sent to every native state their representative who was called resident commissioner, or just resident in common parlance. His duty was to send confidential reports about the state to the viceroy as to how the administration was being run, the conduct of the maharaja towards his subjects, his popularity with his subjects, the state's economy, and so on. The resident was also required to state in his confidential report about the extent of the maharaja's loyalty towards the British Crown. All the maharajas were afraid of the residents and always tried to be in their good books.

Our textile mill worked in all three shifts—twenty-four hours a day. Most of the workers lived in the quarters provided by us; some lived in the town. A long siren was sounded to inform the workers that their shift was about to start. Thereafter, at the exact time when the new shift started, the mill would sound another whistle.

The resident commissioner's house was not far from the mill. The siren blown in the early morning disturbed his sleep and that of his household. He sent word to the maharaja that something should be done about it. During one of his meetings with father, the maharaja mentioned the complaint. He asked father if something could be done about this complaint. Father said that there was hardly anything which he could do. The mill had to sound a whistle, otherwise the workmen would not know that their shift was about to commence. He asked the maharaja to remain firm and to explain the position to the resident. If worst came to the worst, the resident could be advised to shift his house to some far-off locality. The maharaja agreed with father and related to the resident what father had said. The resident also realized that there was nothing that could be done in the matter and reconciled himself to the situation. The maharaja thus was not cowed down by the resident.

I have written somewhat elaborately about my father and Madho Maharaja for that was the beginning of our relationship with the House of the Scindias.

After the death of Madho Maharaja, his son Jiwajirao became the maharaja of Gwalior. I often visited Gwalior with father. I met Maharaja Jiwajirao a number of times. He, like his father, was an enlightened ruler. After independence, when the reorganization of the states took place, Sardar Patel was deputy prime minister. He was very friendly with father.

When the question of Raj Pramukh for Madhya Pradesh was being considered, father suggested the name of Jiwajirao to Sardar Patel. Owing to father's efforts, Jiwajirao was made the Raj Pramukh of Madhya Pradesh. On merits too, he deserved this post.

Madhavrao was born in 1945. As he was the first born male child of Jiwajirao, who was then the maharaja, he was automatically named Yuvraj. He went to school and college in Gwalior and the United Kingdom and also took an MA degree from Oxford University. He was thus an Oxonian. Jiwajirao expired in 1961. The same year saw Madhavrao crowned as the maharaja of Gwalior.

He first got elected to the Lok Sabha in 1971. Thereafter, he got elected to the Lok Sabha in each successive election. This was no mean feat. His constituency was Gwalior or Guna. The last time he was elected was to the thirteenth Lok Sabha in 1999. This was his ninth term. So popular was he that he never lost an election. He made history of sorts by remaining unbeaten throughout his political career from 1971 to 2001.

Madhavrao, when he entered politics, joined the Jan Sangh. The first election he won from Guna was as a Jan Sangh candidate in 1971. Madhavrao, however, did not like being a part of the Jan Sangh outfit which he thought was a communal party. He started drifting towards the Congress. When the elections were held in 1977 he stood as an independent candidate supported by the Congress (I). Finally he joined the Congress (I) party in 1980.

I met Madhavrao in the early 1980s. I was in Delhi at that time. Madhavrao had heard, as he later said to me, that I took active interest in politics. He, therefore, sent me a message that he would like to meet me. I sent word to him that I would be happy to meet him and that he need not take the trouble of coming to my place; I would call on him. But he insisted that he would like to meet me at my house. So Madhavrao came to Birla House. It was a very pleasant meeting. I was highly impressed by him. I could immediately detect the clarity of mind he possessed. When we started talking about politics I could notice that his analysis was very sound. Madhavrao took a liking to me.

I was elected to the Rajya Sabha in 1984. That was my first term. For all practical purposes, I was a Congress (I) MP and always voted for the party. Belonging to the same party, we naturally became even closer. As time passed, our relationship went on deepening till we started regarding each other almost as members of the same family. This relationship continued right till his sad demise in a plane crash on 30 September 2001.

New Delhi, 1999: At a party hosted by Hindustan Times
management on completion of 75 years—with Sonia Gandhi,
Madhavrao Scindia and my daughter Shobhana

Madhavrao was a man of high principles and noble character. Human
memory is proverbially short. Let me therefore narrate how he resigned
from the civil aviation ministry when he need not have done so. He
joined P. V. Narasimha Rao's Cabinet in 1991 and was responsible for
introducing the open skies policy. The ministry functioned very well under
his directions. He, however, resigned after a plane crash, owning moral
responsibility. People instantly equated him with the late Lal Bahadur
Shastri. I was in Delhi at that time. After I heard about his decision I had
some kind of a colloquy with him on the matter. I said to him that if after
every rail accident the railway minister had to resign and if after every
air crash the civil aviation minister, no one would accept the charge of
these ministries. I told him that the ministry under his charge was a well-
administered one. If a plane crashed owing to human error, how could he
be held responsible? Where was the necessity for him to resign, I queried.
He said: 'KK Babu, I deliberately did not consult you on this matter as
had I consulted you before resigning, you would not have permitted me
to resign.' It was a call of his conscience, he said.

In 1995, he was re-inducted into the Union Cabinet by Rao. But, owing
to differences, he resigned in 1996. Rao, who was the president of the
Congress (I) Parliamentary Party and also headed the party, denied him a
ticket in the 1996 elections. Madhavrao consulted all his friends, including

myself. I urged him to stand for the elections. 'You are sure to win,' I said. All his friends advised him similarly. Madhavrao did stand for the Lok Sabha elections in 1996 as an independent candidate and came out victorious.

As a minister, Madhavrao performed extremely well. I came constantly in touch with him. He excelled in whatever ministry and capacity he was placed. During 1984–86, he was Union minister of state for railways. That was the first time he joined the government as a minister of state. As one of my companies was manufacturing wagons, I came constantly in touch with Madhavrao. He was always fair in his decisions. Though we were good friends he never showed any favour towards my company. That was commendable. It was exactly what I had also wanted. In whatever position Madhavrao worked, the performance of the ministry under his guidance showed remarkable improvement.

Rao's term as prime minister came to an end in 1996. For some time, Sitaram Kesri was the president of the Congress (I) party. Sonia Gandhi became the party president in March 1998. Sonia-ji was new to politics; but after she settled down, she discovered that amongst the galaxy of stalwarts of the Congress (I) party, the man whom she could thoroughly trust on matters of integrity and sound wisdom, was Madhavrao. He thus became very close to Sonia-ji.

His demise in a plane accident in 2001 was a national calamity. There is no doubt at all that had he been alive he would have risen even higher in politics. In the Congress (I) hierarchy he was one of the senior leaders at the top after Sonia-ji. He was prime ministerial material.

Apart from politics, Madhavrao was very fond of cricket. During 1990–93, he was the president of the Board of Control for Cricket in India (BCCI). There was a keen tussle between Madhavrao and Jagmohan Dalmiya, then a member of BCCI, for the post of president of the board. Before Madhavrao decided to contest, I had promised my support to Jagmohan who is also very close to me. This support was more of academic than of any real value, as I could not influence any of the voters. But Jagmohan wanted my moral support which I promised him. Then I came to know that Madhavrao was also contesting. He too wanted my moral support. My daughter, Shobhana, and her husband, Shyam, were also very close to Madhavrao. They approached me and said that my moral support should be for Madhavrao. I was on the horns of a dilemma. On the one hand, I had promised support to Jagmohan, and on the other Madhavrao, who was also very close to me, claimed mine. I discussed the matter with Shyam and Shobhana and decided that in such a crucial and delicate situation the best course was that I remain neutral. I sent for Jagmohan and told him how the situation had developed. I said that under the circumstances he should permit me to remain neutral. Jagmohan, sportsman as he is, agreed to my proposal. Madhavrao also appreciated my stand.

In August 1999, I underwent heart bypass surgery. I was eigthy-one years old; not a young age at all. I discovered that it was a very painful operation and that the post-operation recovery was very slow. In fact even one month after the operation I could walk only at the rate of about a mile an hour; I also found that I could not climb down the stairs by myself. There was always the danger of my stumbling.

After the operation I came back to Delhi by a British Airways flight. Shobhana and Shyam came to the airport to receive me. It was almost midnight. But apart from them, Madhavrao was also there at that odd hour. And how did he meet me? He hid himself in a corner. After Shyam and Shobhana had met me, Madhavrao suddenly made his appearance and shouted, 'KK Babu.' I was certainly pleasantly surprised to see him at the airport at that odd hour. This showed Madhavrao's warmth and affection and also his sense of humour.

As Madhavrao was one of the senior leaders in the Congress (I) after Sonia-ji, I frequently came in touch with him. He was a man of unimpeachable integrity and his circle of friends was very wide. He was an excellent speaker and a very good writer. I remember, once I was asked by the organizers of a function to send a message. I get many such requests. This is a formal matter. In such cases, I ask someone in the organization to prepare a suitable message. In this case I asked Shobhana, who is the vice chairperson of the *Hindustan Times*, to have a message prepared for me. I said that after the preliminary drafting had been done, I would correct it and modify the message where necessary and then send it to the organizers of the function. When the message came to me I was surprised to see how well it was drafted. Both from the point of view of language and thought it was an excellent draft. I told Shobhana that she should give my high appreciation to the person who had drafted it. Shobhana smiled and said that she was having dinner with Madhavrao when she casually mentioned about the message I required. She said Madhavrao had himself penned it.

Madhavrao took special interest in the promotion of education. He was the president of the board of governors of Scindia School and made it one of the finest public schools of the country. Madhavrao was also very fond of wildlife and was a member of the Wildlife Society.

I was in the United States when Madhavrao died. Suddenly one day I got a telephone call from my secretary in Delhi—Jyotsna Sud—saying that she had very sad news to convey to me. She then gave the news of the plane crash. I was stunned; it was a personal loss to me. But I consoled myself by the thought that one has to bow before God's will. His demise was a profound loss not only to the Congress (I), but to the entire nation. He provided invaluable support to Sonia-ji and there is no doubt that the party, which has done very well in the last few years, would have achieved even greater heights had he been alive to lend his counsel.

His son, Jyotiraditya, is a very promising young man. He contested the Lok Sabha elections after Madhavrao's death and was returned by the loving public with a vast majority.

When I was born in 1918, Madho Maharaja was still living and was quite active. It is a matter of pride for me that from Madho Maharaja to Jyotiraditya, it is the fourth generation of the royal House of Scindias with whom we enjoy and share a warm friendship. It is also a matter of deep satisfaction that today our relations with the House of Scindias are as intimate as they were between father and Madho Maharaja.

Madhavrao's name will be written in letters of gold in the history of the country for the nobility of his character, his administrative acumen, his high principles in life, and his contributions to various fields during his lifetime. It is sad that cruel hands of destiny snatched him away at the prime of his life; there is not the least doubt that had he been alive, he would have soared very high indeed in the political firmament. His name will be remembered by posterity as long as human beings cherish and admire selflessness, integrity and dedication.

Pandit Madan Mohan Malaviya

Madan Mohan Malaviya, or Malaviya-ji as he was respectfully addressed, was born in Allahabad on 25 December 1861. Though he wanted to study for his master's degree, poverty compelled him to take to earning his living. He was appointed as a teacher in his old school on Rs 40 a month and soon became popular among his pupils. Public life however had a great attraction for him. As there were no rules in those days debarring government servants from attending political meetings, he attended the second Congress session held in Kolkata in 1886 with his Sanskrit professor, Pandit Aditya Ram Bhattacharya. He spoke at the Congress session with conviction and his speech held the audience spellbound. A.O. Hume, the general secretary of the Congress, made an appreciative reference to it in his annual report.

Soon after his return from Kolkata, he was offered the editorship of the Hindi weekly, *Hindustan,* published from a small town called Kala Kanker at a salary of Rs 200 a month. Later, he left the paper and became a lawyer.

Malaviya-ji became a high court lawyer in 1893, but the flow of litigants began from the days when he was studying law. Cases began to pour in from the very start of his legal career. His fame as a lawyer spread quickly throughout the province. Yet he always gave preference to public work over his legal work. He virtually withdrew from the legal profession in 1909, but made an exception in 1922 in regard to the appeal of 225 persons condemned to death in connection with the Chauri Chaura riots (in the Gorakhpur district of Uttar Pradesh) on account of which Mahatma Gandhi suspended the civil disobedience movement, and saved 153 accused from the gallows.

Father came in touch with Malaviya-ji in the early 1920s. He was greatly attracted to Malaviya-ji's transparent sincerity, simple manners, profound erudition in Hindi and Sanskrit and of our ancient texts, as also his high moral character.

Malaviya-ji started the *Hindustan Times.* All the finance needed was provided or arranged by father. Malaviya-ji became chairman of the paper. Most of the shares were purchased by father. A few shares were in Malaviya-ji's name. Even today they stand in his name as nobody came for transfer of these shares after his demise. Malaviya-ji was chairman of the board of directors of the *Hindustan Times* from 1927 to 1946.

In 1909, Malaviya-ji was elected to the Imperial Legislative Council, of which he soon became one of the most important members. The Banaras Hindu University, perhaps Malaviya-ji's greatest achievement, will remind future generations of the keen interest that he took in training and enlightening the mind and the spirit of the young. It was his deep love for Hindu culture and the spiritual ideas embodied in Hindu religious books that gave birth to the idea of establishing the Banaras Hindu University. The importance that he attached to the economic development of the country made him combine the teaching of science and technology with that of religion. The colleges of agriculture, engineering, mining, metallurgy and geology, the ayurvedic college and an allopathic hospital, which was named after Pandit Sunder Lal, the first vice chancellor of the university, were started soon after the establishment of the university. This made the university pre-eminent among the then existing universities.

The scheme drawn up by Malaviya-ji to establish Banaras Hindu University was the result of discussions with his friends and the valuable cooperation of Mrs Annie Besant, of my father, the maharajadhiraj of Darbhanga and the maharaja of Banaras. The foundation stone of the university was laid by the viceroy, Lord Hardinge, on 4 February 1916. The university buildings were declared open by the Prince of Wales (later Duke of Windsor) on 13 December 1921. Malaviya-ji collected a great deal of funds for the Banaras Hindu University. All the princes held him in high esteem. Most of them regarded him as their guru and would touch his feet whenever he called on them. Malaviya-ji had a knack for collecting funds. He also went to Kathmandu and collected some funds from the king of Nepal. At the time of departure, Malaviya-ji blessed the king. Suddenly he said that he had forgotten to bless the queen. So the king of Nepal took him to the queen who also gave him a handsome donation. Malaviya-ji related this to me. Malaviya-ji became the vice chancellor of the Banaras Hindu University and held this office from 1919 to 1938.

There were several well-known writers of Hindi during the latter part of the nineteenth century, for instance, Bharatendu Harishchandra, Raja Shiva Prasad and Balmukund Gupta. Because of this phase there was a cultural awakening among the Hindus at the time. Malaviya-ji also wrote poems and articles in Hindi when he was young and valued Hindi as a vehicle for educating the masses. In those days the language of the courts in Uttar Pradesh (then called North Western Provinces and Oudh) was Urdu. Malaviya-ji advocated the use of the Devanagari script along with the Persian script in the courts.

Malaviya-ji was a conservative in social matters. He believed in the varnashrama dharma (caste system). He was, however, prepared to adjust himself to changes in the social mores of the country to a reasonable extent, but wanted to take the leaders of the Hindu community and the pandits of Kashi along with him in matters of social reform. He felt strongly about the injustice done to the depressed classes in connection with temple entry, and pleaded their cause before the pandits in 1936, and took out a procession in favour of temple entry which was joined by the well known pandits of Banaras and the members of the depressed classes. In the 1920s, he persuaded the pandits of the Oriental faculty of the university to agree to the reclamation of those members of the depressed classes who had been converted to other religions and began their *shuddhi* (purification) himself by making them recite the mantra 'Shri Ram, Jai Ram, Jai Jai Ram' after a bath in the Ganga.

Malaviya-ji was easily accessible and helpful even to the humblest Indian. Even when he could give no help to the sufferers from injustice, he comforted them by listening patiently to their grievances and saying a few words of sympathy. The appeal of poor students, whether Hindu or Muslim, for financial help to complete their education always touched a responsive chord in his heart, and not infrequently he went beyond the university regulations to help them. A Muslim student once complained to him of the unsatisfactory mess arrangements in his hostel. Malaviya-ji was greatly pained to hear this and said, 'My kitchen is always open to you.'

I came in touch with Malaviya-ji around 1925, the same time that I came in touch with Gandhi-ji. Malaviya-ji would often visit father but whenever he came he always found some time to spend with his children. Whenever he visited Kolkata or Delhi he always stayed with us. Once I remember, when he came to visit father, he called me, Madhav Prasad, Basant Kumar and Ganga Prasad. He asked us what we were studying. Then he picked out Madhav Prasad and myself and wanted us to recite a Hindi doha (poem) turn by turn. This went on for about half an hour. The question was who would say that he had no more poems to recite. But Malaviya-ji would not let any of us be defeated. After half an hour he stopped us and said that he was very happy that we could recite so many poems. Both of us were happy because both of us had exhausted our stock of poems committed to memory.

Whenever Malaviya-ji came to Delhi and stayed at Birla House, I would spend ten to fifteen minutes with him each day. Once he came to Delhi just to meet the viceroy. He said he desperately needed funds for the Banaras Hindu University and for that reason he had come to meet the viceroy. Before going to meet the viceroy he said, 'Krishna Kumar, in case you are free I would like you to accompany me. You can wait with the viceroy's ADC (aide-de-camp) when I go to meet him.' I readily agreed. We went together to the Viceregal Lodge (present-day Rashtrapati Bhavan). The viceroy did not keep Malaviya-ji waiting. He soon called him in. I waited with the ADC. Malaviya-ji came back after about twenty minutes. When we were in the car, he said very happily that he was able to get a large donation from the viceroy.

Whenever I visited Banaras I would go to the Banaras Hindu University and call on Malaviya-ji. Knowing he was a very saintly person, I once asked him if he ever had any divine experience or intimations. He remained silent for a minute or so and then said that once he had organized a *yajna* in the university compound. He said that when the ghee was being poured in the yajna cauldron the thought suddenly struck him—how is it that during such an occasion he could not see gods or ancient rishis! Malaviya-ji said that as soon as this divine intimation came to his mind he immediately felt the presence of old rishis as if in a trance. They were all in divine form, like ethereal beings hovering in the atmosphere around him. He said that during the whole yajna ceremony when ghee was poured on the holy flames he saw these ethereal beings or rishis smiling as if thoroughly satisfied with the performance of the yajna. As Malaviya-ji was a very saintly person, there was no room for doubting what he recounted.

Malaviya-ji expired on 12 November 1946. Amongst the leaders of that time, he and Gandhi-ji were the only two persons who had supreme and total faith in God.

T.T. Krishnamachari

T.T. Krishnamachari, or TTK, as he was generally called, was born of a Vaishnavite Brahmin family on 26 November 1899. In 1936, TTK decided on entering politics. In 1942, he formally joined the Indian National Congress as a member. In 1946 he became a member of the Constituent Assembly and participated in its deliberations during 1946–48.

When India became a republic in 1950, TTK joined the Union Cabinet as minister of commerce and industry. In 1956 he became minister of finance. The Unit Trust of India was his brainchild.

While he was finance minister, the unfortunate Mundra episode rocked the country. Feroze Gandhi alleged in Parliament that TTK had extended favours to one Haridas Mundra, who sold counterfeit shares and the M.C. Chagla Commission report led to his resignation from the Cabinet in 1958. But Pandit Nehru's confidence in him was not destroyed. So he joined the Cabinet again and functioned as minister without portfolio.

I came in touch with TTK some time in 1952, soon after he became minister of commerce and industry. He was a man of strong likes and dislikes. He was regarded as a good friend but a bad enemy. He was short-tempered. I was only thirty-three years of age when I came in contact with him. Father was fifty-eight years old. Father and TTK were of the same age group. Father was highly impressed by TTK's sharpness, his analytical mind, and his integrity and honesty. Father was much senior to TTK in politics. TTK knew of father's close association with Mahatma-ji and friendship with Sardar Patel and Pandit-ji. They became good friends. Another person who was a common friend was Ramnath Goenka. The three often met together for discussions.

TTK developed a soft corner for me. Then came the question as to how I should address him. As he was close to father, I was inclined to address him as 'uncle'. Ramnath-ji however said that TTK would feel happier if I addressed him as 'Sir'. Hence I started addressing him as 'Sir'. This pleased TTK. I had no objection in addressing him thus as he was much senior to me. He is the only minister whom I ever called 'Sir'.

All the secretaries and members of the bureaucracy were very much afraid of him. First, they knew that they could not fool him. He was very intelligent and knew the subject of his portfolio well. Secondly, they knew that he was a strong-willed person, had a mind of his own as well as a quick temper. Once it happened that one of my companies—Texmaco—had some problems with its banker, which was the State Bank of India. When the problem could not be resolved between my executives and the bank authorities, my chief executive related the details to me. It appeared that the State Bank of India officials were unjustifiably taking a tough line towards my company. I decided to meet TTK. I related to him the whole matter and said that my company on the whole was sound but that it had some temporary problems owing to depressed market conditions. I said that under such circumstances the bank should stand by the client and not become authoritarian. TTK asked me to meet him the next day, and went to attend a meeting. Within two hours of our talk I got a phone call from the chairman of the State Bank of India. He said that if there was any problem which his juniors were creating for my company, I could have approached him and he would have immediately set the matter right. Soon there was a sea change in the attitude of the State Bank of India towards my company. Next day, I met TTK, and when I told him the whole story, he smiled.

For some reason or the other, TTK took a dislike to Hindustan Motors. My uncle BM was its chairman. Uncle would often brief me to have a talk with TTK about this company. This I did. Father too spoke to TTK on behalf of Hindustan Motors. He softened his stand slightly but his prejudice against Hindustan Motors did not totally vanish.

After retiring from Lal Bahadur Shastri's Cabinet, TTK went back to Chennai (then called Madras) and settled down in his house near the airport. In those days I used to visit Chennai twice or thrice a year. Every time I went to Chennai I would call on TTK I always found him full of affection for me but otherwise in a depressed mood. He was always happy to meet me. I told him that he should not be so morose and glum. He should be active and guide the innumerable people who called on him to seek his advice. But TTK had lost all zest for life. He would say: 'KK, what have I to live for now?' Having served Pandit-ji's Cabinet as minister in charge of various ministries, he felt he had no more ambition in life. I always tried to comfort and cheer him. He passed away on 7 March 1974. He made a gift of his valuable library of nearly 5,000 books to the Vivekananda College, Chennai.

TTK, though a businessman operating on the strength of immense capital, officially fell in with Pandit-ji's socialist policies and introduced budgets which became famous for heavy direct taxation. When he finally took leave of the Cabinet, he had become a bitter man. He spoke in Parliament of 'man-eaters' on the prowl. He may be considered to be a fair mix of capitalism in practice functioning under the garb of socialism in the brew called mixed economy which Pandit-ji prescribed for India.

PART II

INDIRA GANDHI: REMINISCENCES

13

Family Ties

Father was very close to both Gandhi-ji and Sardar Patel. In those days he was not that intimate with Pandit-ji. Nonetheless, their relationship was cordial. Father knew Pandit Motilal Nehru also fairly well. Though Jawaharlal-ji's leanings were towards Fabian socialism, on a personal level there was great cordiality between him and father.

Father used to relate an incident. All members of the family would visit Varanasi regularly to meet my grandparents, who had retired to that holy city around 1918. During one such a trip in the 1920s, father decided to go to Allahabad and take a dip at the holy Sangam (confluence of three holy rivers). Father was an intellectual but also a devout Hindu. For a pious Hindu, a dip at the Sangam is the fulfilment of an ambition. Father went to Prayag Raj (Allahabad), had a dip at the Sangam, and started on his return journey to Varanasi. On the outskirts of Allahabad, the car in which father was travelling broke down. The chauffeur did his best to get the car started, but try as he might he did not succeed. Most chauffeurs in India are poor mechanics and our chauffeur in Varanasi was no exception. Father had no alternative but to go back to Allahabad to arrange for transport there. The question was whether he would be able to find a car to take him from Allahabad to Varanasi. In the 1920s, finding a dependable taxi was not easy. While in that predicament, father suddenly thought of Pandit Motilal Nehru whom he knew well and who was a prince among men. He went straight to Anand Bhavan. Motilal-ji was not in but Jawaharlal-ji was at home. Father asked the peon to inform him that Ghanshyam Das Birla had come and wanted to meet him. Pandit-ji, somewhat taken aback by the unexpected visit, immediately came to the drawing room. Father narrated the difficulty he was in, and said that he needed a car to take him to Varanasi, because his parents would start worrying if he got delayed. Without a moment's hesitation, Pandit-ji lent his car to father who went back to Varanasi in it.

After the Sardar's death, father came in closer touch with Pandit-ji and in course of time their relationship developed into such a steadfast intimacy that Pandit-ji, at father's invitation, visited Pilani thrice in 1950, 1953 and 1961; he also visited our factory at Hindalco, Renukoot, at father's invitation.

BITS, Pilani, 1950: Jawaharlal Nehru rides a horse with my father

On all the visits Pandit-ji was accompanied by Indira-ji. I was present with father on those occasions. Father remained engrossed in conversation with Pandit-ji, and I looked after Indira-ji as best as I could. Owing to my acquaintance with Indira-ji, I prided myself in regarding it as my exclusive prerogative.

During their first visit to Pilani, when Pandit-ji alighted from the plane along with Indira-ji, she gave me a glance of recognition along with her usual charming smile. Seeing this, father was a bit surprised. He enquired about how I knew Indira-ji. I related to him with a certain amount of elation that I had been meeting her off and on whenever I called on Pandit-ji.

Each time Pandit-ji visited Pilani, he would spend a night with us. Father would personally look after all the arrangements, assisted by me and other members of the family. As I knew Indira-ji, I would take the initiative in finding out from her about Pandit-ji's requirements and about her own comforts, and advise father accordingly.

Thus my acquaintance with Indira-ji gradually ripened.

It was in the early 1950s that I had first met Indira-ji, quite by chance. I had sought an appointment with Pandit-ji, the then prime minister of India. I was almost certain that my request for an appointment would be refused. I was a mere youth in my early thirties.

There was a generation gap between Pandit-ji and myself. Besides, father used to meet Pandit-ji quite frequently. Pandit-ji knew that for any important decision to be taken on behalf of the family, father was the ultimate authority. Where then was the question of a busy person like Pandit-ji, who had to carry the burden of the entire country on his shoulders, and who had grown into an international celebrity finding time to see an 'unknown' person like me? So I reasoned, and so I feared. But Pandit-ji was a remarkable man, a real democrat. To my surprise and delight, he agreed to meet me. Pandit-ji enjoyed universal respect. He was held in high esteem even by his critics. Had he chosen not to see me, I would have quite understood his position. But when he agreed to meet me I was thoroughly bowled over by his generosity! And because Pandit-ji agreed to meet me my respect for him purely on that consideration increased tenfold. Selfish, perhaps, but that was the way it was.

The appointment was fixed at the PM's House in Willingdon Crescent. M.O. Mathai was then secretary to Pandit-ji. While I was waiting in Mathai's room, Indira-ji walked in. Mathai introduced me to her. I bowed to her with hands folded in the traditional Indian style of offering 'namaskar'. She responded with a disarming smile. That was how I first met Indira-ji.

My meeting with Pandit-ji lasted just a few minutes; I did most of the talking. I endeavoured to give him my views on the prevailing economic conditions in the country, the problems that some of the industries faced, and on other related matters. He must have felt amused at a young man daring to give views and suggestions to the prime minister of the country. But just as age commands respect, youth commands tolerance. Pandit-ji was kind enough to give me a patient hearing. He interjected a few words to seek clarifications of some points made by me. But otherwise he remained silent. I discovered that he was a good listener. I felt Pandit-ji was impressed by me. Before taking leave, I thanked Pandit-ji for having given me time to meet him and asked whether I could meet him again. He was magnanimous and gave his consent.

Feeling greatly elated and satisfied with myself and my performance, I returned to Mathai's room and narrated to him what transpired at the meeting with Pandit-ji. I also told him triumphantly that Pandit-ji had very kindly agreed to see me again. Mathai was slightly annoyed by this and gave me a short 'sermon', saying that a busy person like Pandit-ji should not be bothered without any justifiable reason. After a while he calmed down and said that I could meet Pandit-ji again, but not before six months. I thought that was good enough. Six months later I met Pandit-ji again. This time, I told Mathai that I would like to meet Indira-ji also, just to pay my respects. Mathai agreed and arranged for me to call on Indira-ji.

After this, it became a routine matter for me to ask for an appointment with Pandit-ji every few months. Pandit-ji, I felt, had taken a liking to me. He wanted to meet and encourage young people and he found me acceptable. During one of my visits I told Pandit-ji that I had started a factory in Kolkata called Texmaco and requested him to visit it. Surprisingly, he agreed to that also.

When I went home, I informed father and other members of the family about it. The fact that Pandit-ji had agreed to visit the Texmaco factory caused great excitement in our circle, as never before had Pandit-ji visited any factory of our group.

Kolkata, December 1953: Jawaharlal Nehru takes a round of Texmaco factory

True to his promise, during one of his trips to Kolkata, Pandit-ji visited Texmaco along with Dr B.C. Roy, chief minister of West Bengal. From Raj Bhawan, Pandit-ji travelled with Dr Roy in an open car to the Texmaco factory which is situated at Belgharia, a suburb of Kolkata. Both sides of the road leading to the factory were lined with throngs of cheering multitudes. On his arrival at the factory, Pandit-ji was garlanded by representatives of the workers and me. He made a quick round of the factory and later drove round the colony along with Dr Roy and myself in an open car amidst shouts of '*jai*s' and '*zindabad*s'.

The news regarding Pandit-ji's liking for me soon got around and gave me improved status in the business circles and in the bureaucracy. I was taken on a number of committees including the Central Advisory Council of Industries and was also invited to join the board of the State Bank of India.

Whenever I called on Pandit-ji I would ask Mathai to fix an appointment for me with Indira-ji too. It sometimes happened that Indira-ji had other engagements and so could not meet me; in such cases she would give me time the next day to call on her. However, on most occasions that I met Pandit-ji, I would meet Indira-ji too. So started my association with her.

14

Vishwayatan Yogashram Trust

Apart from Indira-ji, whom I came to know fairly well, I knew Lal
Bahadur Shastri quite closely.

One day, sometime in 1961, Lal Bahadur-ji called me to his house in
Delhi. He was then the minister for commerce and industry. After a casual
chat and exchange of pleasantries, he asked me to join a yogic trust
called the Vishwayatan Yogashram Trust as its trustee. He explained
that a certain Dhirendra Brahmachari was the moving spirit behind the
Trust. He said Brahmachari was endeavouring to make yoga popular
and since the Vishwayatan Yogashram Trust was doing good work it
deserved support. He revealed that both Indira-ji and he were its trustees,
and invited me also to join the trust. I was surprised at the proposal and
wanted to know whose idea it was. Lal Bahadur-ji explained that my
name had been suggested by Indira-ji. I gave my consent.

After some time, Lal Bahadur-ji again sent for me. He said that Indira-
ji felt the need for funds for the Trust, and that she had sought my assistance
for collecting donations. I agreed to collect funds, and enquired how
much was needed. Surprisingly the amount was not big. Lal Bahadur-ji
indicated that if I could collect about Rs 1 lakh or so, it would suffice. I
replied that for so small a sum there was no need to approach other
businessmen, as I could myself donate that amount. Lal Bahadur-ji said
that Indira-ji felt that instead of accepting the full amount from one
individual, it would be better if the money were to be collected from a
number of persons, so that more people came to know about the Trust.
Under the circumstances, Lal Bahadur-ji suggested that I donate a part of
the amount and that I collect the balance from other businessmen. I acceded
to this, adding that I would be happy if either he or Indira-ji could come
to Kolkata, from where I promised to collect the needed sum. I disclosed
to him that my plan was to organize a dinner either in his or Indira-ji's
honour and collect the required amount from the invitees then and there.

Lal Bahadur-ji sounded Indira-ji on the matter and later advised me to meet her, which I did. I assured her that I could collect Rs 1 lakh from businessmen provided she visited Kolkata. Indira-ji agreed, and wrote in her own hand confirming the arrangement.

The text of the handwritten letter is reproduced below:

Prime Minister's House,
New Delhi-11
12 September 1961

Dear Shri Birla,
Thank you for your letter of the 7th Sept.

It is good of you to help the Yogashram. I shall come to Kolkata on the 25th Sept. and return to Delhi on the 26th Sept. by the evening plane. I shall be staying at the Raj Bhawan.

Actually it is not at all easy for me to go out of Delhi as I have so much touring to do but I must keep my promise to you and to the Trust.

With regards,

Yours sincerely,
Indira Gandhi

P.S. I shall reach Kolkata by the morning plane.

Kolkata, 1950s: Indira Gandhi with us during a private visit

Indira-ji visited Kolkata in September 1961. I again asked her about the amount she wanted me to collect. She repeated what she had said earlier: Rs 1 lakh. There was a small gathering at the airport to receive her. I played the role of master of ceremonies, as it was at my instance that she was visiting Kolkata. Along with a few of my friends and associates I received her at the airport and presented her a bouquet. I had requested Indira-ji to stay at my house but she felt that the governor would not approve, and so she put up at the Raj Bhawan.

Indira-ji, however, did come to my house in accordance with her promise. I do not recollect whether it was an early dinner or late tea. I invited a number of businessmen to meet her. They came gladly. Who would not like to meet the prime minister's daughter? In a brief speech I explained the aims and objects of the Vishwayatan Yogashram Trust and appealed to the guests for the necessary donations. As the amount involved was not large, the money was promised on the spot. I was able to get promises for donations totalling Rs 1,05,701 against the target of Rs 1 lakh. Indira-ji was fully satisfied.

From my residence, Indira-ji drove straight to the airport to catch the flight to Delhi. Even today, I remember the incident vividly. On reaching the airport we were told that the flight was considerably delayed. Indira-ji was required to wait in the VIP lounge for a few hours. After half an hour, I told Indira-ji that I would wait in the main lounge at the airport while she could take rest in the VIP lounge. She was in fact, feeling very drowsy. Indira-ji appreciated the suggestion but insisted that I go back home and not wait for her plane to depart. I protested that as she had come to Kolkata entirely at my invitation I regarded it my duty to see her off and that I would wait at the airport until her flight took off. Indira-ji would not listen to that. She said that she would not stand on formalities, and pressed me to return home as it was getting late. The governor had sent his ADC to the airport to see her off. She spoke to him and also to the police officer on duty and asked them to wake her up in time for the plane's departure. She then reclined on the sofa and went off to sleep. I returned home. The next time when I met her in Delhi she told me how happy she was about the collection that was made. She expressed her appreciation for my efforts and wrote to me accordingly. A copy of the letter is reproduced here:

PRIME MINISTER'S HOUSE.
NEW DELHI-11.

September 30, 1961.

Dear Shri Birla,

      Thank you for your letter and
even more so for the trouble you took over
my visit.

      I am glad everything went off
well and do hope that your estimate of
Rs.1 lac will be proved correct. You will
have the blessings and the gratitude of
the Ashram.

            With kindert regards,

            Yours sincerely,

I was pleased with the letter, more with the postscript added in her handwriting, which shows how informal she was.

The story of Vishwayatan Yogashram Trust did not end there. One day, Lal Bahadur-ji sent for me again. I went to his house, wondering what was in store for me this time. Lal Bahadur-ji said that both Indira-ji and he desired that I should become chairman of the Vishwayatan Yogashram Trust. That came as a bombshell to me. After regaining my composure, I firmly declined to accept the suggestion. Seeing my reluctance, Lal Bahadur-ji hastened to assure me that both Indira-ji and he would continue as trustees under my chairmanship. I told him that whatever money was needed for the Trust or, for that matter, any assistance needed of me was there for the asking; but that I would not like to shoulder the responsibility of the chairmanship. Even otherwise, I explained that I would suffer from an inferiority complex since both Indira-ji and he were much bigger personalities compared to me and, under the circumstances, I would not be able to function well as chairman. On his suggestion, I met Indira-ji too and explained to her my reasons for not accepting her proposal. She tried to persuade me to become chairman but ultimately accepted my viewpoint. My association with the Trust continued for a number of years.

*

My association with Indira-ji continued to grow in strength. On the death of her husband, Feroze Gandhi in 1960, I sent her a letter of condolence. I received a reply; it was a printed letter with her signature. A copy of the letter is given below:

नई दिल्ली ।

आपकी संवेदना और मेरे पति के कार्यों की
सराहना के लिये मैं अनुगृहीत हूँ ।

इंदिरा गांधी

Once I wrote to her about the photograph of her grandfather, Pandit Motilal Nehru. Some of our concerns were major shareholders in a company called Associated Journals which published a newspaper called *The Leader*. In the 1920s and 1930s, *The Leader* was an institution in itself. Pandit Motilal Nehru was one of the founders of the company. Some of the minutes of the board meetings of the company make interesting reading and show how he participated in those meetings. The management of *The Leader* approached me to write to Indira-ji to obtain a photograph of Pandit Motilal Nehru. I wrote accordingly to her. She replied promptly. The reply is unsigned. Perhaps after dictating it, she went out and her secretary despatched the letter without her signature. The text of the letter is given below:

> *Prime Minister's House*
> *New Delhi*
> *5 April 1961*

Dear Shri Birla,
Your letter about a photograph of my grandfather. Dr B.C. Roy also wrote to me.
   I have no good photograph with me and those which were available at Anand Bhavan, Allahabad, have been collected by Shri Mohanlal Saksena. As you perhaps know, he is Secretary of the Central Committee. Therefore I passed on your request to him. He has asked Shri Atulya Ghosh to see those photographs.
   With kind regards

> Indira Gandhi

In May 1964, Jawaharlal-ji died. It was a great loss for the country, in fact for the entire world. I was not in Delhi at that time but rushed to the capital and called on Indira-ji to convey my condolences. She appreciated the gesture. Though her loss was great she kept her poise. After Pandit-ji's death, Indira-ji's importance on the national scene suffered a setback. This was natural as she was no longer the prime minister's daughter or the hostess at the prime minister's house. However, I maintained my relationship with her.

After Pandit-ji's death Lal Bahadur-ji was elected leader of the Congress party. Not much was then known about Indira-ji's ability as an administrator or as a statesman. So she very wisely kept out of the contest. Morarji-bhai was keen to stake his claim to the prime minister's post but, seeing the mood of the MPs and of the country, he did not contest the election. More out of gratitude the country owed to Pandit-ji and due to the close personal relationship that Lal Bahadur-ji had with him, the new leader selected Indira-ji as one of the ministers. She was allotted the ministry of information and broadcasting. She ran the ministry very well, much to the pleasant surprise and satisfaction of her friends and well-wishers, including myself.

After Pandit-ji's death I met Indira-ji more frequently. I would meet her every two or three months. There was no business to talk about during those meetings except general politics and current affairs in both of which I was deeply interested. My calls on her were more in the nature of social visits.

Indira-ji was a little surprised that I had maintained my contacts with her as in the past, even after Pandit-ji's death. One day she even remarked that after Pandit-ji's death few people met her; for example, the various chief ministers and ministers who used to call on her when Pandit-ji was alive had stopped doing so.

It is in the nature of man to bow before the rising sun; to curry favour with those who wield power. They see which way the wind blows. Why blame them? This is human nature with a few exceptions. Who knew then that one day Indira-ji would become the prime minister of the country and that her contributions and services to the nation and the world would match those of her father's?

15

Indira-ji Becomes Prime Minister

Indira-ji continued to play a low-key role on the Indian political scene for some time. Suddenly, one day in January 1966 came the shocking announcement of Lal Bahadur Shastri's death in the USSR (Union of Soviet Socialist Republics). I was in Geneva at the time. One of my relations who was also in Geneva telephoned me to give the stunning news.

I had known Lal Bahadur-ji since he was an MLA and a junior minister in Uttar Pradesh. In state politics, he was regarded as a back-bencher, and did not have much of a following. He had neither a personality nor was he very presentable. But he had some priceless possessions—sincerity and limpid honesty. The way in which he handled the war with Pakistan which was thrust on India immediately transformed his image into that of a leader of immense ability and tremendous courage. My relations with Lal Bahadur-ji were consistently cordial. When he moved to Delhi, my association with him continued as before. Even after he became prime minister he was very informal with me. Once when I called on him, he asked if instead of chatting in the drawing room I had any objection to taking a stroll with him in the garden. After his heart attack, doctors had advised him to take a brisk walk every day, he explained.

When, therefore, I heard about Lal Bahadur-ji's death I was saddened, not only because I had lost a valued friend, but more because his death could spell uncertainty for the future of the country. At least so everyone thought.

From Geneva, I immediately returned to India and rushed to Delhi. Morarji-bhai, being one of the senior-most politicians, had staked his claim for the prime minister's post. He had, in fact, wanted to contest for the post after Pandit-ji's death; but he realized that the consensus at that time was in favour of Lal Bahadur-ji. This time he felt his claim should not be bypassed and so decided to contest for the leadership of the Congress party.

The majority of the businessmen sided with Morarji-bhai. They were sanguine about the fact that he would win the contest. But many also viewed the prospect with trepidation. They argued that though Morarji-bhai always preached to others to be fearless, he was so stubborn himself that he invariably tended to force his views on others. Thus he could neither maintain the loyalty of friends nor countenance their differing with him. The moment anyone differed with him, he was immediately snubbed. That was the reason most of the Congress leaders of Gujarat, who at one time or the other were his followers, gradually deserted him.

When I called on Indira-ji, I asked her what the prospects of her winning the contest for the prime minister's post were. She admitted that it would be a tough fight. She asked me to speak to my friends amongst the Congress MPs to support her. I gave her my assurance for what it was worth. But I felt uneasy. To displease Morarji-bhai required no little courage. Many friends advised me that, being a businessman, I should keep myself aloof from these controversial matters. Though friendly with Indira-ji, I was not as close to her then as I later became in the 1970s. However, my loyalty was to her and so I decided to be in her camp. I had many MP friends in the two Houses of Parliament and decided to persuade them to support Indira-ji. I knew that by doing so, I was bound to be at loggerheads with many business friends and perhaps even with some of the members of my family. I, therefore, decided to consult father and have a frank talk with him.

Father was quite active in public affairs as long as Pandit-ji was alive. After Pandit-ji death there was a marked change in him. With the departure of Pandit-ji from the scene, father felt as if people of his generation had left the earth. He gradually reduced his meetings with politicians and ministers, most of whom were much junior to him in public life.

I told father that I had made up my mind to speak to all Congress MPs whom I knew, to support Indira-ji. I asked for his forgiveness if he was supporting Morarji-bhai, for then my decision was going to be against his wishes. To my pleasant surprise, I discovered that father, too, felt that it was in the interest of the country that Indira-ji and not Morarji-bhai got elected. Father and Morarji-bhai were very close at one time. But father, a strong-willed person himself, also could not stand Morarji-bhai's didactic attitude and sermonizing demeanour. I could speak freely with father as I felt sure that even if he favoured Morarji-bhai as prime minister, he would be tolerant enough to permit me to go my own way in supporting Indira-ji, because he knew that I was close to her. A close disciple and associate of the Mahatma and a friend of Pandit-ji and Sardar Patel, father was a large-hearted man. He gave me permission to act according to my heart's dictate. Under the circumstances, when I came to know that father too agreed with my views, it gave me a big boost in my endeavour. What I needed was moral support from father. That I received in abundant measure.

Indira-ji won owing to her own popularity and because the MPs realized that after the death of Jawaharlal-ji and Lal Bahadur-ji, she was the only person who could steer the country clear of its problems and pitfalls. When I met her after she had won the election, she was generous enough to thank me and to say that if she won it was largely because of the efforts of all her friends and well-wishers. That was truly magnanimous.

*

Indira-ji became prime minister for the first time in 1966, after Morarji-bhai was defeated. After some time a compromise was struck between them, whereby Morarji-bhai was made the deputy prime minister in March 1967. Morarji-bhai knew that my first loyalty was to Indira-ji and that I had worked against him in the contest. But that did not affect his personal relationship with me. He was generous on that count.

People knew that the compromise arrangement would not last long. A distinct tussle for power came to the fore when President Zakir Hussain died in office on 3 May 1969, necessitating the election of a new President. Indira-ji supported V.V. Giri for the Presidential election. Morarji-bhai and his group supported N. Sanjiva Reddy. It was a tough and bitter contest. Though Giri won the election, it left behind a trail of rancour and created a cleavage in the Congress party. To have dissidents within the party was not acceptable to Indira-ji. A parting of ways became inevitable. Indira-ji decided to go in for elections. In a most unexpected and dramatic move, she decided to nationalize the major Indian banks with assets totalling over Rs 3,307 crore, through an ordinance issued on 19 July 1969. Banks with deposits of Rs 50 crore and above were nationalized. That stunned me.

I met Indira-ji soon after the banks were nationalized and expressed quite frankly my deep disappointment and concern over the measure. She was not very communicative. She tried to avoid any discussion on the subject. To me, the whole thing appeared to be an election stunt. After the bank nationalization, an Indira wave swept the country. Indira-ji, shrewd politician that she was, ordered general elections. They were held in 1971.

16

I Contest an Election

The Swatantra Party was established in 1959. Amongst its founders were Piloo Mody, Minoo Masani, Raja-ji and Professor N.G. Ranga. My uncle BM was neither a founder nor even an ordinary member of the party but the leaders knew that they had his support, looked to him for guidance and regarded him as the godfather of the party. All the businessmen in the country were in fact ardent supporters of this party. I too lent my support to the Swatantra Party, which was regarded as conservative. I did not regard this as any insincerity towards Indira-ji. The Swatantra Party had no chance of winning the election. It could, at best, secure only a few seats and thus posed no threat to the Congress party. In my opinion, therefore, there was no contradiction in being a supporter of Indira-ji and also being a member of the Swatantra Party.

The Swatantra Party fought the elections to the Lok Sabha in 1962. It could win only eighteen seats; but this was regarded as quite a good performance for a party that started from scratch. In the next election in 1967, the Swatantra Party vastly improved on its position, winning forty-four seats. In Rajasthan, it got the support of all the royal families as well as businessmen, and the party did fairly well, winning eight seats in Parliament and forty-nine seats in the state Assembly.

When the 1971 elections were due, the Swatantra Party made preparations to contest it. Though the party leaders knew that they could never dream of forming a government, their ambition was to win a good number of seats so as to make their voice heard at the Centre. That was good enough, they thought.

I was approached by the party stalwarts to stand for election from the Jhunjhunu constituency in Rajasthan, which included Pilani. They first approached father, but he kept aloof. They then approached my uncle. Uncle was all for businessmen contesting elections and taking an active part in politics. Uncle always supported me in politics and encouraged me, much more than father, to play an active role in public life. He had a great liking for me. A word from him was adequate. I, too, was keen to enter Parliament. Hence I decided to contest the election and enter the arena of politics in a more direct manner.

The announcement of the election was made on 19 January 1971. I was abroad at that time but on hearing the news, rushed back home. Both the Jan Sangh (predecessor of the Bharatiya Janata Party) and the Swatantra Party approached me to contest the elections under their banners. Though I had many close and even intimate friends in the Jan Sangh, its aims and election manifesto did not impress me. The Swatantra Party was considered to be a right-of-centre conservative party. It believed in the encouragement of the private sector and was opposed to government controls. Many of my friends were members of this party. So I decided to stand as its candidate.

Before submitting my nomination papers, however, I wanted to meet Indira-ji and consult her, lest I should be misunderstood. But by the time I returned to India, she had started her election tours and so I could not meet her. I made a couple of attempts to meet her during the brief periods she spent in Delhi in between her election tours, but did not succeed.

I campaigned vigorously in the Jhunjhunu constituency. An understanding had been earlier arrived at amongst the leaders of Jan Sangh, Swatantra Party and Congress (O) that they would not put up candidates where any member of one of these parties contested. The Congress (O) was virtually unknown in Jhunjhunu district but the Jan Sangh had a fairly strong base; it supported me. Many leaders from these parties came to my constituency to deliver speeches in my support. The topmost leader among the opposition parties was Atal Bihari Vajpayee, who is indisputably the best orator in Hindi. He delivered forceful speeches in my constituency. Among others who came were Tarakeshwari Sinha, Rao Birendra Singh, Kumbha Ram Arya and Maharana Bhagwat Singhji of Udaipur. I worked twenty hours a day.

Indira-ji toured the country extensively. She was a tireless worker with amazing stamina and capacity to withstand strain. She also came to Jhunjhunu and spoke strongly in favour of her candidate but she did not criticize me even once. Even though she did not like my standing for the election against her party nominee, owing to my long association with her, she never said that a 'capitalist' had to be defeated. That was in sharp contrast to the attitude of local Congress leaders whose main line of attack against me was that I was a capitalist and hence an 'untouchable' even though otherwise I might be a 'saint'.

I contested the election in right earnest. There was, however, a very strong pro-Indira wave in the country, partly due to her personal popularity but mainly owing to the bank nationalization. The Indira wave engulfed the country, sweeping the entire opposition before it. Her party won a thumping majority. In the process, I lost. The Swatantra Party was practically wiped out from the political map of the country.

I was present when the counting of votes took place. In the ballot boxes there were sheaves of ballot papers lumped together, which clearly showed that there had been rigging on a massive scale. I had, in fact, heard about it during the contest.

After the elections were over and results announced, many friends advised me to file an election petition. I declined to do so. I thought it best to take the defeat gracefully. Basant Kumar, Sarala and my young nephew, Aditya, helped me a lot during the elections. They worked tirelessly and were very disheartened over my defeat. Aditya was particularly sad. He almost broke down; that was the saddest day in his life, he declared, with all sincerity. But I took the defeat stoically and consoled the members of the family, my friends and my supporters.

I had joined the election fray with great enthusiasm and expectation. But I was totally disillusioned during the election campaign. I discovered that a man has to prostrate himself before the voters in order to win votes. Leaving aside the giants among political leaders, whose victory could be taken for granted, all others (even some of the ministers) virtually had to beg the voters to vote for them. This went completely against my grain. Throughout my life I have endeavoured to avoid arrogance and to practise humility. How far I have succeeded in my efforts is for others to judge. But humility, which I value, is one thing; humiliating oneself quite another. I do not believe in begging for favours.

During the election campaign, on many occasions, I was asked by my supporters and organizers to walk with folded hands in the villages. It is against my nature to do so and I balked at it. At times I was compelled, much against my wishes, to fall in line with what my supporters advised me to do. Seeing all that, I had come to the firm conclusion that if such humiliation had to be suffered to contest the Lok Sabha elections, I would rather be out of it for all time to come. That apart, I came to know that if I won the Lok Sabha election, people from my constituency could come at any time and insist on meeting me. This again is quite alien to my nature. I believe in discipline, not in mob rule; in attaining results, not in failure; in efforts, not in lethargy. Considering the matter from all angles, therefore, I decided never again to contest for the Lok Sabha. It was a new experience for me. That was the only consolation.

17

I Meet Indira-ji After My Defeat

My defeat in the election cast a shadow of deep gloom over the members of the family, my friends and supporters. Though greatly disheartened, I tried to take the defeat valiantly. I returned to Delhi from Pilani. The first thing I did was to try and meet some of the leaders, ministers and, of course Indira-ji.

The ministers received me with apparent cordiality; but a coldness was discernible in their attitude. Most of them were friends of long standing, but on that occasion they too thought it fit to sermonize. Why did I, of all people close to Indira-ji, decided to contest against the Congress (I)? Why did I not endeavour to get a Congress ticket which, I was assured, would have been granted to me merely for the asking?

Among others, I met P.C. Sethi and Yashwantrao B. Chavan. Both were my intimate friends. Chavan told me it was foolish on my part to have stood for election against the Congress (I). He said that if I had won, it could have been explained away, even if not justified. But the defeat, he asserted, had given a big jolt to my status which, before the election, was very high among both the politicians and the bureaucracy. Sethi too gave me a sermon. I realized it was no use arguing with them and others as I knew I could never make them understand or appreciate my viewpoint, the raison d'être for contesting.

I thought I would endeavour to explain my position only to Indira-ji. I, therefore, listened to these reproofs without countering them.

After meeting all those leaders I sought an appointment with Indira-ji. There was no response to my request. Never before in the past had a request for appointment been refused by her. It was clear that she was annoyed with me. There was nothing more that I could do but wait for better times. At one time I thought of returning to Kolkata and making an effort later to meet her. But after due consideration, I decided to stay on in Delhi for some more time.

While I was brooding over the situation, help came in an unexpected manner. One day I received an unexpected phone call from Sethi asking me to meet him. I had no idea why he sent for me but I called on him at his residence. He spoke very feelingly and started with a sermon. Having exhausted himself, he asked me whether I had met Indira-ji. Sethi offered to intercede with her on my behalf and said that he would personally take me to her. He said that everyone makes mistakes at one time or the other. He assured me that he would first prepare the ground and then arrange a meeting for me with the prime minister at her residence at 1, Safdarjung Road.

I do not know whether Sethi spoke to me on his own or whether Indira-ji, kind-hearted as she was and fond of me, after reflecting that I had been sufficiently 'punished', decided to rehabilitate me politically. I never sought a clarification from Indira-ji or from Sethi in this regard.

A couple of days later, Sethi telephoned me and said that a meeting had been arranged which, however, would not be at Safdarjung Road but at 1, Akbar Road, which was the dewan-e-aam of Indira-ji, where anyone could go and meet her in the morning hours, without appointment. It was clear that this was meant as a snub to me to show that a private meeting with her at 1, Safdarjung Road was being denied and that I had to stand in a queue like anyone else to meet her. However, Sethi assured me that he would arrange a private meeting for me even if it was at 1, Akbar Road. The fact that Indira-ji had agreed to meet me even if it was at Akbar Road was of some solace to me. Beggars, in any case, cannot be choosers.

So I went to 1, Akbar Road. Sethi was kind enough to join me there as promised. There was a large crowd as usual. Sethi and I sat down in a corner.

After a while, Indira-ji came. She passed by the assembled people, met them one by one, as was her practice, enquired about their problems and difficulties and gave instructions to her staff after hearing their grievances. When she came to the spot where Sethi and I were standing, I offered my namaskar. She gave me a smile but there was a definite taunt in it. She did not speak, nor did I. Sethi, however, spoke. He said that he had brought me there and would be grateful if the prime minister could spare a few minutes for me separately. She asked us to wait. After she had met all the others, she beckoned me to follow her and took me to one of the rooms in the house.

She asked me, in Hindi how I was. I remember the exact words, 'Kahiye, Krishna Kumar-ji, kaise hain?' I told her I was miserable; not so much because of the defeat but because of the fact that she was cross with me which was apparent in the way she had declined even to meet me. She asked me in a scolding tone, 'Why did you stand in the election against my party, especially when I was struggling for my political survival?' Her contention was that I should have supported her and not opposed her partymen. She even said that had I asked for a ticket she would, in all probability, have considered the request favourably.

I said: 'Indira-ji, I would not like to enter into any argument with you, but did you, even for a moment, think that there was any chance of the Swatantra Party or of the Opposition parties winning the election and forming a government?' I asked her if there was any doubt in her mind about the vigour of the Indira wave which swept the country. I queried if businessmen should not stand for election to Parliament and make their contribution to the national effort in uplifting the country in case they were elected. She had known me for quite some time, and no matter to which party I belonged, how could she ever doubt my personal loyalty and attachment to her, I asked. I told her I had made several efforts to meet her before the elections but did not succeed as she was not in Delhi and was touring about the country. Was that my fault, I queried.

I was so emotionally moved that even in the presence of the prime minister of the country, I could not restrain myself and spoke with great vehemence. Words spoken with sincerity, without guile, always have an effect. I could see that she too was moved and felt convinced about my sincerity. Though Indira-ji sometimes gave an impression of a cold exterior, she was, at heart, a noble, gentle person. After hearing me, she immediately softened. A perceptible change came over her. Everyone makes mistakes, she said softly, but cautioned me not to make such a mistake ever again in future. I promised her that I would always stand by her. God was kind to me. He gave me strength so that I stuck to my promise and was throughout by her side, even during the period of her 'exile' from 1977 to 1979. Within three months of the election, I regained her warmth and affection.

18

Sanjay and His Maruti

I had not known Sanjay Gandhi at all till 1971. He played no part in the 1971 elections. I do not remember when exactly we first met, but it was towards the end of 1971 or early 1972. The first meeting came about suddenly. One of our senior executives in Delhi who knew Sanjay, informed me one day that he wanted to meet me. I was taken aback by the request. In those days I used to stay in the Hotel Oberoi Intercontinental when I was in Delhi. Sanjay met me there.

Sanjay was dressed plainly, in pyjama and kurta. I found him to be a man of few words. After an exchange of pleasantries he came to the point quickly—the purpose of his visit. He talked to me about his 'people's car' project and asked me if some of our companies could make investments in it. I tried to discourage him by saying that big investments were needed to start a car factory, and unless there was a big demand for his cars, which would enable mass production methods to be adopted, the project was not likely to succeed. Sanjay, a strong-willed person, had his own views. He appeared to be very confident of himself. He had no doubt, he declared, of making a success of the project in the manner he had conceived. When I found him determined to proceed with the project, I assured him of my support in a small way to start with. Thus started my association with Sanjay.

After the first meeting, Sanjay met me from time to time. Most of the times he would come to my hotel to meet me. But sometimes I would go to the prime minister's house and meet him there. Though there was a generation gap between us, we took to each other. On many occasions, we had dinner together at the Oberoi. Gradually we became good friends.

In one of the meetings with Indira-ji, I thought it proper to mention Sanjay's meetings with me. She said that Sanjay had no experience in business and enquired about my views about his project's success. I told her of my misgivings. I said that, first, to make a success of a car project copious funds were needed. Secondly, only when there was a substantial demand could modern production technology be adopted; without adopting such techniques the cost was likely to be prohibitive. Thirdly, I said, Sanjay should have gone in for foreign collaboration rather than endeavouring to design a car all by himself. Indira-ji asked me whether I had informed Sanjay of my views and misgivings. I told her that I had done that but that he was confident of achieving success in spite of all the handicaps I had pointed out. It was clear that Indira-ji was uneasy about Sanjay's project. But there was hardly anything she could do to dissuade him, and she knew it. Sanjay was a man of strong and fixed views and was obdurate enough to yield to neither pressure nor persuasion. Indira-ji asked me to give him whatever guidance I could.

One day, Sanjay invited me to visit his factory. I went there but was hardly impressed by what I saw. The buildings were massive but mostly bare. Sanjay was losing money heavily in his project. From time to time, there was criticism by public leaders about Sanjay and his project. It was evident that most of the criticism was levelled merely because Sanjay happened to be the prime minister's son. I thought that was unfair. A prime minister's son has every right to launch his own business. It is only essential that he does not exploit his position. In that regard, Indira-ji was very careful. She kept herself scrupulously aloof from Maruti Limited affairs.

One day, Sanjay telephoned me for an urgent meeting. He was very upset and said that three leaders of the party had gone to his mother and advised her that she should 'order' him to close down Maruti for good. They had said that Maruti was giving a bad name to his mother. The three were Rajni Patel, Devkanta Barooah and Siddhartha Shankar Ray. All three were very close to the prime minister and, as chance would have it, close friends of mine too. Sanjay asked me for my advice.

I told Sanjay that there was nothing wrong in a prime minister's son launching his own business so long as he did not enjoy any special privileges as a result of it. However, the way his factory was being run, I pointed out, gave cause for anxiety, as he was losing money heavily. I also cautioned him that in case the factory closed down, it would give him a bad name and also create unfavourable international reaction for his mother. In spite of my advice, Sanjay was confident of himself as usual and wanted some more time to prove that he could make a success of the car project. What worried him was the fact that his mother, under pressure from the trio, had asked him to close down the factory! Sanjay was very irritated and asked me to speak to his mother so that he could continue with the factory. After some persuasion, I agreed to do so, but asked him to fix a time limit within which either he made a success of Maruti or voluntarily closed it down. Sanjay thought that was a reasonable suggestion and agreed.

As promised, I met Indira-ji and pleaded with her not to compel Sanjay to close down the factory. I told her that so long as she kept herself aloof from the affairs of the company—as she, in fact, had done—no one could point a finger at her. I also apprised her of the assurance that Sanjay had given me—that in case the factory was not made a success in a few months' time he would himself close it down. Indira-ji thought that this was reasonable and accepted my advice. Maruti continued to function.

Suddenly, another day, Sanjay came up with a 'brilliant' idea. He asked me to accept the chairmanship of Maruti—a post held at that time by M.A. Chidambaram, a leading industrialist of south India and a friend of mine. I had no intention of taking on the onerous responsibility. I declined the offer but assured Sanjay that whatever advice or assistance was needed of me would always be given to him merely for the asking, as I had been doing all along.

After this, whenever I was in Delhi I would visit the Maruti factory once or twice as desired by Sanjay and give him my advice.

During one of these visits, Sanjay showed me the prototype of the car which he had made. When I enquired about the stability of the car on the road, Sanjay asked me to enter the car. He drove me round in the car at breakneck speed on a track which had been prepared at the factory for testing cars. The speed at which he drove was frightening; I certainly became nervous. But Sanjay never lost his nerve. Fortunately no mishap occurred. The car stood the speed test well. After we got out of the car, I told Sanjay that I did not caution him to slow down while he was driving as it would have been unwise to disturb a driver zooming at a reckless speed but that I would never again sit in a car which he was driving. Sanjay laughed at my 'timidity'.

During the discussions on how to improve the performance of the factory, an idea struck me to help reduce the losses of his company. The suggestion in fact cropped up during a casual chat with my cousin Ganga Prasad, who was chairman of Hindustan Motors at that time, and a brilliant and pragmatic person. I advised Sanjay to drop the idea of manufacturing a car, at least for the time being, and concentrate on building bus bodies in the Maruti factory! Sanjay was surprised at my suggestion. He did not take enthusiastically to the idea. His argument was that the main purpose of his establishing the factory was to produce a car and that he would never deviate from that goal. I told him that, as a businessman, he should first endeavour to cut down his losses and make the project a viable one—through diversification, if necessary. I pressed the point and said that if he cut down the losses, it would be a great relief to him. Later, when Maruti started making money from the manufacture of bus bodies, he could proceed with the scheme of manufacturing cars. After much argument and persuasion, Sanjay ultimately accepted my advice (much against his better judgement, he declared). He started making bus bodies in the Maruti factory. That brought him some profit. This made Sanjay a wiser person. He increased the manufacture of bus bodies. The losses were substantially reduced. I also suggested the adoption of certain reports and management proformas which I furnished to Sanjay for better control of the work at Maruti. Sanjay accepted that advice as well. As a result of this, Maruti turned the corner and started doing well.

Maruti Limited went on progressing till the Janata Party came to power in 1977. That was a troublesome period both for Indira-ji and Sanjay. The company started losing money again, and after Sanjay's death had to be wound up. The company did not produce a single car during his lifetime but was revived after his death when Suzuki Motors joined the Government of India in a joint venture. The first car from Maruti Udyog rolled out in December 1983.

Rajya Sabha Elections of UP and My Defeat

Nothing of significance occurred between 1971 and 1974. My association with Indira-ji and Sanjay continued as before. I would meet Indira-ji every four to six weeks; Sanjay I would meet more frequently—once or twice a week—whenever I was in Delhi.

In 1974, elections for the Rajya Sabha from a number of states were to be held. Sanjay knew of my interest in politics. He also knew that after contesting the 1971 Lok Sabha election, I had decided never again to contest for a seat in the Lower House. At the same time, he was also aware that I was keen to enter the Rajya Sabha.

In one of the meetings with Sanjay, the question of my standing for Rajya Sabha elections from Uttar Pradesh cropped up, with Sanjay making the suggestion. He said the Congress (I) did not have any surplus votes but if I had any friends among the Opposition members and won the election with their help, that would be a good thing. I told Sanjay that C.B. Gupta or Chandra Bhanu-ji, who was then leader of the Congress (O), was a good personal friend and that many other Opposition leaders in Uttar Pradesh were good friends of mine. With their support, supplemented by my own efforts and the assistance of the Congress (I), I stood a good chance of getting elected.

Sanjay discussed the matter with Indira-ji. He reverted to me and repeated what he had said earlier—that in case I could muster Opposition support, I should certainly stand for election as an independent candidate. He also said that his sympathy and that of the party would be with me along with whatever support the party could provide. It was a difficult task but I was sanguine about getting elected. I agreed to go to Lucknow to contest the election. To help me win, Yashpal Kapur, a man of great dynamism and a confidant of Indira-ji, was deputed to go to Lucknow.

I worked very hard, almost eighteen hours a day. Many of my friends in the Opposition helped me. Chandra Bhanu-ji, one of the cleanest politicians that I have come across, openly supported me. After spending a few days in Lucknow, I assessed the situation and felt certain of victory. But I had not taken into account one factor—the hostility of the chief minister, Hemvati Nandan Bahuguna of the Congress (I). I had known him since the early 1960s. He was one of the most astute politicians I have come across. Initially, our relationship was very cordial. But for one reason or the other we could not get on well together. In 1974, it was an unfriendly and hostile Bahuguna who was at the helm of affairs in Uttar Pradesh.

The election was to be held on 28 March 1974. For some time before the election, Bahuguna had been confined to a hospital in Delhi for the treatment of a heart ailment. However, about a fortnight before the elections he was released from hospital and came rushing to Lucknow. After reaching Lucknow, he started issuing statements almost every day maligning me. That came as a surprise and shock to me. There could be no justifiable logic behind Bahuguna's vilification campaign against me except his personal hostility. If an Opposition candidate got defeated, and I won as an independent, the Congress (I) party should have had reason to feel happy. Surely, the Opposition could not be closer to them than an independent. Therefore, there could be no logic behind Bahuguna's open opposition towards me, more so as I enjoyed the support and confidence of Indira-ji and Sanjay. But owing to personal prejudices and hostility, Bahuguna started a tirade against me and made public statements that it should be the common aim of all parties, Congress and the Opposition, to get me defeated.

I met Yashpal Kapur every day during the period of the elections. Shocked to the extreme, I enquired of him what was happening. Was the Congress supporting me as promised or was it opposing me? I told him that I was prepared to fight the election even if the Congress (I) remained neutral; but here was a situation where the party was being openly hostile towards me. Kapur, who was no friend of Bahuguna, was himself nonplussed.

I dashed to Delhi to meet Sanjay and Indira-ji. I could not stay in Delhi for more than a day because every day counted during the election period. I could not meet Indira-ji at such short notice. That was understandable as the prime minister had a tight schedule. I could not meet Sanjay either, try as I might. It was clear that he was avoiding me, and was, in fact, feeling too embarrassed to meet me. I only got a message from him wishing me the best of luck. Disappointed and disheartened, I returned to Lucknow.

There was no let-up of efforts on my part, though I was feeling thoroughly disgusted. In spite of this, I was quite optimistic and confident of victory. There was general optimism in my camp too. How could I be defeated with all the support that had been promised me by the large number of friends I had among the Opposition parties? And yet there was a lurking fear in my mind—a premonition that I would be defeated.

On election eve, I was definitely depressed over the chief minister's attitude. I met Kapur around midnight. There were one or two persons with him when we met. I was feeling very tired after a hectic day. Kapur, however, helped keep up my flagging spirits by saying: 'Where is the question of sleep for the candidate and his supporters on election eve?' We discussed the prospects of my winning the election the next day. I told him that though I was confident of winning I had a premonition of an ominous outcome. He cheered me up and said that after the elections he would be the first to congratulate me for my success.

Full of confidence and yet uneasy at heart, I went the next day to where the polling was to take place. The voting commenced. Within half an hour, however, I became totally disillusioned. I discovered that there was open voting, which was contrary to the Constitution and the rules framed under it. It was suspected that Bahuguna had manoeuvred it to be so. That was his trump card. The pattern was set in motion by elaborate pre-planning. Every voter would show the candidate the ballot paper before putting it in the ballot box to assure him that he was voting for him. Where then was the question of some of the Opposition MLAs voting for me? Observing the open voting, I immediately protested to the election commissioner, and also sent word to Kapur about what was happening.

The election commissioners in elections to the Rajya Sabha are the judicial secretaries of the state governments. At the time of polling, they are expected to act as independent officers; but at other times they are just like other government officers seeking instructions from the ministers. They are, therefore, under the influence of the ministers and the chief minister. My protest to the election commissioner fell on deaf ears. I also spoke to some friends in the Congress who were in the booth. I sent word to Kapur. He came, but he obviously could not enter the place where the polling was taking place. He sent word to me from outside that there was hardly anything that he could do about the matter. I stayed on for some time but it became abundantly clear that, barring ten or eleven votes of the Congress (O), which had openly decided to support me, I was not likely to get any other vote. Out of sheer disgust, I left the polling area and returned to the Carlton Hotel where I was staying. Many of my supporters had gathered there by then. Everyone knew who had engendered the open voting which was being resorted to for the first time in a Rajya Sabha election in the country and was against the provisions of the Constitution. My supporters were bitter. But there was hardly anything they could do. There was no use my staying in Lucknow any more. Without waiting for the announcement of the result I took the evening flight and returned to Delhi.

The next day, I sought appointments with Indira-ji and Sanjay. I was feeling highly dejected and also irritated. Sanjay met me immediately. I was very upset and related to him what had happened. He had already received the news of the machination of Bahuguna. I asked him: 'If the chief minister of a state were to betray the party boss, what was the idea of encouraging me to stand for election?' Sanjay had no answer. But he was full of sympathy for me. He tried to console me and said that Bahuguna had betrayed the trust reposed in him by his mother. Sanjay, in fact, was furious.

At this time, I was the vice-president of FICCI and, in a few weeks' time, I was scheduled to become its president. I told Sanjay bitterly that with such a defeat behind me I would not like to stand for that post. I said my prestige had been shattered and there was no balm for injured pride. The first defeat in 1971 was bad enough for a man of my status. But I had taken it stoically. To get defeated a second time was thoroughly humiliating.

Sanjay repeatedly consoled me and said that I should never think of declining the post of FICCI president. He consoled me further by saying that amongst businessmen I was closest to his mother. He advised me not to take any hasty decision and tried to assuage my hurt feelings.

The next day I met Indira-ji. I was sore at my defeat and made no pretence to hide my feelings. Indira-ji was very unhappy at what had happened and was very kind and sympathetic to me. She consoled me and assured me of her continued support. She told me that she had heard from Sanjay about my idea of declining the FICCI president's post which, as vice-president, I was automatically due to fill. She strongly urged me, as Sanjay had done, not to refuse the post. Regarding Bahuguna, Indira-ji said that he had not only played mischief with me but had, in fact, also betrayed her. Her kind words greatly soothed my anguish and I tried to settle down to my routine as best as I could.

After a few days, Sanjay sent for me and said that he had been asked by his mother to enquire whether I would accept the membership of the

Planning Commission! I was overwhelmed by the kindness and affection of Indira-ji for this gesture. But I declined the offer. I said that even a minister's post, if offered, would not be acceptable. Sanjay was surprised. I explained to him that whereas I certainly wanted to enter the Rajya Sabha, accepting a minister's post would have meant complete dissociation with my business, which I could not afford. All the same, I thanked Sanjay profusely for the warm thoughts he and his mother had for me.

Sanjay was a man of inflexible resolve. He considered the opposition of Bahuguna to his mother's wishes a treachery. Neither he nor Indira-ji ever forgave Bahuguna, with results that everyone knows.

After my defeat in the Rajya Sabha elections, the warmth of Indira-ji and Sanjay for me increased. I came closer to them. I accepted the FICCI president's post as advised by them. In that capacity, I travelled throughout the country and visited almost every state. Everywhere I met businessmen and addressed them. I listened to their grievances, met chief ministers of various states, cabinet ministers at the Centre and endeavoured to sort out the problems of the business community. I completed my one-year tenure and when its annual session was due in early 1975, I was keen that Indira-ji should inaugurate it. Indira-ji was hesitant to do so as she considered the inauguration of the FICCI annual session to have become a sort of ritual for the prime minister. I, however, pressed her to inaugurate the session during my tenure. She did not wish to disappoint me; so she agreed. In her opening remarks, she paid me a compliment, saying: 'Let us try to be positive and be willing to keep pace with changing times. Your wide-ranging speech, Mr President, made my task easier because by and large it is constructive.'

All the businessmen, as well as I, were happy at the way Indira-ji responded to my speech. Many thought that the presidential speech that I delivered was good in content, thought, substance and language (as enclosed in Appendix I).

20

Indira-ji Loses Election Petition in Allahabad High Court

A n election petition had been filed against Indira-ji in the Allahabad High Court. The plaintiff in the case was Raj Narain, an erratic man known for his hostility to the Nehru family. The lawyer who appeared on his behalf was Shanti Bhushan, one of the foremost lawyers of the country who had become law minister during the Janata Party regime. The trial was held in the court of Justice Jagmohan Lal Sinha. From the proceedings of the case as reported in the papers, it was clear that the case was going against Indira-ji. I spoke to Indira-ji a number of times about the case being not well conducted. I even offered my services to oversee the matter with the assistance of my solicitors, Messrs Khaitan & Co., one of the country's leading firms of lawyers. But Indira-ji thought it best not to disturb the arrangements that she had already made.

Then came the momentous day when the judgment was to be delivered. Everyone waited with suspense, almost with bated breath. The verdict, not unexpectedly, went against Indira-ji and she was debarred from being an MP for six years! The country was stunned by such a severe judgment.

I was in Mumbai at that time. I immediately sent a telegram to Sanjay asking him to convey to Indira-ji my deep concern at the defeat and discomfiture suffered by her. I also rushed to Delhi to meet Indira-ji and Sanjay and offered my sympathies and support in their hour of gloom.

Indira-ji filed an appeal with the Supreme Court and was able to obtain a stay against the execution of the judgment. Our law is clear in such matters. Once a stay has been granted, status quo ante prevails. Indira-ji, therefore, continued as prime minister. She was perfectly entitled to do so until the appeal was disposed of by the Supreme Court. But that was not acceptable to the Opposition. Unfortunately, they did not take an objective view. Their sole aim was to dethrone Indira-ji. The Opposition organized processions and held demonstrations against her continuation as prime minister and demanded that she stepped down immediately. Even a veteran and respected leader like Jayaprakash-ji whom I regarded as a saintly person was persuaded by the Opposition to support them.

The Congress (I) stood solidly behind Indira-ji at that time. It organized processions in support of her. I was all for Indira-ji and I informed her that I too was going to organize a procession of businessmen to demonstrate our solidarity with her. Accordingly, I led a procession of businessmen, which marched to the prime minister's house on 22 June 1975. About 500 businessmen belonging to different industrial and trade associations of Delhi participated in the march. Indira-ji came out of her house to meet the members of the procession. It started raining; I held an umbrella over her head. Indira-ji addressed the gathering.

First, I presented an address on behalf of the industrial and trade associations to her. The address praised Indira-ji for the progress the country made during her tenure and described that as an eloquent tribute to her able and dynamic leadership. In the address, she was lauded for the liberation of Bangladesh. It also commended her for the stimulus given to the pursuit of science and technology, which resulted in India exploding a nuclear device and launching the earth satellite Aryabhatta. It stated that all these achievements had raised the stock of India very high in the world community. After recounting her achievements, I came to the main theme of the address and stated that under no circumstances should she resign under pressure from the Opposition and that there was no valid reason for her to resign as the Supreme Court had granted a stay against the Allahabad High Court order. I appealed to the people, particularly to the business community, to rally round her. Indira-ji replied suitably to the address and thanked me and the business community for standing by her in that hour of crisis.

The Opposition parties organized all types of demonstrations in a big way. Law and order were defied with impunity. I remember that one day I was in Jaipur when it was announced that Jayaprakash-ji and others would come and address a meeting, defying any ban on processions and assemblies. The people knew it would precipitate trouble. In case a large section of the people challenged law and order, such defiance could result in a clash between the police and the mob and might lead to firing and bloodshed. That was exactly what happened at a number of places in the country.

We had won our independence through civil disobedience movements launched under the leadership of the Father of the Nation. After attaining independence, defiance of law and order should have been abandoned, and opposition to the government should have been voiced only in Parliament or in the state Assemblies. It was sad to see that some parties believed in settling scores in the streets.

Lawlessness went on increasing in the country with the police being compelled to use force. When the situation looked like getting out of hand, the prime minister declared a state of Emergency throughout the country on 26 June 1975.

21

Emergency Declared

I have never been an admirer of the Emergency. No one likes suppression of civil liberties and excessive restrictions imposed on society. However, considering the way the law and order situation in the country was deteriorating, Indira-ji was perhaps left with no choice. People thought the Emergency would be withdrawn in a few months. It lasted two years.

Soon after the Emergency was declared on 26 June 1975, all the important Opposition leaders were arrested. Surprisingly, immediately after the declaration, peace and calm returned in public life, law and order were fully restored, discipline in every walk of life became noticeable, strikes and lockouts were greatly reduced, punctuality in the running of trains vastly improved, government servants—particularly railway employees—became very courteous to the public. Alas, if only all this could have been achieved without resort to a declaration of Emergency!

Jayaprakash-ji was a man of great integrity and morality. Even then some of his utterances were absolutely impractical and, if accepted by the people, would have caused great disturbances in the country. Behind the shield of ethics he called for total revolution. He asked the police and the soldiers not to carry out instructions, if those were against their conscience. By total revolution he meant revolution in all walks of life and talked about a partyless democracy. He toured throughout India and was able to gather large crowds wherever he went. Inspired by his speeches, bandhs and gheraos were held throughout the country. The correct version of what Jayaprakash-ji said was that the army and the police should not obey orders that were, in their opinion, illegal or unjust. He also called publicly for Indira-ji's resignation.

Looking at the movements of Jayaprakash-ji, Indira-ji felt that if she resigned under a threat, it would lead to lawlessness and anarchy in the country. She consulted Siddhartha Shankar Ray, the then chief minister of West Bengal, Om Mehta, who was deputy minister in the home ministry

and very close to Indira-ji, Sanjay and also Bansi Lal, then the chief
minister of Haryana, who had the reputation of being a strong man in the
party. Fakhruddin Ali Ahmed then was the President. On 25 June 1975
Indira-ji met the President. The Emergency order was drafted by Ray and
P.N. Dhar and the President signed it. Indira-ji addressed the nation
justifying the proclamation of Emergency. She also promised to withdraw
Emergency as soon as possible. The situation so developed that, according
to Katherine Frank whose biography of Indira Gandhi is unquestionably
the best book on her, dissidence had started in the Congress (I). Indira-ji
therefore thought that there was no alternative but to declare a state of
Emergency.

I met Indira-ji soon after the declaration of Emergency. She told me
that she was not happy, but that she was left with no other choice. I said
that I hoped the Emergency measures would not last long and that they
would be lifted as early as possible. Indira-ji said that was her desire too.

At first things worked well. However, after some time, reports started
coming of excesses being committed in certain areas. There were reports
of vasectomies having been forcibly performed to check population growth,
particularly around Delhi and western Uttar Pradesh. Instances of even
young people being forcibly sterilized were brought to my notice by reliable
persons. In some instances, even newly married men were sterilized,
against their wishes.

One day an acquaintance of mine from a village in Haryana met me.
He informed me that vasectomy had been forcibly conducted on a person
known to him, who got married only six months earlier. This meant that
the couple could not have any children. The victim, my acquaintance
said, was highly depressed after this incident and his wife lapsed into
hysterics. According to this acquaintance, the entire village was shocked
over the deed. He requested me to relate the incident to the prime minister
so that, at least in future, such harsh instances of forcible sterilization
could be avoided.

I knew that family planning operations were being carried out at
Sanjay's instance. I, therefore, spoke to Sanjay. He was, no doubt, sorry
when he heard about the incident, but said that when so many operations
were being performed, some such stray cases were bound to occur owing
to the overzealousness of some people in the government. This did not
satisfy me, and so I asked Sanjay to have an enquiry conducted into the
case to see that the guilty were punished. Later, I spoke to Indira-ji about
the matter. Nothing came of it.

The entire concept of using force for sterilizing people is immoral and, therefore, repugnant. Demolition of unauthorized structures in and around Delhi was also carried out on a large scale. No mercy was shown to anyone.

I met Indira-ji a number of times and apprised her of the excesses. Unfortunately, no action was taken to put a stop to them. I discovered that Indira-ji was not fully informed about the excesses. When I informed her about the reports which had come to my notice, she said that that was not what she had heard.

When the Emergency was declared, and the law and order situation improved, when there was a perceptible change in the attitude of government servants, particularly the police and the railway employees, the people had welcomed the Emergency. But after excesses started being committed there was great public resentment. There was, unfortunately, no attempt by the government to allay people's apprehensions and anger. People panicked and became determined to revolt against the Emergency measures at the earliest opportunity.

Had Indira-ji withdrawn the emergency order after, say, three months or so, and gone for general elections, she would have won the elections hands down. Indira-ji would have gone down in history as a lady of strong personality and the best prime minister that India ever had. My impression is that Indira-ji did want to withdraw the emergency after a few months, but Sanjay prevailed on her not to do so. Under pressure from Sanjay, the emergency continued and the popularity of Indira-ji and Sanjay plummeted. As a result, when the elections were finally held in 1977, the Congress (I) lost heavily. Both Indira-ji and Sanjay were defeated in the elections.

*

The term of the Lok Sabha which was elected in 1971 was to have ended in March 1976. The government, however, was not keen to hold the elections on time. Under the circumstances, the term was extended by a year. Thus, elections were put off till March 1977. In 1977, Sanjay was in favour of further postponing the elections. But Indira-ji was advised by many people, including myself, not to do so. She was confident of winning. But for the excesses committed during the Emergency—which made the government unpopular—Indira-ji would have won the elections.

I was abroad when the elections were announced. I had left India in the early hours of 18 January 1977. On the same evening, the announcement about elections was made. I was in Zurich when P.C.

Sethi who, apart from being a minister was also the treasurer of the Congress (I), telephoned and asked me what my programme was. I told him that I had heard about the elections and was re-scheduling my programme so as to return to India immediately.

Funds are needed for contesting elections. The Congress (I) applied itself to finding ways and means for raising funds from the people. The problem was how to raise funds from businessmen. Knowing my sympathy for the party and my close association with Indira-ji, she requested me to raise funds for the elections. Rama Prasad Goenka, who is a leading industrialist and friend of mine, also got associated with me in this task.

Under the Companies Act, companies were debarred from giving any donations to political parties. I felt that if the law could be changed, I could approach companies whose managements were pro-Congress for donations. The Company Law Board gave some clarification, but it did not satisfy me. I explained the position to Indira-ji. Giving donations to political parties on behalf of the corporate sector was, therefore, out.

Meanwhile, the All India Congress Committee (AICC) had decided to bring out ninety special souvenirs in all the important regional languages. In addition, the Pradesh (state) Congress Committees (PCCs) also decided to bring out their own souvenirs. Advertising in these souvenirs was not illegal. I consulted some of the leading solicitors, who concurred with this view. Having satisfied myself on this point, Rama and myself undertook the task in right earnest, without, however, putting pressure on anyone.

As soon as the elections were announced, all the top Opposition leaders, who had been held behind bars, were released. I was considered a close ally of Indira-ji. I, therefore, came in for severe criticism. Chaudhury Charan Singh criticized me in several public meetings he addressed.

Indira-ji fought the election with her usual zeal. She worked very hard. But when the results started pouring in, it became clear that Congress (I) was going to lose heavily. That was precisely what happened. Not a single seat was won by the Congress (I) in Bihar, Haryana, Himachal Pradesh, Nagaland, Punjab and Uttar Pradesh. The party suffered a crushing defeat in almost all states, barring south India. Then something unimaginable happened; both Indira-ji and Sanjay lost in their constituencies.

My analysis of the reasons for the debacle is that Indira-ji lost the elections for only one reason—the excesses committed during the Emergency. People in our country want security and peace. They desire to have a government sympathetic towards their problems. Even former Punjab chief minister, Pratap Singh Kairon, was popular in his state in spite of charges of corruption against his sons. Why? Because he provided good governance. When the Emergency was declared, the immediate reaction of the people was one of fear. After a time, when the people discovered that the declaration of Emergency brought in its wake discipline in our lives, courtesy amongst the government servants, and that corruption diminished, they heaved a sigh of relief and in fact welcomed the Emergency. However, during the Emergency, when forcible operations for sterilization and demolition of unauthorized buildings started taking place, the people became scared and their feelings got outraged. If Indira-ji did not lose the elections in the south, it was only because no excesses were committed there.

I was in Kolkata when the election results started pouring in. I was certain that in spite of the excesses, Indira-ji would be able to win the election, though with a much reduced majority. My expectations were completely belied. As the results were announced, it became clear that my assessment was wrong and that the Congress (I) was going to be routed in the election. I immediately rushed to Delhi. When I reached Delhi late in the evening, at the airport itself I heard that both Indira-ji and Sanjay had been defeated! I could not believe my ears. Their defeat was a defeat of the party and, as I was close to Indira-ji, I regarded it as my defeat, as well as a defeat for all who supported her. This was the spirit in which I took the election results.

I wanted to drive down to the prime minister's house from the airport itself. But as it was very late and, as I myself was badly shaken by the reverses in the election, I went to meet Indira-ji and Sanjay early the next morning. I went without an appointment. This was not an occasion to seek an appointment with her. I merely walked in. I reached the prime minister's house and sent word to Indira-ji through R.K. Dhawan, her special assistant, that I wanted to meet her. There was a large crowd of Congressmen and her supporters, all feeling very dejected. Indira-ji met me after some time. Though dazed by the defeat, she retained her composure. I was conscious of the fact that it was pointless to analyse the causes of the defeat at the time and to tell Indira-ji that she had lost, nay, that we had lost the election owing to the excesses committed during the Emergency. This was no occasion for finding fault. I told Indira-ji that as long as she was prime minister, I had been the recipient of kindness and affection from her; under the circumstances, now that she had lost the prime minister's post, she could count on my being even closer to her and that I was always at her disposal if I could be of any assistance to her in any way. She was visibly moved and deeply appreciative of what I said.

I called on Sanjay too and reassured him of my support in the same vein. I was absolutely sincere in what I said. Unlike his mother, Sanjay was crestfallen. Perhaps he realized that he was the root cause of the defeat of his mother and the party.

22

Closeness to Indira-ji Grows Stronger during Adversity

Indira-ji remained at her residence—Safdarjung Road and Akbar Road—for a few days. The new Janata Party government, though full of venom and hatred towards her, did not disturb her for some time. Later, since she had lost the election and was not even an MP, she was asked to vacate the house. Indira-ji complied with the request promptly and shifted to a smaller house, much too small in fact, which was allotted to her—12, Willingdon Crescent. The Opposition felt that as she had lost the elections the government should not provide her any accommodation. But considering the past positions held by her, it did allot her a house. I personally felt that, looking to her past services, to the position held by her, and looking to the services rendered by her father who was held in veneration by all—even the Opposition—a much better house should have been provided to Jawaharlal Nehru's daughter.

I met Indira-ji from time to time and maintained close contact with her throughout the period she was out of power. Many business friends, in all sincerity, advised me that, as I was primarily a businessman, I should not try to annoy the government of the day. They cited the example of *The Times*, London, which traditionally supports the government in power. I was grateful to those friends for the friendly spirit in which they gave their advice, but I could never agree to desert Indira-ji after her defeat. She had been kind and considerate to me while she was in power. Now that she was out of power, I thought it would be the height of ingratitude to desert her. I knew that continuing to support Indira-ji was tantamount to clashing with the government. This was not a happy thought, but I was prepared to face the consequences. That apart, over the years my relationship with Indira-ji had become so close that I began respecting her as a family elder. I knew I enjoyed her warmth, affection and trust.

Where, then, was the question of my deserting her in her hour of need?

I had some friends in the Opposition. They too advised me to stop calling on Indira-ji. I disregarded their advice. My house was under watch by the police and my phone was being tapped; but I continued to meet Indira-ji and Sanjay.

Once when I met Sanjay he told me that as the house where he and his mother stayed was under constant surveillance by the police, it would be better for us to meet elsewhere. I was not afraid of going to his house but Sanjay insisted that we meet at an unknown place—out of the range of police observation. He suggested that we drive in separate cars towards Rohtak in Haryana, and that he would join me in my car at a deserted spot. We could then discuss whatever matters we had in our minds. I rejected this idea. Ultimately, we decided to meet at an independent place—the house of Sanjay's mother-in-law Mrs Anand. We always met after dusk. I would leave my car about a furlong away from Mrs Anand's house and walk the rest of the distance. This arrangement continued throughout the period that Indira-ji was out of power.

I would meet Indira-ji, about once or twice every month at her residence. On 3 October 1977, she was foolishly arrested. She faced the situation courageously. By sheer chance, I had met her about two weeks earlier. After her release, I met her again. She was none the worse for her experience. But the people were shocked at her arrest. It was clear to the public that this was nothing but an act of vendetta against Indira-ji on the part of the Janata Party government. It was that and other similarly foolish acts on the part of the government that led to its fall.

I knew that the Congress (I) was passing through a period of difficulties. I also knew that the party was short of funds. Therefore, from time to time I arranged money. Indira-ji appreciated that but asked me to keep the money, saying that the party would get it from me as and when it was needed.

I had come to know Indira-ji in the early 1950s. The acquaintance had gradually matured into a close relationship. In 1971, came a slight chill when I stood for election from Jhunjhunu for the Lok Sabha on a Swatantra Party ticket. This, however, did not last long and in a few months' time the relationship was normalized. From 1974 onward, my closeness to Indira-ji further strengthened. After her defeat in the 1977 election, when she was deserted by a large number of her followers, the relationship deepened considerably and she started regarding me as a member of the family. The relationship continued so till her tragic assassination in 1984.

Indira-ji was always kind and considerate towards me and even indulgent at times. She did not mind my expressing personal views frankly whenever I differed with her. In fact, many years earlier, when she was prime minister I once had a frank talk with her. I sought her permission to speak freely. I told her there was no point in my always seconding what she said, that it was better that I spoke to her openly about whatever

New Delhi, 1981: My wife and I were invited to a private tea with Indira Gandhi, then prime minister

I felt; I also asked her permission to tell her what the public reaction was to her statements, speeches and actions. I told her that so long as she accepted me as a friend she should not mind if, sometimes, she found that my ideas and advice ran counter to her own views. Indira-ji agreed with me. She was liberal and noble, and I always felt at ease in her presence. I would sometimes even make observations in a humorous vein. She did not mind it at all and was very informal with me.

*

My warm relationship with Indira-ji was not liked by many high-ups in the Janata Party. The government, as a result of pressure by some of its ministers, began persecuting her friends and supporters.

An astrologer used to visit my house in Kolkata from time to time. I have had mixed luck with astrologers. Sometimes, I found their predictions came true but on most occasions, I found them to be wrong. One evening in July 1977, the astrologer met me. I had been hearing wild rumours about my safety, and out of sheer curiosity I asked him what the future had in store for me. He studied my horoscope. He felt rather ill at ease in answering. On my pressing him to tell me frankly what he foresaw, he said that I would be entering a troublesome period very shortly. Curiosity goaded me on to know a little more. So I again asked him after how many days the 'bad' time would start. He replied that my troubles would begin within a week. According to him, there was apprehension of my being arrested and imprisoned on political grounds. But he also assured me that God was with me and that in spite of the effects of 'malignant' stars no harm would come to me, though there was a lot of harassment in store. My wife and other members of the family grew very depressed. Though I was also nervous, I tried to cheer them up and asked them to have faith in God.

Soon after this I went to Delhi. There, I heard a rumour that all those who had sided with Indira-ji were to be harassed in some way. I also heard that the wrath of the government was likely to fall on me soon. But I maintained a cheerful exterior. I soon discovered, much to my dismay, that my income tax cases were being reopened.

In cases where the government cannot find anything prejudicial but still desires to harass businessmen, reopening their past assessments under the Income Tax Act is the simplest thing to do. That was the weapon used against me. I received a letter from the Income Tax Department making all sorts of queries.

Questions were asked about the name and style of the HUF (Hindu Undivided Family) to which my father and uncles belonged, particulars of its total assets and properties, when it was partitioned, whether the partition was a complete or a partial one, the date of the partition, and so on. Besides, I was asked to furnish the names and the income tax file numbers of the partners of the HUF to which father belonged and full particulars of the properties which came to my HUF from father's HUF, which the income tax officer termed as the bigger HUF. I was further asked whether this bigger HUF had received assets from an even larger HUF. If so, I was asked to furnish details and evidence. I was also asked to furnish a list of all the furniture, refrigerators, air-conditioners and typewriters I possessed along with the dates of their acquisition. Further, I was told to give details about the number of servants, cooks, bearers, durwans under my employ and also to state whether these servants were provided full board by me or whether they paid for their own food. There were several other queries.

I sought an appointment with Morarji-bhai, who was prime minister. I told him about the questions that were put to me by the income tax department. I told him that the government should not be vindictive towards those who had supported Indira-ji. Morarji-bhai, despite being stubborn and obdurate at times, had the reputation of being a man of sterling character and I had hoped that he would stop the Income Tax Department from harassing me in that fashion. Once earlier, when he was the finance minister during the days when Indira-ji was prime minister, some such roving enquiry had been initiated against me. I had approached Morarji-bhai at that time and he had intervened. The late T.P. Singh was then the finance secretary and Morarji-bhai had telephoned him in my presence to stop the roving enquiry. But this time he refused to intervene. He told me frankly that he was not prepared to move in the matter and that he thought it best that the law took its own course. I pleaded with him that the law taking its own course meant undue harassment of an innocent person. But Morarji-bhai was adamant and refused to budge.

I met Indira-ji and narrated to her how the government was out to harass me. She was sorry to hear about my plight. She repeated what she had said in the past—she was a politician, whatever was to happen to her would happen, but I should take care of myself and my business interests. I thanked her for her advice but I ignored it.

I then sought an interview with H.M. Patel, the finance minister. I had known Patel for a long time. We often met when he was working in the government. He was as fond of books as I am and we would often exchange notes on the latest books published. He would also recommend good books that he had read.

After retiring from the government, Patel joined the Swatantra Party. As I was also a member, our closeness continued. But our relationship cooled when I became close to Indira-ji. Yet I held Patel in high esteem.

I met Patel at his office. I showed him the letter that I had received from the Income Tax Department and told him I was certain that ultimately I would get justice from the Income Tax Appellate Tribunal or the court. But I said the government should not harass a person by going into questions like how much furniture he possessed or what his expenses were. I told him my father and uncles had separated in the late 1920s or early 1930s. I pointed out that the income tax department could not reopen a case beyond eight years and that it was nothing but sadistic for the department to probe incidents that had taken place forty or fifty years earlier and that there should be a certain amount of decency and fairness in whatever action the government took and that it was nothing but a blatant example of political persecution of one who happened to be Indira-ji's friend.

Patel went through the letter from the income tax department and agreed with my views, much to my pleasant surprise. He said that the information sought was completely uncalled for. To be fair, I told him that I had met Morarji-bhai, but that he had refused to intervene. I clarified that I thought it proper to tell him that so that he might not later say that I had kept him in the dark about my talk with the prime minister. Patel appreciated my 'frankness and sincerity', as he termed it. He was fair enough to agree that it was nothing but a case of harassment. Patel then immediately took up the phone and asked for the chairman of the Central Board of Direct Taxes (CBDT). In my presence, he told the chairman that he had seen the letter received by me, that most of the queries were irrelevant, and that no roving enquiry should be initiated against me with the intention of harassing me. He further said that if the department could lay its hands on any legitimate and substantial grounds for action, that would be perfectly in order, but that there should be no witch-hunt. I felt satisfied at Patel's intervention. A man much smaller in stature than Morarji Desai, he showed a much greater sense of fairness and courage than the then prime minister.

My troubles, however, did not end.

Ugly rumours of impending persecution by Chaudhury Charan Singh, who was home minister, were in the air. I sought an appointment with T.C.A. Srinivasa Varadan who was then the home secretary. I asked him frankly whether the government had anything against me. Varadan was quite polite but, being a seasoned bureaucrat, was inclined to be reticent. To talk on such a sensitive matter was an onerous task. He must have thought it prudent to keep silent. Another reason for Varadan's reserve might have been that what was being proposed in my case was not at his instance. He might have felt a certain sense of helplessness while carrying out the directions of a higher authority—Chaudhury Charan Singh. So I thought it best to meet Chaudhury Saheb himself.

I had known Chaudhury Charan Singh since the 1940s, ever since he was a minister in Uttar Pradesh. Without being a fanatic, he was a staunch Hindu and had great regard for our ancient culture and heritage. I, too, am a devout Hindu and I, too, am not a fanatic and have great regard for our ancient culture and heritage. Thus we had much in common. Chaudhury Saheb was also absolutely honest in financial matters. His private life was without blemish and his habits simple. He had a genuine love and concern for the poor, particularly for the farmers. Owing to all these qualities, I had always held him in high esteem. His one weakness was his unbridled ambition for power. There is nothing wrong in being ambitious. But in the case of Chaudhury Saheb it overshadowed his other noble qualities.

During the election campaign in 1977, Chaudhury Saheb was highly critical of me. In a speech delivered in Saharanpur on 28 February 1977, he had said: 'This house was nearest to the Nehru family and it was not surprising that one of its scions led a deputation of industrialists to Mrs Gandhi to extend their full support to the government for imposing the Emergency.'

On 13 March 1977, in Delhi, Chaudhury Saheb repeated the same thing: 'It is not surprising that in 1975 Birla, along with a few other industrialists, went to the prime minister and expressed their complete support for the Emergency.'

When I met Chaudhury Saheb, he was very cordial. He first gave me a short sermon and said that as a businessman I should have been more pragmatic, that in order to safeguard my business interests I should have kept all the parties happy.

Chaudhury Saheb then asked me why I had led a delegation of businessmen to Mrs Gandhi to show our support for the Emergency. I told him that he was completely misinformed and what he had said during his speeches was absolutely incorrect. I said I had led the delegation but on 22 June 1975 before the Emergency was declared on 26 June 1975. The delegation, I said, had only assured Indira-ji of the support of businessmen to her continuing as prime minister after she had got a stay from the Supreme Court on the Allahabad High Court judgment which had held her guilty of adopting corrupt electoral practices and had nullified her election. Chaudhury Saheb appeared to be a bit taken aback, as he was sure that the procession of businessmen that I had led was in favour of the Emergency. I told him to check his facts.

Chaudhury Saheb then asked me a number of questions. Why did I get involved in politics? Why was I still siding with Indira-ji? Had I no duty towards my present business? Could a businessman afford to incur the displeasure of the government?

I explained to Chaudhury Saheb that I had no wish to quarrel with the government but that my relations with Indira-ji were a personal matter and that he should not confuse my personal relationship with Indira-ji with my activities as a businessman. It would have been sheer opportunism on my part, I said, to desert Indira-ji at that juncture, when I was with her all along while she was in power. I also told Chaudhury Saheb that I treated Indira-ji as a family elder and there was no question of my deserting her, and joining any other camp.

Then Chaudhury Saheb asked me a staggering question. 'Can you give me any clue regarding Indira-ji's wealth? Where has she hidden it?' I was taken aback by the question. After a short pause, I told him to pose this question to Indira-ji. I said sarcastically that Indira-ji had never taken me into confidence about the extent of her wealth or where she kept it. I also added that had Indira-ji taken me into confidence about her wealth I would not have betrayed her, just as I was not deserting her now. The meeting ended indecisively. Chaudhury Saheb was obviously not satisfied with my replies. He thought I knew many of Indira-ji's 'secrets' but was not obliging enough to divulge them to him. He was visibly annoyed.

Chaudhury Saheb thought up yet another way to harass me by trying to confiscate my passport. However, that was not in the hands of the home ministry as passports are issued by the external affairs ministry. Of course, the home ministry is consulted about the credentials of the applicant, but the ultimate issuing authority is the external affairs ministry.

Under the directions of Chaudhury Saheb, the home ministry informally requested the external affairs ministry to confiscate my passport. I got scent of it and immediately met Atal Behari Vajpayee, the external affairs minister, who then directed his ministry not to take any action. Ultimately Chaudhury Saheb personally spoke to Atal-ji to confiscate my passport. Atal-ji did not agree to oblige Chaudhury Saheb, unless a specific charge to justify the confiscation could be levelled against me. When Chaudhury Saheb pressed him, he told him that he would not do so but that in case Chaudhury Saheb desired my passport to be confiscated, the home ministry should write officially to his ministry to do so.

Earlier I had informed Atal-ji that if my passport was confiscated without any rhyme or reason, I would not hesitate to go to court to seek justice. Despite the fact that Atal-ji was a friend, I made my intention clear. That, in fact, strengthened Atal-ji's hand in being firm with Chaudhury Saheb, since written directions from the home ministry for the confiscation of my passport would have rendered it liable to action if I took the matter to court.

I met Chaudhury Saheb again thrice to impress upon him that whatever policy he followed towards those who were close to Indira-ji should be fair and that nothing should be done out of malice or vengeance. As later events will show, my pleas fell on deaf ears.

At that hour when my fortunes were in the dumps, all the important leaders of the Janata Party were hostile to me and often downright rude.

However, two leaders who had always been friendly with me remained so during this period. They were Atal-ji and Chandra Bhanu-ji. Even people like Piloo Mody, who had all along been friendly to me, turned indifferent. Piloo and I at one time belonged to the same party—the Swatantra Party—and so were very close to each other. When I sought an appointment with Piloo, he was even hesitant to meet me. Later when he did agree to meet me it was in a stealthy manner so that others may not come to know.

Another exception was Madhu Dandavate, who was the railway minister. I had not known Dandavate earlier. I came to know him only after he became a minister. He met me whenever I asked for an appointment and was always courteous. I found him a thorough gentleman.

I knew Indira-ji had no liking for Chandra Bhanu-ji but he was very friendly with me and had supported me when I contested for the Rajya Sabha election from UP in 1974. I informed Indira-ji that I was seeking his help wherever I faced difficulties with the Janata regime. I thought it proper to keep her informed of the matter.

Many of my industries were facing problems and hardships. Even genuine grievances were not being redressed by the bureaucracy, which knew that the government was hostile towards me. I would, therefore, seek Chandra Bhanu-ji's assistance whenever I had any problem. He was

New Delhi, 9 December 1999: With Atal Bihari Vajpayee, then prime minister

friendly, but I discovered that he would not or could not help me in the least. Perhaps age and failing health had started telling on his vitality and vigour. All that he did was to tell Morarji-bhai once or twice that I was a friend of his. That, as was to be expected, had no effect on Morarji-bhai.

I had known Atal-ji, who later became prime minister, also since the late 1950s. When I contested the Lok Sabha elections in 1971, he had visited my constituency at my invitation and had spoken at two or three places in my support. Atal-ji is a gentleman to the core.

Atal-ji enjoyed a very high status in the Janata government. Apart from being the external affairs minister, he was also the leader of the erstwhile Jan Sangh. I called on him.

Atal-ji did not like my continued friendship with Indira-ji but when I explained to him my viewpoint, he appreciated the fact that I had stood by Indira-ji, when she was no longer a political force to reckon with. Though Atal-ji was in the Opposition camp, he did not approve of the manner in which Indira-ji was being persecuted.

When I met Atal-ji, I told him that I did not expect or demand any favour from the Janata Party; the only point I was trying to make, I said, was that natural justice should not be denied to me and to my business, and that the unnecessary harassment being meted out to me should cease.

Atal-ji, perhaps more to test me rather than question me seriously, asked whether I was prepared to desert Indira-ji's camp and join the Janata camp. I told him that was not possible. Atal-ji did not press the point.

When I met Indira-ji I informed her of Atal-ji's views and also how he felt unhappy about her persecution by some of the leaders of the Janata Party. She felt happy that Atal-ji displayed a sense of fairness.

On one occasion, after the incident over the proposed impounding of my passport, I got a message from the external affairs ministry that the government wanted to inspect my passport. That was a strange request. As I was required to go out of the country several times a year I became concerned as to why the government wanted to inspect my passport. I was suspicious that it might be with the intention of impounding it. I immediately sought an appointment with Atal-ji, but, as luck would have it, he was out of the country. Being the external affairs minister, he was frequently out of the country—perhaps more often than was necessary. I then telephoned Shiv Kumar, his devoted secretary, and explained the position to him. Shiv Kumar spoke to the concerned people in the ministry and the idea of 'inspecting' my passport was dropped.

There was yet another instance when I was penalized by the

government. I was a director of Industrial Credit and Investment Corporation of India. ICICI was established as an industrial development institution in the private sector and it made a significant contribution to the industrialization of the country by helping a large number of projects. The majority of its shares were held by companies in the private sector or by the general public. Father was one of the promoters.

When Indira-ji nationalized banks in 1969, the character of the ICICI changed because a number of banks held shares in the company. With bank nationalization, the majority of the shares of the ICICI thus came to be held by the public sector. In spite of that, the Government of India, while Indira-ji was prime minister, did not make any major change in the composition of the board and tried to retain the private sector identity of the organization.

After Indira-ji's defeat, when I became anathema to the Janata Party government, I realized that it was only a question of time before I would be asked to resign from ICICI. That was what happened.

In early 1979, when I went to Mumbai to attend a meeting of ICICI, Jagdish Saxena, who was the then chairman of the Industrial Development Bank of India (IDBI) and also a director of ICICI in that capacity, called me aside after the meeting was over. Saxena was a fine person, a thorough gentleman, and a friend of mine. He said that if I were to submit my resignation from the board of ICICI, it would be appreciated. He asked me not to put any queries to him about the matter. I had no intention of asking any questions and embarrassing him as it did not require much wisdom to guess what prompted him to make the suggestion. I, therefore, submitted my resignation, as desired by the government. Had I not resigned, I could have continued as a director till my term expired in the normal course and would, in all probability, have been re-elected. However, I did not want to stay on when the government did not want me to be on the board. But the action showed the pettiness and the vindictiveness of the Janata government.

*

The Janata Party won the elections in March 1977 and pressures were brought to bear on me during the latter half of 1977.

After the Janata Party came to power, many people were baying for my blood. In fact, soon after the elections, in one of the meetings of the Janata Parliamentary Party many members were highly critical of me. An atmosphere of hostility was generated and I realized that if this resulted in a cloudburst I might be swept away—temporarily at least. My problem was to defend myself without compromising on my principles and without abandoning my friendship with Indira-ji. When the situation further deteriorated I thought of meeting Jayaprakash-ji.

I knew Jayaprakash-ji intimately since childhood when he started working for my father. As secretary to father, Jayaprakash-ji stayed at our house in Kolkata. Even when Jayaprakash-ji entered active politics and acquired fame, I kept up my connection with him. On many occasions, he wrote to me for donations for some institution or the other, or recommended people for employment. Whenever he came to Kolkata, he would invariably visit me. I always showed him the greatest respect. Though he knew that I was close to Indira-ji, our personal relationship continued to be cordial and warm.

During the Janata regime it came to my knowledge that many people went to Jayaprakash-ji and tried to poison his ears against me to prevent him from intervening in case the government took action against me. I was told that Ramnath Goenka, the proprietor of *Indian Express,* was particularly annoyed with me.

I had known Ramnath-ji since 1946. He was a fearless man. He was a good friend and a bad enemy. Barring a few occasions, I always had the good fortune of enjoying his trust, confidence and affection.

Before the Indian Iron and Steel Co. (IISCO) was nationalized, it had started losing money heavily. The chairman of the company was Sir Biren Mookerjee. He too was a dauntless man but, unfortunately, never tactful. He could not get on well with the powers that be in Delhi. In spite of his efforts, Sir Biren could not get assistance and resources for modernizing IISCO. The condition of the company therefore started deteriorating, to the disadvantage of its shareholders.

As the share prices fell very low, Ramnath-ji found the price very attractive. He, therefore, purchased a large number of shares. He might have had the nobler objective of putting the company in better shape after acquiring it, but his move did not find favour in West Bengal where Sir Biren was held in high esteem. Ramnath-ji, however, went on cornering the shares and acquired a large number of them. Ultimately, he lost heavily on the venture but he took it in his stride and never regretted having embarked on that gamble. That shows his mettle.

During the Emergency, *Indian Express* was in trouble and clashed with the government. Ramnath-ji had been a family friend. I was able to bring about an informal understanding between him and the Congress (I) high command. One of the points of the understanding was that the chairman of his newspaper companies would be someone acceptable to both Ramnath-ji and the high command. According to the understanding, I was made the chairman of his companies. My name, in fact, was suggested by Ramnath-ji himself. The experiment, however, did not succeed. My relationship with Ramnath-ji became somewhat sour, though it was restored to normalcy after some time. The story went round that he too wanted to see me 'punished' for my 'misdeeds' of the past.

Ramnath-ji was very close to Jayaprakash-ji. Among all the public figures Jayaprakash-ji regarded Ramnath-ji as closest to him. I was told that Ramnath-ji too had spoken against me to Jayaprakash-ji. The story was that Ramnath-ji had told him not to come to my assistance and that he was going to 'finish' me off. I did not believe this story. I knew however that Ramnath-ji was a good friend but a bad enemy. I certainly became nervous. I conveyed to Indira-ji what I had heard. She had no advice to offer. What was to be done?

I was very close to Ramnath-ji's son, Bhagwan, and telephoned him in Chennai to persuade Ramnath-ji not to harm me. Both Bhagwan and his wife, Saroj, promised to help me. Bhagwan was a great sport; he assured me that in case he found that his father was out to harm me he would stand by me and publicly oppose him. I then tried to talk to Ramnath-ji on the phone but as soon as he heard my voice, he put the receiver down. However, after a few months he calmed down and again became friendly with me. Behind that is a story.

There is, no doubt, that during the Emergency Ramnath-ji was under all types of pressures from the government. Yet I tried to maintain a cordial relationship with him. Ramnath-ji had been a family friend. I always desired to maintain a good relationship with him, irrespective of our divergent political views and affiliations. Ramnath-ji was anti-Indira and anti-government—just the opposite of what I was.

Towards the end of 1976 when I learnt that Ramnath-ji was very annoyed with me, I exchanged some correspondence with him. Ultimately, the misunderstanding was resolved and Ramnath-ji wrote me a nice letter on 4 December 1976, the text of which is reproduced below:

My dear Krishna Kumarji,
I am very grateful to you for your letter of 25th ultimo. I am very glad to know that the information given to me by friends and acquaintances that 'you were sore and that you had been let down

by me' was untrue. I am sorry I had to tell them in defence that what you were saying was not correct.

Please take it from me that hereafter if anybody makes a statement like the one mentioned above, I shall tell him to mind his own business and not to discuss the matter with me.

Your letter has completely relieved me and be assured that I shall continue to have the same regards for you as in the past.

Yours sincerely,

R.N. Goenka

Hence when I heard that Ramnath-ji was bitterly hostile towards me, I sent a common friend to him with a copy of this letter. My friend reminded him that I had endeavoured to maintain a friendly relationship with him at a time when he was passing through difficult times and I was in a commanding position, being in the good books of the government and prime minister. What had happened since to make him antagonistic towards me? I do not know whether this common friend did converse with Ramnath-ji or not. But after some time Ramnath-ji cooled down and the old cordiality was restored between us. Ramnath-ji had a lot of respect for father. That might have been one of the reasons for his cooling down.

In any case, I met Jayaprakash-ji and told him that in the event of the government trying to harass me, I would seek his intervention. Jayaprakash-ji was a man endowed with a noble heart and warm sentiments. He readily agreed to help me. However, in actual fact, I did not seek his assistance.

Another person with whom I came in touch during the Janata regime was Chaudhury Devi Lal, a Jat leader from Haryana. In those days, he was regarded as being quite close to Chaudhury Charan Singh. Devi Lal sought an appointment with me. Knowing that he was very friendly with Chaudhury Saheb, I readily met him in the hope that he might come in handy in ensuring that I was not unnecessarily harassed by Chaudhury Saheb and the home ministry.

Devi Lal met me at my house in Delhi. He said that he had heard about my troubles and offered his good offices to help me in those critical days, subject to one condition. I was to persuade some Congress (I) MPs to defect and support the Janata Party. He said that he had definite information that there were fifteen or twenty MPs in the Congress (I) Parliamentary Party who were very close to me. He emphasized that now was the time for me to assure Chaudhury Saheb of my support and demonstrate it by taking this group of MPs to his residence and assuring him that, as their first loyalty was to me, they were now deserting Indira-ji and accepting Chaudhury Saheb as their leader.

I felt rather amused over Devi Lal's naïvety. I knew it was no use reasoning with him over the absurdity of the proposition. So I kept mum and changed the topic.

Not satisfied, Devi Lal met me a second time and repeated his proposal. When I did not respond favourably to his 'sound advice', he felt sorry for my 'foolishness' and left. I met him a number of times after that. He always had a grouse against our paper the *Hindustan Times*. Our personal relationship, however, remained cordial.

23

I Flee India

Rumours had been circulating for quite some time since June 1977 that I was in deep trouble and could be arrested any day. Such news emanated from a number of sources. What was my offence? It was said that I should be arrested and prosecuted as I had helped in getting advertisements for the souvenirs published by the Congress party. The actual reason for harassing me was, of course, that I was close to Indira-ji. The entire family became worried, most of all my wife, who spent sleepless nights. The general atmosphere in our family was one of deep gloom.

In view of such persistent rumours, I consulted my solicitors. I was advised to apply for anticipatory bail. That I declined. I did not like the idea at all. I felt that if the government did arrest me, it would be a wrong move on its part. I argued that as the government was bent on doing mischief, let it be the first to make the wrong move. That, according to my thinking, would expose the government and enable me to win public sympathy. At that stage, I felt I could take the matter to the court and seek justice. In other words, my approach was, let the government arrest me first; I would then apply for bail.

The matter drifted in this manner for some time. I went to Delhi from Kolkata which was my headquarters. I first met Atal-ji and asked him if he knew how matters stood. He confirmed that the situation was grave, and that I could be arrested any day. Chaudhury (meaning Charan Singh), he said, was a tough man and was determined to arrest me. Atal-ji, friend though he was, expressed his helplessness and said that if Chaudhury did get me arrested there was hardly anything that he could do to protect me.

I tried to gather more information through some of my own sources. I got the same feedback. My being taken into custody, I was told, was now merely a question of time. I met Indira-ji and informed her of the position. She was genuinely sorry to learn that I was being put to difficulties owing to my association with her. She advised me to apply for anticipatory bail, which, I told her, I did not like. After I elaborated my reasoning, she agreed with my approach and said that she had suggested applying for anticipatory bail only in case I lost my nerve. Nervous I was, but it was supreme faith in God that stood by me.

I held discussions with my friends and advisers and, wherever necessary, with lawyers too. All the strategies required to counter the arrest were discussed. The simplest course was to apply for anticipatory bail. That I firmly rejected. I felt that to pray for anticipatory bail was to admit one's weakness. I had done no wrong, so where was the question of my applying for anticipatory bail or showing any weakness, even if the government wanted to prosecute me? Another alternative discussed was to go underground and apply for bail after the warrant against me was served. That proposal, too, I turned down. I did not want to go underground like a fugitive. The third alternative was that I take no action, permit the government to arrest me and then apply for bail. This appeared, by elimination, the only course open to me. There was no stigma attached in case a man was jailed for political reasons. But I must admit that I was none too keen to spend a few nights in prison before bail was granted to me. That apart, there were larger considerations regarding my wife and father.

My wife did not keep good health, but irrespective of that no Indian wife could bear the thought of her husband being arrested even if it were for political reasons. I knew that if I were arrested, it would put her under tremendous mental anguish. Father was a very bold and courageous man. But when it came to the question of comforts or discomforts of his children he would become very nervous. Try as I did, I could not find any solution to the predicament I was in. Then one day I suddenly got a telephone call from Atal-ji.

I met Atal-ji on 10 September 1977. He informed me that Chaudhury was likely to take action against me very soon. He wanted to know what I had planned to ward off the impending danger. I told him that I had decided to do nothing but wait and watch, and allow Chaudhury Saheb to make the wrong move. Atal-ji asked me whether I had any plan to go abroad. A very seasoned politician, he had certain plans in his mind when he posed the question to me.

I told Atal-ji of my intention to go abroad towards the end of the month. Atal-ji then came out with his plans. He asked if I had to go abroad why could not I leave immediately? I wondered how that would help matters. If Chaudhury Saheb wanted to arrest me he would do so on my return—or even perhaps before I left. But Atal-ji was insistent. He wanted me to leave immediately. One thing bothered me and this was the question of my prestige. I abhor timidity and cowardice and am a believer in Arjun's philosophy.

Arjun had taken two vows—no cowardice and no fleeing from the battlefield. Was there a stigma attached to fleeing the country, I wondered. I gave it deep thought. After considering the matter in all its aspects and after discussing it with some of my friends I came to the conclusion that to flee the country under political persecution could not be regarded as cowardice; it was a strategy. It was not like the fleeing of an ordinary criminal. My friends gave me the examples of Netaji Subhas Chandra Bose and Jayaprakash-ji. I occupy a much lower rung of the socio-political structure of the country compared to the position of these two giant personalities and brave sons of India. My friends, however, cited these examples to impress upon me that to flee the country in the face of political persecution (which in fact it was) was no act of cowardice. Follow the big men they said: the route that the big men took is the path to follow.

I consulted my wife and father and other members of the family. I informed them of the advice that I had received from Atal-ji. Both father and my wife strongly urged that it would be advisable to leave the country immediately. As things developed later, it appears their advice was sound.

I went to Indira-ji and explained to her what Atal-ji had advised me. She too concurred with Atal-ji's advice. Accordingly, I made preparations to leave India around 22 September 1977. Around 14 September, Atal-ji again sent for me and said that he had heard that I was likely to be arrested on or around 18 September, and that instructions had been issued to arrest me on the charge of collecting advertisements for the Congress (I) souvenirs. I told Atal-ji of my plan to leave around 22 September. Atal-ji took so much interest in my safety only because of his long friendship with me. He insisted that I leave immediately. I informed my wife about what had transpired at my meeting with Atal-ji. She felt miserable on hearing of the government's plan. Since a date had been indicated for my arrest, I advanced my arrangements to leave Delhi, and decided to leave on 16 September with my wife.

Around 14 September, a rumour spread that I was to be arrested the next day itself, that is, 15 September or a day prior to my departure. A suggestion was again made that I go underground, apply for bail when the warrant was issued, and then reappear after the bail had been granted. I stuck to my earlier decision, as I did not like the idea of taking shelter under any subterfuge. There was, however, an atmosphere of intense gloom prevailing in my house. We waited anxiously for the arrival of the police. Fortunately, nothing happened. The rumour of my arrest turned out to be false, as most rumours are.

Then came the day of my departure. Thorough preparations were made to face the situation in case I was arrested at the airport. Father, feeling very restless, wanted to come to the airport himself. But I persuaded him not to do so. I knew that in case I was arrested at the airport he would not be able to bear the sight. He then sent a large contingent of people to see me off. They included half a dozen lawyers, some senior executives of our companies, and some public relations men. The idea was that in case I was arrested at the airport, a bail application be moved immediately.

Though I had got reconciled in my mind that there was no timidity in fleeing, I was still feeling uneasy. I somehow did not like the idea of leaving the country like a fugitive. On 15 September, in spite of the pleadings of my wife, I sent word to Chaudhury Saheb and also to the home secretary that I was leaving the country the next day. I conveyed to them that if they wanted to arrest me they should do so at my house rather than at the airport and create a scene there before hundreds of people.

There was general apprehension in our camp that I would be arrested at the airport. Nothing, however, happened. I learnt subsequently that the papers required to effect my arrest could not be completed in time; hence I was not arrested. In government, matters move slowly. Businessmen always criticize the government for this. This tardiness, however, came to my rescue on this occasion.

I boarded the plane safely. It was an Air France flight. My wife heaved a sigh of relief when the plane took off. I told her, in all sincerity, not to feel elated, for so long as the plane was flying over Indian territory, it could be ordered by the government of India to return to Delhi. It was only after the plane left Indian air space that my wife was able to finally shed the gloom that had descended on her. We both prayed to God in the plane itself.

The Air France plane landed at Paris. From there we went to London and then to the United States. A meeting of the Indo-US Joint Executive Committee was scheduled to be held in Washington while I was there. I was chairman of the Indian section of the committee. I did not participate in the meeting, as that might have embarrassed my friends.

About a fortnight after I left the country, a first information report (FIR) dated 3 October 1977 was lodged against me by the police in Delhi.

In fact, two FIRs were filed by the Delhi Special Police Establishment Fraud Squads. The FIR filed by Fraud Squad II was against P.C. Sethi, D.P. Chattopadhyay, K.D. Malaviya, H.R. Gokhale, R.K. Dhawan, R.P. Goenka, M.V. Arunachalam, Yashpal Kapur and myself. The main charge was collection of advertisements, which the police construed as political donations under the garb of advertisements. On the same day another FIR was recorded against Indira-ji, Sethi, R.K. Dhawan, Jit Paul, and some others, charging them with the purchase of jeeps for use in furthering political activities. The charge against Indira-ji, Sethi, Dhawan and others was that they had pressurized industrial concerns to purchase jeeps for use in election work. Usually, FIRs mention some complainant. In these cases, there was no complainant. The FIR was put up on the basis of information collected by the Delhi Special Police Establishment; the Central Bureau of Investigation (CBI) too had taken cognisance of the matter.

The charge in the FIR filed by Fraud Squad II was curious. It was stated that since political donations by companies were prohibited under Section 293A of the Companies Act, a scheme was devised by the accused persons to disguise the collections for political purposes as contributions for advertisements to a large number of souvenirs proposed to be published by the AICC and the various PCCs. Companies and industrialists were induced to release advertisements in the souvenirs and these constituted merely a device to collect funds for the Congress Party and for political purposes.

In pursuance of this scheme, the FIR said, Sethi and two other former Central ministers—D.P. Chattopadhyay and K.D.Malaviya—obtained contributions by way of advertisements. A copy of the FIR is enclosed as Appendix 2.

The FIR was filed when I was out of the country. As mentioned earlier, I could have obtained anticipatory bail but I did not desire to take the first step. I left it to the government to take the first step; let them make a wrong move, I had argued to myself. Applying for anticipatory bail was tantamount, in my opinion, to an admission of guilt. Now that the government had made a move, this was what I was waiting for. After the FIR was filed, my solicitors in Kolkata immediately applied for bail.

The matter came up for hearing before the Calcutta High Court on 10 October 1977. Siddhartha Shankar Ray appeared on my behalf.

The advocate appearing for the state said that since the petitioner—myself—was away from the country, no such application for anticipatory bail should be entertained by the High Court. The judges disagreed and said that they found no substance in the argument. A copy of the judgment is enclosed as Appendix 3.

Two bail petitions were moved, because the CBI had also filed another FIR in which the accused were Indira Gandhi, P.C. Sethi and others. In that FIR, the accused were charged with procuring jeeps for election work without making payments for them. Since I had supplied some jeeps to the Congress (I), my lawyers thought it wise to file a petition for anticipatory bail against that charge also. Even though my name was not specifically mentioned in the second FIR, since the term used was 'Smt Indira Gandhi, former Prime Minister of India, P.C. Sethi and others', my lawyers felt that the scope of roping me in by using the term 'others' was so large that as a matter of abundant caution two separate bail applications should be moved. The necessary action was taken accordingly.

The Calcutta High Court found both the petitions fit for consideration for allowing anticipatory bail. The judges hearing the petition remarked that they found no substance in the argument of the advocate appearing for the state, that since the petitioner (that is, myself) was away from the country no such application should be entertained. The High Court, therefore, allowed the petition and granted me anticipatory bail.

In New York, I came to know that Atal-ji was due to come to attend one of the United Nations meetings. When he arrived, I called on him. I thanked him for his advice and for the friendship maintained by him when nothing but dark and ominous clouds hovered around me. Atal-ji enquired about my programme, which was to return to India soon. He again showed his friendship and concern for me, and advised me not to return to India till I got a clearance from him. He suggested that I ask one of our senior executives to meet him in Delhi when he returned to find out what the situation was.

After Atal-ji returned to India, one of our executives met him. Atal-ji made enquiries and confirmed that Chaudhury Saheb could do no further harm. I returned to India on 4 November 1977, after staying abroad for about seven weeks. It was one of my longest stays abroad in recent years. I can never forget the kindness and affection shown by Atal-ji and the help rendered by him when I most needed it. He helped me not purely because I was a friend but mainly because he knew that an innocent person was being harassed.

India Today, in its issue of 16–31 October 1977, published the news of my escape from the country. The text of the article is as follows:

BILLIONAIRE'S TIP

The billionaire industrialist was reportedly tipped off about his impending arrest. His trip abroad for 'business purposes' seems more than coincidental. What has made Home Minister Charan Singh more angry is the report that the industrialist's name had been in the list of 54 persons whose passports were to be impounded. Somewhere along the line, the list was shortened and he retained his passport.

Apart from some senior executives of his various firms, a journalist from one of the newspapers owned by the billionaire also escorted him to the airport. The journalist is reported to have used his considerable influence to keep his boss well informed.

Chaudhury Saheb made some comments about me at a press conference he held on 4 October 1977. As it might be of interest to readers, relevant portions of his statement are reproduced as follows:

The Hindustan Times
T.P. message from Head Office

4.10.1977
1400 hrs.

Urgent
For Mr Shekhar Mishra
Calcutta Office

This is further to our message regarding Shri Charan Singh's press conference. The text as creeded by Samachar regarding Shri Birla is as follows:

Quote
DELHI 15 GEN
GANDHI: BIRLA

New Delhi, Oct. 4 - The Home Minister, Mr Charan Singh, said here today that no special favour had been shown to Mr K.K. Birla, one of the industrialists accused having colluded with some Congress ministers for the collection of advertisements for the party souvenirs before the Lok Sabha elections.

He said that Mr Birla has now gone abroad and remarked, 'I

think he is coming here soon.'

A correspondent asked if Mr Birla had met him before going abroad.

The Home Minister replied in the affirmative and humorously added, 'but I did not ask him to go out of the country, he is no friend of mine.'

'Why was not his passport impounded, since the investigations into the souvenir affair had been going on for long ?' asked another correspondent.

The Home Minister said that there were many other persons whose passports had not been impounded and investigations were going on.

Mr Birla, Mr R.P. Goenka, Duncan Brothers of Calcutta, Mr M.V. Arunachalam of Madras and Mr Sudhir Sareen, businessman and relative of Mr Yashpal Kapoor have been charged by CBI of having helped in these shady transactions.

The Ex-ministers involved in the episode are, Mr K.D. Malaviya, Mr H.R. Gokhale, Mr P.C. Sethi and Mr D.P. Chattopadhyaya (Samachar).

On returning to India I met Indira-ji and related to her how Atal-ji had helped me throughout the period of my difficulties. Even after Indira-ji came back to power in 1980, I informed her that I was maintaining my contact with Atal-ji owing to the great warmth and consideration which he had shown to me throughout the period of my crisis.

Though I had received anticipatory bail (which I always carried with me in my pocket wherever I went as per the advice of my solicitors), Chaudhury Saheb was not sitting idle. Some of the companies connected with me had released advertisements, as stated earlier, in the souvenirs. I had also spoken to some friends who had sought my advice on this matter and some of them, after talking with me, had also published advertisements for the souvenirs. That was a sore point with Chaudhury Saheb. He was not prepared to 'excuse' me for this. He directed the CBI to enquire into the matter.

On my return from abroad, I was told that the CBI had been making enquiries about me. I immediately sent an express telegram to C.B. Narasimhan, director of CBI: 'This is to inform you that myself have returned to India today from abroad stop Offer my fullest co-operation in any investigation that you desire stop Thanks and kind regards.'

I received a summons to appear before the CBI in that connection and on 14 November I appeared before V.R. Lakshminarayanan, joint director, for interrogation. Before going to the CBI office, I informed Indira-ji of the position. I had never faced any such interrogation before. In spite of that, surprisingly I was calm and composed as I knew that I had not committed any breach of the law. Indira-ji too encouraged me not to lose my nerve.

Apart from Lakshminarayanan, Ishwar Chandra Dwivedi, DIG (Investigation-I) and F.C. Sharma, superintendent, were also present. Though I was grilled vigorously, all the three persons were cordial. I had no complaints.

At the very outset, I told the CBI that I would like to make two points. One, that I was seeking protection guaranteed by Article 20(3) of the Constitution to every citizen of India of not being compelled to be made a witness against himself. I assured the interrogators that, subject to that, they could fully depend on my unreserved cooperation. The second point was to express the hope that when I left their chamber they would feel that they had met an honest person.

The CBI people queried about the advertisements given for souvenirs by our companies. I explained that such advertisements given to souvenirs brought out by political parties did not constitute any violation of Section 293A of the Companies Act, that there was a high court judgment to that effect, and that the Company Law Board and the CBDT too had issued clarifications from time to time maintaining that advertisements in souvenirs brought out by political parties did not amount to giving donations to political parties (which was not permitted).

The CBI officers then asked me whether I was aware of the fact that the jeeps which were purchased for our companies were loaned to AICC on the advice of P.C. Sethi, and that they had been sent to the then prime minister's house. I replied that I was not aware of the fact, but only knew that jeeps were required by the AICC for a short period and that as some of our companies required some jeeps they had purchased them and had placed them at the disposal of the AICC for a short while. During the interrogation, they asked me if I was aware of the fact that lending jeeps for election purposes attracted Section 293A of the Companies Act, which meant that the action was tantamount to giving donations for political purposes. I told them that, on the contrary, I was advised that lending jeeps in that manner did not amount to giving financial assistance to political parties. The interrogation lasted for about fifty-five minutes. Immediately on my return, I drafted a record of the proceedings from memory. As this might be of interest to readers, I reproduce it here:

Statement given by Shri K.K. Birla on 14.11.77 at 2.30 p.m. at New Delhi before:

V.R. Lakshminarayanan, joint director, CBI, Ishwar Chandra Dwivedi, DIG (Investigation-I), F.C. Sharma, superintendent.

Lakshminarayanan was slightly late in attending the meeting. Hence I.C. Dwivedi and F.C. Sharma started the interrogation.

K.K.B.: I am entirely at your disposal and I am in no desperate hurry. We could easily wait till Shri Lakshminarayanan joined.

I.C.D. and F.C.S.: We appreciate this.

(V.R. Lakshminarayanan joined around 2.40 p.m. The entire proceedings lasted for about fifty-five minutes.)

K.K.B: I understand you would ask me questions regarding advertisements in souvenirs. At the outset I would like to make two points. One is that I am seeking protection guaranteed under Article 20(3) of the Constitution of India whereby a person cannot be compelled to be a witness against himself. Subject to that you may depend on my full cooperation in the deliberations. The second point that I wish to make is to express a hope that when I leave your room I may be successful in leaving an impression on you that you have met an honest man.

V.R.L.: Who gave you this advice?

K.K.B.: My lawyers. The second point is my own.

V.R.L.: What else did the lawyers say?

K.K.B.: The lawyers asked me to speak nothing but the truth. I was very happy at this as this is exactly my approach also. I, therefore, offer my full cooperation to you in whatever query that you may have.

V.R.L.: The lawyers should have told you that according to Section 25 of the Indian Evidence Act, which, in fact, is an earlier Act, any evidence that a person tenders cannot be held against him.

K.K.B.: I greatly appreciate this gesture on your part.

V.R.L.: Mr Birla, I am rather pained that you should have at all telephoned to me from Calcutta about your safety, particularly when I had conveyed to you through Shri Dutta, our DIG in Calcutta, guaranteeing your protection.

K.K.B.: I never doubted your word. But Shri Dutta, out of sheer consideration for me, had himself suggested that I should contact you.

V.R.L.: I appreciate this. Could you now briefly tell us about your role in the jeeps affair?

K.K.B.: Sometime towards the end of January 1977, I met Shri P.C. Sethi. Besides jeeps, Shri Sethi requested me for advertisements to the large number of souvenirs that AICC was bringing out. I told him that I would have to discuss the matter with the executives connected with my firms. Thereafter I went to Calcutta. While I discussed with a number of executives in Delhi and Calcutta the question of releasing advertisements to souvenirs, as far as the matter relating to jeeps was concerned, I discussed it only with one Shri S.N. Gupta, secretary of Shree Services & Trading Company Ltd, which is a service company.

V.R.L.: What did you discuss with Shri Gupta?

K.K.B.: Shri Gupta, inter alia, mentioned to me that advertisements in the souvenirs brought out by political parties did not attract Section 293A of the Companies Act. As far as I can remember, he mentioned three reasons for that. First, he said that there was a judgment of the Calcutta High Court on this issue. Secondly he said that the Company Law Board and the Central Board of Direct Taxes had issued clarifications on this point from time to time holding that advertisements in souvenirs brought out by political parties did not amount to political donations. Thirdly, Shri Gupta referred to some commentary on this matter which also upheld this view.

V.R.L.: Who is Shri Gupta?

K.K.B.: Shri Gupta is the secretary of Shree Services & Trading Co. Ltd.

V.R.L.: I would like to know something about Shree Services & Trading Co. Ltd.

K.K.B.: To be brief, Shree Services & Trading Company render a number of services to a large number of our companies, which include advice on taxation and legal matters, advice on the Companies Act, purchase of stores on behalf of our sugar mills, sale of sugar on behalf of our mills, release of advertisements, etc.

Now, coming back to your query about the jeep affair, when I discussed the matter with Shri Gupta, he informed me that we did require jeeps from time to time for our sugar mills. But he said that diesel jeeps were preferable as they were more economical to run. Shri Gupta said that delivery of diesel jeeps took usually very long and in case we could get the diesel jeeps earlier we should certainly purchase them as they were required by the sugar mills and we could also give them on loan to the AICC for a few weeks. Shri Gupta asked me how many jeeps were required by Shri Sethi. I said that Shri Sethi had mentioned 6 or 7 jeeps. Shri Gupta told me that it would be possible for us to purchase 7 jeeps. On my return to Delhi I reported this to Shri Sethi. He said that if we could place orders with Mahindra & Mahindra he would arrange for immediate delivery of diesel jeeps. I conveyed this to Shri Gupta.

V.R.L.: Didn't Shri Sethi use the words 'Make payment by cheques to Mahindras'?

K.K.B.: Shri Sethi mentioned placing the order with Mahindras. I was more concerned with the substance rather than with the details. I don't recollect his being specific about the payment part.

V.R.L.: What precise role was played by Shri Gupta in this matter?

K.K.B.: Shri Gupta had in fact reported to me two-three days back that CBI had questioned him on this matter. If you refer to some of your assistants you may get to know what Shri Gupta had said.

V.R.L.: Who were the officers who questioned Shri Gupta ?

K.K.B.: I am not aware of all these details. Shri Gupta reports to me only on important matters; as far as details are concerned, I leave it to him.

(Laxminarayanan asked his officers to find out who had met Gupta and to submit a report to him.)

V.R.L.: Are you aware of the fact that the jeeps were sent to the then PM's house?

K.K.B.: Shri Sethi never informed me as to where the jeeps were to be sent. I was only concerned with the fact that the jeeps were required by the AICC for a short period and that subsequently they would be returned to us.

V.R.L.: How is it possible that the fact that the jeeps were used at the PM's house was not disclosed to you by Shri Sethi?

K.K.B.: It is for Shri Sethi to answer why he did not disclose this to me.

V.R.L.: We have definite evidence that the request for jeeps was made to you by Shri R.K. Dhawan.

K.K.B.: This is not a fact.

V.R.L.: Did you meet Shri Dhawan frequently?

K.K.B.: Generally I did not meet Shri Dhawan on my own

initiative. Whenever I went to see the then Prime Minister or Shri Sanjay Gandhi, as a matter of courtesy, I called on Shri Dhawan also. I was always particular in meeting the Prime Minister at her house rather than at her office as the atmosphere in the house was more informal compared to that in the office. For seeking an appointment with the P.M., I used to make a request to Shri Dhawan.

(Lakshminarayanan took out a register in which was recorded the dates on which I met Sanjay and Dhawan respectively.)

V.R.L.: The dates on which you met Shri Sanjay Gandhi and Shri Dhawan do not tally. This shows that you must have met Shri Dhawan independently.

K.K.B.: It might have happened that sometimes I met Shri Dhawan only. But it was very seldom.

V.R.L.: What was the nature of your talks with Shri Dhawan when you met him?

K.K.B.: As I have mentioned earlier, most of my meetings with Shri Dhawan were when I met the Prime Minister or Shri Sanjay Gandhi. But sometimes I met Shri Dhawan independently merely to convey certain ideas or thoughts to the PM on the prevailing economic situation in the country.

I shall elucidate this point further. Let us assume that I met the PM, say, on the 1st of a month. It would have been very unfair on my part to have again asked for an appointment with the PM, after ten days, on the plea that when I met her earlier, something could not be conveyed to her at that time. If some such thing did happen, I sought an appointment with Shri Dhawan and conveyed through him, to the Prime Minister, my views on economic matters.

V.R.L.: Did you derive any personal benefit from such meetings?

K.K.B.: I would most emphatically say 'No'.

V.R.L.: Could you tell us about your relationship with Shri Sanjay Gandhi?

K.K.B.: I know him well.

V.R.L.: How many times did you meet Shri Sanjay Gandhi?

K.K.B.: There was no hard and fast rule.

V.R.L.: What was the nature of the talks in such meetings? Did you have any talk with him about the parliamentary elections?

K.K.B.: Shri Sanjay Gandhi's talks with me were mostly about Maruti. But we discussed other matters also.

V.R.L.: Did Shri Sanjay Gandhi listen to your suggestions?

K.K.B.: He did so sometime.

V.R.L.: How is it then that Maruti is in financial troubles in spite of your advice to Shri Sanjay Gandhi?

K.K.B.: When Shri Sanjay Gandhi originally came to me with the small car project, I told him clearly that it was only if the project was properly implemented that it might turn out to be a paying proposition. But it did not. In fact, at a certain stage when he sought my advice I suggested to him to drop the proposal altogether. (This talk was in a light-hearted manner.)

V.R.L.: Perhaps, the small car projects would have succeeded had the petrol prices not gone up.

K.K.B.: Yes, I agree with you that the rise in petrol price was a very important factor.

V.R.L.: Did you offer any other advice to Shri Sanjay Gandhi regarding Maruti?

K.K.B.: I had been to his factory several times. Though I am not a technical man, as a businessman it struck me that there was considerable space in the factory which could be utilized for bus body-building. I said this to Shri Gandhi. I also pointed out to Shri Sanjay Gandhi that a number of machines were lying idle in his factory and expressed my opinion that to keep them idle was a criminal waste. I, therefore, advised him to organize his sales department better so that the sales of his products could increase and that the machines could be put to some use.

V.R.L. (reverting to S.N. Gupta): Could our officers again go and meet Shri Gupta in case there is need for any further enquiries?

K.K.B.: Shri Gupta would always be available provided timely intimation is given to him.

V.R.L. (coming back to the jeeps affair): How many jeeps are still to be returned by the AICC?

K.K.B.: According to Shri Gupta, four jeeps had been returned while three are yet to be returned.

V.R.L.: Where were these jeeps returned?

K.K.B.: They were returned in Delhi.

V.R.L.: What action is being taken by you for the remaining jeeps?

K.K.B.: Shri Gupta had consulted me about the matter and this is being hotly pursued.

V.R.L.: To the best of my information, AICC has declined any knowledge about the jeeps.

K.K.B.: If this be so, I shall strongly suggest to Shri Gupta to hand over the matter to the police.

V.R.L.: What has the police to do in such matters?

K.K.B.: Just as police help is being taken in the case of an absconding person, we shall report to the police that our jeeps had been stolen and seek their help to trace the jeeps.

V.R.L.: You should write to Shri Sethi in the matter.

K.K.B.: Shri Sethi, to the best of my information, is no longer the treasurer of AICC. However, I shall ask Shri Gupta to write again to AICC. If their reply is in the negative I shall suggest to Shri Gupta to consult our solicitors and thereafter to have the jeeps traced and 'arrested' by the police.

V.R.L.: Did Shri Sethi offer to pay any depreciation for the jeeps?

K.K.B.: No.

V.R.L.: Were you charging any rent for the jeeps?

K.K.B.: No.

V.R.L.: It is rather strange that you did not ask for rent.

K.K.B.: If we had asked for rent it would have appeared very petty. Assuming that the rent is charged at Rs 50 per jeep per day (without expenses on petrol and driver) the total amount would work out to Rs 1,500 per month per jeep. For two months, which was the maximum period for which we thought the jeeps would be required, the amount comes to Rs 3,000 per jeep. Thus for seven jeeps the amount would be Rs 21,000 spread over a number of our companies. It would have looked very petty on my part to insist on that.

V.R.L.: Did you supply any drivers for the jeeps?

K.K.B.: No. The services of drivers were neither asked for nor offered. Even if the services of the drivers were to be asked, we would have declined as I know that the drivers experience a life of hell at the time of elections.

V.R.L.: How do you know this?

K.K.B.: I have myself fought one election and hence I know about this.

V.R.L. (laughing): So, you know the tricks of the trade. Had you supplied the drivers, you would not have lost the jeeps.

K.K.B.: This might be correct. But I am still hopeful that we shall be able to recover our jeeps with the help of the police.

V.R.L.: The reason why I had asked about the supply of drivers is that a number of companies had supplied drivers also along with the jeeps.

K.K.B.: As far as we are concerned, the request was neither made nor did we ourselves offer to supply drivers.

V.R.L.: Are you aware that giving jeeps for election purposes attracts Section 293A of the Companies Act?

K.K.B.: On the contrary, I am firmly of the view that it does not attract the mischief of Section 293A. That apart, when I discussed the question with Shri Gupta, he categorically told me that giving the jeeps on loan did not amount to political donation and hence did not at all attract the mischief of Section 293A.

V.R.L.: Did you sell off the jeeps?

K.K.B.: There is no question of selling the jeeps as they are required by us. In fact they are being used by us.

V.R.L.: Why did you oblige Shri Sethi by lending the jeeps?

V.R.L.'s assistants (in a chorus): Mr Birla, why did you lend the jeeps at all?

K.K.B.: The matter is very trivial. As I mentioned earlier the total amount involved by way of depreciation, etc., is so small that when Shri Sethi made a request for loan of jeeps we acceded to it.

At this point V.R.L. asked his assistants whether they had any further questions to ask. They repeated some of the questions to which I gave the same replies as mentioned earlier.

V.R.L.: Did you meet Shri Sethi on your own or were you sent for by him?

K.K.B.: As chance would have it, I left India in the early hours of 18 January 1977. On the 18 January morning, the announcement about Lok Sabha elections was made. I was in Zurich when Shri Sethi telephoned to me and asked me what my programme was. I told him that I had heard about the elections in India and that as this was a very important event taking place in the country, I was rescheduling my programme so as to return to India as early as possible.

V.R.L.: Are you aware of the fact that the jeeps were purchased sometime in the third week of February?

K.K.B.: I do not know the exact dates.

V.R.L.: Well, thank you, Mr Birla, for your cooperation. We have no further questions to ask.

K.K.B.: You have not asked me any questions in connection with the advertisements in the souvenir.

V.R.L.: Since you are leaving today for Calcutta, we shall meet again on some other date.

K.K.B.: There is plenty of time today itself as my flight takes off in the evening and so I am at your disposal.

V.R.L.: I would prefer to examine you on this matter on some other date.

K.K.B.: Could I meet you again during one of my subsequent trips to Delhi in case I require your assistance?

V.R.L.: You could always meet me while this case is going on and even after the case is over.

K.K.B.: I am grateful for it. I would like to thank you and your colleagues for the courtesy shown to me.

A file, once opened by the government gets closed only when a case is completed. The CBI had started a file on me, and it was not closed even after my interrogation. Though the interrogation by the CBI in my case was thorough, some extra-smart officials felt that further interrogation was needed. A year later, on 18 November 1978, I was again summoned by the CBI. On that occasion, I was interrogated by Ramanathan and Mukherjee, both deputy superintendents and Vellingiri, inspector.

During the interrogation, I was asked more about the role of Sethi in securing the advertisements. I was asked if he had pressed me for the advertisements; whether or not it was proper to advertise in the souvenirs and whether I had advised other members of the family also to release advertisements to the souvenir.

I replied that there was no question of any pressure being put on me for releasing advertisements; that the advertisements given to the souvenirs were justified; that I had not pressed any family member to advertise in the souvenirs, although when anyone asked me whether I had advertised in these souvenirs, I replied in the affirmative.

The CBI wanted to establish that Sethi had misused his position as a minister by trying to collect advertisements for the souvenirs of the AICC. Their game was to catch me off guard so that I might blurt out that Sethi did misuse his position and had collected advertisements. Had I said that under pressure or out of sheer nervousness, I would have been unfair to Sethi. But God gave me strength and I was able to stand up to the onslaught of the CBI officials. I clarified that Sethi, besides being a minister was also the honorary treasurer of the Congress (I) and it was in that capacity and not as a minister that he had approached me for advertisements.

On this occasion, too, I drafted out a record of the proceedings which is given here for the readers' interest:

CROSS EXAMINATION OF SHRI K.K. BIRLA
CONDUCTED BY THE CBI AT NEW DELHI ON
SATURDAY, 18 NOVEMBER 1978
AT 3.00 P.M.

Present: 1. Shri Ramanathan, Dy. Superintendent, CBI
2. Shri Vellingiri, Inspector
3. Shri Mukherjee, Deputy Superintendent, CBI
(joined later).

R.N.: Mr Birla, all the questions that I shall be putting to you will relate to the period 1976 and 1977, i.e. up to April 1977.

Could you please tell us the names of the companies with which you are connected either as Chairman or as a Director?

K.K.B.: It is difficult for me to give you the complete list of such companies off hand. If you so desire I could send it to you.

R.N.: Could you in any case inform me the names of those companies which you could remember?

K.K.B.: The names of the companies that I recollect are as under. I am the Chairman of the following companies:

1. Texmaco Ltd.
2. Zuari Agro Chemicals Ltd.
3. Birla Cotton Spinning & Weaving Mills Ltd.
4. Sutlej Cotton Mills Ltd.
5. Hindustan Times Ltd.
6. Upper Ganges Sugar Mills Ltd.
7. Oudh Sugar Mills Ltd.
8. Gobind Sugar Mills Ltd.
9. New India Sugar Mills Ltd.
10. Bharat Sugar Mills Ltd.
11. New Swadeshi Sugar Mills Ltd.
12. India Steamship Co. Ltd.
13. Ratnakar Shipping Co. Ltd.

I am director of the following companies:
14. Birla Bros. (P) Ltd. I am one of the managing directors.
15. I.C.I.C.I.

I would like to mention again that if you so desire I shall send you a complete list as early as possible.

R.N.: Please do so. Please also tell us which are the public bodies or chambers of commerce with which you are connected.

K.K.B.: I am connected with the following bodies:

1. Federation of Indian Chambers of Commerce & Industry as a committee member
2. Indo-US Joint Business Council as its co-chairman
3. I was also a member of Board of Trade

R.N.: Are you still a Member of the Board of Trade?

K.K.B.: I do not think I am now a member of the Board of Trade. I would like to mention however, that normally when the membership ceases, one receives a letter of appreciation from the Government of India. I have not received any such letter from the government. This would imply that my membership of the Board of Trade has not ceased. But all the same, I do not think that I am now a member of the Board of Trade.

R.N.: Are there any other companies in whose affairs you could have any influence?

K.K.B.: I am a shareholder in a number of companies, but I cannot influence their affairs except as a shareholder.

R.N.: My purpose of enquiry was to know whether you have any large holding in any company and whether you could influence its affairs as a large shareholder?

K.K.B.: There is no such case. But I may mention that I am also an executive in the following three companies:

1. Birla Bombay (P) Ltd.
2. Zenith Distributors and Agents Ltd.
3. Rameshwara Jute Mills Ltd.—Birla Gwalior division

R.N.: Could you tell me names of the companies in which your brother Mr. B.K.Birla is chairman and/or a director?

K.K.B.: Only my brother will be able to answer this question. But some of the companies that I could recollect in this connection are:

1. Kesoram Industries & Cotton Mills Ltd.
2. Jayshree Tea & Industries Ltd.
3. Century Enka Ltd.
4. Century Spinning & Manufacturing. Co. Ltd.

R.N.: What were the circumstances under which you gave advertisements to the souvenirs brought out by the Congress party in 1976 or in 1977?

K.K.B.: I do not at all recollect anything pertaining to 1976. Let us, therefore, confine for the present to 1977. I believe whatever be the circumstances in 1977, the same must have prevailed in 1976 also.

R.N.: Alright, let us confine ourselves to 1977. We shall later come to 1976. In 1977, did you call on Shri P.C. Sethi or did he call you?

K.K.B.: As chance would have it, I left for abroad in the early hours on the 18 January 1977. The same night, the announcement regarding the dissolution of the Parliament, with a view to holding fresh elections, was made. Within two-three days of that announcement I got a call from Sethi-ji at Zurich.

R.N.: What did Sethi-ji say ?

K.K.B.: Sethi-ji asked me whether I had heard about the elections and enquired as to what my programme was. I told him that the news about the elections had appeared in all the European papers also and that I was planning to return to India as early as possible.

R.N.: Did Sethi-ji press you to return to India ?

K.K.B.: The question did not arise since as soon as I came to know about the impending elections, I decided to return to India, and I told him so on telephone.

R.N.: What happened then?

K.K.B.: On return to India towards the end of January 1977, I called on Sethi-ji. Sethi-ji said that he was talking to me in his capacity as the treasurer of AICC and also as chairman of the souvenir committee of AICC regarding advertisements for certain souvenirs that AICC was proposing to bring out. He said that AICC was bringing out many souvenirs in several languages which would have a wide circulation. He said that the souvenirs would contain articles on the achievements of the government in the recent past and that there would be articles on the subjects like socialism, secularism, democracy, etc. He said that it would be in the interest of our companies to advertise in these souvenirs to the maximum extent.

R.N.: Did Sethi-ji press you about any amount?

K.K.B.: No.

R.N.: Did he give you any literature regarding the souvenirs?

K.K.B.: No literature was given. The request was made to me only orally.

R.N.: What was your answer?

K.K.B.: I told him that I shall have to discuss the matter with the executives of the companies with which I am connected.

R.N.: What happened then?

K.K.B.: I held discussions with these executives, some of whom were in Delhi and some in Calcutta. In Delhi, discussions were held with Shri G.N. Dalmia in respect of Sutlej Cotton Mills Ltd. and with Shri Santosh Nath for the Hindustan Times Ltd. In Calcutta, I held discussions with Shri R.C. Maheshwari, general manager of Texmaco Ltd. for Texmaco and with Shri S.N. Gupta, secretary of Shree Services & Trading Co. Ltd., and with Shri H.K. Pachisia, an executive of Shree Services in respect of the sugar mills with which I am connected.

The request of Sethi-ji for advertisements was conveyed to them for their advice. All the executives felt that the souvenirs proposed by the AICC were bound to have a wide circulation and that it was in the interest of the companies to advertise in these souvenirs. They said that by such advertisements, the products of the companies would receive good publicity and that the companies too would be able to project a good image about themselves, thereby earning the goodwill of the public.

R.N.: I had heard about this service company. What exactly are its functions?

K.K.B.: Its functions are varied. They include the purchase of stores required by our mills, sale of sugar, arranging for finances from the banks, looking after the public relations work in Delhi, etc. As I had mentioned in an earlier meeting, while discussing the question of releasing advertisements to the AICC souvenirs, Shri Gupta had made three further points. First, the CBDT and the Company Law Board had issued circulars from time to time holding such advertisements in the souvenirs brought out by political parties, to be permissible under the law and not treating them as political donations. Secondly, a well known publication containing commentaries on Company Law, written by the noted author, Mr Ramayya, held that such advertisements did not amount to political donations and so did not attract the mischief of Section 293A. Thirdly, Shri Gupta mentioned to me about the Calcutta High Court's judgment of 1975, wherein the High Court had held that advertisements were meant to promote business and that in the absence of any improper or oblique purpose, the expenditure on advertisements was deemed to be wholly and exclusively for business purposes.

R.N.: Did Mr Gupta give this opinion at that time or later?

K.K.B.: He gave this opinion twice, once at the meeting which was held towards the end of January 1977 and secondly, soon after Shri Shanti Bhushan had made a public speech during the elections wherein he mentioned that advertisements in the souvenirs of political parties amounted to political donations.

R.N.: You say that by advertisements the companies were to acquire goodwill. What do you mean by that?

K.K.B.: What I understand by goodwill is that our products get popularised amongst the public for their quality and the company side by side earns a good name.

R.N.: Mr Birla, had you been informed that the number of copies of the souvenirs to be published would be very limited and that in some cases the number would be so small that they could give only voucher copies to the advertisers, would you have still advertised in the souvenirs?

K.K.B.: Certainly not. In such a case, I would not have agreed to any advertisements being released to these souvenirs. I have however no reasons to doubt what Sethi-ji had said, namely, number of copies of the souvenirs to be published will be large.

R.N.: Did you know that the souvenirs that were published and particularly those published in 1976 were very few in number?

K.K.B.: I did not know that nor were the executives concerned aware of that.

R.N.: Did you know that some of the souvenirs brought out by the   CC in the past also, had no circulation at all?

K   .B. I n no aware of that.

R   .: Did you ive any advice to your brothers and cousins regarding the advertisements?

K   B. As far a my recollection goes, once or twice when the members of the family met, I was asked as to what I was proposing to do about the advertisements to the AICC souvenirs. I said that I had consulted the senior executives of some of the companies with which I was connected in the matter and that they had advised me that it was in the business interest of the companies to advertise in these souvenirs and that, therefore, these companies were releasing advertisements to these souvenirs.

R.N.: Were your brothers and cousins also approached by Sethi-ji?

K.K.B.: I do not know. It is quite possible that he might have approached them.

R.N.: What was the basis on which the advertisements were released?

K.K.B.: Advertisements that were released depended on a number of considerations, such as the size of the companies, the products to be advertised, etc. In such cases there can, however, be no yardstick.

R.N.: Did it happen that as a result of discussions with Sethi-ji, some lump sum amount might have been agreed to by you which you later on divided amongst your various companies?

K.K.B.: No, it did not happen like that.

R.N.: How many times do you think you met Sethi-ji?

K.K.B.: I met him quite frequently as I was interested in knowing out of sheer curiosity how the elections were going on. In fact, amongst the senior leaders, very few were in Delhi at that time.

R.N.: Did Sethi-ji ask you to request your friends also for advertisements?

K.K.B.: I never forced my views on others. Some businessmen however sought my advice in the matter. On such occasions, I told them that after consulting the executives concerned, the companies connected with me were releasing some advertisements to the souvenirs that were being brought out, as it was felt by the executives that such advertisements were in the business interest of the companies. As to whether the friends should release advertisements or not, I gave my views and I told them that it was for them to decide what to do.

R.N.: Are you aware that FICCI sought a clarification regarding Section 293(A) of the Companies Act and were you connected in any way with it?

K.K.B.: I was never connected with this. I saw FICCI's circular only after it was issued.

R.N.: FICCI had first sent a letter to the Company Law ministry to which there was no reply and thereafter a letter was addressed directly to law minister. Are you aware of this?

K.K.B.: Only FICCI can answer this question.

R.N.: Were you aware of the advertisement rates for the souvenirs published in 1977?

K.K.B.: I was not aware of the rates. This matter was being dealt with by the executives.

R.N.: Are you aware that there is a big disparity between the rates of advertisements in 1976 and in 1977?

K.K.B.: I am not aware of that.

R.N.: How is that in case there was a big disparity in the advertisement rates even then you advertised in the souvenirs in 1977?

K.K.B.: I do not think any of the executives compared the rates like this as to what the rates were in 1976 and in 1977. I would, however, like to point out that had the executives felt that the rates for advertisements were very high and exorbitant, they would have taken the initiative and would have sought my advice.

R.N.: Do you know Mr R.P. Goenka ?

K.K.B.: Yes, I know Shri R.P. Goenka very well.

R.N.: Did you meet him with Sethi-ji?

K.K.B: While I was with Sethi-ji, Shri R.P. Goenka did drop in and vice versa.

R.N.: Let us now come to the advertisements released to the souvenirs published in 1976. What was the procedure followed in 1976?

K.K.B.: I fear I do not recollect what exactly happened in 1976. But I could tell you that either someone must have approached me for the advertisements or the executives might have received circulars. The procedure in any case in 1976 would have been the same as in 1977.

R.N.: Who gave the cheques to Sethi-ji in 1977?

K.K.B.: As per my recollection, on some occasions the executives had given the envelopes containing the cheques to me with a request to hand them over to Sethi-ji since I come to Delhi frequently. It is also possible that in some cases the executives themselves might have given the cheques either to Sethi-ji or to his secretary.

R.N.: We find that in some companies two-three cheques have been given. Does it imply that pressure was put by Sethi-ji to give more and more?

Note: Before K.K.B. could answer this question Ramanathan left the room and on his return he did not pursue this question.

R.N.: Mr Birla, I have no further questions to ask. If you have any queries, you may please raise them.

K.K.B.: In my opinion, this matter should not be permitted to remain in suspense like this. In case, the government thought that they had a good case to prosecute the persons concerned, they should do so. On the other hand, if they felt that they had no case, then the matter should be dropped. This sort of indecisiveness is not good.

Mukherjee, who joined the meeting late, did not have any additional queries.

At the end of the interrogation I suggested to the inquisitors that the final outcome of the enquiry should not be allowed to remain in suspense. I said such suspense caused mental anguish and if the government felt that they had a good case against me, let them prosecute me; I was prepared to face the music. If, on the other hand, they realized that there was nothing against me, the matter should be dropped. I tried to impress upon the CBI officials that indecisiveness and allowing the matter to drag on was not good for either side. In spite of that, the case remained pending. It was ultimately dropped after a few years when Indira-ji returned to power.

Coming back to Chaudhury Saheb, politics apart, my relations with him remained cordial. In fact, when father died in 1983, Chaudhury Saheb was among the first to call on me to offer condolences. It is the politician in him that sometimes led him astray. Otherwise, he was a man of convictions and basically good and gentle at heart. I always maintained a high regard for him in spite of the treatment meted out to me. In course of time he, too, mellowed and stopped harassing me. After going through a period of anguish and trauma my troubles at last came to an end. God was kind to me.

24

Indira Stages a Comeback

The period between 1977 and 1979 was one of vicissitudes for Indira-ji and all her supporters. But she braved all the hardships and encouraged others like me not to lose hope.

From early 1979, it became increasingly apparent that the Janata Party was heading towards a crisis. There was constant bickering among the party leaders. In fact, soon after the elections in 1977, which brought the Janata Party to power, there was an unseemly tussle for the post of prime minister. There were three aspirants: Morarji Desai, Charan Singh and Jagjivan Ram (who was earlier with the Congress). Jagjivan Ram would probably have proved the ablest of the three but, on the intervention of Jayaprakash Narayan and some others, a contest was avoided and Morarji-bhai was chosen prime minister.

Most of the top Janata leaders contended that there should be collective leadership. How can collective leadership in a government function efficiently and effectively? It is a ludicrous idea. Leadership has to be provided only by one person, not by a group of persons. A government needs to be strong and effective. In a democracy this is possible only if the prime minister enjoys the love, affection, respect and confidence of party members and the people. In a way, it was good that the Congress split in 1969, when Morarji-bhai and some others left and formed another party. Those who then remained with Indira-ji were her true followers.

Leaders of the ruling party started fighting each other. H.N. Bahuguna, in a letter to Morarji-bhai dated 10 July 1978, described Charan Singh as a dictator. He said that the interest of the Harijans and Muslims were not safe in his hands. Charan Singh, in a letter to Morarji-bhai dated 2 April 1979, called Bahuguna a KGB (Soviet secret service) agent! It was a free-for-all.

As the in-fighting in the Janata Party increased, it became evident that Morarji-bhai might have to resign. Numerous people in the Janata

Party then began dreaming of becoming the next prime minister. It became apparent that the party would not last long as a cohesive force.

Indira-ji, assisted by Sanjay, played her cards exceedingly well. The result was that Morarji-bhai lost the majority and Charan Singh became prime minister. It is said that N. Sanjiva Reddy who was then President did not give Morarji-bhai a fair opportunity to prove his majority. He had his own scores to settle with Morarji-bhai, having been one of the aspirants for prime minister's post in 1977. And why not? No one from the south had, till then, become prime minister, he argued. Sanjiva Reddy could not forgive Morarji-bhai for having ignored his claims.

However, Charan Singh also could not last long; Parliament was dissolved and fresh elections were ordered. The strategy of Indira-ji and Sanjay succeeded. The Janata Party, which had won the 1977 elections impressively, collapsed like a house of cards. Dissensions among the leading members of the party put an end to its hopes of survival in power.

Indira-ji prepared for the elections with her customary zeal and vigour, touring the country extensively. It was clear from the beginning that victory would be hers. Human memory is proverbially short and our people are tolerant by nature. They gave a chance to the Janata Party, having developed abhorrence for the excesses committed by the Congress (I) during the Emergency. The Janata Party proved a flop. The people wanted peace, stability and good administration. They also felt that Indira Gandhi could never repeat the Emergency and so there was no harm in voting her back to power. As a result, Indira Gandhi was elected with a thumping majority.

I had remained in close touch with Indira-ji and Sanjay. When the question of allotting party tickets arose, Sanjay sent for me and offered me the seat from Jhunjhunu. I told him that I had no desire to contest any Lok Sabha election. Sanjay, however, pressed me to accept the seat. I met Indira-ji and expressed my inability to consider the offer as I had made a firm resolve never again to contest any Lok Sabha seat. Standing for a Lok Sabha seat was not to my liking, I explained to her. Sis Ram Ola, an eminent leader, was subsequently asked to contest from that constituency. He did so, but lost. He should have won but he was betrayed by some of his close friends—not an uncommon practice unfortunately during elections. After the elections Sanjay reproached me for this defeat and said that had I stood for the seat, I would, in all probability, have won. I told him that the question of winning or losing a Lok Sabha election did not arise as far as I was concerned. My determination not to stand for a Lok Sabha seat after my experience in Jhunjhunu in 1971 was unshakable, I explained.

I was in Delhi when the results started pouring in. Indira-ji's house was besieged by admiring crowds. The police arrangements were not adequate. I went to her residence to congratulate her. She received me with her usual warmth. As people were pouring in, I remember her telling Dhawan when I went to congratulate her to close most of the doors of the house and to keep only one door open.

The next day my wife and I along with our daughter, Shobhana, who, too, is politically inclined, took bouquets to Indira-ji. She kindly agreed to have her photo taken with us.

There was general rejoicing around the country over Indira-ji's victory. Sanjay emerged as a leader in his own right. But at the height of his glory befell sudden tragedy—Sanjay's death in an air crash.

25

Sanjay Dies in Air Crash

I was in Delhi when Sanjay died in an air crash on 23 June 1980. I had just returned from my morning walk when the telephone rang. It was Naresh Mohan, one of the senior executives of the *Hindustan Times*, who later became the executive president of the company. He asked me whether I had heard the news. 'What news?' I asked unconcernedly. He then broke the news to me of Sanjay's death. I was stunned. I had met Sanjay only two days earlier. And I was scheduled to meet him again that very afternoon.

I immediately rushed to 1, Safdarjung Road. Indira-ji and the entire family were at the hospital. I wanted to go to the hospital but later decided not to disturb the family there. Instead I waited at Birla House for Indira-ji's return, keeping in touch with her house on an hourly basis. She returned late in the evening and I rushed to meet her. There was a large gathering at the house. People appeared to be confused. Indira-ji was kind enough to receive me separately. I offered her my sincere condolences and asked her to be brave. I told her that if she broke down all her friends and followers would lose heart. I could say no more. I myself was too upset emotionally. Indira-ji was, in fact, the most composed person in that atmosphere of gloom and darkness. Indeed, she consoled others, including me. I laid a wreath on Sanjay's body.

The funeral took place on 24 June. As a large gathering was expected, I telephoned the prime minister's house and spoke to an assistant. I requested the assistant to enable me to reach the spot where the cremation was to take place. After consulting the prime minister, the assistant phoned back. I was provided with an escort and a special permit for the car to go right up to the cremation ground.

In Sanjay's death I lost a valued friend. He was, no doubt, impulsive and had pronounced likes and dislikes. But he was a good friend. I had known him since 1971. He was always kind and considerate to me. His demise was therefore a personal loss.

My association with Sanjay was a long one. I came to know him before he sprang into the limelight. It is not easy to make a correct assessment of Sanjay's good qualities and foibles. He was a good friend and a bad enemy. He stood by his friends through thick and thin. He would go to any length to help a friend in difficulty. Sanjay was a man of intense likes and dislikes. He would endeavour to push up in life those he fancied, but woe betide anyone he took a dislike to.

That I was close to Indira-ji and enjoyed her trust and warmth was known to many. People would often approach me for some recommendation or other. Many bureaucrats too would approach me from time to time with their difficulties and problems. I was very selective in entertaining such solicitations. Only where I felt that the case was a deserving one, would I recommend it. It was, however, not always possible to meet Indira-ji at short notice. Therefore, on some occasions when there was anything that I wanted to be conveyed to Indira-ji I would speak to Sanjay about the matter to be passed on to his mother.

Once, in 1976, a top businessman's brother got into trouble. The government decided to arrest him under COFEPOSA (Conservation of Foreign Exchange and Prevention of Smuggling Act). When the businessman came to know of it, he naturally became very nervous. He hesitated to approach me at first though he knew me well; that was because we were in opposite camps in the politics of business, specifically, FICCI politics. When he asked his friends for advice on how to avoid the impending danger, they told him that perhaps I could be of assistance. The businessman was diffident about approaching me but ultimately, brushing aside the false sense of prestige, he met me. After hearing his story, I assured him that irrespective of business politics I would do my best to help him.

It was difficult to meet Indira-ji. So I met Sanjay and requested him to discuss this man's problems with Indira-ji, and to prevent his arrest. Sanjay knew that the man was opposed to me in business politics. He was, therefore, surprised to find me pleading for him and said so in so many words. I told Sanjay that if a person was in difficulties and approached me for my help, I completely disregarded his past coldness towards me, and had no hesitation in helping him. This was my nature, I said.

Sanjay too had a dislike for the man and was not very happy to take up the matter with his mother. But I insisted and said that the proposal to arrest the brother of the man was perhaps based on wrong information. In any case, I assured Sanjay that even if the man's brother was guilty of any serious economic offence, I would take the responsibility that no such offence was committed by him in future. After all, I said, if a man got reformed and learnt a lesson our objective was achieved, and under the circumstances there was no point in keeping such a man behind bars. Ultimately, I was able to persuade Sanjay to intercede on behalf of this man and speak to his mother. He did so and told Indira-ji about my talk with him and, as a result of this, the matter was ultimately dropped, much to the relief of the businessman concerned.

Once I was approached to intercede on behalf of Viren Shah, chairman and managing director of Mukand Iron. Viren Shah, along with George Fernandes, was held under the Maintenance of Internal Security Act (MISA) around 1975. When I was in Mumbai, Pravin Gandhi, a leading city businessman, telephoned me quite unexpectedly and said that he would like to meet me. He sought my assistance to get Viren Shah released from jail. I was a bit surprised at his making such a request and asked him how he was interested in the case. Pravin disclosed that he had come to see me at the behest of Viren's wife and that Viren was also related to him. Pravin assured me that Viren was innocent and was implicated on wrong premises.

Viren, at one time, belonged to the Swatantra Party. I had not relinquished my membership of the Swatantra Party till it got absorbed in the Janata Party even when I had come quite close to Indira-ji. I had a soft corner for all those who were members of that party. I told Pravin that only two persons could help Viren—Rajni Patel or Sanjay Gandhi. I was close to both of them. As I was then in Mumbai, I went to see Rajni Patel. That day there was no power in the area. Rajni Bhai's flat was on one of the upper floors of the building and I would have had to climb the stairs. The other alternative was to return home. I reasoned that if I could be of any assistance to someone who was behind bars, that should be a matter of satisfaction to me even if it meant some personal hardship. Hence I climbed the stairs all the way. Rajni Bhai was surprised to see me. He asked me how I could come to his residence when there was a power failure. I explained to him that considering the seriousness of the matter I did not mind the trouble of climbing up to his flat. I told him about Viren's detention and requested him to use his good offices in getting him released. Rajni Bhai assured me he would do his best in the matter, but added that he was not optimistic as his earlier attempt to help Viren at the behest of some others had ended in failure.

From Mumbai, I went to Delhi and met Sanjay. He was furious when I told him that I had come to plead for Viren. He asked me how I could recommend the case of a man who was suspected of being involved in a criminal conspiracy against his mother. I pleaded with Sanjay and said that the information which he had must be wrong, and that Viren could not be guilty of any such offence. Sanjay vehemently refused to speak to his mother in the matter in spite of my pleading. I related the failure of my mission to Pravin. He thanked me all the same for my efforts to do whatever was possible under the circumstances.

Viren was released along with other political prisoners in 1977. He became quite powerful during the Janata regime. He could have helped me during the Janata rule by ensuring that I was not harassed. That I was friendly with Indira-ji was well known to the Janata government. I neither sought nor expected any favour from them. I was only hoping that I would not be harassed and in that I expected help from Viren Shah. He repaid the kindness that I had shown him by advising Morarji-bhai not to have anything to do with me. That came to my knowledge through Chandra Bhanu-ji. When I related to Chandra Bhanu-ji what I had done for Viren, he was very surprised. Viren came to know that I was feeling very unhappy with him. One day he met me after a FICCI meeting which both of us had attended. He assured me of his cordiality towards me but defended his conduct in speaking to Morarji-bhai in unfavourable terms about me. It was a matter of principle with him, he asserted. So much for Viren Shah and his principles.

In fairness to Viren, I may say that as the governor of West Bengal he proved to be very popular. He became governor in 1999. He was an active member of the BJP; yet the West Bengal government also approved of his appointment. He visited all parts of West Bengal and would meet a large number of people. Whenever anyone brought any grievance to him, he would take up the matter and would try to resolve it through discussions with the government.

Sanjay was a staunch anti-communist. No power on earth could make him change his views as far as his hostility to communism was concerned. Hence, he developed a dislike for those who had leftist leanings even though some of them were very loyal to his mother. P.N. Haksar, secretary to Indira-ji, and D.P.Dhar, an important leader from Kashmir who later became a minister, fell in that category. Both of them were confidants of Indira-ji and loyal to her. Like Haksar, DP was a man of character. Sanjay, however, developed an aversion to them, with the result that both fell from grace.

I was very close to DP. I had known him ever since he was a minister in Jammu and Kashmir when Sheikh Mohammad Abdullah was chief minister. Once while he was a minister, he met father in Delhi and told him to do something for the backward state. Dhar suggested that we start some industries there. Later, at his instance, Pandit-ji too spoke to father on the subject. Father put me in touch with Dhar. I, accordingly, set up a textile spinning unit at a place called Kathua near Jammu .

After some time, Dhar fell out with Sheikh Saheb. Later, Indira-ji took him in as a Cabinet minister at the Centre. Dhar was a good orator and had a good command over the language. He was, in fact, an intellectual.

My relationship with Dhar was very close and he would seek my views on many matters. Friendship between us became so deep that on many an occasion, when I went to DP's residence, I would meet him in the bedroom where DP, in a dressing gown, would have tea and offer me a cup too.

DP did not hide from me the fact that Sanjay had a dislike for him. One day, he told me that he was being sent to the Soviet Union as ambassador. DP was very unhappy at this decision and was not at all keen to go. He was a heart patient and did not like to go to a very cold country. He spoke to me and said that probably Sanjay had whispered something against him in the ears of his mother, as a result of which he was being packed off to the Soviet Union. DP asked me to intervene on his behalf. On his request, I did speak to Sanjay. But, as mentioned earlier, Sanjay was a man of strong preferences. He did not change his opinion about DP who, therefore, had to go.

I have described elsewhere how, during the Emergency, Ramnath Goenka got into trouble with the government. Owing to my efforts, an informal understanding was arrived at between the government and Ramnath-ji, according to which I became chairman of the *Indian Express*.

After becoming chairman, the first job that I had to attend to was who should be the editor of the paper. S. Mulgaonkar was editor but he was not liked by the government. I had always held Mulgaonkar in high esteem. He was a man of great rectitude and was a fearless journalist. In spite of his stubbornness I liked him. He had worked with father and myself in the *Hindustan Times* for a number of years. I was keen that he should continue as editor. But this had to be approved by the government as well. I consulted Indira-ji. As she was busy, she did not have time to meet Mulgaonkar herself but she directed Sanjay to meet him and report to her. I called Mulgaonkar and briefed him in the matter. I gave a lecture to Mulgaonkar on the virtues of flexibility and following a middle course in life. I admired Mulgaonkar's upright stance but told him that since the country was passing through a period of Emergency, there should be an element of compromise also. On my persuasion a meeting was arranged between Mulgaonkar and Sanjay. Mulgaonkar met Sanjay but the meeting proved to be infructuous. Mulgaonkar was firm in his views and so was Sanjay. When two stubborn people meet, where was the chance of a compromise?

Sanjay was a man of few words, but with pronounced likes and dislikes. On one occasion during the Emergency, he saw a report from one of the correspondents of the *Hindustan Times* to be distorted and not to his liking. The report was highly critical of the government. When I met Sanjay after this report had been published, he was visibly annoyed. He asked me to get rid of the man. I told Sanjay that it would be improper to do so, and besides, it was also not possible to do so under the Working Journalists' Act. His next suggestion was to send the reporter either to Mizoram or Nagaland! I explained that the *Hindustan Times* had no correspondent in either of these areas. I knew after some time he would cool down, which he did. That was the end of the matter.

Indira-ji was completely in the grip of Sanjay. Sanjay was a good friend and a bad enemy. In case someone opposed him, he would not accept that the person was acting out of a concern for public good. He would come down on the opponent with great vengeance. As related before, Siddhartha Shankar Ray, the then chief minister of West Bengal, Rajni Bhai, Devkanta Barooah, who was president of AICC for a long time and Haksar, who was a gem of a person, told Indira-ji that Sanjay's involvement in the Maruti project was doing harm to her reputation. Sanjay got the news as Indira-ji would not keep anything secret from him. Instead of recognizing that the purpose behind the advice was to save her reputation, he took it as personal animosity towards him. He wanted to get rid of Ray as chief minister, but Indira-ji did not agree. Rajni-bhai, who was very close to Indira-ji was pushed into the background; the same happened to Devkanta Barooah. Haksar also had to give up his post as secretary to Indira-ji.

Not only that, Haksar's house was raided by the income tax authorities. When they asked Haksar to open the safes and almirahs, he threw his keys to them and said in a challenging mood, 'You can open them.' Nothing objectionable was found nor any unaccounted for money. Haksar had the reputation of being a very clean man. But he was publicly humiliated. Devkanta Barooah had made a name because of famous speech in which he said, 'India is Indira and Indira is India.' Because he had the audacity to advise Indira-ji to keep Sanjay in check, he had to leave.

Sanjay took a dislike to Ray. The dislike was, perhaps, mutual. The story goes that when Sanjay visited Kolkata during Siddhartha Babu's tenure as chief minister, the latter did not give him adequate attention. In my opinion, Sanjay should not have harboured any dislike for Siddhartha Babu, who was much senior to him in age and had studied in the same institution as his mother when they were students. Besides, whatever advice Siddhartha Babu gave Indira-ji was well intended.

Be that as it may, soon after that Sanjay wanted his mother to appoint someone else as the chief minister of West Bengal. When I came to know of that I told him that it was not a correct move. I pointed out that Siddhartha Babu was functioning well and should not be disturbed. I reminded him of the antecedents of Siddhartha Babu and pointed out that his maternal grandfather, C.R. Das, was, in his days, the undisputed leader of Bengal. Even otherwise, I said that Siddhartha Babu, in his own right, could boast of a good image in West Bengal, and therefore, it would be highly improper to remove him. Sanjay, however, was adamant even though Indira-ji did not accept his advice.

Sanjay was keen that A.B. Ghani Khan Chowdhury should become the chief minister of West Bengal. I told Sanjay that Ghani Khan Chowdhury too was a close friend of mine but that he would not be acceptable to the people of West Bengal. At last, Sanjay dropped the idea of trying to push the name of Ghani Khan Chowdhury with his mother. He asked me, however, whether there could be any substitute for Siddhartha Babu. I again advised Sanjay not to think of removing Siddhartha Babu, but when he pressed me hard to suggest an alternative name, I told him that the only other person I could think of was Dr Gopal Das Nag. Sanjay might have met Dr Nag but did not know him well enough to have formed any opinion about him. Sanjay desired to meet Dr Nag and asked me to arrange a meeting.

I came to Kolkata and had a talk with Dr Nag, who agreed with my views that there was nobody in West Bengal of the stature of Siddhartha Babu. However, he agreed to meet Sanjay. Both of us went to Delhi. I made an appointment with Sanjay for Dr Nag and went along with him. Dr Nag created a good impression on Sanjay. Towards the end of the meeting, Sanjay enquired to whom he owed his first loyalty. I had cautioned Dr Nag about the possibility of such a question being put and had advised him that he should say, provided he felt that way, that his first loyalty was to Indira-ji. Dr Nag agreed and told me that his first loyalty in fact was to Indira-ji who was the head of the party. During the interview, however, Dr Nag got nervous when the question was put to him and blurted out that his first loyalty lay with Siddhartha Shankar Ray. The interview came to an abrupt end. Later, Sanjay gave me a good scolding. Had the Congress (I) won the elections in 1977 in West Bengal, I have no doubt that Sanjay would have put pressure on his mother to get rid of Siddhartha Babu. How far he would have succeeded is another matter.

Sanjay's weakness was that he did not care much for guidance from Indira-ji. He was very independent minded and had tremendous confidence in himself. Had he listened to Indira-ji, the excesses that were perpetrated during the Emergency would have been avoided, in which case Indira-ji, it is certain, would not have lost the 1977 elections. I believe in the strong being humble.

In 1980, the service contract of Hiranmay Karlekar, who was editor of the *Hindustan Times*, ended. The question was who to make the new editor. As I had no one in mind, I consulted numerous friends for their suggestions. I consulted Sanjay too. Sanjay said he had a good name to suggest. When I asked him who he had in mind, he recommended the name of his wife, Maneka! I was taken aback. I told Sanjay that he must be joking. But Sanjay was serious. He said Maneka would brighten up the paper and increase its circulation. I told Sanjay the suggestion was totally unacceptable to me. He wanted to know the reasons. I said, first, he being a friend I would not like to have his wife as the editor of the paper. Secondly, I said Maneka was impulsive and not mature enough to be the editor. Sanjay still disagreed; he said Maneka was very dynamic and would give a new look to the paper. I, however, remained adamant and so the matter was not pursued any further. I must say in all fairness to Sanjay that he did not take amiss my frank views about Maneka.

One excellent quality in Sanjay was his love for trees. Under his guidance, a large number of trees were planted in various states. An observant traveller cannot but notice clusters of trees planted at several places along the road, particularly in areas around Delhi. We have to thank Sanjay for all this greenery that has come up under his loving care.

Sanjay had an excellent memory but overconfidence led to disorderliness in his conduct. During the days when he was actively involved in Maruti I would give him many suggestions whenever we met. During our subsequent meetings, I found that he forgot some of the earlier suggestions. I told Sanjay to cultivate the habit of jotting down points, and keeping them in a file so that he could refer to them later to refresh his memory and review from time to time which suggestions had been implemented and which not. But Sanjay would not listen. He would depend only on his memory. During my meetings with him I always took a file with me. It contained all the points covered in earlier discussions. I could, however, never convince Sanjay that this was the proper method of working.

When familiarity between us deepened, he told me that I did not have to make any appointment to meet him. I had merely to walk in at his residence and he would meet me in case he was free. Otherwise, he said, I could go back. I noted the advice, but never made use of it. I always met him after making an appointment unless I was compelled by the exigencies of the situation to act differently. That happened once.

After it was announced that elections would be held in 1977, all the political parties started making preparations in all earnestness to contest. One day while in Delhi, I was informed that a couple of businessmen had dropped in even though no appointment was fixed with me. They apologized for having intruded upon my time without appointment but said that as it was an important matter, they had taken the liberty of dropping in and taking a chance to meet me. They informed me that they had heard that the prime minister was likely to announce the nationalization of a large number of industries like jute, textiles, sugar, paper, etc., as an election stunt so that she could win the forthcoming elections with ease. These businessmen pressed me to do something immediately about the matter. I was greatly concerned when I heard that. I told them that, in my opinion, their information could not be correct. All the same I assured them that I would immediately move in the matter.

I rushed to the prime minister's house. It was difficult to meet Indira-ji without an appointment but I was able to meet Sanjay. He was surprised to see me, because though I used to meet him quite frequently, I always did so only after making an appointment. I told Sanjay what the rumour was and pressed him to arrange a short meeting with Indira-ji urgently. I also asked Sanjay to use his influence with his mother to prevent the rumoured nationalization. Sanjay had a lot of faith in the private sector, and believed in centrist policies. In fact, policy-wise, he could be called right-of-centre. He did not at all subscribe to the socialist philosophy. He, therefore, very willingly arranged for me to meet Indira-ji. It was a short meeting and I apprised her of the wild rumour that I had heard. She heard me with patience but did not respond. Nothing, however, happened and no industry was nationalized. Heaven only knows whether or not the rumour had any basis.

Barring one or two occasions when he really got annoyed with me,

Sanjay showed a lot of respect for me and my views. In spite of his many whims, Sanjay was a good friend. He would show a lot of tolerance towards me. Throughout my association with him, he remained a steadfast friend. His sad and sudden demise was a personal loss to me.

26

Rajiv Enters Politics

After Sanjay's death, I continued to be in Delhi for some time and called on Indira-ji many times. After the first shock was over and Indira-ji had settled down, she consulted me in a general way about Sanjay's estate duty, and also posed a few queries on related matters. I answered them to the best of my ability, telling her at the same time that I was no expert on the subject. She then asked for my advice on certain specific matters. I told her that though broadly I knew about matters concerning income tax and estate duty, I would study the matter referred to by her and then advise her. That I did.

About a fortnight after Sanjay's death, during one of my meetings with Indira-ji, I broached the subject of persuading Rajiv to give up his career as a pilot in the Indian Airlines and enter politics. It was generally said that Rajiv was reluctant to give up his occupation and join politics. I told Indira-ji that after having lost one son in an air crash it was necessary that Rajiv be withdrawn from the hazardous profession of flying. Indira-ji agreed with me but said that Rajiv's heart was in flying and that he was reluctant to give it up. I was amazed when I heard that. The future post of prime minister was assured for Indira-ji's son and Jawaharlal-ji's grandson. Whereas people fight for power and position, here was a man, I said to myself, who cared nothing for the august position of prime minister!

I asked Indira-ji whether I could have a talk with Rajiv. She replied that she had already asked many of her friends to speak to Rajiv and persuade him to give up his job in the Indian Airlines and join politics. She said I too should have a talk with Rajiv. I agreed to meet Rajiv and discuss the matter with him. But as I did not know Rajiv and as I assumed he knew nothing about me, I suggested to Indira-ji that before I met him she might brief Rajiv about my relationship with her. She agreed to do so and advised me to meet Rajiv after a couple of days so that, in the meantime, she would have the opportunity of talking to him about me.

I met Rajiv after two or three days, my first formal meeting with him. Earlier, once when I was sitting with Sanjay both Rajiv and Sonia-ji happened to drop in. Sanjay had then introduced me to them. Apart from exchanging pleasantries, no discussion took place at that brief meeting and after speaking to Sanjay for a few minutes, they left.

My meeting with Rajiv lasted about fifteen minutes. After a little casual talk, I told him about my friendship with Indira-ji. I explained to him how for me she was like a family elder and how she always showed me considerable warmth and consideration.

After prefacing my conversation thus, I said that as I considered myself to be like a member of the family, I thought I should urge him to give up the profession of a pilot and take to assisting his mother in politics. Rajiv showed me great respect and courtesy. He said that many other people had given him the same advice and that he was seriously considering the suggestion. I thought that was a good beginning for the first meeting. I was highly impressed by Rajiv. I found him to be a man of great charm and magnetism. The impression he created was that of a thorough gentleman, a man of character and rectitude. I felt he was a man of great promise and that if he could be persuaded to join politics, the future of the country was assured.

The first meeting made apparent the one big difference between Rajiv and Sanjay. To Sanjay, the end justified the means. Not so with Rajiv. Thus if family planning was good and essential, according to Sanjay, it did not matter if force had to be used to introduce it effectively. On the contrary, the image that I formed of Rajiv after my first meeting, which was confirmed further by my subsequent association with him, was that for him even where ends were justified, the means adopted to achieve them too had to be noble. This in fact is what our scriptures and saints teach.

A few days later, I met Indira-ji and told her about my meeting with Rajiv. She told me that he too had mentioned to her about our meeting. I met Rajiv a second time soon, when apart from discussing other matters I brought up the earlier subject about his entering politics. This time he appeared to be more receptive. After a few days, Indira-ji informed me in one of my meetings with her that Rajiv had agreed to give up his flying career, but only after some time. She said that his ambition was to give up flying after becoming eligible to fly an Airbus. It was good that Rajiv decided to enter politics, much to the relief of all his friends and well-wishers—in fact, much to the relief of the entire nation.

New Delhi, 1986: Rajiv Gandhi with me when he was
prime minister

Rajiv was a man of character and would tolerate honest differences. I remember an incident towards the end of 1980. The *Hindustan Times* wrote a strong editorial criticizing some government policy. Indira-ji was usually not disturbed by such editorials. She was too liberal and noble to take notice of such editorials so long as she felt that the criticism was constructive and well intentioned. But someone close to her criticized the editorial. This man telephoned me and said that such an editorial should not have appeared in our paper. I did not enter into any argument with the gentleman. I knew that some of the people surrounding Indira-ji were sycophants and it was no use arguing with them. However, during one of my meetings with Rajiv I raised the matter with him. I explained to him that the policy of the paper was to offer constructive and critical support to Indira-ji's government. I said if the paper never criticized the government even when, in its opinion, such criticism became necessary, it would be regarded as a mere mouthpiece of the establishment. I told Rajiv that was not the way that I desired to run the paper; I added that such a policy of the paper would also not help Indira-ji as any paper which deferentially toed the government's line was bound to lose credibility. Rajiv fully appreciated my viewpoint. He told me very categorically that he did not like sycophancy himself and that the paper would be able to play its proper role only when it took an impartial view of things. I then sought his permission to refer his views to the gentlemen who had found fault with the editorial. Rajiv had no objection to my doing so. This shows how, unlike those who cannot stand criticism, Rajiv was tolerant of the views of others. He was truly a broad-minded person.

Unlike Sanjay, Rajiv did not have strong likes and dislikes. He was a fair-minded person. Thus, if even a friend made a mistake, he had, in Rajiv's view, to be accountable for it. There is a saying in Hindi that a good ruler should ensure that a lion and goat could drink water together on the same bank of a river. This applied to Rajiv to a great extent. He would not unduly protect a friend who was guilty of misdemeanour; likewise he did not like to persecute or harass a foe for the pleasure of it.

After the 1980 elections, Indira-ji designated me a member of the National Integration Council. It was the first time that any businessman was made a member of this prestigious body. It appears, when the question of reconstituting the National Integration Council arose, she asked Bhishma Narain Singh, the minister for parliamentary affairs, to suggest nominations to the Council. Indira-ji also suggested that businessmen too should be associated with the august body. Whether she suggested my name or whether Bhishma Babu did so, I do not know. But both J.R.D. Tata and I were nominated to the Council. When I went to thank her, she only said that she thought that I would prove to be a good choice and so she had included my name in the reconstituted Council. I was also nominated to the Asian Games Committee; that too was done at Indira-ji's instance.

Around the same time, some high-ups told me that Indira-ji wanted me to join the board of directors of the Reserve Bank. I thought that, considering my age and the status I enjoyed in society, and in view of the trust and warmth that I enjoyed from Indira-ji which, I believe, was well known to all including the bureaucracy, this position was not what I should aspire to achieve. I had been a director of the State Bank of India and of ICICI for a number of years in my younger days. I was on the Central Advisory Council of Industries and on the Board of Trade too for quite some time. I had also served on the governing body of the Council for Scientific and Industrial Research (CSIR) for a number of years. The prime minister was the chairman of that body. In fact, many people including members of the bureaucracy who had problems, often approached me to put in a word to the prime minister on their behalf, and where I felt that some injustice was being done, I would intercede on their behalf. Directorship of the Reserve Bank of India, therefore, appeared to me to be below my status.

I then heard that there was also talk about nominating my nephew, Aditya Vikram, to the body. I thought him to be eminently fit for such a nomination. I met Indira-ji and told her that for me the mere thought that I enjoyed her trust, confidence and warmth was ample reward. Indira-ji was keen that I join the board of the Reserve Bank, but when I explained to her my viewpoint she agreed with me. The idea of nominating me on the board was, therefore, dropped and Aditya was made a director.

Sometime in 1976, Sanjay had mentioned to me that his mother had asked him to sound me out whether I would be interested in accepting the Padma Bhushan award. I declined the offer. Sanjay was amazed. I explained that I was not enamoured of titles. That apart, I said that I considered Padma Bhushan too insignificant an honour to be attracted by it. Sanjay reported my views to his mother. He thought that if a higher award was offered to me, I will accept it. He, therefore, came back and suggested that I could accept Padma Bhushan initially, and after a year or two he would arrange for the award of Padma Vibhushan to be conferred on me. That also I declined. I explained to Sanjay that my father was awarded Padma Vibhushan a few years back. For me to receive the same award and be equated with father, I explained, would be an act of disrespect on my part to father. I, therefore, asked Sanjay to convey my thanks to his mother but to excuse me from accepting the honour.

In April 1980, a shocking incident happened when someone attacked Indira-ji with a knife. On 15 April 1980, I wrote to Indira-ji expressing my concern to which I got a reply dated 24 April 1980 from her. The text of both these letters is reproduced here:

15th April 1980

My dear Smt Indira-ji,
I was shocked to read in the papers about the dastardly attack that someone attempted on you. I do not know whether it was a well-planned conspiracy or whether it was merely a thoughtless act of a lunatic. Be that as it may, it was a matter of great relief that you were not hurt.

The country needs your wise leadership for years to come and I join the rest of the countrymen in tendering our gratitude to the Almighty for having protected you.

Kind regards

Yours sincerely,
K.K. Birla

24 April 1980

Dear Shri Birla,
I appreciate your message of concern at the recent knife throwing incident. Thank you for your good wishes.

Yours sincerely,
Indira Gandhi

Indira-ji would often call me to dinners which were hosted by her in honour of some foreign dignitary. When the British Prime Minister Mrs Margaret Thatcher came to India on 29 September 1982, Indira-ji was kind enough to invite me to dinner which she had hosted for Mrs Thatcher. All the guests arrived on time. After some time, Indira-ji came in with Mrs Thatcher and introduced the guests to her. A group of guests swarmed around Mrs Thatcher, and another around Indira-ji. It is not in my nature to intrude or push my way to meet a VVIP. I, therefore, remained in the background. Suddenly, Indira-ji spotted me in a corner. After exchanging a few pleasantries she asked me whether I had an opportunity to talk to Mrs Thatcher. I told her that as Mrs Thatcher was surrounded by a number of people, I did not think it proper to butt in. Indira-ji then herself took me to Mrs Thatcher and once again introduced me to her. She said that I was a member of the Birla family, which was one of the two biggest business organizations in the country in the private sector. I was somewhat taken aback by those kind words. I acknowledged her kindness by saying to Mrs Thatcher that my greatest satisfaction was that our prime minister was always kind to me and that I enjoyed her trust and confidence.

*

There was a gap of a few months after Sanjay's death before Rajiv started taking an active interest in politics. He proved to be of great assistance to his mother. Rajiv dedicated himself to the task of helping his mother to the maximum possible extent. Indira-ji gradually began leaving many tasks entirely in his care.

The Asiad or IX Asian Games was an event in which Rajiv took a lot of interest. After India had agreed to host the Asiad, there was genuine apprehension that the several sports events may not be properly organized, leading to confusion and chaos. But after the Asiad was over, there was general applause for the manner in which Rajiv organized the sports meet. Remaining in the background, he organized the entire show remarkably well. I was a member of the executive board of the Special Committee and also of the Special Organizing Committee of the Asian Games. Sardar Buta Singh was the chairman. Rajiv did not participate in any of the meetings of the committees. But everyone knew that behind the scenes, he was organizing the whole show. At every stadium and for every event, rehearsals would be held twice or thrice under Rajiv's direct supervision. Every event was planned with meticulous care and to the most minute detail, directly under his guidance. Though I did not meet Rajiv in any of the committees formed for organizing the games, I met him at some of the social functions and parties organized in connection with Asiad. At one such party held towards the end of Asiad, I congratulated him for the very fine organization that had been set up to conduct the games. Rajiv replied with his usual modesty that he was happy that things had gone off well. I had heard that, for a fortnight prior to Asiad, Rajiv worked right till 2 a.m. Once at a social function, I asked him whether that was true. He confirmed it. Later, I wrote to Rajiv congratulating him on his successful handling of the Asian Games. I also sent to him some cuttings from the foreign press, commending him for successfully organizing the Asiad. I promptly received a reply from him. The text of the letter is given below:

12 January 1983

Dear Shri Birla,
Thank you for your letter dated the 7th December 1982 about the successful completion of the Asian Games and the appreciative comments in the Foreign Press.
With best wishes,

Yours sincerely,
Rajiv Gandhi

In a similar manner, he also helped his mother in organizing the Non-Aligned Movement (NAM) meet. He accomplished that also very successfully. Remaining in the background, Rajiv would assist his mother in whatever sphere she needed his help.

His stature grew steadily. He possessed qualities of leadership and he won over his critics through his personal charm. Without being hasty, Rajiv insisted on efficiency and performance.

Gradually I came to know Rajiv fairly well. I always received the greatest courtesy and warmth from him. Knowing how busy he kept, I never sought frequent interviews with him though at our meetings he was good enough to say that I could meet him whenever I so desired.

After 1980, excepting for the Punjab imbroglio and to some extent the problems faced in Assam, our nation kept faring well in every sphere until the big tragedy struck engulfing the country in enormous gloom—the sad and cruel assassination of Indira-ji.

27

Indira-ji's Assassination

I had gone abroad in October 1984 and returned on 19 October. After a
hectic schedule abroad, I was tired and decided to take a short holiday
in Shillong, the lovely capital of Meghalaya. My wife and I reached
Shillong on the evening of 29 October. I had gone to Shillong with the
idea of spending about a fortnight there. There are beautiful drives all
around Shillong which have an invigorating effect on the health of a
person, both physical and mental.

We had spent just two days at Shillong when I got some shocking
news around 10.30 a.m. on 31 October. I was talking to my nephew
Aditya Vikram in Mumbai on some business matter. During the
conversation, Aditya told me that something had appeared on the teleprinter
about an attempt on Indira-ji's life. Aditya said that was the first flash
and that the news was yet to be confirmed. I was stunned. I went on
hoping against hope that the news would turn out to be false. But something
told me that my worst fears were likely to be confirmed.

I immediately telephoned our people in the *Hindustan Times* in Delhi.
They confirmed the news. Till then it had not been announced whether or
not Indira-ji had succumbed to the injuries caused by the bullets fired at
her. However, the *Hindustan Times* staff told me in confidence that their
information was that Indira-ji was no more. They said it in a very guarded
manner but there was no mistaking the fact that they appeared to be sure
of the news they had received.

I prepared myself for the worst. I told my wife about what I had heard
and about my worst apprehension. Both of us prayed to God for Indira-
ji's life.

My wife greatly admired Indira-ji. She had met her on a few occasions
along with me. Though Indira-ji did not know much about her, she knew
that my wife did not keep good health. Often, Indira-ji would enquire
from me about my wife's health. That such an important person like

Indira-ji should enquire about her health had always touched my wife and myself. Deep gloom descended on us.

There was no direct flight from Shillong to Delhi. I looked up the Indian Airlines timetable and found that it was impossible to catch the flight that very day for Delhi from Guwahati, which is a three-hour drive from Shillong. I, therefore, immediately sent my secretary to purchase tickets for Delhi for the next day.

We left Shillong next morning and reached Delhi by the evening. Immediately on our arrival, my wife and I went to Teenmurti Bhawan where the body of the late prime minister was kept to enable the people to pay their last respects and offer floral tributes. We placed a wreath on the body.

After that I immediately contacted the prime minister's house and informed an assistant that I would like to call on Rajiv to convey my condolences to him personally. I was advised to do so after the funeral was over.

The funeral of Indira-ji was organized on 3 November. I went to Rajghat. There were lakhs of people lined up all along the route to pay homage to their beloved leader. The arrangements were perfect. Many in the crowd were weeping unabashedly. The funeral was performed in traditional Hindu style amidst the chanting of Vedic hymns. After the funeral was over, I returned home with a heavy heart.

Soon after Indira-ji's death, the massacre of the Sikhs unfortunately commenced in Delhi, Haryana, and in several other parts of the country. It was a tragedy in which numerous innocent Sikhs were killed in the mob fury.

Soon after Pandit-ji's death, Indira-ji had emerged as the most popular leader in the country. She not only maintained the traditions set by her illustrious father but also initiated new moves in a number of other directions. Indira-ji played an important role in the country's life as well as in the arena of international politics and relations. She was very popular with all sections of the people. Women, in particular, were especially proud that one of their kind should be adorning the high post of prime minister.

Every morning, Indira-ji would meet anyone who wanted to see her at 1 Akbar Road, when people could place their problems before her. She would attend to their queries and try to help them as far as was possible. Young and old, irrespective of caste, creed and religion, barring perhaps a few fanatics, everyone loved her. Even those Sikhs who did not agree with her policy on Punjab affairs, held her in high esteem.

After her assassination, people went wild with rage and helpless Sikhs became targets of attack. In their fury, the Hindus forgot that the sins of a few cannot be blamed on an entire community. The Sikhs are a brave people with a glorious tradition. By and large they are guileless and peace-loving. There could be no graver crime than to attack innocent Sikhs, resort to arson, and commit other heinous acts against them.

When Rajiv got the news, he swung into action to control the situation. Even before the funeral took place, Rajiv who had now become the prime minister, moved against all those who indulged in violence. He took command of the situation and started giving directions to scotch the disturbances. He sent word to all the chief ministers to maintain law and order at any cost and personally went round various areas in Delhi to ensure that innocent lives were not lost. The lieutenant governor of Delhi, P. Gavai, was changed. Though a good man, he had been in indifferent health and was not in a position to do justice to his onerous task. The situation demanded that a more dynamic person be put in charge. That was precisely what Rajiv did. He appointed M.M.K. Wali as the new lieutenant governor. It was only owing to the supreme efforts made by Rajiv that the situation was brought under control and normalcy restored.

After Indira-ji's funeral, I wanted to make a condolence call on Rajiv. Accordingly, I made a request to the prime minister's house. One day, late in the evening, my telephone rang. Someone said that he was speaking from the prime minister's house and asked me whether I had sought an appointment to call on the new prime minister. I replied in the affirmative. I was asked how long I would take with the prime minister. That, I thought, was a curious question. I told the caller that it was a condolence call and should not take more than a few minutes. I was asked to reach Akbar Road the next day at an indicated time.

I went to the prime minister's house the next day. Security had by then been tightened very rigorously. Metal detectors had been installed. I was permitted to go inside the house after a thorough search. There was a large crowd there. Some persons were going in and some coming out, after meeting Rajiv. I went to a room as directed. There were about eight or ten persons standing there. Rajiv was also in the room. He talked with each person for a few minutes. When Rajiv came to me, I offered him my condolences.

During the brief meeting, Rajiv sought my cooperation in two directions. One was that I speak to the editors of our papers—*Hindustan Times* and *Hindustan*—that no news should be published which could fan bitterness between the Hindus and the Sikhs. Rajiv said that he was against suppression of news, but felt that a certain amount of restraint had to be exercised by newspapers at that juncture when feelings ran high. I readily agreed with his suggestion. The other request was that for some time we publish a mid-day edition of *Hindustan Times*. He said that all sorts of rumours were being spread, causing panic amongst the people. If the mid-day edition could be brought out, that would go a long way, he said, in restoring peace and confidence by scotching rumours. I pointed out to Rajiv that we had an evening edition which came out around 5 p.m. and asked him whether any other edition was needed. Rajiv said that he was aware of the evening edition, but what he wanted was that *Hindustan Times* bring out one more edition around 2 p.m. I assured him that we would do that.

On returning home, I immediately called the editor and other executives of the paper over to Birla House and told them about my conversation with the prime minister. They told me that owing to continued arson and violence in and around Delhi, attendance was as low as 20 per cent of the normal attendance, and that bringing out a mid-day edition of the paper in addition to the evening edition would pose serious problems. I told my people that I knew of their difficulties but I had no heart to tell the prime minister about our problems, particularly as he was making vigorous efforts to quell the disturbances. I, therefore, urged all my executives to strengthen the hands of the new prime minister by bringing out a mid-day edition of the paper. My staff was inspired by the prime minister's efforts to restore peace in the capital, and all rose to the occasion in spite of the difficulties. From the next day itself, the mid-day edition came out. I sent a copy specially marked for Rajiv, and got a message from his secretary that he was happy that the needful had been done.

*

Indira-ji was a very gentle-hearted lady. She was deeply moved whenever any part of the country was hit by natural calamity. Once Morvi town and a village called Lilapur in Rajkot, Gujarat, were affected by floods. Indira-ji immediately issued an appeal for donations to help the inhabitants of the flooded areas.

In response to her call, I asked the management of the *Hindustan Times* to start a fund for the relief of these areas. I asked the management to contribute handsomely and to appeal to readers to send liberal donations to this fund. This was done and we were able to collect Rs 2 lakh. As chairman of *Hindustan Times,* I sent a cheque for this amount to Indira-ji. She was quick to acknowledge the letter and wrote thanking me for the donation. A copy of her letter is given below:

16 June 1980

Dear Shri Birla,

Thank you for your cheque for Rs 2,00,010.40 p for the rehabilitation of the flood-hit people of Morvi Town and Lilapur Village in Rajkot. I am sure this donation will be greatly appreciated by the people of Gujarat.

Yours sincerely,
Indira Gandhi

Once I told Indira-ji that knowing of my close relationship with her, my daughters and sons-in-law were keen to meet her along with my wife and myself. I asked her, considering she always had a tight schedule, if that was possible. She immediately agreed and gave instructions then and there to Dhawan to fix an appointment for all of us to call on her. This we did. Indira-ji was very kind to all of us. Tea was served and Indira-ji talked with everyone for a few minutes much to the delight of my daughters and their husbands.

Once I received some unusually large *langra* mangoes from a farm very close to our sugar mills. I sent a few of them to Indira-ji. She was surprised to see such huge mangoes and immediately wrote to me, saying how delicious they were. The text of her letter is given below:

17 July 1982

Dear Shri Birla,

Thank you for the Langras.

I ate one last evening. It was quite the most delicious I have had this year.

Yours sincerely,
Indira Gandhi

When Sanjay's son, Varun, was born, I was abroad. I immediately sent a cable of congratulations to Indira-ji. There was an equally immediate response from her saying how thrilled the entire family was with the arrival of the newest member of the family. The letter is given below:

17 March 1980

Dear Shri Birla,

Thank you for your cable of good wishes on the birth of my grandson.

We are all thrilled with the newest member of the family.

With good wishes,

Yours sincerely,
Indira Gandhi

Indira-ji was full of tact. She had a very subtle way of doing things.

After her electoral victory in 1980, she wanted to make the National Integration Council somewhat more active. She also desired that I should be taken in as a member of the Council. I had not become a member of Parliament then. Indira-ji thought that to include only me in the Council might give rise to criticism. If a businessman for whom she had a liking was to be included in the Council, tact demanded that there should be at least one more businessman so that no one could say that she had shown favour to one particular industrialist. Accordingly, J.R.D. Tata was also invited to join the Council.

Indira-ji, however, had no great fancy for JRD, though she had respect for the House of Tatas. JRD, too, though he might have supported the government as a matter of prudence, was no admirer of Indira-ji. He had admitted so in his book and in his interview published in the *Illustrated Weekly of India*. The coolness perhaps was mutual.

I have always held JRD in high esteem. Both of us were members of the Central Advisory Council of Industries for a number of years. We often differed in our approaches to problems. Though JRD did not like my differing with him, he was good enough to tolerate it. But, in spite of such differences, the relationship between us was cordial. On two occasions we also played bridge at the house of S. Mulgaonkar, a former editor of the *Hindustan Times*.

JRD was a sport. When my acquaintance with him deepened, he asked me not to address him as Mr Tata but call him simply Jeh (abbreviation for Jehangir—his first name). I felt embarrassed and said that as he was much senior to me both in age and position, I would rather address him properly than only by his first name. But he insisted on my calling him

Jeh and since then I addressed him in this way both in conversation and correspondence.

Both JRD and I attended the first meeting of the National Integration Council. Our seats also were side by side. Indira-ji, who was the chairperson of the Council, presided over the meeting. The meeting started in the morning and went on till 9 or 10 p.m. It is remarkable that Indira-ji sat throughout the meeting; she conducted it with great aplomb. Everyone was given an opportunity to speak. She would call the speakers one by one. Suddenly she called on me to speak and said: 'Mr Birla, I believe you have some other engagement and would like to leave early.' I caught the hint and spoke. There is no doubt that JRD, being much senior to me from every consideration, should have been given an opportunity to speak before I was called upon to do so. And yet I was asked to speak first. This was nothing but showing indifference to JRD, who was given his chance to speak quite late in the afternoon.

I realized how subtle Indira-ji could be when the situation demanded. But she could be very blunt too; her repartees in Parliament while answering the Opposition were, on many an occasion, devastating.

When Nani Palkhivala, who too was a friend of mine, became active during the Janata regime, Indira-ji got a shock. Palkhivala was one of the best legal brains of the country. He was very close to the house of Tatas. In all legal matters, the Tatas were guided by his advice. He was also a very upright person. He was clearly on the side of the Janata government. At one time, there was talk of his being offered a ministerial post, but later he was made the ambassador of India to the United States. Indira-ji thought that she had been betrayed by the house of Tatas.

During the Emergency, the *Indian Express* was very critical of the government's policy. Vidya Charan Shukla was the minister for information and broadcasting. Messages were sent many times to Ramnath-ji and/or his son Bhagwan not to contravene the directions of the government and the paper was instructed to remain within the Emergency guidelines stipulated for newspapers. At one time, it even appeared as if the government would take drastic action against the paper. The powers of the government during the Emergency were boundless. Later, an informal understanding was arrived at, in which I played no mean part. As mentioned earlier, it was agreed that the chairman of the company would be someone acceptable to both the government and Ramnath-ji. My name as the chairman was then proposed by Ramnath-ji and accepted by the government.

Before the understanding was reached, many persons had suggested to Indira-ji that Ramnath-ji be put behind bars under MISA. Some high-ups had also made similar suggestions to Indira-ji. I then thought it proper to meet Indira-ji. I told her that Ramnath-ji was a family friend and that some solution other than putting him under MISA should be devised. The commendable fact was that in spite of the pressure put on Indira-ji by many of her advisers to arrest Ramnath-ji, she steadfastly resisted it. Indira-ji was a kind hearted person and even where politically she differed with anyone, she would endeavour to keep personal relations cordial. Ramnath-ji was not arrested.

*

After Indira-ji's assassination and when the period of mourning was over, Rajiv started functioning as the full-fledged prime minister. His first aim and task was to hold the general elections, which were due to be held before the first week of January 1985. Rajiv did not consider it prudent to keep people guessing about when the elections would be held. He, therefore, announced elections between 24 and 27 December 1984.

Rajiv worked tirelessly for the success of the Congress (I) in the elections. He travelled throughout the length and breadth of the country much in the same way as his mother had done in earlier years. He toured the majority of the constituencies and worked non-stop.

The Congress (I), as expected, was returned to power with an overwhelming majority. It was a landslide victory for Rajiv Gandhi and the party. Whereas Indira-ji's name and martyrdom undoubtedly played a very important role in the victory of the Congress (I), it has to be simultaneously appreciated that the Indian voter is very mature. Sentiments, no doubt, played a significant role in the elections, but the electors also had to see in whose hands they were entrusting, for the next five years, the destiny of the country fraught with problems. In the short period that Rajiv had functioned as prime minister, the elector had seen him show promise of his abilities, and had arrived at the conclusion that if there was anyone who could keep the country intact and lead it along the path of progress and prosperity, it was only Rajiv.

Rajiv emerged as a mature statesman within a short period, even though he was quite young. He showed commendable qualities. He had a modern outlook and abhorred underhand practices.

After the general elections in 1985, Rajiv applied his mind to eradicating corruption in public life. He thought he should make a beginning in the political sphere where unfortunately many members, particularly of the state Assemblies, would resort to political horse-trading. Hence the currency of the words 'Ayaram' and 'Gayaram'. Rajiv thought that if corruption had to be eradicated, a beginning had to be made by cleansing the country's political life. Thus, soon after elections, he introduced the Anti-Defection Bill.

What was highly commendable was that he consulted the Opposition before bringing in the bill, and accepted many of their suggestions. Rajiv, however, did not want to take any chances and sent word to all the party MPs not to leave Delhi even if there was a pressing need so that the bill could be passed smoothly. I had won the election to the Rajya Sabha as an independent MP, supported by the Congress (I). H.K.L. Bhagat, then minister for parliamentary affairs, requested me to be present in Delhi, if possible. There was a wedding in the family but in view of the importance of the matter I stayed back in Delhi until the bill was passed. As a result of Rajiv's effort, the bill was in fact passed unanimously, a creditable and rare achievement. An endeavour was made for the first time to eradicate corruption that had crept into our political life.

Another very wise step undertaken in the domestic sphere was the Ganga project to free the Ganga of pollution. This project was viewed as good from all angles. The name Ganga has a tremendous evocative hold on the Indian mind in general and the Hindu mind in particular. Uttering the name makes the devout Hindu conjure up hallowed visions of the holy river along with a belief that Mother Ganga will wash away all his sins. Making Ganga pollution-free will help the entire country. The project, therefore, received universal acclaim. The expectation was that if the Ganga project succeeded, the government would sanction schemes to make other major rivers free from pollution.

Unfortunately, however, the Ganga project has not shown much success. Ganga continues to be highly polluted. Unless and until all such works of national importance receive full cooperation of the public and until there is a general awakening amongst the people that fighting pollution is as much their responsibility as it is of the government, matters cannot improve.

28

My Election to the Rajya Sabha

Sanjay Gandhi requested that I contest the Lok Sabha elections from Jhunjhunu in 1980. After I declined, he sent word to me to reconsider my decision. My mind, however, was fully made up not to stand for a Lok Sabha seat. When I met him I thanked him for offering me the Lok Sabha seat but told him to keep me in view for the Rajya Sabha election.

After Indira-ji's impressive victory in 1980, I felt that there was a good chance for me to get elected to the Rajya Sabha from Rajasthan. I had wide contacts in Rajasthan and told Sanjay so. Sanjay was equally keen to see me contest the election and promised full support. However, to review the position finally, he had asked me to meet him on 23 June 1980 at 2 p.m. That very morning, he died.

The elections to Rajya Sabha from Rajasthan were to take place on 4 July 1980. Though Indira-ji took the loss of Sanjay very courageously, I thought it would be the height of selfishness on my part to go and request her for a Rajya Sabha seat in view of the great tragedy that had taken place. There could, therefore, be no question of my talking to Indira-ji about my discussions with Sanjay during her bereavement. Many of my friends, including some VIPs from Rajasthan, pressed me to approach Indira-ji and get her approval to stand for the election. I thanked them but told them it would be very improper on my part even to broach the subject at that time. The matter was thus dropped.

After my defeat in the 1974 election, Sanjay was anxious to see me elected to Rajya Sabha at the first possible opportunity. But victory eluded me every time. Elections to the Rajya Sabha are held every two years. After my defeat in 1974, in 1976 there was no safe seat for me; in 1978 Indira-ji was out of power and so the question of my getting elected did not arise; in 1980 Sanjay unfortunately died.

The next elections to the Rajya Sabha were due in 1982. I spoke to Indira-ji sufficiently in advance and asked her if she would be prepared to give me a seat from Rajasthan. Indira-ji said that she would sound out her colleagues in the Congress Parliamentary Board and thereafter send word to the chief minister of Rajasthan. She appeared to be confident that, as her colleagues and partymen knew that I was close to her, there would be no problem in her securing the Parliamentary Board's consent to support me. With Indira-ji's support I did not anticipate any difficulty in getting either a Congress (I) ticket or at least the promise for the surplus vote of Congress (I) to be cast in my favour.

It soon became clear, however, that there was some confusion somewhere which came in the way of my getting the nomination of the Congress (I). The last date for filing the nomination papers was 19 March 1982. Till 15 March, I was given no directions as to whether or not I was to file my nomination, either as a Congress (I) nominee or as an independent supported by the Congress (I). I waited but no word came from the Congress High Command. I was greatly perplexed. On the one hand, I knew that I had Indira-ji's support to stand for the election; on the other, there were no directions for me from the party. There were, however, rumours that Chief Minister Shiv Charan Mathur was against a seat being given to me; he wanted some nominee of his own choice.

With only a day left for filing the nomination, I became restless and called on Dhawan. I explained my predicament to him and requested him to arrange a short meeting for me with Indira-ji. Dhawan told me categorically that my name had been cleared by Indira-ji and that I should proceed to Jaipur without any delay and file my nomination.

Though Dhawan spoke in all sincerity, I had a premonition that all was not well. I telephoned a few friends in Jaipur and asked them to find out how matters stood. They made enquiries from the chief minister who said that he had not received any directive concerning me. He said that he had sounded out some people in the party, but they were not happy over my name being considered. He was non-committal.

With that information I again met Dhawan and urged him to find out from the prime minister what the correct position was. Dhawan again consulted the prime minister and advised me to proceed to Jaipur forthwith and file my nomination. I was, however, very reluctant to go until I knew for certain what the actual position was. Dhawan then advised me to meet Pranab Mukherjee and discuss the matter with him.

Pranab Babu was a very powerful minister during Indira-ji's time. Among all the Cabinet ministers, he was regarded as the closest to her and was the number two person in the Cabinet. In those days, I was not close to him, though now we are good friends. I called on Pranab Babu, and he confirmed what Dhawan had said. Pranab Babu also advised me not to lose any time but to proceed immediately to Jaipur. That was around 9 p.m. on 18 March 1982. I came back to Birla House and again telephoned some of my friends in Jaipur, who in turn got in touch with the chief minister once again. He still maintained that he had not received any clear instructions in the matter. I went again to Pranab Babu. By now it was around 10 p.m. Pranab Babu once again confirmed that the prime minister desired that I should contest from Rajasthan. To me it appeared that I was being made to run from pillar to post to no avail.

At the meeting with Pranab Babu, I told him very categorically that unless I was promised definite support by the Congress (I) and the chief minister was given clear instructions to that effect I was not prepared to go to Jaipur to file my nomination. The time was now well past 10 p.m. It was too late to meet the prime minister but I took a chance and went to the residence. Fortunately, Dhawan was there. It was my third meeting with Dhawan that day. I told Dhawan frankly that till the matter became clear, I was not prepared to proceed to Jaipur to file my nomination. Dhawan repeated his earlier advice to proceed to Jaipur next morning to file my nomination. I reiterated to Dhawan that if there was any uncertainty about the party supporting my nomination, I would not like to proceed to Jaipur. I also pointed out that as I enjoyed a certain status in society, if I went to Jaipur and returned empty-handed without filing my nomination papers, that would give rise to unnecessary and unsavoury speculation, which I wanted to avoid. Dhawan then spoke to Pranab Babu over the phone in my presence and said that, in all fairness, I should be told frankly what the actual position was. Dhawan also told Pranab Babu that unless the position was made clear to me I was not prepared to go to Jaipur. After his talk with Pranab Babu, Dhawan advised me to meet Pranab Babu again.

I called again on Pranab Babu. It was now well past 11 p.m. I told him that I was not prepared to file my nomination unless a clear picture about the support from the Congress (I) to my candidature emerged. I asked him to relate to me exactly his talk with the chief minister. Pranab Babu said that the chief minister was told that for the three seats for which there was to be contest, one name was being proposed by the Centre, and that the choice of candidate for the second seat was being left to the chief minister. As regards the third seat, Pranab Babu said that he had told the chief minister that the final decision was also being left to him but that the High Command would be happy if I was nominated for this seat either as a Congress (I) candidate or as an independent candidate supported by the party. Pranab Babu said that the chief minister would surely take the hint that the High Command wanted me to be nominated for the third seat. He then advised me to proceed to Jaipur.

As I got into the car, Pranab Babu again sent for me and said that in case the chief minister had any doubt about the matter he could telephone him at Delhi when he would repeat to him what he had said to me.

I thought that was a good enough assurance. I, therefore, decided to proceed to Jaipur the next day, early in the morning. I returned home by midnight and gave instructions to my people who were waiting for me to make preparations so that we could leave for Jaipur next day early in the morning.

I snatched a few hours' sleep and left for Jaipur early the next day. I also sent word to our people in Jaipur to fix an appointment for me with the chief minister.

On reaching Jaipur, I drove straight to the chief minister's residence. I met him and enquired about the position regarding my nomination. For the first two seats, there was no problem. Regarding the third seat, he said that the matter had been left entirely to his discretion. When I apprised him of what Pranab Babu had told me, the chief minister clearly conveyed to me that it was not what he had understood from the High Command. I then requested him to talk to Pranab Babu immediately on the phone. The chief minister was reluctant to do so and did not wish to talk with anyone in Delhi about the matter. It was clear that he was backing a candidate of his own choice for the third seat. He told me clearly that he would not put through any phone call to Delhi but that in case the High Command had any instructions they could as well telephone him. Ultimately, on my pressing, he promised to have a talk with Pranab Babu. I then left for my residence in Jaipur. After an hour or so, I sent someone to meet the chief minister about the outcome of his talk with Pranab Babu. I did not think it necessary to call on him again personally. The chief minister sent a laconic reply that he could not get through to Pranab Babu.

I could have called Pranab Babu on the phone from Jaipur but after due consideration I came to the conclusion that if the chief minister was not keen on my contesting the election, it was better that I did not file my nomination. I had the unfortunate experience of the 1974 election in mind, when I got defeated purely owing to the hostile attitude of the Uttar Pradesh chief minister H.N. Bahuguna. Hence I thought if Mathur was not enthusiastic about my candidature it was better to refrain from contesting the election. So I returned to Delhi, a disappointed person.

On reaching Delhi, I called on Pranab Babu and related to him my experience. He maintained that I should have filed my nomination papers. I told him that it was not possible for me to do so because I was not prepared to contest an election with a hostile chief minister.

I could not meet Dhawan since he had gone abroad with the prime minister. I did meet him after the prime minister's return and requested him to fix an appointment with Indira-ji, which he did. I related to Indira-ji all that had transpired between the chief minister and myself. Indira-ji was genuinely sorry that I could not file my nomination. I told her that I was not prepared to do so since, without the chief minister's support for my nomination, the chances were that I might have been defeated. Indira-ji did express her surprise that the chief minister did not catch the clear hint that was given to him. I told her not to worry on my account as what had happened had become a thing of the past. However, I told her that she could keep me in mind when the elections were due again after two years.

Soon after that I met Rajiv and gave him details of what had happened. I asked him how such confusion could have arisen. Rajiv was aware that a lot of confusion had arisen over the allocation of seats. He was, however, kind enough to assure me on my request that at the next election for the Rajya Sabha to be held in 1984 he would help me.

I have known Shiv Charan Mathur since 1980. But after that experience, I felt rather sore. I am very sensitive in matters where the question of my prestige is involved. So I decided not to meet him again. I stuck to my decision and stopped meeting him even though he visited Delhi quite frequently. Shiv Charan-ji could sense that I was unhappy with him as earlier I used to meet him quite frequently. Some friends came to know about this estrangement, and spoke to him stating that the misunderstanding should not be allowed to persist. They arranged a meeting between us. I told Shiv Charan-ji that I could have stood for the Rajya Sabha election in 1982 as an independent and perhaps won. However, I decided not to stand for the election unless the chief minister was enthusiastic about my candidature, as I wanted to take no chances. Shiv Charan-ji was somewhat apologetic. He said that there was some confusion about the nomination and that he had not received clear directives. He assured me that had he received clear directions, he would have certainly helped me. Where the misunderstanding arose between Pranab Babu, who maintained that he had telephoned the chief minister and the chief minister who denied it, is anybody's guess.

The next Rajya Sabha election was due to be held in March 1984. I sought an appointment with Rajiv sufficiently in advance. In spite of his busy programme, Rajiv readily agreed to meet me. I asked him whether the Congress (I) would agree to give their surplus votes, as I desired to stand as an independent candidate supported by the party. I assured him that I was hopeful of winning the seat.

From the Opposition it was certain that either Radheshyam Murarka, an ex-MP, or his nephew, Kamal Morarka, would stand for this seat. It was going to be a tough contest but I was hopeful that, apart from the surplus votes of Congress (I), I would be able to obtain a large number of votes from the Opposition or independent members many of whom I knew. Rajiv remembered his earlier promise to support me. He also consulted his mother and at a subsequent meeting promised me the necessary support. He also agreed to speak to Shiv Charan-ji.

I remained in Delhi till the Congress Parliamentary Board met. On the day of the meeting, I was taking a walk in my garden when my bearer came running to inform me about a phone call from the prime minister's house. It was Arun Nehru, who told me that he had been asked by Rajiv to inform me that the Parliamentary Board had decided that the party would contest only two seats for the Rajya Sabha from Rajasthan, and they would cast all their surplus votes in my favour for the third seat. I felt very happy and thanked Arun Nehru. I again resumed my walk in the garden, which is a ritual with me. After a few minutes, the bearer came running again to report that there was another phone call from the prime minister's house. This time it was Rajiv himself confirming that the Parliamentary Board had decided to support me for the third seat. Rajiv, who was general secretary of the AICC, said I must win the seat, and wished me the best of luck. I thanked Rajiv profusely. Soon after that, Makhanlal Fotedar also telephoned and congratulated me and confirmed what Rajiv had said.

Two days later, I left for Jaipur. Before that I wanted to meet Rajiv to thank him personally for his support. He was busy, however, and the meeting did not materialize. I then spoke to Dhawan and told him that I desired to meet Indira-ji just to seek her good wishes. I am sentimental by nature. Some inner voice told me that if I went to Jaipur without obtaining Indira-ji's good wishes, I might not succeed in the election. I told Dhawan of my superstition and pressed him to arrange a meeting with Indira-ji even if it were a short one. Dhawan did so and Indira-ji wished me good luck. It was not a case of mere formality or courtesy. I could perceive a transparent sincerity in Indira-ji when she warmly gave me her good wishes. Of course, I had never any doubt that she was as sorry as I was over my defeat in 1974. She was genuinely happy now that the time was opportune for me to get elected to the Rajya Sabha. Her face betrayed a distinct expression of involvement in my nomination for the third seat.

I proceeded to Jaipur. On reaching Jaipur, I immediately called on Shiv Charan-ji. True to his word, he was very helpful and cooperative. For him the contest had become a prestige issue. If the Congress (I) could win all the three seats that would be a matter of pride for him and would add to his stature. He laboured hard for the victory of all the three candidates. My daughters and sons-in-law also came to Jaipur to help me win. It was a tough contest. Kamal Morarka was, I soon discovered, a formidable opponent.

All of us worked very hard, working eighteen hours a day throughout our stay in Jaipur. Apart from my daughters, sons-in-law, numerous friends and well-wishers and some executives who volunteered to work for me stationed themselves in Jaipur.

Then came the day of polling. We proceeded to the place where elections were to be held. After the formalities were over, the voting started. After the votes had been cast, the counting began. There were ups and downs. Apart from two Congress (I) candidates and myself as an independent, there was Kamal Morarka contesting on the Janata ticket. Visitors could see and hear from outside how the counting was going on. At one time, Morarka who was trailing behind took a lead over me. My second daughter, Jyotsna, who is very sentimental, got so disheartened that she withdrew to the background from the visitors' gallery. But soon I again took the lead over Morarka and reached the top of the list. When the counting was over, I was declared winner with the highest votes—53 in my favour. Shanti Pahadia, a Congress candidate, too was declared victorious. The contest then lay between Bhim Raj of Congress (I) and Morarka. I had been warned beforehand that there was danger for Bhim Raj and so had told all my supporters to cast their second preference votes for him. Had Bhim Raj been defeated, I would have regarded it as my defeat and would have submitted my resignation from the Rajya Sabha forthwith to Indira-ji. Fortunately, as a result of my second preference votes being cast in favour of Bhim Raj, he too won.

It was nothing but God's grace, Indira-ji and Rajiv's support, the good wishes of friends and the hard labour put in by the chief minister which saw me through to victory. So successful was Morarka in making inroads into the Congress (I) citadel, that had he had two more days to organize matters, he would have won and Bhim Raj, perhaps, would have lost. That would have been a sad day for me. I thanked God that both Congress (I) candidates and I won.

The chief minister sent for me as soon as the counting was over. He congratulated me, offered me a garland, sweets and tea, and expressed his happiness at my victory. He was very kind. There was great rejoicing in the Congress (I) camp.

I was surrounded by throngs of admiring crowds. My supporters vied with each other in shouting 'K.K. Birla *ki jai*' or 'K.K. Birla zindabad'. I came to my residence where a large number of people had assembled. Many had come from the villages in Jhunjhunu to greet me. There is a story behind that. Though I was defeated from Jhunjhunu in 1971, I treated the district as if it were my constituency. Under the circumstances whenever there was a drought or famine in the area, I would commence relief operations there. In Rajasthan, there is drought every three out of five years. Hence, I had an opportunity of serving the people of the Jhunjhunu constituency on several occasions. I would travel widely in the area and supervise the relief operation. Since 1971 when I stood for the Lok Sabha election, relief work was carried out in 321 villages. In these villages, 235 rooms were constructed for schools, dharmashalas, etc., seventy-two unserviceable wells were repaired, forty-six new wells dug, two big tanks were repaired and seventy mini waterworks constructed. Some culverts were also constructed and sometimes cattle were fed during the drought. That gave me an opportunity of coming in touch with a large number of people. All those people would say how sorry they were that I was defeated in the election in 1971. Hence when people came to know that I was contesting the Rajya Sabha election, they came in large numbers on the day of polling in anticipation of my victory. They all felt they were well rewarded after my victory and went back happy.

We have a very good pandit in Jaipur, a very religious man. He had blessed me for victory and had performed puja throughout the night before the polling began. Being a devout Hindu I had visited some temples also before the election and I went to these temples again to offer my prayers of thanksgiving to the presiding deities. I also visited some other places of worship.

I came back to Delhi. I was able to meet Indira-ji for a short while to thank her for her support. She congratulated me. I met Arun Nehru and Fotedar also. They were both happy at my victory and congratulated me. After the elections, I could stay only for a day in Delhi. I wanted to stay for some time more in Delhi but had to cut short my stay as all my friends and relatives were insisting that I return to Kolkata without any delay to give them and the staff and workers of our companies an opportunity to greet me on my success at the elections.

Rajiv was not in Delhi at that time; so I could not meet him. I, however, wrote to him thanking him for the support that I had received from him in winning the election. He replied to me conveying his warm greetings on my success. A copy of the letter is given below:

30 April 1984

Dear Shri K K Birla-ji,
Thank you for your letter dated the 23rd April 1984. Please accept my warm greetings on your election to the Rajya Sabha.
   With best wishes,

Yours sincerely,
Rajiv Gandhi

I met Rajiv after some time, when he personally congratulated me.

The next morning I returned to Kolkata. A large number of people from our offices, as well as admirers, friends, relations and all the members of the family had assembled at the airport to receive me with garlands and bouquets. As I was a Congress-supported candidate, many Congressmen had also come to the airport to receive me. They congratulated me on entering Parliament. Everyone was happy. That I succeeded after two defeats was a matter of great satisfaction and rejoicing for everyone.

My only regret was that my uncle BM was not alive. Father was a karmayogi and philosopher. He neither rejoiced over victory nor felt unduly dejected in defeat. But uncle had encouraged me all along in my political aspirations. He loved me like a son. At my hour of victory I missed him sorely. I had no doubt in any case that he must have felt happy in his heavenly abode at my victory. I am sure that both father and uncle showered on me their blessings from their heavenly home.

29

Correspondence with Indira-ji

Copies of some more important correspondence with Indira-ji are reproduced below which may be of interest to the readers.

1 September 1955

Dear Mr Birla,

You must have heard of the hospital founded in memory of my mother—the Kamala Nehru Hospital at Allahabad. The hospital has been doing exceedingly good work and has been expanding its activities. But for some years we have been rather anxious about the increasing deficit in the running expenses as well as the paucity of funds for urgent developmental work. I am enclosing a brief statement containing facts about the hospital and its needs.

In order to help raise funds for the hospital, Shrimati M.S. Subbalakshmi, the well-known singer, has offered to give a recital in Delhi at the time of the Industries Fair. This recital will take place on the evening of Friday the 4th November 1955 at the National Physical Laboratory auditorium in New Delhi.

We are issuing a number of donation tickets of Rs 500/- each. I shall be grateful for your co-operation in disposing of them. Please buy as many as you can, bring your friends and relatives and help to make it a successful evening.

Please let me know how many tickets you would like to have. I shall send them to you. Cheques may be forwarded to me drawn in favour of 'Kamala Nehru Memorial Hospital Fund'.

Thanking you,

Yours sincerely,
Indira Gandhi

5.9.55

My dear Smt Indira-ji,

On my return from the Continent I have just seen your kind circular dated 1st September regarding the Kamala Nehru Memorial Hospital Fund. As desired therein, I have pleasure in sending to you herewith a cheque for Rs 500/- being the cost of one donation ticket.

The ticket may please be sent to me at your convenience.

With kindest regards,

Yours sincerely,
K.K. Birla

6 September 1955

Dear Mr Birla,

Thank you very much for your cheque for Rs 500/-, for a donation ticket. The tickets are not yet ready but will be sent to you soon.

I am grateful for your prompt reply.

Yours sincerely,
Indira Gandhi

PART III

MY LATER LIFE

30

Shree Radha Krishna Temple

O ur family has constructed temples and dharmashalas in many parts of the country. My uncle, Jugalkishore, was a very devout Hindu. He constructed temples at Delhi, Patna, Kurukshetra, Vrindaban, among other places. The temple at the Banaras Hindu University was also constructed with his advice and guidance. The major cost of the construction of that temple was borne by him. Father constructed an exquisitely beautiful marble temple for Goddess Saraswati at the BITS campus at Pilani. Other members of the family too have constructed temples at many parts of the country. I have constructed one temple as well as a dharmashala at Ayodhya and the only dharmashalas at Rudraprayag and Vindhyachal. It was also my ambition to construct a temple at Kolkata, my business headquarters. I received full support and encouragement from my father and my wife towards achieving this objective.

My wife and I, therefore, commissioned a temple at Kolkata. The construction began in 1970, and took twenty-five years to complete—an unduly long time. When the work was started, the construction work was expected to take five to seven years. However, we obviously underestimated the difficulties of executing the kind of work that was involved. It took us this long as the intention was to see that the temple became an exquisite work of art and beauty, beckoning all residents and visitors as a landmark of the City of Joy.

A year or so after the work began, it became clear that the construction would take a long time to complete. We could have finished the temple earlier had we sacrificed executing some of the intricate artistry inherent in the whole architectural design. But it was my firm resolve that the aim with which we had started the construction, namely that the temple should be a model of our ancient temple architecture, should not be abandoned under any circumstances. Jagmohan Dalmiya, who is an eminent figure

A view of Radha Krishna temple in Kolkata at night

in the cricket world and who was formerly the president of the International Cricket Council, played a very significant role in the construction of the temple. By God's grace, the temple has now become a landmark of Kolkata. Some tourist guides for India published in foreign countries have started mentioning our temple as one of the must-see sights in Kolkata.

The temple was constructed with stones quarried from areas near Panna in Madhya Pradesh and the inside panelling was executed in marble.

The main temple is of Shree Radha Krishna. I have been an ardent devotee of Lord Krishna since my childhood. His teachings in the Gita have greatly fascinated and inspired me, as they did my father. I have found peace and tranquillity of mind by reading and reciting the Gita and trying to imbibe the significance of its teachings. We talk about national integration as essential for the unity of the country. National integration is possible only if there is amity amongst people of various states and different religious faiths, castes and creeds, who must become imbued with a spirit of tolerance towards each other. It is the desire to see various people intermingle and congregate in a spirit of peace and serenity that inspired me to construct the temple of Shree Radha Krishna.

The temple rises to an imposing height of 160 feet and covers an area of nearly 22,000 square feet at the base. With its shimmering sandstone exterior and marble interior the temple is regarded as an exquisite work of art, embellished with intricate patterns of carvings. The main deities are Krishna and his consort Radha, flanked on either side by Durga and Shiva. Outside, on the spacious plaza, are the temples of Ganesha and

Hanuman and the ten avatars or incarnations of Vishnu.

The construction began in 1970 and the *pran pratishtha* (ceremony of consecration of the deity) was performed on the morning of Wednesday, 21 February 1996, by Swami Chidanand-ji Maharaj. The temple was inaugurated by Dr Karan Singh, the renowned scholar and exponent of our ancient culture, heritage and philosophy. The temple objectifies the message enshrined in our religious scriptures, which I got inscribed on a marble slab near the entrance of the temple. It reads:

> On this auspicious occasion the prayer of the entire Birla Family is:
>
> May this Temple spread the message of the Vedas, Upanishads, Gita and other religious scriptures, of our saints and holy people; may it lead people along the path of piety and dedication to God;
>
> May it inculcate the script of adherence to the principles of humanitarianism, compassion towards the poor and needy, and of amity and goodwill among mankind.

My wife and my eldest daughter, Nandini Nopany, look after the daily ministrations and needs of the temple. It is estimated that 1,500 to 2,000 devotees visit the temple every day; on public holidays the number goes up to 80,000, and on special occasions like Janmashtami or the New Year the number of visitors goes up to as many as 1,25,000 devotees.

31

Rajiv Gandhi Loses the Election

Rajiv Gandhi won the general election in 1984 with an overwhelming majority. The Congress (I) got 403 seats out of 515 Lok Sabha seats where polling was held. This was a record victory for the Congress (I) and requires some comment.

Rajiv administered the country well but unfortunately during his tenure, the issue connected with kickbacks paid in the purchase of the Bofors field gun cropped up. The Opposition pounced upon it and alleged that about Rs 64 crore had been siphoned off. The needle of suspicion pointed towards Ottavio Quattrocchi, an Italian national who was reportedly very close to both Rajiv and Sonia. But in 1989, the Congress (I) suffered a humiliating defeat in the general elections and a coalition government was formed with the Janata Dal leader V.P. Singh as prime minister and the elected leader of the National Front with outside support from BJP and four Left parties. After the election many of the old faithful deserted the Congress (I) party.

During one of my meetings with Rajiv, he asked me what, according to me, was the reason for his defeat. I believe in the dictum that if an opinion is sought of a person he should speak honestly and frankly; more so if he is the opinion seeker's well-wisher. Basking in the warmth and goodwill of Indira-ji, and Rajiv, I always regarded it as my bounden duty to give what I thought was the correct picture about any matter on which my opinion was sought. Thus, when Rajiv asked me what the reason for his defeat was, I told him that the discussions on Bofors—the vociferous and well-orchestrated demonstrations by the Opposition parties in Parliament—had unfortunately sullied his image, and that was the only reason for his defeat. I also told Rajiv that I had absolutely no doubt that all the rumours that were being spread were trash and without any vestige of truth in them and that he was being made a target for political reasons. Rajiv was well aware of the reason but in spite of that he asked me for my view as he knew that I did not believe in flattery and sycophancy and would give him an honest diagnosis of the matter.

Rajiv then said that his impression was that all the noise that was being made by the Opposition concerning Bofors was confined to Delhi and/or the major cities which were served by newspapers. He said that 75 per cent of Indians lived in villages. Therefore, how could he lose when 75 per cent of the voters did not know much about Bofors? I told Rajiv that he was not well-informed in this regard. I said that Hindi and other Indian language newspapers were published from almost all the towns and were circulated in the villages also. Thus the propaganda about Bofors had reached the villages too and everybody felt that large sums of money had changed hands in the purchase of the guns. Thus the defeat of Congress (I) was not unexpected.

In a February 2004 judgment, a bench of the Delhi High Court completely exonerated Rajiv in the Bofors case. Rajiv was a man of noble and honourable disposition. He was a man of great integrity and rectitude. All the same, his name got sullied by the politicians and the media, much to the discomfiture and annoyance of the members of his family and his supporters in the Congress (I).

During one of my talks with Rajiv, I suggested that I would arrange dinner parties for him where I would invite journalist friends and some intellectuals to meet him. I said that I could organize such parties every month and that would give him an opportunity to disabuse the mind of these journalists about any misconception that they might have harboured in respect of Bofors. Three or four such parties were arranged in 1990. Some of the eminent people connected with the media who attended the dinners were Aveek Sarkar, proprietor of the *Telegraph*, Dilip Padgaonkar of the *Times of India*, Aroon Purie, proprietor of *India Today*, Malini Parthasarathy of the *Hindu*, Vir Sanghvi, then editor of *Sunday*, Shekhar Bhatia, then executive editor of the *Telegraph*, Girilal Jain and H.K. Dua who was at the time the editor of the *Hindustan Times*. I had also invited some other public figures and eminent leaders of the Congress (I) party, namely Dinesh Singh, Vasant Sathe, P. Chidambaram, N.K.P. Salve, P.V. Narasimha Rao, V.N. Gadgil, Madhavsinh Solanki, H.K.L. Bhagat and a few others.

Rajiv's frank talks with these eminences helped to erase some of the stigma that had got stuck to his name. In the 1991 general election, the Congress (I) did better than in 1989. Rajiv worked very hard and I had no doubt that the party would have formed the government under his leadership. However, Rajiv was assassinated in the midst of the campaign.

That was a tragic blow to the Congress (I) and the country.

People say that Rajiv's assassination generated a sympathy wave for him and helped his party. I do not subscribe to this view. The Congress (I) did better owing to the efficient leadership provided by Rajiv during this time.

I heard the following story relating to Rajiv's assassination from some reliable sources. It appears His Holiness Jagadguru Shankaracharya of Kanchi Kamakoti Peetham, Shri Chandrasekharendra Saraswati, who was called the Paramacharya, had sent word to Rajiv through a reliable source asking him not to visit Tamil Nadu for electioneering. The Paramacharya also said that if he did decide to visit the areas near Chennai, he should first visit Kanchipuram to meet the Paramacharya. Rajiv, who was a noble soul, somehow or the other did not heed the Paramacharya's advice. Perhaps this happened because he was short of time. Be that as it may, all the devotees of the Paramacharya, including myself, believe that had Rajiv got the blessings of the Paramacharya before he went to Chennai, he would have survived the bid on his life.

32

My Second Term as Elder

In April 1990, there were elections to the Rajya Sabha from several states, including Rajasthan. My term as an independent MP supported by the Congress (I) was ending. I approached Rajiv and asked him if he was satisfied with my performance and added I should be sent to the Rajya Sabha for a second term. I also told Rajiv that instead of being nominated as an independent supported by the Congress (I) I would like to be nominated for the Rajya Sabha on behalf of the Congress (I). Rajiv, much to my satisfaction, said that he appreciated my performance and would certainly like to nominate me as a Congress (I) MP.

There were, however, several other VIPs who wanted to be in the Rajya Sabha. I was aware of the fact that Rajiv had a liking for me and would, ultimately, nominate me in preference to others. All the same, Rajiv asked me what my opinion was since there were so many other important leaders who wanted to enter Parliament through the Upper House. I told Rajiv that I had fought the 1971 Lok Sabha election and during the campaign, I had felt that I was unequal to the task. My nature was such that I did not find it congenial to go round my constituency to plead for votes with folded hands. I told this to Rajiv and said I had given up the idea of fighting any Lok Sabha election after 1971 and that this fact was known to Indira-ji and Sanjay. I also told Rajiv that Indira-ji and Sanjay were keen that I should contest the Lok Sabha elections held in 1980 as a Congress (I) nominee from Jhunjhunu but I had told them of my firm resolve. Rajiv, too, was aware of this fact. All the same, he said that he would take the final decision shortly before the nomination papers were to be filed.

Meanwhile, I sought meetings with all the people who were keen to contest the the Rajya Sabha election. Most of them were my friends. I met them one by one and told them that I was aware that they were keen to get elected to the Rajya Sabha and that I, too, was keen to do the same.

I said each of us should certainly try to get nominations of the Congress (I) party. But in making these efforts we had to be careful, I said, not to create bad blood and that whoever was nominated by the Congress (I) high command should be gracefully allowed by others to stand for the election.

After a lot of discussions the Congress Working Committee/Parliamentary Board of the Congress (I) took the decision to field me as one of its nominees for the Rajya Sabha elections from Rajasthan. I went to Jaipur and filed my nomination, and there was no problem in my getting elected.

Amongst the aspirants was Nawal Kishore Sharma. When he was denied the nomination, he took it sportingly. I had talked to him earlier and he stood by his word. I had also talked to Rajesh Pilot, who was also a friend. Rajesh was one of the top leaders of the party with a large following. When I met Rajesh he said that a person of his position did not want to stand for the Rajya Sabha but would be contesting the Lok Sabha elections. In spite of that, when I was made a Congress (I) nominee he did not take it in the right spirit.

The Rajya Sabha election of 1996 had some interesting features. P.V. Narasimha Rao was the prime minister and also president of Congress (I). My second term in the Rajya Sabha had started in 1990 and was coming to an end in 1996. On the strength of its membership, the party could win only one seat in the Upper House.

I met Narasimha Rao and said that as the president of the party, it was for him to decide whom he would like to nominate for this one seat. I explained that technically I had completed only one term as a Congress (I) MP. Conventionally, a Congress (I) MP whose performance was good was allowed to serve a minimum of two terms. I told Narasimha Rao that I had regularly attended the Rajya Sabha sessions throughout the year. As for my performance as an MP, I told him that I spoke regularly on the budget, offering constructive suggestions for amendments and participated in discussions on other important matters too. Besides, I regularly put questions and sometimes also made special mentions. I also said that I had regularly attended the meetings of the party. Narasimha Rao appeared to be satisfied and he said that he would consider all these points while selecting the next nominee. The last date of filing nominations was 9 February. Narasimha Rao, who was and is a shrewd politician, said that he would make his decision known just a day or two prior to the filing of the nomination. He, however, did not reveal what was on his mind.

When only three days were left for filing the nomination, I met Narasimha Rao again and asked him what his decision was. He said that he had not yet made up his mind but would do so the next day, that is only two days before the filing of the nomination. However, he said that I should go to Jaipur and await his decision there. I told him frankly that I would not play the game which he was toying with and would not go to Jaipur unless I was nominated by him. Narasimha Rao even then would not reveal his mind. He again advised me to go to Jaipur.

When he insisted that I go to Jaipur, I concluded that he was going to nominate me. I reached Jaipur just two days before the last date for filing nomination. Next day, just a day prior to the filing of nomination, there was again kite-flying as to whom Narasimha Rao was likely to nominate. It was only late in the evening that the message came through from Narasimha Rao that he was nominating me for the seat. What followed next was simple. Accompanied by a large number of Congress (I) MLAs and other friends, I filed my nomination and was declared elected without any hassle.

33

End of My Rajya Sabha Innings

I was first elected to the Rajya Sabha from Rajasthan in March 1984 as an independent supported by the Congress (I). My term ended in April 1990. During the first few months of my first term, Indira-ji was prime minister. She greatly appreciated my standing by her when she lost the elections in 1977 and Morarji-bhai became the prime minister. After this, she started treating me like a member of the family. At the time of my second term, Rajiv Gandhi was the leader of the Congress (I) party. When the time came for fresh Rajya Sabha nominations he decided to nominate me for one of the two seats to be filled, without any hesitation.

In 1996, there was only one person to be nominated on behalf of the Congress (I) from Rajasthan. Some people opposed my name on the ground that I had completed two terms in the Rajya Sabha. There has been a convention in the Congress (I) that as far as possible a person should be nominated to a Rajya Sabha vacancy only for two terms. But there were also many exceptions to this convention. Sitaram Kesri, for example, had been nominated five times. That apart, technically I had served only one term as Congress (I) nominee; in my first term I was an independent MP supported by the Congress (I). Narasimha Rao, who was then the prime minister, was a friend of mine. I enjoyed his trust and confidence. He knew that my performance as an MP of Rajya Sabha was up to the mark. After due consideration, he nominated me in 1996.

In 2002, when elections were due again, I wondered whether I should seek renomination. The argument in favour of my seeking nomination was that I felt that I had discharged my duties as a Rajya Sabha MP honestly and sincerely. I regularly attended the Rajya Sabha sessions. When the session was on, I spent a great part of my time in the House. I meticulously followed the directions of the party. Whenever there was any whip I always followed it scrupulously. I remember when, in February 1991, my grandnephew Yash Birla's wedding was fixed in Mumbai, I had informed Yash's father, my nephew Ashok, that I would certainly attend the wedding. But an important vote came up and Rajiv sent word to me not to leave the House till the voting was over. Discipline has always played an important role in my life. It is like second nature to me. The head of my party had given a direction and I had to follow it. I telephoned Ashok and explained to him the position. I also assured him that I would take the first plane after the voting was over. I reached Bombay by a very late flight. By the time I reached Birla House at Mumbai, the venue of the wedding, I found that the ceremony was over and the reception too was more or less over. Most of the guests had left; only a handful remained. Ashok, aware of my difficulty, did not misunderstand.

Let me revert to the thoughts that were flowing in my mind as to whether or not I should endeavour to obtain nomination for the Rajya Sabha again. There were some other favourable points for my seeking renomination. I participated in the discussions in the Rajya Sabha on all occasions. I also took active part in the proceedings of the Standing Committee for Finance, of which I was a member, whenever its meetings were held in Delhi. I enjoyed the respect of all the members. Even the members of other parties held me in esteem. These were the plus points.

The points against my seeking re-election were two. First, my age: in 2002 I was eighty-four. To do justice to the job for the next six years would undoubtedly be difficult at my age. But a more important consideration was my wife's health. Manorama has never enjoyed good health. In October 1992, she had a heart attack when she was in Delhi. I was not there at that time. But she telephoned my daughter Shobhana and my son-in-law Shyam. It was owing to the immediate and timely action taken by them that Manorama could be taken to the Escorts Hospital. She recovered but her heart was slightly damaged. In December 2001 she developed atrial fibrillation, in which the pulse rate goes up and there is abnormal rhythm in the heart. This was a dreaded setback to her health. Soon after this, she collapsed one day. The attending doctor said it was a case of cardiac arrest. He massaged her heart very vigorously so that respiration could be resuscitated. By God's grace her heart revived and she recovered. When that happened, I decided not to stand for the Rajya Sabha during the next election.

After considering the pros and cons, I decided that if the party were to renominate me I would make it clear that I would not be able to attend as many meetings of the Rajya Sabha as in the past. My attendance would depend upon Manorama's health. This decision gave me great mental relief. I am a great believer in God and my feeling is that God guided me in taking this decision.

Having decided thus, I sought an appointment with Sonia-ji. That was in December 2001, more than three months before the nominations were to be filed. I always believe in frankness and honesty. I told Sonia-ji that if she decided to renominate me she should keep in mind that I was already eighty-four years old and that by the time my term came to an end I would be nearing ninety. I did not expound further. I wanted Sonia-ji to make up her mind and, in case she decided to renominate me, then only would I tell her about my attendance being dependent on my wife's health. I further told Sonia-ji that I would not meet her again before the election, adding that I did not want to create an impression that, at my age and after having completed three terms as an MP, I was still hankering for renomination.

As the time for the elections came near, various people wanting to get into the Rajya Sabha started making the necessary noises. I had informed Sonia-ji that I would not meet her but in order to keep in touch with what was happening regarding the nominations, I had asked Vir Sanghvi and my daughter Shobhana to keep in touch with Sonia-ji. Vir Sanghvi was the editor of the *Hindustan Times* and he has been a friend since his Kolkata days, when he was editing *Sunday* magazine, which was part of the *Ananda Bazar Patrika* group. I however was firm in my resolve that in case Sonia-ji did decide to renominate me, I would tell her that my attendance in the Rajya Sabha would be governed by the health of my wife.

Sonia-ji applied her mind very keenly to this problem. Ultimately, she sent for Vir and told him that, in view of the ground realities, as I had mentioned to her, it was best that I was not renominated.

There was one thought which kept crossing my mind at that time and that was that in my place my daughter, Shobhana, could be nominated. I would have felt very happy had that happened. But Shobhana, who is totally involved in the management of the *Hindustan Times,* was very clear on this point. She said that for the present she did not entertain any thought about entering the Rajya Sabha.

On 19 March 2002 after nominations for the Rajya Sabha were completed I wrote to Sonia-ji as under:

19 March 2002

My dear Smt Sonia-ji,
My term as a Member of the Rajya Sabha is coming to an end on 9th April, 2002. I shall be completing three terms. In the first term

I was elected as an Independent supported by the Congress. Two subsequent terms I won as a Congress (I) nominee. I thus had the privilege of working as an MP under the leadership provided by Indiraji, Rajiv and yourself.

Our connection with Nehru/Gandhi family goes back to 80 years. Father knew Pandit Moti Lalji since 1926. Once when he came to Kolkata, Father had invited him to tea at our house and introduced me to him. I touched his feet and received his blessings. Father was very friendly with Pandit Jawahar Lalji too. Panditji was kind to me also and on my invitation visited my Engineering company called Texmaco in Kolkata in 1950s. Panditji has also visited Pilani twice on Father's invitation. I was present on both the occasions. I was quite close to Indiraji and after the Emergency when her Government fell, I stood by her. After that our relationship got very much cemented. She treated me like a member of the family. Rajiv was always very kind to me and so are you. I do not think any other family, barring relations of Nehru–Gandhi household, has had such a long relationship with your family as our family had.

On the eve of my retiring as a Member of the Rajya Sabha I wish to convey my gratitude and my deep appreciation for all the kindness and courtesies shown to me by you.

Kind regards

Yours Sincerely
K.K. Birla

My letter of 19 March to Sonia-ji and Sonia-ji's letter dated 17 March 2002 to me crossed each other. Sonia-ji wrote to me as under:

17 March 2002

Dear Shri KK Birla

I would like to convey to you my deep appreciation of the great distinction with which you have served the Nation, Parliament and the Congress Party, during your long tenure as a member of the Rajya Sabha.

Your wisdom and ability, your expertise and experience in so many fields, have been invaluable for us, and have won you widespread respect and admiration. You brought stature and honour to the institution of Parliament with your dignified and dedicated commitment to your responsibilities.

I hope that we will continue to benefit from your wise counsel for many years to come.

With warm personal regards

Yours sincerely,
Sonia Gandhi

I replied to her on 23 March stating:

23 March 2002

My dear Smt. Sonia-ji

I am in receipt of your kind letter dated 17th March. I have to thank you for your words of appreciation on my performance as a Member of Parliament, Rajya Sabha. After having completed three terms in Rajya Sabha (18 years) I could not have expected a better gift from the party than your generously worded letter as its Chairperson. I am grateful.

After retiring from the Rajya Sabha I am shifting my headquarters to Kolkata. I shall, however, be visiting Delhi quite frequently and once in a while I shall take the opportunity of calling on you. I sincerely hope that in the next general elections the people of India will vote our party to power under your able leadership.

Indiraji treated me like a member of the family and after the emergency when I stood by her, our relationship got further strengthened. The affection and regard that I have for your family can never change.

Kind Regards

Yours Sincerely
K.K. Birla

A few days later, I met Sonia-ji. She received me very warmly and again thanked me for the services rendered by me to the party as an MP. I had a suspicion all along that there was something more to not renominating me. I had heard that Sonia-ji was determined not to give a seat again to S.B. Chavan (since deceased) who held a number of posts, including that of home minister in the Congress (I) regime or to N.K.P. Salve, who also held many posts when the Congress (I) party was in power. Her problem was that in case she declined seats to these two veterans it would have been difficult for her to accommodate me. I asked Sonia-ji as to whether what I had heard was correct. She did not deny it. I assured Sonia-ji that what she had done was the correct thing. I said that it would not have been possible for me to follow the rigorous Congress (I) regimen; had I been re-elected, perhaps after a year or two, owing to my age and my wife's health, I would have failed to perform as I did before. I also told Sonia-ji that my visits to Delhi would become less frequent but once every three or four months I would call on her. This I have been doing.

34

Educational Institutions at Pilani

The Birla Institute of Technology and Science (BITS), Pilani, is a reputed institute for higher education and is a deemed university. I have been associated with this institute ever since its inception, first as a member of the board of governors and later as its chairman.

Pilani has become a centre of education. When my father, who was born here, was a young boy of six or seven, his grandfather Shivnarayan was concerned about his education. Shivnarayan was a very charitably disposed person. It struck him that, like his grandson, many other children did not have the benefit of education. So he decided to construct a pathshala at Pilani. The pathshala started with one teacher in 1901. It is here that father and his elder brother, my uncle Rameshwardas, received their preliminary education. That is how the seed of education was sown in Pilani.

The pathshala evolved slowly and steadily into a high school in 1925 and became an intermediate college in 1929. The Birla Education Trust (BET) was founded in the same year, to start colleges to impart education in the humanities, sciences and engineering. The intermediate college developed into a degree college in 1943. In 1947, this college was raised to the level required for imparting education in postgraduate classes. In fact three colleges were started to impart education: art and science; commerce and pharmacy; and general.

Father was a man of clear vision and he thought it best to separate all the colleges from the other faculties and make them part of a separate institute. That is how BITS was founded in 1964.

Father's ambition was to make BITS one of the premier institutes in the country. It was clear that it would not be possible to do so by changing or modifying the then existing colleges. What was needed was a new campus where the buildings and various wings of the institute could be constructed on a planned basis. A large area of land was, therefore, acquired at Pilani and a multi-structural blueprint drawn up by the best architects. BITS came up in this area with all modern facilities. As soon as one enters BITS campus one is highly impressed by the majestic beauty of the layout, the modern hostels and the very imposing building for the institute itself.

I was helping father even before BITS was established and when BET was running the engineering college. When BITS was born in 1964, I was taken on the board of governors from the very first day. While all decisions were taken by the board of governors under father's chairmanship, the detailed management of the institute father entrusted to me.

From the very beginning, we decided not to seek any help from the Central or state governments or the University Grants Commission for recurring expenses so that there could never be interference in the functioning of BITS by any of these authorities. The institute accepts only special aid earmarked for special purposes. Thus it is a wholly privately financed and owned institute, fully residential, admitting both boys and girls. There are separate hostels for the girls.

The primary objectives of the institute are to provide for or otherwise promote education and research in the fields of technology, science, humanities, industry, business and public administration and to collate and disseminate effective ideas, methods, techniques and information as are likely to promote the material and industrial growth and welfare of India and also to train young able and eager men and women to create and put into operation such ideas, methods, techniques and information as are necessary for the purpose.

The institute was registered as a society on 13 May 1964. Subsequently, by notification in the Gazette of India dated 27 June 1964, the ministry of education declared that the institute being an institution for higher education should be treated as a deemed university. This institute started functioning with effect from 1 July 1964 with father as its chairman.

A public school was also established in Pilani. My brother Basant Kumar and I had been assisting father in running BET, including the colleges, from the time it was established. The admission process for BITS Pilani and Goa campuses commences in January every year and about 1400 students are admitted annually. BITS has acquired such name and fame that for these 1400 admissions the number of applicants who write the admission test runs into about 70,000. The BITS admission test, known as BITSAT, is a unique online computer-based test which is spread over a period of 35 days and the candidate has a choice of specifying his centre and also the date. The system is fully transparent and the score is displayed to the candidate soon after the test. The system of admission is totally merit-based, the merit being decided on the score obtained by the candidate in the BITSAT. Such is the demand for admission that I get requests from very high-ups, including ministers, for admission of their relatives and wards at BITS. I also receive numerous letters at that time. I give them only one reply: there is no quota for the management of the institute and that all admissions are strictly on merit.

Once R.K. Dhawan sent for me. Dhawan's designation was special assistant to the prime minister but Indira-ji had so much confidence in him that he became more powerful than any minister. I went to the prime minister's office and met him. Dhirendra Brahmachari, who used to teach

Pilani, early 1950s: Indira Gandhi at BITS during her visit with Jawaharlal Nehru

yogic exercises to Indira-ji, was with Dhawan. I knew Dhirendra Brahmachari very well. They said that the prime minister wanted two students to be admitted at BITS. I explained the position to Dhawan and expressed my helplessness in the matter. Dhawan said that I as the chairman should have some seats at my disposal—a sort of discretionary quota. Dhirendra Brahmachari supported Dhawan vociferously, declaring that it was unthinkable that the chairman of an institute should not have any seats at his disposal to fill according to his discretion. I felt it was fruitless to discuss this matter as they were only carrying out directions given to them by the prime minister. I requested Dhawan to fix an appointment for me with Indira-ji to allow me to explain the position to her. The appointment was fixed at a short notice and I called on Indira-ji. I explained the position to Indira-ji, who appreciated it but asked me an exploratory question—can nothing be done in the matter? I said: 'Indira-ji, there is a simple solution provided you accept it.' I told her that I was prepared to place five seats at the disposal of the prime minister. These could be regarded as the prime minister's quota. My only stipulation for this quota would be that the recommended person should not have obtained less than a certain percentage of marks, say 70 per cent. On this basis, five students would be accepted. At the same time I also said: 'Indira-ji, for these five seats you will receive 500 requests for admission.' Indira-ji smiled and said that I was a clever man to have passed the buck to her.

Apart from engineering subjects, higher degrees are offered in biological sciences, chemistry, economics, English, mathematics, physics and management. What is known as MBA in other institutes is known as MMS at Pilani.

Education is the most important single factor in achieving rapid economic development and technological progress and in creating a social order founded on the values of freedom, social justice and equal opportunity. Programmes of education are the basis of efforts to forge bonds of common citizenship, to harness the energies of the people, and to develop the natural and human resources of every part of the country. What one sees in BITS today is the dream come true of my father and founder chairman Ghanshyam Das Birla, who was a visionary.

The aim of education is not merely to impart knowledge but also to instil appropriate habits of thought and action, inculcating in students at the same time a sense of social responsibility. According to Dr S. Radhakrishnan, in order to complete this training, education must be humane; it must include not only the training of the intellect but also the refinement of the heart and the discipline of the mind and spirit. Our effort at BITS, Pilani, is to ensure harmoniously blended development of the students' physical, intellectual, aesthetic, social and spiritual powers and not merely to impart theoretical knowledge and skills. Our efforts are in conformity with the aims and functions of education as universally visualized.

In the early days of its expansion BITS, Pilani, had an active collaboration with Massachusetts Institute of Technology (MIT), Boston. Faculty members from both institutes used to visit each other's campus for training and exchange of ideas. BITS adopted all the best traits of the American system of education, namely, semester system, modular and flexible curriculum, continuous and internal evaluation and university–

industry linkages. BITS, Pilani, also developed many unique features like dual degree, practice school for all disciplines and off-campus distance-learning programmes. The practice school programme emphasizes the need for integrating theory and practice. We have our students undergoing practice school work in France, Italy, Germany and the United States.

It is as the result of the high level of technical education which is being imparted by IITs and IIMs and private institutes like BITS that there is keenness on the part of various foreign companies in the US, UK, etc., to outsource their requirements. India is their first choice for such outsourcing. This will lead to a big increase in the employment opportunities for our educated youth and this is certainly a matter of pride for the country. Such outsourcing will also benefit the foreign countries if their final products become cheaper. If the cost of the final product is lower, that will lead to increased demand. Those states in the United States which are clamouring for a ban on outsourcing are taking a very short-sighted view of the matter. Today, BITS is the only university in India which runs these programmes successfully. Based on the success of our interaction with industries through our practice school programmes, BITS, Pilani, also ventured into participation in human resource development programmes of the corporate sector through off-campus collaborative and distance learning programmes. We started with just fifty students in 1989 and today we have about 8,000 students in this programme.

After I became chairman of the institute, I realized the need to accommodate many more aspiring good students. I realized that this was very important for our national development. Five years ago, we decided to increase the total number of students at BITS Pilani, from 2,500 to 4,000 and we have allocated about Rs 30 crore from our own funds for this expansion plan. Today, we have a strength of 4,000 students. BITS is bigger than any IIT. As a part of the expansion plan, we have built an extensive library complex which is probably the biggest in any university in India. The building of the library was planned on the model of Rajasthani architecture. It is one of the prettiest buildings of its time. We have also networked the entire campus so that internet and other communication facilities are available for each student in his or her room as well as each faculty member in his house. This computer connect is done jointly by the institute and by the contribution of an innovative project—'BITS-Connect'—by a large number of alumni of BITS from the United States.

In 2000, we decided to establish a campus in Dubai. It was essential to promote our education abroad and also to help the people in the Gulf

Goa, 5 May 2006: Prime Minister Manmohan Singh
inaugurates the new BITS campus

area. Since Dubai has a large population of Indian expatriates, it enables
them to have access to good education. We run three engineering degree
programmes in Dubai and plan to add a few more programmes in the
coming years. At present, we have about 500 students there and we hope
this number will double in the near future.

Some time in 2001, we had also planned to have a campus in Goa to
replicate BITS, Pilani. This has been built in an area of about 180 acres
of land leased by Zuari Industries, a company in our group, at a nominal
lease rent and this campus will have an annual intake of 600 students. It
is one of the most modern state-of-the-art institutes. The entire institute,
including the classrooms, are air-conditioned. This is an over Rs 100 crore
project. The Goa campus started functioning in 2004. Its formal inauguration
was done by Prime Minister Manmohan Singh on 5 May 2006. Construction
work on a campus at Hyderabad has also commenced. This campus too
will have a capacity of 2,500 students. Admissions will start in July 2008.
All this has been financed by us without any government aid.

We have come a long way in our contribution to the educational
development in India since 1964. Today we enjoy an excellent reputation
and when various magazines from time to time write about educational
institutes there is always special mention of BITS. These magazines also
say that BITS ranks at par with IITs. While this gives us a good brand
image, we are sure that we have to do much more to enable our

contributions to have everlasting impact on national development. We have a committed faculty and motivated students. I am glad to state that in the educational atmosphere prevailing at BITS, Pilani, our students are disciplined and give us full cooperation. Our students also take part in various cultural activities which is a matter of satisfaction to us.

Such is the reputation of BITS that before the boys graduate, a large number of people from both the public and private corporate sectors visit Pilani and slot about 95 per cent of the students in suitable positions through campus selection. All important business houses in the private sector send their talent scouts to BITS.

35

Kanchi Mutt Honours Me

The Kamakoti Peetham at Kanchipuram is a very honoured seat of the ancient tradition of the Shankaracharyas. Shri Adi Shankaracharya was considered a divinity. He was one of the ablest and most astute brains ever born on this earth. Born in 509 BC, Adi Shankaracharya is regarded by Hindus as an incarnation of Lord Shiva. He travelled throughout the country and founded four main mutts or seats of learning in the four corners of India, namely, Sarada Peetham at Sringeri in the south, Jyotir Mutt near Badrinath in the Himalayan region in the north, Govardhan Mutt at Puri in the east, and Dwaraka Mutt in Gujarat in the west. After establishing the four mutts, Adi Shankaracharya came to Kanchipuram, established the Kanchi Kamakoti Peetham in 482 BC and himself presided over this mutt. He attained 'samadhi' at Kanchipuram in 477 BC at the young age of thirty-two. Though Adi Shankaracharya had established only four mutts, the Kanchi Kamakoti Peetham enjoys the same importance as the other mutts. Shri Shankaracharya of this mutt has the same status as those of the other mutts established by Adi Shankaracharya.

Before the present Shankaracharyas, the Shankaracharya at Kamakoti Peetham was His Holiness Shri Chandrasekharendra Saraswati. He was a very holy person, regarded by many as a 'living God'. People say that Adi Shankaracharya was the incarnation of Lord Shiva and His Holiness Shri Chandrasekharendra Saraswati was an incarnation of Adi Shankaracharya. I had the good fortune of having darshan of Shri Chandrasekharendra Saraswati on several occasions. Whenever I went to him I always felt like I was in the midst of an atmosphere of bliss, peace and holiness. I felt as though I was in a state of ecstasy, feeling the divine presence of a supreme power all around holding me in a trance.

There are at present two Shankaracharyas at Kanchi Mutt—His Holiness Shri Jayendra Saraswati and His Holiness Shri Sankara

Vijayendra Saraswati. Shri Jayendra Saraswati however is the main Shankaracharya.

All the Shankaracharyas are held in high esteem. They are all scholars of Sanskrit and of the sacred texts.

The present Shankaracharyas of the Kanchi Mutt—Shri Jayendra Saraswati and Shri Sankara Vijayendra Saraswati—happened to be at Haridwar in August 1997. The director of BITS then was Dr S. Venkateswaran. (The designation of the director has been changed to vice chancellor. Likewise, my designation of chairman has been changed to that of chancellor.) When Venkateswaran came to know about the Shankaracharyas being at Haridwar, he went there and invited them to visit Pilani. The two Shankaracharyas came to Pilani in November 1997. They stayed there for a few days and were impressed by the role played by the institute in spreading higher education. The Shankaracharyas were also happy to learn of the high reputation that BITS enjoyed and to know that BITS alumni held several high posts in government and industry. The two Shankaracharyas also felt elated to know that a large number of alumni of BITS have settled in foreign countries where they were spreading the name of the institute.

Some time later, the Shankaracharyas sent word to Dr Venkateswaran that they desired to confer some honour on me. Dr Venkateswaran spoke to me and said that the Shankaracharyas had mentioned that in case I found it difficult to visit Kanchi Mutt they were prepared to go to Chennai and confer the title on me there. I told Venkateswaran that there was no question of their Holinesses going to Chennai just to confer this title on me. I would myself go to Kanchi Mutt, I said, to receive the blessings of the Shankaracharya. Accordingly, a date was fixed—13 August 2002—for conferring the title which they called 'Vidya Seva Ratnam' The ceremony was held at Kanchi Kamakoti Peetham. There was a large gathering. Conferring the title, the senior Shankaracharya said: 'The way Dr Birla had been running the Birla Institute of Technology & Science, Pilani, proved his devotion to giving high-quality education to the people of the country. This is one institution where there is no donation, capitation or recommendation. And the engineering courses are not specific to just one speciality but are so comprehensive and well-rounded that we get engineers who are proficient in different fields.'

His Holiness praised BITS for its unique standards that had enabled it to produce scientists and engineers who had brought laurels to the country. He added that the university run by the Kanchi Mutt had benefited a lot by its association with BITS. He said: 'Not only are our teachers trained there but our course content, method of teaching and other important educational inputs have been done in consultation with BITS. This has helped our Chandrasekharendra Saraswati Viswa Maha Vidyalaya to develop on lines similar to BITS.'

The title of the citation praised me for making Pilani, particularly BITS, 'one of the largest national reservoirs of talent and technology'. The citation further said: 'The education that the Birla institutions offer kindles the spirit of enquiry, encourages and fosters innovation and ennobles life.'

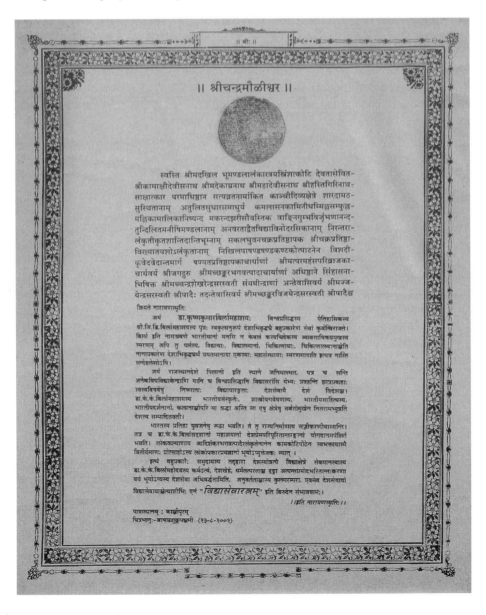

CITATION awarded to Dr K.K.Birla

Dr Krishna Kumar Birla, son of legenday Shri G.D. Birla carries on with missionary zeal and conviction the monumental task of national development through the institutionalization of the core sectors that influence human development, a task the late Shri G.D. Birla immersed himself in, all his life. Dr K.K. Birla has brought the place of his birth, Pilani in Rajasthan to world attention through a number of schools and institutions run by the Birla Education Trust. The Birla Institute of Technology & Science (BITS) is one of the largest national reservoirs from where the technology talent of young minds is harnessed and channelized for the country's progress. The education that the Birla institutions offer kindles the spirit of enquiry, encourages and fosters innovation and ennobles life. Dr K.K. Birla's interests in Indian literature, scientific research, Indian philosophy, Arts and culture and sports saw the creation of K.K. Birla Academy, which undertakes research on scientific, culture and historical subjects.

Vast new human potentials are being unleashed by the swift removal of barriers, the opening of walls both real and self imposed. Geography, alliances and relationships are being rearranged not just on maps, but more importantly in our minds—in how we think about ourselves and others. The power and the potential of the Indian youth to face the world of the morrow is sown in the nurseries energized by the undying spirit and devotion of people like Dr K.K. Birla.

In its quiet, unobtrusive way, the Kanchi Mutt truly symbolizes the spirit of Hinduism—A way of life. In these times of decay, disparity, moral rejuvenation is the key to progress. The Mutt, conscious of its responsibility in this endeavour has been encouraging exceptional human efforts bereft of greed and self aggrandisement, that leave a positive impact on the society by conferring the traditional mutt honours and titles to these social leaders, a practice that has been in vogue from times immemorial.

Pleased with the work of Dr K.K. Birla in the fields of education and health care, Their Holiness Jagadguru Sankaracharyas Sri Jayendra Saraswati Swamigal and Sankara Vijayendra Saraswati Swamigal confer on Dr K.K. Birla, the title 'VIDYA SEVA RATNAM'. May his efforts continue and be crowned with success at all times.

Given at Kanchipuram on this, the 13th day of August 2002.
NARAYANA SMRUTHI

The citation also recorded 'Dr Birla's interests in Indian literature, scientific research, Indian philosophy, art and culture and sports that saw the creation of the K.K. Birla Foundation which encourages outstanding achievements in these fields.'

The citation, as reproduced above, was in Sanskrit along with an English translation. In my acceptance speech, I thanked Kanchi Peetham and said that BITS had developed into a transnational organization with collaborations in Dubai, Nepal, Indonesia and Malaysia and had more than 10,000 students in India. I praised the Shankaracharya for his efforts in spreading the message of humanism, spirituality and harmony and promised to support national reconstruction through education. I also praised the Shankaracharya for his efforts to find a peaceful solution to the Ayodhya issue. I sought the blessings of the two Shankaracharyas.

The conferment of this award was publicized throughout the country and more particularly in Tamil Nadu.

36

K.K. Birla Foundation

I have established a number of charitable trusts. These are all private trusts in the sense that donations are not sought; if someone voluntarily gives a donation, it is accepted.

In 1990, I thought of creating a wide-spectrum fund which would encourage endeavours in different aspects of art and culture. I established the K.K. Birla Foundation. The symbol of the Foundation is adopted from a motif sculptured in the Sanchi Stupa I of the Sunga era. It depicts a lotus in full bloom in a pot and is accompanied by another blossoming lotus and leaves. Above the central lotus is the *srivatsa* symbol which, according to mythological belief, God Vishnu carries on his chest. The symbol signifies creation, knowledge and prosperity.

From time immemorial, Indian literature has been in the forefront of efforts to propagate the fundamental values of life. Even today this aspect of our cultural movements finds eloquent expression in the various languages of our multilingual country, and provides the same life-giving force as it did in the past. Despite the diverse traditions of our languages, the basic ethos of Indian literature will be found to be the same. The comprehension of this reality, however, presents practical difficulties, which are often accentuated by political and social factors. We are acquainted with foreign literature, mainly through English, but have scant knowledge about the volume and variety of literary creativity in our own languages. Acquaintance with outstanding writers like Gurudev Rabindranath Tagore, Sarat Chandra, Premchand and others whose works, transcending the boundaries of languages in which they were created, have permeated the thoughts of the whole country, is rare. In the interest of national unity, it is imperative to lift our outstanding creative works out of their respective narrow linguistic bounds and place them on the pedestal of national knowledge.

The Foundation presently operates four high-level annual awards:

- Saraswati Samman: Given for an outstanding literary work in any Indian language;
- Vyas Samman: Given for an outstanding work in Hindi literature;
- Bihari Puraskar: Given to a writer belonging to Rajasthan; and
- Vachaspati Puraskar: Given for an outstanding work in Sanskrit.

There are many more awards and fellowships that the Foundation grants which I shall describe later.

Of the four, the Saraswati Samman is the most prestigious and is given every year to an outstanding work of an Indian citizen in any of the languages mentioned in Schedule VIII of the Constitution of India. Thus books in eighteen languages published in a ten-year period preceding the award year are considered.

The total award money for the Samman is Rs 5 lakh. In view of its intensely meticulous process of selection, which is made as objective as humanly possible, the Samman has come to be recognized as the highest literary award of the country.

Like the Saraswati Samman, the Vyas Samman is also given every year for an outstanding work in Hindi published by an Indian citizen during a period of ten years preceding the year of the award. The award money is Rs 2.50 lakh.

In order to ensure fairness in the Saraswati Samman, the chairman of the Chayan Parishad, which is the apex body in a three-tier arrangement for taking the final decision, is always a retired chief justice or a retired judge of the Supreme Court.

At the Saraswati Samman presentation ceremony held on 5 September 2003 to honour Mahesh Elkunchwar, I raised the following pertinent question while addressing the chief guest (BJP leader Dr Murli Manohar Joshi, who is himself a scientist):

Honourable Joshi-ji, you are a scientist and also have a deep understanding of literature. And that is the reason why I would like to take this opportunity to repeat a thing or two from what I have been saying about the relevance of our literature. The twentieth century has been hailed for vast progress of science and technology. The achievements in these fields have certainly provided a high standard of living created by an extraordinary productivity and physical comforts. But unfortunately this progress has also produced a monster of destruction. Is it not true that today mankind is scared of its very existence and is losing faith? It is a tribute to Man's indomitable spirit that it is determined not to accept defeat; it refuses to lose hope for the future. And the biggest companion and inspiration for this grit displayed by us is literature. Science can provide material comforts but is not endowed with competence to arouse human sensitivity and inner consciousness of Man. It is the inherent strength of literature which keeps the inner eye awake in the face of the densest darkness and does not allow hope to stumble. It is literature which enables Man to remain Man. Science can be a lifestyle, not values.

I had one more objective in view. The need for strengthening the process of rapport between the literatures of different languages is constantly growing. Keeping this perspective in view I endeavour to provide impetus and encouragement to research in comparative Indian literature.

Following this announcement I decided in 1993 to institute a scheme of fellowships for the study of comparative Indian literature. The scheme provides for two fellowships every year and was welcomed by the literary world. At one of the functions to reward a Saraswati Samman scholar I said:

> It is, in fact, a part of our wider activity to encourage the study of comparative literature in order to strengthen the ties between our languages. In this background I had said that we intended to initiate schemes on research, translations, publications, etc. I am happy to say that our programmes in these fields are making steady progress. Last year, we started a new scheme to award high-level fellowships for the study of comparative Indian literature. It was gratifying to know that many eminent and well-known litterateurs came forward to work under this programme and that the two of them selected are well-known literary figures in the country. Certainly, the scheme has been widely welcomed in the literary and educational circles.

Under another scheme, the Foundation has also provided assistance for publication of translations of outstanding works from one Indian language to another. As a result of this encouragement Tulsidas's *Vinayapatrika*, Jaishankar Prasad's *Kamayani*, and selected poems of 'Nirala' have been published in other languages. Similarly, works of prominent poets like Balamani Amma, K. Ayyappa Paniker, E. Neelakanta Singh have been brought out in Hindi. Twenty-two books have been translated with the Foundation's assistance.

According to my understanding, literature defines the cultural values of human lives. It does not merely impart intellectual colour, but introduces perceptions and moral encouragement and self-restraint. In other words, literature is intimately connected with the cultural life of the country. With this background, in 1992, the Foundation instituted the Shankar Puraskar, named after Adi Shankaracharya, for a book in Hindi on Indian philosophy, culture and art.

In 1991, the Foundation had instituted a scheme relating to scientific research called the G.D. Birla Award for Scientific Research. The main objective of the scheme is to accord recognition to high-calibre scientific research undertaken by Indian scientists ordinarily below the age of fifty, resident and working in India. Like other awards, it is given every year and is available in any branch of science including medical science, basic as well as applied. The emphasis here is on the work done by scientists during the last five years. The award has been particularly welcomed by the scientific community because while there are many awards for scientists at higher levels this is the only award for upcoming scientists.

In 1991, the Foundation started a programme to provide talented journalists opportunities to develop their capabilities through study and research. The idea was that promising journalists need to be encouraged to take a break from their routine to enrich their intellectual capabilities. The programme called the K.K. Birla Foundation Fellowship for Journalists covers three sections—Hindi, other Indian languages, and English.

In 1996, the Foundation started a scheme of fellowship in economics. The object of this fellowship is to provide opportunity to eminent scholars in the subject, teachers and others concerned with economic administration in the Central and state governments to undertake in depth study of serious aspects of economics. The duration of the fellowship is one year.

The Foundation is also encouraging the publication of books, especially for adult literacy programmes. Over the years it has given a grant of Rs 3 lakh to the National Book Trust for this purpose. So far, 114 books have been published in various languages under this programme as a result of assistance given by the Foundation.

The Foundation also organizes two annual series of lectures. One series is by an eminent Indian scholar in Hindi and the other by a foreign writer or scholar.

Another scheme known as the K.K. Birla Foundation Award for sports was started in 1991 to encourage the outstanding performance of sportspersons. The selection board is presided over by former Test cricketer Sunil Gavaskar.

Apart from these awards the Foundation gave a special award of Rs 2.50 lakh to tennis player Leander Paes for bringing glory to the country by winning the bronze medal in the Atlanta Olympics. In 1999, the Foundation announced a cash award of Rs 1.50 lakh to cricketer Anil Kumble for his splendid performance of taking all ten wickets in the second innings against Pakistan in the second test of the Pepsi Challenge Trophy in Delhi. Over and above the annual awards, the Foundation gave, as a one-time reward, two awards, one for an all-time great and the other for living legends to the late Dhyan Chand, the hockey wizard, and Gavaskar. It also gave an award to Viswanathan Anand, the outstanding chess champion. These selections were made by a special committee chaired by the late Madhavrao Scindia.

The Indian Centre for Philanthropy, an independent organization, the mission of which is to foster a sharing and caring culture, writes as under about the Foundation:

The K.K. Birla Foundation is an example of this kind of private philanthropy. A private family Foundation set up by a leading business family of India, it is one of the few large foundations in the country dedicated to promoting the cause of literature, education, literacy, higher learning, research and sports.

The four high-level awards in literature and one in Indian philosophy, culture and art instituted by the Foundation are regarded as among the most prestigious in the field. The rigorous and impartial process of selection of awardees and the wide search for meritorious works have helped enhance the prestige of these awards.

In addition, the Foundation also offers fellowships in journalism, comparative Indian literature and economics.

The Birlas not only poured money into their hometown Pilani, but in every place they inhabited. Few families in India have undertaken welfare and development activities as well as the promotion of literature and culture on a scale matching the Birlas. To their credit, it must be said that their services have not been restricted to any single creed, race or region. Hundreds of institutions, new and old, have benefited by their largesse and serve as monuments of their dedication.

The main objectives of the Foundation are charitable and welfare activities, particularly in the fields of education, higher learning, literary output and culture, art and music, scientific research, economics, sports, journalism, etc. The Foundation considers that successful implementation of well-thought-out programmes in these fields will make a significant contribution to the academic and cultural progress of the country.

As stated earlier, the Saraswati Samman is the most prestigious of the Foundation's awards and is awarded every year to an outstanding literary work by an Indian citizen published during the last ten years in any of the eighteen languages of India recognized in the Constitution. The people who have been honoured with the Saraswati Samman since the inception of the Foundation are:

Year	Author	Book
1991	Dr Harivansh Rai Bachchan	Autobiography [Hindi: In four volumes]
1992	Ramakanta Rath	Sri Radha [Oriya: poetry]
1993	Vijay Tendulkar	Kanyadaan [Marathi: play]
1994	Dr Harbhajan Singh	Rukh te Rishi [Punjabi: poetry]
1995	Balamani Amma	Nivedyam [Malayalam: poetry]
1996	Shamsur Rahman Faruqi	Sher-e-Shor Angez [Urdu: literary criticism]
1997	Manubhai Pancholi	Kurukshetra [Gujarati: novel]
1998	Sankha Ghosh	Gandharba Kabita Guccha [Bengali: poetry]
1999	Dr Indira Parthasarathy	Ramanujar [Tamil: play]
2000	Manoj Das	Amruta Phala [Oriya: novel]
2001	Dr Dalip Kaur Tiwana	Katha Kaho Urvashi [Punjabi: novel]
2002	Mahesh Elkunchwar	Yugant [Marathi: play]
2003	Prof. Govind Chandra Pande	Bhagirathi [Sanskrit: poetry]
2004	Sunil Gangopadhyay	Pratham Alo [Bengali: novel]
2005	Prof. K. Ayyappa Paniker	Ayyappapanikerude Kritikal [Malayalam: poems]
2006	Dr Jagannath Prasad Das	Parikrama [Oriya: poems]

The Foundation is of the view that the success of such programmes depends upon help and cooperation of universities and other institutions of higher learning, eminent scholars, teachers, literary, cultural, scientific and sports organizations. Our experience in this field has been very happy and encouraging.

37

My Daughters and Sons-in-law

I have three daughters. By the grace of God, all of them are happily married. The two eldest—Nandini and Jyoti—live in Kolkata whereas the youngest, Shobhana, lives in Delhi.

The eldest, Nandini, is married to Bimal Kumar Nopany of the well-known Nopany family which has established many charitable institutions as well as a public school at Ranchi and a high school in Kolkata named Nopany Vidyalaya which has been certified by the Government of West Bengal as the best school in the state. Nandini is endowed with inborn qualities of leadership. She is associated with Belle Vue Clinic, which is a leading nursing home of Kolkata and the Birla Planetarium. Under the guidance of her mother, Nandini also looks after Shree Radha Krishna Temple at Kolkata, besides some charitable trusts, and the biggest sugar mills in my group, namely, the Upper Ganges Sugar & Industries Ltd. All the three daughters are deeply attached to each other. Nandini, being the eldest, bosses over the other two in their mutual dealings. She has one son and one daughter.

My second daughter, Jyoti, is very fond of sports, particularly of cricket. She has brought out a book called *Cricketing Memories*. The book contains articles by leading cricketers of the world and memoirs of Mushtaq Ali, Ian Chappel, Denis Compton and others. It also contains lovely cartoons by leading cartoonists of the country, including the three famed cartoonists—R.K. Laxman, Mario Miranda and Sudhir Dar. While Jyoti was compiling this book she happened to go to Australia. She sought an interview with Sir Donald Bradman, the best cricketer our world has produced. Bradman sent word that in view of his advancing age he did not meet anyone except his intimate friends. Jyoti then sent him a sample copy of her book and requested Sir Donald to write the Foreword. Sir Donald said that he had stopped writing Forewords but he agreed to meet Jyoti. He was highly impressed by the contents of the book and by Jyoti's

A photograph of Mahatma Gandhi
taken by me in 1945

Dr Rajendra Prasad relaxes at Birla House,
New Delhi, in 1942

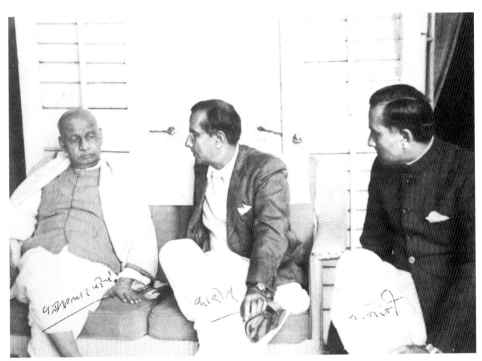

I took this photograph of Sardar Vallabhbhai Patel at Birla
House with my father and uncle in 1930

With Babu Jagjivan Ram at a function in the mid-1950s

With Asoka Mehta at a function

A big welcome for me at Durgiana temple in Amritsar in the 1950s

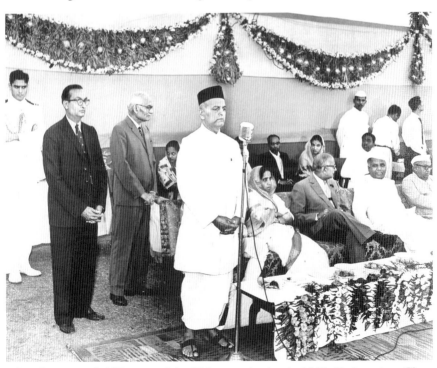

At a function to mark 100 years of the Birla organization in 1962. Yashwantrao Chavan, then chief minister of Maharashtra, can be seen along with my father and uncle, R.D. Birla

Then President of India
R. Venkataraman inaugurated
a memorial to my father on
9 September 1990

Inauguration of the
Radha Krishna temple at Kolkata
in February 1996. My wife and
I are performing a puja, with our
daughter Nandini

Guru Hanuman, famous teacher
of wrestling, receiving me at a
function he had organized

personality. After the meeting, he agreed to write the Foreword.

Jyoti has also founded a trust to help young cricketers in getting proper training so that in course of time they could emerge as worthy players. This trust tries to scout for young promising players all over the country and then give them financial assistance for their training. Sachin Tendulkar was one such youngster who was helped by Jyoti when he was an unknown person in the cricket world. In a book on Sachin called *The Making of a Cricketer: Formative Years of Sachin Tendulkar in Cricket* his brother Ajit Tendulkar wrote: 'Sachin toured the UK twice with the Star CC in 1988 and 1989. The Young Cricketers Organization of Calcutta, established by the Birla Trust, sponsored him in the first year. Jyotsna Poddar took the initiative for the sponsorship.'

Kolkata, 10 December 1977: Wedding of my youngest daughter
Shobhana with Shyam Bhartia. Kanyadan was done by
Gangaprasad and his wife Nirmala as my eldest daughter
Nandini tries to tie the knot

Though Shobhana is the vice chairperson and editorial director of the Hindustan Times Ltd, her instructions are that no publicity is to be given to her. Hence the paper gives her publicity only when it becomes essential to do so. Being in the newspaper business and with her temperament, she has a large number of friends in all sections of society. She has numerous friends even in the United States, which she visits once a year to keep in touch with the progress in journalism. She is a good organizer and possesses great ability. For these qualities she has been able to win the love and affection of all her friends and acquaintances as well as her staff members.

My three sons-in-law are as devoted to me as my daughters. Each possesses his own individuality and personality. Bimal rightfully prides himself in the fact that he has been able to provide his son and daughter the highest education. Both of them are MBAs from foreign universities. While the son, Chandra Shekhar, got his MBA degree from Carnegie Mellon University at Pittsburgh, his sister Shruti did her MBA from the European University at Geneva. Incidentally, Chandra Shekhar's wife, Shalini, a very able girl, is also an MBA. While Chandra Shekhar was studying for MBA at Carnegie Mellon University, Shalini did her MBA from the University of Pittsburgh. Shalini is the granddaughter of Rai Bahadur Gujarmul Modi and daughter of Satish and Abha Modi.

Saroj Kumar Poddar, my second son-in-law, has extensive contacts with businessmen not only in India but in foreign countries as well. He is a successful businessman and owns equity in a number of world-class and multinational companies. He is the chairman of Gillette India Ltd. I call him an encyclopaedia owing to his vast knowledge of things in general. Impressed by his encyclopaedic knowledge, the global giant GEC Alstom, now renamed Areva T&D India Ltd, has made him the chairman of its Indian subsidiary.

Saroj was the president of FICCI during 2005–06. As the president of FICCI he did a remarkable job. Saroj, during his presidentship, visited ten countries. Some visits were:

a. When the prime minister, Dr Manmohan Singh visited many countries and took businessmen with him, Saroj, in his capacity as the president of FICCI, was the leader of the delegations of businessmen;

b. When, likewise, Shri Kamal Nath, Minister of Commerce & Industry, led delegations to some foreign countries.

c. A number of times Saroj, as the president of FICCI, led delegations to foreign countries. In all he met twenty-seven heads of states—Presidents and prime ministers—in India or in their countries.

No other president of FICCI in the last twenty years has done so much work as Saroj has for the business community through FICCI and through his personal efforts.

My youngest son-in-law, Shyam Sundar Bhartia, is a very successful businessman. Starting from scratch, he established Vam Organic Chemicals, now called Jubilant Organosys Ltd, which is the largest company of its kind in India. He became the managing director of Vam Organic Chemicals at the young age of twenty-five. After the company was established, he approached financial institutions and banks for loans to put up the plant. All these financial bodies were hesitant to give loan to a company whose managing director was so young. They expressed their doubts to young Shyam. Shyam then told them to ask him any question concerning the company and after that if they were dissatisfied with his answers, they were free to express their opinion. After discussing the matter with Shyam they were so impressed that they immediately agreed to his managing the company. I always say of him, of course in a lighter vein, that he can make money from anything that he touches. He possesses what we call the Midas touch.

I am fortunate in having talented daughters and able sons-in-law. I have six grandchildren—four boys and two girls. I am proud of all the grandchildren. I have seven great-grandchildren also—four boys and three girls. They too are very cute and sharp.

38

My Heart Bypass Surgery

The only time I missed office was due to an illness in 1942. It is not that I never fall ill. Sometimes I do get low fever, which lasts two or three days. My work, however, does not suffer and I continue with my daily routine. I got high fever once when I was visiting one of our sugar mills. The temperature shot up to 102 degrees. As I had important work to do, I took an aspirin and continued my normal activities.

I take a walk daily for thirty-five minutes or so and exercise regularly for twelve minutes. The exercise includes two yogasanas also. I have thus developed a sturdy constitution. So when I developed a heart problem, it came as a shock not only to me but to all my relations, friends and well-wishers.

The first indication of the trouble came when I was on a visit to London. On 4 June 1999, I was taking a brisk walk in the park of Grosvenor Square. Suddenly, I experienced pain in my left arm. I felt somewhat uneasy. There are many benches in the park. I did not sit down, but held the back of the bench and remained standing. I thought it might be muscular pain. After two or three minutes, the pain subsided. I recommenced my walk. This time I deliberately walked very briskly. The pain reappeared. However, there was no pain at all at a slower speed. I became certain that the pain had something to do with the heart. I did not want to consult any physician or cardiologist in London before consulting my physicians in India. Whenever I am out of India, my wife telephones me every day. I did not inform her about this trouble lest it overly upset her. She is a heart patient. I stayed in London for a fortnight more and then returned to India on 19 June. My wife, who was in Mussoorie, had come down to Kolkata as a grandson was born to my eldest daughter Nandini and a granddaughter was born to Jyotsna, my second daughter. I did not inform my wife about my trouble.

My wife usually spends the summer months in Mussoorie. I also join her sometime in the third week of June for my annual holiday and stay there for about three-and-a-half weeks. Accordingly, I went to Mussoorie with my wife on 26 June. Even in Mussoorie, I did not inform her about the pain. During all this period, since the time the pain first appeared, I did not experience any pain except when I walked fast. It was certainly foolhardiness on my part not to have informed my doctors in Kolkata or my wife about this ailment. I was supremely confident about my health, and since I did not have any pain when walking slowly, I did not take the matter as seriously as I should have.

On 20 July, while in Mussoorie, I informed her and our two physicians—Dr Sunil Sanon and Dr Aditya Prasad, who regularly attend on us—in Mussoorie about the pain. Both are very able physicians. Dr Sanon, apart from being a general physician, is also a good cardiologist. Dr Aditya Prasad is the son of the late Dr Jwala Prasad, whom we had known since 1949. When they heard my story, they told me that on my return to Kolkata I should immediately take a treadmill test. I, therefore, telephoned our family physician Dr Sushil Mishra in Kolkata to fix an appointment. I reached Kolkata on 26 July. The tests were conducted on 27 July. The first test was echocardiography. The results were normal. The doctors felt confident that the treadmill test too would show no major defect in the heart. However, I could not complete the test as about halfway through the doctors stopped the machine. They had sufficient evidence that there was something wrong with the heart.

That very evening, a meeting was held with my doctors along with two cardiologists. These doctors had seen the report of the treadmill test and asked me to go immediately to London for heart bypass surgery. I told them that it was impossible for me to leave India before the end of August, as I had to take many important decisions connected with my companies. I explained to the doctors that only I could take the decisions and any abrupt departure to London would affect the performance of my companies for the next many months.

Some decisions concerning the sugar mills had to be taken immediately. Operations of sugar mills being seasonal, it was important that the decisions were taken in time. The doctors and my wife then posed a question to me: What is more precious—my life or my work? I explained that it was not a question of my life; the real question was what was the importance of life if a man did not fulfil his obligations at a crucial time. I said that if the companies did badly as a result of my sudden departure from India without taking the important decisions, there would be a major setback in the performance of these companies, and that would give me a bad name. So I told the doctors that I would prefer death to disrepute. The doctors, my wife and members of the family stopped trying to persuade me when they saw my determination.

The doctors meticulously chalked out a programme for me so that my condition would not deteriorate till I reached London. They gave me a large number of medicines to protect the heart and keep the blood thin. The doctors also gave me a spray and said that in case I felt any pain in the left arm or chest I should immediately apply this spray. I told my wife that I could leave around 30 August. My heart at that time did not give me any trouble except when I walked fast. My wife said that we may as well leave after another four or five days as Shree Krishna Janmashtami was being celebrated in our temple in Kolkata on 2 September. I agreed with her. The preliminary meeting with our cardiologist in London was fixed for 6 September and the operation was fixed for 7 September.

Surprisingly, whereas I had not felt any pain in my arm from 4 June till 20 July except while walking fast, I started feeling pain even when not walking from about the end of July. The four doctors were again consulted. They were unhappy at this development. I too had become cautious by that time.

I had some urgent work in Delhi. So I went to Delhi on 18 August. The pain would occur almost all the time. I was required to take the spray to protect the heart almost every 10–15 minutes. I called Dr Aditya Prasad from Mussoorie to be close to me. I defied my doctors in Kolkata, but it was necessary that every precaution be taken so that my condition remained stable while I was in India. My heart condition, however, went on deteriorating.

Once while I was in Delhi, the pain surfaced in the chest also. Dr Aditya Prasad said that whether the pain was in the arm or in the chest, it was the same thing. He said that the pain was related to the heart.

The deterioration of my heart condition deeply worried me and all the members of the family. It was one thing to delay the operation so long as the heart was not affected. But I was keen that the operation take place before it could affect the heart. By this time, I had to take the spray every ten minutes. I certainly realized that if owing to delay in the operation the heart got affected, I would have to be extremely cautious all my life. Owing to the deterioration in my condition, my wife, all my daughters, sons-in-law and grandsons came down to Delhi. My wife immediately came along with Dr Anil Mishra, who is one of my cardiologists in Kolkata and head cardiologist of the B.M. Birla Heart Research Centre. Dr Mishra examined me and said that considering the condition of my heart we should leave for London immediately. There should not be any delay of even one day. I told my doctors that it would not be difficult for me to leave on 26 August as I had almost finished all my pending work and what little work was left to be attended could be finished in the next two days. The problem, however, was of air and hotel bookings at such short notice. My daughters working very strenuously arranged this and so we left for London on 26 August. My daughters and their husbands also left at the same time, travelling by different planes.

My younger brother, Basant Kumar and his wife Sarala, also reached London just when we reached there. So did Priyamvada Devi Birla, wife of my cousin, the late Madhav Prasad. My cousin Ganga Prasad, who was to have visited the United States, also adjusted his itinerary so as to be in London along with his wife, Nirmala Devi, soon after the operation. He also arranged to send Dr Mishra to accompany me to London. Anil stayed for about ten days right till the operation was performed and I was permitted to return to my hotel. Though we brothers and cousins had separated a few years back, the bond of affection and warmth never deserted us. Almost the entire family was in London during the operation. I was overwhelmed by this unprecedented show of familial sympathy for me.

We arrived in London in the early hours of 26 August. My four family physicians from India were also there—three had accompanied me in the plane while the fourth, Dr Rajiv Sharma, came from Mumbai. The three doctors who accompanied me had taken a number of medicines and oxygen cylinders so that they could attend to me if there was any problem on the plane. Fortunately, nothing happened and I reached London safely. That very afternoon I had an appointment with Dr Anthony Rickards, one of the leading cardiologists of London, who enjoys a worldwide reputation. My daughters, sons-in-law and four physicians accompanied me.

Dr Rickards examined me and after hearing how I had been keeping good health except for the sudden affliction a few weeks ago, felt I might not need surgery. He said that considering my age—I was eighty-one at that time—he would make his best efforts to see if angioplasty would suffice instead of bypass surgery. Everything, of course, depended upon the angiography for which an appointment had already been made for the next morning.

Before coming to London, in fact, as soon as my treadmill test was done, we had discussed whether I should have the operation performed in London or in Cleveland. Cleveland enjoys the reputation as being the best heart centre in the world. The entire family including myself, however, opted for London. First, because London is more homely; secondly, it is closer to India; thirdly, we had full faith in the doctors of London who are considered more careful and conservative. Someone remarked that doctors and surgeons in Switzerland also were very good. We finally opted for London.

In London, a special hospital called the Heart Hospital had been constructed by a Singapore group of businessmen called the Glen Eagle Group. Some doctors in London too had invested in the Heart Hospital, Dr Rickards being one of them. Next day, I went to the Heart Hospital accompanied by all the doctors, my daughters and sons-in-law. I found the Heart Hospital to be an excellent hospital befitting its reputation. I was put under sedation when angiography was done. The result was very frightening. The main artery was blocked to the extent of 99 per cent, the second artery to the extent of 95 per cent, the third to the extent of 75 per cent, and the fourth to the extent of 50 per cent. Dr Rickards, who had been keen to avoid bypass surgery before the angiography, opined that angioplasty was out of the question. He said it was surprising that I did not suffer a massive heart attack with such low supply of blood to the heart. The doctor fortunately found my heart to be in excellent condition but said that the operation had to be performed post-haste, that very day.

Bypass after implantations is regarded as a major surgery. When Dr Rickards had told me earlier that he might be able to manage with angioplasty I was very happy. Now when I was suddenly told that the operation had to be performed immediately I was downcast and completely flabbergasted. I pleaded with the doctor to give me three days time to prepare myself for such a major operation. Dr Rickards said that he would give me only four hours time and that too because he had to find a surgeon for performing the operation at such short notice. What is more, even for these four hours I would have to be shifted immediately to the emergency ward. When I again pleaded for three days' time, he said that if I insisted he would agree but only on one condition—that all this time be spent in the intensive care unit (ICU) under twenty-four-hour observation so that the operation could be performed at a moment's notice, in case of an emergency.

I have always had very great respect for English doctors. They are a very dedicated lot. Hence I could not brush aside the advice of Dr Rickards. Considering this near ultimatum, I consulted my family and family physicians and decided that there was no point postponing the inevitable. The operation was performed at 5 p.m. on 27 August. The surgeon was Dr Charles W. Pattison, one of the top cardiac surgeons in London. The doctors had told me that the operation would take between four and four-and-a-half-hours. Actually, it was completed in three hours.

While the operation was in progress, all my relations and most of my senior executives in India kept awake. I was shifted to the ICU at 9 p.m. British time, which meant 1.30 a.m. in India. It was only when these people in India got confirmation that the operation had been successfully performed that they retired to bed, with much relief. I was quite touched by so much warmth shown by all the members of the family, my executives and secretaries.

Before I left India, I had been assured by a few friends who themselves had undergone heart surgery not to have any fear regarding the operation even though it was a major one. They said that I would be kept for two days in the ICU under heavy sedation and on the third day shifted to my room reserved in the hospital for me, and I would feel quite cheerful once I was moved to my room.

Before the operation I had visited the ICU where I was to be kept for two days and also my room where I was to be shifted subsequently. The ambience of the room was pleasant and homely. The ICU was a large hall with no windows and so no view. I am a claustrophobic person. The ICU appeared to be gloomy and cheerless to me. However, as my friends in India told me that I would be kept under sedation for two days I got reconciled to the idea of staying in the uncongenial room.

After the operation, when the effect of anaesthesia wore off, I woke up. I was aware that I was in the ICU. It was about midnight. I found that I was alone; there was no nurse near me. Later I was told that there was one nurse for two patients. After some time the nurse did come. She was with me for five minutes. I tried to speak to her to request her to put me under heavy sedation. But I found that I had lost my voice and could only whisper but could not speak. I must have kept awake for ten or fifteen minutes. Being claustrophobic, I was feeling miserable. But I knew there was nothing that could be done about it. I bore the mental suffering bravely. After some time I dozed off but again woke up twice or thrice during the night. The next morning, my wife and the members of the family came to see me. They told me that as the operation was successful and my condition was good, the doctor had permitted me to be shifted to the room reserved for me on Sunday.

Meanwhile, as this was a very major surgery my wife and family members had arranged for a number of prayer meetings to be held and pujas to be performed in Kolkata. My wife, who is a very pious lady, had also taken the video of 'Maha Mrityunjay Jap' prayer which, as the name denotes, is regarded the most effective prayer for a person whose life is in danger. She arranged for this 'jap' to be played throughout the period non-stop from the time that I was put in the operation theatre till the time I was shifted to my room in the hospital. Belief in the efficacy of prayers is a universal phenomenon. It is not just a superstition. Tennyson had said that more things are wrought by prayer than the world can dream of. At any rate, both my wife and I are great believers in the efficacy of prayers offered to God with sincere devotion.

After the operation, recovery was normal. After I was shifted to the room, my surgeon and the cardiologist asked me to start walking. Like me there was another person who had undergone heart surgery the same day. His room was also very close to my room. Whenever I took my walk in the morning and in the evening I would offer my greetings to the other man and he reciprocated. I was a bit surprised to find him always very cheerful. This was the second time that he had undergone heart bypass surgery. One day while walking I dropped in on him in his room. I asked him how he was always so cheerful, whereas I was still feeling somewhat gloomy. In a hushed tone he said that he would take me into confidence. The secret was he said that every night his wife would bring a bottle of whisky for him.

After the surgery, I became very weak. The muscles lost their strength and normal ability to act. For the first six weeks I could walk only at a quarter of my normal speed. Gradually, however, I improved. It was a slow recovery. The doctors said that in this type of operation, I should not look for day-to-day but rather week-to-week progress.

My recovery was satisfactory. My family physicians from India, however, said that I should not return to India until five weeks after the operation.

The heart bypass surgery has been a major event and experience of my life. Now when I look back and think about the operation I recall the words of Dr Rickards with trepidation that one week's delay could have resulted in a massive heart attack. I now realize how kind and merciful God has been to me.

Viewing the overall situation, therefore, it was only God's blessings and the loving care with which my wife, my daughters, their husbands, my brother, cousins and their wives and other members of the family looked after me and good wishes of my friends, staff members and well-wishers and my self-confidence that saw me through this major crisis in my life.

39

My Career as an MP

I was a member of Parliament (MP) in the Rajya Sabha for three terms. From 1984 to 1990 I served as an independent MP supported by the Congress (I) party. For the subsequent two terms I was a Congress (I) MP.

I did not miss any sitting of the Rajya Sabha for more than two or three days in a session and that too only if very urgent work cropped up.

My timings for attending the Rajya Sabha were:11 a.m. to 1 p.m. in the House itself; 1 p.m. to 2 p.m. in the Central Hall, having tea or coffee with other MPs or ex-MPs; from 2 p.m. to 4–4.30 p.m. again in the House.

In the event of a speech being delivered by any important MP or minister, I would spend the entire afternoon in the Rajya Sabha.

During these three terms, I spoke on a number of subjects. I would always speak on the Union budget and other financial matters. I spoke on a number of occasions on the railway budget also, and on many other topics. Some of the discussions in which I participated were on:

The Kashmir situation	26 July 1984
Motion of thanks to the President	4 March 1986
Economic situation in the country	3 December 1986
Drought conditions	6 August 1987
Motion on Bofors	11 August 1987
Protectionist measures by various countries for foreign trade	27 April 1989
Diamond reserves in Rajasthan	28 April 1989
Working of the ministry of external affairs	28 April 1989

I also made special mentions on a number of subjects:

Smuggling activities on Indo-Pak and Indo-Bangladesh borders	4 March 1986

Reported deaths of two children in stormwater drain in Delhi	11 March 1986
Inaccurate, irrelevant information in textbooks	25 April 1986
Reported increase in Sati cases	17 November 1986
Reported premature failure of engines of Dornier planes	10 March 1987
Acute water shortage in Delhi	6 May 1987
Terrorizing of Indians in USA	8 March 1988
Severe water crisis in Delhi	25 April 1988
Constant decline in value of rupee	19 December 1988

I took part in most of the calling attention motions. Some of these were:

Happenings in Gujarat	29 April 1985
Mercenary school of terrorism in Alabama	25 July 1985
Flood and drought conditions in the country	6 November 1986

All my important speeches during my first and second terms were printed in the form of books. The first book contains the speeches delivered during my tenure as an MP from 1984 to 1990. The Foreword was written by P. Shiv Shanker who was then the leader of the Congress (I) in the Rajya Sabha. I quote some paragraphs from it:

Shri Birla's contribution to the Rajya Sabha debates was not confined to economic issues alone. When discussions on other major issues affecting the well-being of the people cropped up, he was prompt in offering his considered observations. He provided grist to the mill of Parliamentary debates. This may have amazed those who saw him only in the role of an industrialist but it did not surprise me as I was aware of his active interest in diverse spheres. His views on Kashmir, Gorkhaland, Fiji, etc., are proof positive of his active interest in matters of vast range.

What has endeared Birla-ji to all the sections of the House is his sincerity and simplicity of nature. Though born with a silver spoon in his mouth, he bears true humility.

While writing this Foreword to Birla-ji's select speeches, I congratulate him on his excellent performance in the Rajya Sabha, and wish him many more fruitful years in his parliamentary career. I have no doubt that looking back, he should feel satisfied with himself.

In my second term from 1990 to 1996 I spoke on topics such as the Russian President's decision to suspend transfer of rocket technology to India on 27 April 1992 and the need to preserve historical monuments of the country.

I was very distressed when I found that Indian girls and women were being exploited on the promise of jobs in West Asian countries. I made a special mention on the issue on 22 December 1992. Some of the subjects on which I spoke were danger of the spread of the Thar desert on 23 December 1993, working of the ministry of defence on 26 April 1994 and drug smuggling in Tihar Jail on 16 August 1995.

The Foreword of the book containing my important speeches during the second term was written by Dr Manmohan Singh, who was then the leader of the Opposition in the Rajya Sabha. What gladdened my heart was that he went through all the speeches that I had sent him. This is clear, as in his Foreword, he has made various references to my speeches. The full text of the Foreword is reproduced here:

Foreword

I am very happy to write a Foreword to this volume which is the second collection of some of the speeches of the veteran industrialist and distinguished parliamentarian Shri K.K. Birla in the Rajya Sabha.

Shri K.K. Birla brings to the Rajya Sabha the immense knowledge and wisdom of one of India's foremost captains of industry. Thus his views on the management of our economy and in particular on the problems of industry and trade are of great public interest.

This volume which consists of some of the speeches delivered by Shri Birla in the Rajya Sabha from 1990 to 1996 contains a wealth of information and analysis of contemporary macro economic issues. Readers of this volume will find particularly instructive Shri Birla's speeches dealing with the General Budget of the Union Government, the Railway Budget and the Finance Bill. These speeches highlight Shri Birla's analytical abilities as well as his abiding concern and commitment to accelerating the process of social and economic development. Shri K.K. Birla rightly emphasizes that we can find meaningful solutions to the problems of mass poverty only through a rapidly expanding economy. His speeches on the union budgets from 1991 to 1996 ably deal with the challenges our economy had to face during this period and how we grappled with those challenges. Serious students of India's economic development in the 1990s will find these speeches highly informative.

Readers of this volume will also greatly benefit from Shri Birla's speech on the price rise delivered in the Rajya Sabha on 8th August 1990. In this speech, Shri K.K. Birla foresaw the gathering economic crisis which overtook the country a few months later. Similarly his speech on the power crisis delivered in the Rajya Sabha on 15th July 1991 contains many useful suggestions which are relevent even today.

Shri K.K. Birla's deep knowledge of India's economic problems is known all over India. But he is a multi-faceted personality and he is equally concerned about wider societal issues having a bearing on our people's well being. His concern to preserve and protect India's vast cultural heritage comes out loud and clear in his intervention on 26th November 1992 on the need to preserve the historical monuments of the country. His intervention on 23rd December 1993 on the Danger of Spreading the Thar Desert shows his deep concern for the environment and ecology. Similarly, other interventions included in this volume point to Shri Birla's abiding concern about the welfare of women and children and the evils of drug smuggling. His speech in the Rajya Sabha on 6th April 1994 on the working of the Ministry of Defence is yet another indication of Shri Birla's wide ranging interests in the functioning of our Public Administration.

Shri K.K. Birla came to Rajya Sabha in 1984. He is now a very senior and respected member of the House. In view of the vast reservoir of experience, knowledge and wisdom that he possesses, his views on important aspects of public affairs should be of great interest to the people as a whole. I am therefore very happy that Shri Birla has brought out this volume. I commend this volume to all those interested in understanding India's economic policies in the 1990s.

30 September 1998   Manmohan Singh M.P.
                                    Leader of Opposition in the Rajya Sabha

In my third and last term from 1996 to 2002, I spoke on every Union budget that was presented in Parliament and most of the railway budgets. I also spoke on the working of the ministry of external affairs on 9 July

1998, on the sugar policy on 9 December 1998, and on the slowdown in the economy on 16 August 2001. My speech on the slowdown of the economy was widely applauded.

My life as an MP was laborious. Whenever I made a speech, I had to study a lot. I had to prepare myself thoroughly before asking questions as well, which I did frequently. As a result, my sleeping time was reduced to only five hours a day. I would retire at around 12.15 a.m. and get up at 5.15 a.m. After getting ready, I would study all matters of Parliament for about an hour and a half before reaching Parliament at 11 a.m.

When Rajiv was prime minister, he organized a Dandi Yatra in March 1988 in memory of the historical Dandi March undertaken by Mahatma-ji on 12 March 1930, which ended on 6 April 1930. The Dandi March was in protest against the salt tax imposed in India by the then viceroy, Lord Irwin, who decreed that salt-making would be the monopoly of British companies. Gandhi-ji undertook the march from Sabarmati in Gujarat to Dandi, a small fishing village off the Gujarat coast, covering a distance of 365 km. Gandhi-ji and his followers covered this distance in twenty-three days.

Rajiv Gandhi's Dandi Yatra was symbolic. It was a one day yatra from Mahatma-ji's Sabarmati Ashram to Chandola where Mahatma-ji broke the Yatra for rest, on the first day.

Rajiv invited Congress supporters, including all party MPs, to undertake this yatra but said that only those MPs should come whose health permitted them to complete the yatra. I was then seventy. Many people asked me not to undertake this yatra. As I kept good health and exercised regularly, I was confident of finishing the yatra. I took a spare pair of shoes as shoes sometimes start pinching during long walks. As it was very hot and sunny, I did not put on any dark attire, because dark cloth absorbs heat more. Thousands of people joined the yatra. All of them were full of enthusiasm. However, many dropped out owing to the heat. I was accompanied by a few friends including Shiv Shanker-ji and Amar Singh, who was then in the Congress but is now with the Samajwadi Party. As a matter of caution, I had asked my chauffeur to follow us at a reasonable distance so that I could return to Ahmedabad in the car if I could not complete the yatra. However, I was determined not to fail. From time to time I would take a sip of water to keep my throat cool. Fortunately I was able to complete the yatra.

I completed my third term on 9 April 2002. I was then eighty-four. Life as a party MP was hard. Every week there were three or four functions which I had to attend. Sometimes there were parties hosted by the leader of the party. In every session there was a party by the vice president for all MPs. Whenever there was any wedding in an MP's family, and if he invited me, I would attend, even if the MP was not a close acquaintance. Sometimes even if an MP whom I did not know sent a card and pressed me to come, I went. Once a sibling of an MP was getting married at a distance of almost 30 km from Delhi. Coming and going took two hours. I was in no mood to go, but when the MP pressed me I could not say no.

Whenever any foreign dignitary came, both lunch and dinner parties were thrown by the President and the prime minister. I was invited on most of the occasions. When the United States President Bill Clinton came to India, a dinner party was given in his honour. Many MPs and other VIPs made efforts to be invited to this dinner party. I regard it beneath my dignity to lobby for an invitation. Fortunately, the President did invite me to the dinner which I gladly attended. During the drinks before dinner, the invitees get an opportunity of meeting the invited guests. I was able to talk to President Clinton for a few minutes before dinner. I was also present when he addressed both the Houses of Parliament. He spoke well and was full of praise for India. He made a deep impression on the Indian public. Likewise, when Pakistan's General Pervez Musharraf came, I was invited for the dinner hosted by the President.

Whenever the leader of my party made a public speech, I attended the function. I attended many public speeches made by Sonia-ji. I remember once she spoke in the summer. I attended her meeting. I put a bottle of water in my pocket and took sips from time to time. Once Rajiv, when he was the leader of the Opposition, decided that as a protest on some issue, all Congress (I) MPs should show their dissatisfaction by sitting out in the open continuously for twelve hours. During this period, they were not expected to stand except to have food and refreshments or to go to the toilets. Hundreds of MPs or leaders of the party sat there under a shamiana for twelve hours. There were no chairs. Everyone had to sit on the carpets. It was an exacting experience. Many people who could not stand it left after seven or eight hours on one pretext or the other. But I had no intention of 'cheating'. I sat there the entire time.

In addition, there was a major setback in the health of my wife in 2001. Once she suffered a cardiac arrest, but as the doctor was with her, he was able to revive my wife by massaging her chest. I began to feel that the type of life which I had been leading for eighteen years, was getting tougher. My health was very good but I felt that I could carry on in this way for two more years at the most. Taking all this into consideration I met Sonia-ji and told her that if she nominated me again I would be ninety years of age by the time I completed my next term. Also, that I would not be able to lead the life of a disciplined member after perhaps one-and-a-half to two years and that my attendance in Parliament also would become irregular. I retired on 9 April 2002 after completing my third term. It was perhaps the best period of my life. I liked my work as an MP and I have at least this satisfaction that my attendance was very high and that I actively participated in the proceedings. The other point of satisfaction was that I received love, affection and respect from other MPs, irrespective of party affiliation.

40

My Business Activities

I made a beginning in business in 1938, looking after the sugar mills in our group. At present, there are seven sugar units under my charge. These were very tiny when I took control in the early 1940s. For example, the biggest sugar unit—the Upper Ganges Sugar and Industries Ltd—was a tiny factory with a capacity to crush about 1,300 tonnes of cane per day. Today, it is a robust unit of over 10,000-tonne crushing capacity. Likewise, all the sugar units have expanded their capacities eight to ten times.

My father started our textile unit in Okara some time in the 1930s. This was a very well-planned unit. Father had purchased equipment from Reiter, a famous textile machinery manufacturing company of Switzerland. After the country's partition in 1947, Okara became a part of Pakistan. After partition, many people advised us to sell off the mill. Father, however, did not agree and carried on. All the Hindu employees were evacuated to India. The general manager was a man called Gajanand Dalmia. On the advice of the Government of India, he left this unit just for a short period. After a few days, we sent him back to Okara. Gajanand, brave as he was, went cheerfully without any fear. We had many Muslim officers there. They all offered their full cooperation to run the mill efficiently. The Government of Pakistan, under pressure from our government, agreed to provide full security. Gajanand was a very helpful man, popular in the area. He started meeting government officers. He met all the top people in the district of Okara as well as in the capital. The mill ran quite efficiently and paid good dividends. As the Pakistan government was already short of foreign currency, it could not freely permit remittance of dividends. We did receive dividends in India, but after long delays. The mill continued to function well, till the 1971 war over Bangladesh. After the war the authorities seized the mill as enemy property.

In my opinion, the Government of India did not show enough courage.

After the 1971 war, we had Pakistan under our thumb. We could have cleared up all these matters with Pakistan.

With some funds that we had received from Pakistan sent by remittances, I thought Sutlej Industries should start a spinning unit in India. After careful consideration, we decided to put up a unit in Rajasthan at a place called Bhawani Mandi in Jhalawar district. The plant went into production in the mid-1960s. We placed the order for modern machines. This unit is doing well.

After some time, we decided to expand this spinning unit. While plans were being prepared, Kashmir Chief Minister Sheikh Abdullah happened to drop in at Birla House in New Delhi to meet father. He pleaded that

Srinagar, 1979: Sheikh Mohammad Abdullah, then chief minister of Jammu and Kashmir, at the stone-laying ceremony of Birla Sarai

we should start some industry in Jammu and Kashmir. After that I had several independent meetings with Sheikh Abdullah and we decided to establish a spinning unit at a place called Kathua. We called it Chenab Textile Mills, the name selected by Sheikh Abdullah himself. This unit has expanded considerably. As this was the first major industrial unit in the state, Sheikh Abdullah appreciated our action in setting up this unit. Whenever we had any problem, we had only to approach the chief minister. Sheikh Saheb and his wife Begum Saheba became good friends of mine. They said that when we had any problem I need not personally telephone

Sheikh Saheb; our chief executive could go and meet him. Sheikh Saheb and later his son, Farooq, always helped in resolving the problems faced by this unit. We expanded this unit and it has now become a major textile unit in the country. The Government of Jammu and Kashmir has always been helpful.

Sutlej Industries is one of the best-run textile units in the country. Starting as a small unit, today it has grown into a major textile company. It has two textile units—one at Bhawani Mandi and the other at Kathua. Its capacity is 155,000 spindles. It also has looms with a capacity to produce 42 lakh metres of fabric per year. Its total turnover in 2006–07 was Rs 719.53 crore.

Texmaco went into production sometime in 1940. Unfortunately, the Second World War started before we could do much. Texmaco had some very impressive machines on its floors. The government insisted that we produce military equipment in this company. We had no option but to fall in line. However, after the war it started manufacturing textile machinery and also wagons. It had many ups and downs but whenever there was any problem we were able to find ways and means to save it. In course of time, the textile machinery manufacturing business started flourishing. We had a tie-up with a Japanese company called Howa.

Later, the demand for textile machinery also dropped considerably. Bad times beset the company and eventually we had to approach the Board for Industrial and Financial Reconstruction (BIFR), a body constituted by the government to help sick units recover. I took a personal interest in the matter; but our experience with the BIFR was a disaster. I, along with our chief executive Ramesh Maheshwari, attended a number of meetings of BIFR. The members of the bench where we appeared were very rude and officious. I told our people that we had gone to BIFR with great expectations but the treatment we received was hardly sympathetic. We, therefore, decided to exit from BIFR. Accordingly, we approached the Kolkata High Court in 1995. We won the case and extricated ourselves. Unfortunately, at a time when we needed full sympathy from banks and financial institutions, we found their attitude very harsh. I sent Maheshwari to meet the heads of these institutions and asked him to convey to them that if they felt that our management was good they should try to help us. I told Maheshwari to convey to these bodies that every industry suffers periods of setback. If the institutions felt that we were on the right track, they should help us.

At that stage, I brought my son-in-law Saroj Kumar Poddar also into the picture. Saroj was to act like a managing director and Maheshwari as the executive president. Saroj is a brilliant man. His knowledge of law and finance is superb. He has the qualities of leadership. As the chairman, I held meetings with them almost every month. Ultimately, as a result of these efforts, we were able to turn the company around. We also went for diversification and today the company is manufacturing wagons, structurals, sugar mills machinery, boilers, hydro-dam gates etc. It is flourishing once again and has a bright future.

Texmaco has an excellent steel foundry also. Its capacity is about 9,000 tonnes and this is being increased. We want to produce world-class goods. The company also manufactures agro machines for fertilizer companies.

In 1953, it had occurred to me that I should invite Pandit Jawaharlal Nehru, who was then prime minister, to visit Texmaco and see for himself what our house was doing without any foreign technical assistance. I spoke to father. He welcomed the idea and advised me to meet Pandit-ji. M.O. Mathai was then the secretary to Pandit-ji. He was very friendly with me, and arranged my meeting with Pandit-ji. After some persuasion Pandit-ji agreed to come to the factory. I spoke to father about it; he was naturally delighted on my success. I told him that he should be present on that occasion. But the great man that father was, he said, 'Nothing doing. It is your baby and it is best that you show Pandit-ji round the factory.' Pandit-ji accordingly visited Texmaco on 14 December 1953. There was

Kolkata, December 1953: I accompany Jawaharlal Nehru on a round of Texmaco factory

a large gathering. Dr Bidhan Chandra Roy was then the chief minister of West Bengal. Pandit-ji, Bidhan Babu and I sat in one car. Knowing Pandit-ji's preference, we drove in an open car. In those days there were many cars, the hoods of which could be opened. As was the habit of Pandit-ji, when we reached the vicinity of Texmaco factory, he stood up to receive the greetings of the crowd. He was sitting on one side of the car on the back seat. I was sitting on the other side. Bidhan Babu was in between. When Pandit-ji stood up, as a courtesy I also stood up. Bidhan Babu then told me to sit down. I told Bidhan Babu that that might suggest disrespect to Pandit-ji. He spoke strongly in Bengali, 'Boso, boso, boso (sit, sit, sit).' So I sat down. Pandit-ji enjoyed the sight of the gathering and being driven in the car with people cheering all around. His visit was a great inspiration to me. He spent quite some time in going round the factory, inspecting the machines and observing how people worked.

Texmaco acquired a good name for its management and labour relations. The factory was well laid out and there was plenty of greenery at the site. A mark of its excellence was that whenever any foreign dignitary came to Kolkata, the West Bengal government would arrange a visit to Texmaco. Thus when Nikolai Aleksandrovich Bulganin, chairman, Council of Ministers of USSR, and Nikita Sergeyevich Khrushchev, secretary of its Communist Party, visited Kolkata in 1955, the West Bengal government arranged a visit to Texmaco. However, as a huge crowd had gathered all along the road, the visit had to be cancelled for security reasons. Bidhan Babu, however, arranged my meeting with both these VVIPs. I met them at the Government House and explained to them what Texmaco was doing. Haile Selassie, emperor of Ethiopia, also visited Texmaco in the same year.

Texmaco is the biggest producer in India of wagons and hydro-mechanical equipment. It participates in foreign tenders also and exports a sizeable volume of its products. One out of every four wagons of the Indian railways rolls out of Texmaco. Consequently, it has the largest market share. It is the only engineering concern that can build the most complicated wagons. Texmaco has made significant contribution to core infrastructure—power generation, irrigation, agriculture and flood control. It is famed for manufacturing the most robust industrial boilers besides various types of process equipment to international standards. It has a sprawling campus. It has set up an Estate School. It boasts a fine club with facilities for playing tennis and a modern swimming pool.

Special mention must be made of Ramesh Maheshwari. He joined me in 1962. None of my other executives has put in so many years in our organization. Maheshwari came through a common friend. He is a great believer in astrology and he is regarded as a competent astrologer himself. He made a special request through this common friend that I should see him only at some particular time which, according to his knowledge of astrology, was auspicious. I was a bit amused but I met Maheshwari during the time that he had indicated. He joined as a middle-level executive; but in course of time by dint of hard work and ability he became the chief executive. I found Maheshwari very dynamic and a very able executive. He can write well and speak well; he has a very clear brain and a knack for handling labour properly. In the last forty years there has been no major labour trouble in Texmaco. When other industries hear about it they are amazed, because 'gherao' tactics were the brainchild of some people after the Left Front government came to power in West Bengal.

The last major labour trouble in Texmaco, a strike lasting about four months (April–August), took place in 1968. At that time the labour union of the company worked under the guidance of Jyoti Basu, before he became the chief minister of West Bengal. There were many labour unions in our company but the majority of the workers followed CITU. The trouble took place as usual on some minor issue. But it appeared that the workers were bent on going on strike. After about four months they were exhausted. Texmaco too came under a great financial strain. But I said that we were not in a position to come to any understanding with the workers except on our own terms.

Whenever such strikes take place, there are always some people who act as intermediaries. One day one such person came to me and said that it would be a good idea if Jyoti Babu and I met at some common friend's place. There was a well-known lawyer, Snehanshu Acharya, who belonged to the Communist Party but was a very liberal-minded person. Most of the industrialists were his friends. Acharya was a good friend of mine also. The meeting was arranged at his residence. The meeting—in fact, perhaps three meetings—were held at Acharya's place, each lasting more than an hour. I was always accompanied by Maheshwari. I found Jyoti Babu to be a very reasonable man. A labour leader who sees only the interests of labour and does not see the viewpoint of the management can never succeed. Jyoti Babu, while presenting the labour point of view, also saw our viewpoint and our capacity to pay. Ultimately an agreement was reached.

This was the first time that I came in touch with Jyoti Babu. After that I met him frequently and I often went to his house. Our friendship continued even after he became chief minister. Then I used to meet him at the

Writers Buildings. Later, when I took to active politics and joined Parliament, I maintained contact with Jyoti Babu. We met mostly at his residence at Salt Lake.

There are seven sugar units in my group—four in Uttar Pradesh and three in Bihar. Till the early 1930s, India was a major importer of sugar. All this sugar came from Java, which was then a part of the Dutch Empire. The sugar units in Java under Dutch management were efficiently run and were the biggest exporters of sugar to India. In the late 1920s, there was a public outcry as to why a large country like India should depend for its requirement of sugar on foreign countries and why it could not produce its own sugar. The expert opinion was that Uttar Pradesh, Bihar, Karnataka, Tamil Nadu, Maharashtra and, in fact, the entire country was suitable for sugar cane plantation. The soil of these states and climatic condition were fit for production of sugar cane. The government, bowing to public pressure, steeply raised the import duty on sugar so that sugar cane could be planted in the country on a massive scale and sugar units be established here. Thus, in the 1930s a large number of sugar units were put up in the country and, within a period of five years, with protection given by the government, India became self-sufficient in sugar. At that time we also established sugar units in Uttar Pradesh and Bihar.

The entire economy of India changed with the establishment of these sugar units. The sugar industry plays a very important role in the improvement of the economy of the rural areas. My group is the biggest producer of sugar in the private sector in the country. All our sugar units try to improve the quality of the sugar cane and spend huge amounts of money on sugar cane development.

The sugar units have had their ups and downs. There were periods when sugar was completely controlled. During such periods prices of both sugar cane and sugar were fixed by the government. The policy of the Governments of Uttar Pradesh and Bihar was to give as high a price as possible to the sugar cane cultivators and in order to safeguard the interest of the consumers, keep the sugar price as low as possible. During such periods, industry suffered.

The condition of the sugar units in Bihar is not very good. Apart from other things, north Bihar gets flooded almost every year owing to high rainfall in Nepal from where water rolls down. Once when the sugar industry in Bihar was in deep trouble, some of the sugar units could not make the sugar cane payment to the farmers in time. Karpoori Thakur, the then chief minister, was a friend of mine. He had strong socialistic views. One day he suddenly decided to nationalize the sugar industry in his state. He did not consult the industry about it and as a populist measure came out with a notification on nationalization of the sugar units in Bihar on 29 October 1978.

I was reading my morning papers in my house in Kolkata. As soon as I got this news from our people in Patna, I rushed there to find out what the facts were. I met Karpoori Thakur and upbraided him for taking this step without discussing the matter with the industry. I told him that my relationship with him was very cordial and that before taking such a hasty step he should have discussed with me the problems which he thought his state or its farmers were facing from the sugar industry. After prolonged discussions, Karpoori Thakur realized that he had taken a hasty step. 'But what can I do now? What has been done is done,' he said. I told him that we would fight out the matter in court and the only reason why I met him was to urge him not to have a vindictive attitude.

When I went to Patna, I had taken our solicitors with me. The owners of all the sugar units in Bihar had rushed to Patna with me. They were depending on me to provide the leadership and save the sugar industry of Bihar. After studying the matter in Patna, I came back to Kolkata. We filed a writ petition in the Calcutta High Court and obtained a stay order. The state government had by then realized its mistake. The government knew that it would lose the case. Ultimately, the notification was withdrawn.

There are two fertilizer units in my group—one at Zuarinagar, Goa, and the other at a place called Gadepan, near Kota in Rajasthan. The first fertilizer company that I started was Zuari Agro Chemicals Ltd (now Zuari Industries Ltd). This was started in 1967 and went into production in 1973. The company had some initial problems, particularly concerning pollution. However, we took proper steps and today no waste water of Zuari Industries situated in Goa goes out to the sea. The company is functioning well.

Chambal Fertilizers was established by me in 1985. Some four years earlier, Indira-ji, who was then the prime minister, had sent for me. She said that India's requirement of fertilizers was enormous and that the country would like to become self-sufficient in the sector. Indira-ji knew about the able manner in which Zuari Industries was being run and the contribution that it made in terms of employment and generation of wealth in the country. She asked me to establish another fertilizer plant. She reassured me that I would be granted the licence for setting up a unit anywhere in north India including Uttar Pradesh, Punjab, Haryana and Rajasthan. I selected Rajasthan and the plant was established at Gadepan.

Kota, Rajasthan, January 2001: With villagers during a visit to
the Chambal Fertilizers and Chemicals factory

We received full assistance from the Central and the state governments.
Chambal's fertilizer plant is world class. I was keen to make it one of the
best industrial units in the country. Hence the architect was told to provide
a lot of greenery in the area and to design a layout that would be the
pride of the country. We selected one of the best architects and laid out
the garden according to the advice of garden experts. I dare say that
Chambal's plant is one of the best-laid-out units in the country and perhaps
in the world. After watching its progress and looking to the need for
fertilizers in the country, we established another unit in the same campus.

We also acquired Paradeep Phosphates Ltd, the largest producer of
phosphoric acid and di-ammonium phosphates (DAP) in the country from
the government in partnership with Office Cherifien Des Phosphates (OCP)
of Morocco. This was a sick unit in the public sector situated in Orissa
and was acquired by our group as a result of the government's
disinvestment policy. The two units in the group cover almost all the
states of north and south India, and with Paradeep Phosphates making its
contribution, almost the entire country will be covered.

All my fertilizer units are being looked after by H.S. Bawa. He joined
my group in 1979. He is a very able man and I will count him among the
top executives of the country.

It is the constant endeavour of the companies in my group to follow
global standards of corporate conduct towards their shareholders,

customers, employees, etc. My companies believe in achieving organizational excellence leading to increasing employee and customer satisfaction and shareholder value along with serving the people in the areas where our units are situated.

The primary objective of corporate governance is to create and adhere to a corporate culture of conscience and consciousness, transparency and openness, and to develop capabilities and identify opportunities that best serve the goal of value creation. Thus, my units are fully committed to carrying out corporate social responsibilities.

All the industrial units under my chairmanship are also deeply concerned about conservation of water and planting of trees to prevent recurrence of droughts. Thus, rural development, water conservation, community service, health care, education and general improvement of the quality of life of our people in the areas where these units are situated are their prime concern. Our units also provide medical care, undertake infrastructure development, promote sports, cultural and social activities and infrastructure development activities in the villages, which include installation of new hand pumps, deepening and upkeep of existing tube wells, providing water storage tanks and building check dams. In Rajasthan, where there is a drought in three out of five years, there is a real problem of shortage of drinking water. This is receiving our special attention.

Thus all units in my group, fertilizer units, sugar mills, textile units or my leading engineering complex Texmaco, take care to discharge their social obligations. They are doing the best they can.

God has been kind to me. All my units are doing well. There are always ups and downs in an industry. All the units under me had to face a bad period at times; but with proper guidance and good work done by the top executives, they are on the whole doing well.

PART IV

VIGNETTES

Our Top Executives

We have many top executives who could be considered as belonging to an all-India cadre of officers with the finest qualities of leadership and discernment in every sphere of commercial activity. An executive must have many qualities in order to be efficient and able. Some qualities which I always try to look for when I appoint an executive are: honesty, ability, vision, strength of character, maintaining discipline, human touch and capacity for hard work.

I treat my executives as members of a big family. I now make some comments on some of them.

Father's senior-most executive was Durga Prasad Mandelia. He hailed from Pilani. His father, Gauri Dutt Mandelia, looked after our zamindari at Ranchi in the 1920s when we were children. Gauri Dutt-ji was a lovable character and we were very fond of him.

Father had a knack of selecting good and efficient people with the potential to develop. He selected Durga Prasad and took him under his wing. Durga Prasad was first put in charge of our textile mills at Gwalior, known as Jiyajeerao Cotton Mills. His performance was outstanding. Later, when father was growing old, he entrusted the management of all his companies to Durga Prasad's care. He looked after these companies very well and was regarded as father's right-hand man. People would often say that just as Hanuman was completely devoted to Lord Ram, so was Durga Prasad devoted to father.

Tara Chand Saboo was also a senior executive during father's time. He too hailed from Pilani. He looked after Birla Jute Mills (now a division of Birla Corporation). He was a very popular figure. Apart from being attached to father, he was a close friend of my elder brother Lakshmi Niwas.

Murali Dhar Dalmia, another top executive, joined Birla Jute Mills when I was fifteen or even younger. He was put in charge of the stores department of the mills. Within a short duration, the stores department became famous for its cleanliness, orderliness and efficiency. Many people would visit Birla Jute Mills just to see the stores and then say that it was a kind of a drawing room of Birla Jute Mills.

Murali Dhar was suddenly transferred to Birla Cotton Mills in Delhi. This is how it happened.

The chief executive of Birla Cotton Mills was a person called Jwalaprasad Mandelia. Jwalaprasad suddenly died of some ailment in 1935. Lakshmi Niwas was looking after Birla Cotton Mills in those days under father's overall supervision. Bhai-ji sent a wire to father who was then in London asking his advice as to who should be given charge of Birla Mills. Father, who had a high opinion about Murali Dhar, immediately replied that he be given the charge. Bhai-ji had some reservations about it, but father overruled him and told him firmly to appoint Murali Dhar as chief executive of Birla Cotton Mills immediately. This was done and the performance of Birla Mills, which was then an ailing unit, soon improved and it became a healthy unit of the group.

I was a student in Hindu College when Murali Dhar took charge of the mills. I often came in touch with him. I developed a liking for him as a person and also admiration for his abilities. In 1938, when I had fallen ill and stayed at Almora for five months, on the advice of Mahatma-ji, Murali Dhar, whose health was rather frail in those days and who also needed a change, visited Almora and stayed with me for about a month.

Owing to his ill health, Murali Dhar had to retire from his work for a few years. Father asked him to take leave with full pay till he got well. Simultaneously, Father entrusted the work of Birla Cotton Mills to me. This was sometime in the late 1940s. At that time Ram Prasad Poddar was working as a senior executive in the mills. I took charge but even though Murali Dhar was not well I constantly consulted him about the management and important decisions.

Father's system of organization was simple. In the textile units under him he would keep two chief executives of equal rank. One would look after the entire technical side including production, quality control, stores, time office and also public relations. The other executive would look after the entire commercial side such as purchase of cotton, marketing of cloth and finance.

After some time, when Murali Dhar was well, he resumed his duties as chief executive. Poddar was then transferred to Century Spinning & Manufacturing Company Ltd—a major company in the group. He too turned out to be an able man. He was also a man of very high principles. After Murali Dhar took charge of Birla Mills, he came directly under me.

During the Emergency, Murali Dhar also got into difficulties and was sent to prison. Chaudhary Bansi Lal, who was then chief minister of Haryana, took a dislike to Murali Dhar on an insignificant matter. Murali Dhar, while looking after Birla Cotton Mills, was also in charge of the textile mills that we had in Bhiwani. There is also a college at Bhiwani, called Technological Institute of Textile & Sciences (TIT), for imparting education and awarding degrees to students in textile technology. Bansi Lal got annoyed with Murali Dhar concerning some matter connected with TIT. He sent a message to Murali Dhar making certain requests for taking action against the principal of TIT. Requests coming from the chief minister were treated by most people of Haryana as orders. Murali Dhar showed courage and defied Bansi Lal as he felt that the principal was not at fault. This made Bansi Lal furious and he wanted Murali Dhar to be arrested. Murali Dhar, who had a fine legal brain, fought the case right up to the Supreme Court. He lost the case in the Supreme Court and so surrendered to the Haryana police. They put him in prison but he was treated like a political prisoner. Thus he also became one of those who were victimized during the Emergency.

Murali Dhar is an excellent bridge player. In 1984, when I got elected to the Rajya Sabha and when Delhi became my headquarters, I used to play bridge regularly on Saturdays, Sundays and holidays. Murali Dhar, being the president of Delhi Bridge Association, would organize the game for me.

Murali Dhar is a man of versatile qualities and tastes. He has a very clear brain. He is in his nineties but is keeping fit for his age. His brain and memory are normal. He was one of the ablest executives who worked under father and also under me.

Ram Prasad Poddar worked for a very short time with me. He was a very able person. Apart from that, he was a very pious man and honest to the core. As chief executive of Century Mills, Poddar worked very ably and the firm acquired fame for its products; so good was the quality of its products that the majority of them were exported.

While working in Century Mills, Poddar had a presentiment of his death. He called his sons and told them that the company's house which he was occupying should be returned within one month of his death. After his demise, his sons came to my younger brother, Basant Kumar, who was and is the chairman of Century Mills, told him what their father had told them but added they would be grateful if the period was extended, to which Basant Kumar readily agreed. Poddar was a man of noble character.

When I joined business in late 1938, my uncle BM put me in charge of the sugar mills in our group. There were three sugar mills managed by him—Upper Ganges Sugar Mills at Seohara was the largest. When I went to Seohara in December 1939, Gopichand Dhariwal was in charge of the mills. Dani was assistant secretary, the No. 2 man. When I reached Seohara by train all the senior executives of the mills were there at the railway station to receive me. Dani was one of them.

Dani was an able executive. He had a keen sense of humour. He was a good social figure and was endowed with a certain magnetism which helped him to draw friends around him. In course of time, he became like a member of the family. In due course, I made him the top executive at our sugar mills at Seohara. Dani worked very sincerely. He was a true sportsman, a good conversationalist, and very witty. He did not have any children. Rather than toiling and drudgery, he thought of living a carefree, peaceful life and so he pressed me for early retirement. I tried to persuade him not to do so and to continue with us for a few more years. He said he could not refuse me but that his heart was not in the work. I then let him retire but as I valued his counsel I made him an advisor to the group of my sugar companies. Whenever I went on holiday in India I would ask Dani to accompany me. My wife, my daughters, sons-in-law and everyone took a liking for him, so delightful a person was he.

Dani died of cardiac arrest on 26 August 1993. He had to be admitted to hospital for his heart ailment. He came to have dinner with me at my residence in Delhi the day before he was to be admitted to hospital. I had a presentiment that Dani would not survive in the hospital. I started talking about his long association with me. Dani also got emotional and expressed his devotion to me. Two days after being admitted in the hospital, he expired. His body was cremated at Garh Mukteswar. Shortly after his demise, my wife and I went to Moradabad to call on his wife and other members of the family.

Mohanlal Khandelia was the ablest among the sugar mills executives. I engaged him at New India Sugar Mills in 1949. He worked for twenty-seven years in our sugar mills in Bihar. In 1976 he was transferred to Upper Ganges Sugar Mills. Mohanlal worked very honestly and sincerely. In his later years, one of the valves of his heart was damaged. Mohanlal, therefore, had to lead a cautious life. Later he was advised to have an operation performed on the valve.

He decided to have the surgery done in a famous hospital in Chennai. I had a premonition that Mohanlal may not survive this operation. Before his departure for Chennai, Mohanlal came to see me. We talked about old times. Something prompted me to see Mohanlal off. I, therefore, went right up to the main door of the house to see him off, which I had never done in the past. Mohanlal too noticed it. He realized something was worrying me. As I feared, Mohanlal did not survive the operation. His family members were very sore about the absence of proper care in the hospital.

All throughout Mohanlal's association with me, he helped me not only with the work of the sugar mills but in solving any other problem I had. Thus, when I fought two elections from Rajasthan for the Rajya Sabha in 1984 and 1990, Mohanlal was all along with me. His early demise was an irreparable loss.

In my method of organization, a lot of power is delegated to the executives. My main companies could be divided into three groups. These are:

- **Fertilizers:** There are three units in India: Chambal Fertilizers & Chemicals Ltd, Zuari Industries Ltd and Paradeep Phosphates Ltd. One unit, Indo Maroc Phosphore SA (IMACID) is in Morocco in 50:50 partnership with a company belonging to the government of Morocco called Office Cherifien des Phosphates (OCP).
- **Spinning units:** The spinning units are under my company Sutlej Industries Ltd. These are situated at Bhawani Mandi in Rajasthan and Kathua in Jammu and Kashmir. There is also a spinning unit under Chambal Fertilizers at a place called Baddi in Himachal Pradesh. Though this belongs to Chambal, for better administration its management has been given to Sutlej Industries.
- **Sugar mills:** There are seven sugar units in my group, four in Uttar Pradesh and three in Bihar. They are situated in the districts of Bijnore, Lakhimpur Kheri, Sitapur and Shahjahanpur in Uttar Pradesh and Gopalganj, Champaran and Darbhanga in Bihar.
- That apart, there is one major engineering company in West Bengal called Texmaco.

Each of these companies has its own chief executive called either managing director or executive president. There is also a head for each group of companies

My System of Organization

I believe in decentralization. Once I asked Pandit Govind Ballabh Pant, when he was chief minister of Uttar Pradesh, how strong his hold over the administration was. 'Krishna Kumar,' he said, 'not a leaf in my state moves without my approval.' What he said was correct. The state did not move whereas the rest of India marched forward.

The administration of an organization is an art. To organize the management properly one must, in my way of working, give ample powers to the chief executive. At the fountainhead is the principle of decentralization. I am a great believer in this principle.

Every three months, I hold a meeting of the company concerned and spend about four or five hours going through the performance of the unit, its future plans, financial position, marketing and labour relations in great depth. All the senior executives of that unit join in such meetings. After that, decisions are arrived at by general consensus. If an occasion arises when a consensus is not reached, I give the final ruling. But this rarely happens.

After a decision has been reached, the concerned executives are asked to implement it and show me the results. Subject to the approved budget, they are at liberty to place the order for equipment, negotiate the price and finalize the order. (My approval is obtained for more costly equipment.) If there is any vacancy, within sanctioned limits, they can fill it. I interview candidates for senior posts.

Once all these formalities are over, the executives are left free to organize the performance of each unit and show me results. The next meeting is held after three months. In between the management sends me daily reports of all important functions so that I keep in touch. Again after three months we meet and discuss how the actual results compared with the estimates.

The advantages of this method are many. First, I give an opportunity to the executive to show his performance. Secondly, I do not ask him to meet me from time to time and thus waste his time and mine. I have before me in the file copies of the estimates and other decisions taken. I keep a watch as to how the company is performing. Thirdly, the executive knows that he has got to satisfy me with his performance. He also knows that if he were to give any explanation it will be very closely scrutinized. I tell my executives that I want results from them, not explanations.

My executives tell me that the amount of liberty that they enjoy is not bestowed in any other organization. I also find that this type of organization is giving me good results. What is more, by this method I simplify the execution of work. I spend five to six hours every three months even on major companies like Chambal Fertilizers. That way, if many other companies are added to my group, that does not bother me, for what I am required to do is just to spend five or six hours in every quarter and thereafter to keep in touch with the progress. There is, however, a catch in this way of working. This system works only where the top executives are very able persons. Hence I pay my top executives handsome salaries and try to get the best person available to fill that post. Some of my top executives are:

H.S. Bawa: He is the senior-most executive of my fertilizer units. Bawa is a highly qualified and professional man. He is a man of great ability and integrity. In my opinion, he is one of the best administrators in the country.

Navratanmal Gupta: He is the senior-most executive of my spinning units. He is, like me, from the Maheshwari caste. I do not know why he has taken the surname of Gupta, which is not a Maheshwari surname. The Gupta surname is used by Agarwal families. Navratanmal is a very able and efficient person. He is a finance and commerce man. Yet he has considerable technical knowledge. Because of his organizational ability and skill in working, all the spinning units in my group are running successfully. He is regarded as one of the best administrators in the spinning units.

Suresh Khandelia: Suresh Khandelia is the son of Mohanlal Khandelia. He is a chartered accountant and a brilliant administrator. Under Navratanmal's overall control, he looks after the two units at Kathua and Baddi.

Chand Bihari Patodia: Chand Bihari Patodia is the chief executive of my sugar units. He is a commercial-cum-finance man. Though he is not a technical man, he has made an in-depth study of sugar technology with the result that no sugar technologist can fool him. On the other hand, where some unit is not working properly, he is able to direct the technicians about what ails the company and what should be done to improve the performance. He is, in my opinion, the best chief executive in the sugar industry.

Ramesh Maheshwari: Ramesh Maheshwari is an outstanding administrator. By training, he is a lawyer endowed with a strong common sense. He is a good orator and excellent conversationalist. He is also a very good astrologer. He is deeply devoted to me and his performance as the chief executive of my engineering unit Texmaco is commendable.

Maheshwari joined Texmaco in 1962. Owing to his long association and his deep devotion towards me he has become a kind of member of the family. Texmaco has made remarkable progress under Maheshwari's management. Along with Maheshwari, my second son-in-law Saroj Kumar Poddar has also made valuable contribution to the success of Texmaco. The reason why the organization is at present functioning very successfully is that I, as the non-executive chairman, am consulted by Saroj and Maheshwari in case there is any major development. Thereafter, Saroj is in constant touch with Maheshwari who has an absolutely free hand in running the company. This has paid rich dividends in the performance of Texmaco.

Dr S. Venkateswaran

In running Birla Institute of Technology and Science, Dr S. Venkateswaran, vice-chancellor, has been of a great help to me. He had been at Pilani for thirty-two years and became director of BITS, Pilani, in the year 1989. Later, when the designation 'chairman of the board of governors' was changed to 'chancellor', Venkateswaran was re-designated as vice-chancellor in September 2003. Venkateswaran is a man of great ability, integrity and also has organizational skills. He retired from the vice-chancellorship in July 2006; but looking to his experience and ability he has been made professor emeritus-cum-advisor.

Encounter with the Police Commissioner in Delhi

When I was a student in Hindu College, Delhi, I was very fond of driving and I went by car to college. A chauffeur would sit by my side. I used to drive quite fast, but I was a good driver. I started driving when I was about seventeen or eighteen years of age. I gave it up after reaching the age of seventy-five, realizing that at that age when the reflexes were not very alert it was unwise to drive a car and get involved in an accident. My habit was to drive the car cautiously in a crowded street but where the road was clear I would drive fast.

Once, in 1936, while going to college, I saw another car ahead of me. I could make out that it was a government car. I had overtaken other cars, but the question was whether or not I should overtake this car. I knew that it was a government car but not overtaking it, I thought, would be timidity on my part. What will my chauffeur think, I argued—that his boss was afraid of overtaking a government car! After taking all the pros and cons into consideration I pressed my foot on the accelerator and overtook the other car. Horn blaring, it soon overtook me, the chauffeur got down and asked me to stop. In pre-independence days, all the important posts in the government were filled by the British. A British officer came out of the car and said that he was the police commissioner of Delhi and that he was going to charge me with exceeding the speed limit. Being a student and full of spirit, I started arguing with him, but he would not listen. He asked me for my driving licence. He took down some details and said that I would soon receive a summons. He asked me for my address. I gave the address of Birla Cotton Mills Ltd. In my youthful bravado, I was undaunted and decided to face the situation when the summons came.

When the summons came, I consulted Murali Dhar Dalmia. He found that the summons was incomplete. I was addressed merely as 'Birla, son of Ghanshyamdas-ji'. So I did not go to the court on the appointed date. Instead, a lawyer was sent who said he was representing Birla Cotton Mills Ltd. He said that Birla Mills could not be and was not the accused, but who the accused was, was not clear. The magistrate asked the public prosecutor the full name of the person who was being charged. As the prosecutor could not furnish the details, the case was dismissed.

Ustad Bismillah Khan

Bharat Ratna Ustad Bismillah Khan was the country's best shehnai player. The shehnai is usually played at weddings or receptions. Playing classical tunes on the shehnai is a very difficult task. Ustad Bismillah Khan, who hailed from Varanasi, achieved this.

I had known Ustad Bismillah Khan since the early 1960s. I greatly admired him as he was an outstanding artiste. Once I had also invited him to play at a reception I held after the wedding of one of my daughters.

On 17 July 2002, Ustad Bismillah Khan wrote to me about his granddaughter, Manisha Raza. He said that she had passed her higher secondary examination and requested that she be admitted at BITS, Pilani. I replied to him on 21 July stating that I would have gladly helped her in view of the fact that she belongs to such a well-known family whose head, the Ustad, had served the country with his unparalleled shehnai recitals and who had also given performances outside the country, thus enhancing the country's reputation abroad. I wrote, 'I have been hearing your shehnai for over forty years and have been your admirer.'

Proceeding, I said that at BITS Pilani all the admissions were made strictly on merit and this would preclude me from doing anything special for his granddaughter. I suggested that there were some institutes in Karnakata and Tamil Nadu which accepted students on payment of capitation fee. I promised to pay some amounts towards such capitation fee. I also said that we had an institute at Dubai called BITS, Pilani, with a good reputation. I explained to the Ustad that there were separate hostels for boys and girls there. I offered to have his granddaughter admitted there and also offered to bear all the expenses for her education. Ustad Bismillah Khan replied that he wanted to have his granddaughter admitted at Bangalore. I replied that I would pay Rs 1.50 lakh towards her education expenses. His granddaughter wrote to thank me. I also received a very nice letter of thanks from Ustad Bismillah Khan. Copies of these are reproduced:

25 September 2002

My dear Birla Sb

Namaskar

Kindly excuse me for intruding in your busy moments with these few lines.

Thank you very much for the draft of Rs 1.5 lakhs (One lakh fifty thousand rupees) for Manisha Raza. I cannot forget the most touching and emotional moments that I had shared with Birla's family. I pray to Almighty God to give you all long life and strength. Apologizing for putting you to this inconvenience.

With many thanks again from,

Yours sincerely
Bismillah Khan

8 August 2002

My dear Birla Sb

Adab Arz.

Kindly excuse me for intruding in your busy moments with these few lines. I received your kind letter dated 21 July 2002.

I have decided to admit my grand daughter at RVCE or MVIT Bangalore. You know that I am a humble artist who has spread Indian classical music in every corner of the world. I am really very frustrated that Manisha did not get admission at Pilani. But I am very confident that you will offer full help to admit her at RVCE or MVIT Bangalore. I would request you to kindly help her by paying some amount as a capitation fee. I would be very thankful to you. I am anxiously awaiting for your kind response.

With regards,

Bismillah Khan

Mahatma Gandhi's Funeral

Gandhi-ji died on 30 January 1948 at Birla House, New Delhi. Father and I had gone to Pilani the previous day to take Pandit Govind Ballabh Pant and his son K.C. Pant (Raja) around BITS. It was here that we got the sad and shocking news of Gandhi-ji's assassination. Father, Pant-ji and Raja immediately left by father's plane for Delhi. As it was a small plane, all of us could not be accommodated. So I left for Delhi by car, along with some other people.

From the early morning, lakhs of people started gathering around Birla House to take part in the funeral procession. In such a rush, the arrangements for the funeral were found wanting in many respects. I was then about thirty years old. I thought if I informed father of my resolve to attend the funeral he would try to dissuade me from going as the arrangements made by the police and the administrators were not very effective for the management of a highly volatile crowd that was likely to gather. I, therefore, very quietly slipped out and joined the procession. It had been decided that, barring some top leaders, everyone would walk from Birla House to the cremation ground, which was about four and a half miles away. The people in the procession walked at a snail's pace. This was not unexpected. It took us more than two hours to reach Rajghat.

After the funeral pyre was lit, everybody started dispersing from Rajghat. I had asked one of our senior executives of Birla Cotton Mills to send a car to the cremation grounds and be on the lookout for me so that I could return by car. The executive to whom I spoke forgot to give the necessary instructions. The result was that after the funeral function commenced and the people started leaving the cremation grounds, I found that there was no car for me.

In the funeral procession three or four of us were together, including Basant Kumar's father-in-law the late Brijlal Biyani, who was called Berar Kesri. He too had no vehicle to take him back. Both of us and three or four other people who were with him started walking back. Somewhere on our way back we hailed a tonga. We reached Birla House five or six hours after we had left for the funeral.

Soon after I left, father discovered that I was not at Birla House. He made anxious enquiries. Nobody knew where I was. But father guessed rightly that I must have gone to the funeral. After waiting a couple of hours, when I did not return, father's anxiety grew. He asked many of our executives to make enquiries in various hospitals. I could not be traced at the hospitals either. Father was very concerned and he became nervous. When I returned in a tonga late in the evening I found father waiting at the gate of Birla House with more than a dozen servants and executives. He was greatly relieved to see me but gave me a piece of his mind for attending the funeral without letting anyone know. He said I should have gone in such a disorganized procession after making proper arrangements. I told father that I had spoken to one of our senior executives. On enquiry, it was learnt that the executive who was awake the whole night completely forgot about the matter. He had been so tired that after reaching his house he immediately fell asleep. Father was irritated with Brijlal also. He said: 'Brijlal-ji, Krishan always indulges in such hazardous adventures. But how could an elderly person like you not take care to see that he reached the house in time?' Brijlal tried to explain that at that time no conveyance was available owing to the milling crowds on the road. However, after a few minutes, father calmed down and was his normal self.

Mahatma-ji's funeral cortege being taken from Birla House to
Rajghat

Presidents of India

I was an MP from 9 April 1984 to 8 April 2002. During this eighteen-year
period, there were four Presidents: Giani Zail Singh, R. Venkataraman,
Dr Shankar Dayal Sharma and K.R. Narayanan. They were all very
cordial towards me. But I was closest to Venkataraman, because I had
known him since he was a minister. He had started as an active member
of the Congress Party in the state of Madras (now Tamil Nadu). As minister
of industry and labour of erstwhile Madras, he did a remarkable job.
Whenever any industrial unit had any problem connected with the Centre,
Venkataraman would visit Delhi and take up the problem personally
with the ministries concerned in order to have it resolved as early as
possible.

After he came to the Centre in 1980, he became the finance minister
and later the defence minister. As finance minister, his performance was
outstanding. Later he became the vice-president of India in August 1984
and after that President in July 1987.

342   KRISHNA KUMAR BIRLA

Venkataraman was a great devotee of the Paramacharya of Kanchi, like me. Whenever there was any function connected with the Kanchi Kamakoti Peetham, Venkataraman would speak to me to give some assistance for a noble cause. I always carried out his wishes.

Once I decided to attend a function at the Kanchi Mutt. I told Venkataraman that I would go to Chennai and from there to the Kanchi Mutt. At that time he had retired from the President's office. The government had granted him a suitable house in Chennai along with proper security guards and an official car. Venkataraman was very happy when he heard that I was going to visit the Shankaracharya and said that he also wanted to go. He invited me to travel from Chennai to Kanchi Mutt with him in his car. I agreed.

After reaching Chennai, I went to Venkataraman's residence. Escorted by the security car, we travelled the distance in the shortest possible time. After offering our obeisance to the Shankaracharya, we went to the guest house where we had a meal. A notable characteristic of the south Indians, particularly the Brahmins, is that however high they may rise in life, they never forget our ancient culture. They feel proud to follow our traditional ways. Venkataraman, a religious Brahmin as he is, ate simple food along with me. Rice and yoghurt are essential items of south Indian food. I can eat any type of food so long as it is prepared in ghee and does not have garlic and onion. I enjoyed my meal with Venkataraman and then we returned to Chennai.

I call on Venkataraman even now. Though he is about 97 years of age, he keeps good health and has a fairly good memory. The last time I met him was in 2003. He embraced me and was very happy to meet me. He made one or two requests for the Kanchi Kamakoti Peetham which I fulfilled.

My relations with late K.R. Narayanan were also very good. He was a man of a very simple nature without any ego. I was also close to Dr Shankar Dayal Sharma. Narayanan also had served as the vice-president before becoming President. I came to know him more intimately after he became President. I visited him often at Rashtrapati Bhavan. I did the same with Dr Shankar Dayal Sharma.

Shankar Dayal-ji was a very sentimental man. Once when he was the vice-president and chaired the Rajya Sabha, an MP made some rude remarks questioning his impartiality. Shankar Dayal-ji broke down in tears. Many MPs rushed to console him. I was one of them. After he had recovered somewhat, he said that in case his impartiality was in question, he would not like to occupy the chair. It was only when leaders of all the parties assured him that they had full faith in him that his composure returned.

I held Narayanan in great esteem. He was one of the best Presidents our country has so far had. An interesting incident happened during his tenure. I am not elaborating it but I am reproducing below my letter dated 18 February 1999 to him. This will be found to be interesting.

18 February 1999

PERSONAL & CONFIDENTIAL

My dear Shri Narayanan,

This is regarding a personal matter concerning which I am taking the liberty of writing to you.

Ever since we attained Independence I have been calling on the Presidents, starting from Shri Rajendra Babu who became the first President of independent India right up to Dr Shankar Dayal Sharma. I have called on all the Presidents once every 3-4 months. That is because I knew all the Presidents even before they were elected to that high office.

After you became the President I wanted to call on you too. Unfortunately, no appointment has been given to me till now.

I have worked under your Chairmanship of the Rajya Sabha. Even in those days when you were the Vice President, I used to call on you both in your office and at your residence from time to time. You were kind enough to have presided over one or two functions of K.K. Birla Foundation also. Under the circumstances when my requests for appointment to meet you were denied, I was naturally a bit surprised.

I wanted to meet you purely as a gesture of courtesy. I must have made at least 8-10 attempts to call on you since you became the President. Every time that I put in a request, there was no response from your office. My secretary made repeated enquiries but all the time she was told that the time to call on you will be indicated later. No appointment, however, ever materialized.

I assumed that you were so busy that you had no time to meet even Members of Parliament. I, therefore, kept silent about the experience. Later some friends opined that perhaps my requests for appointments did not reach you and that some of the people in your Secretariat themselves took the onus of deciding that you had no time to meet me. Under the circumstances I thought of acquainting you with the matter.

It does sound strange to me that the President should have no time to meet a senior Member of Parliament-cum-Industrialist. However, that is a matter for you to decide. If you are really very busy, I shall be the last person to upset your busy schedule; but if on the other hand my requests are not being accorded due consideration by the people in your Secretariat, I thought you should know about the matter.

Kind regards,

Yours sincerely,
K.K. Birla

Soon after that, I received a message from the President's secretariat that I could meet him whenever I found it convenient. I never had any problem after that in meeting the President. Not only that, Narayanan would invite me to all important parties when he invited foreign VIP guests. I met President Bill Clinton and President Pervez Musharraf at the dinner parties given by him when they visited India.

When I met Musharraf, I said: 'Mr President, I got my Honours degree from the Punjab University, Lahore.' He was interested when he heard this and picked up conversation with me. I then told him that we had a textile unit at Okara in Montgomery district and that we did not sell off this unit even after the partition and we ran it successfully. I said that our chief executive and one or two people were Hindus and all others including the senior executives were Pakistanis. The General asked me: 'Dr Birla, are you still running that unit?' I replied: 'No, Mr President. After the war of Bangladesh in 1971, our unit was seized by the Government of Pakistan as enemy property. We were sorry to lose this unit as the mill was functioning well and we received full assistance from the Government of Pakistan.' I also said that our top executive was Gajanand Dalmia. He was a brave man and he stayed on in Pakistan. I further said that he was very popular both with the workers and the government officers. Musharraf was very happy when he heard this.

Kanhaiyalal Maneklal Munshi

Kanhaiyalal Maneklal was born in Bharuch in south Gujarat to an upper middle-class Bhargava Brahmin family. He received his primary education at home under the supervision of his mother Tapi-ben and his secondary education in the Khan Bahadur Dalal High School at Bharuch. After matriculating in 1901, he joined Baroda College. He got his B.A. degree in 1906 and LL.B degree in 1910 from Bombay University.

Sri Aurobindo, Gandhi-ji, Sardar Patel and Bhulabhai Desai made a profound impression on Munshi-ji's thinking and way of life. He was also greatly influenced by Vedic and classical Sanskrit literature. He had copiously studied English, French and German literatures and the histories of various countries. With his versatility in learning, he made his mark in various fields—political, social, educational, cultural and religious.

Before Sri Aurobindo took up the spiritual vocation, he was a revolutionary. He happened to be a professor at Baroda College where Munshi-ji studied. Munshi-ji was drawn towards the revolutionary movement and even took an interest in the technique of bomb-making. But after his arrival in Mumbai around 1915, he drifted towards the Home Rule League and became its secretary. In 1927, he was elected to the Bombay Legislative Council from the university constituency.

With the Bardoli satyagraha in 1928, he became a convert to Gandhi-ji's creed of politics. He resigned from the Legislative Council on the Bardoli issue. He then joined the Congress, participated in the salt satyagraha (1930) and was arrested. In December 1933, he started the movement for creating a parliamentary wing of the Congress, and in the following year became the secretary of the Parliamentary Board. In 1937, he was appointed home minister in the B.G. Kher ministry in Mumbai. In 1940, he offered individual satyagraha and was arrested. In 1941, he went on a tour of the country campaigning for Akhand Hindustan (United India). That very year he resigned from the Congress on account of a difference of opinion in taking recourse to violence in self-defence. Between 1943 and 1945, he argued several cases connected with the Quit India Movement.

In 1946, he rejoined the Congress on Gandhi-ji's advice and was elected to the Constituent Assembly. Nehru appointed him to the expert committee for drafting the Constitution of India. In 1948, he was appointed Agent-General of the Government of India to Hyderabad and in that capacity handled an extremely dangerous and volatile situation of accession very tactfully until the state of Hyderabad joined the Indian Union. In 1952, he was appointed food minister in the Central government. However, Pandit-ji did not trust him. He was, therefore, sent to Uttar Pradesh as Governor, a post he held from 1953 to 1958. In 1960, he resigned from the Congress and joined the Swatantra Party, and became the vice-president of the party.

Munshi-ji's greatest contribution by far to the academic and cultural life of the country is the foundation of the Bharatiya Vidya Bhavan in 1938, a centre with branches all over India and abroad. The Bhavan promotes varied activities including establishment of colleges in arts, science, engineering, journalism as well as faculties for the study of Sanskrit, dance, drama and music. It conducts special courses on the Gita. It had undertaken and completed the project of publishing the *History and Culture of the Indian People* by historians selected by the Bhavan. Bharatiya Vidya Bhavan has now become one of the world's top cultural institutes with interest in education, development of culture, publication of books etc. Munshi-ji was also associated with the Sahitya Samsad, the Gujarati Sahitya Parishad, and the Hindi Sahitya Sammelan.

Munshi-ji stood for creating a composite Indian culture, which was a happy blend of orthodoxy and modernism. He believed that traditional values could subsist side by side with liberal and forward-looking attitudes. He was a follower of the Sanatan Dharma (orthodox Hindu religion) and yet he was of catholic taste and advocated adoption of an outlook based on tolerance and goodwill.

He was a champion of the unity of India and opposed the formation of linguistic states, which he felt would undermine the country's essential oneness.

Munshi-ji was a journalist from his youth. His articles were first published in *East and West* and the *Hindustan Review*. He started a Gujarati monthly, the *Bhargava*, a caste magazine, in 1912. He was a joint editor of *Young India* in 1915. He started the *Gujarat*, an illustrated Gujarati monthly, in 1922. In 1936, he founded The Hans Ltd for pooling prominent literary outputs in Indian languages through Hindi. He started *Social Welfare*, an English weekly in 1940, and finally *The Bhavan's Journal* in 1954. The *Bhavan's Journal* is now being published in several languages.

Munshi-ji was also an accomplished speaker. The Banaras Hindu University, Sagar University, Osmania University and Vallabh Vidyapeeth, Anand, conferred honorary doctorate degrees on him.

He lived in style, at once elegant and cultured. He wrote many books in English but attained special eminence as a novelist in the Gujarati language. He wrote historical novels and social dramas.

Munshi-ji was one of the eminent lawyers of the country and rose to be one of India's most eminent jurists. With his business background, he could expertly grasp matters concerning income tax which either made or marred business activities. We took advice from him on all taxation matters relating to our companies. Munshi-ji was never in favour of evasion of tax, for that, in the eyes of law, was a crime. He would give advice to be guided by those sections of the Income Tax Act which when correctly applied enabled a company to avoid paying excess income tax. We followed his advice. And though, on rare occasions, the income tax officers objected to what the companies did, ultimately the companies always won on appeal.

The Bharatiya Vidya Bhavan has developed and blossomed into a large and prestigious institution. In the early 1950s when Munshi-ji became food minister, I came very close to him. Munshi-ji told me about the Bhavan and requested me to organize funds for it. I told him that I could help him only in respect of Kolkata. I made out a list of several industrialists in Kolkata and requested Munshi-ji to visit Kolkata for two days to contact them. When he did so, I made appointments with the leading industrialists of the city and Munshi-ji called on them, accompanied by me. We met a dozen or so industrialists in this way. Later I hosted a dinner party where I invited many more industrialists. I spoke to the guests for a few minutes, introduced Munshi-ji and the Bhavan's activities. There was a positive response from invitees.

Munshi-ji asked me to take more interest in the affairs of the Bhavan, and, in fact, hinted that in due course I should take over the Bhavan's activities. I declined to do so because my field of activities lay between Kolkata and Delhi and, therefore, looking after a big institution like Bharatiya Vidya Bhavan with its headquarters in Mumbai was not a practical proposition. He, however, made me a trustee of the Bhavan. While Munshi-ji was alive, I regularly attended the meetings of the Trust. After his demise, I stopped attending these meetings. I was a trustee of the Bhavan till 2004. The Bharatiya Vidya Bhavan will always remind posterity of what a splendid institution Munshi-ji was able to set up. It now enjoys international repute, and is a standing monument to his far-sighted greatness.

India and Morocco

Chambal Fertilizers & Chemicals started a joint venture corporation in Morocco called Indo Maroc Phosphore SA (IMACID) to manufacture phosphoric acid in collaboration with the government-owned OCP. I had been to Rabat, Morocco, in April 1998 at the time of the inauguration of this venture. I had called on the prime minister and many other ministers. The newspapers gave my presence there very good publicity.

After this, whenever the ambassador of Morocco has had any problem with the Government of India he would meet me and seek my assistance in the matter. After one such meeting, I wrote a letter dated 6 July 1998 to Vasundhara Raje, who was then minister of state for external affairs, which is reproduced below.

Personal

6 July 1998

My dear Vasundhra

I understand an agreement is under negotiation between the Govt. of the Kingdom of Morocco and the Govt. of India regarding reciprocal arrangement and protection of investments. I also understand the agreement has been unduly delayed as on certain points clarifications were needed by the Ministry of Finance of our Government and that there has been undue delay in that.

As you are aware, we are putting up a plant for the manufacture of Phosphoric Acid in Morocco. Morocco is a friendly country. It is also a stable country. I am sure in course of time some other industrialists too will start ventures in Morocco. It will, therefore, be in the interest of both the countries and in the interest of the businessmen of India if such an agreement is finalized as early as possible.

I shall be grateful for your comments.

Kind regards

Yours sincerely,
K.K. Birla

When I did not receive any reply from Vasundhara, I sent her a reminder on 5 August. To this I got a prompt reply dated 17 August reproduced on page 349.

The problems enumerated by the ambassador were resolved. I got a letter dated 12 August from the ambassador of Morocco thanking me for my support. The letter is reproduced on page 350.

NO. V.456/MOS (VR)/98

MINISTER OF STATE FOR EXTERNAL AFFAIRS
INDIA
विदेश राज्य मंत्री
भारत

VASUNDHARA RAJE

August 17, 1998

Shri Birlap

    I have received your letter of August 5, 1998 regarding relationship between India and Morocco.

    An Agreement regarding reciprocal arrangement and protection of investments between India and Morocco has been signed recently. It is heartening to know that you are starting a chemical unit in Morocco and it sounds well that the relationship between India and Morocco will go a long way. We would, on our part, provide all required assistance towards strengthening the bond of friendship between India and Morocco.

Yours sincerely,

(Vasundhara Raje)

Shri K.K.Birla,
Member of Parliament (RS)
Birla House,
7, Tees January Marg,
New Delhi 110 011.

    The news reached King Hassan II of Morocco also. Unfortunately he expired in July 1999. Later, when his heir King Mohammed VI came to India in February 2001 he honoured me with two prestigious medals.

Embassy of the
Kingdom of Morocco
New Delhi

سفارة المملكة المغربية
نيودلهي

No. 588/98

August 12, 1998.

Mr.K.K.Birla ,
Chairman,
Birla Group of Companies,
7 Tees January Marg,
New Delhi – 110 011.

Dear Sir,

With reference to your letter dated July 6,1998, I am pleased to inform you that the Agreement between the Government of the Kingdom of Morocco and the Government of the Republic of India regarding the Promotion and Protection of Investments has been finalised in Rabat and initialed during the end month of June 1998.

I would like to take this opportunity to thank you for your valuable support and cooperation.

Thanking you,

Yours sincerely,

Mohammed Belmahi
Ambassador

CC: Mr Mourad Cherif

Director-General, OCP

33, GOLF LINKS, NEW DELHI - 110 003, INDIA.   TEL. : 91-11-4636920/21/23/24   FAX : 91-11-4636925
E-mail : sifamand@giasdl01.vsnl.net.in

My Relationship with the House of Tatas

My relationship with the House of Tatas has always been very cordial. I knew J.R.D. Tata and Naval Tata since the early 1940s. J.R.D. was a noble person. It was on his insistence that I had started calling him by his first name, Jeh. I was more friendly with Naval whom I used to run into at meetings called by official bodies.

I reproduce here the letter that I had written to Ratan Tata on 18 April 2004 and his reply dated 23 April. These will be found to be of interest to the readers.

18 April 2004

Dear Ratan,
You may find this letter of interest. But first some preliminary remarks.

I do not think I have met you more than on three or four occasions. The last time I met you was many years ago at the house of Shri Jaswant Singh, the present Finance Minister. Shri Narasimha Rao was then the Prime Minister. Shri Jaswant Singh was a Member of Parliament. I had gone to meet him at his residence. You and, if I remember correctly, Nusil Wadia were there. Jaswant Singhji introduced both Nusli and yourself to me. I told him that was not necessary as I knew both of you.

Your father Shri Naval Tata was a dear friend of mine. We addressed each other by first names. I knew Shri JRD Tata also very well. When Smt. Indira Gandhi was the Prime Minister we went together in a number of delegations. That apart many times when JRD came to Delhi Shri S. Mulgaonkar, the then editor of our paper Hindustan Times arranged a game of bridge in the evenings at his residence which was followed by dinner. Mulgaonkar used to invite JRD and myself. Hence on many occasions we played bridge at Mulgaonkar's house and later had dinner there. JRD was such a magnanimous person that after he came to know me more closely, he insisted that I called him 'Jeh' and not Mr Tata even though there was a generation gap between us. The last time I saw JRD was just a few weeks before his demise. Both of us were travelling together from Bombay to Delhi. When we reached the Delhi airport I got in the bus provided by the Indian Airlines. To my surprise I found JRD was also in the bus. I said

'Jeh—I am shocked that for a person of your stature Indian Airlines did not provide a car'. JRD was a noble soul. He merely said 'KK—I never ask for a car for myself'. I told him 'What you say is in keeping with the nobility of your character but Indian Airlines, without your asking for a car, should have used their discretion'.

As you may be aware I retired from the Rajya Sabha in 2002, after serving as an MP for three terms. I am now in my 86th year and am leading a semi-retired life. I, however, am absolutely fit both physically and mentally. Hence, I continue as Chairman of some of the companies in my group. I am also the Chancellor of Birla Institute of Technology & Science (BITS), Pilani. In that capacity I am happy to state that the House of Tatas offer employment to a large number of our students. They send their representatives for campus interviews at Pilani, as do many other industrialists of the country. This year 83 students got employment in companies run by the House of Tatas.

The reason why I thought of writing to you is this.

Many books have been written on father late Shri G.D. Birla. Recently a book has been published, written by a person named Medha M. Kudaisya who is teaching as a Professor or Assistant Professor at the National University of Singapore. This lady has done tremendous research on father before writing this book which has been published by the Oxford University Press. In her research Kudaisya was assisted by my younger brother Basant Kumar and his wife Sarala who possess father's correspondence with most of the important leaders of those days. Some of the facts brought out by Kudaisya were even unknown to me also.

Kudaisya ended the book by summing up father's life in the following words:

'His was a life which was shaped by some of the most momentous events of the twentieth century. As he himself said, he had been born in the Victorian age and lived on to see India progress into the nuclear age. Undoubtedly, he must be regarded as one of the greatest Indians of the twentieth century, for his outstanding leadership of business, his political sagacity, his multi-faceted philanthropy and, above all, his vision of India for which he worked tirelessly.'

In this book on father there are several references to the House of Tatas and to JRD but I am giving only a select few in the enclosure to this letter. I thought of writing to you as many facts

mentioned in the book may be of interest to you.
Kind Regards,

Yours Sincerely
K.K. Birla

23 April 2004

Dear Dr Birla,
Thank you so much for your letter of April 18th.

I am deeply touched that you have taken so much time to write me such a warm and interesting letter covering your close friendship with my father and with Jeh. My father often spoke of you.

Also, thank you for your thoughtful gesture of sending me the extracts from Ms. Kudaisya's book relating to Tatas.

Yours has also been a life of achievement and contribution to public life. I feel privileged to have received your letter.

With personal regards and best wishes,

Yours sincerely,
Ratan

Along with my letter to Ratan, I had enclosed extracts giving the references to J.R.D. or the House of Tatas in the book by Medha M. Kudaisya on father. I am giving here a summary of these enclosures:

- Tata Iron and Steel Co Ltd (TISCO) was set up by Shri Jamshedji Nusserwanji Tata in 1907. Ever since its establishment, it was enjoying protection from foreign imports. In 1927, the Government of India introduced a Bill to extend this protection for a further period of seven years. At the same time, however, it also introduced the principle of imperial preference which proposed significantly lower duty for British steel imports in contrast to imports from other countries. Father was then a Member of the Central Legislative Assembly. The Members were called MLAs, equivalent to present-day MPs. Father and his friends in the Assembly raised a storm in the Assembly and opposition to imperial preference soon became their battle cry. Father led the campaign, arguing that imperial preference must be opposed tooth and nail. In those days even if the Assembly adopted some Resolution, the Government could overrule it. Thus, even though Father was greatly supported by Lala Lajpat Rai and Pandit Motilal Nehru, the imperial preference proposed by the Government became a reality.

- After the famous Quit India Resolution was passed in the Congress Working Committee meeting in Mumbai on 14 July 1942, all the top leaders of the country—Mahatmaji, Jawaharlal Nehru, Sardar Patel, Rajendra Babu, etc—were arrested. Father wanted a group of businessmen to meet the Viceroy, Lord Linlithgow. Lord Linlithgow declined to give time to this delegation. Father then, along with fellow businessmen including J.R.D. and Sir Purushottamdas Thakurdas, sent a strong representation to the Viceroy.

- By 1943, father was confident that the days of the British Raj were numbered. He was convinced that the business community would be invited to play a crucial role in the post-war set-up of the Indian economy. Accordingly, on 11 December 1942, father, J.R.D., Kasturbhai Lalbhai, Lala Shri Ram, Sir Purushottamdas Thakurdas, A.D. Shroff and a few others met at the Mumbai office of the Tatas to discuss what later came to be widely known as the Bombay Plan. The Bombay Plan was the precursor to the five-year plans started by Jawaharlal Nehru after Independence. This plan was discussed and then finalized by the top leaders of the Indian business community. It was very well received by the country.

- After Mahatma-ji's sad assassination, Jawaharlal Nehru and Sardar Patel called father and asked him to make a collection from the business community for a fund that was established and was called Gandhi Memorial Fund. The target of collection was Rs 5 crore. Father met all the important industrialists to seek their support. Father approached J.R.D. and requested him to make contributions from his group and also to secure collections from other industrialists who were connected with the steel industry. J.R.D whole-heartedly supported father. The total collection made was Rs 5.27 crore, exceeding the target.

The Move against Charitable Trusts

The Budget presented on 28 February 2002 by Yashwant Sinha, then finance minister, came down somewhat heavily on the running of charitable trusts. Till that time, charitable trusts were required to spend 75 per cent of their income in the year of receipt and were allowed to accumulate the balance 25 per cent. The finance minister proposed in his Budget that the trusts will be required to spend the entire amount of income in that year and could not accumulate 25 per cent to strengthen their resources.

The proposed steps would have proved to be very harsh on the trusts. A number of representations were made by top business organizations like FICCI and the Confederation of Indian Industry (CII). I was then still an MP. A large number of businessmen wrote to me to take up the matter with Prime Minister Atal Bihari Vajpayee. I then discussed the matter with Atal-ji and pointed out the difficulties which would be created by the proposals. I said that the government should encourage people and companies to set up trusts to serve the public. What the Budget was proposing to do would greatly harm the trusts and would discourage people from establishing charitable trusts in future. The prime minister was quite sympathetic.

I then wrote a letter dated 15 April 2002 to Brajesh Mishra, principal secretary to the prime minister, which is reproduced here. Subsequently the matter was satisfactorily sorted out.

15 April 2002

My dear Shri Brajeshji,
In the Union Budget presented by the Finance Minister on the 28th February some proposals have been made which will be highly detrimental for establishment and running of charitable trusts. I may explain the position.

Till the amendment proposed in the Finance Bill 2002 charitable trusts were required to spend 75% of their income in the year of receipt and balance 25% of the income the trusts were permitted to accumulate. The trusts were also permitted that if for any reason 75% of their income could not be spent, the unspent portion could be spent the following year after certain formalities were completed with the Income Tax Department. As per the Finance Bill 2002 it is proposed that 100% of the income of trusts be spent that very year. This amendment will prove to be very harsh on the trusts. I would like to offer the following comments:

The question as to whether a charitable trust should spend 100% of its income or 75% has been a subject matter of discussion for quite a long time. Upto 1974 a charitable trust was required to spend 100% of its income. This created lots of problems for the trusts. By the Taxation Law (Amendment) Act, 1975 it was provided that only 75% of the income be spent by the trust in the year when income is generated. Since 1975 this provision has been working to the satisfaction of all concerned.

The change in 1975 was made after due deliberations. Now suddenly the Finance Minister desires that 100% of the income of the trusts should be spent that very year. As a consequence, a piquant situation has arisen.

If a trust pays more than its income its funds get depleted. If it cannot spend 100% of the income it gets taxed. Either way it is a loser.

It is not right to tax the income of the trusts. If public spirited men or corporates under their management desire to set up charitable trusts the Government in fact should encourage such people and corporators to set up the trusts and serve the public. The Government's proposal to tax trusts will act as discouragement to people to start charitable trusts. Besides, this measure will not add to the income of the Government. Why then such drastic steps?

Charitable trusts are playing an important role in rendering social service. Apart from hospitals, educational, art and research institutes that these trusts run, whenever there is a calamity like drought, floods, etc. the charitable trusts play a key role. Public trusts big or small are thus in the country's interest. The proposed amendment is therefore not in the country's interest. Some problems relevant to the proposal I may narrate as under:

1. Unless a charitable trust is allowed to accumulate 25% of the income, sufficient capital cannot be generated in a trust to take care of future needs and exigencies.

2. If 25% of the income is disallowed to be accumulated it will make it difficult for the charitable trusts to look after the future needs and exigencies of society and prevent the trusts to grow. Thus they will be deprived from the benefits of the economies of scale. Some charitable trusts like medical trusts or educational trusts require huge capital expenditure to be incurred for replacement of medical equipment or construction of buildings, hostels, purchase of furniture, books, etc. If funds are not permitted to be accumulated how will these trusts be able to meet heavy capital expenditure ?

3. In the case of every individual, firm or any other taxable entity, there is emphasis on saving for the future. Similar emphasis should be on charitable trusts for keeping 25% of their income

as reserve for future needs and exigencies.

4. In some years due to certain natural calamities or due to some
    other reasons like economic slow down the trust may not
    receive any income or donation and unless there are
    accumulated funds its charitable activities will come to a
    grinding halt.

Considering all these factors I request that the present system of
allowing charitable trusts to accumulate 25% of their income to
continue unhindered. I hope the foregoing matter will receive your
kind consideration.

Kind regards

Yours sincerely,
K.K. Birla

Good and Bad Luck

In the late 1970s, there was a period when nothing that I did turned out
right. After repeated failures, on the advice of my wife and friends, I
consulted some astrologers in Kolkata. The astrologers said that the bad
spell through which I was passing was owing to the planet Saturn (Shani).
They said that in the life of almost every man there is a period when
Shani casts its evil influence. Such a period lasts for quite a long time —
seven and a half years. According to the astrologers of Hindi-speaking
areas, this is called 'Shani ke dasha, sadhe saati'. I am not a great believer
in astrology though some forecasts have turned out to be correct in my
life. At any rate, when father found that I was passing through a difficult
period, he sent me the following poem by Arthur Hugh Clough:

For while the tired waves, vainly breaking,
seem here no painful inch to gain,
far back, through creeks and inlets making,
comes silent, flooding in, the main.
And not by eastern windows only,
when daylight comes, comes in the light,
in front, the sun climbs slow, how slowly,
but westward, look, the land is bright.

I felt great relief after reading this poem. The fact that father was concerned about the bad times through which I was passing, also gave me a lot of comfort.

Visit to Niagara Falls

In 1954, my wife and I visited the United States for the first time. I was advised to definitely include the Niagara Falls among the places I visited. When we reached the township called Niagara Falls, we enquired from the hotel staff how to visit the Falls. They gave all the assistance that we needed. Describing the view of Niagara Falls as fascinating, they added that a much better view of the Falls could be had from the Canadian side. This advice was not given to us when our travel agent made our itinerary and we thus had no Canadian visa. Our United States visa was only for a single entry, as were most visas in those days. The hotel staff advised that I could try my luck with the immigration authorities to get a permit to cross into the border of Canada, have a good view of the Niagara Falls and then re-enter the United States. Accordingly I went to the border and had a discussion with the immigration officers. The particular officer whom we met was a rather difficult type. He made it plain to us that under no circumstances would he permit our re-entry in the United States in case we crossed over to Canada.

I argued with the officer concerned that my wife and I were there as tourists and that it would be a great disappointment to us if we failed to see the great Niagara Falls from the Canadian side. But the officer was adamant. I even suggested to the officer that he keep our passports with him, permit us to cross over to Canada, and return our passports when we came back. I added that we would not spend more than forty-five minutes to see the Niagara Falls from the Canadian side. I was later told that most immigration officers take a lenient view in such matters. But this particular officer was stubborn as a mule. He said sarcastically: 'Going to Canada is your concern; but when you return I am the final authority. You are young—I am warning you that under no circumstances will I permit you to re-enter the States.'

Dejected, we came back to the hotel. I met the manager and asked him whether he could help us in any way. Then the manager got an idea. He said that there was a doctor of Indian origin who had settled in the United States and that he was quite influential with the customs officials. He gave me his address and suggested that I try my luck with him. I went to the doctor at his residence. There was no use trying to telephone him and seek an appointment. I rang the bell. It was some time around 6 p.m. or 7 p.m. The doctor had just returned home after work. I related our problem to him. He was very sympathetic. He said that he knew one of the customs officers fairly well.

The doctor telephoned the officer. The first thing he did was to ask when the shift would change and a new set of officers come to the immigration department. After making enquiries, the doctor said that in case we were prepared to visit the Niagara Falls after 10 p.m. he would be able to help us. My wife and I jumped at the opportunity. We went with the doctor to the border after 10 p.m. Before entering the Canadian side, I requested the doctor that I would not feel happy unless and until he could obtain approval of the immigration people for visiting the Niagara Falls from the Canadian side. I said that under no circumstances would I like to face the ticklish situation of crossing the border and finding that we could not get back into the United States. The doctor was very helpful. He talked in my presence to the customs/immigration people. They agreed to this proposal. The doctor was kind enough to arrange our visit to the Niagara Falls from the Canadian side. There was no problem when we returned to the American side. I thanked the doctor profusely. How could he ever be happy, he said, if he could not help a fellow Indian in such a simple matter?

Pikes Peak

One of the tourist attractions in the United States is the area near Colorado. Colorado is at the base of the Rocky Mountains and Pikes Peak is the highest peak in this mountain range. Its altitude is 14,110 ft. My wife and I hired a car for going to Pikes Peak. After we had driven about half the distance, it started snowing. That was not unusual, as snowfall is a common phenomenon in the high altitudes.

Our chauffeur, however, had not taken snow tyres along. It became impossible for the car to proceed any further. We were both very disappointed, particularly me, as I am very fond of natural beauty. I told my wife that she should sit in the car while I walked up a short distance just to enjoy the scenery. After I had walked for about five minutes, two people came in a car and seeing me walking they stopped the car. They asked me what I was doing there. I told them that my wife and I were from India and that we wanted to go to Pikes Peak, but there were no snow tyres in the car. I said that I had decided to walk for about half an hour or so, so that I could get a better view of that area. Americans are very helpful in these matters. The man driving the car said that he would take us to the Pikes Peak as he had snow tyres. I told him that I would not go alone. We would have to go back to pick up my wife. I occupied the back seat and the car went back to pick up my wife. She also was very happy that we could get a lift and so both of us went to Pikes Peak as a result of the kindness shown by the passing Good Samaritan.

After reaching Pikes Peak, the driver of the car showed us around for about 15-20 minutes. After that I suggested that we all have tea together. We went to a restaurant and had tea and snacks. After this, I requested the driver of the car to drop us back at our car. We thanked him profusely, and I offered him a tip of $20. The driver was polite and he said that that was not necessary. I thanked him again and we got into our car to return to Colorado. On the way, I told my chauffeur that the driver of the other car was a very decent gentleman, that he took us to Pikes Peak, explained to us the attractions in that area, that we had tea together and then had dropped us to our car. I said what surprised me was that I offered him a tip of $20 which I thought was quite handsome in those days. I added that the driver of the car had refused to take this tip and that this was somewhat surprising. Our chauffeur then explained that the driver of the car refused to take the tip as he was none other than the sheriff of the area. No wonder!

No Petrol in the Car in UK

I had a very interesting experience in London in the early 1950s. There was an exhibition in one of the northern cities of England, perhaps Manchester. I used to drive the car myself in those days, both in London and in the countryside. We hired a car and decided to take about a week's round trip going to some distant places and also to Loch Lomond in Scotland.

We got our hotel reservations; but in Manchester we could not get any accommodation whatsoever. All the hotels were full owing to the exhibition. As a last resort, we took lodgings in another hotel which was about thirty miles away from Manchester. Our programme was to visit Manchester for two days. So we booked a double bedroom in that hotel which was in the countryside of Manchester.

On the second day of our stay, around 6 p.m. when we left Manchester for our village hotel, I told my wife that there was no petrol in the car and we should have our petrol tank filled up before we proceed any further. Just as we were searching for a petrol pump, two people raised their thumbs. In those days picking up hitch-hikers was a common practice. Nowadays it has become dangerous to take any unknown person in one's car. Many cases of assaults have been reported from such rides. But England was a safe place in the early 1950s. The two people got in. I told them that before we proceed further I had to get some petrol in the car. They said not to worry as there were two petrol pumps on the way from where we could get petrol. Accepting their advice we proceeded towards our village hotel.

After driving a short distance, we saw a petrol pump. I stopped the car there. The man who was looking after the pump said that unfortunately he had run completely out of petrol and so could not help us. This frightened me. My two companions reassured me and said that we would be able to fill up at another petrol pump, which was perhaps only three or four miles further on. After going for about two miles the car stopped. The petrol was completely exhausted. I asked them what was to be done. They said that the second petrol pump was only about a mile away and that by pushing the car (which was a small one) up to the petrol pump, we were sure to get petrol there. My wife knew driving, though she was not an expert. She took the driver's seat and the three of us pushed the car towards the petrol pump. After pushing the car for about half a mile we reached the pump. We were exhausted. When we reached the pump we found that the owner had retired for the day. The pump was closed. There was no one there. By then it was approaching 11 p.m.

There was nothing to do but to find some place to rest for the night. I informed our two companions that they could accompany us and spend the night at the hotel which we might locate. The two persons said that there was a small hotel just opposite the road where we could go and find shelter. They said that they would walk about forty-five minutes to one hour; they would be able to reach their destinations. It was clear they did not want to spend the night away from their homes lest they were misunderstood. We parted company.

I locked the car and my wife and I walked across the street to a small hotel that was located there. We rang the bell. After some time a stout woman in her early forties opened the door. We related our plight and asked her to accommodate us for the night at her hotel. She replied that the hotel was full. I pushed my way in and said that even if the hotel was full we would spend the night sitting in the lounge of the hotel. It was quite cold outside and we said that there was no other alternative but to spend the night in the lounge of the hotel if necessary.

By this time the proprietor, as we later discovered she was, had a good look at us. It appeared that when she first refused entry to us she was not sure what type of people we were. At that time of night, vagabonds also on many occasions tried to find lodgings in hotels. She was able to judge that we were not vagabonds, more importantly we were not drunk. She said that there was one room vacant and took us there. Next morning, after paying the hotel bills, we went to our car. The petrol pump had opened and so after filling the car we drove to our destination.

Case against Rajiv Gandhi

A case against Rajiv Gandhi and some others concerning Bofors was pending in the Delhi High Court. Some time in early February 2004 the High Court exonerated the late Rajiv Gandhi. I wrote to Sonia-ji on that occasion. The text of my letter and her reply are reproduced here:

5 February 2004

My dear Smt Soniaji,
I am at present in London and I am sending this fax letter to you from here through my Delhi Office.

I am very happy that Delhi High Court has completely exonerated Late Shri Rajiv Gandhi. I had never any doubt that attempts were made to vilify Rajiv for political and selfish reasons.

It is a great day for all of us that he has been completely absolved of all charges in the Bofors case. I completely share your joy on this occasion.

With kind regards,

Yours sincerely,
K.K. Birla

12 February 2002

Dear Dr Birla,
I was touched by your kind words on the Delhi High Court Judgement clearing Rajivji's name in the Bofors case.

The verdict is a vindication of truth, of my husband's honour and of the fundamental principles of our democracy. It took 17 long years for justice to be done, but my husband always had full faith that, ultimately, the truth would triumph.

I deeply appreciate your good wishes and support.

With good wishes.

Yours sincerely,
Sonia Gandhi

Rajiv Gandhi Memorial at Sriperumbudur

Rajiv Gandhi was assassinated on 21 May 1991 at Sriperumbudur. The general elections were on at that time and he was campaigning for the Congress. A memorial named Rajiv Gandhi Ninaivakam was built to perpetuate the memory of this great son of India. The memorial has been constructed at Sriperumbudur. A very beautiful publication was brought out on this occasion.

I took the copy of this publication to Sonia-ji. She very kindly autographed it for me and mentioned:

To
Dr K.K. Birla
With fond and respectful regards.

Sonia Gandhi
24.6.02

Life After Retirement

After retirement, owing to my advancing age, I started taking more holidays. I spend about three and a half months abroad and about two months of holidays in India. For the rest of the time, I work as hard as before.

I read a number of magazines, both political and economic. Whenever an interesting book on current affairs is published, I try to read it.

I maintain good health and walk briskly every day for about thirty-five minutes. That apart, I do yogic and free hand exercises for ten minutes daily. God has been kind to me. I believe in leading a healthy life. In this respect I have been very fortunate. Since 1941, I missed office due to illness for only one day, excluding the time I had to undergo operations. I attribute this also to God's blessings.

My Interest in Sports

I have a keen interest in sports, particularly football and tennis. Football has been the most popular game in Bengal and ever since I was a young man of thirty years I have been taking interest in the game. I was an admirer of the Mohun Bagan Club and when in Kolkata I would never miss any good match that it played.

Later, I started taking interest in the Rajasthan Club of Kolkata. This club was started by my father in the 1920s. In those days it was called the Marwari Club. After I started taking interest, I changed the name to Rajasthan Club. It was in the fourth division in those days. With three or four friends who also took active interest we brought it up to third division, then second division and then to first division.

Our ambition was that the Rajasthan Club should win the IFA Shield. We made many attempts, but as there were a number of strong teams we did not succeed. Ultimately, the Rajasthan Club won the IFA Shield in 1955. After that the Rajasthan Club got politicised. That, unfortunately, is a characteristic of Indian society. In whatever field we are, we indulge in politics. That is the reason why there are forty-four parties in the Lok Sabha. This trait is present also among the Indians abroad. In the United Kingdom there are so many associations. Some look after the interests of the non-resident Indians (NRIs) who come from Gujarat, others of those who hail from the Punjab, and so on.

After the Rajasthan Club won the IFA Shield many people wanted to take control of this club. I was not interested in such politics. So I left the Rajasthan Club for good the next year itself.

I also used to take a lot of interest in tennis. The South Club in Kolkata was the hub of tennis in the country. Whenever any important tournament was held, we would leave the office at around 2 p.m. and return to the office after the matches were over. In those days Ghaus Mohammed was the topmost player in the country. He remained at the number one position in Indian tennis continuously for five to six years.

I am, to a great extent, secular in my outlook. After I entered the Rajya Sabha a large number of Muslim MPs became my good friends. But when, year after year, Ghaus Mohammed became the champion and was loudly cheered by the Muslim spectators, we yearned that a Hindu should come up to defeat Ghaus Mohammed. The cynosure of all the spectators was Sumanta Mishra. His father Sir L.P. Mishra was the general manager of Hindustan Motors. Sumanta was a brilliant player. The only defect was that he was moody. But his style was what the modern style is. Thus whereas Ghaus Mohammed used to play tennis from the base line, Sumanta would play from somewhere upfront. Then in 1946, both Ghaus Mohammed and Sumanta reached the final in an all India tournament. We went to see the match at the South Club. The spectators' gallery was full to bursting. It was a well contested match, but ultimately Sumanta won. We all rushed to greet and congratulate him. The magic of Ghaus Mohammed was broken.

Later, I became president of the All India Lawn Tennis Association (AILTA) and remained in that position for five years from 1980 to 1985. In that capacity, I took active interest in tennis. I would play an important role in the selection of the teams for the Davis Cup. To deal with the players, most of whom were moody, was a problem. But I enjoyed their trust and with my persuasion I was able to create a good atmosphere.

I love bridge also, which I play regularly on Saturdays, Sundays and on public holidays.

Budget 1998 and Educational and Medical Institutions

The Union Budget for 1998 came down heavily on educational and medical institutions. Earlier, institutes which were run by societies established by business houses were not required to file any income tax return. The arrangement worked very satisfactorily since independence till 31 March 1998. In the 1998 Budget, the finance minister amended the

Act and these institutes were required to file income tax returns and pay tax on the surplus. What the businessmen found very irritating was the provision that if these surpluses were invested or deposited in some public sector companies then they were not required to pay taxes. But in case they made such investments in the private sector, they were required to pay taxes and file income tax returns. I sent a letter dated 21 December 1999 to Atal-ji who was then the prime minister.

I also met the prime minister and the finance minister. After all these efforts, the finance minister further amended the proposed Act and the rigours were considerably reduced.

My Uncles

Jugalkishore-ji and Juhari Devi: My eldest uncle was Jugalkishore. Being the eldest of his generation, he was called Bada Babu-ji. He started business in Kolkata when only thirteen. In those days, trading was the main business of families from Rajasthan. There were organized markets for trading where persons could purchase goods for ready delivery or futures.

Bada Babu-ji had no formal education. He knew Hindi, simple arithmetic, and had a good head for accounts. In course of time, he improved his Hindi and, being of a religious bent of mind, he also acquired an elementary knowledge of Sanskrit (Dev Bhasha).

Bada Babu-ji was excellent at trading. He traded in a large number of commodities including gold, silver, oilseeds, cotton, jute, hessian, shares etc. His principle was to swim with the current. If the market was buoyant he would buy goods. If dull he would sell. The main principle of futures trading is to go along with the current, not against it. The story goes of a Simple Simon who had purchased some shares in the stock exchange and over-sold some other shares. When the market went up he profited in the shares he had purchased and lost in the shares which he sold. The net outcome was neither plus nor minus. He said to himself: 'I have got good profit in the shares that I have purchased. Let me book this profit'. This he did. He said: 'As for the loss I have suffered in shares, well, I shall watch the situation'.

Babu-ji deeply loved his brothers and nephews, but he had most confidence in father. Babu-ji was a very kind-hearted person and so was his wife, my Bada Badima, as we called her. Badima was as pious as Babu-ji and under her advice Babu-ji sent instructions to the manager of our haveli at Pilani that no one should ever go hungry in the village. Every evening, one Surjan Das, who was a disciple of the mahant of the temple would go around the village and ask if anyone was hungry. The hungry people would then be fed at the haveli.

From his early boyhood, Babu-ji started developing qualities of piety. As he grew up he became more and more religious-minded. He devoted all his time to the uplift and propagation of Hinduism and endeavoured to bring about a spirit of unity among the different sects of the Hindu community. Babu-ji was a devout Hindu, but in no way fanatic. His definition of Hinduism was very liberal encompassing the grouping of a wide variety of sects under the banner of Hinduism. He was known for the catholicity of his views. He regarded all the religions originating in this country—Jainism, Sikhism, Buddhism—as branches of a giant tree, which could be called Arya Dharma. Babu-ji was firm in his view that Hinduism did not endorse untouchability and strongly believed in abolishing the practice, in opening the doors of all temples to all Hindus, including untouchables, and treating the untouchables like any other Hindu.

Because Babu-ji regarded Buddhism to be a part of Hinduism, he regarded the Japanese, who follow both Shintoism and Buddhism, the Chinese, Thais and Sri Lankans very close to him. Likewise, he had a great regard for the Sikhs who, he said, valiantly fought many battles in defence of the Hindus. Babu-ji constructed a number of temples where untouchables (or Harijans as they later came to be called, after the name that Gandhi-ji gave to them) were freely permitted entry.

Babu-ji constructed the Laxmi Narayan Temple known as Birla Temple at Delhi and other temples at Patna, Kurukshetra and Vrindavan. These temples were kept spotlessly clean. Babu-ji constructed dharmashalas also in most of the temples. Not only Hindus but people of other religion were also welcome to visit these temples. Hindus irrespective of their caste could stay in the dharmashalas. The Laxmi Narayan Temple was inaugurated by Mahatma-ji, who had a very high regard for Babu-ji and was happy that the temple was open to followers of all religions.

During the Second World War, Babu-ji shifted to Delhi and stayed there till his demise in 1967. In the afternoon, from 3 p.m. onwards, people from all walks of life would come to meet him. Many came to seek his help, but groups of people from many societies such as the Arya Samaj, Sanatan Dharma organizations, Gurukuls and pro-Hindu politicians would flock to him. He would spend three hours meeting people.

Those who were with Babu-ji when his end came said that at the last moment even when he was in a coma, his hands rose as if in prayer. The general belief is that at the last moment he had a darshan of Bhagwan.

Rameshwar Das and Sharda Devi: My uncle Rameshwar Das, whom we also addressed as Babu-ji, was a very kind-hearted person. He believed in altruism—showing unselfish concern for the welfare of others. He was a financial wizard and whenever father wanted to launch a new company or arrange finances for an existing company he would always consult Babu-ji. Babu-ji was extremely fond of father. Though he was senior to father by three years, he cherished a great affection for father from his very childhood.

Babu-ji was quite sturdy in his young age, unlike father who was physically weak. So fond was he of father that when they went to the pathshala opened for them by their grandfather, he would often carry father on his shoulders or piggy-back. Babu-ji's affection for father remained unflagging to the end.

Babu-ji was held in great esteem by the entire business community of Mumbai, which would consult him whenever there was any problem, respecting his acumen in financial matters. He was in the trading business but put up some industrial units also.

His greatest contribution to society is the Bombay Hospital. Babu-ji felt that a large city like Mumbai should have a modern hospital. He called a meeting of a large number of businessmen from the Rajasthani community and disclosed his views about establishing the hospital. Everybody approved and contributed towards the construction of this hospital, though the bulk of the donations came from Babu-ji and other members of the family. After the hospital was completed the suggestion was to call it Marwari Hospital since it was funded entirely by the Marwari community. The idea was not that the hospital was to be reserved for Marwaris alone, but merely to indicate that the hospital was a contribution of the Marwari community for the social welfare of the general public. Sardar Patel advised him not to give any communal tag to the hospital but to name it simply as Bombay Hospital.

Sardar Patel was a leader of unimpeachable integrity. After he became the deputy prime minister, whenever he visited Mumbai, he would stay at our house with Babu-ji and not with his only son, Daya Bhai. During his last days, when Sardar Patel suffered from kidney trouble, he went to Mumbai to consult doctors and stayed with Babu-ji. He died at Birla House, Mumbai.

My aunt, Sharda Devi, was Babu-ji's second wife, his first wife having died when Babu-ji was around thirty. Badima, as we called her, was a very philanthropic person. She was greatly devoted to Babu-ji as was Babu-ji towards her.

I was fortunate to enjoy the blessings of both Babu-ji and Badima. I reproduce here the letter which Babu-ji had sent to me. This was perhaps the last letter that he sent to any member of the family before he passed away. In this letter he has blessed me and said that God was always with me. What greater boon could I expect?

इंडस्ट्री हाउस,
१५९ चर्चगेट रिक्लेमेशन,
बम्बई.

दि० १६: ४: ७३

चि० कृष्ण,

तुमने आम भेजे सो मिल गये. आम बहुत अच्छे थे, इतने अच्छे आम यहां पर नहीं मिलते, सब को मैंने बांटा और सबको बहुत पसंद आया. टेलीफोन लाइन नहीं चलती है इस लिए मैं तुम्से बात नहीं कर सका.

तुम्हारी फैक्टरी दस मई तक चल जायगी यह जान कर बहुत खुशी हुई.

तुम्हारी तबियत अच्छी होगी. तुम ज्यादा फिरने का नहीं रहना. फिरने से शरीर घिसता है. एक जगह रहने से भी जर लगता है. इस लिए जितनी आवश्यकता हो इतना घूमो और काम करो.

ईश्वर का स्मरण तो तुम करते हो सो इस बारे में मुझे कुछ लिखने की जरूरत नहीं है. भगवान हमेशा तुम्हारे साथ है.

श्री कृष्णकुमार बिरला,
कलकत्ता.

B.M. Birla and Rukmini Devi: My youngest uncle was Braj Mohan, or Uncle BM, as we lovingly addressed him. I had the good fortune of enjoying his love and affection to an unusual extent. In our generation there were six of us—brothers and cousins—including his son Ganga Prasad. He loved me as much as he loved Ganga Prasad. In fact, when I started my business career, uncle had discussions with father and took me under his tutelage. There were three sugar mills under him in our group— at Sidhwalia (Saran district), Hasanpur (Darbhanga) and Seohara (Bijnore in Uttar Pradesh). After giving me some preliminary training he placed all the three mills under my supervision. He was the chairman of these companies but so large-hearted was he that after some time he insisted that I take over their chairmanship. In spite of my vehement protestations, he resigned from the boards of all these companies. He put Orient Paper Mills under Ganga Prasad. He kept another company, NEI, to himself. But the biggest company that he founded was Hindustan Motors. Established in 1942, this is the oldest automobile company in India. It was a pioneering effort which he launched.

The socio-political atmosphere in the country at that time was such that every young man and woman believed in the philosophy of socialism without bothering to find out what true socialism stood for. The popular concept of socialism was that all the major industries, particularly the core industries, should be taken over by the state. The businessmen of the country knew that the policy followed by the Congress governments was not leading the country on the path of progress. The same Congress party, after P.V. Narasimha Rao became prime minister, made major changes in that policy. It realized the importance and worth of the private sector and began laying emphasis on that.

Though a supporter of the Congress, uncle did not like this trend at all. He realized the importance of there being a party which was right of centre in its thinking. Thus the Swatantra Party was born.

Uncle never held any position in this party, but for all practical purposes he was the godfather of the Swatantra Party. Under his inspiration the Swatantra Party did fairly well. It was born in 1959 and continued as an independent party till 1977 when it merged with the Janata Dal.

Under uncle's inspiration, a large number of businessmen stood for election as candidates of this party. The golden period of the Swatantra Party was 1967 when forty-four MPs got elected to the Lok Sabha as this party's nominees. However, in 1971, when there was an Indira wave in the country, the Swatantra Party was almost wiped out. I too stood for election in 1971 as a nominee of this party and was defeated.

Uncle's mental faculties were very sharp. The condition of the country and its economic problems always worried him. But his was a lone voice in the wilderness. Uncle was twelve years younger than my father. There was a great bond of affection between them and uncle was greatly devoted to father.

Of all of uncle's contributions in the sphere of social welfare, two were outstanding. One was the Birla Institute of Technology started by him at Ranchi which is now an autonomous university, and is doing well. The second was the establishment of Calcutta Hospital, which has become one of the premier hospitals of the country.

In the 1970s, uncle suffered a heart attack. He was not all that old, but doctors advised him to lead a less active life. In spite of that uncle led a fairly active life till 1980. Towards the end of 1981, the condition of the heart deteriorated.

Even when uncle knew that his end was near, he cared about others. Such was his noble nature. He knew that one of my companies was in difficulties. Even when he was in his death bed he spoke to Ganga Prasad and his grandson, Chandrakant, to try to help me. This they related to me after he expired. What a great soul uncle was.

This sad event occurred on 11 January 1982. So devoted were father and uncle BM towards each other that father found it a torture to remain in Kolkata when uncle was in a critical condition. We also knew that if father remained in Kolkata for long, he would brood over uncle and that would adversely affect his health. Father himself was nearing eighty-eight. We advised him to go to Delhi or some other place. Knowing he would not be able to suffer the loss of his younger brother passing away before his very eyes, father remained out of Kolkata when death came peacefully to uncle. I was away on tour too. However, I had a premonition that uncle's end was drawing near, so I rushed back. I reached Kolkata just in time, a day before the end.

Thus passed away a great personality who led a very active and fruitful life in commercial, financial, political and social fields, a personality clear in his vision regarding the country's needs, a personality who did a lot for the business community and his fellow countrymen. A copy of a letter sent to me by uncle dated 8 July 1930 is given here.

8 July 1930

My dear Madho Krishna,

No letter from you for a long time. What is the matter? Has the cool climate of Mussoorie given you such a sound sleep that you find it difficult to rise.

At least in Calcutta we are not having such a nice time. Calcutta has also discarded its wait and see policy and is giving great support to Gandhiji's Movement. Foreign cloth is almost impossible to sell. So are other foreign things. Daily the feeling amongst the people is gaining ground and the spirit is just marvellous.

How is your spirit in Mussoorie? Have you all gained weight and are getting fat? Or simply like Krishna reading books and spoiling your eyesight.

What about monkey? Is he still calling Chanki, or changed to Chandrakala?

Hope you all are well. With love to all.

Yours sincerely
Braj Mohan

Others of My Generation

In the earlier chapters I have written about my grandfather, grandmother, father and my uncles. The idea was not so much to describe their lives but to portray their personalities and characters. Father was one who achieved greatness in everything he did. My uncles too were great achievers in their own spheres.

My father had three brothers. Uncle Jugal Kishore had no children. My younger uncle, Rameshwar Das, had four daughters—Savitri, Satyavati, Luxmi and Radha—and two sons—Gajanan and Madhav Prasad. Gajanan was a fine sportsman. He was an excellent tennis player and was, at one time, considered one of the ten best players of the country. He was a very sporting type of person in his habits and had wide contacts amongst a cross-section of the social elite. He did not take much interest in business. He was a very popular figure in Kolkata and was regarded a very generous person. He died in 1969.

I had an elder brother Lakshmi Niwas and have a younger, Basant Kumar, who is two years younger to me. Lakshmi Niwas or Bhai-ji, as we all called him, was a man of saintly disposition. He was very dutiful to my father and always anxious to do his every bidding. His son is

Sudarshan—or SK, as he is familiarly known. He again is a boy with very wide contacts. Basant Kumar possesses brilliant business acumen. I had three sisters—Chandrakala, Anusuya and Shanti. While Chandrakala was elder to me, the other two sisters were younger. In the last five years both Chandrakala and Anusuya expired. All my sisters were/are amiable and affectionate.

A copy of the letter sent by Bhai-ji on the occasion of Diwali which was celebrated by him in Mussoorie, is reproduced here which will be found to be interesting. In the same letter, Ganga Prasad had also sent his Diwali greetings as well as my sister-in-law the late Sushila Bhabhi. It appears from Bhabhi's letter that it was written when Sudarshan was a small child of about two years, or about sixty-nine years back. No date has been given on this letter.

॥ श्री ॥

Amongst us three brothers, father loved Basant Kumar the most. There were several reasons for this. First, Basant was the youngest and so, after mother's demise, greater care and affection naturally devolved on him. Secondly, he was so handsome that he immediately attracted attention. He was a chubby boy. There has existed a great bond of affection between Basant Kumar and myself.

Basant Kumar's wife is Sarala. Their engagement and wedding had the full blessings of Mahatma-ji and Jamnalal Bajaj and naturally the blessings and approval of father. Sarala is the daughter of Brijlal Biyani, a man of great courage and rectitude. He was from Rajasthan but owing to his selfless services and qualities of leadership he became the undisputed leader of Berar. Basant Kumar was married on 30 April 1942 at Akola. So popular was Brijlal that the wedding was attended by thousands of people from far and near.

When the barat was to leave for Akola, I developed high temperature. I have a frank nature but I thought it best to keep this matter a secret. It was only when the train left Mumbai for Akola that I informed my father and uncles of my temperature. By taking aspirin to keep the temperature down, I was able to stand the journey and actively participate in the wedding.

Like her father, Sarala is a born leader and a very popular figure, enjoying the respect of all the members of the family. She is a and o strong personality and is a great source of inspiration to Basant Kumar.

Apart from business, Basant Kumar started many institutes, the two most important ones being the Sangeet Kala Mandir at Kolkata, which has become famous for music, dance and our ancient culture and is perhaps the best of its kind in India, and the Birla Academy of Art and Culture, Kolkata. Basant Kumar was very fond of purchasing Indian paintings. He has donated these to this institute. Sarala is very active in both the institutes. A letter sent by Basant Kumar and Sarala on 3 July 2001 to my wife and myself on the occasion of our diamond jubilee wedding celebration is given here, as is a letter sent to me on my eighty-fifth birthday and my reply to this letter.

ॐ

स्नेही भाई कृष्ण - भाभी मनोरमा
सप्रपदी के आलोक में दो पवित्र प्राणों -
दो निर्मल जलधाराओं के संगम जैसा
दो अन्तरात्माओं की मिलन यात्रा का
स्नेह मिश्रित साथ शरद्, साथ हेमन्त,
एवं साथ वसन्त के सायुज्य में
कृष्ण-मेघ की तरह अमृत वर्षण करता हुआ
सृजन-श्री के छन्द रचता हुआ
दाम्पत्य जीवन की षष्टि-पूर्ति पर
निरन्तर श्रद्ध-सिद्ध मधुमान हो
'शतं जीव शरदो वर्षमान :
शतं हेमन्ताम्
शतं वसन्तान -
वर्द्धिनशील सौ-शरद्, सौ हेमन्त और
सौ वसन्त ऋतुओं तक दीर्घायु-शतायु
होने की शुभकामनाओं सहित
                      प्रांजलि प्रणाम .

                                भाई वसन्त
                            सूरतगढ
                          अक्तूबर्ड २००९

ॐ

My dear Bhai Krishna
        Our best wishes and Pranams
to you on the happy and Auspicious occasion
of your completing 85 years of very happy
fruitful and successful life. You are the h[ead]
of the Birla family. There is complete affinity
love and affection amongst the family
members. For this the credit goes to the whole
family, specially to Bhabhi and you. All the
members of the family have great love
respect and confidence for both of you.
        Our sincere prayers to God
to give many many more years of active
and healthy life to you.
तु-श्री भाईजीसी सरलाके सादर-प्रणाम।

                              भाई वसन्त   9.92.07

My dear Basant and Sarala,

I am in receipt of a very warm and affectionate letter from both of you.

By Grace of God there exists affection amongst all the members of the Birla family. Amongst four of us—Sarala, yourself, Manorama and myself the bond of love and affection is very strong. You and Sarala have always been of immense strength to both of us.

Both of you form a remarkable couple. The contribution that you have made in several spheres such as art, culture (Birla Academy, Sangeet Kala Mandir), spread of education (number of schools established by you), spread of religion (your close relationship with our religious leaders particularly Swami Chinmayananda, Swami Akhandanandaji, Ram Kinkerji, etc.) and construction of Dharamshalas at a number of holy places in the Himalayas are remarkable.

I shall soon be entering my 86th year. Some time back I said to Chandrakala Bai and Lakshmi Bai that at their age they should be fully prepared to leave this world without notice. The same applies to me. I have made all preparations to leave this world whenever God ordains. I only offer two prayers to Him—one whatever be the time that is left to me I may spend in peace. My second prayer is that God may guide me like a shepherd does his flock to follow the path of righteousness and not deviate from it in any way.

Yours affectionately,

Krishna

Ganga Prasad is the chairman of the Birla Institute of Technology, Ranchi, the Calcutta Medical Research Institute, the B.M. Birla Heart Research Centre, Kolkata, and the B.M. Birla Science and Technology Centre, Jaipur. He is a remarkable man with a lot of constructive work to his credit, which is a reflection of his social consciousness and vision. He has constructed temples at Jaipur, Hyderabad and Bhopal. These temples are uniquely situated and attract a large number of visitors all the year round. He has built planetariums at Hyderabad, Chennai and Jaipur. Ganga Prasad has also started a number of research institutes. In view of the services rendered by him in several fields of activities, the government conferred the award of Padma Bhushan on him in 2006. Copies of the citation and the award are reproduced on page 377.

SHRI GANGA PRASAD BIRLA

Shri Ganga Prasad Birla has been spearheading various organisations actively involved in promotion of education, including for weaker sections, medical welfare, scientific and economic research, development of industry, preservation of culture & heritage and social welfare.

2.   Born in August 1922, Shri Birla is a Science graduate from Calcutta University. After his retirement from active participation in business, Shri Birla is devoting time to social welfare and cultural activities. The Trusts and Societies with which he is closely associated as Chairman/President have established various institutions for promoting public welfare, include: Birla Institute of Technology, Ranchi (B.I.T.), a deemed University, having extension centres at various places within the country and abroad; Birla Institute of Science Research, Jaipur which has been conducting multi-disciplinary research at its different Centes including research in Bio-technology and Water Management; The Calcutta Medical Research Institute, Kolkata and B.M. Birla Heart Research Institute, Kolkata, Premier Medical Centres in Eastern India; Modern High School for Girls, Kolkata and Rukmani Birla Modern High School, Jaipur, renowned educational centres; Birla Archaeological & Cultural Research Institute, Hyderabad which conducts research in the fields of Archaeology, Museology and Science. Various Trusts with which Shri Birla is associated have taken up projects for slum clearance, building houses for weaker sections, schools for education of the children of slum dwellers and in rural areas; establishing places of public worship which have architectural beauty; and renovation of ancient historical monuments of archaeological importance, maintaining original ambience at different places in India.

गंगा प्रसाद बिरला

मैं, भारत का राष्ट्रपति, आ.प.जै. अब्दुल कलाम, व्यक्तिगत गुणों के लिए आपके सम्मानार्थ, पद्म भूषण प्रदान करता हूँ।

नई दिल्ली
दिनांक   29 फाल्गुन, 1927
          20 मार्च, 2006

राष्ट्रपति

His son is Chandrakant. Chandrakant is a very sweet-tempered and affable young man. Hindustan Motors, of which he is the chairman, is his flagship company. He is a man of great humility and is highly respectful towards elders, particularly towards me. He is very affectionate by nature and eager to help others. His wife, Amita, is the daughter of Lord R.K. Bagri, who is a very successful NRI businessman in London.

Sudarshan's son is Siddharth who is also coming up well. He is a very frank, outspoken and sincere person. He is my favourite.

Basant Kumar's son was Aditya. He possessed qualities of leadership in abundance. He inherited the major companies of father and looked after them very efficiently. After father, in my opinion, he was the most brilliant member of the family. He died quite young.

Though all the brothers and cousins had legally separated in the early 1930s, substantial cross-holding of shares always existed. After father's demise, we thought it best to terminate the cross-holdings. Hence each member acquired shares of his company from the other members of the family. This was regarded by the businessmen of the country as a partition in the Birla family. Call it partition or whatever, it was, in fact, a re-allotment of the shares and investments in the family groups. What is remarkable is that the entire business of changing the shareholding pattern was effected very smoothly, without any hitch or bitterness. We brothers and cousins might have put forward different views about the valuation of shares but the whole transaction was carried out without any rancour, unlike what happens in other families who quarrel over such matters openly. The result is that even after the so called partition, the silken bond of love and affection among the members of the family has remained intact. And today the Birla family is as united as ever.

Bhai Madhav Prasad: Madhav Prasad or Madho Babu as we called him, who passed away on 30 July 1990, was my cousin but he was just like a brother to me. We grew up together from childhood.

When young, there was keen competition between us in studies, games and in all other spheres of mutual interest. But the silken bond of love and affection between us was never adversely affected by any ill feelings of one-upmanship. This bond in fact grew stronger with the passage of time.

At Hare School, we took part in various games. We were particularly fond of football. Apart from playing football, we greatly enjoyed watching this game. Mohun Bagan was our favourite team. I remember once there was an important match in the Kolkata football league between Mohun Bagan and Durhams, which was a British military outfit. It was anticipated that there would be difficulty in obtaining the tickets for the match, as there would be a huge crowd waiting for tickets. We, therefore, went to the Maidan almost four hours before the match started and cooled our heels waiting for the tickets! Such was our enthusiasm for football.

Madho Babu and I got married into the same family—the Tapuriah family—which is one of the oldest families of Kolkata, respected for its culture and elegant tastes. Madho Babu was married to Priyamvada Devi, daughter of Mangtulal Tapuriah. Mangtulal-ji was a man of excellent refinements. He was universally acclaimed as a *rais* (aristocrat). I was married to his grand-daughter, Manorama. After the school days were over, the rivalry between Madho Babu and myself ceased. Only the bond of affection remained. This bond of affection got further strengthened through our marriage ties.

Time passed in this way. We left behind our boyhood days, became youths, then adults, and finally passing our salad days, entered the evening of our lives.

After 1982, a great transformation had come over Madho Babu. He became very religious and tolerant. He became extremely considerate towards his colleagues and staff members. He always had good words for all who met him. Owing to indifferent health, he gradually withdrew from business. But Priyamvada Devi rose to the occasion and started deputizing for Madho Babu by ably looking after their business interests. This was a matter of satisfaction to him and to all other members of the family.

Madho Babu was suffering from a heart ailment. We never talked to him about his health. But during this illness he developed a sixth sense; he could guess that owing to his heart's condition he did not have much longer to live. Yet he maintained absolute composure in the face of imminent death which is the ultimate truth of life. Only a saint can face death with such stoicism. He would often recite the famous sloka of the Gita which translates as, 'A man discards old clothes and puts on new ones; likewise the soul discards the old body and takes on a new one.'

In view of this philosophical and stoical outlook which God enabled him to develop, he started taking a detached view of life. At the same time, his love for my daughters grew in intensity. He virtually pined for their company and would feel very lonely when they returned to their homes at the end of the day. His attachment for my wife and myself also grew.

Madho Babu had a philanthropic nature. Belle Vue Clinic and the

Birla Planetarium, which he established in Kolkata, are examples of his benevolent concern for the people of the city. Both the institutions are well run and have become familiar landmarks of the city. They will perpetuate his memory. After his demise, Priyamvada Devi took the reins of running the numerous companies of the M.P. Birla group in her own hands. She expired on 3 July 2004 owing to kidney trouble.

Kumar Mangalam Birla: Kumar Mangalam is my grand-nephew. He is Basant Kumar's grandson and the late Aditya's son. Like his grandfather and late father he is a very able person. He is a person of great warmth,

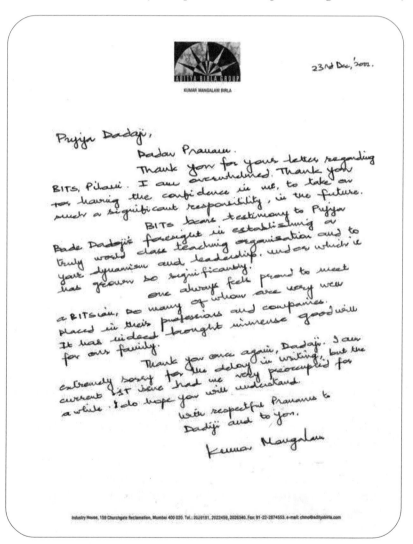

of very pleasant nature, soft spoken and man of high principles. All his industrial units are doing well. His group is called Aditya Birla Group after his father. Reproduced on page 380 is his letter dated 23 December 2002. How charming a letter Kumar Mangalam had sent me will be clear after a reading.

Also given below is a letter sent to me when Kumar Mangalam was three or four years old. He had gone to Corbett National Park and had then sent me this letter. Whenever I read this letter I get a strong impulse to rush to him and give him a warm hug.

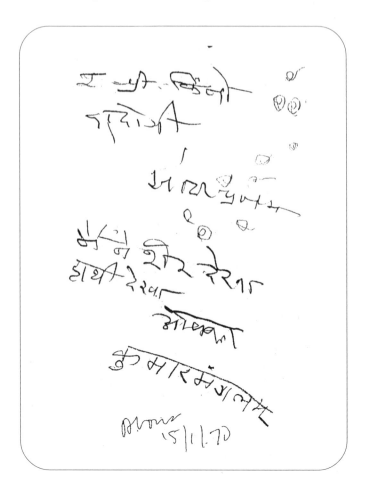

Khushwant Singh

Khushwant Singh was the editor of the *Hindustan Times* from May 1980 to April 1983. His name was recommended to me by Indira-ji. I asked Khushwant Singh to come and meet me. I did not know much about him though I had met him earlier on two or three occasions. I was told that he was a very upright person and wrote fearlessly.

When Khushwant Singh joined the *Hindustan Times* he started a column 'With malice towards one and all'. It became very popular and he agreed to write this column in the *Hindustan Times* on a regular basis even after he left the paper.

Once in this column he wrote a piece about me and our family. That piece is reproduced below.

Without any hoo haa

- - - - - - - - -

Two books of R N Jaju, *G. D. Birla* and *Eloquent Reflections of Sarala Birla* (Vikas) made me realise how little I know about this family with which I have been associated for over 20 years, as editor of K K Birla's *The Hindustan Times*, and thereafter as a syndicated columnist. To the best of my knowledge, of the dozen who edited the paper before and after me, the only one who could be described as 'friend of the boss' was late Sri Mulgaonkar. He treated everyone with great courtesy, occasionally invited one to dinner (vegetarian, cooked in *desi ghee,* no alcohol), invariably served you tea or coffee when he sent for anyone of his staff and saw them off to their cars when they were leaving.

Birlas have been among the top three industrial houses of the country for almost a century. They have always been a very conservative and close-knit family. They have never been involved in any financial scandal. They treat their employees well and earn their loyalty. They do not make a big *hoo haa* about the temples, schools, colleges, hospitals and plantations they raise. In short, few know anything about their private lives.

The closest I came to befriend one of the Birla clan was a short association with Manjushree Khaitan, daughter of B.K. and Sarala Birla and sister of Aditya Vikram who was well on the way of getting to the top of the ladder of Indian industry till death cut his brilliant career short five years ago. Jaju's book is about Aditya

Vikram's mother, Sarala. As I expected, it reveals nothing about the lady but is a collection of speeches she delivered on different topics at different places in English and Hindi. Readers will get an idea of what she thinks, but not what she is.

I then sent a letter dated 1 August 2000 to Khushwant Singh and received a prompt reply from him:

1 August 2000

My dear Khushwant Singh,
I have read with interest a short appreciative piece which you have written about our family in your *Malice* column dated 29th July. I have also read with interest when you say that the only 'friend of the boss was late Mulgaonkar'. It is a fact that I had a great liking and respect for late Mulgaonkar. I liked Mulganokar for his fearless writing and for his strength of character. He often invited me to his house for dinner and for a game of Bridge. He was one of the top players of this game in the country. Twice I played Bridge with Shri J.R.D. Tata or 'Jeh', as I called him, at Mulgaonkar's place.

However, I have had very cordial relationship with you also and have always held you in high esteem. I have always enjoyed reading your *Malice* column. Particularly I have enjoyed the 'hoax' which you have played on the public by pretending that you are fond of pretty women and wine. You have tried to create an impression as if you enjoy worldly pleasures. However, the public has not been taken in by your pretences and they hold you in high respect. As for myself I have always admired you for the principled life that you lead.

I hope God will grant you a long and healthy life so that you could continue to serve the people with your writings and with your wit and humour.

Kind regards,

Yours sincerely,
K.K. Birla

4 August 2000

My Dear Ann-Data,

That is how I used to refer to you when I was editor of H.T. That is how I see you today as much of my sustenance still comes from H.T. because of you.

It would be presumptuous on my part to claim your friendship but I am very beholden to you. It was very kind of you to write on me for K's book and to me about my note on Jaju's book on your sister-in-law. I wish he had done more homework.

I hope this finds you in the best of health.

Yours
Khushwant Singh

Lord Paul of Marylebone

I have known Lord Paul for almost forty years now. Both my wife and I are very fond of Lord Paul, Swraj Paul-ji as we call him, and his wife Lady Paul or Aruna-ji. Aruna-ji was born and brought up in Kolkata. She had her education at the famous girls' school and college, Loreto House, which is perhaps the best educational institution for girls not only in Kolkata but perhaps in the whole country. Our association with Loreto House goes back to around seventy-five years when my cousin, Ganga, joined it. After that, all the daughters of the Birla family including my three daughters were educated there. So did my daughters' daughters and now my great grand-daughters. Under the circumstances, all my daughters know Aruna-ji very well.

Swraj Paul settled in London after the sad demise of his daughter in London many years back. She died at a very young age of leukaemia. He has built up his business empire in London and is today one of the topmost industrialists of the United Kingdom. He has steel units in a number of countries including the United States. He started in a big way in India too, where his units make components for the automobile industry and are doing very well. Though a businessman, somehow he became a supporter of the Labour Party of which most of his friends were members. In course of time, he was made a Peer and is called The Rt Hon. The Lord Paul of Marylebone.

Swraj Paul is a great philanthropist also. He has given large donations to various institutes. Once the London zoo faced financial difficulties. The British press said that unless someone gave a big donation, the zoo would have to be closed down. The London zoo consisted of two parts—the main zoo and the children's zoo. The children's zoo boasted all varieties of animals but only one or two of each type. Swraj Paul came to the rescue of the zoo. He gave a large donation (perhaps one million pounds) for the children's zoo, which was named after his late daughter Ambika.

As a Member of the House of Lords, Swraj Paul takes his work very seriously. He hardly misses a session of the House and attends all the meetings. He participates in all discussions. Whenever my wife and I go to London we meet him over a cup of tea in the House of Lords. After one of my visits to London he sent me a very warm letter on 18 December 1999, as follows:

My dear KKji

I really do not know where to start. Both Aruna and I have had so much of your hospitality, affection and welcome from the moment we arrived.

First of all, it was nice to see you in such good form. The celebration of the 75th year of HT and the dinner yesterday was wonderful. Your looking after so many people personally is a lesson to us. For me, you are a great man and I am proud to have you as a good friend.

The highlight always is the quiet time we spend at London. Thank you so much. We are looking forward to see you in London on 7 January of the New Year.

It was nice to see Shobhana and Shyam. Shobhana is making her name and you can see the responsibility she is taking up. Please convey our good wishes to her.

In Vir you have made a good choice. He will bring you the glory, you well deserve.

Kindest regards and wish you a very happy Millennium.

Swraj Paul

Professor P. Lal

Professor P. Lal is a renowned literary figure of Kolkata, as well as of India. He has established an institution called 'Writers Workshop'. The Workshop holds literary sessions every Sunday morning. Many notable literary figures like Mulk Raj Anand, Pearl Buck, Nirad C. Chaudhuri, W. Norman Brown, Karan Singh etc. have attended these. It has published over 2,500 books since 1958. Prof. Lal is a poet as well. The Workshop has brought out *Srimad Bhagwad* under his guidance. It contains fifty-six original paintings by folk artistes of Orissa. I have known Professor Lal for over twenty-five years. He has taught my daughter Nandini also. I hold Professor Lal in high esteem owing to his erudition and the high principles that he follows in his life.

I sent him two or three chapters of this autobiography and asked him his impression of these chapters. He wrote back on 16 November 1999 a comment which is reproduced here and on the jacket of this book.

What a family! Simple and complex, traditional and modern, religious and rational, money-minded and money-renouncing, Indian and international, fiercely individualistic and inspiringly loyal and familial . . .

I am, however, very impressed by the brevity of your style. It is stark, honest, clear. You never use an extra word. Bernard Shaw said that 'effectiveness of assertion is the alpha and omega of style'. I am myself learning from the bare-bones simplicity of your style-less style. You will notice that whatever changes I make, are done respectfully, to maintain the quality of your transparent manner of presentation.

P. Lal

I received another letter dated 24 October 2006 from him, a copy of which is also reproduced on page 387. This too will be found to be very interesting.

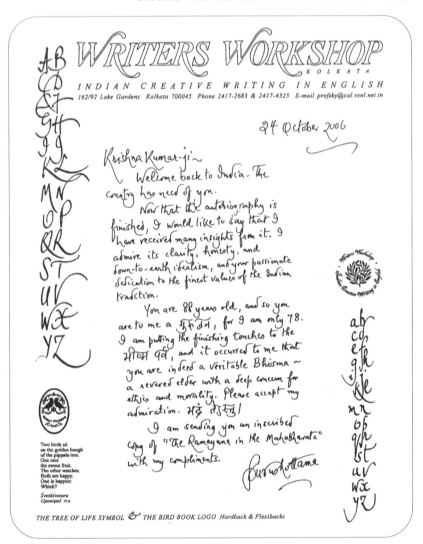

Dalai Lama

Elsewhere, I have written about His Holiness the Dalai Lama. Upset by the threat of the Chinese government, he left Tibet and came to India. He stayed at our house at Mussoorie for over a year.

When the government made arrangements for the Dalai Lama to shift to Dharamshala, he sent a very cordial letter dated 29 April 1960 to me. A copy of the letter is reproduced on page 388.

Personal

Birla House,
Mussoorie
29 April 1960

Dear Mr Birla,
On the eve of my leaving Mussoorie for my new residence at
Dharamsala, I wish to write and convey to you and to your family
the deep gratitude of myself and the members of my party for the
generous hospitality that you extended to us when we arrived in
India last year. Time has passed very quickly indeed and it seems
to be only such a short while ago that we arrived in India from
Tibet under unhappy circumstances. It is, however, over a year
now since we came and started living in your beautiful and
comfortable House and surroundings. You and your family have
been the very personification of kindness and generosity and we
cannot adequately thank you for all that you have done for us. We
shall, however, always cherish happy memories of your hospitality
and shall always wish you and your family, the very best in life.
    With kindest regards,

Yours sincerely
DALAI LAMA

Gandhi Memorial Fund

After Gandhi-ji's death, Jawaharlal Nehru and Sardar Patel felt that a
large amount of money could be collected from industrialists to set up a
Gandhi Memorial Fund. Father called captains of industry from all over
India and Nehru and Patel addressed them. It was decided at that meeting
to raise a sum of Rs 5 crore from the business community. Father, who was
ably assisted in this collection drive by Kasturbhai Lalbhai, told businessmen
that they should donate money generously. It was decided that the fund
would be collected industry-wise, and so industry-wise quotas were worked
out. Father entrusted the work of collection from the sugar industry to me.
The target of collection was fixed at Rs 50 lakh. Our group was at that
time the largest producer of sugar in the country and I was then the deputy
chairman of the Indian Sugar Syndicate Ltd. This Syndicate was a limited
body recognized by the governments of Uttar Pradesh and Bihar as the sole
representative of the sugar industry of those states. These two states produced
80 per cent of India's sugar up to the mid-1940s.

After receiving father's instructions, I started collecting funds vigorously. I drew up my strategy on the basis of the capacity of each unit. Most of the sugar units gave their contributions which I had fixed against each unit after consulting all the leaders of the industry in Uttar Pradesh and Bihar. Some units did not contribute the amount fixed by me out of sheer jealousy. They did not like the idea of a young industrialist like me being given such an important role. I was then only thirty-one years old. However, I knew how to handle the dissidents. In the case of Uttar Pradesh, as a last resort, I took help from Pant-ji, who was then the chief minister of the government of Uttar Pradesh. The text of my letter to Pant-ji dated 17 February 1949 is reproduced here:

THE INDIAN SUGAR SYNDICATE LIMITED

8 Royal Exchange Place
Calcutta

My Dear Pujya Shri Pantji,
We are finding it extremely difficult to realise the dues of the Gandhi Memorial Fund from the following factories in U.P.:

(a)	The Lord Krishna Sugar Mills Ltd., Saharanpur (Dist. Saharanpur)	Rs 49,506-14-0
(b)	Seth Shiv Prasad Banarasidas Sugar Mills Ltd., Bijnor (Bijnor Dist.)	Rs 45,970-6-0
(c)	Diamond Sugar Mills Ltd. Pipraich (Dist. Gorakhpur)	Rs 11,970-5-0

I shall be extremely grateful if you could kindly ask the District Authorities to collect this money. I know for certain that all these three factories can make the payment of their contribution to the Gandhi Memorial Fund if the District Authorities put pressure on them. They are not hardpressed for money like Dhampur. I am sorry to give this trouble to you but since you had promised to assist us in our difficult task and since Pujya Shri Sardarji is very anxious for the early remittances to the Fund, I have no other option left but to trouble you.

In U.P. & Bihar, 32 factories have not as yet paid their contribution. Before I submit more names to you, I am trying to collect the money voluntarily from them.

With kindest regards

Yours sincerely,
K.K. Birla

With Sardar Patel as the patron of the fund which was for a very noble cause, all those whom I contacted fully cooperated with me. As to those who declined to remit donations as fixed by me, Pant-ji took immediate action. As a result of this, the sugar industry was able to collect more than its quota.

The total amount that father could collect was Rs 5.27 crore. This was a big amount in those days. Father was happy that the funds collected by him exceeded the quota fixed by Pandit-ji and Sardar Patel.

M.O. Mathai

M.O. Mathai was special assistant to Pandit Jawaharlal Nehru from 1946 to 1959. He was born in Kerala and was a very bright person. I came to know Mathai soon after he joined Pandit-ji's employment. On the occasion of Pandit-ji's sixty-seventh birthday, I had conveyed my felicitations to him. Though I knew Pandit-ji, I thought it better to write to Mathai. That way I was certain my letter would be placed before Pandit-ji. The text of that letter dated 12 November 1955 is reproduced here:

12 November 1955

My dear Mr Mathai

I shall be grateful if you could kindly convey to Pandit-ji my heartiest felicitations on the happy and auspicious occasion of his 67th birthday.

It is my proud privilege and honour to join the vast multitude of well wishers, friends and admirers of Pandit-ji all the world over in their sincere and humble prayer to Almighty to grant him a long life so that he may continue to guide and lead not only our country but humanity throughout the world.

With kind regards

Yours affectionately
K.K.Birla

In course of time, I got very close to Mathai. He was very close to Pandit-ji and was as good as a member of his family.

Pandit-ji had started the *National Herald* newspaper. It was badly managed and so was always in financial difficulties. Mathai approached us for special advertisements for the *National Herald*. Some extracts from Mathai's letter dated 20 November 1956 addressed to me is reproduced on page 391 for the interest of readers:

Personal & Private

My Dear Krishen Kumar,

When you met me this morning, I spoke to you about the help rendered by Braj Mohanji and Ghanshyamdasji by way of special advertisements for the *National Herald* for the calendar year 1956. In fact, Braj Mohanji arranged rupees two lakhs by way of special advertisements from concerns under him and, later, Ghanshyamdasji produced a similar amount from others, both in Bombay and Calcutta . . .

The best course would be for you to send me the names of the companies concerned and the amount each company is prepared to give in the form of special advertisements. Then, I shall have proper bills sent to you. On receipt of these bills, you might kindly arrange to send me cheques drawn in favour of the Associated Journals Limited, Lucknow. Thereafter, I shall have formal receipts sent to the companies concerned through you. This was the procedure we adopted last year.

I was interested in what you had to say regarding some of the editorials or write-ups which appeared in the *National Herald*—which in your opinion, were against the policy of the Central Government. Please send me cuttings of these. I myself have very little time to go through newspapers in any great detail. On receipt of the cuttings from you, I shall take up the matter with the Editor, who is a very able and fine person. However, nobody is free from shortcomings or faults just as Durgadas is not! . . .

Yours affectionately,

M.O. Mathai

I found Mathai to be a very warm-hearted person and very active. Whenever I had any problem, he would examine it dispassionately and if he was convinced that it genuinely deserved the prime minister's attention, he would place it before Pandit-ji.

Mathai created many enemies, owing to his closeness to Pandit-ji. He thought that Pandit-ji would publicly protect him against the attacks by the critics. Pandit-ji, however, was a very shrewd person. He chose not to take sides in the battles between Mathai and his critics. Ultimately, Mathai had to leave Pandit-ji's service. Thereafter, he became a bitter man which is reflected in his autobiography.

Sheriff of Kolkata

I was made the sheriff of Kolkata on 20 December 1960. This was done at the instance of Dr B.C. Roy, then chief minister of West Bengal.

While I was the sheriff, Queen Elizabeth II visited the city. I received a letter dated 13 February 1961 from N.K. Sengupta, Under Secretary to the Government of West Bengal, asking me to be present at the airport on 17 February to receive the queen and Prince Philip, Duke of Edinburgh. A copy is reproduced below:

> Sir,
> I am directed to state that Her Majesty Queen Elizabeth II accompanied by His Royal Highness, the Prince Philip, Duke of Edinburgh and her entourage will arrive at Dum Dum Airport from Panagarh by air at 15.40 hours on the 17th February, 1961 and leave Dum Dum Airport for Madras by air at 12.30 hours on the 19th February, 1961.
>
> I am to request that you may kindly make it convenient to be present at the airport on the 17th February, 1961 to receive the Royal dignitaries on their arrival and again on the 19th February, 1961 to bid them farewell at the time of their departure.
>
> You may kindly arrive at the airport at 15.00 hours on the 17th and at 11.15 hours on the 19th February.
>
> A copy of the pamphlet containing the programme of ceremonies on arrival and departure at Panagarh and Dum Dum Airports, convoy of cars and seating plan, composition of the party etc. is enclosed for your information.
>
> One car Park Sticker is also sent herewith for your use.
>
> Yours faithfully,
> N.K. Sengupta.

I was then forty-two years of age. As the sheriff, it was a part of my duty to escort the High Court judge to the court. There was a seat for the sheriff on one side of the judge. Many old records of the sheriff's office were lying packed in trunks. For lack of space they could not be put in any book shelf. I got the trunks opened in the presence of my staff and went through all the letters and notes that I could lay my hands on. One of the oldest records was a petition in May 1874 signed by a number of citizens of Kolkata. One of the resolutions suggests that some sort of a memorial be raised to the memory of Justice Dwarka Nath Mitter. Among the persons who had supported this were Pandit Iswar Chandra Vidyasagar and W.C. Bonnerjee—both personalities of national fame.

National Integration Council

Indira-ji made me a member of the National Integration Council in 1980. On 9 October 1980, I received a letter of invitation which is reproduced below.

Dear Shri Birla,
Linguistic and regional tensions which have arisen in various parts of our country and the recrudescence of communal and caste conflicts indicate the work of divisive and disruptive forces. In a similar situation, in 1961 it was decided to set up a National Integration Council as a permanent forum for people of differing categories and views to discuss and devise measures to fight the evils of communalism, casteism and regionalism which were weakening our unity and integrity. In 1968 the Council was reconstituted and made more broad-based. A note on the working of the Council is attached.

There has been a demand in Parliament to revive the Council. Hence it is proposed to reconstitute the Council broadly on the pattern of its earlier composition but keeping in view the changes that have since taken place in the national scene. A list of the Members of the National Integration Council is enclosed.

I have pleasure in inviting you to be a Member of the National Integration Council. I seek your cooperation in making the Council a useful and effective institution. Your suggestions on the scope and functioning of the Council would be welcome. We shall, of course, have a detailed discussion of the Council's programme of work at its first meeting which I hope to call soon.

With good wishes,

Yours sincerely,
Indira Gandhi

From the business community there were only two members—J.R.D. Tata and myself.

J.R.D. was a very outspoken person. He was a highly respected and internationally renowned leader of the business community. That apart, he was an elderly person. There was a generation gap between us. I therefore knew my own limitations. I knew that whereas he could afford to speak in a strongly critical language, I would have to put the same thing in a milder manner.

Indira-ji would often ask me to speak before J.R.D. I always felt awkward, but I knew Indira-ji did not have much liking for him.

The National Integration Council, after Parliament, is the most important body of the nation. As will be seen from the list of membership attached to the letter of Indira-ji, apart from three important ministers of the Central government, all the chief ministers were its members as well as important leaders of political parties. I served on the National Integration Council for two terms.

After formation of the government by Dr Manmohan Singh, I have again been invited to join the Council.

Commemorative Stamp

A commemorative stamp in memory of father was issued by the Government of India through my efforts. A copy of the First Day Cover of the stamp is reproduced here.

I Try to Learn the Computer

The computer is an innovative development which has brought about a revolution in the work ethics in offices, stores etc. All the important statements that a company has to present to shareholders like profit and loss statements and balance sheets are now computerized. They take much less time. Bookkeeping has improved. A revolutionary change has come in the stores department of the corporate sector whereby at any given time one could know the stock of each item in the stores department. There is, in fact, an all-round improvement.

I had tried to learn computer operations but I found that it is difficult to learn new things after the age of seventy-five. While I personally do not know much as to how to use the computer, I know what the benefits are of the computer. I have accordingly computerized all my companies on a massive scale so that they are not left behind in the competitive world.

I discovered that my daughters, grandsons and their wives have all learnt how to handle computers. I was a bright student in school and college and I stood eleventh in the matriculation examination from the Calcutta University and fifth in the Intermediate Science from the Delhi University and also fifth in Hindi Prabhakar (Honours) from Punjab University. I, therefore, thought that if I tried to acquire computer literacy, a man of my 'brilliance' would be able to learn it within a short period. But just as Arjun forgot the art of warfare and found himself unable to protect the women of the Yadav families after Lord Krishna had departed from this world, I discovered that it was difficult to learn computers when I was approaching my eightieth year. With great effort I was able to just use the computer for elementary work; but I could not do complicated work.

Once when Shobhana and her husband Shyam came to have dinner with me, I told them that the performance of my companies was good because I had computerized them on a vast scale; at the same time I said that it was a matter of disappointment to me that I could not learn much about the computer except its elementary data.

All my daughters are very affectionate and always helpful. Shobhana said that her younger son, Shamit, would be able to teach me how to use the computer in about a week's time. After that it was a matter of practice. This was a fair enough proposal and I agreed to be taught by my grandson!

Shamit tried to teach me how to use the computer for four-five days. I could not pick up much. Shamit, out of respect for me, did not say that my brain was not agile. On the sixth day, when he found that I had made very poor progress, he said very humbly but sweetly, 'Nana-ji, you do not have to learn how to use a computer. You have already introduced computers in all your companies. That is good enough. It is the job of the managers and your secretaries, whenever any information is needed, to get it from the computer and place it before you. A man of your position does not have to learn how to use a computer. After all, you are interested in the end results. Why should you waste your time in learning computer work? If you have to do it, then what are your managers and secretaries for?'

I realized that what my grandson was saying was basically correct. I said, 'Beta, I realize what you say is correct. Now tell me what should I do with this very expensive computer which your mummy has purchased for me? Shall I ask your mummy to send it back to the store from where she purchased it and get a refund?' Shamit said, 'Nana-ji, that will not look proper. This computer was purchased about a fortnight back and it has been used by you and me.' 'Then what shall I do with it, son?' I asked him. He said, 'Nana-ji, I am prepared to take it so that you can get rid of your worries and problems.' This is how I learnt about the functioning of the computer.

Messages from the Presidents

Whenever the President went to the state which I represented as an MP, he would write to me about it so that, in case I wanted to attend any function concerning the President's visit, I could do so. Dr Shanker Dayal Sharma was very particular about this. He would also invite MPs from each state for breakfast. On my birthday also I regularly received his letters of good wishes. A copy of his letter dated 11 October 1994 reads as follows:

11 October 1994

Dear Shri Birla,
On the joyous occasion of your birthday on 12 October 1994, I offer you my congratulations and wish you many happy returns of the day. May you be blessed with a long and happy life in the service of the people.
    With kind regards,

Yours sincerely,
Shanker Dayal Sharma

K.R. Narayanan was also particular to write me a letter of congratulations on my birthday. He was kind enough to send me a very

nice letter on our diamond wedding anniversary on 3 July 2001. The text
of his letter is reproduced here:

2 *August 2001*

Dear Dr Birla,
I thank you for your letter dated July 31, 2001.

Usha and I are happy to know that your Diamond Wedding
Anniversary was celebrated on 3rd July.

We send our warmest greetings to you and your wife and wish
both of you many many happy returns of the day. Our nation will
always remember your contribution for the progress of the country.
With kind regards,

Yours sincerely,
K.R. Narayanan

Narayanan would invite me to each and every dinner that he gave in
honour of any visiting dignitary. I attended all of these banquets if I was
in Delhi. If there was any special VVIP I would change my programme so
as to be present in Delhi at that time. For example, Shri Narayanan gave
a dinner in honour of General Pervez Musharraf, President of Pakistan,
and Begum Saheba Musharraf, and invited me to the banquet held on 14
July 2001. Sometimes he would send me a letter of thanks in his own
handwriting when I sent him some fruit from our gardens or *sherbet* or
thandai made by my wife. Once he sent a short letter (date not given), a
copy of which is reproduced below.

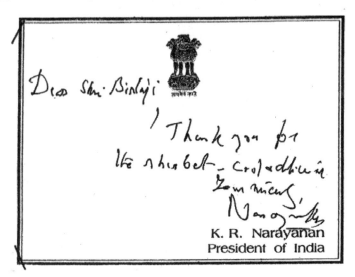

Shri Narayanan was kind enough to invite me to the dinner hosted by him in honour of President Clinton on 21 March 2000. Many people tried to secure an invitation to this dinner. I never made any such effort which I thought was beneath my dignity. Not only would Shri Narayanan invite me to all important functions, he gave me a very high position in the seating arrangements. He also sent me a letter after I had undergone bypass surgery in London:

2 November 1999

Dear Dr K.K. Birla,
I am relieved and glad to learn that you have been gradually recovering from the bypass surgery performed on you. I wish you a speedy recovery to your normal health.
    With regards,

Yours sincerely,
K.R. Narayanan

Narayanan was a great humanitarian. Perhaps he was the best President that we have had in the last twenty years.
    Dr A.P.J. Abdul Kalam also would invite me to dinners but by that time I had ceased to be an MP. I found that in the seating arrangements I was given a very low position. I made enquiries and then was told that ex-MPs have no special privilege. Having enjoyed sitting next to VVIPs as an MP, I did not cherish the idea of sitting so low on the table. I then sent a message to the secretary of the President asking him not to invite me any more. Thereafter, I stopped going to the President's banquet altogether.

Correspondence with the Prime Ministers

P.V. Narasimha Rao: Rajiv Gandhi was assassinated on 21 May 1991 while he was campaigning for the general elections. In those general elections, the Congress got 224 seats out of 516 seats for which elections were held. Though the Congress missed the majority by a small margin, it was invited to form the government, being the single largest party. Had Rajiv been alive he would have undoubtedly become the prime minister again. After his assassination there were two contenders for the prime minister's post—Narasimha Rao and Sharad Pawar. Ultimately, Narasimha Rao was elected the prime minister. The general impression was that he had the support and good wishes of Sonia Gandhi.

I was quite close to Narasimha Rao and used to meet him quite frequently. Whenever any industry had a problem, they would approach me for bringing the facts and condition of the industry to his knowledge. Some time in July 1991, I was informed by some businessmen that the government was thinking of changing the mode of valuation of unquoted shares. I wrote to Narasimha Rao on 1 August 1991 pointing out that Rule 12 of Schedule III of the Wealth Tax Act was sought to be amended to provide valuation of the shares by adopting a break-up value method after taking into account the market value of each asset owned by a company. This, I pointed out, would cause havoc for the income tax assesses. The letter is reproduced here:

1 August 1991

My dear Shri Narasimha Raoji,
This is concerning the proposed changes in the mode of valuation of the unquoted shares. I had explained that such changes will cause lot of hardships to the shareholders of these companies. You had kindly agreed to have the matter examined and had asked me for a note.
I am accordingly enclosing a note herewith.
Kind regards

Yours sincerely,
K.K.Birla

Narasimha Rao acknowledged this letter in his letter of 9 August 1991. The proposed change in the valuation system was dropped. A copy of the letter is reproduced below:

9 August 1991

My dear Birlaji,
Thank you for your letter of 1st August, 1991 regarding valuation of unquoted shares.

I am asking the Ministry of Finance to examine the matter in the light of your suggestions.

With regards,

Yours sincerely
P.V. Narasimha Rao

On 16 July 1992, I wrote to Narasimha Rao urging that Rajasthani should also be made one of the languages recognized in the Eighth Schedule of the Constitution. I wrote:

16 July 1992

My dear Shri Narasimha Raoji,

As an M.P. from Rajasthan I am taking the liberty of making the following suggestion to you for your kind and sympathetic consideration.

From time to time, representations have been made to me to approach the Government of India for their recognising Rajasthani as one of the languages in the Eighth Schedule of the Constitution. I had made efforts in this direction in the past but did not succeed.

The Government of India, from what I hear, are shortly going to include some more languages in the Eighth Schedule of the Constitution including Manipuri and Nepali. Population of Rajasthan is much larger than that of Manipur. Rajasthani is a rich language and many books have been and are being written in Rajasthani. Hence I plead that along with Manipuri and Nepali, Rajasthani also be included in the Eighth Schedule of the Constitution.

In case Rajasthani is recognised in the Eighth Schedule of the Constitution, this will be a matter of great satisfaction for the people of Rajasthan and will greatly enhance the image of our Government in Rajasthan. From every angle, therefore, this will be a step in right direction.

I shall be grateful if the matter could receive your kind attention.

Kind Regards,

Yours sincerely,
K.K.Birla

After sending this letter, I met Narasimha Rao. He told me that there would be no problem in recognizing Rajasthani as a national language, but the initiative had to come from the government of Rajasthan. The state government unfortunately took no action though I wrote to it repeatedly.

Some time in early 1994, Maharashtra was hit by a major earthquake. Narasimha Rao appealed for donations to the Prime Minister's National Relief Fund. I contributed towards that and also collected funds from many of our companies in which I was the chairman. I had sent cheques for Rs 75 lakh to Narasimha Rao. A copy of his reply dated 6 April 1994 is quoted below.

6 April 1994

Dear Shri Birla,
Thank you for your letter of April 5, 1994 enclosing a cheque for Rs 75 lakhs for the Prime Minister's National Relief fund.

Please convey my deep sense of appreciation to all the donors for their kind gesture towards the quake victims of Maharashtra.
With regards,

Yours sincerely,
P.V. Narasimha Rao

Narasimha Rao was undoubtedly one of the best prime ministers that we have had since independence.

H.D. Deve Gowda: Deve Gowda was prime minister for a very short period of ten months—from June 1996 to April 1997. I had known Deve Gowda fairly well even before he became prime minister. I had invited him for tea on several occasions. He was kind enough to accept my invitations and visited my house. He wrote me a very nice letter dated 20 April 1997 when he gave up his office. It is reproduced below.

Dear Shri Birla,
On the eve of my demitting office of the Prime Minister of India, I would like to place on record my deep sense of gratitude for your invaluable cooperation during the last 10 months.

When the United Front Government assumed office in June 1996, we made certain promises to the people of India. We pledged to preserve the secular nature of our heritage, to strengthen the forces of cooperative federalism, to achieve rapid economic growth coupled with enhanced social justice, and to give a responsible and responsive Government to the people of India, a clean Government which is open and transparent in its decision making. Today, I can say with legitimate pride, that my Government was largely able to redeem these pledges.

About 10 moths ago, a great responsibility was placed upon me. I tried to fulfill this responsibility to the best of my ability with your cooperation both inside and outside the House. I thank you for the trust you reposed in me and for your cooperation during this period. I bid you farewell with the belief that our great country shall continue to progress and that all its citizens will have the opportunity to enjoy freedom, have access to justice and a high quality of life.

Yours sincerely
H.D. Deve Gowda

Atal Bihari Vajpayee: Atal Bihari Vajpayee became the Prime Minister on 16 May 1996 for the first time. My relationship with him all along has been very friendly. I have the privilege of knowing Atal-ji for over thirty-five years. He came to Pilani to canvass for me when I fought the Lok Sabha elections from Jhunjhunu in 1971 on behalf of the Swatantra Party. BJP was functioning in those days as 'Jan Sangh'.

Our friendship has continued ever since. Even after he became the prime minister, Atal-ji remained free from ego. He retained his humility and always talked very politely with whoever met him. He is a man of noble nature. A copy of his letter to me dated 11 January 1999 is given on page 403. This concerns the Saraswati Samman given to the best book published in India in the last ten years. That Atal-ji attended this function is a matter of honour to me.

At the time of Kargil War in 1999, I organized a collection for the National Defence Fund from the companies under my control. A letter was sent to Atal-ji on 10 August 1999 on page 403:

प्रधान मंत्री
PRIME MINISTER

नई दिल्ली
11 जनवरी, 1999

प्रिय डॉ. बिरला,

श्री मनुभाई पांचोली को 'सरस्वती सम्मान' दिये जाने के संबंध में आपका 7 दिसम्बर, 1998 का पत्र मिला, धन्यवाद।

मुझे इस समारोह में सम्मिलित होकर खुशी होगी। समारोह का आयोजन 15 मार्च, 1999 को सांय 6.00 बजे किया जा सकता है।

शुभकामनाओं सहित,

आपका

(अटल बिहारी वाजपेयी)

डॉ. कृष्ण कुमार बिरला
संसद सदस्य
'बिरला हाऊस'
7, तीस जनवरी मार्ग
नई दिल्ली - 110 011

10 August 1999

My dear Shri Atalji,

As I had mentioned to you when we met on 22ⁿᵈ July, two of the major companies in my Group—Messrs Chambal Fertilizers & Chemicals Ltd and Zuari Industries Ltd—have contributed Rs 30.00 lakhs and Rs 10.00 lakhs respectively to the National Defence Fund. This is for the welfare of the families of our brave soldiers who laid down their lives in defence of the country in the Kargil war as also for those soldiers who got disabled.

I had also mentioned that I shall be arranging some further

404   KRISHNA KUMAR BIRLA

contributions. I am glad I have been able to organize Rs 10.00 lakhs more for the Fund. This includes a contribution of Rs 2.50 lakhs from myself and an amount of Rs 1 lakh from my wife Smt Manorama Devi as also an amount of Rs 2.50 lakhs from one of my trusts.

Staff and workers of Chambal Fertilizers and Zuari Industries and some other companies have also contributed about Rs 7.50 lakhs. Cheques for all these amounts along with a list of the donors are enclosed.

I shall be grateful if the receipts for all these donations are sent to me, to be forwarded to the respective donors.

Kind regards,

Yours sincerely,
K.K. Birla

I sought an appointment with Atal-ji and gave the cheques to him. Likewise at the time of the Orissa super-cyclone, I made a contribution to the Prime Minister's National Relief Fund. Here is a copy of Atal-ji's reply dated 24 December 1999:

24 December 1999

Dear Dr Birla,

Thank you for the contributions from Chambal Fertilizers & Chemicals Ltd, Zuari Industries, Sutlej Industries and Hindustan Welfare Trust towards Prime Minister's National Relief Fund. I appreciate the gesture of the donors.

The amounts will definitely contribute towards promotion of various schemes for extending relief to those affected by the Super Cyclone in Orissa.

With regards,

Yours sincerely,
A.B. Vajpayee

We have an apple orchard in Kulu. We grow both types of apples there—red delicious and golden delicious. Likewise in Uttar Pradesh, one of our sugar factories has a farm where langra mangoes of high quality are grown. Very good gur (jaggery) is manufactured in the area of one of our sugar mills. I send apples, langra mangoes and gur as also chandan sherbet and thandai prepared by my wife to a large number of friends, including many ministers and, of course, to the leader of my party, Sonia-ji. Some of the ministers did not care to reply or send me a letter of thanks. This practice I have been following for the last thirty years and I am keeping it up even now, though since my retirement from the Rajya Sabha in April 2002 I have been leading a semi-retired life. Whenever I sent these gifts to Atal-ji, when he was prime minister, I always got his letter of acknowledgement and thanks. A copy of one such letter dated 24 August 2001 is reproduced here:

प्रधान मंत्री

Prime Minister

नई दिल्ली
24 अगस्त, 2001

प्रिय डॉ. बिड़ला

सप्रेम नमस्कार!

आपके द्वारा भेजे गए सेब प्राप्त हुए। सेब बहुत मीठे एवं स्वादिष्ट थे। आपका बहुत-बहुत धन्यवाद।

शुभकामनाओं सहित,

आपका,

(अटल बिहारी वाजपेयी)

डॉ. के.के. बिड़ला,
संसद सदस्य,
7, तीस जनवरी मार्ग,
नई दिल्ली - 110 011.

Atal-ji is the greatest statesman in India and is, in fact, regarded as a politician and diplomat of world class. I consider myself to be fortunate to have enjoyed his friendship and warmth.

Dr Manmohan Singh: Manmohan Singh became prime minister on 22 May 2004. He is a very old friend and I have known him for over forty years now. In fact when the book containing my speeches during my second term as a Rajya Sabha MP was published, he was kind enough to write the foreword.

When the tsunami hit India and many countries of Asia, I collected a large amount of money from our various companies and contributed Rs 84,02,837 to the Prime Minister's National Relief Fund. A copy of my letter dated 2 February 2005 written to Dr Manmohan Singh and his reply dated 8 February 2005 are reproduced below:

My dear Dr Manmohan Singhji,

I was in London where I had gone for my medical check up when the Tsunami hit many countries of Asia. It was not merely a national disaster but an Asian calamity. I immediately asked my various companies to get their Boards' approval for sending donations to the Prime Minister's National Relief Fund. My wife was with me in London at that time. Both of us felt that as a large section of humanity has been hit we should make personal donations also. Accordingly I decided to make a contribution of Rs 10.00 lakhs and my wife Rs 5.00 lakhs to the Prime Minister's National Relief Fund. From my various companies also I have collected donation cheques.

The staff and workers of our fertilizer companies—M/s Zuari Industries Ltd and Chambal Fertilizers & Chemicals Ltd—have made some contributions. So have the staff and workers of another company under us called Paradeep Phosphates Ltd. Another two companies—Zuari Seeds Ltd and Simon India Ltd—in my group and their employees have also responded promptly.

These cheques are worth a total of Rs 84,02,837/- details of which are given in the enclosure.

I shall be grateful if you could kindly arrange for the receipts to be sent to me in the name of the donor companies and trusts.

Kind regards,

Yours sincerely,
K.K. Birla

8 February 2005

Dear Dr Birla,

I write to convey my thanks to you and your wife and the staff and workers of the various companies in your group for their generous contribution to the Prime Minister's National Relief Fund.

Your gesture of support will contribute to relief and rehabilitation efforts being undertaken in the disaster-affected areas.

With warm regards,

Yours sincerely,
Manmohan Singh

Gujarmul Modi: Gujarmul Modi was a self-made man. The family originally came from Haryana. They later settled in Patiala. From there his family shifted to Modinagar where Gujarmul-ji established a sugar factory. Though not highly educated, Gujarmul-ji was a very pragmatic and dynamic person. Starting from scratch he was able to build an empire at Modinagar. The large number of industries he founded flourished well while he was alive. As Modinagar was getting too crowded, Gujarmul-ji set up another township, Modipuram, where he started new industries.

Gujarmul-ji was a fearless man. Once, a delegation from the sugar industry wanted to meet Morarji Desai when he was prime minister. I was asked to lead the delegation, but knowing Morarji-bhai's nature I suggested the name of Gujarmul-ji, who accepted it gladly. I warned him in advance that Morarji-bhai, though a man of great integrity and character, had the bad habit of giving sermons when people went to meet him. Gujarmul-ji told me not to worry. I was eager to see the battle royale when these two 'warriors' met. When the delegation went to meet Morarji-bhai, he, as was his habit, started preaching. Before he could finish Gujarmul-ji started interrupting him. This went on for some time. Morarji-bhai continued in his inimitable style. Gujarmul-ji then said, 'Mr Prime Minister, we have not come to meet Morarji-bhai. We have come to meet the person who is occupying the Prime Minister's chair. We bow to the chair. So long as you are sitting in this chair we bow to you. Once you leave this chair we will never come to meet you.' Morarji-bhai found his match in Gujarmul-ji and fell quiet.

Gujarmul-ji was very fond of Mussoorie, where he had a house. He went there almost every year. As I also visited Mussoorie every year, he would often invite me for tea. I found in him a very dependable friend. After Gujarmul-ji's demise, his family got separated. Gujarmul-ji had five sons. His younger brother was Kedar Nath Modi who was also a very powerful and influential man. He too was very friendly with me. My eldest grandson, Chandra Shekhar Nopany, is married to Gujarmul-ji's son Satish Modi's eldest daughter Shalini. She is a gem of a person.

Asoka Mehta: I had known Asoka Mehta since the early 1940s. Asoka Mehta and Jayaprakash Narayan, both staunch socialists, were, at one time, members of the Congress party. During the civil disobedience movement in 1932, Asoka-bhai was sent to prison for two and a half years. While in detention he came in touch with Jayaprakash-ji, Dr Ram Manohar Lohia and Achyut Patwardhan. In 1934, a division took place in the Congress. The socialist bloc separated and formed the Congress Socialist Party. The leaders of the Congress Socialist Party were Asoka-bhai, Jayaprakash-ji and Lohia. Each of them was a great personality in his own way.

I came in touch with Asoka-bhai when he became a cabinet minister in the 1960s. He was the minister of fertilizers. We were then in the process of commissioning our factory Zuari Agro Chemicals at Goa. Asoka-bhai called me and said that he would like the plant to be established as early as possible and that in case there was any difficulty or problem, I should immediately meet him. He said this in all seriousness. I would therefore meet him quite frequently. The remarkable thing about him was that whenever I met him with any problem, he would give me time and try to understand what my problem was. Thereafter he would give his decision then and there.

In the first two or three cases, he consulted his secretary. Thereafter, he took a liking to me. He was convinced that what I was telling him was the truth without trying to exaggerate anything or trying to hide the weak points of my case. He would, therefore, accept my word and give his decision immediately. Zuari's commissioning in fact got delayed by about six months. Had it not been for Asoka-bhai, the delay might have lasted ten months.

Asoka-bhai was a good orator and skilful parliamentarian. One could always see honesty in his conduct. Once Pandit-ji had asked him to speak on an important matter. Asoka-bhai told Pandit-ji that he had not prepared himself and was not in a position to participate in the discussions. In spite of that, when Pandit-ji insisted that he speak, he got up, spoke for about three or four minutes and sat down rather abruptly. He told Pandit-ji to excuse him as he was not in a position to make any contribution to the discussion. Such was the honesty of this man.

After retirement from active public life owing to his indifferent health, Asoka-bhai shifted to the house of the maharani of Patiala. They were very fond of each other and the maharani looked after him.

I had great respect for Asoka-bhai and so I often called on him. He was very fond of me. I had called on him a few weeks before he died. From the way his health was deteriorating, he knew and I also knew that it was only a question of a few weeks before he would leave this world. But he was a fearless man, not afraid of death. I asked him with great respect and humility, 'Asoka Bhai, I wish you a speedy recovery and good health. I do not know when I am next going to meet you. You are a man of high principles and I respect you for that. What is your final advice to me?' I used the word 'final'. He understood it. He said, 'Krishna Kumar, I like you. I have only one advice to give to you. Stick to high principles in life. Never give them up. Even if the prime minister were to speak to you, never compromise on principles. Even if you have to suffer as a result of that, bear it peacefully.' I was deeply touched by Asoka-bhai's advice. A few months later he died. I always remember his parting advice. He was a great man.

Sonia Gandhi: Once when I was with Sanjay Gandhi, Rajiv and Sonia-ji dropped in. That was just before Indira-ji lost power. Sanjay introduced me to them. I spoke to both of them for a few minutes. I called Rajiv by his first name and addressed him as 'tum' as I used to address Sanjay. That was my first meeting with Sonia-ji. Though I addressed Rajiv with the more informal 'tum', I addressed Sonia-ji with the more formal 'aap'.

I came to know Rajiv more intimately after Sanjay died. Gradually our friendship developed. He was a thorough gentleman. But I did not get an opportunity to meet Sonia-ji in those days.

When the Congress came to power in 1991, after Rajiv was assassinated during the election campaign, all the members of the Congress Party in Parliament wanted Sonia-ji to become prime minister. Sonia-ji, however, declined to accept this responsibility and Narasimha Rao became the prime minister. He was also elected as the President of AICC. From that time on, I started meeting Sonia-ji. I met her once every month except when I went abroad.

In the general elections in 1996, the Congress was defeated very badly. Narasimha Rao, therefore, had to quit.

Sonia-ji became the president of the All India Congress Committee (AICC) in 1998 and also the leader of the Congress Party in Parliament. She used to address the Congress MPs once or twice every session. I attended all such meetings. Many times she would hold public meetings in different parts of the Capital. Being a party MP, I attended these meetings. Sonia-ji is a very pleasant and able person. In all her actions there is a sense of propriety and fairness.

Even after I retired as MP, I meet Sonia-ji, who is the chairperson of the

United Progressive Alliance (UPA). I have always found her to be a person of great charm. She tries to follow a policy based on equity and fairness.

After Rajiv's assassination in 1991, a foundation called Rajiv Gandhi Foundation was started. It is a large organization and has been doing very good work. Sonia-ji is its chairperson. Even though she never requested for contribution towards this foundation, I have been sending her donations from time to time. On 29 November 1991 I sent her a donation of Rs 25 lakh. A charming reply came from her on 13 December 1991, which is reproduced below:

13 December 1991

Dear Shri Birla,
Thank you for your kind and generous donation to the Rajiv Gandhi Foundation. We enclose a brochure describing the aims and objectives of the Foundation. Your contribution will be most valuable in implementing Rajiv Gandhi's vision of a new and modern India. We seek your continued interest and encouragement. A formal receipt is enclosed.
    With good wishes.

Yours sincerely,
Sonia Gandhi

My relationships with Indira-ji and Rajiv were informal. In course of time, my relations with Sonia-ji also became informal.

Once at the end of a meeting of the Congress Parliamentary Party, a peon came to me and said that Sonia-ji wanted to meet me in her room in Parliament House. I immediately went to her room where Sonia-ji had the issue of the *Hindustan Times* of two or three days earlier on her table. There was an article which was somewhat critical of the Congress in Parliament. Sonia-ji showed me that piece and expressed her displeasure that such an article should have been published in our newspaper. 'Being a member of the Congress Party, Birla-ji, your paper should have taken a more balanced view,' she said. I told Sonia-ji that as the chairman I had laid down the policy that the paper had to follow. Within the framework of that policy the editor had full liberty to write editorials and have articles published. I said, 'Sonia-ji, I do not interfere with the functioning of the editor so long as he follows the policy of the paper as laid down by the Board of Directors under my chairmanship. If we started interfering with the editor and if the paper carried only pro-Congress Party articles, it will lose its credibility. This is a principle which I have been following,

Sonia-ji,' I said. I also told her that I would convey her views to our editor, Vir Sanghvi.

Later I spoke to Vir and my daughter, Shobhana, who is the vice-chairperson and editorial director of the paper. Vir is not only an outstanding editor but also a man of great integrity and objectivity. He is also a friend of mine. Vir met Sonia-ji and, in his own inimitable style, told her that she should have been more polite with a senior person like me. Sonia-ji sincerely felt unhappy at the somewhat harsh attitude she had shown to me. She immediately telephoned me and said that, if she had in any way hurt my feelings, her apologies should be accepted. That was her greatness.

In February 1992, the *Hindustan Times* held an exhibition of cartoons drawn by young amateur cartoonists. I sent a copy of the book containing the cartoons to Sonia-ji. Her reply dated 28 February 1992 is reproduced below:

राजीव गांधी संस्थापन

RAJIV GANDHI FOUNDATION

Sonia Gandhi
Chairperson   February 28, 1992

Dear Shri Birla,

        Thank you for your letter of 24th February. The books of cartoons and caricatures are delightful. The Hindustan Times has evidently made an excellent efforts to encourage cartoonists.

        I send you and the Hindustan Times my warm good wishes.

                        Yours sincerely,

                        Sonia Gandhi

ShriKK Birla
M.P. (Rajya Sabha)
Birla House
7, Tees January Marg
New Delhi - 110 011

जवाहर भवन, डा. राजेन्द्र प्रसाद मार्ग, नई दिल्ली-110 001.
JAWAHAR BHAWAN   DR. RAJENDRA PRASAD ROAD   NEW DELHI 110 001   INDIA

At the beginning of the summer season in 1993, I sent her chandan sherbet and thandai. The sherbet and thandai that I send to most of my friends are specially prepared under the supervision of my wife Manorama. The recipes that she uses for preparing these cold drinks are excellent. Many of our political friends do not care to reply. But Sonia-ji sends a reply every time. I got a very nice letter dated 26 April 1993 from Sonia-ji which runs as follows:

26 April 1993

Dear Smt & Shri Birla,
Thank you for the 'Sherbet' which you so thoughtfully sent. We all enjoyed it.
    With best wishes.

Yours sincerely,
Sonia Gandhi

I got a letter dated 25 October 1994 from Sonia-ji asking me to be one of the speakers at a function which she was organizing on behalf of the Rajiv Gandhi Foundation. This was a programme on 'The Literate Child— Towards Fulfilling A Promise' and was held at Vigyan Bhavan. Amongst the many speakers, apart from Sonia-ji, were the prime minister, chief justice of India and the finance minister. The text of the letter is given below:

25 October 1994

Dear Shri Birla,
As you know, the Rajiv Gandhi Foundation is commemorating the 50th birth anniversary of my late husband with a series of events highlighting his vision of a strong and self-reliant India.

One of his chief goals was to make primary education available and indeed mandatory for all children. The Foundation has therefore decided to seek the help of the Jawahar Bhawan Trust, UNICEF and the Ministry of Human Resource Development to support the establishment of Universal Primary Education in India by the year 2000.

As a first step, a document is being prepared which will affirm our joint commitment to the children of India. This will be released at 1600 hours on 14 November in a function at Vigyan Bhawan in commemoration of Jawaharlal Nehru's birth anniversary.

To make this function a significant event we invite you to be one of the speakers. As you will see from the attached programme, other speakers will include Finance Minister Dr Manohan Singh, Human Resource Development Minister Shri Arjun Singh, Chief Justice Ahmadi and luminaries from various fields such as industry, academia, non-governmental organisations and the media.

Such a coming together of diverse bodies to affirm their commitment to this important cause will help to establish Universal Primary Education as one of the most important development imperatives. I look forward to hearing from you.

Sonia Gandhi
Chairperson

I attended the function and made a short speech of about ten minutes. As this speech was highly appreciated by the audience and Sonia-ji, it is reproduced here:

Speech delivered on 14th November 1994 at Vigyan Bhavan, New Delhi
On 'The Literate Child—Towards Fulfilling a Promise'

Smt Soniaji, Honourable Ministers, fellow Parliamentarians and friends,

I am very happy the Rajiv Gandhi Foundation is commemorating the 50th birth anniversary of Shri Rajiv Gandhi in a befitting manner by trying to highlight his vision of a strong and self-reliant India. I am grateful to Soniaji for giving me this opportunity to address this august gathering not only because the subject which is being discussed here is of such importance, but also to seriously analyse the work done by our great leaders in building the foundations of the India of their dreams—an India where poverty and ignorance is being replaced by prosperity and knowledge.

Soniaji, you have correctly stated in the letter which you wrote to the speakers in today's function that one of the main goals of Shri Rajiv Gandhi was to make primary education available and indeed mandatory for all children in order to make India a strong nation. The people of India could make no nobler commitment than this to the future generations of our land.

India has taken great strides in all spheres, be it economic, scientific or social. We are in the select group of nations that have successfully implemented a satellite programme. We rank sixth in the world in terms of purchasing power parity. Our pool of scientific personnel is now the second largest in the world. We have a vibrant capital market with over 6500 listed companies, the second highest in the world. We also have one of the largest manufacturing sectors in the world, spanning almost all areas of manufacturing activities.

The progress of a country towards prosperity and strength and its educational programme go hand in hand. The Rajiv Gandhi Foundation has rendered yeoman's service by organizing this function today to highlight this endeavour.

Even though India today has a technically qualified manpower, which rates among the best in the world, both in terms of quality and quantity, in the area of universal primary education, we still have miles to go. It is internationally accepted that "Every child should be given a fair chance of growing up sound in mind and body, and making the best use of its natural faculties." A literate child holds promise for taking India to new heights of achievement and glory. Children have a right to education, a right to acquire literacy. This is even more imperative because there is incontrovertible evidence that human capital is the driving force of modern economic growth.

The role of universal education has always been emphasized by our great seers and saints. Education for all without any distinction of class or creed is brought out by the fact that Shree Krishna the prince, and Sudama the poor boy, studied in the same Gurukul.

Education combats poverty and social evils. One year spent additionally in a mother's education has been associated with a 90% decrease in under five mortality. The children of better educated mothers are healthier.

The 20th century, which will shine in history as a century memorable for freedom attained by all subjugated nations, is coming to a close and the advent of the 21st century is only a few years away. The way our country has progressed and is progressing,

I expect the demand of all items of consumption to double in about 8 to 10 years' time when the 21st century will still be in its infancy. A high challenge lies before the country to meet this demand. This will not be possible unless substantial progress is made in the field of education, in the sphere of science and technology. We have to create a big pool from where experts could emerge. It is not possible to have a Newton or an Einstein or a CV Raman and Tagore unless the pool is large enough to throw up geniuses. This leads to the conclusion that primary education should be mandatory for all children.

Our national leaders were quite conscious about this aspect of social development. Free and compulsory education for all children up to the age of 14 years was included as a constitutional obligation in the chapter on 'Directive Principles of State Policy' in the Constitution. In pursuance of that in the first stage, universal education should be provided to all children till they reach the age of eleven years and in the second, this age limit should be raised to fourteen years.

The Indian Industry and Business Enterprises should effectively supplement the efforts of the government. I in fact would be happy to call upon my colleagues in the industry to target specific areas around their industries to promote projects on primary education in partnership with the government, NGOs and the local community.

While providing Universal Primary Education is indeed essential, in my opinion, a very important aspect should be to define 'education'. Merely acquiring the ability to append one's signature does not make a person educated. Primary education should lay down the foundation which helps a person become educated and not just literate. The education of a child must go hand in hand with the building up of character.

If this does get accomplished, it will be a glorious day for India.

I received a letter dated 6 February 1997 from Sonia-ji on the occasion of the wedding of her daughter, Priyanka. It is an excellent letter:

SONIA GANDHI
10 Janpath, New Delhi-110 011

February 06, 1997

Dear Birla ji,

It is with great pleasure that I write to you to convey the good news of my daughter's wedding. Priyanka is getting married to Robert Vadra, who is the son of Rajinder and Maureen Vadra. The wedding is to take place on 18th February, 1997. Though it is my desire to share my happiness with all the friends and well-wishers of my family, in particular those who have given us so much affection and support through the years, I believe that such events ought to be held on a moderate and intimate scale. I therefore plan to have a small celebration with a limited number of close family members from each side. I trust that you will understand my sentiments and that Priyanka and Robert will have your good wishes and blessings for their new life together.

with warm regards

Sonia Gandhi

Mr K K Birla
Birla House
7, Tees January Marg
New Delhi - 110 011

I received a letter dated 30 October 1999 from Sonia-ji which will be found to be interesting. Both that letter and my reply are given here:

30 October 1999

Dear Shri Birla,
On the auspicious occasion of Diwali, may I take this opportunity to send my good wishes to you and your family.

This beautiful Festival of Lights also celebrates the spirit of fidelity and fraternity, of steadfastness and selflessness, of courage and grace in the face of adversity. On this Diwali, let us rededicate ourselves to these values, in the service of our nation, our party, and our secular, democratic ideals.

All of us in Parliament have a Sacred trust to fulfill—the faith and confidence reposed in us by the people. Let us also pledge to fulfill that trust, and do our utmost to meet their needs and aspirations.

Yours sincerely,
Sonia Gandhi

8 November 1999

My dear Soniaji,
I am in receipt of your kind letter dated 30th October along with your good wishes for Diwali. I am grateful for your greetings which I heartily reciprocate. I had sent a Diwali greeting card to you a few days back which you must have received.

Though our Party could not get a majority in the elections it still has not done badly, considering the circumstances prevailing. Our Party has a very important role to play as the principal Party in Opposition. I am sure, the Party will do well under your able leadership.

I am still recovering from the heart bypass surgery which I had undergone in London a few weeks back. I had met you before I left for London. The operation was successful though it will take another four months for complete recovery.

I shall call on you when I am next in Delhi.
Kind regards,

Yours sincerely,
K.K. Birla

I also wrote a letter to Sonia-ji which is interesting.

17 March 2000

My dear Smt. Soniaji,

In my opinion the present practice that our party has adopted of not giving Rajya Sabha tickets to the defeated Lok Sabh candidate for a period of two years needs reconsideration.

When two persons fight one is bound to be defeated. The question is what the margin of the defeat is. If the margin of the defeat is high, it is a rout. Such candidates should go through the 'penance' of waiting for two years before their names could be considered for nomination to the Rajya Sabha. On the other hand where there is a close contest such candidates should not be debarred from being nominated for the Rajya Sabha. By getting defeated such candidates suffer a set back in their political career. They fight for their party and if they get defeated by a small margin it implies they did well. Such candidates need a pat on the back. They should have the satisfaction that though defeated the party is solidly behind them. If on the other hand such candidates are denied tickets for Rajya Sabha, it amounts to double punishment for them.

As to what the margin of defeat should be for such consideration is an open question. This is a matter for you to decide. In my opinion the percentage should be somewhere between 80 to 90. This means that in a contest if the winner gets say 10 lakh votes and the Congress (I) candidate gets 9 lakh votes, he should certainly be eligible for nomination to the Rajya Sabha. As to whether this figure should be 9 lakhs or be reduced to 8 lakh votes is a matter which needs consideration. My main theme is that those who get defeated by a small margin should not be excluded from the race for the Rajya Sabha seats.

Kind regards,

Yours sincerely
K.K. Birla

I received a reply dated 28 March 2000 from Sonia-ji, which is also reproduced here.

28 March 2000

Dear Shri Birla,

Thank you for your letter of March 17. As you know I greatly value your views and I shall certainly keep in mind your suggestions regarding the nomination to the Rajya Sabha of those candidates who have lost.

With warm regards,

Yours sincerely,
Sonia Gandhi

In August 2000, Priyanka gave birth to a baby boy. I wrote a small letter dated 29 August 2000 to Sonia-ji and received a charming reply dated 2 September 2000 from her. A copy of her letter is reproduced below:

2 September 2000

Dear Dr Birla,

Thank you for your kind letter on the birth of my grandson. I am touched that you share our happiness.

Priyanka and the baby are doing well, and she and her husband are filled with delight and wonder at becoming parents.

A newborn child always fills one with hope and deep gratitude for the gift of life. I feel very blessed and happy to be a grandmother. I only wish Rajivji were with us to share our joy.

Yours sincerely,
Sonia Gandhi

She also wrote a very nice letter dated 10 December 2000 in response to my letter of greetings on her birthday. A copy is reproduced below:

10 December 2000

Dear Dr Birla,

Thank you for your kind greetings.

I am overwhelmed by the affection and blessings I have received on my birthday.

Yours sincerely,
Sonia Gandhi

I am also reproducing my letter dated 14 December 2001 to Sonia-ji and her reply dated 18 December 2001.

My dear Smt Soniaji,
Dr Manmohan Singhji, Leader of our party in the Rajya Sabha had a few days back sent to me and to other MPs of Congress Parliamentary Party copies of letters sent by you as the Congress (I) President to the Prime Minister and a few letters to the Congress (I) Chief Ministers. I am sure this move would lend cohesiveness to our party MPs' views in the Parliament.

All your letters to the Prime Minister and the Chief Ministers of Congress ruled states were very well written. I have also gone through the speeches made by you in the Lok Sabha which too were very appropriate. From the numerous letters which you have sent to the Prime Minister it is clear that every significant matter of national importance has been taken up by you with the Prime Minister. My hearty compliments.

I do not know, however, what was the reaction of the Prime Minister to the suggestions that you made. It would have been better had the party MPs been informed about that also. In the papers sent by Manmohan Singhji there is only one letter from the Prime Minister sent to you dated 12th October.

I have no doubt that our party will continue to function well as a responsible opposition party, under your dynamic leadership.
Kind regards,

Yours sincerely,
K.K. Birla

Dear Dr Birla,
Thank you for your letter of December 14, 2001. I have taken note of its contents. I am happy that you found copies of my correspondence to be useful. On many of my letters, substantive response is still awaited.

Yours sincerely,
Sonia Gandhi

My brother Basant Kumar and his wife Sarala had brought out a book called *Immortal Icons* which contains correspondence that father had with many leaders of his time including Motilal Nehru, Jawaharlal Nehru, Madan Mohan Malaviya and Lala Lajpat Rai. I spoke about this book to Sonia-ji. She asked me to send her a copy, which I did. Her reply dated 1 April 2002 is reproduced below:

Dear Dr Birla,
Thank you for your letter of 27 March 2002 enclosing a copy of the book 'Immortal Icons' containing the important correspondence of your father, Shri G.D. Birla. I look forward to reading it with interest.
  With good wishes.

Yours sincerely,
Sonia Gandhi

Once it came to my notice that the income of the Rajiv Gandhi Foundation had gone down and their investments were not substantial. Returns from the money deposited with some of the government companies were not satisfactory and the Foundation was in dire financial straits. I sent a letter to Sonia-ji about it. She not only took notice of my letter but sent the secretary general of the foundation, Moni Malhoutra, to meet me personally. A copy of her letter dated 10 April 2003 is reproduced below:

Dear Dr Birla,
Thank you for your letter of 29th March. I much appreciate your concern about the Rajiv Gandhi Foundation's investments. The Foundation now has an Investment Adviser as well as an Investment Committee consisting of four of our Trustees—Dr Manmohan Singh, Shri P Chidambaram, Shri RP Goenka and Dr V Krishnamurthy.
  I would, however, welcome your advice on our investment policy and our current portfolio of investments. I have asked the Secretary-General of the Foundation, Shri Moni Malhoutra, to meet you personally and share these details with you. Could your office please telephone him and arrange a mutually convenient time to meet?
  With kind regards,

Yours sincerely,
Sonia Gandhi

I got the matter of investments studied by a committee of experts. This committee consisted of some senior officers of my own group. Then

I sent a detailed letter to Sonia-ji and again received a nice reply dated 29 May 2003, a copy of which is given below:

Dear Dr Birla ji,
I have received your letter of 24th May apprising me of the findings of your examination of the investment portfolio of the Rajiv Gandhi Foundation. I appreciate the trouble you have taken. I am forwarding your observations to the Secretary General of the Foundation.
    With good wishes,

Yours sincerely,
Sonia Gandhi

I got two important letters from Sonia-ji—one dated 6 June 2003 and, after some correspondence, another letter dated 17 January 2004. The text of the letters is given here:

6 June 2003

Dear Dr Birla,
Thank you for your letter of 24th May on RGF's investment portfolio. I am grateful to you and your financial executives for examining the portfolio so meticulously and for the advice which you have given. I am asking our Investment Committee to consider the recommendations carefully.
    With kind regards,

Yours sincerely,
Sonia Gandhi

17 January 2004

Dear Dr Birla,
Thank you for your letter of 22nd December regarding RGF's investments in the light of your recent experience of balanced mutual funds.

I have brought your letter to the attention of our Investment Committee. With the market as high as it already is, they echo your advice of caution, but will keep the matter under review.

I am grateful for your continuing interest and advice.
    With kind regards,

Yours sincerely,
Sonia Gandhi

When the Delhi High Court cleared Rajiv's name in the Bofors case, I wrote a letter to Sonia-ji. I got a nice reply dated 12 February 2004:

12 February 2004

Dear Dr Birla,

I was touched by your kind words on the Delhi High Court Judgement clearing Rajivji's name in the Befors case.

The verdict is a vindication of truth, of my husband's honour and of the fundamental principles of our democracy. It took 17 long years for justice to be done, but my husband always had full faith that, ultimately, the truth would triumph.

I deeply appreciate your good wishes and support.

With good wishes,

Yours sincerely,
Sonia Gandhi

In 2006, Sonia-ji had submitted her resignation from the Lok Sabha on the issue of holding an 'office of profit'. She enjoyed certain facilities as chairman of the UPA and felt that there was a danger that these might be construed as her holding an 'office of profit'.

Almost all the parties felt that both the Houses of Parliament could pass a Bill so that many institutions are exempted from the list of 'office of profit'. Knowing full well that it might not be necessary for her to resign, Sonia-ji, being a highly principled lady, took the more honourable course of resigning voluntarily. Sonia-ji then sought re-election on 8 May 2006 from her constituency of Rae Bareli, which she won by a record margin. I sent her a letter of congratulations on her victory. A copy of her reply is given below:

22 May 2006

Dear Dr Birla,

I was touched to receive your warm letter of congratulations.

I am deeply moved by the renewed expression of faith in me by the voters of Rae Bareli. Their support has only strengthened my conviction that our wise electorate values and responds to principles and ethics in political life.

With my good wishes,

Yours sincerely,
Sonia Gandhi

Invitations from VVIPs

Whenever any important dignitary came to India, the President or the prime minister were always kind enough to invite me to lunch or dinner. Thus, in May 1984 when the present United States President, George Bush's father, George W. Bush, then the vice-president of the United States, came to India, Indira-ji hosted a lunch for him to which I was invited. A copy of the table plan of the lunch hosted by Indira-ji in honour of Mr George Bush is also reproduced below:

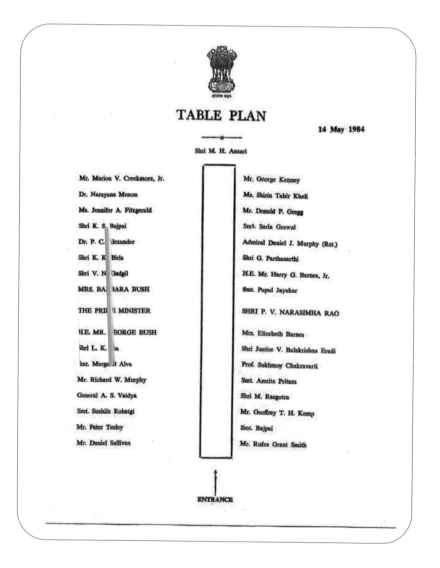

In November 1986, Rajiv invited me to lunch when the prime minister of Italy Bettino Craxi came. Some of the others invited to the lunch were: B.G. Deshmukh, Krishna Sahi, K.C. Pant, Sarala Grewal, B.K. Modi, S.S. Grewal, K.P. Singh Deo, Arjun Singh, Balram Jakhar, Ashok Gehlot, R. Prabhu, Prof. M.G.K. Menon and S. Venkitaramanan. When the prime minister of the Netherlands, R.F.M. Lubbers, came to India, Rajiv again invited me to the dinner. In April 1990, R. Venkataraman, the then President, invited me for a lunch he hosted for Toshiki Kaifu, prime minister of Japan. In December 1991, R. Venkataraman invited me for lunch when the Chinese prime minister, Li Peng, came to India. In Decmeber 1993, Dr Shankar Dayal Sharma invited me to dinner when King Birendra Bir Bikram Shah Dev, King of Nepal came to India. He also invited me for dinner in March 1995, when Mrs Chandrika Bandaranayke

TABLE PLAN

15th April, 1981.

—o—

Mr. Ranjit Mathrani.	Mr. Tim Lankester
Shrimati Ansari.	Shri J. R. Hiremath.
Mr. M. K. Ewans.	Prof. R. N. Dogra.
Shri R. D. Sathe.	Shri Sita Ram Singhania.
Shri Hari Krishna Shastri.	Shrimati Khurana.
Shri K. K. Birla.	Shri Mohd. Shafi Qureshi.
Shri Rajiv Gandhi.	Shri B. P. Maurya.
Shrimati Jha.	Shrimati Pupul Jayakar.
H.E. Sir John Thomson.	Shri Frank Anthony.
Shrimati C. P. N. Singh.	Shrimati Maneka Gandhi.
Shri Y. B. Chavan.	Dr. V. A. Syeid Muhammad.
Shrimati Sheila Kaul.	Dr. Charanjit Chanana.
Shri L. K. Jha.	Shri Pranab Mukherjee.
MR. DENIS THATCHER.	Miss Carol Thatcher.
THE PRIME MINISTER.	Shri Bal Ram Jakhar.
THE RT. HON'BLE MARGARET THATCHER MP.	Shri R. Venkataraman.
Shri P. V. Narasimha Rao.	Shrimati Saroj Khaparde.
Shrimati Gurbrinder Kaur Brar.	Shri C. P. N. Singh.
Shri S. L. Khurana.	Shrimati Mukherjee.
Shrimati Chanana.	Shri Mohd. Yunus.
Shri Jagan Nath Kaushal.	Shrimati Sonia Gandhi.
Shrimati Anthony.	Sir John Graham.
Shri C. R. Krishnaswamy Rao Sahib.	Shri Ebrahim Sulaiman Sait.
Mr. Bernard Ingham.	Shrimati Sathe.
Shrimati Dogra.	Shri Madan Bhatia.
Shri H. D. Bhalla.	Dr. V. N. Tiwari.
Shri M. H. Ansari.	Mr. Michael Alexander.
	Shri C. R. Gharekhan.

↑

ENTRANCE

Kumaratunga, who was then the President of Sri Lanka, came to India.

Indira-ji used to invite me to dinner even when I was not an MP. On 15 April 1981 she invited Margaret Thatcher, who was then the prime minister of Great Britain and Northern Ireland, for dinner. The other invitees were R. Venkataraman, Narasimha Rao, Y.V. Chavan, Rajiv and Sonia-ji, Pranab Mukherjee and Balram Jakhar. A copy of the table plan is given on p. 425.

This was a very important dinner. Mrs Margaret Thatcher is regarded amongst the three top politicians ever born in the UK, others being Queen Elizabeth I and Churchill. She completely changed the social atmosphere of UK by passing several laws to keep peace and discipline in the country. To be invited for dinner even when I was not an MP was a great honour indeed.

I had also received an invitation card from Indira-ji when Rajiv was married to Sonia on 25 February 1968. A copy of that is also reproduced below:

मेरे सुपुत्र राजीव का विवाह सोनिया माइनो से २५ फरवरी १९६८ को होना निश्चित हुआ है । हम आपके आशीर्वाद के अभिलाषी हैं ।

इन्दिरा गांधी

१ सफ़दर जंग रोड नई दिल्ली

मधु वाता ऋतायते मधु क्षरन्ति सिन्धवः। माध्वीर्नः सन्त्वोषधीः॥६॥
मधु नक्तमुतोषसि मधुमत्पार्थिवं रजः। मधु द्यौरस्तु नः पिता ॥७॥
मधुमान्नो वनस्पतिर्मधुमाँ अस्तु सूर्यः। माध्वीर्गावो भवन्तु नः॥८॥

There are some *slokas*, perhaps from the Vedas, in the invitation card.

Emergency and My Visit to London

I was one of those who had supported the declaration of Emergency. But I had all along felt that it should last only for three or, at the most six, months. I repeatedly requested Indira-ji to withdraw the Emergency after the first few months. She was inclined to do so but Sanjay was insistent that it should continue.

One day Indira-ji sent for me and said that I should go to London. She said that the declaration of Emergency and the circumstances preceding it were not fully appreciated by people in Britain. Indira-ji had a lot of respect for Great Britain, but she felt that the situation she faced and how the country had become a land of anarchy, should be explained to the businessmen and politicians in London. She further observed that if the situation had been allowed to deteriorate further and the Emergency not imposed, India would have gone the Pakistan way in which case, who knows, the military could have taken over the country.

I did not quite agree with Indira-ji. In July 1976, I repeated to Indira-ji what I had said earlier—that the proper course for her would have been to have called off the Emergency after three or four months and to have declared elections. As it is, thirteen months had elapsed since the Emergency was declared.

Indira-ji agreed with me but said that Sanjay was not in favour of withdrawing the Emergency. I told Indira-ji again that it was she and not Sanjay who was the prime minister. Sanjay, I said, was a young man and did not have the maturity that she had. I again pleaded with her. She said, 'You first go to London and try to explain the situation to the people there. After that come and report the matter to me.'

Accordingly, I went to London. B.K. Nehru was then the high commissioner for India in London. He was as old as my father, but, in spite of that, we were good friends. I held BK in high esteem and BK treated me with great warmth. On 9 August 1976, the Indian Chamber of Commerce of Great Britain gave a luncheon party for me. This was attended by over fifty people. On 12 August 1976, one of my business friends threw a cocktail party. Close to seventy or eighty people came. BK also arranged for me to meet many ministers and MPs. I could meet the following:

- Edmond Dell, secretary of state for trade
- Evan Luard, minister of state, foreign affairs

- Reginald Maudling, shadow foreign secretary
- Lord Limerick, president, Association of British Chambers of Commerce,
- Sir Ralph Bateman, outgoing president, CBI
- Lord Nelson of Stafford, chairman, General Electric
- Lord Inchcape, chairman, Inchcape Group
- A.W.B. Hayward, chairman and managing director, Shaw Wallace Co
- W. Bowey, managing director, Port of London Authority
- Sir Michael Parsons, managing director, Inchcape & Co. Ltd
- A.B. Marshall, managing director, P & O S N Co.
- Lord Barnetson, Chairman, United Newspapers Ltd;
  Chairman, Reuters;
  Chairman, Council of Commonwealth Press Unit; and
  Chairman of several industrial companies
- Evelyn De Rothschild, chairman, the *Economist*
- P.C. Roberts, deputy chairman and chief executive of *Mirror* group
- A.V. Hare, managing director, *Financial Times*
- M.J. Hussey, managing director and chief executive, Times Newspapers Ltd
- Ian C.Trafford, managing director, the *Economist*
- Brian Nicholson, managing director, *Evening Standard* and director of Beaver Brooke Newspapers Ltd
- H.M. Stephen, managing director, *Daily Telegraph*
- H.C. Thompson, director and general manager, Times Newspapers Ltd
- Douglas Long, deputy chief executive, *Mirror* Group
- Frank Barlow, director and general manager, Westminster Press Ltd
- Andrew Knight, editor, the *Economist*
- Roy Wright, editor, *Daily Express*

It was a long list. Most of the people who came had heard about me and knew that I was a friend of Indira-ji. This received good publicity in England. One paper stated that 'there has not been such a distinguished gathering in London to hear a private individual'. I was asked about the press censorship. I said, 'it was imposed as is normal under the Emergency anywhere, in Britain too. It had since been relaxed to self-censorship by papers'. I was also asked when the Emergency was to be lifted. I said, 'Mrs Gandhi had said publicly that she would lift the Emergency as soon as the Opposition agreed to act constitutionally.' Trade Minister Edmond Dell said that he could not comment on India's internal matters but he congratulated India on the remarkable economic progress made by it in recent months. He also congratulated me on my clear account of the pre-Emergency and post-Emergency periods. Concluding, Dell said that he was impressed by India's remarkable progress and expressed his best wishes for her greater prosperity. BK said that my assessment as a private individual should have more impact than what he, as an official representative, could expect. He agreed entirely with what I had said. Referring to my father, whom he knew very well, BK said that my father had, for more than half a century, devoted his life and work to India's development though he had not always received due recognition for it.

I came back and met Indira-ji. She said that she was very happy over my visit. She had received a full report from BK in which he had praised me and my performance. BK also mentioned that my speech had been received well by the media in Britain.

I told Indira-ji that there was a general feeling in Britain that the Emergency should be lifted as early as possible. Indira-ji promised to keep my suggestions in view. Actually the Emergency was lifted on 21 March 1977. In the elections held soon after, the party lost heavily. Had the Emergency been lifted in six months, it would have been quite another story.

Some Correspondence with Mahatma Gandhi

At the time of my wedding, Mahatma-ji too had sent his blessings. A copy of his letter is reproduced on p. 430:

सेवाग्राम   SEVAGRAM,
वर्धा सी.पी.   WARDHA. C.P.

२२-६-४१

Mahatma-ji's letter is legible but its English translation is also given below:

21 June 1941

Chi Krishna Kumar
I received your letter. My blessings will positively be with you on the day of your wedding. May God fulfil all your benevolent wishes. If one enters Grihasthashram as a part of dharam then much philanthropic work can be done.

I received your cheque. This will be used for the welfare of harijans.

Bapu's Blessings

I also sent a letter on 25 August 1938 to Mahatma-ji. This was to know his views on ahimsa (non-violence). I was then only twenty years of age. Mahatma-ji had come to know me as whenever he stayed at Birla House in Delhi, I made all the arrangements in accordance with instructions from my father. It was greatness on Bapu's part that he chose to send a reply to the letter of a youngster like me. Owing to his busy schedule he could not do so immediately, and sent his reply after nine months, as reproduced on pages 432 to 434.

On the first page, Bapu writes about some trouble that had taken place in Rangoon (now called Yangon). I am not offering any comments on that; but he says that non-violence could be effective even in such an instance. Non-violence with its attached virtues should be of a very high degree. Bapu says that he has not been able to achieve non-violence of that standard yet, but 'I am making efforts towards that. By God's grace it may come'. Mahatma-ji was able to achieve non-violence and other virtues that are attuned to it. He was a saint and karmayogi of the kind that are born only once in a millennium. It is out of sheer modesty that he has written that he has not been able to attain non-violence of the required standard but that by God's grace it may come.

In the letter, Bapu says the war between Lord Ram and Ravan should be regarded as non-violent. For proper explanation, Bapu says, see *Lanka Kand*. I think what he probably meant was what Bhagwan Shree Krishna said to Arjun:

• Any action that you take should be for a good cause. Fight with the

spirit of a *stithpragya* (a man with a very high degree of equanimity).
- When you take an action, do not look to the results.
- Fight for a good and just cause.
- If you fight for a good cause, then you do not commit any sin.

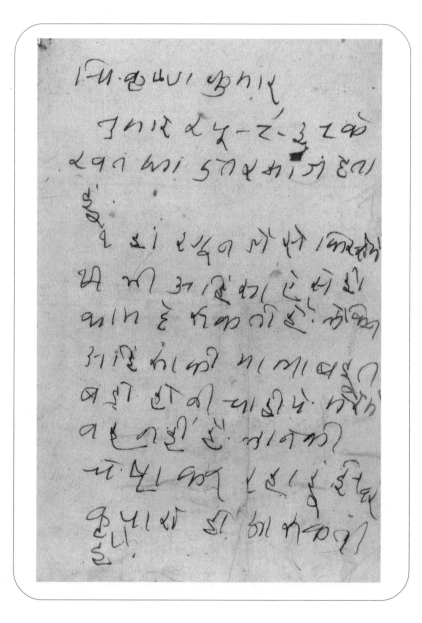

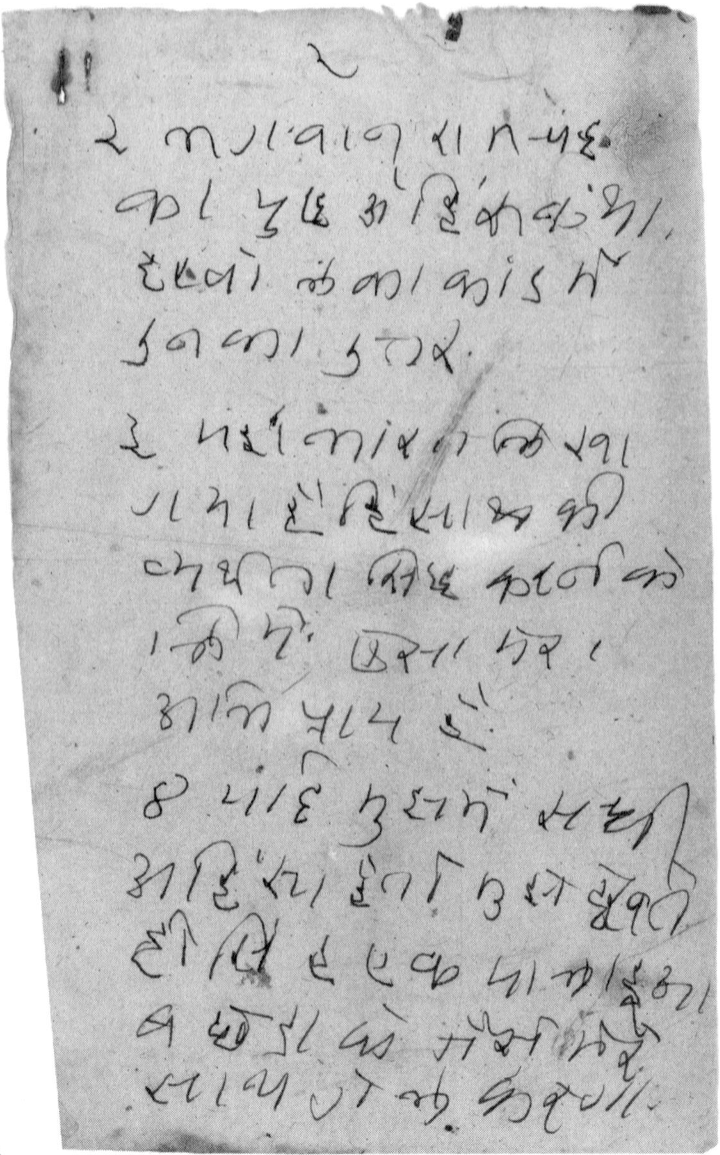

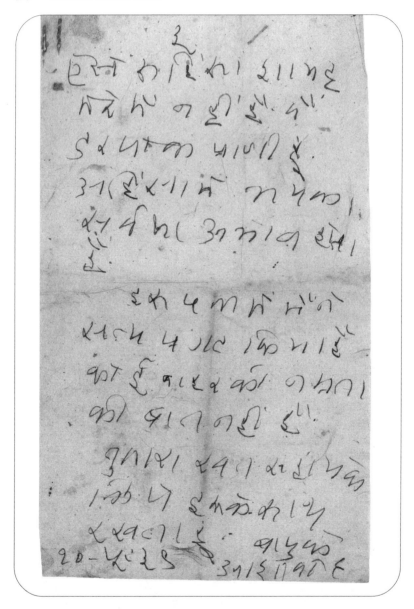

Bapu says, 'If there is full non-violence [*ahimsa*] in me, then even a lion will behave like a calf of a cow'. Bapu's letter is dated 10 May 1939. This was in reply to my letter dated 5 August 1938. Bapu writes that owing to his tremendous workload he could not reply earlier.

I had written another letter to Bapu. It was a letter of the kind a young man would write to his father and grandfather about his general well-being. Mahatma-ji's reply dated 31 January 1942 is reproduced below:

The English translation is as under:

Chi Krishna Kumar

I should have written to you earlier. But I was so busy that I forgot to reply. I am sorry for that. I hope Manorama is well. May God protect her.

Bapu's blessings

Expressing his regret for the delay in replying! Such was Mahatma-ji's greatness.

Visit to Pondicherry

My visit to Pondicherry was, in a sense, accidental. A very good friend of mine, Lokenath Dhandhania, lived in Bhagalpur. Apart from being a fairly well-to-do person, he was very fond of art and culture. He also loved gardening. He had two sons. His younger son, Kishorilal, came under the influence of the Mother at Pondicherry and he declared that he would settle down there and join the Mother's organization. Lokenath was highly perturbed by this. He came to me with a request that I should go to Pondicherry, talk to his son and try to persuade him to leave the ashram, return and join the family business. Lokenath added that he would be grateful in case I could meet the Mother also if necessary. I told him that there was no problem in my going to Pondicherry and meeting the Mother, but that I had doubts if his son would agree to return to Bhagalpur or Kolkata and rejoin business. But I agreed to go as Lokenath was feeling very dejected over his son's departure.

At Pondicherry I met his son and had a detailed discussion with him. He said that he was not at all willing to go back to Patna, Bhagalpur or Kolkata. Ultimately, on my persuasion he agreed that if the Mother wanted him to leave the ashram he would do so and return to Bhagalpur.

An appointment had been fixed with the Mother for me. I met the Mother and was highly impressed by her personality, charm and magnetism. I told her about the boy, about Lokenath, about their family background and begged the Mother to permit the young man to go back and join his family business. The Mother said that in case the boy wanted to return she would not stand in his way, but that she would not instruct him to go back to business. He was a free soul and he could decide as he thought best. Thus a stalemate occurred. Kishorilal said that he would not go back to his business unless the Mother asked him to do so. The Mother, on the other hand, said that he could go back to his business provided he wanted to do so. I thought I should now return to Kolkata, but the Mother said that she would like to have another fifteen minutes with me. My discussion with the Mother about Kishorilal had lasted for about forty-five minutes. Hence, I was a bit surprised when she said that she would like to have another fifteen minutes. I did not understand what this was about but since she desired so, I sat facing her. The Mother then asked me to look straight into her eyes and stared instantly at me. Before I met the Mother, many of her devotees had told me that she might ask me to gaze into her eyes. In case she asked me to do so, they said, I should regard myself as a fortunate person. They said that in this way the Mother would pass her blessings on to me. I, however, had my own views. When the Mother asked me to look straight into her eyes, I immediately realized that she had a hypnotic power. I had read a lot about hypnotism and knew that many people had the power to hypnotize others. But I had no intention of being hypnotized. So I looked at her eyes for a few seconds and then looked away. After a few seconds I again gazed at the Mother. This game of hide and seek went on for fifteen to twenty minutes. Then the Mother too probably realized that I was difficult to hypnotize.

Once in London a doctor had told me that hypnotism is good medicine for certain ailments. Out of sheer fun, I went to a hypnotist along with my wife and asked him to try to hypnotize me. He tried for half an hour and then said that hypnotizing me was beyond his power. When I met the Mother I was confident that she would not be able to hypnotize me. But all the same, I realized that the Mother had a very strong personality. Spiritually, too, she was at a very high level. As I had no intention of being hypnotized, I played the game in my own manner.

I returned to Kolkata and told Lokenath what had happened. He was very sorry to note that the Mother would not let his son return to him, but all the same he was very grateful to me. He also said, 'Babu, it was my good fortune that the Mother could not hypnotize you.' I told him that as soon as the Mother had asked me to gaze in her eyes I became suspicious and was on my guard.

Conferment of D. Litt.

I got a message from the Pondicherry University that they wanted to confer the degree of 'Doctor of Letters [Honoris Causa]' on me. The function was to be held on 10 September 1997. I had made all preparations for visiting Pondicherry but I had to cancel my programme at the last moment owing to some unavoidable reasons. The vice-chancellor of the university was Dr A. Gnanam. I am not quoting the full citation but only two paragraphs from it.

> Shri Birla's contribution to educational development is not a whit less than his contribution to the nation's industrial expansion. Under

his vigilant care, Birla Education Trust, Pilani runs several residential and non-residential schools. Birla Institute of Science & Technology, Pilani imparts excellent higher education in Engineering and Science. K.K. Birla Academy, New Delhi and K.K. Birla Foundation promote research and propagate the Indian heritage.

Birla, the man, is as fascinating a figure as Birla, the industrialist. A simple and unassuming person, to whom humility is wisdom, he goes about doing his chosen task with missionary zeal and works for eighteen hours a day even at the age of seventy-nine. He keeps himself busy managing his industries, promoting sports and fine arts, lecturing and writing articles and books on religion, economics, current affairs, and contemporary social issues, besides being a member of our Parliament. One of the top industrialists of the country, he is non-pareil.

Gajanand Dalmia

Gajanand Dalmia was a very brave person. He was the manager of the textile unit of Sutlej Cotton Mills at Okara in Pakistan. In May 1958, he and two other Indian officers of the mills were arrested by the police on charges of evasion of income tax and consequent loss of revenue to the Government of Pakistan. It was a politically motivated case. Some Pakistani employees of the mills could not relish the idea that officers from India should look after the mills. They wanted a Pakistani officer to be elevated to the post of general manager. We then made a representation to the government of Pakistan. I am reproducing below three paragraphs from that representation:

> If, however, unknown to the Company or its Managing Agents, there has occurred any breach of any law or regulation by any employee of the Company or there has been any loss of revenue to the Government of Pakistan by any act of contravention by any employee of the Company such as by way of incorrect packing and/or marketing, sale of stores and/or other consumable goods, under-invoicing etc., then in view of these circumstances and in view of the most sympathetic attitude of the authorities concerned and the declared benevolent policy of the Government of Pakistan, the Company offers a sum of Rs 2,50,000/- [Rupees two lacs fifty

thousand only] as a gesture of its goodwill, sincerity and cooperation. A cheque for this amount is being enclosed herewith.

The Company submits that the Central Board of Revenue, Government of Pakistan, will be kind enough to accept this amount on the understanding that the Company and/or its Managing Agents are absolved of all consequences of any contravention of the rules and regulations prevalent in Pakistan, in case any such contraventions have taken place.

The Company and the Managing Agents assure the Government of Pakistan that they are always prepared to give their utmost cooperation and to take all such steps as are possible for the observance of all rules and regulations of Pakistan.

This representation was made after some people, whom we had sent to Pakistan, had come to an understanding in this connection with the authorities concerned.

Correspondence with Harish Salve

Harish Salve is one of the topmost counsels at present in the Supreme Court. He had accepted our brief in the Rajendra Lodha matter, but subsequently returned it and took the brief on behalf of Lodha to fight against us. Our lawyers say this is the only case in their knowledge of a counsel accepting a brief from one person and returning it to accept the brief from the former client's adversary.

I had some interesting correspondence with Harish in connection with the Lodha case. Copies of letters exchanged are reproduced below which may be of interest to the readers.

Personal & Confidential

25 July 2005

My dear Harish,

I am writing this letter to you in connection with the recent correspondence that has taken place between you and Ms. Gauri Rasgotra. In your last letter to Gauri dated 18th July you have stated 'I will certainly meet Mr Birla—although as far as the retainership is concerned, my decision is final'. I am not making any effort of any type to persuade you to change your decision. If you have taken a decision the chapter is closed. But all the same I thought of writing to you this letter from two points of view.

The first point is that I played an important role while the recent negotiations with you were in progress. Hence some comments on what you have written in your letter to Gauri are necessary. However, I would not have written to you had this been the only point in my mind. There is another point much more important which prompted me to write this letter to you. That point I shall explain later in this letter.

Coming to the first point of the role that I played, I would like to state as under: It was some time on the 1st of July and I was on holiday in Mussoorie. Our people telephoned to me from Kolkata on the 1st of July and said that Shri Rajendra Lodha was in London, that you were also in London, and that Rajendra was making serious efforts to persuade you to give up our brief. When I heard this I asked my secretary to try to locate you and ascertain from you the convenient time when I could telephone to you. I was informed that I should telephone you at 11.00 p.m. IST. I accordingly telephoned you from Mussoorie at 11.00 P. M. on the 1st of July. I first introduced myself and then asked you what the position was about the Lodha matter. You told me that now-a-days you do not appear in the Court when there are four or five lawyers appearing on behalf of a party. I fully appreciated your view and I explained our position. I said that cases have been instituted against Lodha by us both on civil and criminal matters. On civil matters I said only two persons would appear from our side—Shri Arun Jaitley and yourself. You said that you had no problem in working with Arun. I gave you a firm assurance that if we engaged a third lawyer it would be subject to your approval and that nobody would be engaged from our side without your prior approval. You said this was perfectly in order. I therefore regarded our talks as satisfactory and conveyed this to our people in Kolkata.

Suddenly on the 13th of July I got news that you were having a rethink on the matter. I was told some correspondence had taken place between you and Gauri. When I got this news I again got in touch with you on the telephone. You repeated what you said to me at Mussoorie, that namely, you do not accept briefs when there are too many lawyers. I repeated what I had said in Mussoorie that there would be only two lawyers on the civil side to represent us—yourself and Arun. 13th July was a Wednesday. To me it looked as if you were not fully satisfied. Hence I said I would be in Delhi on Saturday and Sunday in the following week when I would meet you at your residence. You said that it was alright. I was confident in my mind that when I met you at Delhi I would be able to dispel all your doubts. I accordingly asked my secretary in Delhi to seek an appointment with you at your residence either on the 23rd or 24th July as per your convenience. When my secretary telephoned your secretary the next day to enquire if you had indicated any time she was told that the time would be indicated after a few days.

After our talk I asked our people to place before me the entire correspondence that took place between you and Gauri. In one of your letters to Gauri you had given the names of a number of lawyers who have been engaged. Khaitan & Co. assured you that there were going to be only two lawyers to represent us. Your reaction, if I have understood you correctly, was that this would amount to a breach of retainership. Side by side, you also mentioned that the seniormost counsel would obviously lead from our side and that this was not acceptable to you. This is what I was going to discuss with you to dispel any doubts that you may have had in your mind. Our idea was to have only two lawyers. About the other lawyers whom we had sent retainership fees, it was our problem as to how to handle the matter.

In the list that you have sent to Gauri there are many names with whom we have no connection whatsoever and no retainership has been sent to them. For example, we have not given any brief to Messrs Soli Sorabjee, Mukul Rohatgi, Virendra Tulzapurkar and Janak Dwarkadas—the names that have been mentioned by you in your e-mail dated 7 July to Gauri. In this letter you have also mentioned that you were told that the charge of the Birla case was no longer under me but was under my younger brother Basant Kumar who was now handling this case. Gauri has replied to this letter, but let me also state that your information is not correct. We brothers and cousins are working in close consultation with each other. There is abundant affection and warmth amongst all of us. All the members are considered equal. I am at present the head of the Birla family and in that capacity I am the first among equals. Be that as it may, the fact is that no important action is being taken by the family or our lawyers without first getting my approval.

My idea of writing this letter to you is this: When an understanding had been reached between us, first when I telephoned to you from Mussoorie on the 1st of July and secondly when I telephoned to you from Kolkata on the 13th of July, was it proper for you to write to Gauri that the decision taken by you was final? I would not like to enter into any controversy with you. I leave the matter to your judgement.

As I have mentioned at the very beginning of this letter, there were two reasons for me to write this letter to you. It is the second reason, which is of much more importance, that has prompted me to write this letter to you. The reason of my writing to you even after the chapter has been closed is because I had a special relationship with Shri N K P Salve, your father. I am therefore writing to you not as a client but more like a close friend of your father. Shri N K P Salve and I were together in the Rajya Sabha for three terms or 18 years. Not only that, I had known your father even before I joined the Rajya Sabha in 1984. I have known him since the late 70s when on several occasions he was kind enough to accept my invitation to visit Birla House and have a cup of tea with me. In the Rajya Shabha we were very close to each other. Our views, almost on all matters, were similar and this resulted in a deep bond of friendship. Many times during the lunch recess we used to have coffee or snacks together at the Central Hall. If you speak to Salve Saheb I am sure he will confirm what I have written.

It is this reason—that my sentiments have been hurt by the son of Shri N K P Salve and he should give up our brief and accept a brief from Lodha—that induced me to write this letter to you. I felt very unhappy when I read your letter dated 18th July which you sent by e-mail to Gauri, where you wrote that you would be prepared to meet me at your house if I so desired but that your decision of relinquishing the brief was final. I feel greatly hurt by the position that has now emerged.

Now that you have given your final decision that you are giving up the brief I am not going to make any effort to dislodge you from your decision but I can not restrain myself from writing to you my views.

Kind regards,

Yours sincerely,
K.K. Birla

His reply was as follows:

29 July 2005

My Dear Birlaji

At the outset, let me say that I understand and appreciate the sentiment underlying your letter.

I always have—and continue to—hold you in high esteem for your contribution towards nation building and also for the reason that you have been my father's friend. I am distressed at this situation caused by what has transpired in the past year.

I have been publicly decrying this relatively new practice of 'blocking' counsel. It brings a bad name to our profession, making us look like commodities on sale.

It is no longer in doubt that while I was assured (by the solicitors) that the retainers would be confined to those seniors who are to be actually briefed to argue the case, it is now clear retainers were being handed out on behalf of the 'family'.

As you correctly point out, it is not proper to think of any one member handling the dispute—it relates to the family and you being the senior most would obviously have a decisive say in matters. In fact, it was for precisely this reason that I found little comfort in the explanation that some members had handed out these retainers.

When the article in *India Today* said that a rash of retainers had been handed out, I sought a clarification, and was told that it was simply not true.

For the first time, it has now been candidly accepted that retainers have been given to others, including some senior counsel who are senior to me.

In order to limit my work, one rule I scrupulously follow is that I do not accept second briefs—I feel this also respects the high office I had the privilege to hold during 1999-2002.

As I tried explaining to you in brief on the telephone, the situation that comes about by this kind of handing out of retainers, creates a great deal of embarrassment for me vis-a-vis other professional colleagues.

After I spoke to you at Mussoorie I made certain further inquiries and personally ascertained that retainers had been accepted on behalf of the Birla family by a number of other seniors including Mr Soli Sorabji.

The unalterable situation then was that either there would be the other senior counsel also appearing in the matter, or there would be a breach of retainer if they were not so briefed. For such breach of retainer, irrespective of what they are told, they would hold me responsible.

Most of all, the situation was contrary to the assurance that had been given to me, and it was obvious that the information that was being given to me had been knowingly distorted. I hasten to add that you did not personally give any such information, yet the fact is that I accepted the retainer on being misled in this manner.

It is in this context that I had informed Gauri that the situation had now become unalterable and that I had little choice other than to return the retainer.

I was looking forward to explaining this to you in detail when we met personally, and I was sure that you would understand the delicate situation in which I was placed, for there are nuances that I could have explained to you which are best not put on paper.

I am happy that you articulated your views in your letter and I thought my doing the same would help clear the air.

With regards,

Harish N. Salve

Personal & Confidential

10 August 2005

My dear Harish,

Please refer to your letter dated 29th July. I am grateful to you for your compliments for the contribution of the Birla Family towards nation building. I also highly appreciate the comprehensive manner in which you have dealt with points raised by me in my letter of 25th July. I wanted to close the correspondence with your reply; but, there are a few points in your letter which need clarification. I would, therfore, like to offer the following observations:

1. About the new practice of 'blocking' a Counsel and creating an impression as though Counsels are commodities, I would like to emphatically state that what you have stated was never our intention. What we did was out of sheer necessity. We had sent retainer fees to only four senior Counsels as under:

1.   Yourself.
2.   Shri Arun Jaitley
3.   Shri F.S. Nariman
4.   Shri K.K. Venugopal

The Lodha matter is in the Calcutta High Court. After that it will go to the Supreme Court. By the time the final verdict comes it may take a few years. When we decided to retain some Counsels we had to take a long term view. In such an important case to retain four senior Counsels was a wise step purely as a safe-guard against any unforeseen development.

As the situation has evolved, the step we had taken, of retaining four Counsels, stands vindicated. As you have decided to return our brief we are now left with only three senior Counsels—Arun, Fali and Venugopal.

I had already written to you in my earlier letter that the four Counsels whose names were mentioned by you were never approached by us. They were:

1.   Shri Soli Sorabji
2.   Shri Mukul Rohatgi
3.   Shri Virendra Tulzapurkar
4.   Shri Janak Dwarkadas

I may also state that Lodhas too have engaged four senior counsels. They are:

1.   Shri Shanti Bhushan
2.   Shri Gopal Subramaniam
3.   Shri Anil Diwan
4.   Shri C.A. Sundaram

According to our reports, you have accepted Lodha's brief. I understand both Shri Shanti Bhushan and Shri Anil Diwan are senior to you. Thus a peculiar situation has arisen. I may be excused if I say that according to my reports in the last 30 years there has not been a single instance where a Counsel has returned the brief of a client and accepted the brief from the opposite party to fight the first client.

There is no question of regarding the Counsel as a "Commodity". Counsels enjoy a very high stature in the society. We, the members of the Birla family, are modest by nature. We cherish humility in life, and do not stand on ego. We give the greatest respect to our lawyers. When we gave retainership to four Counsels, it was as a matter of abundant caution as explained above.

You have mentioned in your letter that you said that you have 'personally ascertained that the retainers had been accepted on behalf of the Birla family by a number of other seniors including Mr Soli Sorabji'. I am afraid your information is absolutely incorrect. No brief has been given to Shri Soli Sorabji by any member of the family.

You have stated that you wrote to Gauri 'that the situation had now become unalterable and that I had little choice other than to return the retainer'. I may again be excused if I write that when I, as the head of the Birla family [eldest member], had talked to you on the phone not once but twice, there was no necessity at all for you to have written to Gauri. When talks were being held at the highest level—yourself and myself—no talk should, in fact, have been held with Gauri. This is my view.

You have mentioned in your letter 'I was looking forward to explaining this to you in detail when we met personally.' Permit me to state under:

I talked to you on the telephone from Kolkata on 13th July when it was agreed that we should meet in a few days. Next day i.e. on 14th July I asked my Secretary to contact your Secretary to fix an appointment for me for 23rd or 24th July as per your convenience. Instead, you wrote to Gauri on 19th July, just four days before I sought an appointment (for 23rd /24th July) that, as far as the retainership matter is concerned, your decision was final.

If you were looking forward to meet me, you could have surely waited for four more days for our meeting. I state with all sincerity that I was indeed looking forward to meeting you. But the meeting would have been fruitful only in case you met me with an open mind. If you had already taken a full and final decision, there was no point of my meeting you.

Let me say that there is no bitterness in my mind and that I regard this chapter as closed. Even though this is not a happy ending, I shall certainly retain warmth for you as after all you are the son of an old friend—Shri N.K.P. Salve. I hope that we too could be friends in the future. With these words I close the correspondence.

Kind regards,

Yours sincerely,

K.K. Birla

My Daughter Shobhana Becomes a Member of Parliament

I have written elsewhere in this book regarding my youngest daughter Shobhana. She was born in the year 1957. Shobhana and her husband Shyam Sundar Bhartia are both brilliant in their own fields. Shyam is a very successful businessman. Shobhana has proved to be a very able administrator in her own right. She shuns publicity. Shobhana is a highly principled girl.

Gujarat was affected by severe drought when Atal-ji was prime minister. I collected funds for the Prime Minister's National Relief Fund from all my companies including the *Hindustan Times* of which I am the chairman. I suggested to Shobhana that we go together and present the cheques to the prime minister. A photographer was present on the occasion. A photographer is always available at the prime minister's house whenever a person goes to meet him. After presenting the cheques, Shobhana said that she would not like to be photographed, and she moved away. That is the sort of girl she is.

Shobhana also told me that she did not want to give the money she raised through the *Hindustan Times* to the Prime Minister's National Relief Fund, but that she wanted to use it to adopt a village on behalf of the newspaper. I readily agreed to this. Hence when we went to meet the prime minister and presented the cheques, the money collected through the *Hindustan Times* was not there. Later, the *Hindustan Times* did adopt a village and completely rebuilt it with the funds raised. It turned out to be a remarkable village. Shobhana received blessings from the villagers.

When my Rajya Sabha term ended in 2002, it is quite possible that, with some effort, I would have received Sonia-ji's consent to take Shobhana in my place. But Shobhana very firmly said that on sentimental grounds she would not like to contest that year and that someone else could get elected to the seat that I vacated. After the elections were over, I had a talk with Sonia-ji, who said that she would try to find a seat for Shobhana in the Rajya Sabha as early as possible. Shobhana could have contested from Rajasthan in 2004. Santosh Bagrodia had completed two terms and so I thought Shobhana had a good chance of being nominated on behalf of the Congress party. But when I met Sonia-ji she told me that Bagrodia had said that for his first term he fought the election as the seat had fallen vacant owing to the demise of the sitting MP and so in the first term he did not get a full term of six years. Hence Sonia-ji said that she had promised the seat to him. I did not press the point though I did say to Sonia-ji that Bagrodia did not deserve the third term. Later I discovered that in his first term, Bagrodia was short of the six-year term by only two months.

I told Shobhana that there was no chance for her contesting from Rajasthan in 2006. With its reduced strength in the Rajasthan Assembly, the Congress could get only one MP elected from the state. That seat, I said, would in all probability be given to Rama Goenka who was close to Sonia-ji and who had finished only one term. Hence I made no efforts for Shobhana's entry to Rajya Sabha from Rajasthan that year.

Shobhana, in any case, never tried for a Rajya Sabha seat. I have been meeting Sonia-ji from time to time. A friend told me that she had great respect for me and that she had said so to this friend. Sonia-ji said that she knew that I was close to Indira-ji, and that I stood firmly by her when she was out of power. Sonia-ji also knew that I was close to Rajiv. Sonia-ji's warmth for me was evident from her instructions that whenever I went to 10 Janpath I would not have to pass through the security. Instead a car would be waiting for me and take me straight to Sonia-ji's residence. Not only that, after every appointment when I took her leave she would always come up to the door and make sure that there was a car waiting for me to take me back to the main gate of 10 Janpath. Sonia-ji had also told me that she was very fond of Shobhana and that if Shobhana got elected to the Rajya Sabha, she would be of great help to her.

Nowadays I go to Delhi only when there is some meeting or the other. In that sense Delhi is no longer my headquarters. One day Sonia-ji sent for Shobhana and said that she was very happy with her for her ability, nature and personality. Sonia-ji said to Shobhana, 'I had promised your father that I shall try to get you in the Rajya Sabha as early as possible. In pursuance of that I have recommended to the Prime Minister to forward to the President your name for being nominated as a member of the Rajya Sabha. Please inform your father that I am very happy with you and that I have kept my promise.' Shobhana thanked Sonia-ji for that and conveyed this to me. I was very delighted. I told her that I would meet Sonia-ji as soon as her nomination went through.

To contest an election and enter Parliament is the work of a politician. I was a politician. I had served for three terms in the Rajya Sabha. I, therefore, meticulously followed all the instructions given by the Congress Parliamentary Party, that is, by Sonia-ji, and, before that, by Rajiv. Thus whenever Sonia-ji spoke in public I went there. Once Rajiv decided that all the Members of Parliament should try to do the *Dandi March* up to the first night's halt that Mahatma-ji had made when he made the famous '*Dandi Yatra*' in the year 1930. I did that too and walked all the way from Ahmedabad to the first night's halt of Mahatma-ji.

Shobhana, on the other hand, has been elected not as a politician but is the President's nominee for the services rendered by her to the public. This is regarded as a very high honour. The entire family was delighted when she was nominated. When she was sworn in, I watched the ceremony from the visitors' gallery along with Shyam, Shobhana's two sons and her daughter-in-law.

On the day that she decided to take the oath as MP, I had a quiet talk with a senior person in the editorial department of the *Hindustan Times*. I suggested to him that he send a photographer and a correspondent who could wait for us at Gate No. 12 of Parliament House (from where the Rajya Sabha members enter Parliament). I also told him to keep this to himself as both of us knew that Shobhana does not want publicity. I told him that I would accompany Shobhana right up to the lobby of the Rajya Sabha. From there on she could go to the House. I would go to the visitors' gallery. All these arrangements were made very quietly. I also told this staff member not to speak a word about it to Shobhana.

In the evening that senior staff member telephoned me and said, 'Sir, Mrs Bhartia has given instructions that her photo, when she went to the Rajya Sabha to take oath as an MP, is not to be published in the paper and that as far as the swearing in ceremony is concerned, a very nominal publicity should be given.' Later, I sought an appointment with Sonia-ji and thanked her profusely for being kind to Shobhana.

BITS—Goa Campus

The Birla Institute of Technology and Science, Pilani, is a deemed university. It is one of the topmost institutes of engineering in the country. It is regarded on par with the IITs. The institute was established in the year 1964.

I had approached Dr Manmohan Singh, to inaugurate the Goa Campus of BITS, Pilani and he very kindly agreed to do so. Excerpts from the speech delivered by me on the occasion are given here:

The Pilani Campus was blessed with the visits of many distinguished personalities, significant among them being Pt Jawaharlal Nehru, the then Prime Minister (three visits—1950, 1953 and 1960), Dr Rajendra Prasad, the then President (1951), Dr S Radhakrishnan, the then Vice President (1956) and Dr R Venkataraman, the then President (1990). We are fortunate to have you, Mr Prime Minister, as the first distinguished visitor to our newly established Goa Campus.

Under the lead provided by you, India is fast emerging as a powerful nation both politically and economically. It is a matter of satisfaction that all the countries of the world—the United States, the Russian Fedration, the EU and the countries of Asia and Africa—are now eager to have friendly ties with India.

Education has always enjoyed a very high degree of regard and respcet in the Indian society. Starting with the *'Vedas'* and *'Upanishads'* of pre-historic times and oceans of knowledge (ज्ञान) of all types, we had the Gurukul system under which the rich and poor, Krishna and Sudama, sat at the feet of the same Guru as equals. In ancient India when the Magadha emperors ruled the country for over a thousand years we had the University of Nalanda where over 10,000 students sought knowledge in various faculties from over 1500 teachers and learned people.

It is said in our scriptures.

मात देवो भव।
पित देवो भव।।
गुरुः देवो भव।।।

Mother, Father and Guru are just like God. That inheritance is cherished today also, and the present-day Indian too is keen for enlightenment.

Prime Minister, Dr Manmohan Singh-ji, I shall explain what our philosophy and our aims are. May I say however that the Indian media have for years been placing BITS, Pilani at the same level as the IITs. I shall speak more about this later.

A significant fact to note is that all admissions at BITS are made on an all-India basis, purely on merit, judged through a unique and transparent computer based on-line test held at various centres across the county—the only one of its kind in the country.

Our prime consideration has been to prepare young men and women to act as leaders for the promotion of the economic and industrial development of our nation and to produce leaders who in the political field can play a creative role in guiding the destiny of the country. We feel proud to see that students of BITS, Pilani have found a niche for themselves in the society and are occupying high positions in various walks of life, not only in our country but also abroad. In fact, amongst the Government employees at the Centre and the States and even amongst the MPs and MLAs, there are BITS alumni. This is a matter of pride for us. Alumni of BITS can be found in a large number of countries. Many of our alumni send us donations from time to time for some specific causes.

Prime Minister, Dr Manmohan Singhji, not only are we involved in quality education in BITS but we are also conducting several research and development programmes. The Pilani Campus houses many research laboratories in all areas of science and engineering.

Mr Prime Minister, BITS, Pilani was started as a small 'Pathshala' way back in 1901 by my great-grandfather, Shri Shiv Narainji to educate his two grandsons, my uncle Shri Rameshwar Dasji and his younger brother, my father, Shri Ghanshyam Dasji. With the passage of time this tiny 'Pathshala' blossomed into three separate colleges of Arts; Science, Commerce & Pharmacy; and Engineering under the Birla Education Trust. It was my father's vision to establish a modern university of international standards to foster the scientific temper. Thus, in 1964 the three then existing colleges were merged to constitute the present institute called the Birla Institute of Technology & Science, which was simultaneosly recognized as a deemed university under the UGC Act. I was able to see the vision of my father, Shri G D Birla, unfolding since I and my younger brother Basant Kumar were deeply involved and closely associated with father in running the earlier Birla Colleges and the current institute, BITS, since its inception along with a number of other educational institutions which were and are still being run by the Birla Education Trust [BET]. In fact BET, which is being run under the guidance of my brother Basant Kumar, is the biggest educational trust in the private sector in the country.

Dr Manmohan Singhji, after I became the Chairman and later the Chancellor of the Institute, I realized the need for expanding the Institute to accommodate many more aspiring meritorious students. We have increased the total number of students at BITS, Pilani from 2500 to 4000 and we allocated about 30 crore rupees from our own funds for this expansion plan.

In the year 2000 we decided to establish a campus in Dubai called BITS, Pilani-Dubai Campus. It was essential to promote our education abroad and also foster goodwill between India and the Gulf countries. BITS, Pilani-Dubai Campus has acquired a good name in that entire zone. I am happy to state, we have some students from Bangladesh and Pakistan also at the Dubai Campus.

Now let me come to the Campus at Goa. We could accomplish this 130 crore-rupee project last year with our own resources. Sprawling over 188 acres of land leased by Zuari Industries, of which I am the Chairman, the Goa Campus boasts several modern buildings. The location of this campus is unique in its scenic beauty and panoramic view of its picturesque surroundings encompassing the Zuari River, hollocks, waterway, forests and landscape. From the infrastructural perspective, it is perhaps the finest campus in the country. The entire building, except the hostels, is air-conditioned. In addition, the entire campus has been provided, as in Pilani, with a fibre optic networking with internet connection to every hostel room, every faculty cubicle, all classrooms and faculty houses. At present the campus has about 1200 students and by the time the first batch of students graduate in another two years, it will attain a student strength of 2500.

Consequently, the total strength of all the three campuses of BITS—Pilani, Dubai and Goa—will rise to 8000. On this occasion I am happy to announce that on invitation from Shri Rajasekhara Reddy, Chief Minister of Government of Andhra Pradesh, we are planning to open a Campus in Hyderabad and for this purpose we have already acquired 200 acres of land from the Andhra Pradesh Government. When this campus becomes fully functional, the total on campus student strength of BITS will rise to about 11000.

We have 10000 students who are receiving education of a high order through Off-Campus and Collaborative Programmes. Our total strength of students will soon become 18000 and in another two years' time BITS, Pilani will be turning out 5000 graduates per year, 90% of whom will be engineers. Five years down the line, our roll strength will rise to over 30000, turning out over 7000 graduates, 90% of whom will be engineering graduates.

It is a matter of deep satisfaction to us that our students get absorbed in all the important industrial houses of the country. That their market evaluations are at par with those of IIT students, is a matter of no less satisfaction.

Mr Prime Minister, may I add, ours is the only university, which offers admission in both the semesters, is privately funded, has an affordable fee structure where, a student, once admitted is required to pay the same fees throughout the course of his/her study there, which offers scholarships to 22% of its students from its own budget.

The system attracts the best young minds from the country and, every year, about 17 Board toppers from among the 26 examining Boards, join BITS. The Institute's education system has a unique component by which students spend about seven months as interns in industries—a concept similar to medical interns—before they graduate through innovative programme of Practice School. For this purpose the Institute has an extensive network of linkages with about 100 industrial units throughout the country.

The popularity of the institute could be judged by the fact that for 1400 seats (800 in Pilani, 600 in Goa), 48000 students or over 34 times the required number appeared for the admission test last year. Twenty five per cent of them were girls.

Having had the privilege of enjoying your friendship for over 40 years now, Dr Manmohan Singhji, may I take the liberty of adding a few words on a personal note and express a few thoughts about the future of BITS.

Firstly, let me state, Dr Manmohan Singhji, the satisfaction that I derived in running the Birla Institute of Technology & Science, Pilani and its campuses, first as its Chairman and later as its Chancellor, was far greater than the satisfaction I obtained from running my industrial units.

With God's grace, good wishes of friends and with your blessings, Dr Manmohan Singhji, I am hopeful that we shall be able to establish two more campuses of BITS besides the Hyderabad campus in the next five years. That will provide me immense happiness and satisfaction.

Service to humanity should be the supreme aim of life according to Shrimad Bhagwad Gita. I am an ardent devotee of Gita. Indeed Dr Manmohan Singhji it was to serve the people and the nation that I zealously expanded BITS, Pilani. As I have detailed above, when I took charge of the Institute we had only 2500 students. Today the number of students, including those enrolled in our "off campus" scheme, has increased to 18000. In the next five years this number should double, if not more. At the same time my aim is to further improve the quality of education imparted at BITS.

Dr Manmohan Singhji, the law of universe is that the old generation goes and the new generation steps in. As the poet Tennyson wrote 'The old order changeth yielding place to new'.

That is the eternal truth. Owing to my advancing age, therefore, I may not be able to personally guide the affairs of BITS for long to achieve these aspirations. My grand-nephew Kumar Mangalam who is the Pro Chancellor of BITS, who is a very able and successful young man and who will take over the reins of BITS after I retire, will, I am sure, make my dreams come true. Any achievement of BITS will add to the glory of my esteemed father.

It is my sincere prayer that God, the Supreme Being, may shower His choicest blessings on us and guide us on the path of:

टसतो मा सद्गमय ।
-    From untruth lead me to truth.
तमसो मा ज्योतिर्गमय ।
-    From darkness lead me to light.
     And as a result achieve what the
     Vedas say
म   त्योर्मा‌अम   तंगमय ।
-    From mortality lead me to
     immortality.

The Prime Minister's written speech ran into three pages, but he was so highly impressed by what he saw at Goa that after having read the first few paragraphs of the speech he spoke extempore. The speech was very scholarly. It was heard with rapt attention. We recorded his speech on tape. Some extracts from the speech are given below:

I am delighted to be in Goa for this auspicious occasion to inaugurate this Campus of Birla Institute of Technology & Science. Shri K.K. Birlaji has just now reminded us of how a hundred years ago when his grand father and his great grand father started a school at Pilani, they planted a seed that has long bloomed into a mighty tree of knowledge. I pay tribute to the memory of these great nation builders and all those who have helped him build this great institution that BITS now is.

I am delighted that after establishing your credentials at Pilani, and winning laurels in Dubai, you have established a new Campus in this beautiful state and I am mightily pleased that you do not propose to rest on your laurels that you are raising your sights to establish a new Campus at Hyderabad as well. That's a sort of vision our country needs if it is to meet the challenges of the 21st century.

We are living in an age where human knowledge is growing at an unprecedented pace. The power as well as the wealth of the nation will increasingly depend upon its access to knowledge, its ability to operate on the frontiers of human kowledge, particularly the knowledge of Science and Technology.

It was Winston Churchill who once said that empires of the future are going to be the empires of the mind and if we have to conquer, and to build those empires of the mind, access to knowledge and acquisition of knowledge is the foremost necessity of our nation. Therefore, all those who are engaged in this noble mission of strengthening the nation building, the nation's knowledge base are in their own way great nation builders of our nation.

I compliment the Chancellor Dr K. K. Birla who has been the moving force of this great institution. Yours is an outstanding example of private initiative in the promotion of the national cause of higher education. The late Shri Ghanshyam Dasji Birla wanted to impart education free of dogma; learning that would foster a scientific approach to life, enabling students to remain dedicated to the eternal quest for truth. I am happy that BITS has lived up to this noble vision in discharging its duties to our people and our nation at large. You have set a shining example of what the private sector can do in developing technological and scientific manpower for our country.

We have in our country splendid example of private initiative in education. Institutions like BITS, Manipal Academy and the Tata Institutes have extended high quality educational facilities to our younger generation. I congratulate Dr K. K. Birla for having been a visionary and a practitioner of this vision in such a magnificent manner. The overwhelming initiative of the private sector will and can act as a propelling force in getting our country moving ahead in social and economical development.

For several years now, BITS Pilani has been a symbol of what the corporate sector has been able to do for higher education in our country. While we are proud of our IITs and other state funded institutions of excellence, we are equally proud of similar institutions in the private sector. In Manipal, in Vellore, in Bangalore, in Pune and many other places, our corporate sector has created institutions that have acquired a global standing. I sincerely hope that more and more business groups will come forward to invest in our knowledge economy.

Our educational system is in the need of both, expansion and improvement. I have repeatedly said that our Government is committed to addressing issues pertaining to increasing access to education, at all levels of the human pyramid. Equally we are also committed to promoting excellence and ensuring that our students and teachers compare with the best in the world. There is no contradiction in pursuing these twin objectives. Some countries like China have done this quite successfully. I dream of seeing an India that is fully literate.

In concluding, once again I compliment the management and the faculty of BITS for their dedication and commitment to the noble task of strengthening this knowledge base of our country. I take this opportunity to join all of you in paying homage to the dedication, the commitment and to the nobility and intense sense of patriotism that has characterized the life and work of Dr K. K. Birlaji. May this example prove true inspiration for all future generations to come. I wish your Institution well in your future endeavours. May your path be blessed.

Letters from Father

Apart from correspondence relating to business interests, I had a lot of correspondence with father on general matters; but, unfortunately, I have not preserved many of his letters. I have only two letters with me which are reproduced on pages 457 to 459.

Father has not mentioned the date in the first letter, but from the text it is clear that it was written when I received good marks in Class VIII of Hare School some time in March or April 1933. This letter is written in a lighter vein.

The second letter is dated 18 October 1938. In this letter father has inquired why I was going to a Japanese hair dressing saloon at Park Street, Kolkata for hair cuts. There used to be a high-quality Japanese hair dressing saloon at Park Street during the British days. I did not mind going there at all. As father was very close to Mahatma-ji, he wrote this letter to point out that this was inconsistent with the 'swadeshi culture'.

My eldest uncle Bada Babu-ji regarded the Japanese as part of Aryan brotherhood as the Japanese were Buddhists. He did not mind at all if I had my hair cuts in a Japanese hair dressing saloon.

BIRLA HOUSE,
ALBUQUERQUE ROAD,
NEW DELHI.

પ્રિય શ્રી ઘનશ્યામ

સવારના પત્રમાં મારા વિશે

ષષ્ઠા ને ધ્યાન થી વાંચી ઘેમ

ખૂબ માન્ય ને દિલ સાથી ખાતરી

અર્ધ સમજાવી છે જ્યા કિન્તુ ખૂબ

તો એનો પત્ર ખુશી પ્રકાશ

થો હ્રદયમાં મળ ખુશાલ ખૂબ

વોધી ખૂ થો ખૂબ અન્ય પ્રિયજન

વાંચે અન્ય છે ગમ ગણો છે

ખૂબ અન્ય છે ખૂબ હોતો હું

સવારના જ ખાવાખાંય જાપ

તો છે વ્હાલા છે ધૈર્ય વિશ્વાસો એ

ખૂબ સાચ્ચા તો વહેતા ખૂબ

વ્હાલા ખૂબ સુખઃખ અનુ છે વાંચો

ખૂબ

ખૂબ નાના ખૂશી અક જિજ્ઞાસો

ખાવા એ અવ અનુ એ ખૂબ રામ

વ્હાલા રમે

વાંચો અલ
ખૂબ રામ

BIRLA HOUSE,
ALBUQUERQUE ROAD,
NEW DELHI.

BIRLA HOUSE,
ALBUQUERQUE ROAD,
NEW DELHI.

(૨)

આની દ્દ 'ખો દ્દિષ્ણ લોદ્ષ્ણ ગ્રાગા ન
ષ્રભણ દ્ગગ ન ષ્ષ્ષ' દ્દિ્ગુખો
ગ્ સ્દ્ બો ગ્ગ ગ્ષ્ષ્ દ્ધ
ગ્ન ગ્ગ દ્દ્ષ્ગ ્ ્ ્ ્ દ્ગ્ગ્દ્ષ્
ગ્રભષ્ગ દ્ધ ગ્ દ્ગગગ્ૂદ્ષ્ ગ્રગ્દ્ધ
ગ્ સ્ગ્દ્ષ્ દ્ન દ્ષ્ દ્ષ્દ્ષ્ગ્ગ
ષ્ગ્દ્ દ્ગ્ ્ષ્ દ્ ગ્ગ્ગ્દ્ષ્દ્ષ્ષ્
ગ્ ષ્ગ્ દ્દ ્દ્ ષ્ગ્ષ્ ૨૦૦
૨ગ્ ૧ગ્ દ્દ્ગ્ગ્દ્ષ્ ગ્

દ્ગ્ ૧૧૧ ્ દ્ષ્ ૨૦૦ ૨ગ્
૧ગ્ દ્ગ્ ગ્ગ્ ૧ ૨૩ ૨ગ્૨
ગ્ગ્ષ્ ૨ ૩ષ્ ૧ ૨ગ્ દ્ધ
ગ્ગ ૨ગ્ગ્ષ્ દ્ધ ષ્ દ્ગ દ્ગ્ગ્ષ્ગ્ગ્ષ્
ગ્ ૧ દ્ગ્ ગ્ષ્ દ્ ખો ૧ ૨ગ્દ્
૨ષ્ ૨ગ્ ૩ો ૨ગ્ સ્ષ્ ૨ષ્ ૨૨ષ્
ગ્ ્ ષ્ગ્ષ્ ૧૨ગ્ દ્દ્ગ્દ્ષ્ દ્ ગ્
૨ષ્ગ્ગ્દ્ષ્ ્ ૨ગ્ષ્ગ્ષ્ ોષ્ષ્
ષ્ગ્ગ્ગ્દ્ષ્ ૧ષ્ ૨ષ્ગ્ગ્ષ્ ્
ગ્ગ્ગ્ગ્ગ્ષ્ગ્ગ્ગ્ ૧૨ગ્ગ્
દ્ ગ્ષ્ગ્ ્ ૨ગ્ગ્ગ્ ગ્ગ્ગ્
૨ગ્ ષ્ગ્ગ્ષ્ગ

Certificates

I took my Intermediate examination from the Hindu College, Delhi. I stood seventh in the university. I also did my Honours in Hindi from Lahore University in 1939, much before the partition. I was amongst the first seven students. A copy of the certificate sent by the Panjab University is also given below.

Roll No.____604.

The University of the Panjab.

ORIENTAL FACULTY.

SESSION 1939
EXAMINATION IN HINDI LANGUAGE AND LITERATURE.

This is to certify that____Krishan Kumar Birla____,

*son of*____Ghanshyam Das Birla____,

*of the*____Montgomery District____,

*(Regd. No.*__39.z.3229__*), passed the* **Prabhakar** *(Honours in Hindi Language and Literature) Examination of this University in* __First__ *Division.*

SENATE HALL,
LAHORE :
The 1st August, 1939.

CONTROLLER OF EXAMINATIONS,
University of the Panjab.

Sardar Vithalbhai Patel and Father

Sardar Vithalbhai Patel was Sardar Vallabhbhai Patel's elder brother. Though not as impressive a personality as his younger brother, Vithalbhai was a member of the Central Legislative Assembly. He was a good parliamentarian.

Father had contested and won the elections to the Central Legislative Assembly held in 1926. Vithalbhai was the Speaker of the House. He conducted the House very well and was a strict disciplinarian. Whatever

law was passed in the Central Legislative Assembly was always subject
to the approval of the Government of India. The Viceroy's Executive
Council had the power to veto and nullify a law approved by the Assembly.
As the use of this veto power gave a bad name to the government, its aim
was to ensure that such situations did not arise and that the Assembly did
not pass a law on which the Viceroy might have to use the veto power.
The government was aware of the fact that if it had to use its veto power
and the Central Legislative Assembly became body without any authority
as a result, it made for bad publicity not only in India but in the
international community. Hence, the government always made its best
efforts to ensure that it did not get defeated in the Central Legislative
Assembly.

Once the Congress party moved an important motion in the Assembly.
Time was allotted for a discussion and for voting in a routine manner.
Father, as chance would have it, had asked for an appointment with the
Viceroy. The Viceroy very artfully gave time to father just when the
voting was to take place. The idea was to keep father, who was an
important member of the Assembly, from reaching the Assembly in time
to cast his vote. Every vote counted and so there was a possibility that the
absence of even one person from the Congress party and its allies may tilt
the balance in favour of the government. When father got the news of the
appointment, he saw through the Viceroy's game. But not to accept the
appointment time or to ask for some other time would have been very
discourteous. Father, therefore, had no option but to accept the
appointment. Father went to Vithalbhai and explained the Viceroy's ploy.
Vithalbhai, as was his practice, first preached a short sermon to father, as
to why he had sought an appointment on the day of the voting. Father
said that he had not specifically asked for an appointment for that very
day; he had merely asked for an appointment, and that the Viceroy had
played a trick to deprive the Congress party and its allies of one vote.

Father told Vithalbhai jokingly that argument or sermon to him could
be deferred to some other day; the need of the hour was that a solution be
found. After discussions, Vithalbhai and father concocted a plan.
Vithalbhai suggested that father should request Pandit Madan Mohan
Malaviya, to whom he was very close, to start speaking just fifteen minutes
before the voting and to continue speaking till father returned after his
appointment with the Viceroy. Vithalbhai said that he would interrupt
Malaviya and remind him that voting was to take place. But he added
that he could do nothing if Malaviya ignored his call and went on speaking

since Malaviya was one of the top leaders of the country. The plan worked very well. The Viceroy had called father just at the time the voting was to take place and the Viceroy went on talking about various matters. Usually, a meeting with the Viceroy did not last more than half an hour or forty minutes. That day the Viceroy very graciously kept talking and discussing matters on all sorts of topics for one hour. The Viceroy was certain that voting would be over by this time. Father took leave and returned to the Assembly. Malaviya was speaking on the evils of the British Raj. He started from the time when the British came to India as traders and by the time father returned he had reached the time of Bal Gangadhar Tilak, the famous nineteenth century leader. Tilak was even prosecuted for some of his writings for stating that 'Swaraj was the birthright of every Indian'.

The Speaker was sounding the bell every two or three minutes. Malaviya was speaking on the atrocities that the British had committed on Indians. On noticing father's return to the Assembly, Malaviya spoke for another ten minutes and then said that he would need another one hour, but as the House was in a hurry, he would speak on that important matter at some other opportune time and sat down. A motion was then moved and the Congress Party won, albeit by a small majority.

The Lodha Affair

Madhav Prasad died on 30 July 1990. He was three months older than me. In his earlier days, Madhav Prasad was a strict disciplinarian and a very strong administrator. The staff of his companies certainly respected him owing to his qualities of equity and justice; but, more than respect, they feared him. In the early 1980s, however, a complete transformation came over Madhav Prasad. From being a tough-minded administrator, he became a remarkably gentle human being. It is difficult for a man to get completely transformed, but there are instances in history. Emperor Ashoka, for example, was completely transformed after his victory in the Kalinga war.

No major event in Madhav Prasad's life could be pinpointed upon as the reason for this transformation. But, one day it dawned on him that he was over sixty-two years of age, that he had already undergone a heart bypass surgery in 1979 and that the doctors had warned him that the arteries would again get blocked after ten years. Doctors had also advised him that if he wanted to have another heart bypass surgery, he should undergo the operation well before the tenth year of the operation. Around

1986, Madhav Prasad was in a dilemma as he could not make up his mind whether to undergo the second heart bypass surgery.

Since they had no children of their own they discussed between themselves and decided to leave everything after their death to charities. Both of them, accordingly, made mutual wills in 1981. Later on, some time in early 1983. Madhav Prasad told me that they had replaced their earlier wills and in 1982 had made mutual wills leaving behind all their assets ultimately to charities. I was made one of the executors of the 1982 will of Madhav Prasad.

The mutual will is where husband and wife make a will, the ultimate objective of which is common. The wills of both Madhav Prasad and Priyamvada Devi had the same wording. Both the wills said that in case one of them died the entire wealth would go to the surviving spouse and after the death of the surviving spouse it would be used for charity (barring some jewellery which was bequeathed to my daughters). Thus the language of Madhav Prasad's will and his wife Priyamvada Devi's will was identical.

Madhav Prasad's assets at that time were valued at approximately Rs 5,000 crore. Today perhaps their valuation may be anywhere between Rs 20,000 and 25,000 crore. Never in the history of India has a person bequeathed his entire wealth for charitable causes. The only other example in Indian history is that of the legendary Bhamashah, who gave away his entire wealth to Maharana Pratap Singh after he was defeated in the Battle of Haldighati and asked him to recruit a fresh army to fight Akbar. Maharana Pratap did that and was able to win back all his forts, excepting Chittor.

Madhav Prasad's health kept deteriorating from the early 1980s. In the late 1980s whenever he met my daughters—who would meet him every day at his house and spend two or three hours with him—he would recite the famous sloka from the Gita—

वासांसि जीर्णानि तथा विहाय
    नवानि गृह्णाति ।
तथा रीराणि विहाय जीणा
    न्यन्यानि संयाति नवानि देही ।।

This means that just as a man discards his old clothes and puts on new clothes, the soul discards old bodies and adopts new bodies. By the time he expired, he had acquired a saintly disposition. His end was very peaceful.

After his death, his wife took up the management of his property.

Later, Rajendra Lodha, who has an audit firm, started calling on Priyamvada Devi on a regular basis. He became her main advisor and offered assistance in managing the affairs of the M.P. Birla Group. Priyamvada Birla died on 3 July 2004. A few days after her demise, Lodha sent word to me to state that he had the latest will of Priyamvada Birla and that he would like to acquaint me with the same. I, therefore, fixed a date and called a meeting of all the members of the family. When Lodha was called, he read out the so-called will, according to which she left her entire property to him.

All the members of the family were stunned when they heard this so-called will allegedly executed on 18 April 1999 as read out by Lodha. Their hearts were full of revulsion and anger. They were furious, and after consultations within the family, the entire family decided to challenge Lodha and the so-called will read out by him, as they felt that this could not be a genuine will.

Members of the family sent for Nand Gopal Khaitan of Khaitan & Co, and entrusted their case to him. Nand Gopal consulted some other lawyers. In the given background of the couple's abiding commitment to charities and otherwise apprised of the circumstances, all felt that the alleged will of 1999 could be challenged on many a cogent ground and not least on the basis of mutual wills executed by Madhav Prasad and Priyamvada in 1982. The deeper we probed into the matter, it became all too clear that the said will was the handiwork of Lodha, who had ingratiated himself into Priyamvada Devi's favour by sheer sycophancy with the ulterior motive of grabbing her estate.

Our resolution to contest the 1999 will was prompted purely by our desire to honour the wishes of Madhav Prasad that he wanted all his wealth to go to charities.

R.P. Pansari, a competent and experienced chartered accountant, who was working for Ernst and Young but had earlier worked for the M.P. Birla group was equally outraged. Out of his past loyalty to Madhav Prasad, he not only shared with us a lot of information, relevant to the ensuing litigations with Lodha on many fronts but volunteered to help us by overall supervision. Nand Gopal Khaitan, who is a bright young solicitor, was entrusted with the responsibility of conducting the litigation. That apart, there had to be a member of the family to guide the case on a day-to-day basis. Devendra Mantri, who is a close relation of the family, came forward to take on this responsibility.

Thus the case started and all the members of the Birla family felt confident, as Goswami Tulsidas had said—

जानकीनाथ सहाय करे जब
कौन बिगाड़ करे नर तेरो।

When Bhagwan Ram is there to help you, who can do any harm to you.

The case is going in various courts. As the matter is subjudice, I am not offering any more comments.

PART V

CORRESPONDENCE

Rafi Ahmed Kidwai

K.M. Munshi

Atulya Ghosh

Lal Bahadur Shastri

Dr B.C. Roy

C.B. Gupta

Jayaprakash Narayan

Prabhavati Devi

Morarji Desai

Asoka Mehta

M.O. Mathai

Pandas and Great-Grandfather
  and Grandfather

Kamlapati Tripathi

Banarasi Das Chaturvedi

Gulzari Lal Nanda

Humayun Kabir

Acharya Vinoba Bhave

Sir C.D. Deshmukh

Viyogi Hari

G.D. Malpani

B.G. Kher

H.K. Mahtab

Justice S.R. Das

K.B. Sahay

Malcolm MacDonald

Major General W.H.A. Bishop

Manibehn Patel

Dr Rajendra Prasad

Pandit Jawaharlal Nehru

Satyanarayan Sinha

Gaganvihari L. Mehta

S.K. Patil

Justice S.C. Lahiri

Sankar Banerjee

Kamalnayan Bajaj

C.C. Desai

V.V. Giri

Dr K.N. Katju

Srikrishna Sinha

Jagjivan Ram

Maharaja of Gwalior

Sri Prakasa

H.N. Bahuguna

Sampurnanand

Mohanlal Sukhadia

Sir Shri Ram

Anugrah Narayan Sinha

Rajkumari Amrit Kaur

Dr S. Radhakrishnan

T.T. Krishnamachari

Ashoke Sen

Justice H.N. Bhagwati

Kaka Saheb Kalelkar

Aruna Asafali

Binodananda Jha

Swaran Singh

Pandit Govind Ballabh Pant

Rafi Ahmed Kidwai

As mentioned earlier, I was very close to Rafi Ahmed Bhai. Some correspondence that I had with him is reproduced here as this might be of interest to the reader.

5 August 1952

My dear Shri Rafi Saheb,
It was very kind of you to have visited us during your recent trip to Calcutta. I felt very much flattered at the informal way in which you dropped in at our House. No doubt you win friends wherever you go.
    Thanking you and with kindest regards,

Yours sincerely,
K.K. Birla

Minister for Food & Agriculture,
17 September 1952

My dear Mr Krishan Kumar
This is about Mohendra Datt Sharma, B.Sc., (Electrical Engineering), Banaras University. He wants to join some engineering firm for practical training. He has no intention of entering into any service because he wants to start his own workshop. I hope it will be possible for you to allow him to join Hindustan Motor Works as apprentice to study the practical working of all the engineering work that your firm is doing. I hope there will be no difficulty. Mr. Sharma's address is:- Baba Khaki, Meerut.

Yours sincerely,
Rafi Ahmed Kidwai

19 September 1952

My dear Shri Rafi Saheb,
I am in receipt of your kind letter dated 17th September. There will be no difficulty about Mohendra Datt Sharma joining Hindustan Motors. But probably if he had joined Texmaco he would have got a kind of variety training. We have both Heavy and Light machines there. But I shall do as you kindly advise me. Please let me know.

With kindest regards,

Yours sincerely,
K.K. Birla

K.M. Munshi

I had a voluminous correspondence with Munshi-ji with whom I was very close. A few letters are given here.

Minister for Food & Agriculture,
18 December 1950

My dear K.K.
I returned from tour only today and I have just seen your letter of the 13th December about the 107 per cent formula in regard to sugar production. I shall look into the matter and write to you again later.

With kind regards,

Yours sincerely,
K.M. Munshi

6 April 1951

My dear Krishna Kumar,
In connection with the Somnath Celebrations to be held at Veraval, I am issuing invitation cards all over the country and as the details about Prabhas Pattan may not be known in several parts of the country, I have given on the invitation card your name as one of the gentlemen who should be contacted for further enquiries in

anticipation of your concurrence so that when any one makes an enquiry to you, you may be able to put them wise as to the quickest method of reaching Veraval and also to pass on to me such other enquiries as you may not be in a position to answer. I hope you will kindly co-operate with me to this extent so that our co-operative efforts may make the function successful.

Yours sincerely,

K.M. Munshi

11 April 1951

My dear Shri Munshiji,

Thanks for your kind letter dated 6th April. I am glad you have given my name as one of those who may be contacted for further enquiries regarding the Somnath celebrations. I am always very happy to be associated with any social or religious function specially in one with which you also may be connected. Kindly, however, send me details about the celebrations and other literature which might have been printed in this connection so that, as far as possible, I may satisfy the enquirers without troubling you. The list of gentlemen to whom invitations have been sent may also be sent to me as that would be better.

    Meanwhile with kind regards,

Yours sincerely,

K.K. Birla

19 April 1951

My dear K.K.,

Thank you for your letter of the 11th April, 1951. The installation ceremony of the Somnath Ling will be performed at 9.47 a.m. on the 11th May when Dr. Rajendra Prasad will attend. At 2.30 p.m. the All India Sanskrit Conference is to be inaugurated by the Congress President, Shri Purshotam das Tandon and under the Presidentship of His Highness the Rajpramukh of Travancore Cochin. The same day in the evening the ceremony of laying the foundation stone of the Dehotsarga monument will be performed by His Highness the Jam Saheb. The preliminary ceremonies will commence on the morning of the 8th and will end on the afternoon of the 12th. I will send you the souvenir as soon as it is ready and such other material as appears to be necessary.

As at the moment decided, invitations are being issued to all Cabinet Ministers, Ministers of State, Deputy Ministers, Judges of Supreme Court, all Ministers of all States, all Chancellors, all Speakers and Presidents of Upper Houses and all rulers and heads of religious institutions. One hundred invitations to the business community will also be issued and the invitation cards will be sent to Ghanshamdasji for distribution. The Chief Minister of Saurashtra will compile a list one hundred names from Saurashtra business community. It may not be possible to send the entire list to you but the above information will give you an idea as to whom the invitations are to be sent.

The railways have agreed to give single-fare concession to the delegates attending the Sanskrit Conference and special steamer service will run between Bombay and Veraval during these days. There is also service by air from Bombay up to Keshod from where after about two hours' journey by rail or road one can reach Veraval.

I hope this information will be enough.

Yours sincerely,
K.M. Munshi

(Personal)

Governor, Uttar Pradesh,
10 July 1952

My dear Krishna Kumar,
I wrote to Ghanshyamdasji about the 'Leader', which I heard was going to be closed. It would be a calamity indeed for Uttar Pradesh if one of its oldest papers is closed down. Ghanshyamdasji says that you are looking after it. What are you going to do about it?

Are you not coming to Lucknow one of these days? I am going down to Lucknow on the 16th.

With kind regards,

Yours sincerely,
K.M. Munshi

2 February 1953

My dear Shri Munshji,
It was very kind of you to have rung me up the other day regarding the 'Leader'. It was very wrong on their part to have given so much undue publicity to the students' view point. The students in our country are unfortunately going in the wrong way and there can be no two opinions that the matter has to be dealt with firmly to ensure discipline.

I immediately rang up the 'Leader' people who, however, assured me that they had no intention whatsoever to support this Movement. That perhaps was correct but it was wrong on their part to have given such wide publicity to the statements made by the students' unions or their supporters. I am, however, putting a stop to this thing and if there is any other way in which we could co-operate with you, you have only to inform me.

Enclosed please find copy of my letter to Rameshwarji Nevatia.

Yours sincerely,
K.K. Birla

11 December 1955

My dear K.K.,
Your letters dated 7th and 9th December.
I will of course be happy to have dinner with you. My Secretary is writing to you about the date.
Looking forward to meeting you,

Yours sincerely,
K.M. Munshi

5 May 1956

My dear Shri Munshiji,
I have got first three books of Bhartiya Vidya Bhavan on Indian history. The fourth book 'Imperial Kanauj' I have not been able to get as yet though I have placed the order for the same.

I, however, wanted to make one suggestion regarding these books. The binding and the size of these books are not at all uniform. One can understand some book being voluminous and the other comparatively containing less pages. But why should the size of the paper and the colour of cover differ? When the books are put side by side, they look very unpresentable. I hope you will kindly speak to the publishers so that in future at least uniformity is maintained. I fear the books cannot be placed side by side in any show case.

I hope you are having good time at Nainital. Any work for me? With kindest regard,

Yours sincerely,
K.K. Birla

(Personal)

13 March 1957

My dear Krishna Kumar,

I would like to keep you posted with the latest developments of the Bhavan, in connection with which we will have to pull our full weight.

The Government of India has a scheme of sponsoring engineering colleges through private agencies. The last Council meeting of the Bhavan decided to go ahead with the scheme of the Bhavan establishing an engineering college, if the Government of India and the Government of Bombay gave it full support.

The scheme has now been fully discussed with the Government of Bombay, and is being taken up with the Government of India. We expect to get the results within a few weeks' time. The position, as it was placed before the Council, was as follows.

An engineering college at our Andheri campus would cost 64 lakhs, non-recurring expenditure, out of which the Government of India would pay us 32 lakhs, and we will have to find half the share. We can easily spare land which would be of the value of 10 to 15 lakhs. In the result, we will have to find another twenty lakhs of rupees as our share.

We are negotiating with the Government of Bombay, and I think that Government will agree to bear all the recurring deficit.

The position, therefore, is that if we can raise twenty, or twenty-five lakhs of rupees, we will be able to have one of the largest engineering colleges in the country, and the only engineering college in Bombay; the value of our assets will be doubled, i.e., our seventy lakhs' assets at present will became almost double.

It is a good opportunity to the Bhavan, and I would like you to think on this question, because we have to do our part of the bit and raise 20 lakhs. If we can get it in one donation, the Bhavan can give the name of the donor to the College – of course with the usual representation on the Trust and the Council which its rules permit. If not, we shall have to pull our full weight in order to get the collection. But this looks like God-sent, and we would be failing in our duty if we did not do our best.

I should, therefore, like to get your reactions early, because I feel that without all of us pulling our weight, it would be impossible to put through the scheme.

With kind regards,

Yours sincerely,
K.M. Munshi

(Personal)

20 March 1957

My dear Shri Munshiji,
I am in receipt of your kind letter dated 13th March and I am very happy to learn about the project of Engineering College which you propose to take up. As you know, I am always at your disposal and would be only too glad to interest myself in any cause you might wish me to pursue.

I may, however, mention that as things are, I am not very hopeful of raising funds on any substantial scale for the project you have in mind at present. I have never seen money market so tight or people passing through such stringent monetary conditions. This is probably the worst financial crisis we are passing through during the past twenty years. There appears to be no money either with the middle classes or with the rich. Companies too are in great financial difficulties and they are short of funds even for rehabilitation or modernization. The present position is largely due to high taxation and unless the taxes are lowered, no savings can be effected, and consequently the tightness in the money market cannot ease.

Apart from this, there has been heavy depression in the share market. Share values have depreciated by about 40% which means that the people have lost to that extent. The total value of shares and stocks in all the markets in India was something like Rs 2500 crores a year back. Of this, about Rs 1000 crores have disappeared owing to recession in prices. In view of these circumstances, it would be preferable, in my opinion, to wait for better times.

Besides, as you know, all my contacts are in Calcutta and U.P. I am not very sure if people in these places would be interested in donating for a College in Bombay. Efforts for raising collections would, therefore, have to be concentrated in Bombay and Ahmedabad. For Bombay, Uncle R.D. would be the best man to approach. If, however, I am needed at Bombay, I shall certainly go whenever you so require. But my contacts in Bombay are rather poor.

With kindest regards,

Yours sincerely,
K.K. Birla

(Personal)

3 May 1957

My dear Krishna Kumar,
The opening ceremony of the Bhavan's Delhi building will be performed by the Prime Minister on the 16th of this month. I hope you will make it convenient to be present. This is a landmark in the life of the Bhavan and I would certainly like you to be there.

With kind regards,

Yours sincerely,
K.M. Munshi

Hotel New Weston,
Madison Avenue At Fiftieth Street,
New York 22, NY,
27 June 1958

My dear Krishna Kumar,
My wife and I are having a good though hectic time here. We hope to complete our tour of the U.S. by the end of June and leave for Southampton on July 2 by QUEEN MARY. Evidently we have been in the same cities without knowing that we are there. L.N. is

here with his wife and we have spent some time together.

I do not know, after the demise of Devadas, who is looking after the affairs of Hindusthan Times. You may remember that the first book in the Bhavan's Book University (started in 1951) was Rajaji's MAHABHARATA which has been originally published by the Hindusthan Times. At that time, we were given permission to do so, subject to due acknowledgement, to Hindusthan Times in our edition. We have since published Rajaji's RAMAYANA as a companion volume to his MAHABHARATA.

The Bhavan would now like to have permission to publish in the Book University Series Rajaji's FATAL CART & OTHER STORIES published by Hindustan Times some years back and which is possibly now out of print. Rajaji has no objection to this. He is giving us another collection of his Stories & Fables. If you give permission to publish the FATAL CART & OTHER STORIES, we will be able to have in our series two volumes of Stories & Fables by Rajaji, Part I being the 'FATAL CART' and Part II being the new collection being given by him.

Will you kindly look into the matter and do the needful. If you will write to me at the Bhavan's address in Bombay, they will redirect the letter to wherever I happen to be at that time.

With kindest regards from both of us,

Yours sincerely,
K.M. Munshi

29 July 1958

My dear Shri Munshiji,

I am in receipt of your kind letter dated 27th June. I was very happy when I was told that you were going round the world. I was ahead by about three weeks. Whereas I arrived here on 2nd of July after a tour of three and a half months, it appears your trip would take longer.

Regarding the permission to reprint of Shri C. Rajagopalachari's book 'Fatal cart & other Stories' by Bhartiya Vidya Bhavan, I understand that the Hindustan Times had previously permitted Bhartiya Vidya Bhavan to reprint Rajaji's 'Mahabharata' at a royalty of 15% on all the sales. It has been the practice that all the royalty received from the publisher is paid to Rajaji, the author of the publication. Same terms could, therefore, be applicable on the book mentioned by you. If there be anything further in this matter, please do write to me.

Not knowing your address, I am forwarding the letter to your Bombay address. I hope they will forward it to you.

With kindest regards,

Yours sincerely,
K.K. Birla

Camp: Bhartiya Vidya Bhavan,
New Delhi,
21 November 1950

My dear Krishna Kumar,

I had been to Madras in the first week of this month. You will be glad to hear that there is tremendous enthusiasm for the Bhavan there and we have set up a fairly influential Provisional Committee there. A copy of the list of the Members of the Provisional Committee is enclosed for your information.

We had also a good function in Madras to celebrate the release of the 100,000-th copy and 50,000-th copy respectively of Rajaji's 'Mahabharata' and 'Ramayana' along with five other new publications in our Book University Series.

Some months ago, you arranged for permission to publish in the Bhavan's Book University Series, Rajaji's 'Fatal Cart and Other Stories' published by the Hindustan Times. Rajaji is now revising it.

When I was in Madras, Rajaji mentioned that his book 'Hinduism: Doctrine and Way of Life', published by the Hindustan Times some time ago is now out of print and he would like it to be re-published in the Bhavan's Book University Series. We shall, of course, give him the same terms as you have been giving him. Will you kindly write to the persons concerned in the Hindustan Times to arrange to give us the necessary permission?

I will be returning to Bombay on the 26th of this month, to be in time for the 21st Foundation Day Celebrations of the Bhavan, which is commencing on December 1. In a few days you will be getting a copy of the detailed programme of the Foundation Day Celebrations. Any likelihood of your being in Bombay during the period—December 1 to 9?

For seven years, the Hindustan Times, on every fortnightly Sunday, published my Kulapati's Letters, which are fairly popular all over the country. Why have I fallen out of favour with the Hindustan Times of late and the Letters dropped?

With kindest regards from both of us,

Yours sincerely,
K.M. Munshi

10 December 1958

My dear Shri Munshiji,

Thanks for your kind letter dated 21st November. I regret I could not reply to it earlier.

I am glad to learn that Bhartiya Vidya Bhavan is thinking of republishing Rajaji's book 'Hindusim: Doctrine and Ray of Life', which was published by 'Hindustan Times' some time ago. Hindustan Times would not mind in the least if the book is published by the Bhartiya Vidya Bhavan. I regard Bhartiya Viday Bhavan as my own and I shall be happy if this book is published by them.

As regards 'Kulpati's Letters', that was always a popular feature in the Hindustan Times' Sunday magazine. We had, however, very reluctantly to stop it as owing to paucity of newsprint the size of the Sunday magazine had to be reduced from eight pages to four pages only. As soon as the newsprint position improves, we propose to start publication of this feature again. But God alone knows when the newsprint position would improve.

I fear I could not visit Bombay during the 21st Foundation Day Celebrations Week.

With kind regards to Mrs. Munshi and yourself,

Yours sincerely,
K.K. Birla

Atulya Ghosh

Atulya Ghosh was the president of the West Bengal Pradesh Congress Committee for a number of years. He never aspired to become the chief minister of the state. But, barring Dr B.C. Roy, he was more powerful than Congress chief ministers. I had a very cordial relationship with him. The following letters will be found to be interesting.

27 November 1952

Dear Sri Krishnakumar,
I am sending to you all relevant letters concerning our Library for which Brijmohonji wrote to us that he will be sending some books.
    This is for your attention and necessary action.

Yours sincerely,
Atulya Ghosh

22 March 1957

My dear Shri Atulya Babu,
I was very happy to learn about your success in the elections. The result was never in doubt as far as you were concerned but all the same, it is heartening to find that people have chosen you as their representative in the Parliament.
    Congratulating you once again,

Yours sincerely,
K.K. Birla

25 September 1958

My dear K.K.
Perhaps you are aware that the districts of Midnapore, 24-Parganas, Maldah, Cooch Behar and West Dinajpore have been seriously affected by Floods and Cyclone this year and thousands of people have been rendered homeless. The local Congress Committees have already started relief operation which requires huge amount of money and other essential commodities. The Pradesh Congress Committee has decided to collect both money and materials for this purpose. The people of West Bengal have always given wonderful response to such humanitarian call and I hope, this year too, they will not fail to extend the helping hands to the distressed people. We shall be obliged if you kindly send your contribution

to us at your earliest convenience for sending relief to the distressed people.

Thanking you,

Yours Sincerely,
Atulya Ghosh

Lal Bahadur Shastri

Lal Bahadur Shastri succeeded Pandit Jawaharlal Nehru as prime minister of India in 1964. Though there were other aspirants for that post like Kamaraj and Morarji Desai, Lal Bahadur-ji emerged from the tussle as the consensus candidate. He acquired great fame when India defeated Pakistan in 1965. At the invitation of the Russian Premier, Kosygin, he went to Tashkent in January 1966 for a summit meeting with General Muhammad Ayub Khan, then President of Pakistan. Lal Bahadur-ji suffered a fatal heart attack after signing a treaty with Pakistan and died there. Before joining the Union Government, Lal Bahadur-ji was in UP politics and was a minister for several years in the state government. The text of a few letters exchanged with Lal Bahadur-ji is reproduced here.

(निजी)

परिवहन एवं रेल मंत्री,
भारत,
1, यार्क प्लेस, नई दिल्ली,
15 जनवरी 1956

प्रिय कृष्ण कुमार जी,

नमस्कार। श्री राधेश्याम पाठक जी प्रयाग के रहने वाले हैं। उन्होंने अपनी कन्या का विवाह पिछली अप्रैल या मई के महीने में किया था। उसमें वह कर्जदार हो गये हैं। उन्होंने पहले भी मुझसे इस सम्बन्ध में कहा था परन्तु मैंने आपको कष्ट देना नहीं चाहा। इधर उनके दो पत्र लगातार मिले हैं जिन्हें मैं इसके साथ भेज रहा हूं। अब वह कुछ अधिक परेशानी में पड़ रहे हैं। ऐसी स्थिति में मैंने आपको यह पत्र लिखना उचित समझा। श्री राधेश्याम जी इलाहाबाद में सन् 1930 से कांग्रेस में काम करते रहे हैं। यद्यपि पिछले कुछ वर्षों से वह प्रजा-समाजवादी दल में चले गये हैं परन्तु उससे हम लोगों के व्यवहार में कोई अन्तर नहीं आया। साधारणतः वह एक अच्छे स्तर से रहते हैं और उन्हें अपने लिए कहने में स्वभावतः संकोच होता है। सम्भवतः उन्होंने कुछ अधिक ही कर्ज लिया होगा। आप उनके पास यदि सीधे ही चेक अथवा रुपया जो ठीक समझें, गोपनीय रूप से भेज दें तो कृपा होगी। आपको कष्ट तो दे रहा हूं परन्तु राधेश्याम जी

की आवश्यकता को देखकर ही ऐसा कर रहा हूं। श्री राधेश्याम जी का पता नीचे दे रहा हूं।
श्री राधेश्याम जी पाठक
जीरो रोड, इलाहाबाद

विश्वास है आप स्वस्थ और प्रसन्न हैं।

आपका,
लाल बहादुर

श्री कृष्ण कुमार जी बिरला,
बिरला भवन, नई दिल्ली,

20 जनवरी 1956

प्रिय श्री लाल बहादुर जी,
सादर नमस्कार,
　　आपका 15 तारीख का कृपा पत्र मिला। श्री पाठकजी के बारे में आपने लिखा, आप जैसा उचित समझेंगे वैसा मैं करूंगा। मैं दिल्ली आ ही रहा हूं, सो आपसे इस विषय में बात कर लूंगा।

आपका विनीत,
कृष्ण कुमार

माननीय श्री लाल बहादुर जी शास्त्री,
परिवहन एवं रेलमंत्री,
भारत सरकार,
नई दिल्ली

All India Congress Committee,
New Delhi,
20 March 1957

Dear Shri Krishna Kumarji,
I am grateful to you for your kind message on my election to the Lok Sabha. Please accept my sincere thanks for the same.
　　With kind regards,

Yours sincerely,
Lal Bahadur

Minister for Communications,
New Delhi,
30 April 1957

My dear Shri Krishna Kumarji,
Many thanks for your message. Good wishes of friends and well wishers are always a source of great strength in the performance of one's duties and I am happy that I carry your affection and goodwill in the new task entrusted to me.

  With renewed thanks,

Yours sincerely,
Lal Bahadur

Minister, Commerce & Industry,
New Delhi,
5 September 1960

Dear Krishna Kumarji,
I have your letter dated 2nd September, 1960. I am sorry that you will not be able to attend the meeting of the Central Advisory Council of Industries. We had to postpone it as the meeting for the National Development Council was fixed for the 12th of September. I would not like to prevent you from going to Amarnath. I know if you are delayed you may not be able to go there at all. I thank you all the same for writing to me.

Yours sincerely,
Lal Bahadur

वाणिज्य एवं उद्योग मंत्री, भारत,
नई दिल्ली,
10 अक्तूबर 1960

प्रिय कृष्ण कुमार जी,
नमस्कार । आपका पत्र मिला । यह जानकर प्रसन्नता हुई कि आप अमरनाथ यात्रा सफलतापूर्वक पूरी कर आये । आपने बड़े साहस से काम लिया । आप सब को इस पवित्र यात्रा से स्वभावतः बड़ा सन्तोष मिला होगा ।

आपको कुछ दिन अवश्य श्रीनगर में रहना चाहिये। इससे आप सब को आवश्यक विश्राम भी मिल जाएगा।

आपका,
लाल बहादुर

श्री कृष्ण कुमार जी बिरला,
जोबी रॉय पैलेस होटल,
श्रीनगर (कश्मीर)

(Personal & Confidential)

24 June 1961

My dear Shri Lalbahadurji,

I am glad you are taking interest in the Assam affairs. I thought of writing to you about the problem of Muslim infiltration which, I find from the papers, has been receiving your attention.

For the last 20 or 25 years Muslims from Bengal have been slowly infiltrating in Assam. After the partition of the country it was expected that perhaps this infiltration will stop. But unfortunately it did not happen. The Muslim from Pakistan, who are infiltrating to Assam, are getting every support and encouragement from the Muslims in India residing near our border. Once, some people of Assam including Shri Prabhudayal Himatsinka, who as you know is a Member of the Parliament, had drawn Sardar Patel's attention to it. But the leaders in Assam at that time were absolutely indifferent to this danger. Hence nothing happened.

I have been going to Shillong almost every year and I also drew the attention of the various Ministers in Assam towards this infiltration but unfortunately I too did not succeed in doing anything. Now after the incident at Hailakandi the Assam Government has suddenly woken up.

It is a matter of satisfaction to every one that you are taking personal interest in this matter. I am sure that with your able tackling, this problem, which is rather alarming, will be solved.

May I humbly suggest that if in the vacant lands near our borders we can settle Punjabi and Sikh refugees, that will be a permanent solution of the problem. After all it is not possible to keep a constant vigilance on the borders, more so when the local Muslims are sympathetic to the immigrants. Hence a permanent solution may

be to settle Punjabi Hindus and Sikhs in that stretch of land. They are sturdy people and I am sure that they will resist any unlawful immigration. I thought of sending this suggestion to you for whatever it is worth.

With kindest regards,

Yours sincerely,
K.K. Birla

4 July 1961

My dear Shri Lalbahadurji,
I am thankful to you for your kind invitation on the occasion of marriage ceremony of your son, Shri Hari Krishna. On this happy and auspicious occasion, kindly convey to the bride and the bridegroom my heartiest congratulations and best wishes for a long, happy and prosperous married life.

With kindest regards,

Yours sincerely,
K.K. Birla

Dr B.C. Roy

Dr B.C. Roy, as mentioned earlier, was a remarkable person. Before joining politics, he was our family physician and friend, very close to all members of the family. As a physician he was outstanding. He was one of the best chief ministers that West Bengal ever had.

Among others, Bidhan Babu's letter dated 20 July 1950 will be found to be interesting, particularly his remark, 'the lawyers were too shrewd for a simple minded like you'.

Chief Minister,
West Bengal,
20 July 1950

My dear Krishna Kumar,
The initials and address of the Manager is
   A.C. Sen,
   Bijli House,
   Shillong.

I have read your letter. I have to find out how the complainant's lawyers got hold of the letter. I have been thinking that the lawyers were too shrewd for a simple minded like you.

Yours sincerely,
B.C. Roy

14 October 1950

My dear Dr Roy,

It was a good thing that you phoned me this morning about wrong report given to Shri Bhupati Majumdar. The position of our staff members who are members of the Territorial Force is this.

Sometime back we were approached by the Government of India, Ministry of Defence, through the Chamber of Commerce to assist the Government in getting recruits for the Indian Territorial Force. The copy of the Circular issued to the staff members is enclosed herewith. You will please find from our notice how we have tried to encourage members of the staff to join the Territorial Force.

In our Texmaco factory, four members of the staff joined the Territorial Force. Along with this, some workers also joined the Territorial Force but this they did on their own independent choice. As you know, the management these days has no control over the workers and so we specifically issued this circular to the staff members only and not to the workers.

Even these four members of the staff who joined the Territorial Force on our pressure found it rather difficult to join the parades etc. regularly.

Some time back Lt. Col. S.N. Sharma of the Territorial Force approached our General Secretary, Mr. Ratanlal, asking him to persuade both the members of the staff as also the workers to join the Ranchi Camp of the Territorial Force. Mr. Ratanlal explained that as far as the workers are concerned, he will ask his Labour Officer to contact them but that for the staff members he would have a chat with them.

The workers flatly refused to join the Ranchi Camp and Lt. Col. Sharma was informed about the same. As about the staff members, they also are very reluctant to go. As an encouragement we offered even to pay Rs 100/- to those members of the staff who decided to go. But unfortunately even then the response has been very poor. I

think out of a total of 37 members of the staff of all our concerns who have joined the Indian Territorial Force, only 13 or 14 are going.

You will thus kindly see that from the very beginning our attitude has been one of extreme encouragement to the staff for their joining the Territorial Force. But you will kindly appreciate that it is a kind of voluntary organization and it is not possible for us to compel the staff members to take more interest.

I hope you will very kindly explain the position to Shri Bhupati Majumdar also.

With kind regards,

Yours sincerely,
K.K. Birla

4 July 1952

My Dear Dr Roy,
I am leaving tomorrow afternoon for Delhi, and shall be away for about a fortnight. Meanwhile, I hope you may very kindly have spoken to Mr. Sen, so that I may have your house during Puja. The Puja this year starts from the 26th September. I will, therefore, be going away round about this time and shall stay at Shillong till the middle of November.

Thanking you and with kind regards.

Yours Sincerely,
K.K. Birla

Calcutta,
8 July 1952

My dear Krishna Kumar,
Your letter dated the 4th July, 1952.
I have told Mr Sen and you will get the house as desired.

Yours sincerely,
B.C. Roy

Camp: Banaras
15 September 1955

My dear Shri Bidhan Babu,

Apropos our discussions, held yesterday, I beg to confirm that it will be possible for us to donate three and a half lacs of rupees by about the 15th of October for the proposed Engineering Foremen's College. As I had explained, sanction of the Boards of Directors of the respective companies would be required before any donations could be made on behalf of such companies and it was very kind of you to have appreciated my point. I am sure, however, it will be possible for us to have all the formalities completed by the 15th of October by which time we hope to send our donations as mentioned above.

As soon as I am back I shall get in touch with you so that this scheme may be finalized and work started.

With kindest regards,

Yours sincerely,
K.K. Birla

26/27 September 1955

My dear Krishna Kumar,

You have to purchase tickets worth Rs 100/- for the Charity Performance in the Rungmahal Theatre to be held in aid of the flood-stricken people of Orissa. You may send your man to Shri Naresh Nath Mookerjee, Ex-Mayor of Calcutta.

Yours sincerely,
B.C. Roy

16 April 1956

My dear Dr Roy,

I wonder whether you know or not that I take interest in sports also. I and a few friends are running the Rajasthan Club which has done a lot to propagate football in this State. This Club also won the I.F.A. Shield, coveted football trophy, last year.

I and some other friends would like to meet you any time

convenient to you regarding the desirability of having another Enclosed Ground in Calcutta. The gentlemen who would be accompanying me would be as under:

1. Mr M. Dutta Roy, Secretary, Indian Football Association.
2. Mr Dhiren Dey, Astt. Secretary, Mohun Bagan Club.
3. Mr G.N. Khaitan, Secretary, Rajasthan Club.

We shall be grateful if you could kindly grant us an interview any time convenient to you.

With kindest regards,

Yours Sincerely,
K.K. Birla

18 April 1956

Dear Krishna Kumar,
Your letter of the 16th April.

We may discuss questions about sports on Monday, the 23rd April, 1956, at 11 A.M. in my office.

Yours sincerely,
B.C. Roy

25/26 April 1956

My dear K.K.,
I am sending you a note regarding the Veda Pracher Samity's work. They are doing very good work in the matter of research in Vedic manuscript. I shall be glad if you can help them with Rs 5,000/-.

I am enclosing herewith all the connected papers.

Yours sincerely,
B.C. Roy

27 April 1956

My dear Shri Bidhan Babu,
I am in receipt of your kind letter dated 25th/26th April, 1956. I am enclosing herewith four cheques from our companies totalling

Rs 5,000/-. I would be thankful if receipts are sent in the names of these companies.

With kindest regards,

Yours sincerely,
K.K. Birla

Camp: New Delhi,
26 September 1957

My dear Krishna Kumar,

I am sending you the details about Sen Gupta, Inspector of Boilers, whom you wanted to employ. Although he was in the service of the Government of West Bengal, he is now on deputation to the Government of India as the Chief Technical Advisor (Boilers) in the Ministry of Works, Housing and Supply. He is due to be superannuated on the 31st December, 1959. Therefore, he has got only about one-and-a-half years more to serve under Govt.

As you know, he is in Government service and, therefore, he is entitled to pension and gratuity on some fixed basic. He is now getting Rs 1785/- inclusive of all allowance but if you require his services, you will have to pay him more.

The best plan would be for us to recall him from the Government of India and then lend his services to you on your preserving his pensionery and gratuity rights and paying him whatever salary you want to give. I will see you when I go back to Calcutta.

Yours sincerely,
B.C. Roy

14/15 September 1960

Dear Sir,

I am informed by a very reliable authority that you will shortly be recruiting a number of members of your staff. May I place before you the proposition that you might consider the persons, who have been retrenched by Messrs Mackninnon, Mackenzie & Co. due to a change of their policy, and give to the old staff of that Company a chance? I hope you will consider the cases of those persons favourably.

Yours faithfully
B.C. Roy

11 May 1961

My dear Krishna Kumar,

I have received a note from your Superintendenting Technologist, Prof. J.M. Saha, who came to see our factory. He has given a long note, but he has not touched the point that I wanted him to comment upon and, that is, to let me know whether it is possible to prepare clean sugar from Khansari sugar and, if so, what would be the economics of it including the cost of the plant and the cost of manufacture.

Will you please ask him to give me the details?

Yours sincerely,
B.C. Roy

(Personal)

12 May 1961

My dear Shri Bidhan Babu,

I am in receipt of your kind letter dated 11th May. I am writing to Prof. Saha to prepare a supplementary note on the point raised by you. Prof. Saha stays at our sugar factory situated near Lucknow. I hope to get his supplementary note within about ten days' time. In case, however, you think that a personal discussion with him is necessary, I could send for him whenever you require him.

With kindest regards,

Yours affectionately,
K.K. Birla

C.B. Gupta

C.B. Gupta was a man of great integrity and character. He was one of the best chief ministers that Uttar Pradesh has had. He was like a member of the family to me. Pandit-ji and Indira-ji, however, did not have a liking for him. But Chandra Bhanu-ji stuck to his principles. A few letters from the voluminous correspondence I had with Chandra Bhanu-ji are given here.

20 November 1950

My dear Shri Chandrabhanuji,

I am writing this letter to you in connection with my talks with you regarding the sugar industry. As I had already explained to you, at present the factories are not able to use up cane from the deep interior. This is so because the cost of bringing such cane to the factory for being crushed is so high that it becomes wholly uneconomic for the mills to crush such cane. And unless some incentive is given to the mills to enable them to bring cane even from distant stations, the production of sugar cannot increase. It is from this point of view the industry suggested the revision of cess, which is at present being levied at a flat rate of three annas, to one anna at the outstations and four annas at the gate. This reduced cess at the outstations while on the one hand will give a margin to the factories to bear the extra cost of transport involved, on the other will not affect the revenues of the State also, since of the total cane crushed, only 30% represents outstation cane. So what the Government losses by reducing the outstation cess from As.-/3/ to /1/-, they will make up the same in the increased cess for the gate from As. -/3/- to As. -/4/-.

I hope, therefore, you will give this matter your earnest and sympathetic consideration and see that this very reasonable demand of the Industry is met.

I also confirm having sent to you the following telegram in this connection:

'REFERENCE MY TALK WITH YOU HOPE CESS BEING REVISED FOUR ANNAS GATE AND ONE ANNA OUTSTATIONS KINDLY WIRE'.

With kind regards,

Yours sincerely,
K.K. Birla

Health & Civil Supplies Minister U.P.,
Lucknow,
23 November 1950

My dear Krishan Kumarji,
I am in receipt of your letter dated November 20, 1950 and also your telegram regarding sugar cess. I have passed them on to the Hon'ble Pant-ji for necessary action.

Yours sincerely,
C.B. Gupta

Lucknow,
25 November 1952

My dear Krishna Kumarji,
Apropos the talk that I had with you in connection with the holding of the 40th Session of the Indian Science Congress, I request you to send a cheque for Rs 25,000/- towards meeting the cost of the session as well as construction of a hostel and buildings for laboratories in the University out of the proceeds that are received on this occasion. I am herewith enclosing the appeal that I have issued to the Patrons of Science. You have agreed to become one of the Patrons and I hope you will attend the Congress on the 2nd of January 1953 when it opens and is inaugurated by the Prime Minister of India, Pt. Jawahar Lal Nehru.

Yours sincerely,
C.B. Gupta

Lucknow,
3 December 1955

My dear Krishna Kumarji,
I am in receipt of your letter dated November 28, 1955. I have given the necessary instructions to the officers concerned regarding the visit of your two officers to the Churk Factory. Sri Thirani came and saw me in connexion with the various questions that you referred to him for my consultation. The question of establishing a pulp factory will have to wait till the Government of India has

received the recommendations of a Committee which it has appointed to consider the availability of resources for the same. When the report is out your case will be most sympathetically considered by us.

Hope this finds you in the best of health.

Love,

Yours affectionately,
C.B. Gupta

Lucknow,
18 May 1957

My dear Krishna Kumarji,

I am in receipt of your letter dated May 14, 1957. I think the figure of Rs 2,56,000/- quoted by you in your letter as donation to the Moti Lal Memorial Society for the purposes of the Birla Hostel is a wrong figure. I had sent for the Accountant of the Society and I had talks with Sri Gopi Krishna Tandon, General Secretary of the Society. They tell me that so far only Rs 2,26,000/- has been received, although the total expenditure that has been incurred upto-date on the construction of the hostel comes to Rs 3,18,894/-

The hostel building is not yet complete. The community hall, the dining hall, the kitchen servants' quarters, outside bath rooms, and lavatories yet remain to be constructed. Perhaps they will cost another sum of Rs 1,25,000/-.

The extra expenditure so far has been met by an overdraft on the United Commercial Bank. It comes to this that so far nearly 93,000/- rupees have been overspent. In order to complete the whole hostel therefore, it is necessary to obtain from you the present extra expenditure amounting to Rs 93,000/-along with another sum of Rs 1,25,000/- for the completion of the hostel.

Birlas, wherever they have constructed public buildings, have spent much more than what has been spent in Lucknow, the capital of this state. Surely I expect much more from younger Birlas and there is no reason why they should not outbid their seniors.

Convey my love to your children and remember me to your wife.

Yours affectionately,
C.B. Gupta

Lucknow,
14 July 1958

My dear Krishna Kumarji,
I thank you for your letter dated 8th July 1958 and am glad to learn that you have come back. I hope and trust this sojourn must have added to your various experiences which you have in the business line. I hope that we shall have occasion to meet soon as you will be on this side in the near future to visit your factories.
   With regards,

Yours affectionately,
C.B. Gupta

Lucknow,
5 September 1958

My dear Krishna Kumarji,
I am in receipt of your letter dated 2 September 1958. I thank you for the same. I will be at Lucknow on the 13th. You may take your lunch with me on that date.
   With regards,

Yours affectionately,
C.B. Gupta

Lucknow,
12 October 1958

My dear Krishna Kumarii,
This is just to bother you in connexion with the appointment of the brother of one of my old private secretary, Sri Rajeshwar Nath, who is now a Deputy Collector and is in charge of a Sub-division here. The applicant's name is Kameshwar Nath whose application is enclosed herewith. He is a B. Com., LL.B. from the Lucknow University and has also undergone practical training in the Chartered Accountant's Course as an Article Clerk for two years. He is very anxious to get some suitable appointment under you.
   I am deeply interested in him and I trust you will try to accommodate this young man in one of your concerns, preferably in Uttar Pradesh or at Delhi.

Hope this finds you in the best of health,

Yours affectionately,
C.B. Gupta

Lucknow,
15 March 1959

My dear Krishna Kumarji,
I thank you for your letter dated March 10, 1959, along with a cheque for Rs 10,000/- on behalf of Oudh Sugar Mills Ltd. Formal receipt for the same along with income-tax rebate certificate will be sent to you in due course. I have forwarded your cheque to General Secretary of the Motilal Memorial Society for incorporation in the accounts of the Society,

    With regards,

Yours affectionately,
C.B. Gupta

Lucknow,
1 June 1959

My dear Krishna Kumarji,
Perhaps you know that I had spoken to you about Shri Banarasi Dasji who was my Parliamentary Secretary. He could not be elected to the U.P. Assembly in the last general elections. He is very energetic and devotes his full time to public work. As such he needs some help to enable him to maintain his big family. He has been speaking to me about taking some paper agency on behalf of some factories which you run. Perhaps you own a Paper Mill and he feels that if he is appointed as an agent of this Mill he could meet his expenses. He is prepared to arrange such securities as are required under rules of the Co. for being appointed as an agent.

    I hope and trust that you will take some interest in him. Perhaps you are not in charge of the Paper Mill but either Madhovji or L.N.Ji are looking after it. They can help him.

    With regards,

Yours affectionately,
C.B. Gupta

(Personal & Confidential)

Lucknow,
17 June 1959

My dear Krishna Kumarji,

I thank you for your letter dated June 8, 1959. I have returned only yesterday from Binsar in the Almora district and consequently I could not acknowledge your letter earlier. I am sorry to learn that you could not accommodate Sri Banarsi Dasji for giving him paper agency. Of course, the other assistance which you have offered shall be taken advantage of to relieve of his present worries. I shall write to you later on about it.

 With regards,

        Yours affectionately,
        C.B. Gupta

20 March 1961

My dear Chandrabhanuji,

I am taking the liberty of addressing this letter to you regarding the Caustic Soda Project in U.P. taken up by Shri Shyam Sundar Kanoria. Shyam Sundar is very friendly with me and he has been seeking my advice regarding the successful implementation of the scheme from time to time. He has now come across certain hurdles and has requested me if I could write to you to help him. The facts stated by Shyam Sundar are as follows:

Kanoria took up this scheme of Caustic Soda in February 1960. As Caustic Soda is an electrolytic industry, electricity would be a major factor in the cost of production and, therefore, the rate at which power is available would have an important bearing on the economy of the plant. The requirement of electricity for the plant is estimated at 10,000 K.W. Kanoria tells me that the Government of U.P. had assured him in writing that they would meet this requirement at economic rates. It was on this assurance that he gave up an alternative site for the plant in Orissa where he was offered electricity by the Orissa Government at cheep rates and where there would have been the additional advantage of nearness of salt which is another raw material required for the process.

Against his requirement of 10,000 K.W., Kanoria has been offered

5,000 K.W. of Rihand power at 2 np. and 5,000 K.W. of thermal power from Mau at 5 np. This power would be made available to him in 1962. He has further been informed that in 1964, the 5,000 K.W. of thermal power would be replaced by the Obra Hydel power which would cost him only slightly more than 2 np. Kanoria's difficulty now is that according to this offer, he would have to take 5,000 K.W. of thermal power for two years, from 1962 to 1964, at a very high rate. With this rate of electricity, he would find it hard to compete with similar plants in South India where power is cheap. In order to overcome this difficulty Kanoria wishes that the power supply from Rihand may be increased from 5,000 K.W. to at least 7,500 K.W. The balance 2,500 K.W. he would take from Mau for 2 years at the high rate before it is replaced by the cheaper Obra Hydel power. Kanoria has already seen you in this connection and he came back with the impression that you were favourably impressed and would agree to his request.

Kanoria has made an application for loan to I.C.I.C.I. of which I am also a director. The matter is still under examination but generally speaking I.C.I.C.I. want to be assured about the competitiveness of an industrial undertaking before they grant any assistance to it. In these circumstances if the I.C.I.C.I. find that the rates proposed to be charged by the U.P. Government are not competitive they may not favourably consider his proposal.

I am confident that with your great interest in the industrial development of Uttar Pradesh and in the light of the circumstances mentioned above you will be kind enough to take a favourable decision in the matter and help the establishment of this factory in U.P. I thought this was a fit case for being brought to your notice. Hence this letter.

With best personal regards,

Yours sincerely,
K.K. Birla

Chief Minister, U.P.,
Lucknow,
30 March 1961

My dear Krishna Kumarji,

I am in receipt of your letter dated March 20, 1961, regarding the establishment of Caustic Soda Project in Uttar Pradesh by Shri Kanoria. In this connection, Shri Kanoria himself has seen me several times.

I may, however, inform you that the whole scheme is under examination of the Government.

Yours affectionately,
C.B. Gupta

Note: Shyam Sundar Kanoria is an old friend of mine. As a result of this recommendation, Kanoria Chemicals got established. It is a flourishing company.

1 May 1961

My dear Shri Chandrabhanuji,
This is to introduce to you Shri Bhagwati Prasad Bajoria and Shri Kashi Nath Tapuriah. Both of them are eminent businessmen of Calcutta. Shri Bhagwati Prasad Bajoria belongs to the well known house of Surajmal Nagarmal. He is the younger brother of Shri C.L. Bajoria, who is the chairman of M/s Macleod & Co., one of the foremost business houses of the country. Shri Kashi Nath Tapuriah is the managing director of M/s Roberts McLean & Co. and is director in a number of concerns of Calcutta. He happens to be my wife's uncle.

Both these gentlemen wish to have some talk with you regarding the management of B.I.C. I shall be grateful if you could kindly spare a few minutes of your precious time to give them a patient hearing.

With kindest regards,

Yours affectionately,
K.K. Birla

*Camp: Birla Niwas,
Mussoorie,
3 June 1961*

My dear Shri Chandrabhanuji,
I understand that your programme has been finalized for visiting

Mussoorie on the 17th and would be staying here till the 19th. I am leaving for Calcutta on the 18th morning. On the 17ᵗʰ, however, I am here.

I do not know your programme for Lunch on the 17ᵗʰ. I know there are a number of other claimants on you. But if it is not inconvenient, I would suggest a quiet family Lunch on the 17th. My wife and children are here and are anxious to meet you. I shall not invite any outsiders. Dani, of course, will be there.

In case you have already fixed up other engagement, then I shall not press you for it. But in case you are free on the 17th, I shall be most grateful if you could kindly have Lunch with us.

Meanwhile, with kindest regards,

Yours affectionately,
K.K. Birla

Lucknow,
6 June 1961

My dear Krishna Kumarji,
Thanks for your letter of 3 June 1961. I am sorry I shall not be able to accommodate your wishes as I shall not be in Mussoorie on the 17th instant. I am reaching there on the 20th of June.

Yours affectionately,
C.B. Gupta

Lucknow,
27 June 1961

My dear Birlaji,
Kindly refer to your letter dated May 29, 1961.

Perhaps the Government of India might grant a license for a composite textile mill for U.P. during the Third Five Year Plan. I would, therefore, advise you kindly to put in an application for the grant of a licence for a composite unit. Perhaps this might go through. I will speak to Sri Manubhai Shah and see if it is possible to get you a licence for a composite unit in U.P.

Yours sincerely,
C.B. Gupta

7 December 1961

My dear Sri Chandrabhanuji,

I am in receipt of your letter dated the 30th November. I am very sorry to note that you feel that there has been a change for the worse in the editorial policy of the 'Leader'. I myself do not read the Leader, but the policy laid down by us for the paper is to give a critical support to the Government. This means that, whereas we have to support the Government on the whole, the same should not be a blind support but should be on logic and merits. This is, as you know, the policy followed by the 'Hindustan Times' also.

Thakur is not the 'Editor' of the Leader. He is the General Manager, and as such has nothing to do with the editorials of the paper of its policy. In case there has been any lapse, as mentioned by you, it is a lapse on the part of the editor, who is Shri R. N. Zutshi. He has been there for the last 30 years or so, but I am sorry to note that his writings recently have not found favour with you. You had also a talk with me on the phone in this connection and you mentioned to me at that time that you would be sending me certain clippings so as to show that the 'Leader' was taking an unreasonable stand on certain issues. I shall be grateful if you could kindly send me those clippings, so that I may go through the same.

I may, however, mention one thing. Thakur had once severed his connections with the 'Leader' about 4 or 5 years ago. Subsequently he apologised and re-joined the paper. During the period of his absence we tried a number of other people as the Manager, including one Gunthe. This latter person was previously working in Hindi Sahitya Sammelan. It was subsequently found out that he was not a very honest person and so we had to part company. Thakur had, in the meantime, apologised and we brought him back. Gunthe, it appears, is a vindictive type of person and he has been carrying on some propaganda not only against Thakur but also against the paper itself. He is also known to Smt. Indiraji and he had also tried to poison her ears. I meet Indiraji off and on and during my interviews with her she was kind and good enough to bring to my notice some allegations which were being made against the 'Leader' and against Thakur. I was able to explain to her the true facts and also how Gunthe was trying to vilify Thakur and the paper. My impression is that Indiraji was satisfied. It is just possible that the report which you have now received might also have been inspired by Gunthe. I merely thought of bringing this fact to your kind notice.

With profoundest regards,

Yours affectionately
K.K. Birla

Jayaprakash Narayan

I have several letters of Jayaprakash-ji with me. A few which might be of interest are reproduced below.

C/o Mrs Sumita S. Morarjee,
Scindia House,
Ballad Estate,
Bombay,
25 May 1955

सर्वोदय आश्रम,
सोखोदेवरा,
(जिला-गया, बिहार)

प्रिय कृष्ण कुमार जी,

आज से एक महीना पहले जब पटने से रवाना हो रहा था तब आप का पत्र और पांच-पांच हजार के तीन चेक मिले थे। चेक मैंने उसी समय सर्व सेवा संघ को भेजवा दिये थे। उनकी रसीदें मिल चुकी होंगी। आप के दान की सूचना हाल में पत्रों मे भी प्रकाशित करा दी थी।

शांतिप्रसाद जी की तरफ से भी 15000 रु. अभी मिले हैं : ऐहनास इन्डस्ट्रीज के 5000 रु. और श्रीकृष्णा ज्ञानोदय सुगर के 10000 रु.। दो-चार दिनों में शांतिप्रसाद जी को देखने जाऊंगा, तब अपील निकालने के विषय में चर्चा करूंगा।

आप दो को छोड़ कर अभी तक और किसी अन्य चीनी मिल मालिक की ओर से दान नहीं मिला है। यदि आप अपने नज़दीक के लोगों से दो शब्द कह देते तो बड़ी कृपा होती। इस सिलसिले में भागीरथ जी को भी लिखा है।

आशा है आप सकुशल होंगे।

सस्नेह,
जयप्रकाश

कैंप : मदुराई,
20 मई 1959

प्रिय कृष्ण कुमार जी,

आप ने अखबारों में देखा होगा कि कुछ सप्ताह हुए सीतामढ़ी सब डिवीजन में अकस्मात् हिन्दू-मुसलमान दंगा शुरू हो गया। दंगा का समाचार मिलते ही सर्वोदय नेता श्री वैद्यनाथ चौधरी के नेतृत्व में शांति सैनिक घटना स्थल पर पहुंच गये। शांति सैनिकों ने उस इलाके में बहुत अच्छा काम किया है। वहां इस काम के संचालन के लिये एक शांति सैनिक शिविर की स्थापना हुई है। इसी शिविर की आर्थिक सहायता के लिये यह पत्र लिख रहा हूं। दंगे से जो लोग पीड़ित हुए हैं उनकी सहायता बिहार सरकार तथा बिहार खादी ग्रामोद्योग संघ जैसी संस्थायें कर रही हैं परन्तु शांति सैनिक शिविर के लिये सरकार से सहायता लेना उचित नहीं माना गया है। शिविर के खर्च के लिए बिहार में कुछ फंड इकट्ठा किया गया है परन्तु अभी कुछ कमी रह गयी है। इसलिए आप से प्रार्थना है कि 1000 रु. इस काम के लिये देने की कृपा करें। रुपये श्री वैद्यनाथ चौधरी, बिहार राज्य भूदान-यज्ञ कमेटी, कदम कुआं, पटना 3, बिहार को सीधे भेज दें।

आशा है आप कुशल पूर्वक होंगे।

आपका सस्नेह,
जयप्रकाश

संस्थापक : जयप्रकाश नारायण

ग्राम निर्माण मंडल
सर्वोदय आश्रम
डा॰ सोखोदेवरा, जिला गया (बिहार)
विभाग

पत्रांक——   दिनांक——

मैसूर
7. 6. 59

प्रिय कृष्ण कुमार जी,

मैं आपको एक खबर देना चाहता हूं। मैं 21 जून को मदुरै पहुंच रहा हूं। वहां 5, 6 दिन रहने का विचार है। श्री वर्गीलांग के मिलना है और मदुरैमी जेलयमेल्ल के मैच में आगवा भाग हूं। यदि एक लोगों के रहने का प्रबंध आपके गत से हो सके तो मैं बहुत अनुग्रहित हो आगा। एक लोग चाट लाएंगे रहोंगे :- श्रीमती मैं, एक अन्य महिला और हमारे सेक्रेटरी। यदि यह प्रबन्ध हो सके तो हमारी सूचना इसे रास्ते में भेजना देंगे। वहां का मेरा पता रहेगा —
c/o. Shiva Nath Prasad, 35, Rashbihari Avenue, Calcutta.। एक लोग 18 जून को रास्ते पहुंच देंगे।

आशा है आप सपरिवार कुशल रहे होंगे।

आपका
स्नेहर
जयप्रकाश

मैसूर,
7.6.1959

प्रिय कृष्ण कुमार जी,

दो-तीन बातों के सम्बन्ध में आपको लिख रहा हूं। पहली बात अपने सम्बन्ध में है। मैं 21 जून को मसूरी पहुंच रहा हूं, वहां 5-6 दिन रहने का विचार है। श्री दलाई लामा से मिलना है और कम्युनिटी डेवलपमेन्ट मिनिस्ट्री के एक कैम्प में भाषण करना है। यदि हम लोगों के ठहरने का प्रबन्ध आपके यहां हो सके तो मैं बहुत अनुग्रहित होऊंगा। हम लोग चार व्यक्ति रहेंगे— प्रभावती, मैं, एक अन्य महिला और हमारे सेक्रेटरी। यदि यह प्रबन्ध हो सके तो इसकी सूचना मुझे कलकत्ते में भेजवा देंगे। वहां का मेरा पता होगा- द्वारा श्री शिवनाथ प्रसाद, 35, रासबिहारी एवेन्यू, कलकत्ता। हम लोग 16 जून को कलकत्ते पहुंचेंगे। दूसरी बात विजय कुमार सिंह के सम्बन्ध में है। उनके सम्बन्ध में काफी दिन हुए एक पत्र लिखा था, उसका उत्तर भी आपकी तरफ से गया था। अभी हाल में जब मैं कलकत्ते गया था तो विजय कुमार सिंह मिलने आये थे। उन्हें अभी तक पिछले महीनों का वेतन नहीं मिला है। आपने लिखा था कि उनके लिए दो सौ रुपये मासिक निश्चित किया गया था परन्तु अभी तक एक मास का भी वेतन उन्हें नहीं मिला है। वह बहुत कष्ट में हैं। उनके भविष्य के सम्बन्ध में आपने मुझे धर्म संकट में डाल दिया है। आपके यहाँ यदि उनके लिए कोई काम न हो तो मैं कैसे आग्रह करूं, दूसरी तरफ उस नवयुवक और उसके परिवार के भरण-पोषण का प्रश्न है, इसलिए निर्णय आप ही पर छोड़ना चाहता हूं। अपने विशाल संगठन में कोई न कोई काम विजय कुमार के लिए निकाल सकें तो मुझे बड़ा संतोष होगा।

एक तीसरी बात अभी ध्यान में आई है, वह स्वर्गीय अनुग्रह बाबू के स्मारक के सम्बन्ध में है। आपको स्मरण होगा कि मैंने आपसे कुल मिला कर 15000 के लिए प्रार्थना की थी, उसमें से साढ़े सात या दस हजार आप श्री बाबू के द्वारा भेजवा चुके हैं। मेरी प्रार्थना है कि बाकी रकम भी कृपा करके उनके पास भेजवा दें। चेक अनुग्रह स्मारक निधि के नाम से होना चाहिए।

आशा है आप सपरिवार कुशल पूर्वक होंगे।

आपका सस्नेह,
जयप्रकाश

3 अप्रैल 1959

माननीय श्री जयप्रकाशजी,
सादर प्रणाम।

आपका 28 मार्च का कृपा पत्र मिला। श्री विजय कुमार सिन्हा के विषय में आपने लिखा, उनका वेतन पहले नियुक्त नहीं किया गया, कारण उनकी कार्यकुशलता के विषय में हम लोग अनभिज्ञ थे। आपका पत्र आने पर मैंने उनके विषय में जांच की है। उनकी योग्यता के विषय में अभी तक जो हम लोग निर्णय कर पाये हैं, उसके अनुसार उनका वेतन 200 रुपये माहवार नियुक्त किया जा रहा है।

हम लोगों के विभागों में आवश्यकता से अधिक आदमी इस समय हो रहे हैं। अधिक आदमियों की भर्ती करने से काम तो खराब होता ही है, साथ-साथ नये आदमियों को क्या काम

दें, इसका प्रश्न रहता है। अतः श्री विजय कुमार सिन्हा के पास भी काम नहीं के बराबर है। ऐसी दशा में एक सुझाव यह भी है कि श्री विजय कुमार सिन्हा को काम से हटा दिया जाय। अतः यदि आपका आग्रह रहा तब तो बात दूसरी, नहीं तो हम उन्हें हटाने का ही विचार कर रहे हैं। बाकी जैसी आपकी आज्ञा होगी, वैसा ही मैं करूंगा।

आपका विनीत

श्री जयप्रकाश नारायण,
कदम कुआं,
पटना

28 मई 1959

माननीय श्री जयप्रकाश जी,
सादर नमस्कार

आपका 20 तारीख का कृपा पत्र मिला। आपके सुझाव के अनुसार मैं 1000 रु. श्री वैद्यनाथ चौधरी को भिजवाने का प्रबन्ध कर रहा हूं। कृपया लिखियेगा कि चेक श्री वैद्यनाथ चौधरी के नाम से भिजवाना है या किसी संस्था के नाम से। मेरे विचार से किसी संस्था के नाम से भिजवाना ठीक रहेगा।

आशा है आप सकुशल होंगे।

आपका विनीत

श्री जयप्रकाश नारायण,
पटना

15 जून 1959

माननीय श्री जयप्रकाश जी,
सादर प्रणाम।

आपका 7 ता. का कृपा पत्र मिला। मसूरी में हम लोगों का एक मुख्य मकान है तथा दो छोटे मकान हैं। यह तीनों मकान ही श्री दलाई लामा के लिये हम लोगों ने खाली कर दिये। मैं स्वयं तीन दिन पहले ही मसूरी से लौटा हूं। वहां कुछ दिन के लिये गया था। हमें भी होटल में ठहरना पड़ा। यदि मकान हमारे पास रहते तो आपको ठहराने में हमें बड़ी प्रसन्नता होती।

श्री विजय कुमार सिंह के बारे में आपने लिखा, यद्यपि उनके लिये अभी कोई काम नहीं है, लेकिन साथ-साथ आपका आग्रह मैं कभी टाल भी नहीं सकता। अतः श्री विजय कुमार सिंह को स्थायी रूप से काम देने का प्रबन्ध करवा रहा हूं। उन्हें अभी तक वेतन नहीं दिया गया था, कारण जब मेरे 13 अप्रैल के पत्र का उत्तर नहीं मिला तो मैं निर्णय नहीं कर सका कि उनके विषय में क्या करना है किन्तु बीच-बीच में उन्हें खर्चे के लिए रुपये उनके वेतन के पेटे बराबर दिये जाते रहे।

मैंने चीनी विभाग के अध्यक्ष को कह दिया है कि वह श्री विजय कुमार सिंह को कह दें कि उन्हें वेतन 200 रुपये मासिक के हिसाब से मिल जायेगा किन्तु हमारे यहां वेतन दो प्रकार से

मिलता है, कुछ तो प्रति मास और कुछ वर्ष के अन्त में बोनस के रूप में। श्री विजय कुमार सिंह को कितना वेतन प्रति मास मिलेगा और कितना साल के अन्त में यह चीनी विभाग के अध्यक्ष उनसे बात कर लेंगे किन्तु साल के अन्त में उन्हें 200 रुपये मासिक की औसत पड़ जाये इसका प्रबन्ध करवा रहा हूं।

अनुग्रह बाबू के स्मारक के विषय में आपने लिखा, इस बारे में एकाध दिन में ही आपको पत्र लिख रहा हूं। चेक भी आपको ही भिजवा दूंगा।

आशा है आप सकुशल होंगे। मेरे योग्य कार्य अवश्य लिखें।

आपका विनीत

श्री जयप्रकाश नारायण,
कैम्प, कलकत्ता

16 जून 1959

माननीय जयप्रकाश जी,
सादर प्रणाम।

अनुग्रह स्मारक निधि के लिये चार हजार रुपये के चेक आपको भिजवा रहा हूं। कृपया रसीदें कम्पनियों के नाम भिजवाने का प्रबन्ध करवा दीजियेगा।

साढ़े तीन हजार रुपये के चेक आपको सितम्बर में भिजवा दूंगा।

आपका विनीत

साथ में 4 चेक

श्री जयप्रकाश नारायण,
कैम्प, कलकत्ता

कैम्प, नई दिल्ली,
28 जून 1959

प्रिय कृष्ण कुमार जी,
आपका 16 जून का पत्र मिला और साथ-साथ चार चेक-कुल मिला के चार हजार रुपये के। ये चेक स्मारक निधि के दफ्तर को भेजवा रहा हूं। वहां से रसीदें कंपनियों के पास चली जायेंगी। आपको बहुत-बहुत धन्यवाद।

आपका सस्नेह
जयप्रकाश

कदम कुआं,
पटना,
2.10.1959

प्रिय कृष्ण कुमार जी,

आपका पत्र यथा समय मिला था। उत्तर में विलम्ब हुआ, क्षमा करेंगे।

अनुग्रह बाबू के स्मारक के सम्बन्ध में श्री बाबू से आपकी जो बातें हुई वह जानकर अत्यन्त हर्ष हुआ। आप अवश्य रुपये उन्हीं के पास भेजें। वह सर्वथा उचित होगा परन्तु रकम के बारे में फिर निवेदन करना चाहता हूं कि 10,000 रु. आप लोगों के लिये थोड़ा होगा। चीनी मिल उद्योग के सम्बन्ध में आपने जो कुछ लिखा है वह ठीक है, परन्तु आप लोगों का बड़ा ऊंचा स्थान है। आप श्री इन्द्र कुमार करनानी को जानते होंगे। उनके पास मैं कलकत्ते में गया था। उनसे पुराना परिचय है। उन्होंने 20,000 रु. देने का वादा किया 10,000 रु. झरिया और 10,000 कलकत्ते के कोटा में। आपको इस हिसाब से 25,000 रु. से कम नहीं देना चाहिए। आप विचार कर लें।

श्री मंगेश्वर शर्मा के विषय में आप ने जो कुछ लिखा वह जान कर भी बड़ी खुशी हुई।

इस पवित्र दिवस पर आप सब की शुभकामना करता हूं।

आपका सस्नेह
जयप्रकाश

CAMP: *Patna,*
30 October 1966

Dear Krishna Kumarji

I am writing to request you to be a member of the Bihar Relief Committee. Your cooperation will be of great help. I do hope you will be kind enough to accept.

Yours Sincerely,
Jayaprakash Narayan
President
Bihar Relief Committee

पुनश्च:
अलग से एक और पत्र भेज रहा हूं ।

CAMP: Patna,
3 November 1966

Dear Krishna Kumarji,

You may have learnt from the press about the terrible calamity that has befallen Bihar. Because floods and droughts have been a normal occurrence in our country, there is danger of this year's drought in Bihar being also treated as a normal affair. The danger is that in that case hundreds of thousands of lives might be lost. Therefore, I am anxious to impress upon you that this is an unprecedented calamity, the like of which has not been known in living memory.

The Bihar State and the Union Governments will certainly do all that lies in their power, but a calamity of the present dimensions cannot be adequately faced by the Government alone. This is an occasion when everyone in the country, rich or poor, has to do his bit to save fellow countrymen from painful death. It is for this reason that I am writing to you and to a few other friends in positions such as yours.

As you may know, all the political parties and voluntary agencies in this State, with the full support of the State Government, have selected me to head and set up a relief organisation. Accordingly, a Bihar Relief Committee has been set up. As President of the Committee, I shall be issuing a public appeal in a few days, yet I felt that a personal appeal to the leaders of the business world should help better to bring home to them the gravity of the situation.

Our need is for all manner of things: money, food-grains, other food-stuffs, clothes, blankets, medicines. These and similar articles are needed as gift. However, there are other things such as water-lifting sets (diesel & electrical) and boring plants from the most elementary types worked by hand to the sophisticated rigs that can cut through rock, which may be given at concessional or market rates. There is also need for private agencies to undertake boring operations and installation of tube-wells, etc.

The Relief Committee is at one with the Union and State Governments that despite the drought every effort has to be made to encourage and step up production of whatever crops are possible in the shortest possible time. As the days pass, in many parts of Bihar, there will be lack even of drinking water. The above machinery is needed to help in this drive for production.

The Relief Committee would soon be formulating concretely these diverse needs, which would be communicated to you and others concerned. In the meanwhile, I hope you will give this matter your earnest thought. I shall be grateful for your advice and suggestions.

Before concluding, I should like to inform you that the Tata Industries in Jamshedpur have already contributed Rs 2,00,000/- towards the Relief Fund, and have promised another contribution of Rs 3,00,000/- later. I hope other industries and business houses will contribute equally generously.

With kind regards,

Yours sincerely,
Jayaprakash Narayan

पुनश्च: हिन्दी में एक पत्र लिख चुका हूँ।

9 November 1966

My dear Shri Jayaprakashji,

I am in receipt of your kind letter dated 30th October. I am usually touring about between Calcutta, Bombay and Delhi. Hence it will be difficult for me to attend any meeting of the Bihar Relief Committee. All the same the cause is so pious that I find it difficult to decline to become a member of this committee particularly if you so desire. I would suggest, however, that you may have the name of Shri K.P. Modi, Secretary of Marwari Relief Society as alternate member so that he may attend the meetings in my place.

With kind regards,

Yours Sincerely,
K.K. Birla

दिनांक : 11 नवम्बर 1966

प्रिय कृष्ण कुमार जी,

पत्र के लिये धन्यवाद। मुझे बड़ी खुशी होगी यदि मारवाड़ी रिलीफ सोसाइटी ही बिहार रिलीफ के लिये कलकत्ते में धन तथा सामान के संग्रह का काम तथा वही उनका वितरण अथवा उनके द्वारा रिलीफ का अन्य आवश्यक काम करे। मेरी कमिटी सोसाइटी को पूरा सहयोग देगी।

परन्तु एक बात का ध्यान रखा जाय। उत्तर प्रदेश तथा मध्य प्रदेश की क्या स्थिति है, मुझे निश्चित रूप से मालूम नहीं परन्तु बिहार की तो भयंकर स्थिति है और बिगड़ती ही जानेवाली है।

इसका अर्थ है कि अब तक जिस पैमाने पर रिलीफ का काम देश में होता रहा है उससे काम न चलेगा। लाखों के मरने की भी स्थिति आ सकती है— भूख और प्यास दोनों से ही। इसलिए सोसाइटी को बड़ी योजना बनानी होगी।

जब मोदीजी यहां आये थे तो तीन क्षेत्रों में काम करने की सोच रहे थे— एक-एक क्षेत्र के दो-दो या तीन-तीन प्रखण्डों में। तो क्या बाकी अकालग्रसित प्रखण्डों में— जिनकी संख्या सैकड़ों है— कलकत्ते के व्यापारियों की सहायता नहीं मिलेगी? कलकत्ते से तो एक करोड़ रुपये की सहायता की अपेक्षा है। रुपयों में ही सहायता चाहिए, ऐसी बात नहीं। कपड़े चाहिए और कम्बल, जीप, ट्रक, दवाएं, कन्ट्रोल के बाहर के अनाज, पम्पिंग सेट, बोरिंग प्लांट, तरह-तरह के स्पेयर पार्ट, चलते वर्कशाप आदि-आदि। यह सब सोसाइटी करे तो बड़ी अच्छी बात होगी।

टेलीफोन पर आपसे एक चलते वर्कशाप (Mobile repair workshop) की याचना की थी। टाटा इंडस्ट्रीज एक दे रहे हैं— अब तक 4,10,000 रु. तो वह दे ही चुके हैं। आपके लिये यह बिल्कुल आसान बात है। रिलीफ के काम के समाप्त होने पर वह लौटा दिया जायेगा। और यही बात बाकी सामान के लिये भी लागू है जो दान में मिलेंगे।

सिद्धराज जी को तो पहले ही तार दे चुका था और वह 15 नवम्बर को सुबह तूफान से पहुंच रहे हैं। आपके यहां आने की प्रतीक्षा उत्सुकता से कर रहा हूं।

हर शुभेच्छा के साथ,

आपका सस्नेह,
जयप्रकाश नारायण

पुनश्चः रिलीफ कमिटी के आफिस के लिये यदि आप एक हिन्दी और अंग्रेजी रेमिंगटन टाइपराइटर और एक विद्युत-चालित गेस्टेटनर दान में या कर्ज दे सकें, तो बड़ा आभार मानूंगा।

जयप्रकाश नारायण

7 May 1967

Dear Krishna Kumarji,
This is to introduce Shri Dharmavir Singh, Manager of the GRAMODAYA weekly, Patna.

The Gramodaya is published by the Bihar Sarvodaya Prakashan Samiti, of which I am the President.

The weekly is being regularly published since 1963 and has a circulation of about 4000 copies. Being a serious views journal it cannot be expected in these days of cheap journalism to have a large circulation.

Shri Dharmavir Singh is going to Calcutta on my behalf to secure advertisements for the GRAMODAYA. This letter is to make a personal request to you to help in this constructive and valuable activity.

Yours sincerely,
Jayaprakash Narayan

29 May 1967

My dear Shri Krishna Kumarji,
I thank you for your support to the GRAMODAYA weekly.

Yours sincerely,
Jayaprakash Narayan

November 1967

Dear Krishna Kumarji,
I am sure you are aware of the good work being done by the West Bengal Gandhi Smarak Nidhi of which Shri Sakti Bose is the Sanchalak. The West Bengal Gandhi Smarak Nidhi in collaboration with the All India Khadi & Village Industries Commission, the Adimjati Sevak Sangh, the Kasturba Memorial Trust, and the West Bengal Sarvodaya Mandal, has undertaken an extensive constructive programme in the disturbed Siliguri Sub-Division. In order to do this good work efficiently they need, among other things, some motor transport. Shri Sakti Bose has negotiated for the purchase of a second-hand Jeep the cost of which, including repairs and maintenance as well as the driver's salary for a year (minus petrol), comes to Rs 15,000/-. I write this to request you for a contribution of Rs 1,000/- for this purpose. The cheque may be drawn in the name of Gandhi Smarak Nidhi (West Bengal) and the money or cheque may be sent directly to Shri Sakti Bose, Secretary. Gandhi Smarak Nidhi (West Bengal), PO: Barrackpore, Distt. 24 Parganas.
With kind regards,

Yours sincerely,
Jayaprakash Narayan

4 November 1968

Dear Krishna Kumarji,
I am writing to recommend the application of Manoranjan Kumar Srivastava for financial assistance in order that he may complete his course of studies. I know his father Shri Mangal Prasad Srivastava of Motihari, Champaran. Mangal Babu is one of the old freedom

fighters whose life has been one of sacrifice and suffering. Therefore, I hope you will be kind enough to help this young man to obtain his M.B.B.S. degree from the Darbhanga Medical College.

Yours sincerely,
Jayaprakash Narayan

Camp: Calcutta,
13 February 1973

Dear Krishna Kumarji,
I am writing to seek your support and financial help for the Students Health Home, Calcutta (142/2 Acharya Jagdish Bose Road, Calcutta-14, Phone-242866).

The Students Health Home, Calcutta, is an organization of a kind that is very rare in this country. More than twenty years ago, it was born of the self-help endeavours of students. The Calcutta Students Health Home has proved by its example the immense possibilities of development and national reconstruction on the basis of self-help and voluntary co-operative effort of common citizens. As a publication of the S.H.H. puts it "the Home believes that popular initiative only can trigger development activities and the people's awareness sustain them."

The Home has been serving the ailing students for the past twenty years and is presently trying to build a 100-bed hospital for the exclusive use of students, and has been able to construct the first three floors wherein a modern Polyclinic and a 10-bed indoor ward have already been put in operation.

Another unique programme that the Home has currently taken up is a 'Walk For Fuller Life' which is to start on the 25th of this month from Dumdum Junction to Tollyaganj, more or less following the proposed track of the underground railway. This programme has been undertaken in collaboration with the National Service Scheme, West Bengal. To quote from the Home's folder 'this walk will be a WALK FOR FULLER LIFE by participating in which the students and youth will demonstrate their concern and support for the developmental and constructive activities now taking shape. We propose to mobilize all sections of people: journalists, teachers, players, writers, actors, social workers and others from all strata and communities of the Great Calcutta Society.'

So much by way of introducing this fine organization. The students who will meet you with this letter will give you further information if needed. I hope you will agree with me that this is a cause and activity which deserve the support and generous help of those like you who are in a position to give both.

Thanking you and with kind regards,

Yours sincerely,
Jayaprakash Narayan

13 March 1973

My dear Shri Jayaprakashji,

I am in receipt of your letter dated 13th February. Though there are numerous demands on us, I always try to support a good cause. Hence I shall certainly give some donation to the Students Health Home. I hope, however, that the people behind this Home are honest and sincere. Sometimes in case the people contacted with an institution are not good people the institution runs into difficulties. I hope, therefore, you have satisfied yourself on that score.

Kind regards.

Yours sincerely,
K.K. Birla

31 March 1973

Dear Krishna Kumarji,

Thanks for your letter of March 13 which I received on my return from Bombay with Prabhavati.

I am happy to note that you will give some donation to the Students' Health Home. I am reasonably sure that the Home is doing commendable work in Calcutta and needs support and encouragement.

Prabhavati's condition is said to be 'static' after her return from Bombay. The line of treatment decided upon by Bombay and Patna doctors through mutual consultations is being followed, and it seems to have arrested further growth of malignancy, at least for the time being.

With best wishes.

Yours sincerely,
Jayaprakash Narayan

Camp: Saharsha,
28 January 1974

My dear Krishna Kumarji,

I am writing to request you for some small assistance to Shri Satyesh Bhattacharya, one of the old freedom fighters from Nadia District. West Bengal. Satyesh Babu met me at Varanasi during my last visit there and related a rather sad story about his struggle to keep alive after his retirement from active work. Satyesh Babu has no family, his wife having died nearly 40 years ago. He also retired from politics along with me after which he found a job as a school teacher in Kathmandu. After his retirement he went to Banaras to spend his last days there on his meager savings which he has now run through. He lives alone in a room given free by a Bengali friend and cooks his own food and washes his own cloths. He is 79 and you can imagine the suffering of an old man who gave the best part of his life to the country's service. I asked him why he had not applied for the Freedom Fighter's pension. He replied that he just could not bring himself to ask for a return of any kind for his national work. I was rather touched by his attitude and I immediately borrowed a thousand rupees from the Gandhian Institute of Studies and gave him the money which will see him through until the end of May after which I have promised to raise more money for him. But, he said he may not live to need more. Be that as it may, my request to you is to be good enough to send a donation of Rs 1,000/- to the Gandhian Institute of Studies which will take care of my debt. The Cheque should be made in the name of the Gandhian Institute of Studies, and sent direct to the Director, Prof. Sugata Dasgupta, Gandhian Institute of Studies, Rajghat, Varanasi-1. I should add that donations to the Institute have the usual income-tax exemption. A copy of the concerned certificate will be sent to you with the receipt. I shall be very thankful for this little assistance to a poor old self-respecting fighter of freedom.

With best wishes,

Yours sincerely,
Jayaprakash Narayan

24 May 1977

My dear Shri Jayaprakashji,
I was very happy to read in the papers that your operation in Seattle was successful. Mr. Abraham too, when I telephoned to him, confirmed it. May God grant you a long life.

I wanted to come and meet you personally, but owing to some unavoidable reasons I will be able to visit Bombay only in early June, when I hope to visit you.

Meanwhile, I am sending an officer from one of our companies to meet you. I hope you will very kindly spare a few minutes for him.

Kind regards,

Yours sincerely,
K.K. Birla

5 June 1978

My dear Krishna Kumarji,
This is about Shri Suresh Singh, son of Shri Shaligram Singh, a valiant freedom fighter who had guided me through the Hazaribagh Jungles after my escape from the prison in 1942.

The boy actively participated in the Bihar movement and also suffered imprisonment. He passed the I.Sc. Examination in the Second Division last year. He now desires to study Engineering and seeks admission in the Birla Institute of Technology, Mesra. I shall be happy and grateful if you can do something in the matter.

As for my health, I am better than before. I hope you are also well.

With best wishes,

Yours sincerely,
Jayaprakash Narayan

14 July 1978

My dear Shri Jayaprakashji.
I am in receipt of your kind letter dated 5th June regarding Shri Suresh Singh s/o Shri Shaligram Singh. The boy's father came to

see me. But unfortunately, it was discovered that the boy has not applied for admission to B.I.T. at Mesra. The date for submitting the application was over long time back and the admission tests were also completed. Hence it was explained to him that it was not possible to do anything now in the matter. He was also told that if the boy submits his application for admission next year well in time, every consideration would be shown to him, particularly in view of your recommendation.

I had telephoned Abraham, who told me that you were feeling better. Kindly look after yourself.

Kind regards,

Yours sincerely,
K.K. Birla

16 February 1979

My dear Krishna Kumarji,
I write this to request you for some financial assistance to Abraham, my Secretary, who is taking this letter to you and whom you know well. He has been working with me for the last fifteen years. He is in distress as his mother is seriously ill and is proceeding to Kerala to make arrangements for her treatment. I shall be grateful for whatever financial help you can provide him.

You have been helping me in the past without my asking, but this is a special request and I am sure you will give Abraham some substantial help.

It was indeed so kind of Shri Ghanshyamdasji to have taken the trouble to come to Patna to see me in December last. I am deeply grateful to him for this as also to you all.

With my best wishes and warm regards,

Yours sincerely,
Jayaprakash Narayan

22 February 1979

My dear Shri Jayaprakashji,
I am in receipt of your kind letter dated 16th February. Abraham is a good man and has served you with great sincerity and loyalty. I

shall certainly discuss his problems with him and shall then do the needful. Please do not worry on this account.

I hope you are feeling better now. I have not been to Patna since I last met you. Meanwhile, if there be any work for me, please do not hesitate to write to me.

Kind regards,

Yours sincerely,
K.K. Birla

Patna,
3 March 1979

My dear Krishna Kumarji,
This is about Sunil Kumar Sinha, who is my own sister's grandson. He passed the I.Sc examination in 1976 in the first division from the Bihar University and now seeks admission in the Birla Institute of Technology, Mesra (Ranchi).

The boy is intelligent enough to merit State scholarship at the B.Sc stage. I shall be very grateful if you kindly do something for him in this connection. His biodata is enclosed.

With very best wishes and regards,

Yours sincerely,
Jayaprakash Narayan

Patna,
5/7 March 1979

My dear Krishna Kumarji,
I thank you for your prompt reply to my letter of 16th February 1979. I am grateful for your financial assistance to Abraham.

Healthwise I am feeling better.

With best wishes,

Yours sincerely,
Jayaprakash Narayan

Patna,
7 March 1979

My dear Krishna Kumarji,
This is about Shri Suresh Chandra Bhatnagar, a brilliant and experienced journalist of twenty years' standing. Unfortunately, he is unempoyed and is in search of a job that suits his abilities and experience. He has approached me through Shri Prakash Koirala, son of Shri B.P. Koirala, to whom he has been very helpful in various ways.

I am writing this to request you to see whether Shri Bhatnagar could be absorbed in the Hindustan Times. I hope he may be an asset to the esteemed journal, considering his abilities as evident from the enclosed resume of his working experience.

I would be very happy and grateful if you can do something for him.

With best wishes,

Yours sincerely,
Jayaprakash Narayan

5 May 1979

My dear Shri Jayaprakashji,
I am in receipt of your kind letter dated 3rd March. At the outset I would like to mention how happy and relieved the entire country is at your miraculous recovery from the illness. It is only God's grace aided by people's prayers and your own virtuousness that have given a new lease of life to you. I have been keeping myself in touch with the progress of your health. Once I telephoned to Abraham, but otherwise I have been ascertaining the improvement through my various sources.

The engineering college at Ranchi is not being looked after by me but by my cousin, Ganga Prasad. I am, therefore, strongly recommending the case of your sister's grandson, Shri Sunil Kumar Sinha to Ganga Prasad. I hope that whatever is possible will be done.

Kind regards,

Yours sincerely,
K.K. Birla

Prabhavati Devi

Prabhavati Devi was Jayaprakash Narayan's wife. I knew both Jayaprakash-ji and Prabhavati Devi well. A copy of her letter dated 20 January 1958 and my reply dated 23 January 1958 are reproduced here.

महिला चर्खा समिति,
कदम कुआं,
पटना - 3,
20.1.1958

भाई कृष्ण कुमार जी,
नमस्कार।

आशा है आप सकुशल होंगे। हम लोग भी अच्छे हैं। कष्ट दे रही हूं क्षमा करेंगे। इस पत्र के साथ जयप्रकाश जी की अपील है, पढ़ने से सब हाल मालूम होगा। मैं आशा करती हूं आप अपना (आशीर्वाद स्वरूप एक सौ रुपया 100/-) ऊपर लिखे पते पर जल्दी से भेजवाने की कृपा करेंगे।

पत्रोत्तर की आशा रखती हूं।

आपकी बहन
प्रभावती

23 जनवरी 1958

प्रिय प्रभावती बहन,
सादर नमस्कार।

आपका 20 तारीख का पत्र मिला। कमला नेहरू शिशु विहार के लिये सौ रुपये भिजवाने के लिये कलकत्ता पत्र लिख रहा हूं।

आशा है आप प्रसन्न होंगी।

आपका विनीत
कृष्ण कुमार

Morarji Desai

Morarji Bhai was a family friend. At one time he was close to father. Morarji Bhai, however, was such a stubborn type of person that he did not attach any importance to what others said. He believed that whatever he said was right. Except for his adamantine stubbornness, Morarji Bhai was a highly principled person. He was prime minister from 1977 to 1979. But the government did not last long owing to internal differences.

Some letters that were exchanged between Morarji Bhai and me are reproduced here.

Chief Minister,
Government of Bombay,
Bombay,
18 March 1953

Dear Shri Birla,
While I thank you for your letter of the 13th March, inviting me to declare open the show-rooms of the Texmaco Ltd. in Bombay, I regret very much that as I do not normally perform opening ceremonies of proprietary concerns, I shall not be able to accept your invitation.

Yours sincerely,
Morarji Desai

21 March 1953

My dear Pujya Shri Morarji Bhai,
I have to thank you for your kind letter dated 18th March. I fully appreciate your position but I hope it would be possible for you to reconsider your decision when I place the following facts before you:-

Texnaco is not a proprietary concern in any sense. It is a Public Limited Company. Its shares are well distributed to public and a large percentage is being held by a number of Trusts. The concern was started as an enterprise for the service of the nation. Birla Bros. have been the Managing Agents but we have voluntarily foregone our entire Managing Agents' commission during the last thirteen years except for one year. Texaco has had to fight against heavy odds as the British Manufacturers who formed a sort of 'combine' had virtual monopoly in this country. I myself would not have approached you if Texmaco had been just an ordinary proprietary concern. As a matter of fact, I had, for this reason, taken Father's advice also before I approached you. I am sure, in view of the above facts, you will kindly agree to perform the opening ceremony of our Show Room.

With kindest regards,

Yours affectionately,
K.K. Birla

Minister, Commerce & Industry,
New Delhi,
18 March 1957

My dear Kumar,

I thank you very much indeed for your congratulations on my election to the Lok Sabha from Surat District.

May God give me strength to be worthy of this confidence reposed in me by the people.

Yours sincerely,
Morarji Desai

(Personal)

5 October 1957

My dear Pujya Shri Morarjibhai,

You have, in my opinion, performed a Herculean task by bringing about unity in the Bihar Congress. It is no doubt a great achievement. But the question which comes before one's mind is: how long will this unity last? Unfortunately provincialism and casteism is rampant in India, Bihar, as you must have discovered by now, is an extreme case and the State has suffered much owing to casteism particularly. There is, therefore, always a danger of relapse. And the only thing which can prevent it is your constant visits to the State and your touch with its activities. Without your personal touch I see no future for Bihar. I hope, therefore, the remarkable results achieved by you will be solidified.

If there is any suggestion regarding 'Searchlight', I am always at your service.

With kindest regards,

Yours affectionately,
Krishna Kumar

10 October 1957

My dear Krishna Kumar,

Thank you for your letter of 5th October which reached me only today. The question whether the unity which has been begun to be achieved in Bihar Congress ranks will really be achieved and whether it will last is natural because several times in the past this difficult problem was tackled, unity was achieved temporarily and things became worse day by day. I cannot, therefore, say whether the present efforts have achieved any permanent result. But there are two new factors this time which were absent on the previous occasions. The agreement arrived at this time between the two factions is completely unconditional and is not based upon any recognition or admission of rival claims. Thirty prominent leaders of Bihar Congress, who can be said to be responsible for this state of affairs to a large extent, have signed a statement admitting their responsibility for the sorry state of affairs that prevailed in Bihar. These two important factors lead one to hope that this agreement is genuine and may last for a long time. Much, however, depends upon how Shri Babu will carry on his work hence forward. I feel that he has a very large heart and is not of a vindictive mind. I have every hope that he will treat all impartially, and will make a supreme effort to create confidence amongst all sections.

Casteism was not the main cause of the trouble. Main cause of trouble was groupism which arose out of conflicting personal rivalries for leadership. If this groupism disappears, casteism can be successfully tackled. At any rate, this is what I tried to impress upon all concerned in Bihar, and I must say, in fairness to all of them, that they all cooperated with me fully and without reservation. Though a very good atmosphere has resulted as a result of these talks, the position will have to be watched carefully and the agreement nursed tactfully for at least a year if permanent results are to flow from this agreement. Ultimately, everything is in God's hands. Man can only make an honest effort.

Hope all of you are doing well. Please give my good wishes to all in the family.

With best regards and wishes,

Yours affectionately,
Morarji Desai

8 August 1958

My dear Pujya Shri Morarji Bhai,
I wish to bring to your kind notice a serious difficulty in regard to the export of textile machinery. The difficulty arises out of the fact

that foreign buyers very often insist on the supply being made on credit extending to several years. To give you an instance, Texmaco recently participated in a tender for the supply of Ring Frames to a textile mill which is being set up in Ethiopia by us in participation with the Ethiopian Government. As our prices were competitive, we have been assured of the order subject, however, to one important condition, namely, that the supply will have to be made on a three year credit basis, 25% of the price will be paid to us against documents and the balance 75% in three equal instalments at the end of the first, second and third year respectively. As the value of the order is about Rs 10 lacs, the supply would involve a credit of approximately Rs 7½ lacs.

This tender, if it materializes, will be India's first opportunity of exporting textile machinery and Texmaco is very keen to take the lead. But the difficulty is about credit. If it cannot arrange credit, the tender will certainly go to Japanese firms who have offered credit not for three but for five years.

According to the present practice, banks discount bills for a maximum period of only six months because they themselves get credit facilities from the Reserve Bank of India for bills of only three months' maturity. I approached the Reserve Bank for treating this as a special case and help Texmaco to make the export by permitting banks to discount the bills for a longer period. The Reserve Bank appreciated the importance of encouraging exports but were unable to do anything in the matter because they were tied down by Section 17 of the Reserve Bank of India Act. According to the provisions of that Section, only bills maturing within ninety days from the date of their discounting are eligible for rediscount by the Reserve Bank or for being held by it as security for advances. Texmaco's bills for the export of textile machinery on a three year credit basis are, therefore, not eligible for extension of credit by the Reserve Bank to the Scheduled Banks.

I am exploring other avenues of credit for enabling Texmaco to make the export and perhaps I shall succeed this time. But this difficulty, I think, is going to become a regular feature in the export of machinery. Texmaco has lately received enquiries for the supply of a large number of boilers, tank wagons, etc., from the Government of China and it is likely that they too may insist on credit terms. In other countries, as you know, the exporters of machinery are in a position to grant long term credit to their customers because they, in turn, themselves receive similar discount facilities from banks of their respective Governments. If Indian exporters of machinery want to compete in the international market, they must be able to offer the same credit facilities to their customers as other foreign suppliers do. It appears, therefore, that unless the Reserve Bank of India Act is suitably amended so as to permit the rediscount of bills of more than three months' maturity, there would be no satisfactory or lasting solution to the problem.

Since the question of exports is so very important in the present context of the country's foreign exchange position, I am referring this matter to you and hope that it will receive your kind consideration.

With my respectful pranams,

Yours affectionately,
Krishna Kumar

16 अगस्त 1958

पूजनीय श्री मोरारजी भाई, सादर प्रणाम।

मैं कल सुबह देहली से वापस लौटा, वहां केवल दो दिन के लिये गया था। 14 तारीख की शाम को मेरा विचार आपके यहां घर पर आने का था। मुझे काम तो कुछ नहीं था, केवल आपको प्रणाम करने के लिये जाना चाहता था। शाम को साढ़े सात बजे पंतजी के यहां हम लोगों की एक मीटिंग थी। हम लोगों को आशा थी कि मीटिंग आधे घंटे में समाप्त हो जायेगी किन्तु पंतजी कार्यवश बाहर चले गये और इसलिये पौने नौ बजे के बाद हम लोगों की मीटिंग प्रारम्भ हुई। मीटिंग को समाप्त होते-होते साढ़े नौ बज गये। 15 तारीख की सुबह मैं चला आया। आने से पहले मैंने प्रणाम करने के लिये टेलीफोन किया था किन्तु आप लाल किला गये हुए थ, इसलिये पत्र द्वारा क्षमा याचना कर रहा हूं।

आपका विनम्र,

पूज्य श्री मोरारजी भाई देसाई,
वित मंत्री, भारत सरकार,
नई दिल्ली

वित मंत्री, भारत,
20 अगस्त 1958

भाई श्री कृष्ण कुमार,

तुम्हारा ता. 16 का पत्र मिला। ता. 14 और ता. 15 को तुम मुझे मिल नहीं सके इसमें तुम्हारा कोई कसूर नहीं था, इसलिए क्षमा याचना का पत्र लिखना जरूरी नहीं था।

ता. 26 की रात को मैं बम्बई पहुंचूंगा और ता. 27 की रात को लंडन के लिये निकलूंगा।
सब कुशल होंगे।

तुम्हारा,
मोरारजी देसाई

श्री कृष्ण कुमार,
8 इंडिया एक्सचेंज प्लेस,
कलकत्ता

Finance Minister, India,
18 December 1958

Shri Morarji Desai has been maintaining satisfactory progress after he underwent an operation on the 16th December and it would be some time before he resumes work. He thanks you very much indeed for your kind enquiries after his health and for your good wishes for his speedy recovery.

Asoka Mehta

Asoka Mehta was one of the founders, along with Jayaprakash Narayan, of the Socialist Party. The Socialists were formerly members of the Congress party.

I have written elsewhere that Asoka Mehta was a highly principled man. When the fertilizer plant of Zuari Industries Ltd was put up, Asoka-bhai was the minister of fertilizers at the Centre. Whenever I approached him with any difficulty, he always tried to help me. Some of the correspondence I had with him is reproduced here.

18 December 1958

Dear Shri Birla,

May I request you to consider the possibility of setting up a weighing station for sugar cane for the cane purchases by New India Sugar Mills at Mahnar Road station? Representations from that area suggest that such a weighing station at Mahnar Road station would be of considerable benefit to the large number of cane growers who are dependent on the factory.

Yours sincerely,
Asoka Mehta

20 December 1958

My dear Shri Mehta,

I am in receipt of your kind letter dated 18th December. I have made enquiries regarding Mahnar road station. I understand there is not much cane on that station so as to justify the opening of a weighing centre. All the same, in deference to your wishes and in the expectation that by opening a weighing bridge centre here we shall assist in multiplication of cane I have issued instructions for doing the needful.

I hope you will find the same satisfactory.

With kind regards,

Yours sincerely,
K.K. Birla

22 December 1958

Dear Shri Birla,

Thank you for your letter of 20th instant. I am grateful to you for your prompt and favourable reply.

Yours sincerely,
Asoka Mehta

30 December 1958

My dear Shri Mehta,

I had sent instructions to our sugar mills at Hassanpur to start making purchases of cane at Mahnar Road. One unexpected difficulty, however, has cropped up and that is about the weigh-bridge. The weigh-bridge to be installed at a cane centre has to be approved by the Weights Department of the Government of Bihar. The latter prefer the improved type of weigh-bridge which has notches on the lever. The slider once fixed in the notch does not shift its position. The ordinary type of weigh-bridge does not have a notch. As far as accuracy is concerned, there is not much difference between the two. But the notch type of weigh bridge is more reliable as the slider is fixed in it, whereas in the ordinary weigh-bridge slider can slightly be moved this way or that way.

The Government of Bihar does not normally approve of the ordinary weigh bridge and insists on the notch type. Unfortunately, all our weigh-bridges of the notch type have been exhausted because we are running a large number of weighing centres at Hassanpur mills—about 25 in all. We have, however, with us the ordinary type of weigh bridge. We are seeking permission from the Government of Bihar to use that weigh bridge at Mahnar Road as a special case. But as you know, Government machinery generally moves very slowly and even the completion of formalities may take so long that it may not be possible to install the weigh bridge in time. If, however, you could assist us in the matter, things perhaps may be expedited. I thought of acquainting you with the situation.

With Kindest regards,

Yours sincerely,
K.K. Birla

M.O. Mathai

M.O. Mathai was private secretary to Jawaharlal Nehru. Later on, he had to give up his post as he created many enemies. He was in any case very close to me and whenever I went to him for any assistance from the PMO he would examine the matter dispassionately and help me where he felt that I had a good case.

29 August 1952

Dear Mr Mathai,

As about the pair of the beautiful Ganesh Lamp you left me in a fix, as I had absolutely no idea as to how much I should give you for the same. Your guess would certainly have been better than mine, but my work was made more difficult as you left the matter entirely to me. Although it is very difficult to assess the correct value of a piece of real art as this pair is, I am sending Rs 2000/- for the pair which, I hope, you will very kindly accept. I have to thank you very cordially for having consented to part with such a beautiful piece of art.

Thanking you,

Yours sincerely,
K.K. Birla

Prime Minister's Secretariat,
New Delhi,
2 September 1952

Dear Mr Birla,

The Prime Minister has received your letter of the 4th August. He has asked to inform you how sorry he is in not acknowledging it earlier. He appreciates the significance of the new industrial development you mention i.e. the manufacture of the first industrial Boiler. But he regrets he is too over-burdened with work to undertake a trip for the formal function.

Today I spoke to him about the talk you have had with me and the possibility of having the firing ceremony in Delhi. He has not committed himself to anything. I think that when you come to Delhi next you might see PM. Don't come simply for that. Other business might take you to Delhi; then you can see him. PM will be out of Delhi from 11th to 16th Sept. He will be away in Indore then.

With all good wishes,

Yours sincerely,
M.O. Mathai

5 September 1952

My dear Mr Mathai,

I have to thank you for your letter dated 2nd September. I think the best course would be to meet the Prime Minister in Delhi. I am coming down to Delhi to attend a meeting of the sugar industry called by Shri Rafi Ahmed Kidwai and shall take the opportunity of ringing you up for an appointment with the Prime Minister.

I hope you have received the previous letter along with Rs 2000/-.
With kind regards,

Yours sincerely,
K.K. Birla

17 January 1953

My dear Mr Mathai,

I am sorry to encroach upon your time but as I value your advice very much, I hope you will kindly not mind the troubles that I am giving you. You may please recollect that when I was in Delhi some time in November, I had related to you how great injustice has been done to Bharat Airways mainly owing to pursuing a policy of favouritism by certain persons. I am sorry to inform you that the same policy is still being pursued at the time of nationalization of the Airways.

As you know, some sort of compensation is required to be paid to the Air Companies for nationalization. A number of formulas could be adopted for this purpose. Some formula may suit some one while other formulas may suit others. It is a curious coincidence that the formula that has been evolved very well suits a particular Company but throws to wind any justice or equity as far as others are concerned. You will be surprised to learn that as a result of this formula whereas the compensation fixed for a Viking plane is four lakhs of rupees, the compensation payable for a Sky master which is a far better plane with four engines and far more accommodation, is only five lakhs of rupees. What could be more absurd. I may also mention that the current market price of a Viking plane is only five lakhs of rupees whereas the current market price of a Sky master is between twenty to twenty two lakhs of rupees. Thus, those having Viking planes will get 80% of the market value whereas we in Bharat Airways will get only 20% of the market value for our Sky master planes. What could be more inequitous? I thought of writing this to you and drawing your attention.

With kindest regards,

Yours sincerely,
K.K. Birla

21 March 1953

My dear Mr Mathai,
I am enclosing herewith copy of a representation dated 19th March addressed by Bharat Airways Ltd. to the Hon'ble Prime Minister of India. You doubtless must have by now received it but I am enclosing herewith an additional copy for your ready reference. In spite of knowing full well how valuable the Prime Minister's time is, the letter has been addressed to him so that looking to the importance of the matter, proper justice may be done. I think personal talk in this matter will be very helpful and I am always

prepared to come and discuss the matter whenever you so desire.
With kindest regards,

Yours sincerely,
K.K. Birla

Bharat Airways Ltd,
Calcutta,
19 March 1953

The Honourable Prime Minister of India,
New Delhi

Subject: Nationalisation of Airlines

Sir,

We beg to be excused for encroaching upon your valuable time, but
our only reason for doing so is that the impending nationalization
of airlines, affecting as it does the vital interests of Shareholders to
whom both the Government and we not unnaturally owe a duty,
should receive the consideration and sympathy it deserves.

We understand the Government have evolved two alternative
methods of evaluating compensation. They are :–

A) The valuation of assets based on the principle of applying a
certain percentage of depreciation to the book value of assets; &

B) Purchase of the shares of a particular company, taking an
average price of shares ranging over a predetermined period of
years before June, 1952.

We have objected to scheme 'A' since its application produces
anomalous and unfair results. For instance, world market price of a
Skymaster aircraft is approximately Rs 25 lakhs. Scheme 'A' would
give us approximately 17% of world market value. On the other
hand, another company with similar aircraft imported into India
about the same time as ours, and which is not in as good a condition
as ours, will obtain about 60% more compensation than us.

In 1948, the then Hon'ble Minister in charge of Communications
was keen to commence air services from India to the Far East and
had promised to give us an agreement on the lines of the agreement
that was entered into for Western Routes, but because of financial
difficulties later on, we could not be given that agreement, and so
we suffered big losses.

We imported three Skymasters in the year 1948. We undertook

all the pioneering work which is required before a scheduled international air route could be opened. We commenced operation from Calcutta to Bangkok and Hongkong in May, 1949, after the Air Transport Licensing Board finally granted us licence to operate this route.

During the development period of this route, we suffered heavy losses. Operating losses combined with development losses totalled a large amount, and as such we were pressing the Government to give us subsidy to cover these heavy losses. Eventually, as a result of the recommendation of Air Transport Inquiry Committee, the Government agreed to give us some subsidy, commencing from October, 1950, on operations between Calcutta/Bangkok and Singapore only.

The subsidy fixed by the Government was so inadequate that it partially covered the operating losses only, leaving the heavy development losses to be borne completely by us. However, we submitted to that, because, planning over a period of 10 years, we would have made good these losses. But, just after operating for 3 years, we will be taken over, thereby nullifying the advantages of long-term planning and operation.

If nationalization of airlines is considered to be in the national interest, we have not only no objection to it, but in fact, the Government can count on our fullest and wholehearted support to their scheme. On the other hand, we submit that when Government take over our undertaking, they should compensate us for the losses which we were prepared to bear in the initial stages as a good business risk, working on the assurance of 10 years' licence, expecting however, to make good these losses, as is the case in any properly planned business, in the latter years when the development stage of the business is over, and the remunerative stage begins.

Our Skymaster aircraft, if purchased by the application of scheme 'A' and without taking into consideration their present world market value, or the initial losses that we had to incur for International operations, would be extremely unfair and unjust, since any compensation to be paid by the Government to a private individual or a company, whose assets the Government wish to take over, should be such as to place them in a similar position to what they would be if they had the choice to dispose of the assets in the open market.

Scheme 'B', whereby the Government would purchase the shares of a company, and thus take over the company as a going concern, would be by far the best method of taking over the undertaking. The Government while agreeing to this alternative method, find difficulty in its application to Bharat Airways, because of the company's preference shares of Rs 100/- each, which carry full preferential rights and cumulative interests at the time of winding up of the company. In fairness, preference shares should be paid Rs 100/- each, together with accumulated dividend. If the Government find this difficult, we would be happy to negotiate between the Government and the Preference Shareholders a reasonable price for these shares. This, we submit, would be quite easy and mutually satisfactory.

If scheme 'A' is applied to Bharat Aiways, the total amount payable to us would be such that it would be entirely distributed to Preference Shareholders, in view of their preferential rights. We have nearly 25,000 Ordinary Shareholders who are also interested in their investment and will lose all their investment which they put on trust at our disposal. The complete loss of their investment would be no fault of ours, but will be due to circumstances explained above.

Having regard to the above, we trust that the question of an equitable basis for computing compensation will receive your earnest consideration.

Thanking you,
We remain, Sir,

Yours faithfully,
For BHARAT AIRWAYS LTD.,
Per Pro Birla Brothers Ltd.,
Managing Agents.

Pandas and Great-grandfather and Grandfather

The Pandas at our holy places have a remarkable way of keeping records of their clients who visit these holy places. I enclose herewith writings of the Panda when my great-grandfather went to Dwarka. His writing is of Samvat 1947 which means the year 1891.

The text reads:

पृष्ठ 70

श्री

सेठ शिवनारायण माहेश्वरी बेटा शोभाराम का पोता उदयराम का गोत्र बिड़ला पिलानी का जिला जयपुर सेठ शिवनारायण, बेटा बलदेव तथा बलदेव का बेटा जुगलकिशोर तथा शिवनारायण का

कबीला साथ में कुदणाबाई दोनों जन द्वारका जाकर आए साथ में दूसरे ब्राह्मण मनसुखराम गौड़ बेटा मोतीराम का गरडू भाई ईश्वर बेटा सूरज तथा ईश्वर का बेटा जानकी संवत् 1947 चैत्रवदी तीज वार सोम को डाकोर जी को आए जब पंडा मेहता अमृतराम मोतीराम तथा दबे रणछोड़ कुबेर को माना है ।

(सही मारवाड़ी में) शिवनारायण

The second writing is regarding grandfather's visit to Dwarka. This is dated Samvat 1978 or the year 1922.

The text reads:

पृष्ठ 92
श्री रणछोड़ राय जी

गाम पिलानी जिला जयपुर वर्तमान बम्बई तथा कलकत्ता के माहेश्वरी बनिया गोत्र बिड़ला सेठ रायबहादुर बलदेवदास जी पुत्र शिवनारायण जी का, पोता शोभाराम जी का, परपोता उदयराम जी का तथा साथ में बेटा रामेश्वर तथा रामेश्वर का बेटा गजानन्द तथा रामेश्वर की माता जी तथा घर में बेटा जुगलकिशोर तथा रामेश्वर तथा घनश्यामदास तथा ब्रिजमोहन तथा रामेश्वर का बेटा गजानन्द तथा माधुप्रसाद तथा घनश्याम का बेटा लक्ष्मीदास तथा किशनप्रसाद तथा राधाकिशन तथा साथ में ब्राह्मण शास्त्री सत्याचरण तथा रामकुमार पंडित तथा नौकर-चाकर साथ श्री डाकोर जी आए द्वारका जाकर। पंडा भवानीशंकर नारणजी तथा माणकलाल अमृतलाल तथा बाबर कुबेर को माना है और हमारे वंश कुटुम्ब के जो आवें वे भी मानें।

संवत् 1978 का वैशाख सुदी 9 शुक्रवार।

(सही मारवाड़ी में) बलदेवदास

Likewise when my great-grandfather went to Haridwar, he made a record of his visit in the Panda's book called '*Bahi*' which is reproduced below. This is dated Baisakh Krishna 4, Samvat 1952, or the year 1896.

My great-grandfather's (Shri Shiv Narayanji] writings in the Panda's '*Bahi*' after his visit to Hardwar

Dated : Samvat 1952 or year 1896 AD]

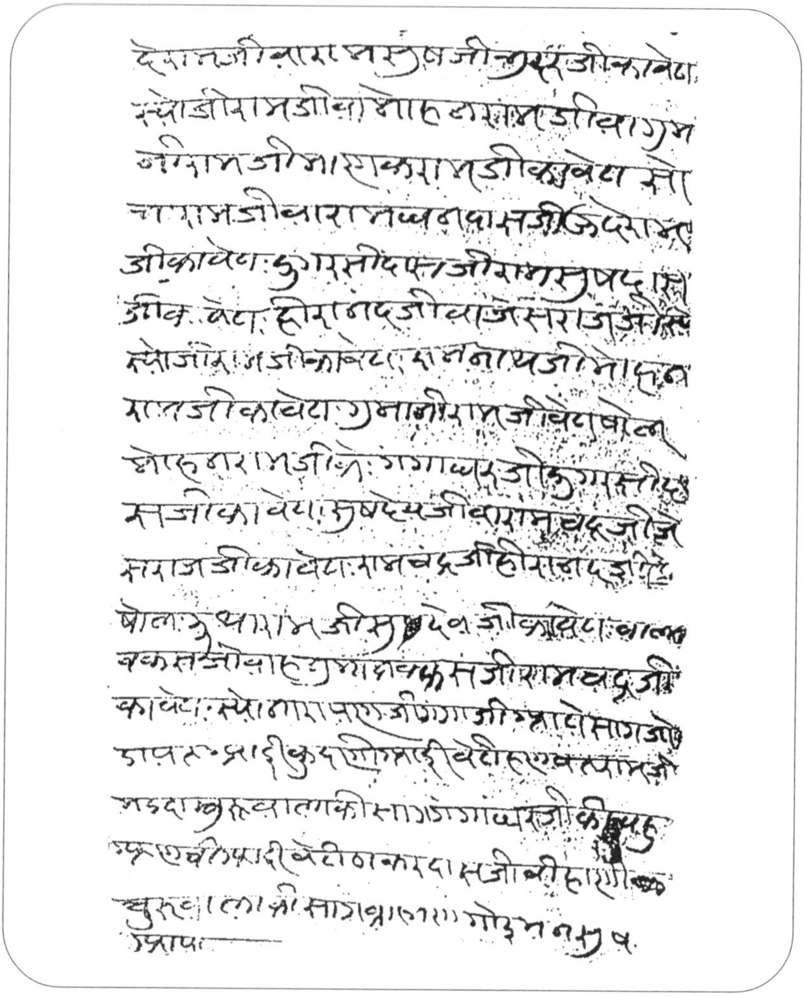

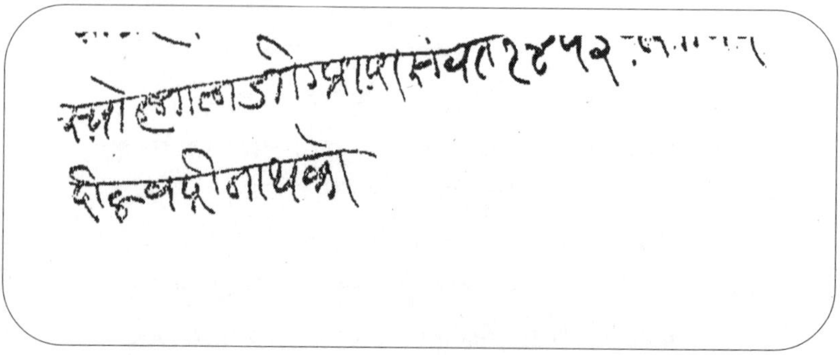

संवत १८५२

Kamlapati Tripathi

I had known Shri Kamlapati Tripathi since the early 1950s. He was for some time a minister in the government of Uttar Pradesh; later he became chief minister. He was also a cabinet minister in the central government. Some of the correspondence I had with him makes good reading.

शिक्षा मंत्री, उत्तर प्रदेश,
लखनऊ,
अक्टूबर 10, 1958

प्रिय श्री बिरला जी,

आप का दिनांक 29 सितम्बर 1958 का पत्र मिला। धन्यवाद। श्री दानी, जब मैंने आप को फोन किया उसके दूसरे ही दिन मिल गये। धन्यवाद।

आशा है आप प्रसन्न हैं।

आपका,
कमलापति त्रिपाठी

श्री के. कुमार बिरला,
8 इंडिया एक्सचेंज प्लेस,
कलकत्ता - 1

3 February 1959

My dear Shri Kamlapatiji,

Through your kind efforts, 'Pradhan' was allotted to Hargaon by Babuji. But after that allotment something happened as a result of which Babuji has decided to review his own decision. This is very strange. Never before in the history of Sugar Industry has a decision given in an appeal been reviewed so shortly. I hope you will kindly do something in the matter. We have put our entire trust and confidence in you.

I am reaching Lucknow on the 9th February on way to Hargaon and would meet you either on that day or on my return from Hargaon on the 12th.

Meanwhile, with kindest regards,

Yours sincerely,
K.K. Birla

20 February 1959

My dear Shri Kamlapatiji,

I am very grateful to you for the kind efforts made by you regarding Pradhan. I could only assure you that you took up a just cause. Babuji's decision has been fair and equitable and I have no doubt that it was owing to very sound and just advice given by you to him.

Thanking you once again and with my very kind regards,
I remain,

Yours Sincerely,
K.K. Birla

Banarasi Das Chaturvedi

Banarasidas-ji was a noted Hindi writer. He was a government-nominated Member of the Rajya Sabha for some time. I give below a letter that I had received from him and also a letter that I had sent to him.

सांसद : राज्य सभा,
99, नॉर्थ एवेन्यू,
नई दिल्ली,
10/9/1958

श्रीमान कृष्ण कुमार जी,
सादर वन्दे।

    जैसा कि मैंने आपके सेक्रेटरी श्री रामकृष्ण जी से फोन पर कहा था अमर शहीद रामप्रसाद बिस्मिल की बहन श्रीमती शास्त्री देवी (पता : पी-6, कोसमा, जिला-मैनपुरी, उ. प्र.) फाके कर रही हैं। उनके विषय में एक अपील मैंने पत्रों में छपाई है। उसकी प्रति साथ में भेजता हूं। उनके पांच बीघा खेत है जो 400 रुपये में गिरवी रख दिया गया है। मेरी आप से करबद्ध प्रार्थना है कि आप जो कुछ भी उनके लिए दे सकें, दें। आप सीधे मनीआर्डर से उन्हें भेज दें या फिर मुझे ही भेज दें, तो मैं उन्हें रवानः कर दूंगा।

    उनका स्थान कोसमा मेरे घर फीरोजाबाद (आगरा) से 36 मील की दूरी पर है। मैं खुद उनके घर की तीर्थयात्रा शीघ्र ही करना चाहता हूं।

    कृपा बनी रहे।

विनीत
बनारसीदास चतुर्वेदी

बिस्मिल का आत्मचरित अभी मैंने छपाया है। आप इस समय जल्दी में हैं इसलिए उसे कलकत्ता रवानः करा दूंगा, वैसे वह २॥) रुपये में आत्माराम एंड संस, कश्मीरी गेट से मिल सकता है।

11 सितम्बर 1958

माननीय श्री बनारसीदास जी,

सादर नमस्कार।

आपका 10 ता. का कृपा पत्र मिला, मेरे सेक्रेटरी ने भी आपसे हुये वार्तालाप का जिक्र मुझसे कर दिया था। श्रीमती शास्त्रीदेवी को 250 रुपये मनीआर्डर भिजवाने का प्रबन्ध करा रहा हूं।

आपका विनीत

श्री बनारसी दास चतुर्वेदी,

नई दिल्ली

Gulzari Lal Nanda

Gulzari Lal Nanda was a Union minister for some time. He was a good friend of mine. He had great faith in astrology. Once an astrologer gave him a conch and said that this was the famous conch called *Panchjanya* which belonged to Bhagwan Srikrishna. Nanda-ji would worship it every day. Some of the letters we wrote to each other, quoted below, will be interesting to read.

Minister for Labour,
New Delhi,
30 August 1958

My dear Krishna Kumarji,

I am enclosing copy of a letter which I have addressed to Brijmohan-ji today.

I am writing this to enlist your personal interest in the activities of the Bharat Sevak Samaj and your support for the collection of funds which are urgently needed for this Organisation.

With kind regards,

Yours sincerely,
G.L. Nanda

29 September 1958

My dear Shri Nandaji,

In continuation of my letter, I am sending herewith four cheques

amounting to Rs 4,000/- for Bharat Sevak Samaj on behalf of
some of our concerns.

With kindest regards,

Yours sincerely,
K.K. Birla

4 October 1958

My dear Krishna Kumarji,
I have received your letter of the 29th September 1958 and the
enclosed cheques. I am grateful for your keen interest in the Bharat
Sevak Samaj and the support that you give from time to time for
its activities.

With kindest regards,

Yours sincerely,
G.L. Nanda

Humayun Kabir

Humayun Kabir was a man of highly nationalistic views. He was a good
friend of mine. He was secretary to Maulana Abul Kalam Azad, who
was a minister in the government of India for a number of years. Later
Humayun Kabir became a minister in the Government of India.

Maulana Azad was a very upright and sincere person. He was a great
scholar also. The following correspondence with Humayun Kabir will be
found to be interesting. It is surprising how the lawyers served notice on
his heir, one Nooruddin, for one of the bills of the suppliers on a complaint
that Abul Kalam Azad had not paid a bill of Rs 1,486.68. I arranged the
payment and Humayun Kabir sent me a very nice letter dated 28 August
1958 which is a pleasure to read.

Minister, Scientific Research & Cultural Affairs,
New Delhi,
25 August 1958

My dear Shri Birla,
I hope you have received my letter of 22nd August 1958 informing
you that the cheque No. OPM-6544 dated 25th June 1958 was
issued by the Orient Paper Mills. I had also mentioned in that

letter that the creditors are pressing Shri Nooruddin for early payment. In fact, Shri Nooruddin has been served with a legal notice by Messrs Kamla Bhel & Company Private Ltd., Scindia House, New Delhi, for payment of Rs 1486.68 N.P. on account of supply of petrol to the late Maulana Azad. I am enclosing a copy of this notice and hope that you would kindly expedite payment of the sundry debts amounting to Rs 7786.98 N.P. out of the purchase price of the car. I am sorry to trouble you, but you will agree that it would be most undesirable that anyone should file a suit for debts against the late Maulana Azad.

With Kind regards,

Yours sincerely,
Humayun Kabir

Minister, Scientific Research and Cultural Affairs, India,
New Delhi,
28 August 1958

My dear Shri Birla,
Thank you very much for your letter of 26th August 1958 forwarding a cheque for Rs 7,786.98 in favour of Shri Nooruddin Ahmed.

I greatly appreciate your promptness and courtesy in dealing with this matter.

Yours sincerely,
Humayun Kabir

Acharya Vinoba Bhave

Vinoba Bhave needs no introduction. The enclosed letters will be found to be interesting.

5 जुलाई 1958

पूजनीय श्री विनोबाजी,
सादर प्रणाम,

आपका 18 तारीख का कृपा पत्र पिताजी के नाम का मिला। पिताजी, जैसा कि शायद पता होगा, विदेश गये हुए हैं। उनकी अनुपस्थिति में उनके सारे पत्र मेरे पास ही आ रहे हैं।

आपने ब्रह्मचारी ब्रह्मदेव जी के बारे में लिखा, मैं उन्हें सौ रुपया प्रति मास की सहायता की स्वीकृति भिजवा रहा हूं। इतना ही रुपया इन्होंने माँगा था। बारह माह के बाद इनका किस

प्रकार काम चलता है यह देखकर आपकी जैसी आज्ञा होगी तदनुसार कार्य किया जायगा।
आशा है आप सकुशल होंगे।

आपका परम विनीत

पूजनीय श्री विनोबाजी,
जयपुर

मुक्काम : वेडछी, गुजरात,
25 अगस्त 1958

लोकनागरीलीपी

श्री कृष्ण कुमार जी,

आपका तारीख 5 जुलाई, 1958 का पत्र अीसके साथ है। ब्रह्मचारी ब्रह्मदेव जी के लीअे सहायता देने की सीफारीश मैंने कीसी पत्र में आपके पीताजी को की थी, अैसा मुझे याद नहीं है। यहां मैं अीतना और जोड़ दूं की अीस पर्कार की व्यक्तीगत सीफारीश करने का मेरा रीवाज ही नहीं। कृपया तलाश करके क्या बात है, मुझे लीखीअेगा। अभी 3-4 महीने मेरी यात्रा गुजरात में चलेगी।

मेरा पता :
मार्फत : 'भूमिपुत्र'
रावपुरा, बरोडा,
बंबई राज्य

विनोबा का
जय जगत्

9 अक्टूबर 1958

पूजनीय श्री विनोबाजी,
सादर प्रणाम,

आपका पत्र मिला। उसके पहले आपके नाम से जो पत्र आया था, वह आपको भिजवा रहा हूं। इस पत्र के अनुसार ब्रह्मचारी ब्रह्मदेवजी को 100 रुपये भिजवा दिये गये थे। इसके बाद ब्रह्मचारीजी के विचार में परिवर्तन हो गया और मासिक सहायता की जगह उन्होंने नौकरी के लिए निवेदन किया। इतना ही नहीं बल्कि 100 रुपये जो उन्हें भिजवाये गये थे, वे भी उन्होंने वापस कर दिये। चूँकि कोई जगह खाली नहीं थी इसलिए मैंने उन्हें तुरन्त नौकरी देने में असमर्थता प्रकट की। अब आपके कृपा पत्र से मालूम हुआ कि सारी चीज जाली है।

आप जैसे महापुरुष के नाम का भी अपनी स्वार्थ सिद्धि के लिए दुरुपयोग करते हैं वो आश्चर्य की बात तो नहीं है परन्तु दुख की बात है।

मेरे योग्य सेवा लिखें।

आपका परम विनीत

पूजनीय श्री विनोबा भावे
मार्फत : 'भूमिपुत्र'
रावपुरा, बरोडा,
बंबई राज्य

Sir C.D. Deshmukh

Sir Chintaman Deshmukh was a very able finance minister. Earlier he was the Governor of the Reserve Bank of India. I had sent a letter to him regarding granting some protection to my company Texmaco Ltd which then manufactured spinning ring frames required by the textile mills. He was a friend of my uncle B.M. Birla. He was a scholar of Sanskrit and in fact after my marriage in 1941 he had sent a letter of congratulations in Sanskrit slokas. I quote below my letter along with his reply which will be found to be interesting.

Calcutta,
14 November 1950

My dear Sir Chintaman,
Uncle had written to me from London about his talks with you regarding Texmaco. He had also asked me to send you a short note on the subject. His letter was, however, received on the eve of my departure for Shillong from where I returned only a few days back. I regret I could not, due to these circumstances, write to you earlier on the subject.

As desired by you, I am enclosing herewith a Brochure on Texmaco which gives a short history and the background of the concern.

Our main difficulty has been lack of sales. The Tariff Board to whom the question was referred to last year, had recommended firstly, increase in the import duty from 5% to 10% and, secondly, (while the difficulties of foreign currency lasted) import restrictions. They had also stated that after the foreign exchange difficulties were over and imports freely allowed, a heavy subsidy should be given to the Textile machinery industry. In view of these recommendations, the imports of ringframes, looms and other parts have been restricted since last year.

A section of the Textile Industry strongly objected to the restrictions placed on imports. There are three important centres of the Textile Industry, viz. Ahmedabad, Bombay and Coimbatore. The attitude of the Ahmedabad Millowners' Association was, on the whole, sympathetic towards us inspite of certain groups there being opposed to the import restrictions. Coimbatore Industry was divided but the majority were with us. The Bombay Millowners' Association was against the import restrictions although there were groups in Bombay too who strongly felt that the national Textile Machinery Industry should be kept alive.

The groups who opposed the assistance to the indigenous textile machinery industry by import restrictions could be sub-divided into three sections: First come those who will never touch anything which is Indian and for whom the Indian goods are a taboo. In the second section fall those groups of the textile industry who, although they are not prejudiced against the Indian goods to that extent, are nevertheless quite unwilling to give them a trial unless and until they have first established a Trade Mark for themselves.

The difference between these two sections is that whereas the first section will not touch the Indian goods unless compelled to do so, the second section is prepared to experiment with them provided they can be had at a low price.

The third section, which is a very strong and influential one, has a different reason for opposition. They are interested in National Machinery Manufacturers—popularly known as N.M.Ms—This is a Company which has been established in collaboration with British Manufacturers in the U.K. after giving them a huge percentage of shares absolutely free and I believe you must be aware of its agreement with them. The N.M.Ms would, for the first two or three years, be more a kind of assemblers than producers. It is only a few parts that they will produce while all the rest will be imported so that their main function would be to import the parts and assemble them into frames. We, in Texmaco, on the other hand, produce all the parts barring very few. You will thus see that whereas we are producers, the N.M.Ms will be more or less assemblers to start with and their interest lies in importing as much as possible. So, our interests clash.

All the three sections of the Industry who, for one reason or the other oppose import restrictions, when they could find no other tangible argument to oppose the Commerce Ministry's decision of resticting the Imports of ringframes and looms to the extent that they were being produced here, found that the easiest way was to decry the quality of the Indian goods. The matter came up for discussion at a Conference called by the Commerce Ministry and the Industries Ministry in the first week of August at which Mr. Lalchand and myself represented the Textile Machinery Industry and Mr Wadia and Mr Nanddass Haridas represented the Textile Industry. We submitted that the question of quality of indigenous industry had been very carefully examined by the Tariff Board who had sent in their Inspectorate to study the quality not only at our Workshops but also at the Mills where our frames were working. Not only that, Mr Wadilal, a prominent Millowner from Ahmedabad, had personally testified before the Tariff Board that the quality of the indigenous products—and specially that of Texmaco—was creditable. Mr Wadia, however, bitterly complained against the spindles and spinning rings manufactured by Texmaco even though he had not used in his Mills a single part produced by Texmaco. I therefore, suggested that although our goods had already been minutely examined by the Tariff Board Inspectorate, yet we were prepared for the Industries Ministry undertaking another inspection of the spindles and the spinning rings.

The net out-come of this Meeting was that both the representatives of the Textile Industry and of the Textile Machinery Industry agreed to the principle that imports should be restricted, and that if there was any unsatisfied demand which the indigenous textile machinery industry could not meet, then only imports should be allowed. Strangely, however, after going back to Bombay, Mr Wadia could not make his Association agree to this formula and, as I am told, wrote many a letter trying to re-open the whole issue.

The matter therefore was re-opened and it ultimately went to the Economic Sub-committee of the Cabinet wherein I was called. This meeting was held on the 9th October, 1950 and was attended by six Ministers and three members of the Planning Commission. The Ministers included—Sri Rajaji, Sri Sriprakash, Dr Ambedkar, Sri K.M. Munshi, Sri N.V. Gadgil and Sri Gopalaswamy Ayyangar. The Member of the Planning Commission present were: Sri G.L. Mehta, Sri G.L. Nanda and Sri V.T. Krishnamachari.

Questions were put to me for about an hour and a half about the quality of our goods, the reasons for prejudice against our goods, and so on. As to what happened after that, you must be knowing better. A formula, more or less on the same lines was evolved whereby imports were to be allowed only to the extent of unsatisfied demand. This, in a nut-shell, is the position.

As to quality, in the first place, we can produce a large number of certificates to prove its high order. Secondly, as I have mentioned above, I had agreed for another inspection of spindles and spinning rings manufactured by Texmaco. Accordingly samples of British goods were sent to the Alipore Test House, and as for the samples of Texamco goods, when the Government Inspector visited our factory, we showed him the whole stock which consisted of a few thousands of spindles and spinning rings and requested that instead of our giving the samples to him, he himself should choose samples at random at his own discretion so that subsequently it may not be said that the samples which we had given were specially prepared. The Inspector was very much satisfied at our suggestion and at his own discretion he chose a few samples from the huge stock. These samples were sent to the Alipore Test House. The Report of the Alipore Test House has been submitted to the D.G.I.S., Government of India, and we have applied for a copy of the same. We have, however, reasons to believe that the spindles and rings manufactured by Texmaco have been certified to be superior to imported spindles and rings. As soon as I receive the report, I shall forward the same to you, if you so desire.

If there is anything else which you would like to know about Texmaco I shall be only too glad to furnish the same.

I am really very grateful to you for having taken so much interest in Texmaco and I shall deem it a great favour if you could kindly visit Texmaco whenever you happen to be in Calcutta next.

Meanwhile with kind regards,

Yours sincerely,
K.K. Birla.

17 November 1950

My dear Birla,

Thank you for your letter of 14th November and the note on Texmaco, which I have read with great interest. I shall be able to get from the I. & S. Ministry the report of the Alipore Test House.

If I have sufficient time during any of my visits to Calcutta, I shall certainly take the opportunity of visiting the factory.

With kind regards,

Yours sincerely,
C.D. Deshmukh

Viyogi Hari

Viyogi Hari was a renowned Hindi poet. That apart, he was a man of great character and saintly disposition. When Mahatma-ji asked father to accept the chairmanship of Harijan Sevak Sangh, a body dedicated to the services and upliftment of untouchables or Harijans, as Bapu used to call them, father requested Viyogi Hari to look after the handicraft teaching section of the Sangh in Delhi. He was just like a member of the family to us. Two of his letters which I have got with me are reproduced below.

हरिजन उद्योगशाला
(अ. भा. हरिजन-सेवक-संघ द्वारा संचालित)

हरिजन-निवास, किंग्सवे,
20.11.1950

चि. प्रिय कृष्ण कुमार,
शुभाशीष!

तुम्हारा 15-11-50 का पत्र मिला। श्री टंडन जी के जाली हस्ताक्षर का जो पत्र तुमने भेजा था उसे तथा श्री सम्पूर्णानंद जी के जाली पत्र की प्रतिलिपि लौटा रहा हूं। श्री टंडन जी को भी इस जालसाजी का कुछ-कुछ पता चल गया है। बम्बई के श्री नारायण लाल पित्ती ने सीधे श्री टंडन जी के पास एक हजार का चेक भेजा था और उन्होंने वह चेक वापस पित्ती जी के पास भेज दिया। टंडन जी ने यह भी कहा कि शायद वह आदमी गिरफ्तार भी हो गया है। इन दोनों पत्रों की नकलें भी टंडन जी ने अपने पास रख ली हैं।

तुम्हें आगे इस तरह के धूर्तों के जाल में नहीं फँसना चाहिए। बहुत सोच-समझकर, जाँच-पड़ताल के बाद रुपया देना चाहिए। संस्थाओं के नाम पर ठगने वाले धूर्त आजकल देश में चारों ओर फैले हुए हैं इनसे बहुत सावधान रहना चाहिए।

आशा है तुम स्वस्थ और प्रसन्न होंगे।

तुम्हारा सस्नेह
वियोगी हरि

हरिजन-सेवक-संघ,
पटना,
17.4.51

प्रिय कृष्ण कुमार,
सस्नेह नमस्कार।

14 तारीख से बिहार प्रांत के दौरे पर हूं। मुंगेर-भागलपुर से आज पटना आया हूं। तूफानी दौरा है - 1 मई को दिल्ली वापस पहुंचूंगा।

वह रुपया दिल्ली में मिल गया था। 2500/- सेफ में जमा करा दिया है, जिसे मैं अपने विवेक से अत्यावश्यक कामों पर समय-समय पर खर्च करता रहूँगा। शेष 2500. चि. मोती लाल की दोनों बहनों की शादियों में तथा एकाध इसी तरह के काम में खर्च कर दूंगा।

तुम्हारे प्रति मेरा जो स्नेह-भाव है उससे प्रेरित होकर बहुत दिनों से एक लम्बा पत्र लिखना चाहता हूं— आगे कुछ दिनों बाद लिखूंगा। ईश्वर तुम्हें स्वस्थ और चिरायु करे— अभी इतनी ही कामना और प्रार्थना। सो. मनोरमा की कैसी तबीयत है लिखना। कष्ट कुछ तो कम हुआ होगा।

चि. गंगा प्रसाद को सान्त्वना का पत्र लिख दिया था। धैर्य पूर्वक, प्रभु की लीला समझकर सब कुछ समझना ही चाहिए।

तुम पटना कब आओगे?

आशा है, तुम्हारा स्वास्थ्य अच्छा होगा।

तुम्हारा सस्नेह
वियोगी हरि

G.D. Malpani

Govind Das Malpani was uncle-in-law of my cousin Shri Gajanan Birla. He was a Member of Parliament for a number of years. He was one of the top leaders of the Congress party in the then Madhya Pradesh. One letter exchanged with him is reproduced below.

राजा गोकुलदास पैलेस,
जबलपुर,
तारीख 17-7-50

प्रियवर कृष्ण कुमार जी,

ता: 8 के कृपा पत्र के लिए धन्यवाद।

मेरा यह कह सकना संभव नहीं है कि दो हजार रुपया कौन सी मिल के बाकी रह गए हैं। तेरह हजार रुपया जहां-जहां से आया है उसकी सूची इस पत्र के साथ भेज रहा हूं। रहे हुए दो हजार कहां से पाना है, यह निर्णय तो आप ही कर सकते हैं।

विश्वास है आप प्रसन्न हैं। कष्ट के लिए क्षमा प्रार्थी हूं।

भवदीय
गोविन्द दास

साथ में :-
1 लिस्ट

LIST OF SHARE DEPOSITS

1.	Hindustan Motors Ltd., Calcutta	Rs. 1000-0-0
2.	Birla Jute Mfg. Co. Ltd., Calcutta	Rs. 2000-0-0

3.	Shree Keshoram Cotton Mills Ltd.	Rs. 2000-0-0
4.	Birla Cotton Spg. & Wvg. Mills Ltd. Delhi	Rs. 2000-0-0
5.	Upper Ganges Sugar Mills Ltd. Calcutta	Rs. 1000-0-0
6.	Bharat Sugar Mills Ltd., Calcutta	Rs. 1000-0-0
7.	New India Sugar Mill Ltd., Calcutta	Rs. 1000-0-0
8.	New Swadeshi Sugar Mills Ltd. Calcutta	Rs. 2000-0-0
9.	Ruby General Insurance Co. Ltd., Calcutta	Rs. 1000-0-0
		Rs. 13000-0-0

B.G. Kher

After Independence, B.G. Kher was the first chief minister of the state of
Bombay. I was quite close to him. Here is a copy of a letter dated 5
December 1950 from him to me which will be found to be interesting. He
has addressed me like an elder brother.

Chief Minister,
Government of Bombay,
5 December 1950

बम्बई,
5.12.1950

भाईश्री।

आपका 30 नोव्हेंबर का खत मिला। पूज्य दादाजी ने मुझे याद कर 'दार्शनिक विचार' नाम की
अेक अध्यात्मिक पुस्तक भेज दी है, यह सुनकर बड़ी खुशी हुई। पुस्तक अभी तक मिली नहीं।
मिलने पर जरूर पढ़ूंगा और अुम्मीद है कि अुसको पढ़ कर लाभ होगा। श्री दादाजी को मेरे
प्रणाम विदित कीजिये।

आपका
बी. जी. खेर

श्री कृष्ण कुमार बिड़ला,
बिड़ला हाअुस, लालघाट,
बनारस

H.K. Mahtab

H.K. Mahtab was the undisputed leader of Orissa in the 1940s and 1950s.
He was the chief minister of Orissa for some time. Then he joined the

Centre and became a minister under the prime ministership of Pandit Jawaharlal Nehru. I have many letters from him; but I am reproducing below only a few.

Minister for Industry & Supply,
28 August 1950

My dear Krishna Kumarji,
I am sorry I could not meet you at Calcutta even though I fixed up an appointment for the purpose. This time too I was in a hurry to come back to Delhi and I could not meet you. I hope you would not mind it. Next time when I go, I shall make it a point to meet and discuss with you.

As regards your Texmaco, steps are being taken to help you as far as possible. But, as you know, several textile mills have complained that the goods manufactured by you are not quite upto the mark. I do not know how this complaint can be investigated, but I suppose you must have materials to prove that your goods are comparable with foreign goods.

Hope you are doing well.

Yours sincerely,
H.K. Mahtab

(Personal)

As at Pilani,
11 February 1951

My dear Shri Harekrishnaji,
As you will find, I am here at Pilani. His Highness the Rajpramukh was here on the 9th to inaugurate the Golden Jubilee Celebrations of the Brila Education Trust and the President and Shri K.M. Munshi are now here. The President in opening the New College Building which, with an area of over 5,50,000 sq.ft., is one the biggest educational buildings in the country.

I was in Delhi just for two days, i.e. on the 6th and till the afternoon of 7th. I tried to contact you during this period eight times, but unfortunately I could not get you. I was told that you were having the lunch or were busy at the breakfast or you had some visitors. There was always some plea or the other. I even spoke to the people at your house that if you were busy for the time being, the message may be conveyed to you that there was a phone call from me and that whenever convenient to you, your assistant could connect you to me. But unfortunately even that had no result. I personally wanted to invite you for coming to Pilani and I also wanted to discuss some other matter with you. To be frank, after trying for eight times, I subsequently lost all hope of contacting you and so left the matter at that.

I am not writing this in any spirit of complaint. With you our relations are more than that of a friend. But I thought that perhaps you would like to know the statement of affairs which may have escaped your notice. When we try to speak to other Ministers, if they are busy we are told at what time we could speak to them. But unfortunately at your end, it is almost impossible to contact you or even send a message to you. You may kindly also visualize that if we people who are so well-known to you are given such treatment, what the plight of others may be, who comparatively are unknown to you.

These days people have developed the habit of seeing the Ministers for any and every thing. I have scrupulously avoided that. That was a matter of fact the reason why I did not trouble you after the satisfactory conclusion of Texmaco's affairs and I contented myself by merely sending a letter of thanks to you. But this time my business was more important.

I am returning to Delhi shortly, but am hesitating to contact you again in view of my experience.

With kindest regards,

Yours sincerely,
K.K. Birla

23 February 1951

My dear Krishna Kumarji,
Your letter dated the 11th February.

I am very sorry that we could not meet in spite of your trying as many as eight times, as you say. If I could have known it somehow, I would have certainly made it a point to meet you. For future, I would request you to just ascertain if I am here at home or in office and you can come at any time to see me. You should not observe formalities in this. I hope you have not taken it amiss for whatever has happened. Apart from my being a Minister now, we are friends and should meet without formalities as often as possible. I am finding out how it happened here that I was not informed of your desire.

I understand from your letter that you wanted to discuss some important matters with me. Will you please write to me all about them so that I may look into them?

Yours sincerely,
Harekrishna

Justice S.R. Das

Justice S.R. Das was a judge of the Supreme Court which was also called the Federal Court in those days. Ashoke Sen, who was a brilliant lawyer and also a minister for some time in the Union government, was the son-in-law of Justice S.R. Das. I had taken Justice Das to visit Pilani.

Later, Justice Das became the chief justice of India. My relationship with him continued to be very intimate. Copies of a few of his letters are reproduced here.

31 March 1951

Dear Krishna Kumarji,
Yours of the 27th instant. Since writing my previous letter I received the registered packet containing the photographs. They are, indeed, interesting and will serve as a memento of our visit to Pilani, I thank you for the trouble you have taken in sending then to me.

Prabhudayal-ji has recovered from his indisposition. I met your good father when I went to see Prabhudayal. To-day there was the annual session of the Federation of Indian Chambers of Commerce & Industry which I attended.

I trust you are keeping well. With kind regards,

Yours sincerely,
S.R. Das

Chief Justice of India,
Supreme Court,
New Delhi,
8 January 1959

My dear K.K.,
Many thanks for the Texmaco diary that you have sent to me. The get up is excellent and the informations contained therein are extremely useful. While I am delighted to accept your present, I am still more beholden to you for the kind thought that actuated you to send it to me.

I was sorry to hear that your revered grandmother had injured herself as a result of an accidental fall. I trust she is now out of danger and all is well with her.

With kind regards,

Yours sincerely,
S.R. Das

13 January 1959

My dear Chief Justice,
I am in receipt of your kind letter dated 8th January. I am glad you liked the diary.

Pujya grand-mother is now better. She had an accidental fall and one of the bones in her legs was broken. But it is amazing that even at her age, the bone responded very well to the medical treatment. As a matter of fact, the doctors said that the response was as satisfactory as it would have been in the case of a child. We attribute it to her religious temperament that God has been so kind to her.

With kindest regards,

Yours sincerely,
K.K. Birla

K.B. Sahay

K.B. Sahay was a very good minister of Bihar. My relations with him were very cordial. Many letters were exchanged between us. I am giving just a few of them which will be found to be interesting.

9 January 1956

My dear Shri Krishna Ballabhji,
I hope you recollect that you had mentioned to me about Shri Brajkishore Memorial. Subsequently Acharya Badrinath Varma too had met Father. He had also brought a letter from the President.

I had explained to you the full position about this matter. But in view of our past talk as also Acharya Badrinath Varma's visit to this city, we have decided to donate Rs 10,000/- for this noble cause. Kindly let me know in what name the cheques are to be made.

With kindest regards,

Yours sincerely,
K.K. Birla

Patna,
14 January 1956

My dear Shri Krishna Kumar,
I am in receipt of your letter dated 09.01.1956. Many thanks to you for your donation. The cheque may be made in the name of Acharya Badri Nath Varma.

Yours sincerely,
K.B. Sahay

Camp: New Delhi,
22 January 1956

My dear Shri Krishna Ballabh Babu,
I am in receipt of your kind letter dated 14th January.

Father had another chat with the President and we are now increasing our donation to Brajkishore Shastri Memorial to Rs 20,000/-. A cheque for this amount we are handing over to the President here.

With kindest regards,

Yours sincerely,
K.K. Birla

18/22 May 1956

My dear Shri Krishna Kumar Birla,
I am in receipt of your letter, dated the 12ᵗʰ May, 1956. I am afraid, the impression that you carried from my talk with you at Calcutta that Bihar Government was not keen to proceed with the Ceiling Bill is wholly incorrect. I can assure you that I am very keen about it. All that I told you was that neither Shri Dhebar nor Shri S.M. Agarwal nor Shri Nanda-ji had pressed for exemption being granted to sugarcane factory farms in the matter of fixation of ceiling.

Yours sincerely,
K.B. Sahay

Hazaribagh,
5 March 1959

My dear Shri K.K. Birla,
I purchased an Ambassador car last year in April which has covered eighteen thousand miles and is in a good condition. All the same I would like it to be replaced by a new Ambassador car giving my present car in exchange at any extra sum that may have to be paid.

Is the arrangement possible?

Yours sincerely,
K.B. Sahay

Malcolm MacDonald

Malcolm MacDonald was the High Commissioner for the United Kingdom in India. He was the son of Sir Ramsay MacDonald who was the first Labour Prime Minister of Great Britain. I had taken him to Pilani. He was a fine gentleman and was full of warmth and wit. The text of two letters that I received from him are reproduced here.

Office of the High Commissioner for the United Kingdom,
18 February 1956

Dear Shri Birla,

I should have written to you sooner to thank you for that excellent visit to Pilani, but got involved in a lot of urgent work over the weekend.

It was very good indeed of your father and you to arrange for the trip, and, having arranged it, to organise such a pleasant company of fellow-trippers. I greatly enjoyed the day.

Needless to say, I was tremendously impressed with the various educational institutions which we saw in Pilani, and with everything about them. The Birlas are doing a great work there, especially for the young people of India and, therefore, for the future of India. I look forward to other visits later on, to see your huge tree gradually bearing more flowers and fruits.

It was especially good of you to spare the time to be our guide, philosopher and friend on the journey. It was a great pleasure to meet you again.

With kind regards,

Yours sincerely,
Malcolm MacDonald

7 October 1958

Dear Shri Birla

It was charming and generous of you to send Mrs MacDonald and me a basket of beautiful fruits yesterday. They really are very fine, and we are already enjoying them.

Thank you very much for this friendly act.

With kind regards,

Yours sincerely,
Malcolm MacDonald

Major General W.H.A. Bishop

Office of the High Commissioner for the United Kingdom,
Calcutta,
10 December 1958

Dear Mr Birla,

Thank you for your letter of the 8th December. Both Mr MacDonald and I were very sorry to miss the opportunity of seeing you yesterday evening but still more sorry to learn that you have not been well for the last few days.

We both greatly hope that you will be fully restored to health very quickly.

With kindest regards,

Yours sincerely,
W.H.A. Bishop

Manibehn Patel

Manibehn Patel was the daughter of Sardar Vallabhbhai Patel. She looked after him diligently. I have received many letters from Manibehn. Copies of a few letters exchanged with her are reproduced below.

बिरला हाउस,
नई दिल्ली,
11 अप्रैल 1956

चि. भाई कृष्ण कुमार जी,

आपका पत्र मिला था परन्तु दादा जी की तबियत ठीक नहीं थी सुना, इसलिए तुरन्त उत्तर न दिया। बाद में तो उनका स्वर्गवास हो गया, इसलिए थोड़े दिन रुक गई।

मैं तो दादाजी के दर्शन कर न पाई, न आशीर्वाद के लिए भाग्यशाली थी। यह मुझे सदा खलेगा।

चि. सौ. मनोरमा तारीख 18 को आती है, ऐसा काशी कहता था। मुझे तो तारीख 18 को मोरारजी भाई के साथ अहमदाबाद जाना है, सो मिलना नहीं होगा। आशा है अब तबियत बिलकुल ठीक होगी। ज्वर नहीं रहता होगा।

मावलंकर की बाल्टी तब साथ दिल्ली भेज देना। उनकी पत्नी उनकी जगह पर लोकसभा में ली गई हैं और कोई खड़ा नहीं रहा। श्री विट्ठल कन्या विद्यालय के बारे में मैं क्या चाहती हूं आपने पूछा है। क्या बताऊं? हमने तो जून से शिक्षिकाओं को तैयार करने के लिए अध्यापन मंदिर (Training College) खोलने का तय किया है। अगर आप पढ़ सके हों तो उसमें वो सब दिया ही है। हो सके तो छोटी-मोटी रकम कई लोगों से लेकर पचास हजार से

लाख तक दे सको तो अच्छा। इतना नहीं बन सके तो जो कुछ हो सके तो कर दीजिए। इस अध्यापन मंदिर के लिए ही डेढ़ लाख तक का खर्च होने का अंदाज है।

आज मुरली धरजी को टेलिफोन करके 1500 रुपये भेजने को कहा है। चि. विपिन एक महीने के लिए चाहता है। उसकी रकम एक मास में आ जाएगी, तब वापस दे देगा। आपको आज इस बारे में लिख दूंगी, यह भी मुरली धरजी को मैंने कह दिया था।

आप राजी होंगे। कब आओगे ?

आपकी
मणिबेन

17 अप्रैल 1956

पूज्य मणिबेन,

सादर प्रणाम, आपका 11 ता. का कृपा पत्र मिला। दादाजी अचानक चले गये, हम लोग भी समय पर नहीं पहुंच सके, उनका स्वास्थ्य तो मार्च के अन्तिम सप्ताह में ही ढलना शुरू हो गया था किन्तु हम लोगों ने यह मान रखा था कि शायद वे ठीक हो जाएंगे। चाचाजी ठीक समय पर पहुंच गये थे तथा उन्हें उनका आशीर्वाद भी मिल गया था, कुछ दिन और यदि हमें उनका आशीर्वाद मिलता रहता तो अच्छा रहता किन्तु परमात्मा की मर्जी कुछ और थी।

मनोरमा की तबियत आशा है मसूरी जाकर ही पूर्णतया ठीक होगी, वह तो 19 ता. को आपसे मिलने के लिये बहुत उत्सुक हो रही थी।

दादा साहब की बाल्टी मैं मनोरमा के साथ नहीं भिजवा रहा हूं कारण वह प्लेन से जा रही है और उसका सामान सीधा देहरादून चला गया किन्तु मैं मई के पहले सप्ताह में दिल्ली पहुंच रहा हूं। उस समय बाल्टी लेता आऊंगा।

श्री विट्ठल कन्या विद्यालय के बारे में मैंने आपसे पूछा उसके जवाब में आप ने लिखा है कि छोटी-मोटी रकम सभी लोगों से कुछ ले लिया जाय, कलकत्ता में अहमदाबाद के लिये कोई दे सकेगा, यह कहना जरा कठिन है। जिसके पास हम लोग जाएंगे वह यही कहेगा, अहमदाबाद में काफी मिल वाले हैं वे क्यों नहीं दे देते! मैंने इस विषय में बसन्तकुमार से बात की थी। उसका भी यही कहना है, हम दोनों भाई इस संस्था के लिये ढाई-ढाई हजार रुपया देना चाहते हैं। यह चेक श्री विट्ठल कन्या विद्यालय के नाम में बनवाकर आपके पास भिजवा दूं या किसी और नाम से चेक बनवाने होंगे। इसके अलावा बसन्तकुमार कह रहा था कि जब आप अहमदाबाद में हों, उस समय हाडा आपके साथ-साथ और कई मिलवालों के पास एक बार चक्कर काट ले ताकि वहाँ से कुछ रुपया इकट्ठा हो सके। मेरे विचार से कस्तूरभाई को इस विषय में याद दिलाना अच्छा रहेगा।

विपिन के बारे में लिखा वह तो छोटी सी बात थी। इसके विषय में लिखने की क्या आवश्यकता थी।

पत्र आपको बिरला हाउस के ठिकाने से ही भिजवा रहा हूं।

आपका

श्रीमती मणिबेन पटेल,
नई दिल्ली

12 May 1959

My dear Manibehn,

I enclose herewith copy of letter from Sitaram Jaipuria son of Mangturam Jaipuria a friend of ours. I am sorry to read what Sitaram writes regarding Bipin. I am sending him a suitable reply but I think when you meet Bipin you should speak to him about it. I do not know how far the facts are correct but if he has started drinking it is very unfortunate. I am sure, however, you will take whatever action is necessary in the matter.

   With my respectful pranams

Yours affectionately,
K.K. Birla

Dr Rajendra Prasad

Dr Rajendra Prasad needs no introduction. Somewhere earlier I have written how close he was to father and myself. A copy of my letter dated 6th February 1950 is reproduced below. I do not have Rajendra Babu's letter of 30th January 1950; but from my letter his warmth will be evident.

6 फरवरी 1950

पूज्य श्री राजेन्द्रबाबू,

आप का ता. 30 जनवरी का कृपा पत्र मिला। आप का पत्र इतना विनय और नम्रता से भरा हुआ है कि उसे पढ़ कर संकोच मालूम होता है। जो हो पत्र आपके बड़प्पन के अनुसार ही है। मैं तो घर का ही आदमी हूं, अतः इस पत्र की आवश्यकता भी नहीं थी।

   मैं यहां कुछ दिन पहले आया था और बीच में चीनी की मिल की तरफ गया था। अब दिल्ली 4-5 दिन हूं और बिना आपके दर्शन किये नहीं जाऊंगा।

आपका विनीत,

Pandit Jawaharlal Nehru

Pandit Jawaharlal Nehru, the first prime minister, was also the topmost leader of India after Mahatma-ji. Mahatma-ji in his lifetime had declared him to be his heir. Both Jawaharlal-ji and his father Pandit Motilal-ji were very close to father. I was too young at the time for Pandit-ji to grant an appointment when I asked for it. Yet Pandit-ji was a true democrat in the real sense of the word. He always wanted to encourage young men and for that reason whenever I sought an appointment with him he always granted it. I was however prudent enough not to seek another appointment within six months of the one granted. Copies of some letters exchanged with him are given below which may be found to be interesting.

4 August 1952

My dear Respected Panditji,
I apoligize for encroaching on your valuable time, especially when you are in the midst of a Parliamentary Session and are preoccupied with matters of great importance, but my only excuse therefore is your known interest in the industrial progress of our country.

We have at Calcutta a factory named 'The Textile Machinery Corporation Ltd.,' (popularly known as Texmaco) and I am the Chairman of its Board of Directors. It has two distinct Machine Shops—one engaged in the manufacture of Spinning Machinery and the other in the manufacture of heavy Railway and Industrial Equipments. In the latter shop, which is considered to be one of the most modern and up to date of its kind in the country, we manufacture Boilers—both Locomotive and Industrial—as also Petrol Tank Wagons for the Railway, Tramcars and several other items of heavy Equipments.

Boilers and Steam raising Appliances are essential factors in modern industrial establishments but India has all along depended on imports for these basic items and to that extent our industrial progress has been slow. The Plant referred to in para 2 above which has been established for the manufacture of Boilers and other allied Steam raising Appliances in technical collaboration with Messrs. Babcock and Wilcox a British firm of great repute and one of the biggest of its kind in the world, is particularly equipped for the production of other heavy Railway and Industrial Equipment.

Though locomotive boilers are being manufactured in India by both Tatas and the Railways themselves, as far as Industrial Boilers are concerned, no one with the exception of Texmaco has ever attempted their manufacture. The manufacture of the first Industrial Boiler is, therefore, a real landmark in the history of Industrial progress in this country, and I fervently wish—and it would be in the fitness of things too—that you may kindly spare a little of your busy time to perform the 'Firing Service' in the first boiler ever manufactured in the country.

I realise that there are multifarious calls on your valuable time but I sincerely trust that you will honour us by accepting our invitation to perform this ceremony which will undoubtedly go a long way to bring home to our people the big strides we have made towards the country's industrialization. Should we be so fortunate as to obtain your acceptance to our invitation, I would request you kindly to fix a convenient date for the ceremony. I further request that the date may kindly be communicated to me about a month in advance, so that the necessary preparations may be made.

I might add that I had intended to make this request personally but on second thought I felt that I would not be justified in taking up your time when you are already overburdened with affairs of State.

With respects,

Yours sincerely,
K.K. Birla

14 November 1952

My dear Respected Panditji,
On the occasion of your Birthday, kindly permit me to offer you my humble felicitations. We hope and pray that you will have many, many happy returns of the day so that you may continue to guide the destinies of our country for years to come. I would have called personally to offer you my greetings, but I felt that it would not be fair for me to encroach on your time when I know that you are busy with matters of great importance.

With respects,

K.K. Birla

19 November 1952

Dear K.K.,
I am very grateful to you for your message of good wishes on the occasion of my 63rd birthday. To be remembered with affection

by so many friends all over the country and abroad is rather an overwhelming thought. At the same time it strengthens, for one has the feeling of a common purpose animating so many of us. I hope that all of us, wherever we might be, will engage ourselves in this common purpose of serving India and humanity to the best of our ability.

I am particularly glad that my birthday was made the occasion for celebrating children's day. Our children are not only dear to us but are the real wealth of our nation. Let us guard this treasure.

Thank you

Jawaharlal Nehru

22 November 1955

Please accept my thanks for your kind message of good wishes on the occasion of my birthday anniversary. I am deeply grateful for the generous affection and goodwill I receive from my countrymen as well as from friends abroad.

Jawaharlal Nehru

Satyanarayan Sinha

My correspondence with Satyanarayan Babu was voluminous. I am giving below the text of only a few letters which were exchanged.

Minister, Parliamentary Affairs,
New Delhi,
Camp – Patna,
14 October 1950

My dear Krishna Kumarji,
I came here day before yesterday. The atmosphere, on my arrival, was very tense. Thank God, things cleared up in our favour and we have won the election by 2/3rd majority, a thumping success indeed.

I had a talk with Sardar about he price of sugar. He will do the needful in the matter.

I am leaving for home this morning and hope to be back to

Delhi by the 25th of this month. If you have to write to me anything, please do it by my home address—Vill & P.O. Sambhupatti.

    With best wishes,

Yours affectionately,
Satyanarayan

23 December 1950

My dear Sri Krishna Kumarji,

The sudden demise of Sardar gave me such a shock that I have not been able to recover from it completely yet. The Parliament session ended yesterday & so I got a little respite. I got a Shahtush from the Kashmir Emporium & Kashi has paid the bill. I think, the Tush which you had sent was returned to Calcutta. Please talk to me on phone between 8 & 9 p.m. on Monday next—or even earlier in the day. I am not in a position to write to you anything more for the present.

    With best wishes

Yours affectionately,
Satyanarayan

16 August 1952

My dear Krishna Kumarji,

Many thanks for your letter dated 26th July, 1952, which I received in time.

    Since the present session of the parliament is over, I am thinking of making best use of the recess period.

    I was very glad to read in the newspaper that you took keen interest in sending a mountaineering team from Pilani to the Himalayas. I only wish many more such teams will proceed in future. But if I may add, the climbing of peaks is not so interesting at present as the exploration of the entire 1500 length of the Himalayas bordering Tibet. This work is necessary from the point of view of the defence of our country, and must be taken very seriously.

    As an enthusiastic youngman, I think, you will take much interest in the study of our defences and the current political tendencies.

Our country is passing through a very critical period, and unless there are some enthusiasts, there is little hope for a bright future.

We may be proceeding to Kashmir, Ladakh and Tibet next week, and I will let you know about the situation there if I find it of some special importance. After coming back, I am thinking of going to my constituency—in other words to Marhowrah. Hope I will meet again Mr Agnihotri and the climate will be suitable to make some good chocolates. That is, of course, a very good stimulant for me, and I am thankful to you.

I hope that I will soon be able to strike a more cheerful note. I do not enjoy complaining, but as in the case of every youngman of our country, for the moment it is difficult to keep one's spirits up.

Thanks once more. With the very best wishes,

Yours sincerely,
Satyanarayan

17 October 1955

My dear Shri Satyanarayan Babu,
I am in receipt of your letter dated 14th October. Everything is all right here. Manorama's foot is in plaster and I hope plaster will be removed by the end of this month.

Yes, Father is here and we are all having very enjoyable time. There were two sessions of Bare Gulam Ali. He sang exquisitely. He is really a master artist, much better, in my opinion than Onkarnath or Patwardhan. On one of the occasions, Shri T.T.K. was also present.

Yes, Jitendra Babu saw me in Calcutta and I thought he must have written to you about the matter. I had a very satisfactory talk with him and he went back fully satisfied. He would be reinstated there with a promotion in position. He would now be called Joint Editor. The Editor would also have instructions to train him up so that in due course of time he may take up that post. He had some misgivings about Binda, but I think he will find him a changed man.

I am not likely to come towards Delhi by the end of this month. But I hope to be there some time in the next month.

With kind regards,

Yours affectionately,
Krishna Kumar

14 December 1955

My dear Satyanarayan Babu,
I was pleasantly surprised to find your article in Kalayn called 'Tulsi ke Ram'. It is a very well written article. I wonder how you did not show it to me when I was in Delhi. In future when you write any other article, please do not forget to send it to me.
    With kind regards,

Yours affectionately,
Krishna Kumar

9 April 1956

My dear Krishna Kumarji,
A few days ago, G.D. telephoned to me from London. I had advised him not to come to India without finishing his programme, because the physical body of the great soul is no more and there is no meaning in his coming to India by interrupting his programme. I am glad that R.D. and B.M. also have advised him similarly, that is what I learn from their letters. I sent a letter to B.M., a copy of which I am sending to you. You will please read it over to M.P., B.K. and G.P.
    I hope Manorama has completely recovered by now. I am getting her medicine ready.
    With love,

Yours affectionately,
Satyanarayan

Note: This letter was written after the demise of Pujya Grandfather. I could not find the copy of the letter that Satyanarayan Babu had sent to Uncle B.M.

11 April 1956

My dear Shri Satyanarayan Babu,
I am in receipt of your kind letter dated 9th April. Your letter to Uncle is really very touching.
    I had originally held that it would have been proper for Father

to have returned to this country. Father, however, mentioned that he would do exactly what grandmother desired him to do. When the question was put to grandmother, she said that if he was required to return to Europe again after coming to India, there was no fun in his coming but that if he was not required to go to Europe after coming here, he may come immediately. What a practical advice.

Grandfather too was an extremely practical man. It is surprising how a man in old age could adapt himself to the changing conditions. And yet this is what Grandfather was. Even two or three days before his death he had sent a cable to father not to worry to return to India but to complete his job which he was doing. We all wish grandfather could have been amongst us for a few more years to bless us. But God willed it otherwise. He went away in full glory. It is for us now to emulate the shining example which he has laid before the posterity.

Monorama has now completely recovered owing to blessings and good wishes of friends like you. Her old ailment, however, is continuing. She is having slight temperature for reasons unknown. She is shortly going to Mussoorie and I hope would be benefited by the good climate there.

With kindest regards,

Yours affectionately,
Krishna Kumar

20 December 1958

My dear Shri Satyanarayan Babu,
Some time back I had written to you about the support given by us to the Bihar Development Loan. I had no desire to bother you and what I had mentioned to you was only for your knowledge. But kind and affectionate as you always are towards me, you went out of your way and the result was that I got a very appreciative letter from the Chief Minister.

As you happen to come from Samastipur and as you are well acquainted with that area, I an enclosing just for your information a copy of letter which I had sent to the Chief Minister on 13th November, 1958. As you will kindly see from it, a great injustice has been done to Hassanpur factory. I understand that some time back when you were at Shambhu Patti, the prominent people of the locality, who came to meet you, also mentioned that injustice was being done to Hassanpur factory. We always had cordial relations with the Samastipur factory. But after the change of management, they have started these pin-pricks. The rumour is that Mahesh Babu's son-in-law is trying to get a hold in the mills on some sort of partnership basis. Perhaps you are already aware of that.

After the despatch of my letter to Shri Babu, I also wanted to talk with him on the phone. I had, therefore, booked a line for him. He was in Patna but it appears he wanted to avoid me. The result was that his secretary after ascertaining as to who was at the telephone, waited for some time and then said that the Chief Minister was not available. Needless to say, I have received no reply to this letter.

I do not want to write again to Shri Babu in this matter. I would be lowering myself unnecessarily if he is not receptive. That this action has been taken at his instance is certain as all the officers like Jhunak Babu and Shri B.N. Sinha, Industries Secretary, have informally told our representative that they are helpless in the matter. At the same time, if there is no remedy, not only will the Hassanpur factory be put to considerable losses every year but we shall also lose a good deal of money which we have given as advance to cultivators in this area.

I do not know whether any redress is possible. But I thought of bringing the facts to your notice.

With kind regards,

Yours affectionately,
Krishna Kumar

1 January 1959

My dear Krishnaji,

I had been away from Delhi for about 8 or 9 days. I had gone to Gwalior and returned here only last night. This morning I have received your letter dated 20th December, 1958, regarding the supply of Narhan area cane to the Hasanpur factory. I know all about it in detail. In fact, I had mentioned about it to you some time ago. It is a clear case of vindictiveness due to M.S.M. Sharma's criticism. However, I shall discuss about it with you when we meet. If possible, try to telephone to me on the receipt of this letter. In the meantime, I am just thinking over the matter as to what should be done in the circumstances without losing dignity.

With love,

Yours affectionately,
Satyanarayan

29 May 1962

My dear Krishnaji,

Enclosed you will find a letter which has been addressed to me. The letter will speak for itself. In fact when I had been to Patna last time, in Sadaqat Ashram some people had drawn my attention to some scurrilous writings against Rajendra Babu. I am trying to get the cuttings of both the dates mentioned in the letter but in the mean time I would request you also to ask the Editor of the Searchlight giving him a gist of my letter to let you know what is the real position. If the Editor is really bent upon carrying on a personal propaganda against Rajendra Babu, he should be removed from that place without any delay.

The Chief Minister of Bihar is expected here along with some of his colleagues. I would take the opportunity of discussing this matter with them also to find out what is really behind all this.

Hope you have got rid of your cough. More in next.

With love,

Yours affectionately,
Satyanarayan

'रमण'

गुलजारबाग (पटना)
26 मई 1962

आदरणीय श्री सत्य नारायण बाबू,

सादर प्रणाम।

गत 13 और 20 मई के 'सर्चलाईट' को देखने का कष्ट कीजिये, तो पता चलेगा कि भारतरत्न राजेन्द्र बाबू पर किस तरह कीचड़ उछाला गया है। बिहारवासी जानना चाहेंगे कि क्या इसीलिए उस तपस्वी को बिहार लाया गया है? जहां उनके घर ही पर एक अशिष्ट सर-फिरा आदमी उन्हें अपमानित करने की हिम्मत करे?

लोगों का ख्याल है, आप जितना प्रधान मंत्री के समीप हैं, उतना ही धन्नासेठ बिड़ला के। इसका क्या प्रायश्चित होगा - बिड़ला जी स्वयं तय करें तो अच्छा होगा। बिहार के सत्ताधारी

आज तक चुप हैं, और चुप ही रहेंगे-ऐसी आशंका हो रही है। यदि यह असभ्य तथाकथित पत्रकार बिहार से वापस नहीं बुला लिया गया तो परिस्थिति वहां बेहद बिगड़ सकती है।

विशेष, आपके औचित्य पर,

आपका
रमण

सेवा में
श्री सत्यनारायण सिंहा,
मंत्री, भारत सरकार,
नई दिल्ली

Birla Niwas,
Mussoorie,
1 June 1962

My dear Shri Satyanarayan Babu

I am in receipt of your kind letter dated 29th May. I was very sorry to read the contents of your letter.

Rajendra Babu is a big man in every sense. The services which he has rendered to the country are very great. He is, therefore, held in the highest esteem. In case, therefore, SEARCHLIGHT has tried to malign him it is most unfortunate. Could you kindly send me some of the cuttings so that I could go through the same? Meanwhile, however, I am writing to the editor but after I get the cuttings from you, I shall write to him again. The second letter of course will be very strong and in case what has been reported to you is correct, the editor will have to go.

The present editor is Kalhan. He was formerly in Hindustan Times. He is, as a matter of fact, only an Acting Editor. Sharda was an excellent editor and was a real gem. He unfortunately died rather young and his place has not been filled up as yet. We are trying to get some suitable person who may increase the prestige of the paper. But there is a big dearth of people and that is why we have not been able to fix up some suitable person as yet.

Who is this man Raman? I do not know whether he is some stranger or whether he is someone known to you. In case he is stranger, one need not notice of him. In case, on the other hand, he is some-one known to you, he should be told and rather plainly that merely because something appears in any paper connected with us, does not mean as if we have any hand in it. As a matter of fact, our policy has been to lay down general policy of the paper and then to keep aloof. It is neither practicable nor desirable for us to look after the day to day affairs of the paper. Knowing our close relations with Rajendra Babu, I wonder, what led Mr. Raman to believe as if we had any hand in what may have appeared in SEARCHLIGHT.

Kind regards,

Yours affectionately,
Krishna Kumar

Gaganvihari L. Mehta

Gaganvihari L. Mehta was a close friend of mine. He used to work as the general manager in Kolkata of Scindia, a shipping company belonging to Shri Walchand Hirachand. Gaganvihari was a brilliant man. After leaving Scindia he went as ambassador of India to the United States and later he was chairman of ICICI for a number of years. Here are copies of a few letters I exchanged with him.

16 July 1952

(Personal)

My dear Krishna Kumar,

I was just wondering whether you have a trained cook who can accompany us to Washington. He need not necessarily know Western type of cooking, but must know some table manners, etc. I have noticed that you have got some men in your offices in Bombay and Calcutta as well as at your place in Delhi and hence this enquiry. If the man has smattering of a little English, so much the better. He must, however, be prepared to stay for 2/3 years abroad. For English or American type of cooking, I propose taking another man and will also have some local cook from time to time, but it is for our type of cooking that we are looking out for a man. Please let me know whether you can help me in this matter without taking too much trouble.

I was wondering whether you left any instructions with your man here regarding some storage of my furniture and luggage. I shall trouble him if it is at all necessary to do so.

I have altered my programme and now propose to leave towards the end of August by plane via U.K. I may be going to Bombay in the first week of August but may have to return here before I go finally. When you come next to Delhi, you might phone to me and ascertain whether I am here.

With kind regards,

Yours sincerely,
Gaganvihari Mehta
Member, Planning Commission

(Personal)

Embassy of India,
Washington, D.C.,
10 December 1955

My dear Krishna Kumar,

In one of your letters you had mentioned that you were going to write something about your visit to the United States and the work of the Embassy and that you would send me copies of the Searchlight and the Leader when these articles appear. I wonder whether you did write and, if so, I would like to see these articles.

I had written to Da Costa on 1st November sending a list of persons to whom the Quarterly Economic Report of the Indian Institute of Public Opinion could be sent. I had also given another list to Laxminivas. I have not had an acknowledgement from Da Costa at which I am surprised. I wonder whether the letter has gone astray or whether he is on tour. Would you kindly find out and ask him to let me know?

I do not know if you went to Delhi and had an opportunity to see Dr. Dhar.

Until now, the winter has not been severe here but it is just the beginning. We have had three or four slight snowfalls.

I hope you and your wife are keeping well.

With kindest regards,

Yours sincerely,
Gaganvihari Mehta

P.S. Just as this letter was about to be posted, I received your letter of 4th December for which please accept my best thanks. I do not know if Mrs. Mehta received your letter. I shall enquire and let you know. Mrs. Mehta wrote to you from Simla but unfortunately, you did not get the letter.

3 January 1956

My dear Shri Mehta,

I am in receipt of your kind letter dated 10th December. I enclose herewith clippings from the 'Leader' of 8th November. I am sorry I could not send these to you earlier as I was touring about in the country. An identical article has appeared in the 'Searchlight'. All the material about this article was supplied by me, but the language and method of presentation is not mine. I hope you will like the article. Please let me have your comments.

I am sorry to learn that you did not get any reply from Da Costa. I am reminding him about it.

I am likely to go to Delhi shortly when I shall certainly meet Dr Dhar.

How is Mrs Metha? I did not receive any letter from her from Simla. Probably it might have gone astray. Kindly convey my kindest regards to her.

With kindest regards,

Yours sincerely,
K.K. Birla

S.K. Patil

S.K. Patil was a very famous man in his days. He had a lot of influence in Mumbai and outer Mumbai and was regarded as the undisputed leader of these areas. A strong man, he was regarded as Sardar Vallabh Bhai Patel's man in Maharashtra. For some time he was a minister of the central government also. The text of a few letters exchanged with him follow.

17 April 1957

My dear Hon. Patil,

I was very happy to learn from the papers about your appointment as Minister for Irrigation and Power, Government of India. Kindly accept my heartiest congratulations on the meritorious recognition which you so richly deserved. I am sure the Union Cabinet will be richer by having a person of your calibre and vast experience.

With kindest regards,

Yours sincerely,
K.K. Birla

18 October 1958

My dear Hon. Patil,

We have opened a Gliding Club at Pilani. Pilani, as you know, has become an educational centre and this is probably the only club in India where students have facilities of learning gliding. In course of time our intention is to make it a full-fledged Flying Club.

Although the Club has started functioning, we have not as yet had the official opening ceremony performed. Now-a-days, it has become customary to have the opening ceremony performed after a beginning has been made so that on the formal occasion one could see something. I am happy to inform you that very satisfactory progress has been made at Pilani and we would now like to have the opening ceremony performed by you. I shall be grateful for your acceptance.

At present the college is closed owing to holidays. November and December are busy months for the students owing to the proximity of the exams. I am, therefore, proposing to have the ceremony some time in January. The exact date we could decide later to suit your convenience. I shall be grateful for your consent.

With kindest regards,

Yours sincerely
K.K. Birla

27 October 1958

Mr dear K.K. Birla,

I have your letter of 18th October, 1958. As desired by you I shall be glad to perform the opening ceremony of the Gliding Club at Pilani in January next on a date convenient to both of us.

I hope this will find you in the best of health and cheer.

With kindest personal regards,

Yours sincerely,
S.K. Patil

Note: He made a brilliant speech at BITS, Pilani.

25 April 1962

My dear K.K.

I am overwhelmed by the warmth of your congratulatory message. I look upon my re-appointment as Minister for Food and Agriculture as one more opportunity to serve my country in a very vital sphere. In this great task I need the blessings and goodwill of friends and well-wishers like yourself.

I shall ever remain grateful to you for your increasing kindness and affection.

With my kindest personal regards,

Yours sincerely,
S.K. Patil

Justice S.C. Lahiri

Here is a letter that I sent to Justice S.C. Lahiri as the Chief Justice of Calcutta High Court along with his reply, when I was the sheriff of Calcutta.

22 May 1961

My dear Justice Lahiri,

I was very happy to learn that you are taking over as Governor of West Bengal in the absence of Miss Padmaja Naidu. Kindly accept my respectful felicitations.

With kindest regards,

Yours sincerely,
K.K. Birla

25 May 1961

My dear Sheriff,

Many thanks for your letter dated the 22nd May, 1961 and the congratulations contained therein on my appointment to act as the Governor of West Bengal during the absence on leave of Shrimati Padmaja Naidu. I hope and pray that it will be given to me to perform my duties to the satisfaction of all.

I am taking this opportunity for conveying to you my thanks for the Dinner you gave last Friday and for the kindness shown to my colleagues and myself.

Thanking you again,

Yours sincerely,
S.C. Lahiri

Sankar Banerjee

Sankar Banerjee was a noted lawyer. He was a good friend of mine. I am reproducing below a copy of his letter dated 27th June 1961 written to me as the sheriff of Calcutta.

27 June 1961

My dear Shri Birla,
I have been requested by some of the Ministers to request you to pay some money to the heirs of the late Shri Amarendra Lal Das Sharma. You will agree with me that it was a most unfortunate case. The deceased has left two unmarried sisters who were dependant on him. If he had lived he would have seen them married; but his untimely death has caused this terrific embarrassment. My Hon'ble friend, Shri Prafulla Chandra Sen, I understand, has also requested you to pay not by way of compensation, but by way of charity for which you and your family are well-known. A sum of Rs 15,000/- (Fifteen Thousand Rupees) will not affect Texmaco in the slightest. May I request you to give the matter your kind consideration.

Yours sincerely
S. Banerji

Kamalnayan Bajaj

He was the son of Shri Jamnalal Bajaj and father of Rahul Bajaj. I was very close to him. A letter written by him, given here, will be of interest.

Camp: New Delhi,
26 March 1957

My dear Krishna Kumarji,
I thank you very much for your heartiest congratulations and good wishes on my election to the Lok Sabha. This has been possible because the people held father in great esteem and affection. They practically overwhelmed me and I feel my responsibility has increased manifold on that account. I need the good wishes of the friends circle to be able to discharge my duties in the Lok Sabha for the task ahead of me.

With kindest regards,

Yours sincerely,
Kamalnayan Bajaj

C.C. Desai

C.C. Desai was an ICS officer and was very brilliant. In course of time he became the Secretary of several ministries. After his retirement he became high commissioner of India in Pakistan. Whenever he came to Kolkata he used to stay with me. I quote below two letters he sent me.

Karachi,
11 March 1957

My dear K.K.,
Naumann came to see me on Saturday and had a long talk. He is coming to Calcutta shortly and will, of course, call on you. He has been very helpful in the matter of import license for some of the essential machinery for the Sutlej Cotton Mills at Okara and I am sure this could not have been done but for his persistence, influence and perseverance. I have also been talking to him about possible line of expansion by you in Pakistan. I feel that there is very great scope here and that you should not be deterred either by the political atmosphere or by the discriminatory practices which sometimes one sees in this country. I have little doubt that all this is a passing phase and that our relations must become normal in due course and that we would not be the despised people in Pakistan as perhaps we are today. In any case you have a problem of surplus capital which also

requires practical attention. I understand that there is the possibility of a licence being given for a rayon mill of 200 looms in East Pakistan which should be entirely within your range and experience. The capital required will be small and this would give you a good foot-hold for industrial expansion in East Pakistan. Whatever may be the feeling in West Pakistan we would always be met with friendly cooperation in East Pakistan. There would be no difficulty in transferring capital from Lahore to Dacca, both places being in the same country. I would, therefore, earnestly urge you to accept this proposal and put in an application for erecting a rayon mill of 200 looms at a convenient place in East Pakistan. Then there also is a possibility of a licence for a sugar mill—one in Khairpur in West Pakistan and one at Comilla in East Pakistan. This again is in your personal line and I would ask you to consider it seriously. I am not suggesting either any export of capital from India to finance these schemes or reduction in the remittance from Pakistan to India by way of dividends on the capital already employed. What I am suggesting is merely the employment of surplus capital and so there will be no financial disability or objection. While I am here I would also do my best to see that these licenses are given to the Sutlej Cotton Mills. We are also trying for additional licenses to make the Okara plant balanced and these efforts would continue.

2. In this connection I would also like to bring to your notice the fact that corruption has become so rampant in Pakistan that a file cannot move from one table to another without consideration for the person concerned. It is a situation which you must recognise. I am sure you must be getting the same report from Jajooji. Some discretion should be given to him for expenditure on these purposes. I would speak to you more when we meet.

3. Lastly Naumann has his father-in-law, Justice Siddiqui, who stays at 28-A Amir Ali Avenue, Calcutta. He is an Indian and has never come to Pakistan. Formerly he was Chairman of the Labour Tribunal and thus he has experience of labour laws and connected matters. Naumann would like and I support that it would be a good thing if you could make use of the special talent and experience of Justice Siddiqui in one of the Birla organizations. You may mention this to G.D. when you meet him next.

4. I was due to come there in the third week of this month but the programe had to be cancelled as the Jarring Mission would be arriving here on the 14th. I have to be here in case I am required

for consultations. I will now make the programme sometime later on when I am free from these entanglements.

5. I asked Jajooji through Shankarlal to send me five books which I require for some confidential work here. I hope he has spoken to you.

6. I am afraid I have written a long letter but I hope you would not mind.

Hope you are keeping fit and all is well.

With kindest regards to you both,

Yours ever,
Chandulal

16 May 1957

My dear K.K.,

This is a note to introduce my friend A.B. Habibullah, who is interested in developing trade between the two countries with particular reference to sugar. He is connected with a firm which has very great influence in the country. They are in a better position to deliver the goods than perhaps any other firm in the country. This would give you an idea of the importance and influence of Mr. Habibullah. I have asked him to stop on the way in Calcutta and have a talk with you about the prospects of export of sugar from India to Pakistan now and in future. I hope you would find time to have a full discussion with him which you can do with absolute confidence.

With kindest regards,

Yours ever,
Chandulal

V.V. Giri

I knew V.V. Giri fairly well. He was a cabinet minister in the central government for a short period and later in August 1969 he became President when the Congress party split. The text of some of the correspondence I had with him is given here.

(Personal)

Governor, Uttar Pradesh,
15 February 1959

My dear Shri Krishna Kumar Birla,
I desire to introduce to you my nephew V.V. Prasad, who has been connected with Journalism during the last sixteen years and is considered very capable in the field in the Delhi circles.

If you give him a chance, he will prove worthy of your confidence, and he can give a very good account of himself and to your entire satisfaction. Other things being equal, you may consider and do what is possible.

With kind regards,

Yours sincerely,
V.V. Giri

30 March 1959

My dear Shri Giri,
I am in receipt of your kind letter dated 15th February. I am sending a copy of your letter to Shri Mulgaonkar, editor of 'Hindustan Times'. I do not know whether there is my suitable vacancy or not. But I am asking Shri Mulgaonkar to look into the matter and do whatever is possible.

With kindest regards,

Yours sincerely,
K.K. Birla

Dr K.N. Katju

Dr K.N. Katju belonged to Uttar Pradesh. A brilliant lawyer, he practised in the Allahabad High Court. He was made Governor of West Bengal and subsequently became chief minister of Madhya Pradesh. Some of the letters I exchanged with him are given here.

(Personal)

9 July 1950

My dear Krishna Kumarji,
You are aware that the United Council of Relief and Welfare of which I am the President has undertaken the responsibility for providing within their limited means relief to the East Bengal refugees and for co-ordinating the activities of the various social welfare organisations working in aid of those refugees. The Council has recently decided to establish work centres for women at various places where there is a concentration of East Bengal refugees with a view to enabling refugee women to earn a living by sewing and spinning work. A large number of women refugees has already been engaged in preparing children's garments out of the donations of cloth received by the Council and they are supplied with sewing machines free of cost for this purpose. The refugee women so employed get their wages from the United Council of Relief and Welfare and the garments prepared by them are distributed by the Council to refugee children as free gifts. This scheme is working very satisfactorily and it is proposed to extend it to provide work to a larger number of refugee women. The U.C.R.W. therefore requires a large number of sewing machines for free distribution to groups of refugee women working in various centres and it has mainly to depend for this purpose on gifts from the generous public. I hope that the ladies of Birla family who are well-known for their philanthropic activities will extend their cooperation to the U.C.R.W. in this noble endeavour and generously contribute a large number of sewing machines for distribution to refugee women. I also hope that they would also take personal interest in this great humanitarian work.
   With kindest regards,

Yours very sincerely,
K.N. Katju

15 July 1950

My dear Shri Katjuji,
I am in receipt of your kind letter dated, 9th July. We ourselves, as a matter of fact, were thinking of donating sewing machines for

the women refugees. I have now the utmost pleasure in sending to Your Excellence a cheque of Rs 5,000/- herewith. The sewing machines as desired may be purchased out of this amount.

With kindest regards,

Yours sincerely,
K.K. Birla

19 July 1950

My dear Krishna Kumarji,

Thank you very much for your letter of the 15th instant. I am very grateful indeed for your generous gift of Rs 5,000/- to the U.C.R.W. for the purchase of sewing machines and their distribution to needy women. I hope you are well.

With kind regards,

Yours very sincerely,
K.N. Katju

Chief Minister, Madhya Pradesh,
6 October 1960

My dear Krishna Kumarji,

Thank you very much for your kind letter dated the 29th September. I am so happy to know that you have successfully and safely returned from your pilgrimage to Amarnath. This visit shall ever remain a land-mark in your own history.

I do not know how to thank you for your kindly remembering me when you were at Amarnath and for your kindly offering flowers on my behalf. May God bless you.

May I expect you to visit Bhopal in the near future? There is so much to talk about between us.

With kind regards,

Yours sincerely,
K.N. Katju

Note: He was then chief minister of Madhya Pradesh.

Srikrishna Sinha

I knew Srikrishna Sinha, who became chief minister of Bihar after independence, fairly well. There were two top leaders in Bihar in those days—Srikrishna Sinha—called Sri Babu, who was a Bhoomihar, and Anugrah Narain Sinha, called Anugrah Babu, who was a Rajput. I was very close to Anugrah Babu. We had a paper in Patna called the *Searchlight*. This paper was started by Dr Rajendra Prasad and some other leaders in pre-independence Bihar. As the paper was losing money heavily, Rajendra Babu requested father to take it over. Hence, as requested by Rajendra Babu, it was taken over by us. In August 1986, the *Searchlight* was taken over by the *Hindustan Times*. It was then called 'Hindustan Times, Patna Edition'.

In those days the editor of the *Searchlight* was a man called M.S.M. Sharma. He was a strong writer and a very honest journalist. He was a great critic of Sri Babu. Sri Babu often complained against him to me. In response to his complaints I had discussions with Sharma several times. After making independent enquiries I was satisfied that the views taken by Sharma on various matters which offended the chief minister were not wrong. Sri Babu, along with his right-hand man called Mahesh Babu, many times approached me to change the policy of the *Searchlight*. I explained to them that their complaint was not against the policy of the *Searchlight* but against the articles that the *Searchlight* wrote against the chief minister. I told them that I found the articles, though critical of him, to be perfectly in order.

The text of some interesting letters is given below.

29 July/1 August 1958

My dear Krishna Kumarji,
I am in receipt of your letter dated the 15th July. I am glad to hear that you have come from abroad. I too feel that the annual conference referred to in your letter serves very useful purpose. I will request Secretary, Industries, to fix a date for holding the conference.

Yours sincerely,
S.K. Sinha

13 November 1958

My dear Srikrishna Babu,

The allocation of areas for the supply of cane to the various sugar mills in Bihar was, as usual, made several months back. Now, when the season is about to start, the Central Sugar Company, Samastipur, are understood to be trying indirectly to have their area enlarged at the cost of one of our mills, namely, the New India Sugar Mills, Hassanpur. This indirect way of approach by Samastipur Mills has caused anxiety to our mills and I thought of writing to you in this connection. I hope you will please not mind this encroachment upon your valuable time.

The sugarcane crop in District Darbhanga, which was quite poor last season, is expected to be still poorer in the coming season due to draught conditions. As an index of the deterioration of the crop, I give below the quantities of cane which our New India Sugar Mills, situated in that district, have received:-

Crushing Season	*Quantity of cane received (in lac mds)*
1956–57	51.5
1957–58	36.9
1958–59	30.0 (expected)

The other mills in the district are also being similarly affected. But in the case of the Central Sugar Company, Samastipur, which are situated adjacent to Hasanpur, there have been additional causes for which these mills are themselves responsible. These mills, unlike Hasanpur, have not helped their cane growers adequately in matters like the supply of seed and manure, sinking of tubewells and purchase of tractors etc. Last year they did not even pay the cane price timely. As a result of this unhelpful attitude, the cultivation in Samstipur area seems to have gone down to a greater extent than in the areas of other mills. But instead of revising their policy and helping the growers to cultivate more cane, the Samastipur mills are trying to make up the shortage in unfair manner. It is reported that they are bringing pressure on the cane department to extend their area at the expense of Hasanpur. To be more exact, they want to oust Hasanpur from a cane purchasing centre named

Narhan which the latter have been operating for the past more than 20 years. I am quite confident that no injustice of that sort will be done to Hasanpur but still I thought it would be better to bring relevant facts about this station to your kind notice. These facts are:–

(1) Narhan is situated on the Railway line between Hasanpur and Samastipur. It is 13 miles from Hasanpur and 15 miles from Samastipur. It is thus closer to Hasanpur than to Samastipur, and falls within the reserved area for Hasanpur.

(2) All stations between Hasanpur and Narhan are operated exclusively by Hasanpur. Similarly all stations between Narhan and Samastipur are operated exclusively by Samastipur. Narhan, however, has been operated by both the mills from the very beginning. Hasanpur has operated this station regularly from 1936-37 with a temporary break of five seasons namely 1942-43 to 1946-47 due to War Emergency.

(3) The reservation of areas for the coming season was announced in July 1958 and so far as Narhan is concerned, the existing position was maintained. Samastipur did not file any appeal against the reservation decisions in the normal way which the rules allow within a time limit of one month. And now, I understand, they are trying to get the whole Narhan area indirectly by bringing undue pressure at the highest level.

(4) The only plea which Samastipur could advance for encroaching on Hasanpur's area is shortage of cane. But shortage of cane affects Hasanpur also. In fact it will hit Hasanpur more acutely because at the suggestion of the Central and State Governments, these mills are expanding their capacity by 50% at an expense of something like Rs 20 lacs. Hasanpur mills have already been bringing cane from distances upto 100 miles and they hoped that in order to meet their increased capacity, they would be assigned a larger area including exclusive use of Narhan station. Nothing has come out of representations made by Hasanpur in this behalf. On the other hand they now face the risk of having even their existing area curtailed to satisfy Samastipur. The latter, as I have pointed out above, are themselves largely responsible for the shortage of cane in their area. At present they draw cane only from areas upto 20 miles distant as against 100 miles of Hasanpur. There is, therefore no reason why they should not bring cane from longer distances as Hasanpur is doing instead of wanting an unfair

slice out of Hasanpur's already meager supplies. Moreover, if they had any good grounds, they should have filed a legal appeal within a month of the order announcing reservations.

I do hope that Hasanpur's apprehensions are baseless. However, if by any chance any question does arise, I trust the above facts would enable a just decision to be taken.

Hoping to be excused for the trouble and with kindest regards,

Yours sincerely,

K.K. Birla

15 November 1958

My dear Krishna Kumarji

May I thank you for the magnificent support you gave to the Bihar State Development Loan, 1970 which was over-subscribed within a few hours of its issue? We are pleased to note that the United Commercial Bank Ltd, made the biggest subscription to this issue, namely, Rs 55 lakhs. Kindly convey my gratefulness to Shri G.D. Birla also.

Yours sincerely,

S.K. Sinha

Note: Father was then the chairman of United Commercial Bank, Ltd.

8 January 1959

My dear Shri Krishna Babu,

As you are well aware, the Sugar Industry in Bihar suffers from a disadvantage of lack of good roads around the factories. The benefits arising out of development of such roads cannot be over-emphasized. If cane-growers have the benefit of good roads, they can bring their cane to the factories conveniently and thus help in increasing the production of sugar which can be exported to earn valuable foreign exchange. It is a well known fact that in the absence of good roads, sugarcane from many places does not reach the factories and growers have either to convert it into 'gur' or to use it as fodder for cattle.

With a view to remove these difficulties, the Government of India formulated a scheme for road development in sugar factory areas during the Second Five Year Plan. Under this scheme, one-third of the cost of construction of pucca roads is to be met by the Central Government, one-third by the State Government and the balance by the factories concerned and the growers. The schemes received a good response.

Some time back, a member factory informed the Indian Sugar Mills Association that the contributions made by them under the road development scheme were not being allowed as expenses for income tax purposes by the income tax authorities. The Indian Sugar Mills Association then took up the matter with the Central Board of Revenue and represented that these contributions should be treated as an item of expenditure. Unfortunately this request has been turned down by the Central Board of Revenue. The latter, however, have offered to treat such contributions as donations under Section 15B of the Income Tax Act. As, however, there is a limit on the amount of donations by a Company for the purposes of income tax and as besides every factory is required to give some donations or the other, this attitude on the part of the Central Board of Revenue will hardly give any relief. Under the circumstances the scheme of road construction is likely to receive a setback.

The Industry shall be grateful if you could kindly take up the matter with Central Board of Revenue so that the contributions made by the factories under the road development scheme may be allowed as expenditure for income tax purposes.

With kindest regards,

Yours sincerely,
K.K. Birla

January 1959

Dear Krishna Kumarji,
I have your letter of January 8 regarding the income tax on contributions made by the sugar factories under the road development scheme. I shall see what can be done in the matter.

Yours sincerely,
S.K. Sinha

7 August 1960

My dear Birlaji,
As in the last year, we are going in for a loan of Rs 3 crores
subscription to which opens on the 29th August 1960. You are aware
of the backwardness of my State and how important it is for us to
fulfill the development plan allotted to us. This year happens to be
the last of the Second Five Year Plan period and we have to finance
a development programme of about Rs 47 crores so as to be able to
execute the Second Five Year Plan for this State fully. Bulk of the
expenditure is on productive and remunerative schemes. You have
shown great interest in the development of this State and subscribed
to its loans in the past. May I request you to do so more generously
in the current year when we are in greater need of funds to execute
a larger development Plan than in any preceding year?

Yours sincerely,
S.K. Sinha

26 September 1960

My dear Birlaji,
May I thank you for the contribution of Rs 5 lakhs made by the
United Commercial Bank Ltd., towards the Bihar State Development
Loan, 1969? Please convey my thanks to Shri G.D. Birla also.

Yours sincerely,
S.K. Sinha

Jagjivan Ram

I was very close to Jagjivan Babu. There are a large number of letters
with me from Jagjivan Babu and from me to him. I am giving here only
some which make interesting reading.

Minister for Railways,
New Delhi
9 December 1957

My dear Krishna Kumar,
This is just to inform you that I shall be reaching Calcutta on the

13th December at 10.00 a.m. by Kalka-Howrah Mail and leaving for Muri on the 15th by Ranchi Express at 8.40 p.m., as per copy of my tour programme attached.

Hoping to meet you,

Yours sincerely,
Jagjivan Ram

23 December 1958

My dear Shri Jagjivan Ramji,

I am in receipt of your kind letter dated 19th December. I am glad to learn that you are coming to Calcutta on Monday the 29th December by Kalka Mail and are leaving for Madras on Tuesday the 30th December by plane.

I believe you will be staying at the Government House. I shall be grateful if you could kindly let me know what time will suit you so that I could come and call on you. Any time in the afternoon will suit me.

I shall also try to come to the station, but I have not been keeping very good health. As a result of that I am not even coming to the office before 12-30 or 1-00 p.m. In case, therefore, I cannot come to the station, I hope you will very kindly excuse me.

With kindest regards,

Yours sincerely,
K.K. Birla

Maharaja of Gwalior

With the princely house of the Scindias we have had a very long association. Elsewhere in this autobiography I have described in some detail about our connection with them. Our relationship with the house of the Scindias is from 1920 or so. Here is one letter which makes interesting reading.

No.789

H. H. The Maharaja Scindia of Gwalior

Jai Vilas,
Gwalior.

8th November, '57.

My dear Mr. Birla

Many thanks for your letter dated the 2nd November, 1957.

I feel grateful for your kindly according the necessary facilities for the training of Students of the Madhav Engineering College, in the workshop of Central India Machinary Manufacturing Co.,Ltd., Birla Nagar, Gwalior.

With kind regards.

Yours Sincerely

MSSi

Shri K. Kumar Birla,
8, India Exchange Place,
CALCUTTA 1.

Sri Prakasa

Born in Varanasi, Sri Prakasa-ji was a product of the freedom movement. Son of an illustrious father—Dr Bhagwan Das, a well-known philosopher and public leader—Sri Prakasa-ji hailed from the Sah family who had been bankers of the East India Company since the middle of the eighteenth century.

When father contested the election for the Central Legislative Assembly in 1927 the contest was between him and Sri Prakasa-ji. Father won the election but that did not cause any animosity between Sri Prakasa-ji and our family. He remained a family friend throughout his life. Sri Prakasa-ji was a man of great character and humility and also had a great sense of humour. Some of my correspondence with him is provided here.

(Personal)

Governor of Bombay,
18 March 1957

My dear Krishna Kumarji,

I duly received your kind letter of March 7 regarding your visit to Bombay and thank you for the same. I must confess I felt a little hurt when you wrote that it would not be fair to me if people like you try to force themselves on me. I fear I cannot include you or any member of your great family among those whom you class as 'people like me', that is yourself. The great kindness and courtesy that I have always received from every member of the family must put you all in a class apart at least so far as I am concerned.

I must therefore request you kindly to let me know in good time when you should be visiting Bombay; and it will be my business to make sure that I do not miss you again. I feel very disappointed that I should have done so last time. I know all members of your family very well indeed, and it is a pity that I have met you only on one or two occasions.

I recollect the very spirited fight you put up against heavy odds in a committee in Delhi presided over by Rajaji at which I was present as Commerce Minister regarding ring frames. I struggled hard for that myself as I did not understand why ring frames that you manufactured at Rs 17,000/- should not be preferred to foreign ones which cost Rs 25,000/-. I was very angry with Bombay industrialists when they wanted me to remove all embargo from imports of ring frames saying that ones that were manufactured by you, were not suitable.

All that is now old story, I however recollect it very vividly, I understand that the trouble is now over, and that your ring frames are in great demand now as they deserve to be. I believe they are manufactured at Gwalior in one of your factories. I think I was shown that, but my memory is now getting very foggy owing to my recent sorrow, and I may be making a mistake.

I am sorry that the climate of Bombay does not suit me. I am actually writing this from Ahmedabad which is hot & dry and is more suitable for my health than humid and clammy Bombay. I am however now nearly 67 years of age, and my health does not deserve much consideration. I am thankful to you all the same for your kind concern and enquiry. My recent tragic bereavement has completely broken me.

Hoping all is well,
I am,
With kind regards,

Yours sincerely,
Sri Prakasa

19 September 1958

My dear Sri Prakasaji,
I was extremely shocked to learn today about the sad demise of your revered father. In his death, the country has lost a great scholar and a great son. On this sad occasion, please accept my heart-felt condolences.

With kind regards,

Yours sincerely,
K.K. Birla

29 October 1958

My dear Krishna Kumarji
On behalf of my beloved mother, my brother Chandra Bhal, myself and other members of the family, I express to you our deep gratitude for the message of sympathy and condolence that you have been good enough to send on the sad occasion of the passing away of my revered father. Doubtless an extraordinary person has left the stage. For me, a great light has been extinguished for ever. At this solemn moment, what more can I write?

Innumerable men and women from all over the land have expressed their affection and sympathy for me and my family. I may only hope that our countrymen will take lessons from the life and teachings of my father, and that the members of my family and myself would ever prove worthy of your confidence and favour.

In deep gratitude,

Yours sincerely,
Sri Prakasa

H.N. Bahuguna

H.N. Bahuguna who hailed from the present Uttaranchal was a very able man. He was for some years a cabinet minister in the Government of India and was also the chief minister of Uttar Pradesh. When I was put up by Indira Gandhi and Sanjay to contest for the Rajya Sabha elections from UP in 1974, it was Bahuguna who manipulated the voting and infused an open voting which was against the Constitution. That led to my defeat. Bahuguna was then a Congress [I] chief minister. As a result of this he completely lost the trust of Indira Gandhi and Sanjay. Some letters that were exchanged with him are reproduced below.

Lucknow,
21 November 1961

My dear Sri K.K.

I am sorry to bother you about the applicant-Sri Ganga Prasad Upadhyaya in whom I am greatly interested. The boy is M.A. (Sociology) and M.S.W. with specialization in Labour. He is well qualified for posts concerning Labour, and I shall be obliged if you are good enough to fix him up in any suitable job in your great Organisation.

I hope you are keeping fit.

With regards,

Yours sincerely,
H.N. Bahuguna

Lucknow,
30 May 1962

My dear Sri K.K.

I am proposing to come to Calcutta in connection with the meeting of the INTUC. I will reach there by plane from Delhi on June 7, 1962, at 9-45 a. m. and will leave for Lucknow by 5 Up Howrah-Amritsar Mail on June 10, 1962. I wonder if it will be possible for me to meet you there, for I think you must be recessing in some hill stations. On reaching Calcutta I shall contact you, if you happen to be in station.

With regards,

Yours sincerely,
H.N. Bahuguna

Sampurnanand

Sampurnanand-ji was an eminent figure in Uttar Pradesh. He was a great thinker, able administrator, a scholar of great merit and was a man with a socialist bent of mind. Sampurnanand-ji wrote books on Indian philosophy and culture and also several books on history, astrology, socialism and other subjects.

Sampurnanand-ji was an active member of the Congress party of U.P. He was a man of great integrity and moral character. He was fearless and sometimes when he differed with Pandit Jawaharlal Nehru, he would write to him about it. He came from a respectable Kayastha family and so was addressed as Babu Sampurnanand-ji. After independence, he was a minister in the government of Uttar Pradesh and later became its chief minister.

Given here is some correspondence I had with him which will be found to be interesting.

Chief Minister, Uttar Pradesh
30 October 1958

My dear Krishna Kumarji,
I understand that some reorganization of the affairs of the 'Hindustan Times' is soon going to take place and that you are now looking after the matter. In this connection I should like to bring to your notice the case of Sri Kapil Varma. He has been in journalism for about ten years now. During all this time he has been in charge of the Lucknow office of the Amrita Bazar Patrika and the group of papers linked with it. He is looking not only after the News but the Business Section also. During the last three years he has been acting off and on for the 'Statesman' as well. During these years he has covered several sessions of the Congress and has been to Europe as a Leader of the Youth Movement. In my opinion he is a thoroughly reliable youngman and a journalist

who can be trusted to be loyal to his paper and to uphold the high traditions of the profession. His relations with the Government have been excellent during all this time and his comments have always been characterised by sympathetic understanding of the problems of the State.

If you should happen to be on the look-out for a good journalist whom you could put in charge of your Lucknow office of 'Hindustan Times', I can safely recommend the name of Sri Kapil Verma. I am sure, he will be happy to contact you whenever you should so desire.

Yours sincerely,
Sampurnanand

3 November 1958

My dear Shri Sampurnanandji,
I am in receipt of your kind letter dated 30th October. Regarding Shri Kapil Verma, I am making enquiries from Shri Durgadas, the Chief Editor of 'Hindustan Times,' whether he needs some one at Lucknow. You may kindly be rest assured that in case we did need somebody for Lucknow, we shall certainly try out Shri Kapil Verma. It will, however, facilitate matters if you could kindly ask Shri Verma to send me a letter mentioning his qualifications and past experience etc.

It is kind of you to have written to me.

With kindest regards,

Yours sincerely,
K.K. Birla

22 November 1958

My dear Shri Babuji,
You may kindly recollect that I had spoken to you about the desperate cane position of Hargaon sugar mills and had sent a note to Shri Kamlapatiji and Gautamji about the same. The reservation order which has been issued has come as a big surprise to me. Instead of providing any relief to Hargaon sugar mills in its desperate cane position, the order has further cut the allotment of

cane to this factory. I sincerely feel that a very grave injustice has been done by this order to Hargaon sugar mills. It is really impossible to understand the basis of such an order. I do not know whether it is the result of some big error or any spirit of vindictiveness against us. I am asking the management of Hargaon sugar mills to file an appeal against this order officially. But I request you to kindly look into the matter personally so that you may know the extent of hardship which will be caused to Hargaon sugar mills and may be able to secure fair play for them.

With kindest regards,

Yours sincerely,
K.K. Birla

20 February 1959

My dear Shri Babuji,

I have just learnt about your kind decision in the matter of Pradhan cane. It has been a great relief to me and I have been so much moved sentimentally that I cannot restrain myself from expressing my gratitude to you for the same. Pradhan and Deokali are vital for the existence of Hargaon sugar mills and this period of suspense had been of extreme anxiety to me. I am glad that you have very kindly gone through the case yourself and are now satisfied about our representations. You must have also kindly noted that our assessment of Hargaon and Gola cane position was accurate and that Hargaon had started suffering from cane shortage pending your final decision while Gola had still plenty of cane in hand.

Thanking you again for your kind decision and the trouble you have taken into the matter.

I remain,

With kindest regards,

Yours sincerely,
K.K. Birla

6 May 1959

My dear Krishna Kumarji,

There is a very important matter to which I must draw your

attention. I wonder if you have noticed the policy consistently adopted by the Hindustan Times towards me. Its correspondent in Lucknow is a person who takes a pleasure in inventing news deprecatory of me and the present U.P. Government and applauding the words and activities of those who are at present opposing us in the field of U.P. politics. Wrong and distorted news are published under big headlines. I do not know how far you are in a position to influence the editorial policy of the Paper. If you think you are not in a position, or do not wish to take any effective action, I would beg you not to do anything. The result of an ineffective move would be that your correspondent here would come to know about it and introduce more bitterness in what he writes. The editor would do likewise.

Yours sincerely,
Sampurnanand

(Personal & Confidental)

9 May 1959

My dear Babuji,
I am in receipt of your kind letter dated 6th May. I feel very much distressed to note what you write regarding the attitude of the correspondent of the Hindustan Times at Lucknow towards you. I, as a rule, do not at all interfere with the day to day policy of the paper. But here it is not a case of interfering with the Editor. This is a case of dealing with the correspondent who as you mention is guilty of supplying distorted versions. I would not only draw the attention of the Editor towards it but would also press him to see that a stop is immediately put to all such matters. I shall, however, be grateful if you could kindly send me a few cuttings so that I could point the same out to the Editor. The Editor at present is Mr. S. Mulgaonkar. Durga Das, who is the Chief Editor, is shortly retiring. Please, however, keep this information confidential for the time being.

I am grateful to you for having drawn my attention to this matter. With kindest regards,

Yours sincerely,
K.K. Birla

(Confidental)

18 May 1959

My dear Krishna Kumarji,

I have received your letter of the 9th of May. In return I would suggest you to ask your Public Relations Officer to turn to the issue of the Hindustan Times for the last four months. Wherever news have been given as coming from the Paper's special correspondent, they have given a distorted version of the facts boosting the opponents of Government and decrying the members of Government, particularly myself. Every effort has been made to paint those resigning from the Government as models of virtue. There is sometimes a funny aspect of these matters which escapes your correspondent. Sri Charan Singh who resigned about a month ago is going about making a public complaint of the fact that a large proportion of the electricity generated at the Rihand Dam site is being given to the Birlas. Your correspondent forgets that he is himself a Birla employee and records such speeches and statements under prominent headlines. I cannot blame the correspondent alone. He does these things because he is sure that for some reason or other the editor likes such stuff and will publish it unquestioningly. There is a gentleman named Sharma on the staff of the Paper in Delhi. He occupies some important position on the editorial staff. Pantji spoke to him once or twice, pointing out how unfair the attitude of the Paper has been all through. Either Sharma did not care to attach any weight to Pantji's words or he is himself not influential enough to do anything. As I said in my first letter, if it is embarrassing for you to take any effective step by intervening in the Paper's editorial policies, you may kindly ignore my letter. I am quite capable of fighting on this newspaper front if the necessity is forced upon me.

Yours sincerely,
Sampurnanand

3 June 1959

My dear Shri Babuji,

I am in receipt of your kind letter dated 18th May. The Special Correspondent of Hindustan Times at Lucknow is a man called P.

Chakravarty. I am happy to inform you that the editor has decided to recall him. We are sending some other person to Lucknow with strict instructions that he should merely do the news reporting and should not view anything with coloured glasses. I hope with the new arrangement you will have no cause for any complaint.

Regarding the man called Sharma, I have made enquiries about him. There is only one man on the editorial staff of Hindustan Times with this name. His full name is Satyanarayan Sharma and he is a sub-editor cum reporter. Our confidential report about him is not very complimentary to him. But he is holding such a junior post that I do not think he could really influence our Lucknow correspondent. Nor do I think this man has come in touch with Pantji. I am, however, making further enquiries about him and would write to you.

I would hasten to correct your impression about the editor. As yet the Chief Editor was Durga Das. He is retiring shortly and is even now out of India. The entire responsibility, therefore, is being shouldered by Shri S. Mulgaonkar whose designation is Editor and who after the retirement of Durga Das will accept the responsibility of the Chief Editor. Mulgaonkar is a straightforward and honest man. He has no axe of his own to grind in running you down. Probably when you mentioned that the editor was taking sides, you had Durga Das in view. I did not know even about Durga Das having taken sides. But now that he is retiring, I hope you will have no complaint against Hindustan Times on that score.

With kindest regards,

Yours sincerely,
K.K. Birla

3 December 1960

My dear Shri Babuji,

I was watching with great concern the political controversy which has been going on in U.P. for some time past and which has now culminated in your resignation. The news of your retirement from active politics is most unhappy as the country can ill afford to lose the guidance of a leader of your eminence and calibre. During my twenty years' association with you, you always extended to me the utmost courtesy for which I am indeed very grateful to you. I do hope that in future also I shall continue to have the privilege of your scholarly guidance and advice.

With kindest regards,

Yours sincerely,
K.K. Birla

6 December 1960

My dear Krishna Kumarji,

I am to thank you for your kind letter. There is only one regret which I have felt in all this episode. Except for one leading article, the attitude of the Hindustan Times has been simply venomous. For one reason or other, everything that it wrote and the way in which it displayed the news, falsifying and distorting them, made it appear as if it were a personal vendetta against me. This surprised everyone. The *badnami* which I had voluntarily invited upon myself when the power contract with your Firm was being negotiated merited more gentlemanly conduct. However, I am not complaining. I am simply bringing the facts to your notice.

Yours sincerely,
Sampurnanand

10 December 1960

My dear Shri Babuji,

I am in receipt of your kind letter dated 6th December. If the Hindustan Times has falsified and distorted the news, I shall feel extremely grieved. I read the Hindustan Times quite regularly. Generally, I go through the editorials and a few features like 'National Affairs', 'Economic Affairs', etc. But I confess I do not go through the dispatches received from state capitals. As far as the authorities are concerned, one of them was rather strong. But, then, in another editorial the paper commented adversely on Chandra Bhanuji also. The editorial which I am referring to had commented on the delay which occurred in your resignation after your repeated offers of resigning before the P.C.C. election. Personally I thought that the editorial was somewhat strong. But the editor, obviously, seems to have thought otherwise. I am, in any case, writing to Mulgaonkar and shall let you know what his views are in the matter.

We are extremely grateful to you for the way in which you defended the agreement regarding power supply to our aluminium factory. The stand taken by you was the correct stand and my impression is that you won the esteem of all right-thinking people by that attitude.

With kindest regards,

Yours sincerely,
K.K. Birla

3 April 1962

My dear Shri Babuji,

I was very happy to read from the newspaper about your appointment as the Governor of Rajasthan. Kindly accept my respectful felicitations.

Rajasthan will be truly lucky to have a leader of your eminence and calibre to guide it on the path of prosperity.

With kindest regards,

Yours sincerely,
K.K. Birla

17 April 1962

My dear Krishna Kumarji,

This is a belated acknowledgment of your kind message. Please accept my sincere thanks for the same.

Yours sincerely,
Sampurnanand

Mohanlal Sukhadia

Mohanlal Sukhadia was one of the best chief ministers that Rajasthan has ever had. I reproduce here some of my correspondence with him.

27 October 1958

My dear Shri Sukhadiaji,
I hope you recollect that we have constructed a Ladies hospital at Sardarshahr in memory of my mother who hailed from that place. The hospital has been named after mother. Though the hospital has been functioning for some time now, we have not performed the official opening ceremony as yet. Now-a-days, it has become customary to have the opening ceremony performed after a beginning has been made so that on the formal occasion one could see something. I am happy to inform you that satisfactory progress has been made by this hospital and it is rendering useful service. We would now like to have the opening ceremony performed by you. I shall be grateful for your acceptance. The exact date we would like to have in January or February to suit your convenience. Meanwhile I shall be grateful for your consent.

Thanking you and with kind regards,

Yours sincerely,
K.K. Birla

5 November 1958

My dear Shri Birla,
This is with reference to your letter of the 27th October regarding the opening ceremony of the Women's Hospital at Sardarshahr. I shall be glad to perform the opening ceremony provided some date is fixed in January 1959. I can confirm the date after I hear from you in the matter.

With best wishes,

Yours sincerely,
Mohanlal Sukhadia

16 February 1959

My dear Shri Birla
Thanks for your letter of the 26th January 1959 suggesting early March for the opening ceremony of the Lady Hospital at Sardarshahr. As you know, the Budget session of the Assembly

will be going on and as such if the ceremony of the Hospital is held some time in April, it would suit me better. I hope this would suit you as well.

Hoping to be excused for the delay in reply,

Yours sincerely,
Mohanlal Sukhadia

21 February 1959

My dear Shri Sukhadiaji,
I am in receipt of your kind letter dated 16th February. April in Rajasthan may perhaps become dusty. Although April would suit me very well, perhaps the general show may not be very good in the dusty atmosphere. I think the better course, in the circumstances, would be that the opening ceremony be postponed till July. If you approve of this, we could fix the exact date after some time. Kindly let me have your views.

With kind regards,

Yours sincerely,
K.K. Birla

2 March 1959

My dear Birlaji,
Thanks for your letter dated the 21st February, 1959.

As suggested by you, we can have the function some-time in July. You can let me know in due course the date that might suit you.

With kind regards,

Yours sincerely,
Mohanlal Sukhadia

30 March 1962

My dear Shri Sukhadiaji,
I am writing this letter to you regarding the Women's Hospital built by us at Sardarshahr. I hope you will recollect about it, since

I had sought your assistance from time to time in that regard. After completing the construction work of the Hospital, we had given charge of it to the Government of Rajasthan. This was in terms of our agreement with them. The Hospital is, therefore, run at present by the Rajasthan Government.

Off and on I have been receiving adverse opinion about the management and running of this institution. I, however, did not like to bother you, as I was hoping that matters would be set right in course of time.

Shri Rameshwar Tantia also hails, as you may possibly be knowing, from Sardarshahr. He came for dinner with us two days back and he stated that the Hospital was in a deplorable condition. The maintenance was very poor. The glass panes of many of the windows were broken and were unfortunately not got repaired. The Hospital was kept in a very filthy condition and, what is worse, there is neither any nurse nor any lady doctor at present. There was a lady doctor sometime back, but she resigned for some reason or the other. The post has not been filled in since then.

Adjacent to this Hospital, there is a Males' Hospital and the doctor of that Hospital visits the Women's Hospital also for some time. That arrangement, however, is not satisfactory, as what is essential is a whole time lady doctor attached to Women's Hospital.

I hope, therefore, you will very kindly have the matter properly investigated and also issue instructions for the appointment of adequate staff to look after the work of the Women's Hospital.

Rameshwarji also said that, in case the Rajasthan Government finds it difficult to run the Hospital, then a Citizens Committee of Sardarshahr will be prepared to look after the Hospital, provided whatever deficit there may be will be made good by the Government.

I shall be grateful for your comments in the matter.

With kind regards,

Yours sincerely,
K.K. Birla

3 April 1962

My dear Krishna Kumarji,

I have received your letter dated March 30, 1962, regarding the Women's Hospital at Sardarshahr. I am asking the Secretary,

Medical & Health to look into the matter and take necessary action regarding the maintenance and management of the said hospital and posting of a Lady Doctor and other staff.

With kind regards,

Yours sincerely,
Mohanlal Sukhadia

Sir Shri Ram

Sir Shri Ram was a leading industrialist of the country. He was one of the founders of FICCI in the year 1927 along with Sir Purshottam Das Thakurdas and my father Ghanshyamdas Birla. Sir Shri Ram was very fond of me and used to often invite me to dinner. Here are some of the letters I exchanged with him which will be of interest.

Express Telegram

16 April 1951

Was extremely shocked and pained to read Sir Shanker Lal's sad and premature demise. In this bereavement kindly accept best condolences and convey same other members of family.

Krishnakumar Birla

23 April 1951

My dear Krishna Kumarji

Your letter of condolence to hand. Please accept my thanks for the same. God in His mercy is trying me and I request my friends to pray that I may not fail in these difficult trials. His will be done.

With kindest regards,

Yours sincerely,
Shri Ram

13 February 1953

My dear Krishna Kumarji,

As requested personally I would be obliged if you would give me the pleasure of your company at lunch tomorrow at my house at

1.15 p.m. when I have invited a few friends to meet the Governors and Directors of the Central Board of the Reserve Bank.

With kindest regards,

Yours sincerely,
Shri Ram

26 February 1953

My dear Krishan Kumarji,

I am enclosing herewith a copy of a letter of date which we have written to the Texmaco Gwalior Ltd., Gwalior. I will be grateful if you will please ask them to do their best to hurry up the supply.

With kindest regards,

Yours sincerely,
Shri Ram

27 February 1953

My dear Sir Shri Ram,

This is just to express my deep sense of appreciation and cordial thanks for the very sympathetic and rational attitude which you adopted towards the textile machinery industry at the meeting held with the Hon'ble Shri T.T. Krishnamachari on the 24th instant. While some members of the textile industry unfortunately did not take a broad vision and examined the thing from a very narrow angle, it was a matter of particular satisfaction to me that you adopted a very reasonable attitude for which I am thankful to you. I hope that you will kindly continue to have the same attitude towards the textile machinery industry. Any suggestions from you for the betterment will receive the closest attention from me.

With kind regards,

Yours sincerely,
K.K. Birla

Anugrah Narayan Sinha

Anugrah Narayan Sinha was the minister of finance, supply and labour, government of Bihar. He was a very good friend of mine. I have many letters written to me by Anugrah Babu. I am giving below only a few of them.

Patna
7 August 1952

My dear Krishna Kumarji,
I am reluctant to trouble you off and on, but there is no help.

I have received a letter from Abhimanyu in which he says that he has met you and you have very kindly recommended his application for loan to the Board of Directors. His Dacota training will start sometime in September and meanwhile he will be sitting idle. He has also met D.G.C.A. who has advised him to get himself appointed as a supernumerary pilot till the time his training starts. I understand there are several such pilots working under the Bharat Airways. Can you appoint him for the present as a supernumerary pilot. I do not know whether it will be possible for you to do this, but I am just making this suggestion for your most sympathetic consideratio .

With kind ·egards,

Yours sincerely,
Anugrah Narayan Sinha

Patna
8 April 1956

My dear Shri Krishna Kumarji,
I was shocked to receive the news of the demise of your revered and saintly grand-father when I had been to Delhi and I took the earliest opportunity of writing to Shri Brimohanji. I am sure, you will gather sufficient courage and fortitude to bear this irreparable loss.

I received your last letter about Mr. Khanna. I enquired from him and he has no objection to comply with your wishes. I have no objection either. The Secretary had pointed out that a reference might be made to the Government of U.P. but on second thought I find it is not necessary at all. If you want to borrow his services not as an employer but as a private business-man, I see no reason why his services should not be spared. If you still need his services, kindly let me know.

Else alright. With kindest regards,

Yours sincerely,
Anugrah Narayan Sinha

Patna
5 May 1956

My dear Shri Krishna Kumarji

I have your note of May 3. It is true I am busy, but for the 'Searchlight' I shall always find time, especially as the request comes from you.

Yours sincerely,
Anugrah Narayan Sinha

7 May 1956

My dear Shri Anugrah Babu,

I am in receipt of your kind letter dated 5 May. I am glad that you have agreed to become a Director of 'Searchlight'. I am now getting the needful done.

With kindest regards,

Yours sincerely,
K.K. Birla

Patna
21 May 1956

My dear Shri Krishna Kumarji,

Last year I recommended a case to your revered father for providing a seat in the Engineering College, Ranchi, and he was pleased to do so. This year also, in his absence, I am recommending to you another case for nomination for a seat in the College. This boy is also distinctly related to prominent families of Gaya. The name of the boy is Shri Birendra Kumar. He is son of Shri Balbir Prasad, Secretary of the Gaya College.

Hope you are doing well. With kind regards,

Yours Sincerely,
Anugrah Narayan Sinha

Rajkumari Amrit Kaur

Rajkumari Amrit Kaur was a member of the Kapurthala royal family. She was however not a Sikh, but a Christian. She was a minister in Pt Jawaharlal Nehru's cabinet. She was very fond of me and as close as a member of the family. She usually stayed with us whenever she came to Kolkata. Copies of a few letters that I exchanged with her are reproduced here.

(Personal)

Minister for Health,
New Delhi,
18 September 1955

My dear Krishna Kumar,

I am so glad to learn from your letter that both of you have arrived back safely and are well. I shall be very happy to meet you when you come to Delhi, but I am leaving for China on the 27th of this month and therefore there are not very many days left for my stay here before I go.

I am also very grateful to your good father for having so readily agreed to help Col. Pasricha. I can vouch for his integrity and the excellent contacts that he possesses in the Medical World in England. Naturally I do not know the amount of work he would be required to do and how often he would have to come up to London because I believe he has bought a house in the suburbs either in Ealing or just outside. If it is a question of his coming up everyday and putting in some hours of work, I plead for £500 or £400 as you suggest plus some transport allowance. I am sure he will be most grateful for any extra help that he can get.

Love and blessings to you all.

Yours affectionately,
Amrit Kaur

(Personal)

New Delhi,
8 November 1955

My dear Krishna Kumar,

Thank you so much for the cheque for Rs 1,000/-. You are wonderfully kind. I trust that this generous help from you will enable us to put out a good Journal of Sports.

I found my trip to China educative and interesting and I have submitted a long Diary to the Prime Minister about it. When you next come to Delhi and see me you shall have a copy also but I just cannot find time to write my impressions in a letter.

My love and blessings to you all.

Yours affectionately,
Amrit Kaur

(Private & Confidential)

New Delhi,
25 March 1956

चि. कृष्ण कुमार,

I am writing to you for a favour to which I hope it will be possible for you to give the consideration that it merits.

The N.S.C.I. Club House at Delhi is unable to pay its way because during the summer months the bed rooms are not air-conditioned and therefore lie empty whereas the staff cannot be reduced and therefore the overheads remain the same. The Regional Committee is of the opinion that if the 19 or 20 rooms upstairs could be air-conditioned the Club would be fully occupied all the year round and I agree with them. I have had an estimate made and the cheapest that is available to us is the tender from Spencers which would enable us to have single air-conditioning units whose price and installation plus some ducts that have to be laid on would come to a total of Rs 50,000/-. Now the question arises as to how we are to find the money. My request therefore to you is to be good enough to consider favourably the loan of Rs 50,000/- straightaway which the Club is fairly sure of being able to return to you in five years at the rate of Rs 10,000/- per annum. In the meantime, if by any chance my efforts at raising some money for the club succeed we may be able to repay you even earlier. As the installation should be put in at once I shall be very grateful for an early reply from you.

I do hope you have good news from your dear father and that he has benefited by the change to Europe and later to the U.S.A. I myself will be going to the U.S.A. for a month or six weeks from last weak of May and if by chance he is there then I shall hope to meet him.

With my love and blessings to you both and hoping that Manorama is now completely restored and the foot is quite well again.

Yours affectionately,
Amrit Kaur

(Personal)

29 March 1959

My dear Rajkumariji,
Thanks for your kind letter dated 25th March. I am sorry to note what you write about the N.S.C.I. Club. I shall try to arrange a loan to the Club from United Commercial Bank. Could you please let me have a balance sheet of the Club showing its assets and liabilities? I hope the Club has not taken any loan from any other body. I also hope it will be possible for the Club to mortgage its property to the Bank till the amount is returned. This formality is insisted upon by Reserve Bank of India.

Father is at present in Europe. He is going to the States in April and should be back in Europe in first or second week of May. I shall let you know about his programme at the time of your departure.

With kind regards from both of us,

Yours sincerely,
K.K. Birla

4 February 1959

My dear Rajkumariji,
Kindly refer to your letter dated 29th January addressed to father. As you must have seen from Krishnan's letter, he wants some agency

in the South, but I fear there is no agency work which we could offer him. As regards his employment in one of our concerns, since we have no industries in the South, I do not think it will be possible for us to absorb him there. But we can pay him a sum of Rs 150/- to Rs 200/- per month for three years. He will not have any particular work to do and he can devote his time to the improvement of his Tennis. I hope within three years' time, it will be possible for Krishnan to find some suitable work for himself.

Kindly let me have your advice in the matter.

With kindest regards,

Yours sincerely,
K.K. Birla

New Delhi,
9 February 1959

My dear Krishna Kumar,

Thank you for yours of the 4th. I have sent a copy of the same to Krishnan and I hope it may be possible for him to accept this help and, in addition, perhaps get a part-time job in Madras.

I am most grateful,

Love and blessing to you all

Yours affectionately,
Amrit Kaur

Dr S. Radhakrishnan

Dr S. Radhakrishnan was one of the finest philosophers produced by India in modern times. He later became the vice-president of India and was the President from the year 1962 to 1967. I was very close to him. We exchanged many letters. I quote below a few of those which may be of interest.

24 December 1955

My dear Sri Radha Krishnan,

I hope you recollect that father had talked to you regarding the foundation laying ceremony of the Temple which the Birla

Education Trust is building at Pilani. You had very kindly agreed to perform this ceremony. We have got the 'Muhurts' looked into and good 'Muhurt' falls on 27th February. The Muhurt is towards the evening. We could, therefore, go to Pilani on the 27th and return on the 28th. I hope this will suit you. On getting your confirmation I shall make the necessary arrangements at Pilani.

With kind regards,

Yours sincerely,
K.K. Birla

New Delhi,
1 January 1956

Dear Krishna Kumar,

I have your letter of the 24th December, 1955.

As you wish me to be there on the 27th evening, I may leave here after 1 o'clock—as I have to attend the Parliament from 11 to 1—and return next morning leaving there at 7.30 a.m. so as to be present for the Parliament work at 11 o'clock on the 28th Feb.

With all good wishes,

Yours sincerely,
S. Radhakrishnan

T.T. Krishnamachari

T.T. Krishnamachari was a brilliant parliamentarian. He worked in various capacities in the cabinet of Pandit Jawaharlal Nehru. The most important portfolio which he held was the finance ministry. Panditji was very fond of him. He was a great friend of father and had a deep liking for me. A copy of the letter that he wrote to me is given below.

Claridges Hotel,
New Delhi,
18 June 1962

Dear friend,

It was good of you to send me your congratulations and good wishes on my assuming a somewhat nebulous and onerous responsibility in the government of India. I am grateful to you for this indication of your good will towards me.

 With warm regards,

Yours sincerely,

T.T. Krishnamachari

Ashoke Sen

Ashoke Sen was a brilliant lawyer. Later he became the Law Minister of India. I quote one of the letters from him. This may be of interest.

21 May 1962

My dear Krishna Kumar,

You would recall the case of Shri Soumendra Nath Dutta who is the son of a very ordinary employee. Shri Soumendra Nath Dutta wants to get admission into Birla Institute of Technology, 56, B.T.Road. I am enclosing herewith a copy of the letter his father had written to you on the 16th inst. I shall be glad if you could assist the boy in getting admission into the Birla Institute of Technology.

Yours sincerely,

A.K. Sen

Justice H.N. Bhagwati

Justice Bhagwati was a renowned judge of the Supreme Court. Later he became the Chief Justice of India. Following are a few letters I exchanged with him which may be of interest.

16 December 1958

My dear Justice Bhagwati,

Kindly refer to your letter dated 11th December addressed to Father as also Father's reply dated 12th December. I regret I could not write to you earlier as it took me some time to find out from our mills whether any of them had a station-wagon.

 I wanted to place a station-wagon at your disposal as I have found that such cars are always helpful and useful. They can take a lot of luggage and there is also ample seating space. Unfortunately, however, we have no station-wagon available. One of our mills has a station-wagon but it is very old and is not at all reliable. It is as a matter of fact not even in working condition and to make it workable would require atleast one month's time.

We have a Hindustan Utility car but I do not know how far it is dependable for long journeys. I am, however, having the matter investigated by experts. If it is found to be alright, well and good, otherwise I shall place a Studebaker at your disposal.

I have discussed this today with my cousin Girdhar who too will write to you about it. I have also asked Girdhar to consult when you arrive here as to whether you will be free for dinner on 1st evening. On getting your consent, I would like to invite some friends to meet you.

Meanwhile with kindest regards,

Yours sincerely,
K.K. Birla

New Delhi,
17 December 1958

Dear Shri Krishna Kumar,
I am in due receipt of your telegram dated 16th December 1958 to hand this morning, which runs as follows:

'REFCE YOUR LETTER FATHER AM ARRANGING EITHER STUDEBAKER OR HINDUSTAN UTILITY CAR KIND REGARDS —KRISHNA KUMAR'

Many thanks for the same. The programme of our tour has already been sent by me to Shri G.D. Birla. I am also sending a copy of the same to Shri G.P. Birla who had written to me in that behalf. We shall be reaching Howrah by the Kalka-Howrah Mail starting from Delhi at 8.45 a.m. on the morning of Saturday, the 20th December 1958, and reaching there at about 10.50 a.m. on Sunday, the 21st December 1958.

Trusting this finds you all quite okay, and with kind regards,

Yours sincerely,
H.N. Bhagwati

Kaka Saheb Kalelkar

Kaka Kalelkar was a staunch Gandhiite. After independence he also became a Member of Parliament for some time. I reproduce here some of my correspondence with him which makes interesting reading.

New Delhi,
5 June 1959

Dear Shri Birla (K.K.):
My son, Dr. B.D. Kalelkar, has forwarded to me your letter of 31st May, regarding the application of Kumari Saradamani Devi.

I have known Kumari Saradamani for many years. She is the daughter of Smt. Ratnamayi Devi Dixit, who has served in our Mahila Ashram Vidyalaya at Wardha.

Kumari Saradamani had a brilliant career as a student in the Delhi University here. She secured a Govt. of India scholarship for one year for advanced studies in England. She is a very earnest and painstaking student with high moral character. I know she will make the best use of any help given to her and she will be an asset to any institution that profits by her services.

Yours sincerely
Kaka Kalelkar

7 June 1959

My dear Kaka Saheb,
I am in receipt of your kind letter dated 5th June. I have to thank you for your opinion about Kumari Saradamani Devi. I shall give her some lumpsum grant towards furtherance of her studies.

With kindest regards,

Yours sincerely,
K.K. Birla

Aruna Asafali

Aruna Asafali was a renowned leader of Delhi. She was a Hindu but married to a Muslim. I knew her fairly well. Some of the letters we wrote to each other are quoted here.

30 Arpil 1959

Dear Mrs Asafali,
Kindly refer to your letter dated 24th April addressed to Father regarding the portrait of Maulana Abul Kalam Azad. I have already spoken to the Manager, Birla House, to send the portrait to you. Regarding the inscription, you may kindly have it arranged. Please also arrange to send me the bill of the same.

As Father is leaving for the States, he has forwarded to me your second letter dated the 25th April also. I am sending a copy of this letter along with cutting of 'Hindustan Times' to Mr Mulgaonkar, the Editor. I entirely agree with you that there should be no misreporting. I am asking Mr. Mulgaonkar to investigate the matter and then write to you.

With kindest regards,

Yours sincerely,
K.K. Birla

Mayor of Delhi
5 May 1959

Dear Shri Krishna Kumar,
Many thanks for your letter dated 30th April. The portrait of the late Maulana Azad is being unveiled by the Vice President, Dr S. Radhakrishnan on 5th of May 1959, at 6.30 p.m.

I am grateful to you for drawing the attention of the Editor Mr Mulgaonkar to my complaint regarding the unfortunate manner in which I was recently misquoted by a correspondent of the Hindustan Times.

I believe he has already taken steps to see that such incidents are not repeated.

With best wishes,

Yours sincerely,
Aruna Asafali

15 May 1959

Dear Mrs Asafali,
Please refer to the letter of Shri Kailash Chandra, Secretary, Department of Parliamentary Affairs, regarding payment of Rs 2,900/- for the portrait of late Maulana Azad. I am attending to the matter.

With kind regards,

Yours sincerely,
K.K. Birla

19 June 1959

Dear Mrs Asafali,
I enclose herewith 5 cheques totalling Rs 2900/- in favour of 'Maulana Azad Portrait Committee'. I hope you will kindly arrange to send me receipts in names of the companies.

With kindest regards,

Yours sincerely,
K.K. Birla

Binodananda Jha

Binodananda Jha was a famous person of Bihar. He was a minister when Shri Srikrishna Sinha was the chief minister of Bihar. A copy of a letter that I wrote to him is given below.

President,   *8 India Exchange Place,*
Indian Sugar Mills Association,   *Calcutta,*
Bihar Branch   *31 March 1959*

My dear Shri Binodanandji,
I am very thankful for your kind letter dated the 20th February 1959. I am sorry I could not write to you earlier as I wanted to do so after the settlement of bonus for the season 1957-58 for which negotiations had been going on.

The Government's attitude of welcoming an industrywise settlement on bonus is very reassuring. In your earlier letter dated 5th January 1959 you had expressed the opinion that the INSMW Federation need not hesitate to settle the question of bonus with the Indian Sugar Mills Association only on the ground that other federations may oppose it. The Labour Department, you pointed out, found it difficult to persuade the other labour federations to accept the same formula for settlement of bonus as agreed to by the INSWM Federation because a number of employers had already entered into individual agreements with their labour unions to pay a higher quantum of bonus. You, therefore, thought that the move for an industrywise settlement would succeed provided the factories refrained from entering into individual agreements with labour unions affiliated to other federations for granting a higher bonus.

But I never intended or desired that the Government should themselves issue any such advice directly and I quite appreciate that it would not be appropriate for them to do so. I shall deal elsewhere in this letter the assistance that I feel we could legitimately expect from the Government of Bihar.

You have made specific mention of two factories, namely, Bihta and Motipur, where individual agreements have been entered into for payment of a higher bonus. It is true that as far as we are aware, the management of Bihta factory hold special views of their own on the subject and have willingly agreed to pay higher bonus. But I fear in doing so they have only acted in an individualistic fashion rather than acting for the good of the industry as a whole. On the basis of their duration, recovery, prosperity or for any other cause, a higher bonus may be justified in the case of Bihta factory. But if every factory started talking in terms of its own limited sphere, it would mean that there would be individual settlements and there will be no uniform basis. In such an eventuality there would be individual bargaining and I fear nothing but chaos will ultimately result from such a state of affairs. Even as far as the quantum of bonus is concerned, those factories where the Unions are strong may get a higher bonus whereas in those factories where the Unions are weak, the labour may get a comparatively unfair deal. I personally think, therefore, that it is very necessary that where we are dealing with a major problem, we should stop thinking in our own individualistic terms and should think of the industry as a whole. Against this background, I am afraid we cannot commend the action of the Bihta factory. Regarding Motipur, as far as our information goes, this factory had no intention of paying a bonus higher than what was agreed to on an industrywise basis but as they did not want to spoil their season, they thought it was better to purchase peace by paying a higher quantum of bonus. In my opinion the factory should have shown great courage and firmness. But as they did not want to take any risk, they thought that discretion was the better part of valour.

I am particularly grateful to you for your clarification regarding the position of the Government on the question of go-slow. Your assurance about the Labour Department's efforts to maintain peaceful relations in the industry is, however, very encouraging.

You will be pleased to learn that a final settlement of bonus with the INSMW Federation has now been arrived at. A copy of the agreement is being enclosed herewith for your information. The agreement covers 50% of the factories in Bihar. This in itself is a clear enough indication that the basis of the settlement is a fair and reasonable one. We all wish and hope that the same basis of settlement may be accepted by the other labour federations as well. But if any Federation chooses to adopt a different attitude and does not accept this fair basis of settlement, we hope the Government would use their influence in order to maintain peace in the industry.

As you advised, the members of the Sugar Mills Association whose labour unions are affiliated to other federations have already been requested to help in this direction by not entering into individual agreements giving higher bonus. It is hoped also that no factories will willingly enter into such individual agreements. But there may be cases where the pressure from the labour Unions might compel some of them to agree to such individual settlements against their will. And it is to avoid such cases that I would seek the help of the Government. If the Government create the necessary confidence among the factories and see that none of them are coerced into paying a higher bonus against their will, the problem will be solved.

With kindest regards,

Yours sincerely,
K.K. Birla

MEMORANDUM OF SETTLEMENT ARRIVED AT BETWEEN THE
REPRESENTATIVES OF THE INDIAN SUGAR MILLS ASSOCIATION,
BIHAR BRANCH AND THE INDIAN NATIONAL SUGAR MILL
WORKERS FEDERATION ON THE 23ᴿᴰ OF MARCH 1959 AT
CALCUTTA

P R E S E N T

Shri K.K. Birla   Representing ISMA, Bihar Branch
Shri R.L. Nopany

Shri Surendra Prasad Sinha   Representing INSMWF

It is agreed that sugar factories in Bihar having labour unions affiliated to the INSMWF would pay bonus for the year 1957-58 at 65% of the normal rates of bonus as per schedule attached.

2. This amount will be paid by the factories by the end of April 1959, or before the close of the crushing season, whichever is earlier, but in no case earlier than 7 April 1959.

3. If any of the aforesaid factories seek exemption from the payment of bonus owing to losses, meagre profits or uneconomic working, they will apply by 10th April 1959, to a Committee consisting of one representative each of the Association and the Federation and the decision of this Committee would be binding on both the parties. All cases of exemption will be disposed of by this Committee as early as possible and in any case within two months from the date of this agreement.

Sd. K.K. Birla   Sd. R.L. Nopany   Sd. S.P. Sinha

SCHEDULE OF NORMAL RATES OF BONUS

On production of sugar up to one lac mds : Nil
On production of sugar over one lac mds : Annas two per md.
and up to 2 lac mds
On production of sugar over 2 lac mds   : Annas four per md.
and up to 3½ lac mds
On production of sugar over 3½ lac mds   : Annas six per md.
and up to 5 lac mds

Swaran Singh

Sardar Swaran Singh was a good friend of mine. He became the minister of railways in the Cabinet of Pandit Jawaharlal Nehru. A letter sent by me and his reply are given below.

11 April 1962

My dear Sardar Swaran Singhji,
I have read with interest that you are now the Minister of Railways. I have had the privilege of meeting you off and on when you were in charge of the Steel, Mines and Fuel Ministry. In Texmaco we are manufacturing wagons for the Railways and I am happy that your new portfolio will afford me greater opportunities to meet you. I sincerely hope that you will make a grand success of your new assignment.
    With kindest regards,

Yours sincerely,
K.K. Birla

20 April 1962

Dear Shri K.K. Birla,
I write to thank you for your good wishes on my taking over the portfolio of Railways. I need hardly add that I greatly appreciate your kind thought in having conveyed these to me on the occasion of my assuming the responsibilities of the new office.
    Thanking you once again.

Yours sincerely,
Swaran Singh

Pandit Govind Ballabh Pant

Pandit Govind Ballabh Pant was the chief minister of Uttar Pradesh for a number of years. Later Pandit-ji asked him to join the Cabinet at the Centre. My correspondence with Pant-ji is voluminous. He was very fond of me and had great confidence in me. Some letters are reproduced here.

Lucknow,
8 September 1952

My dear Krishna Kumarji,
I am in receipt of your message of congratulations on my birthday. I am thankful to you for the expression of goodwill and affection which I value.

Yours sincerely,
G.B. Pant

Nainital,
31 May 1953

My dear Krishna Kumar,
I was glad to receive your letter of 23rd May. The way you are going to rehabilitate Govind Sugar Mills I am confident will prove fruitful and profitable to all concerned. I remember the talk that I had with you in this connection at Lucknow. I should like to extend whatever assistance I can. It is, however difficult for me to send you any definite reply till I have consulted the Finance Department to whom a reference is being made. I hope to be in a position to let you know whether the amount you need namely three lakhs will be available. You have not mentioned the terms though in case the money can be spared there need be no difficulty in settling them.

The temperature has shot up almost everywhere and in some places in our State it has gone up to 116°. Nainital is lovely and almost at its best these days. I wish you could find some time for a change and also for relative rest and escape from your everyday business.

Yours sincerely,
G.B. Pant

आ नो भद्राः क्रतवो वन्तु विश्वतोऽदब्धासो अपरीतास उद्भिदः ।
देवा नो यथा सदमिद्वृधे असन्नप्रायोवो रक्षितारो दिवे दिवे ॥

20 जून	प्रस्थान बारात	6 बजे सायंकाल
	पाणिग्रहण	रात्रिकाल
21 जून	जलपान	5 बजे अपराह्न

उपहार न लाने की सविनय प्रार्थना है ।

सस्नेह अभिवादन ।

मेरे पुत्र चिरंजीव कृष्ण चंद्र का विवाह श्री गोविन्द बल्लभ पाण्डे जी की कन्या आयुष्मती इला के साथ 20 जून, 1957 को नैनीताल में होना निश्चित हुआ है । निवेदन है कि इस शुभ कार्य में सम्मिलित होकर वर-वधू को आशीर्वाद देने की कृपा करें ।

विनीत
गोविंद बल्लभ पन्त

Lucknow,
11-12 September 1953

My dear Krishan Kumar,
I have to thank you for your letter of September 9 about Kumari Nirmala Joshi. I had asked her to see you in Delhi but unfortunately you had left for Mussorie by the time she reached your residence. I have no doubt that she will receive all the help that you can give her and she deserves your sympathy. I think the proposed arrangement will relieve her mind of present embarrassment and worries.

Yours sincerely,
G.B. Pant

Lucknow,
9 January 1954

My dear Krishna Kumar,
I have to thank you for your letters of 4th and 5th instant.
I am glad that Iswara Dutt has joined the Leader at Allahabad. I have seen the cutting attached to your letter. It marks a distinct

change and that for the better. Zutshi was and is a conscientious and responsible type, but he continues to cherish some obsolete notions and has been somewhat stuck up in that rut. I am sure that Iswara Dutt will revitalize the Paper and give it a new and healthy tone. I shall certainly be glad to meet him when he comes here.

I have also received your letter along with your note about the basis of calculation of bonus in the sugar factories in our State for 1952-53. I must confess that I was not aware of all that you have written. I had learnt that the rate had been fixed jointly by the representatives of the Industry and the Labour. I was really gratified to learn that there had been complete agreement between the two and that in fact the decisions were unanimous having been reached with the consent of every member. It is a pity that your Group was not represented. How it happened to be so I do not know. I wish you had been there. In any case we will have to be more careful next year. I have gone through your note with due care and I trust that the mater will receive the consideration it deserves. It will be desirable to settle the principles in advance and not to wait till the eleventh hour next year. There are also certain other matters which are the subject of agitation at present and I am looking forward to some opportunity for discussing them with the leading industrialists. I expect to reach Calcutta on the 19th.

With greetings for all,

Yours sincerely,
G.B. Pant

Lucknow,
5 March 1954

My dear Krishna Kumar,
I was glad to receive your letters of February 26 and 28. I have since had the opportunity of meeting you. I was glad to hear your views about our budget and appreciate the sentiments that you have expressed in your letters about the progress that is being steadily, though perhaps slowly, made in our State. We have had to face many odds and a series of difficulties but still with the active cooperation and goodwill of all concerned we have been, and I think not without some success, trying to improve the economic condition of our people. We are now taking active steps for setting

up the Industrial Finance Corporation. I was glad to receive your heartening assurance and shall be glad to avail myself of your offer of assistance in the matter.

I know Jagat Singh Bora though not very intimately. He has met me more than once in the course of my visits to Calcutta. He has uniformly struck me as an energetic man of good impulses. He has been perhaps occasionally writing to the papers, but I have no correct measure of his talents or capacity. I myself do not very much like the idea of the symposium being associated with me, but I wonder if it can be of much profit. I had asked Jagat Singh to take an interest in the proposed Tulsi Smarak and to secure the assistance of the inhabitants of Bara Bazaar and other smaller areas. We have a heavy programme before us and I really wish that we may soon be in a position to give a decent start to it.

Hope to meet you here again,

Yours sincerely,
G.B. Pant

Lucknow,
15 March 1954

My dear Krishna Kumar,
I was glad to receive your letter of 7th and have noted with satisfaction that the Hargaon factory will be exceeding the mark of fifty lakh maunds of sugarcane crush. I am impressed by the fact that in spite of the higher bonus scale that was fixed last year you have not been deterred from transgressing the fifty lakh limit. This is just what one would have expected from you. The question of bonus has, I understand, been decided with the unanimous consent of all parties in the past. I wonder if all that you had said in one of your letters addressed to me was brought to their notice. The matter will no doubt receive, I trust, due consideration from them when the question is placed before them again next time with regard to the rate of bonus to be paid for the current season.

I am expecting you here on the 18th. Please give my greetings for the Holi to Ghanshyamdas-ji and other members of the family who may be there.

Yours Sincerely,
G.B. Pant

Lucknow,
1 April 1954

My dear Krishna Kumar,
My Secretary has already acknowledged your letters. You have with your usual promptitude taken up the question of raising funds for Tulsi Memorial about which I had occasion to speek to you at Calcutta and again when you were here last. A few copies of the Appeal have been sent to you. As I told you we wish to collect twentyone lakhs for the first phase. There are a number of places sanctified by Tulsidasji's association with them and a befitting memorial as everyone of these would not only serve to remind people of his remarkable gifts and noble character as a self-less devotee who led a dedicated life but also serve the people in general in other quiet ways. Some copies of the blue-print of the scheme if I can get hold of them will also be separately dispatched to you. The names of some of the members appear in the Appeal to which they are signatories. I am the chairman of the Board and Chaturbhuj Sharma one of our Deputy Ministers is the principal Secretary. If my presence is considered necessary I shall try to come for a day, but I doubt if it will make any difference. Moolchandji and some other friends are also I believe taking interest in the matter and if it be of any help to you, you can also speak to them.

I am glad that you are giving serious thought to the question of the desired factory at Bazpur. The people there would welcome your decision and offer you every assistance and cooperation.

Yours sincerely,
G.B. Pant

7 April 1954

My dear Pujya Shri Pantji,
I am in receipt of your kind letter dated 1st April. Your Personal Assistant has sent to me ten copies of the appeal made by you regarding Tulsi Smarak Fund.

If the target of expenditure is going to be Rs 21 lacs, we have to make a vigorous effort to achieve it. I would suggest the following methods for it :-

(a) Something, in my opinion, should come from the Government of India and from those State Governments where Hindi is well understood. List of such State Governments we could compile.

(b) We have to form Committees for important industries for collection and also in important cities.

(c) We have to use the good offices of some of the important papers for making an appeal through them and collecting through the good offices of the newspapers. My experience has been that sometimes good collections could be made through the newspapers.

I shall try my best as far as collection from the Sugar Industry and Calcutta is concerned. But I must have some sort of authority for this as formalities have to be observed. Kindly let me know if I am proceeding on right lines. Please also let me have your suggestions in the matter.

Your coming here will be very helpful but this will be necessary only after the spade work has been done.

Regarding Bazpur, I have received the preliminary report from Dani, our Secretary at Seohara. His report is not very encouraging. Quality of cane, according to him, is very poor and it will take some time before quality and quantity of cane become satisfactory. The mills is not expected to get a recovery of higher than 8.5 for the first four or five years. He also mentions that cultivators of that area are very unruly and are dominated by Communist ideas. They have been giving lot of trouble to the proprietors of Kicha factory. It seems from Dani's report that per acre yield of this area would be high though sugar contents would be low. In other words, it is a good place from the point of view of the growers and bad from the point of view of the Industry. I have not been able to think out a solution, but probably if growers could be persuaded to accept a lower price for the cane till sugar contents of the cane improve, therein may lie a solution. If you could kindly throw some light on the matter, I shall be grateful.

With kindest regards,

Yours sincerely,
K.K. Birla

31 May 1954

My dear Pujya Shri Pantji,
I intend to send an appeal signed by you and other prominent

leaders for raising funds. The appeal would be printed in all the states where Hindi is understood. Collections will be made through the papers. A preliminary draft is submitted herewith but I hope you will be able to improve and touch upon it wherever you feel necessary.

I am still awaiting return of Mangturamji from Kanpur. I am leaving this place for Nainital on the 5th and want to visit some of the friends before I leave this place.

With kindest regards,

Yours sincerely,
K.K. Birla

Tulsidas Memorial

Tulsidas needs no introduction to the people of India. His immortal epic, the Ramayan, is read with religious veneration by the rich and the poor alike, and a copy of the book is prized as a sacred possession in almost every home. To the Hindus, it is even more than the Bible is to the Christians.

Tulsidas lived at a time when the Moghul Empire had been firmly established in India. The military preparedness of the earlier days of invasion and expansion was giving place to a feeling of security and the consequent ease and lassitude was being unmistakably reflected in the contemporary literature. The time had come when a general toning up of the social standards was badly wanted. This work Tulsidas eminently accomplished in a language and style which the common man could understand and appreciate. His writings came to be regarded not merely as priceless gems of literature but also as embodying a code of social and moral etiquette which will continue to be the goal of every right-thinking man till eternity.

Tulsidas has been immortalised in the hearts of the Indian people through the influence his writings had on them. That influence was great indeed. The well-known historian, Vincent A. Smith, writing about Tulsidas, says, 'That Hindu was the greatest man of his age in India— greater than Akbar himself, in as much as the conquest of the hearts and minds of millions of men and women affected by the poet was an achievement infinitely more lasting and important than any or all of the victories gained in war by the monarch'. It is a pity that even an independent India has so far neglected to give material recognition to the services of

BRUSHES WITH HISTORY: AN AUTOBIOGRAPHY 629

such a great Saint although Hindi, the medium of his teachings, has been adopted as the national language of the country. Setting up a suitable memorial to commemorate the greatness of Tulsidas is almost a sacred duty which we must perform. We appeal to every citizen to participate in the fulfilment of this duty by contributing generously to the fund created for the purpose.

Camp Bombay,
24 November 1954

My dear Pujya Shri Pantji,
The news of your joining the Central Cabinet, though a surprise, was received by me with mixed feeling of sorrow and happiness. I was happy as the Government of India would be immensely strengthened by the inclusion of a giant like you in the Cabinet. But I was sorry as you were the greatest cementing force in U.P. and under your able and benevolent administration, U.P. had become one of the best administered States in the country. I have always looked forward to my visit to Lucknow with a great longing and keenness as going to Lucknow meant visiting you. But I think what you have decided is probably the best for the country though I am sure U.P. will be a great loser owing to your absence.

I shall of course meet you in future when I am in Delhi and I hope I shall continue to enjoy your confidence and affection as in the past.

With kindest regards,

Yours sincerely,
K.K. Birla

Lucknow,
8 December 1954

My dear Krishna Kumar,
I thank you for your letter of 24th November and appreciate the sentiments you have been good enough to express. Large number of friends and associates and the people of U.P. in general have always been generous to me, and poured their affection and goodwill that are an unfailing source of strength. Although I am not sure how far I can be successful, I depend on these to overcome the

growing physical handicaps from which I suffer so that I may be able to share the immense burden of others in Delhi.

Your visits to Lucknow have been few and far between but I hope to see more of you in Delhi.

Yours sincerely,
G.B. Pant

Minister for Home Affairs,
New Delhi,
25 January 1956

My dear Krishna Kumar,

I thank you for your letter of 19th January about Tulsi Smarak Samiti. The names which you have suggested are all right and you may ask Satyanarain Sinha to proceed as you propose. I was under the impression that substantial collections have already been made but your letter shows that till now even preliminary stage has not been crossed. I trust you will appreciate the need of putting all efforts to see that leisurely pace of progress is speeded up. I hope to meet you when you are in Delhi.

Yours sincerely,
G.B. Pant

30 August 1956

My dear Pujya Shri Pantji,

I think we should now send Appeal for collections to the different papers like 'Hindustan Times', 'Leader', 'Searchlight', 'Indian Nation', 'Pioneer' etc. I have made out a draft of the Appeal and have sent it to Shri Satyanarain Babu, Chairman of the Collection Committee, for getting your signatures. I hope you will very kindly favour us with it. Would you advise to get signatures of a few others like Tandonji? Satyanarain Babu would, of course, sign it.

With kindest regards,

Yours affectionately,
Krishna Kumar

12 December 1957

My dear Krishna Kumar,

I have to thank you for your letter of 2nd December. I think it will be all right if you remit Rs 50,000/- to the Chief Engineer, Public Works Department, U.P., Lucknow. The organisers are thinking of holing the formal stone-laying ceremony of the Tulsi Smarak at Rajapur some time in the first week of February. Trust you will be able to attend it.

Yours affectionately,
G.B. Pant

17 December 1958

My dear Krishna Kumar,

Chaturbhuj Sharma has written to me to the effect that the Superintending Engineer in charge of the construction of Tulsi Smarak at Rajpur has estimated that the entire work will amout to Rs 2,80,500/-. Out of this you have already remitted Rs 50,000/-. Although the Superintending Engineer has asked him to deposit the balance of Rs 2,30,500/- immediately, Chaturbhuj thinks that at least Rs 50,000/- should be deposited as a second instalment so that the construction work may proceed uninterrupted. Trust you will kindly get the needful done.

The people connected with the Smarak are thinking of having the stone-laying ceremony in the beginning of 1st week of February. As soon as the date has been firmly fixed, I will let you know. Hope you will be able to join.

Trust this finds you all well.

Yours sincerely,
G.B. Pant

5 January 1959

My dear Krishna Kumar,

I saw your letter of 23rd December, only on my return from tour two days ago. I am concerned to learn that you have not been keeping well. Trust there is nothing serious about the matter and the milk diet prescribed by your Physician has acted as a tranquilizer and eased your stomach. The date for the stone laying of the Tulsi Smarak at Rajpur has not yet been finally settled, but people connected with it think that 1st of February would be convenient to all concerned.

With all good wishes for the New Year,

Yours sincerely,
G.B. Pant

15 January 1959

My dear Pujya Shri Pantji,

I hope you will kindly excuse my encroaching upon your valuable time. But as the associations of the sugar mills in U.P. and Bihar desired my taking up the following matter with you, I am writing to you shortly about the problem confronting them regarding the construction of roads.

We remember with gratitude the close interest you took in the development work in Uttar Pradesh while you were the Chief Minister there. One of the items which had engaged your kind attention was the development of roads around the sugar factories. The benefits arising out of development of such roads cannot be over-emphasized. If cane growers have the benefit of good roads, they can bring their cane to the factories conveniently and thus help in increasing the production of sugar which can be exported to earn valuable foreign exchange. It is a well known fact that in the absence of good roads, sugar cane from many places does not reach the factories and the growers have either to convert it into 'gur' or to use it as fodder for cattle.

With a view to remove these difficulties, the Government of India formulated a scheme for road development in sugar factory areas during the Second Five Year Plan. Under this scheme one-third of the cost of construction of pucca roads is to be met by the Central Government, one-third by the State Government and the balance by the factories concerned and the growers. The scheme received a good response.

Some time back, a member factory informed the Indian Sugar Mills Association that the constructions made by them under the road development scheme were not being allowed as expenses for

income-tax purposes by the income-tax authorities. The Indian
Sugar Mills Association then took up the matter with the Central
Board of Revenue and represented that these contributions should
be treated as an item of expenditure. Unfortunately, this request
has been turned down by the Central Board of Revenue. The latter,
however, have offered to treat such contributions as donations under
Section 15B of the Income tax Act. As, however, there is a limit on
the amount of donations by a Company for the purposes of Income
tax and as besides every factory is required to give some donation
or the other, this attitude on the part of the Central Board of Revenue
will hardly give any relief. Under the circumstances the scheme of
road construction is likely to receive a setback.

I have not written about this matter to Pujya Shri Morarji-bhai.
I thought of drawing your kind attention to the matter because you
had taken such a keen interest in this work and since you are well
acquainted with the condition of the Sugar Industry in U.P. and
Bihar.

With kindest regards,

Yours affectionately,
Krishna Kumar

3 February 1959

My dear Krishna Kumar,
I have received your letter of January 29. I am sorry that I missed
you during your recent visit to Delhi. I wish you had dropped in
some time. I had a touch of lumbago, but now it has almost passed
away. It is rather a nuisance while it lasts. I was sorry to learn that
you have not yet regained your health completely and are still on
a restricted diet. I trust you will get over the trouble shortly. I shall
be glad to see you whenever you are in Delhi.

With all good wishes,

Yours affectionately,
G.B. Pant

13 February 1959

My dear Krishna Kumar,

I have received your letter of January 15 and have discussed the question of the expenditure on roads by sugar factories with the officers of the Finance Ministry. They tell me that it would not be possible to treat this as an ordinary expenditure for purposes of income-tax but the contributions that the factory makes for development of roads in the factory area can be treated as capital investment in the undertaking on which depreciation at the usual rates would be admissible.

The scheme for the development of roads round about sugar factory area is a good one and irrespective of income-tax aspect, I trust that the factories will continue to participate in it as it is useful to them as well as to the growers.

With all good wishes,

Yours affectionately,
G.B. Pant

24 August 1959

My dear Pujya Shri Pantji,

I learn from the papers that President Ayub is meeting the Prime Minister on or about the 1st of September. I was wondering if you could kindly put in a word to the Prime Minister so that he may just make a mention about Dalmia's case to President Ayub. I understand our High Commissioner has sent a strong report to the External Affairs Ministry showing how Dalmia and the two other employees of the Sutlej Cotton Mills were sentenced to heavy terms of imprisonment although they were entirely innocent. I shall send you a note on this subject in case you wish to study the broad facts of the case. However, I understand, the high Commissioner has already sent a good summary of the case. We have also deputed some special officers to Pakistan who are trying to seek the intervention of the various high personalities at Karachi. The information that we have is that President Ayub alongwith Mr. Manzur Qadir, the Foreign Minister, who is accompanying him, has been acquainted with this case and I understand he feels that there has been gross mis-carriage of justice against Dalmia and the two others. The atmosphere, therefore, is good. I consequently think that if the Prime Minister could just mention that, in the opinion of the Government of India too there has been mis-carriage of justice in this case, that should be sufficient.

If you think that I should write a letter to the Prime Minister or seek an interview with him to make this request, I shall gladly do so. But I feel that unless a word from you goes to him, he may perhaps not consider discussing this matter with President Ayub. I am, therefore, entirely depending on you for this matter and would do as you guide me.

With kindest regards,

Yours sincerely,
K.K. Birla

(Personal)

29 August 1959

My dear Krishna Kumar,
I have received your letter of August 24. I can quite appreciate your concern about the Manager of Sutlej Cotton Mills, but I am afraid, it will hardly be appropriate for the Prime Minister to mention this case to President Ayub nor will there be time to do so, as their meeting is going to be a short one. So, I do not think that you should write to the Prime Minister about it.

Yours affectionately,
G.B. Pant.

(Personal)

11 October 1959

My dear Krishna Kumar,
Our High Commissioner at Karachi recently had an interview with President Ayub Khan and represented to him the case of Sutlej Cotton Mills. He informs me that the President gave him full opportunity to explain the case and listened to him with attention. While it is not possible to say what the final outcome will be, the High Commissioner thinks that the case has a good chance of

receiving attention. Ghanshyamdasji was here recently and I have shown him the High Commissioner's letter.

Yours sincerely,
G.B. Pant

16 October 1959

My dear Pujya Shri Pantji,
I am in receipt of your kind letter dated 11th October. I am very happy to note that our High Commissioner at Karachi had an interview with President Ayub Khan regarding the case of Sutlej Mills. You have from the very beginning taken a very keen interest in this affair and only just now I have received the good news of Dalmia and others having been released. It is all owing to the sympathetic interest you have taken in the matter. I am really very grateful to you for it.

With kindest regards,

Yours affectionately,
Krishna Kumar

Note: I have written elsewhere in this book that Gajanand Dalmia, the General manager of Sutlej Cotton Mills at Okara in Pakistan, was a very brave man. Even at the time of partition when all the Hindus fled Pakistan, he stayed at the mills and left it just two or three days before the partition took place. He went back soon after and took charge again.

3 May 1960

My dear Krishna Kumar,
I have your letter of 28th April and am thankful to you for your readiness to collect an additional amount of Rs 50,000/- for the Tulsi Smarak. I had also asked Chaturbhuj Sharma who was here a few days ago to make special efforts to collect as much as he can. This is a national monument and I was expecting a heartening response to the appeal for funds at least from that section of our community which has always contributed generously towards all such causes. I am sorry to learn that they have grown apathetic.

This is a sad commentary on their munificent temperament. However, the work has to be completed in any case. The signatories to the appeal have a special responsibility and we should do all we can to raise the necessary funds, and the sooner it is done the better.

Trust this finds you well.

Yours sincerely,

G.B. Pant

10 September 1960

My dear Pujya Shri Pantji,

I am in receipt of your kind letter dated 4th September. I am myself very anxious to collect Rs 50,000/- for the Tulsi Smarak Samiti. After my talk with you, I made efforts in this direction and contacted a few friends. They all wanted to know more about the scheme of the Samiti. Accordingly, I wrote to Sharmaji on the 1st of July to send me a dozen copies of the schemes. On the 11th July, Sharmaji replied that he would be sending me some copies but so far I have not received them. Of my own accord, I reminded Sharmaji on the 2nd September and requested that he should send me the copies of the scheme as early as possible. As soon as I get the copies, I shall contact these friends again.

I have not been to Delhi recently but I am going there this evening. I shall be in Delhi for only two days but I hope to have my usual dinner with you this time.

With kindest regards,

Yours affectionately,

Krishna Kumar

17 October 1960

My dear Pujya Shri Pantji,

I returned here last night from my holiday at Srinagar. I regret I could not meet you as I did not stop in Delhi. My plane from Srinagar reached Delhi at 4 o'clock in the afternoon and I had to take the plane for Calcutta at 6.30 p.m. I therefore had just sufficient time to go to Birla House and to return to the airport after a wash.

I am now starting the work of Tulsi Smarak Samiti and with your blessings I hope to collect Rs 50,000/- shortly as suggested by you. I shall keep you in touch with the progress.

With kindest regards,

Yours affectionately,
Krishna Kumar

Camp: Raipur,
31 October 1960

My dear Krishna Kumar,

Thanks for your letter of 17th instant. I am glad that you took a holiday and trust you have been benefited by your stay in Kashmir. The Executive Engineer in charge of the Tulsi Smarak has written that due to shortage of money the contractor has practically stopped the construction. Hope you will be able to remit the necessary funds as soon as may be feasible.

With good wishes,

Yours sincerely,
G.B. Pant

1 नवम्बर 1960

पूज्य श्री पन्तजी,
सादर प्रणाम।

तुलसी स्मारक समिति के लिये मैंने आपसे पचास हजार रुपये इकट्ठा करने का वायदा किया था। इसमें से 21 हजार रुपये भाई माधवप्रसाद ने उसके नीचे जो कम्पनियां हैं उनकी ओर से भिजवा दिये हैं। और रुपया इकट्ठा करने की हम दोनों भाई चेष्टा कर रहे हैं। आशा है आपकी कृपा से यह रुपया इकट्ठा हो जाएगा।

आपका विनीत

माननीय श्री गोविन्द बल्लभ जी पन्त,
गृह मंत्री, भारत सरकार,
नई दिल्ली

गृह मंत्री,
भारत सरकार
5 नवम्बर 1960

प्रिय कृष्ण कुमार,

1 नवम्बर का पत्र मिला। माधवप्रसाद का भेजा हुआ 21 हजार रुपये का चेक मैंने चतुर्भुज के पास भेज दिया है। तुलसी स्मारक का काम जो स्थगित हो गया था वह चालू हो जायेगा पर, जैसा तुम्हें विदित ही है, हमारी योजना तो 10 लाख की है। मैंने माधवप्रसाद को भी लिखा है कि अगर तुम दोनों भाई इस काम में लगन से जुट जाओ तो इस धनराशि को इकट्ठा करने में अवश्य सफलता मिलेगी। स्मारक का बनना तो नितान्त अनिवार्य है और हम लोग तो एक तरह से वचनबद्ध हैं। चतुर्भुज भी अपनी तरफ से चन्दा इकट्ठा करने में लगे हुए हैं पर उनके साधन तो सीमित हैं।

सस्नेह
गोविन्द बल्लभ पन्त

श्री कृष्ण कुमार बिड़ला,
8, इंडिया एक्सचेंज प्लेस,
कलकत्ता - 1

Note: The money required by Pantji for the Tulsi Smarak Samiti was finally collected by me and sent to Pantji.

Appendix 1

Fortyeighth Annual Session 1975

ADDRESS BY THE PRESIDENT
SHRI K.K. BIRLA

April 25, 1975

FEDERATION OF INDIAN CHAMBERS OF
COMMERCE & INDUSTRY, NEW DELHI

Madam Prime Minister, Your Excellencies, Fellow Delegates, Ladies and Gentlemen:

I have pleasure in welcoming you all cordially to the 48th Annual Session of the Federation.

2. To you, Madam Prime Minister, I am specially grateful for accepting our invitation to inaugurate our session this morning in spite of the numerous demands on your precious time. During the year you were also kind enough to receive my colleagues and myself, from time to time, when we placed before you our thoughts on some of the pressing economic problems confronting the country. Your presence at these annual sessions is always exhilarating and inspiring. It is our conviction that your message from this forum which reaches the entire business community helps to give direction to the national economic effort.

3. This year marks the Twenty-fifth Anniversary of our Republic, a quarter of a century of considerable positive achievements coupled with stress and strain. We have had droughts and wars, violence and disorder, strikes and lockout which gave moments of dismay and anxiety. We have surfaced out of these vicissitudes as a mature nation dedicated to democratic values. What else is this but an eloquent tribute to the visions

of our leaders, and to the institutions they devised and nursed? It is this continuing tradition of imaginative leadership, Madam Prime Minister, which had led to the resolution of the apparently intractable problem of Kashmir, provided an answer to the recent animated Gujarat election issue and the democratic struggle in Sikkim. It is a matter of pride to the entire nation that last year was remarkable for progress in the technological field which promises to give a new dynamism to our developmental effort. The explosion of the nuclear device in May 1974 was followed by the commissioning of the Bombay High Project. This is not all. We have also entered the space age, and our scientific satellite, 'Aryabhatta', is orbiting the earth. These exemplify the technological breakthrough that the country has achieved under your courageous and farsighted leadership. Our nation has aspired high—'A man's reach should exceed his grasp; or what's a heaven for?'

4. It has, however, been a difficult year, and almost every country has gone through sharp ups and downs—from high speed inflation to a perceptible recession. The global inflation–recession syndrome is largely a reflection of the excessive consumerism that has characterized the economies of the affluent countries. A fear psychosis has gripped them now with the realization that the world's natural resources are not after all unlimited. Consequently, their policies, in some respects, have become more inward looking.

5. Take the case of the sharp and dramatic rise in oil prices. Its impact on developing nations is fierce, almost crushing. An additional $20 billion will have to be found—naturally out of the already insufficient developmental resources. It is highly unlikely that the deficits can be made good by increased bilateral and multilateral aid, unless special assistance programmes are thought of—and thought of fast. Time is the essence in this matter—and time is running out. The international community, and more so the OPEC, has to seriously consider ways of recycling the astronomical petro-funds, which have been accumulated, for the benefit of the developing world.

6. That is only a start. I submit that the less developed countries, on their part, must accept the fact that the best help is self-help. We in India are fortunate—we have manpower, technology, skills and resources. We have a viable economic system. Public sector enterprises have shown considerable improvement recently; and quite a few of them have started earning a fair return on their capital. Industry's twin arms—the public and private enterprises—share common problems and have identical goals. The crucial question, surely, is not so much as whether a project should

be in the public or the private sector; the question is whether the social benefit that proceeds from the project is greater than its social cost. I wish to stress one point—social benefit cannot be measured in terms of monetary return alone. That is naive, 19th century thinking. We have to consider the kind of output that will emerge, the level of employment that will be generated, the amount of exports that will be undertaken and the distribution of income that will follow. To talk of production without social justice is as futile as to talk of social justice without production. The two go hand in hand. They should blend, interact and harmonize. It seems to me that a mixed economy operated on this pattern will promote a higher rate of growth and be of greater value to the people.

7. The past is an achievement, the future is only a goal; the present is what we have to act on. The shape of our plicies, therefore, should reflect a synthesis between short term needs and long term objectives. Two dominant features have characterized our economy in the last three years— inflation and stagnation. In the 28 months since June 1972, prices spiralled by as much as 68 per cent. This clearly reflects the difficult supply position, which was more pronounced in agriculture than in industry. The Government took timely, bold and impressively unconventional measures like partial wage freeze, compulsory deposit scheme and credit control, to discipline soaring prices. The FICCI had lent support to these measures, which were aimed mainly at demand management. They did have a distinctly sobering effect; in fact, since October last prices have dropped by about 7 per cent. This is a commendable achievement, but certainly not the end of our travails.

8. Inflation was only one of the aberrations in the development process. The problem was that the process itself was too slow. In a delicate and difficult situation like this, it should not surprise anyone if even the best of policies should give rise to unintended side-effects. What is needed is continuous vigilance, so that the side-effects do not escalate into a major malady. In other words, while directing our efforts to contain inflation, we cannot let the process of growth to falter.

9. Recession has become a worldwide phenomenon whether we call it by that name or use the fashionable phrase 'Demand Slump'. India has been affected by it and several of our industries, such as steel, non-ferrous metals, glass, rayon, cycles, fans, wire and wire ropes, jute, textiles and machine tools, have been passing through a recessionary phase. Automobiles, wagons, and mini steel plants have been the worst hit. Normally, a fall in prices is good provided the fall is due to increased productivity or results from economy in costs. When prices fall because

of distress sales the economy signals danger. Consider the inescapable chain—poor offtake and accumulation of stocks lead to fall in production and the fall in production leads, inevitably, to unemployment. Quite a few industrial establishments have already closed down.

10. Is it not, therefore, time to consider whether the demand management measures which were effective at the time they were introduced should be modified in the light of the prevailing economic situation? In my judgement, demand management policies have played out their role and should not be allowed to outlive their utility. Let us shift the focus now on revival of demand and in particular on supply expansion. That is the answer not only to the vexed question of inflation but also to the problems of poverty and unemployment. We were hoping that the Central Budget would help in bringing this about. The budget does take a look in that direction, but the actual proposals are so diluted that they fail to create the type of impact that is necessary. May I suggest, Madam Prime Minister, that at the present juncture the attention of both Government and the private sectors should centre on reviving the economy and putting it back on a sustained growth path?

11. In our development programmes, the importance of agriculture is vital. I am not denying that agricultural progress in several States has exceeded the national average rate. Nevertheless, the impression prevails that the States as a whole have been rather slow in imparting a genuine dynamism to agricultural development. Perhaps the Central Government should assume greater responsibility in the development of agriculture and in related spheres such as irrigation and power. Agricultural output can be improved by intensive research and development covering potent inputs like seeds and pesticides and by stepping up the production of fertilizers. Organic wastes too can be used to supplement chemical fertilizers to overcome the fertilizer shortage in the country. Research should be the responsibility of not the Government alone. The industries directly connected with agriculture too should play an effective role in this field.

12. Production undoubtedly should receive high priority; but it is no less urgent that the distribution system should meet the requirements of the poorer sections of society. The levy on wheat trade which was introduced last year was an admirable idea then, and it has not lost its validity. It is true that the total procurement from farmers by the Government and the trade came to 3.3 million tonnes only as against 4.5 million tonnes procured by the governmental agencies in the previous year. This figure does not compare very unfavourably with the

performance of the earlier year, specially if all the circumstances are taken into consideration. In my view, the procurement last year would have been much larger had there been greater and timely cooperation from State Governments, had procedural delays been eliminated, and had the trade been permitted to offer higher price to the farmer for his produce. That apart, there was a more basic reason for the shortfall in procurement—there simply was not enough wheat. One cannot, howsoever hard one may try, procure what is not there. The decline in the wheat crop was as much as 2.5 million tonnes. The levy on traders, in my opinion, combines the merits of State monopoly with the advantages of free trade. The National Commission on Agriculture also has recognized the practical advantages of dual pricing, with a public distribution system functioning along with private trade. I hope, Madam Prime Minister, that even at this late stage the Government will consider drawing on the experience and services of normal trade channels in the distribution of wheat.

13. The size of agricultural output and the level of foodgrain prices are the guiding parameters of our economy. In 1966–68 and 1972–74, when agricultural production plummeted, industrial production languished. In the last two years, capacity utilization in industries has been low, and new investment sluggish. These two are inter-related aspects, but they need to be considered separately. For instance, if Railways do not embark on expansion or renovation programmes, the demand for wagons well as for steel gets automatically reduced; this leads to underutilization of capacity in the wagon, steel and ancillary industries. Expansion of capacity in one industry, therefore, becomes a pre-condition for fuller utilization of capacity in other industries. It is heartening that the Government has taken note of this fact, and in the Central Budget an increase of 23 per cent in plan expenditure has been provided

14. Apart from the demand constraint, industry has simultaneously been exposed to acute input shortages, the most which is important of which is power. There are some signs of improvement in power generation in certain areas. Even so, large parts of the country are passing through a power famine, and the gap between requirements and generation was as high as 35 million units a day in February this year. I feel that the question of power generation is not merely one of equating supply with demand. The supply must always be ahead of demand. This is true of all industries, but more so in the case of a crucial infrastructure like power. Of paramount importance is the management of the power generating agencies both at the administrative and the technical levels. I will not go into the details

now, because they have been spelt out from many forums including the Energy Conference that was organized by us last year.

15. I come now to a very sensitive matter. It is disconcerting that the inadequate rise in production has, in some cases, been the result of unhealthy industrial relations. In 1974 the man-days lost due to strikes and lockouts exceeded 31 million, which was about 50 per cent more than the man-days lost in 1973. Increased industrial unrest is often attributed to the troubled state of the economy. In such a situation, I would say that greater restraint has to be exercised by all concerned so that the economy may recover and push ahead more rapidly. We have all to put our shoulders to the wheel. You had suggested some time back, Madam Prime Minister, that there should be a moratorium on strikes and lockouts for at least five years. I hope that this excellent idea will be given a more concrete shape and a fair trial.

16. As mentioned earlier, new investment in industry is not adequately forthcoming. The dimensions of the problem are far larger than is usually realized:

- First, projects have to be economically viable. This is particularly true of industries which are subject to price control.
- Secondly, prices of capital goods have gone up sharply in the last three or four years making it difficult for the new units to compete with the existing ones.
- Thirdly, the existing units find it difficult to replace assets because of inadequate depreciation allowed under the tax law.
- Fourrthly, finance for new investment has become scarce.
- Lastly, the interest rates have risen steeply.

17. These are the reasons that prevent new industries from coming up fast enough, despite the speedier clearing of industrial licences. I know that the Government is not unaware of this serious problem; but I feel that the principal agencies involved in development—I am referring to the Government, industry and financial institutions—should discuss the issues objectively at a common forum and work out a way for evolving acceptable solutions so that economic development is not hindered in any way. Progress is the need of the hour. Allow me to clarify some of my thoughts on this subject.

18. It goes without saying that, if price controls are necessary, the administered prices should be such as to allow a reasonable margin of profit. With the relative improvement in the supply-demand situation,

prices in industries such as vanaspati, tyres and tubes and automobiles have been decontrolled. This is a forward-looking policy; I hope it will be extended to other items. It may be that the system of price control cannot be abandoned in respect of some commodities, and also a thorough revision of prices is found impracticable; even then, the special categories of consumers can be catered to by a dual pricing system, as in the case of sugar. Let me make it abundantly clear, Madam Prime Minister, that our plea for dual pricing policy is primarily meant for meeting the demand of the vulnerable section of the population and other special categories of consumers at a subsidized price, a price which is acceptedly unremunerative. This loss has to be made good by the industry, whether in the public or private sector, or sickness will follow. The open market price which will naturally be higher than the subsidized price will help the industry to recoup losses and earn normal profits.

19. Even today, in some circles, there is considerable misunderstanding about the role of profits. Profits are not gargantuan capitalist returns. Profits are reasonable surpluses that have to be generated—and indeed, they are earned by industry even in centrally-controlled economies—to replace assets and finance new investments after paying a reasonable return to the investors. Profits are one thing, profiteering another. The former is a weapon of economic growth, the latter is an anti-social activity.

20. For quite some time now, new capital intensive industries have been disabled from coming into existence because of the steep increase in capital cost. In my opinion production from these new enterprises, and from undertakings that expand, should be allowed a concession in excise duty. The extent of such concession will vary from industry to industry, depending upon the incidence of capital cost in the final price. Similarly, continued sustenance of industry requires that capital goods which have worn out or become obsolete are replaced in time. In an inflationary situation, the replacement cost of capital goods is far greater than the accumulated depreciation permitted under the tax law. To bring the two on par, depreciation should be based not on the original cost, as at present, but on the replacement value. When I talk of industry I have in mind enterprises both in the public and private sectors. The logic of costs is universal; it transcends sectoral divisions as much as national boundaries. I am sure that the high-powered Committee appointed by the Government will take note of these aspects.

21. Rapid growth also assumes adequate, even liberal finance. I am aware that the Government has been hesitant to launch upon a policy of liberalization of credit for fear it may lead to a relapse of inflation. May

I venture to say that this fear is not warranted? Prices in the last six months have been checked; and are even falling. Agricultural production has revived, and there is considerable unutilized capacity in industry to absorb any excess demand that may be generated. Surely, in this context, selective liberalization of credit would act as an impetus to production rather than push up prices; it will assist the economy to get back on its feet and start moving. The whole process, however, would become stable and cumulative if proper measures are adopted to generate savings in the hands of the people. That is the crux of the matter.

22. The Planning Commission, I recall, had envisaged a net investment of Rs 1250 crores per year, on an average, to be undertaken by private sector industries in the Fifth Plan period. At current prices, this would amount to Rs 1866 crores. A large part of this finance will have to come from the financial institutions, but they themselves are short of funds. If salt loses its savour, how shall it be salted? Why not permit these institutions to utilize the amount out of the resources blocked under wage freeze and CDS measures? After all, the public financial institutions do adhere to the strictest financial discipline; there cannot be any question or doubt about the additional funds being utilized productively. The financial institutions also have to adopt a more flexible attitude on matters like debt equity ratio, the proportion of promoters' contribution and conversion of loans into equity. These constraints have slowed down the revival and improvement of the economy. A liberalization of the policies and procedures would greatly help.

23. In this connection, I would like to refer very briefly to the sharp increase in the rate of interest. The bank rate has been raised to 9 per cent, and interest on bank credit to 18 per cent. In an inflationary situation, the high cost of credit is perhaps justified; but today the high interest rates act as a drag on production and as a disincentive to investment. I hope the Reserve Bank of India will review the situation favourably by the end of the current busy season.

24. Internal development is also a prerequisite for external viability. Our balance of trade position improved from a deficit of Rs 922 crores in 1966–67 to a surplus of Rs 104 crores in 1972–73. For the first time, the country achieved a breakthrough in the balance of trade position; this is a tribute to the pragmatic policy of the Government, and to the competitive salesmanship of the exporters. This silver lining was not without its dark cloud, however. The situation was seriously upset by the hike in prices of oil, fertilizers, and food. This has given a setback to our balance of payments position, but I have no doubt that there is immense scope for

improvement in exports. Special mention may be made of the sugar and the engineering industries. We also welcome and appreciate the efforts of our Government for the establishment of the Association of Iron Ore Exporting Countries.

25. The reopening of the Suez Canal will bring the European markets closer to us. The advantage of the Generalized Scheme of Preference (GSP) can be enlarged if the European countries could be persuaded to accept a five-year arrangement. We must export more—even at the cost of domestic consumption. At the same time, it hardly needs to be reiterated that there is no substitute for business efficiency—we must have the strictest quality control, timely deliveries, attractive packing etc. We have also to explore another important avenue for achieving a favourable balance of trade position. I refer to import substitution. Import substitution demands greater attention and needs to be treated on par with export promotion. That apart, larger foreign loans and re-scheduling of debt repayments have to be sought. And we have to learn to adapt ourselves better to the changing international currency situation.

26. I may mention that the Federation has been keeping close with other countries with a view to promoting goodwill and establishing with them cordial business relationship. During the year, we held our annual India-Japan Business Cooperation Committee meeting at Jaipur, have had the privilege of receiving industrial delegations from Australia, Austria, Iran, Italy, the Republic of Korea, Sri Lanka, Sweden and U.S.A. I had the opportunity of leading an Industrial Delegation to the West Asian countries in January last and it is my impression that the scope for export of Indian goods, technology and skills is tremendous not only in these countries but all over the world. But these markets are by no means easy pastures. We have to face stiff competition from countries which apart from being more advanced, are already in the field. I suggest that our Government should gently persuade the Gulf countries which no longer belong to the traditional third world to extend preferential treatment to goods and technology originating from developing countries like India.

27. 1975 is a crucial year, Madam Prime Minister. With the end of this year the third quarter of this Century comes to a close and the last quarter commences. Very soon we would be looking forward to the 21st century. This inevitably evokes a number of thoughts about the variety, size and range of problems that have to be faced in the context of our fundamental goal of improving the standard of living of the common man in whom the strength of the nation abides. To achieve this goal, the economy has to generate enough income, savings, investment and

production. Through proper planning and coordinate effort of business and government, the task can be made very much easier.

28. It may be worthwhile to fathom the dimensions of the problems and assess the tasks that lie ahead. The demand for essential commodities is influenced by the growth of population and income. Family planning programmes notwithstanding, our population may well exceed 900 million by the end of the century. It is also difficult to make any precise forecast about the growth of per capita income. We can, for practical purposes, take it at 3 per cent annum. On these premises the production of foodgrains will have to be around 238 million tonnes in the year 2001 AD, of sugarcane (in terms of gur) 36 million tonnes, oilseeds 22 million tonnes and cotton textiles 21 billion metres. That is to say, in the next 25 years foodgrains production will have to rise by 129 per cent, sugarcane by 157 per cent, oilseeds by 153 per cent and cotton textiles by 163 per cent. Even for a modest improvement in the standard of living the targets of overall production to be achieved are colossal. It is better that we know what is expected of us and plan accordingly than step into the future with no blueprint in our hands.

29. National development is both a challenge and an opportunity. It is a challenge to the vision of the policy-makers, to the inventiveness of entrepreneurs, and to the innovative capability of managers at all levels. Let me remind you, friends, if it needs reminding, that business thrives only when it serves. It is acceptable only when it identifies itself with the national ethos. Every enterprise has multidimensional obligations—to its customers, workers, shareholders, the Government, and above all to the community. All of us have to be constantly vigilant to ensure that these obligations are fulfilled in the highest measure.

30. While businessmen in general are perhaps conscious of their responsibilities to the consumers, it is agonizing to see a few of them indulging in anti-social acts such as manufacture and sale of spurious goods including food and and medicines. What greater crime can there be against society? Those who play with human lives for their own selfish gains deserve condemnation and the severest punishment. They are not entitled to be called businessmen. At the same time, I would like to say that on mere technical offences, unless they are of a grave nature, businessmen, particularly traders, should not be harassed.

31. It is important that businessmen should regard themselves as true partners with other sections of society in the building up of the country and towards that end dedicate themselves to the cause of national reconstruction. They should derive satisfaction in the thought that

Providence has given them an opportunity of serving the people and so they should make the best use of their resources for the larger social good. There is no greater virtue than that. Even truth, the greatest virtue has been defined as looking after the welfare of others.

येन भुतहितमन्यन्तम्
तनु सत्यं इति धारणा।

32. Before I conclude, I would like to say how grateful I am to you, Madam Prime Minister, to your Council of Ministers, and to the senior officials of Government, for the encouragement and advice they have offered us from time to time. I am also thankful to the Vice-President of the Federation, Shri Harish Mahindra, from whom I received very generous assistance during my tenure of presidentship, to my colleagues in the Committee who have spared no efforts to make my task easier, and to the many constituents, in the different centres that I visited, who received me with warmth and affection.

33. I take this opportunity to offer Shri G.L. Bansal, Secretary-General of FICCI, and Shri P. Chentsal Rao, Additional Secretary-General, and their colleagues my sincere thanks for their valuable cooperation and assistance in the discharge of my responsibilities as President. I would also like to express my appreciation for the staff of FICCI secretariat for the hard, efficient and unremitting work that they have put in with zeal and devotion.

34. With the end of the current session, Shri Bansal relinquishes his office as Secretary-General after completing 33 years of loyal, dedicated and distinguished service. For his contribution towards the building up of our organization to its present position, we owe him a deep debt of gratitude Shri P. Chentsal Rao will assume the office of Secretary-General, and I have every confidence that he will discharge the responsibilities with ability and devotion.

I now request you, Madam Prime Minister, to inaugurate the Session. Thank you.

Appendix 2

DELHI SPECIAL POLICE ESTABLISHMENT
FS II BRANCH
FIRST INFORMATION REPORT
(Recorded u/s 154 Cr.P.C.)

Crime No.R.C.5/77-FS-II Date and time of report 3 Oct, 1977 at 3.00

Place of occurrence
Delhi and other parts of India with State:

Date and time of occurrence: 1976-77.

Name of complainant or information with address:

Source Offence	U/s 120-IPC r/w sec.5(i) (d) & 5(2) of the Prevention of Corruption Act, 1947 and sec. 293A of the Companies Act 1956 and substantive offences u/s 5(i) (d) & 5(2) of the P.C. Act and sec. 293 of the Companies Act.

Name & address of
the accused:

1. Shri P.C. Sethi
2. Shri D.P. Chattopadhyaya & S/S
3. K.D. Malaviya
4. H.R. Gokhale
5. R.K. Dhawan
6. K.K. Birla
7. R.P. Goenka
8. M.V. Arunachalam

9.   Sudhir Sarin
10.   Yashpal Kapur and
11.   Ram Datta Dube & others

Action taken: Investigation taken up.
Investigating Officer: Shri N.L. Ramanathan, Dy. Supdt. Of Police SPE

INFORMATION

Information has been received from very reliable sources that the All India Congress Committee, for strengthening the finances of the party during the year 1976, and towards the end of 1976 and early 1977 for its election propaganda work, decided upon collecting funds from big business houses and industrialists by abusing the official position of some of the leading Congressmen who were also Ministers, aided and abetted by others including some public servants. Since political donations by Companies falling within the purview of Indian Companies Act 1956 were prohibited under section 293A of the said Act, a scheme was devised by these persons to disguise the collections as contributions to a large number of Souvenirs proposed to be published by the AICC and the various State Congress parties, and the companies and industrialists were induced to take out advertisements though such advertisements were not actually required by them. These collections by way of advertisements in the Souvenirs were merely a device to collect funds for the Congress Party and for political purposes. The collections increased in tempo during February 1977 since the Congress Party wanted to raise large funds for its electioneering campaign.

2. The modus operandi adopted was a general appeal by the AICC General Secretary requesting persons to contribute generously to the Congress by taking out advertisements in the souvenirs to be published by the Congress Party both at the Centre by AICC and also by the State Units. Following up this appeal, Shri P.C. Sethi the then Minister in the Central Cabinet personally went about contacting all the leading industrialists and business houses directly and also through the various Chambers of Commerce and Industries bringing his influence as a public servant to bear upon these persons for making contributions. It was made clear to everyone that it was not the advertisement value which was material but the need for contribution to the Congress Party and each industrialist/company should contribute the maximum possible, and very generously. When smaller contributions were offered, Shri Sethi and some

of his other associates demanded of these business houses to pay more and such houses were made to pay more subsequently. Many of these Souvenirs were only on paper and quite a few of them have not appeared at all and none of them had any real advertisement value. Another significant feature was that many of the companies who had thus 'donated' to the party had not taken out similar advertisements in the previous years and this was purely for a political purpose and bulk of it was used for the election fund. It is also alleged that funds thus collected were actually used for political propaganda during the last general elections to the Lok Sabha by the Congress Party.

3. In pursuance of this scheme, apart form Shri Sethi, two other former Ministers of the Central Cabinet took a prominent part in such collections. Shri D.P. Chattopadhyaya, the then Commerce Minister, demanded and obtained large scale donations from textile manufacturers and coffee planters. Shri K.D Malaviya the then Minister for Petroleum, demanded and obtained similar contributions from 'rayon' manufacturers. Shri R.K. Dhawan, in abuse of his official position as Private Secretary to the then Prime Minister, pressurized many industrialists to contribute.

4. Shri Sethi was assisted among others by three leading businessmen Shri R.P. Goenka of M/s Duncan Brothers & Co. Ltd.; Shri K.K. Birla of Birla Group of companies, and Shri M.V. Arunachalam, the then President of the Federation of Indian Chambers of Commerce and Industry, to go round and induce and/or pressurize business houses for making these payments. He was assisted by Shri Sudhir Sarin and Shri Ram Dutta Dube, both connected with the Souvenir collections. It is alleged that Shri Yashpal Kapur, who is a relation of Shri Sudhir Sarin and important Congress M.P. was also assisting them in these collections, knowing them to be illegal.

5. Just before the general elections, doubts were raised in public mind about the legality of such contributions by companies to a political party in the guise of contributions to Souvenirs. At that time members of the Federation of Indian Chamber of Commerce and Industries were nervous and they met Shri P.C. Sethi to get clarification and also an assurance that Government would not take any action against them though it was generally understood that these were political donations. Shri Sethi got in touch with Shri H.R. Gokhale, the then Law Minister in the Central Cabinet who was also in charge of Company Affairs. Shri Gokhale, who was aware of the illegal nature of these transactions, held discussions with FICCI delegation and, in abuse of his official position, directed his office to issue a 'clarification' stating that these contributions would not

fall within the ambit of section 293A of the Companies Act, 1956. This clarification was issued on 8th March 1977 and handed over in person to Shri P.C. Sethi.

6. The above mentioned accused alongwith others have thus contravened section 293A in pursuance of a conspiracy to commit an offence under section 293A with the above objection of swelling the coffers of the Congress Party prior to the General elections to the Lok Sabha in the year 1977.

7. It is said that in pursuance of this conspiracy, substantial contributions of more than Rs 1.00 lakh each from about 190 companies were secured by the AICC in 1976 and 1977. Undue influence was brought to bear on all these companies to make the contributions and they were overawed and pressurized by virtue of the high position occupied by the above accused and other public servants. The total money thus collected amounted to about Rs 8 crores.

8. As the information detailed above discloses the commission of offences under section 120-B I.P.C. read with section 5(i) (d) and 5(2) of the Prevention of Corruption Act of 1947 and section 293A of the Companies Act of 1956 and substantive offences under the aforesaid section 5(i) (d) read with 5(2) of the P.C. Act 1947 and section 293A of the Companies Act of 1956, this case is registered and taken up for investiga:ion.

Sd/-
SUPERINTENDENT OF POLICE SPE
FS II C.B.I. NEW DELHI

END. NO.
COPY FOR INFORMATION TO:
1. The Special Judge, New Delhi
2. Shri C.R. Krishnaswamy Rao Saheb, Secretary, Ministry of Home Affairs
3. Dy. I.P.P.(S) CBI New Delhi
4. Investigation Officer
5. Office copy

Sd/-
SUPERINTENDENT OF POLICE C.B.I.
FS II C.B.I. NEW DELHI

Appendix 3

In the High Court at Calcutta
Criminal Revisional Jurisdiction
The 10th October, 1977

Present:
The Hon'ble Mr Justice A.N. Banerjee & the Hon'ble Mr Justice A.P.
Bhattacharya, Criminal Misc. Case No. 871 of 1977.

K.K. Birla Petitioner
Versus
The State Opposite Party

For Petitioner:

Mr. S.S. Ray,
Mr D.K. Dutta,
Mr Ajay Nath Mukherji,
Mr Ranjit Kumar Dutta,
Mr Ramesh Chaudhury.

For the State: Mr Biren Mitra

This is an application under section 438 of the Code of Criminal Procedure
filed by the petitioner who apprehends that he may be arrested on the
allegation of his having committed a non-bailable offence under section
120B-I.P.C. read with section 5(1) (d) and 5(2) of the Prevention of
Corruption Act, 1947 and section 293A of the Companies Act, case No.
being RC 5/77 of FS(II)-CBI dated 3.10.77.

Having heard the learned Advocates of the respective parties and on a consideration of the application we consider it to be a fit case in which the application for anticipatory bail should be allowed. We find no substance in the argument of the learned Advocate appearing for the State that since the petitioner is, for the present, away from this country, no such application under section 438 of the Cr.P.C. should be entertained. We also find no merit in the contention that since the case has been registered at Delhi, the petitioner who has given his residential address within the jurisdiction of this court, will not be competent to file an application of the present nature.

In the result, we allow this application and hereby order that in the event of the petitioner being arrested anywhere within the jurisdiction of this court, in connection with the aforesaid case, he shall be released on bail subject to the condition that he would fully cooperate with the investigation officer in the matter of investigation of the case.

A.N. Banerjee
The 10th October, 1977   A. Bhattacharya

Typed by: Narayan
Examined by: s/d
Read by: s/d

Index